Free Banking
Volume III

The International Library of Macroeconomic and Financial History

Series Editor: Forrest H. Capie
Professor of Economic History
and Head of the Department of Banking and Finance
The City University Business School, London

Free Banking
Volume III

Modern Theory and Policy

Edited by

Lawrence H. White

Associate Professor
Department of Economics
University of Georgia, USA

An Elgar Reference Collection

Published by
Edward Elgar Publishing Limited
Gower House
Croft Road
Aldershot
Hants GU11 3HR
England

Edward Elgar Publishing Company
Old Post Road
Brookfield
Vermont 05036
USA

British Library Cataloguing in Publication Data
Free Banking. – (International Library of
Macroeconomic & Financial History;No.11)
    I. White, Lawrence H. II. Series
    332.1

ISBN 1 85278 597 7 (3 volume set)

Printed in Great Britain at the University Press, Cambridge

Contents

Acknowledgements

The editor and publishers wish to thank the following who have kindly given permission for the use of copyright material.

American Economic Association for articles: Lawrence H. White (1984), 'Competitive Payments Systems and the Unit of Account', *American Economic Review*, **LXXIV** (4), 699–712; Robert Greenfield and Leland B. Yeager (1986), 'Competitive Payments Systems: Comment', *American Economic Review*, **76** (4), 848–9; Lawrence H. White (1986), 'Competitive Payments Systems: Reply', *American Economic Review*, **76** (4), 850–53.

Bank Administration Institute for article: Fischer Black (1970), 'Banking and Interest Rates In a World Without Money', *Journal of Bank Research*, **1**, 9–20.

Basil Blackwell Ltd for article: Neil Wallace (1988), 'A Suggestion for Oversimplifying the Theory of Money', *Economic Journal*, **98** (390), Conference Supplement, 25–36.

Gary S. Becker for his article: (1957), 'A Proposal for Free Banking', unpublished.

Cato Institute for article: Richard E. Wagner (1986), 'Central Banking and the Fed: A Public Choice Perspective', *Cato Journal*, **6** (2), 519–38.

Duncker und Humblot GMBH for articles: Roland Vaubel (1985), 'Competing Currencies: The Case for Free Entry', *Zeitschrift für Wirtschafts- und Sozialwissenschaften*, **5**, 547–64; Martin F. Hellwig (1985), 'What Do We Know About Currency Competition?', *Zeitschrift für Wirtschafts- und Sozialwissenschaften*, **5**, 565–88.

Elsevier Science Publishers B.V. for articles: Bart Taub (1985), 'Private Fiat Money with Many Suppliers', *Journal of Monetary Economics*, **16** (2), 195–208; Milton Friedman and Anna J. Schwartz (1986), 'Has Government Any Role in Money?', *Journal of Monetary Economics*, **17** (1), 37–62; Karl Wärneryd (1990), 'Legal Restrictions and Monetary Evolution', *Journal of Economic Behavior and Organization*, **13** (1), 117–24.

Free Market Books for excerpt: Ludwig von Mises (1978), 'Monetary Stabilization and Cyclical Policy [1928] in Percy L. Greaves, Jr. (ed.), *On the Manipulation of Money and Credit*, Part II, Chapters 3–4, 131–47.

Heather Foundation for excerpt: E.C. Riegel (1978), 'Toward a Natural Monetary System', *Flight From Inflation: The Monetary Alternative* [1954], 47–63.

Helbing & Lichtenhahn Verlag for article: Roland Vaubel (1984), 'The Government's Money Monopoly: Externalities or Natural Monopoly?', *Kyklos*, **37** (1), 27–58.

Kluwer Academic Publishers for article: Kevin Dowd (1988), 'Option Clauses and the Stability of a Laisser Faire Monetary System', *Journal of Financial Services Research*, **1**, 319–33.

J.C.B. Mohr (Paul Siebeck) and George A. Selgin for his article: (1987), 'The Stability and Efficiency of Money Supply Under Free Banking', *Journal of Institutional and Theoretical Economics*, **143** (3), 435–56.

Ohio State University Press for articles: Benjamin Klein (1974), 'The Competitive Supply of Money', *Journal of Money, Credit and Banking*, **6** (4), 423–53; Lance Girton and Don Roper (1981), 'Theory and Implications of Currency Substitution', *Journal of Money, Credit, and Banking*, **XIII** (1), 12–30; Robert L. Greenfield and Leland B. Yeager (1983), 'A Laissez-Faire Approach to Monetary Stability', *Journal of Money, Credit, and Banking*, **XV** (3), 302–15; Lawrence H. White (1987), 'Accounting for Non-Interest-Bearing Currency: A Critique of the Legal Restrictions Theory of Money', *Journal of Money, Credit, and Banking*, **19** (4), 448–56; John Bryant (1989), 'Interest-Bearing Currency, Legal Restrictions, and the Rate of Return Dominance of Money', *Journal of Money, Credit, and Banking*, **21** (3), 240–45.

Western Economic Association International for article: George A. Selgin and Lawrence H. White (1987), 'The Evolution of a Free Banking System', *Economic Inquiry*, **XXV** (3), 439–57.

Every effort has been made to trace all the copyright holders but if any have been inadvertently overlooked the publishers will be pleased to make the necessary arrangement at the first opportunity.

In addition the publishers wish to thank the library of the London School of Economics and Political Science and the Marshall Library, Cambridge University for their assistance in obtaining these articles.

Part I
Free Banking with a Distinct Base Money

[1]

Excerpt from Ludwig von Mises, in Percy L. Greaves, Jr. (ed.), *On the Manipulation of Money and Credit*, 131–47.

III

THE REAPPEARANCE OF CYCLES

1. Metallic Standard Fluctuations

From the instant when the banks start expanding the volume of circulation credit, until the moment they stop such behavior, the course of events is substantially similar to that provoked by any increase in the quantity of money. The difference results from the fact that fiduciary media generally come into circulation through the banks, i.e., as loans, while increases in the quantity of money appear as additions to the wealth and income of specific individuals. This has already been mentioned and will not be further considered here. Considerably more significant for us is another distinction between the two.

Such increases and decreases in the quantity of money have no connection with increases or decreases in the demand for money. If the demand for money grows in the wake of a population increase or a progressive reduction of barter and self-sufficiency resulting in increased monetary transactions, there is absolutely no need to increase the quantity of money. It might even decrease. In any event, it would be most extraordinary if changes in the demand for money were balanced by reciprocal changes in its quantity so that both changes were concealed and no change took place in the monetary unit's purchasing power.

Changes in the value of the monetary unit are always taking

132   ON THE MANIPULATION OF MONEY AND CREDIT

place in the economy. Periods of declining purchasing power alternate with those of increasing purchasing power. Under a metallic standard, these changes are usually so slow and so insignificant that their effect is not at all violent. Nevertheless, we must recognize that even under a precious metal standard periods of ups and downs would still alternate at irregular intervals. In addition to the standard metallic money, such a standard would recognize only token coins for petty transactions. There would, of course, be no paper money or any other currency (i.e., either notes or bank accounts subject to check which are not fully covered). Yet even then, one would be able to speak of economic "ups," "downs" and "waves." However, one would hardly be inclined to refer to such minor alternating "ups" and "downs" as regularly recurring cycles. During these periods when purchasing power moved in one direction, whether up or down, it would probably move so slightly that businessmen would scarcely notice the changes. Only economic historians would become aware of them. Moreover, the fact is that the transition from a period of rising prices to one of falling prices would be so slight that neither panic nor crisis would appear. This would also mean that businessmen and news reports of market activities would be less occupied with the "long waves" of the trade cycle.[1]

2. Infrequent Recurrences of Paper Money Inflations

The effects of inflations brought about by increases in paper money are quite different. They also produce price increases and hence "good business conditions," which are further intensified by the apparent encouragement of exports and the hampering of imports. Once the inflation comes to an end, whether by a providential halt to further increases in the quan-

---

[1]To avoid misunderstanding, it should be pointed out that the expression "long-waves" of the trade cycle is not to be understood here as it was used by either Wilhelm Röpke or N. D. Kondratieff. Röpke *(Die Konjunktur,* Jena, 1922, p. 21) considered "long-wave cycles" to be those which lasted 5-10 years generally. Kondratieff ("Die langen Wellen der Konjunktur" in *Archiv für Sozialwissenschaft,* Vol. 56, pp. 573ff.) tried to prove, unsuccessfully in my judgment, that, in addition to the 7-11 year cycles of business conditions which he called medium cycles, there were also regular cyclical waves averaging 50 years in length. LvM.

tity of money (as for instance recently in France and Italy) or through complete debasement of the paper money due to inflationary policy carried to its final conclusions (as in Germany in 1923), then the "stabilization crisis"[2] appears. The cause and appearance of this crisis correspond precisely to those of the crisis which comes at the close of a period of circulation credit expansion. One must clearly distinguish *this* crisis [i.e., when increases in the quantity of money are simply halted] from the consequences which must result when the cessation of inflation is followed by deflation.

There is no regularity as to the recurrence of paper money inflations. They generally originate in a certain political attitude, not from events within the economy itself. One can only say, with certainty, that after a country has pursued an inflationist policy to its end or, at least, to substantial lengths, it cannot soon use this means again successfully to serve its financial interests. The people, as a result of their experience, will have become distrustful and would resist any attempt at a renewal of inflation.

Even at the very beginning of a new inflation, people would reject the notes or accept them only at a far greater discount than the actual increased quantity would otherwise warrant. As a rule, such an unusually high discount is characteristic of the final phases of an inflation. Thus an early attempt to return to a policy of paper money inflation must either fail entirely or come very quickly to a catastrophic conclusion. One can assume—and monetary history confirms this, or at least does not contradict it—that a new generation must grow up before consideration can again be given to bolstering the government's finances with the printing press.

Many states have never pursued a policy of paper money inflation. Many have resorted to it only once in their history. Even the states traditionally known for their printing press money have not repeated the experiment often. Austria waited

---

[2]The German term, "Sanierungskrise," means literally "restoration crisis," i.e., the crisis which comes at the shift to more "healthy" monetary relationships. In English this crisis is called the "stabilization crisis."

134   ON THE MANIPULATION OF MONEY AND CREDIT

almost a generation after the banknote inflation of the Napoleonic era before embarking on an inflation policy again. Even then, the inflation was in more modest proportions than at the beginning of the 19th century. Almost a half century passed between the end of her second and the beginning of her third and most recent period of inflation. It is by no means possible to speak of cyclical reappearances of paper money inflations.

3. The Cyclical Process of Credit Expansions[3]

Regularity can be detected only with respect to the phenomena originating out of circulation credit. Crises have reappeared every few years since banks issuing fiduciary media began to play an important role in the economic life of people. Stagnation followed crisis, and following these came the boom again. More than ninety years ago Lord Overstone described the sequence in a remarkably graphic manner:

> We find it [the "state of trade"] subject to various conditions which are periodically returning; it revolves apparently in an established cycle. First we find it in a state of quiescence, — next improvement, — growing confidence, — prosperity, — excitement, — overtrading, — convulsion, — pressure, — stagnation, — distress, — ending again in quiescence.[4]

This description, unrivaled for its brevity and clarity, must be kept in mind to realize how wrong it is to give later economists credit for transforming the problem of the crisis into the problem of general business conditions.

Attempts have been made, with little success, to supplement the observation that business cycles recur by attributing a definite time period to the sequence of events. Theories which sought the source of economic change in recurring cosmic events have, as might be expected, leaned in this

---

[3]*MME*. "Credit expansion," p. 27.

[4]Overstone, Samuel Jones Loyd (Lord). "Reflections Suggested by a Perusal of Mr. J. Horsley Palmer's Pamphlet on the Causes and Consequences of the Pressure on the Money Market," 1837. (Reprinted in *Tracts and Other Publications on Metallic and Paper Currency*. London, 1857), p. 31. LvM.

direction. A study of economic history fails to support such assumptions. It shows recurring ups and downs in business conditions, but not ups and downs of equal length.

The problem to be solved is the recurrence of fluctuations in business activity. The Circulation Credit Theory shows us, in rough outline, the typical course of a cycle. However, so far as we have as yet analyzed the theory, it still does not explain why the cycle always recurs.

According to the Circulation Credit Theory, it is clear that the direct stimulus which provokes the fluctuations is to be sought in the conduct of the banks. Insofar as they start to reduce the "money rate of interest" below the "natural rate of interest," they expand circulation credit, and thus divert the course of events away from the path of normal development. They bring about changes in relationships which must necessarily lead to boom and crisis. Thus, the problem consists of asking what leads the banks again and again to renew attempts to expand the volume of circulation credit.

Many authors believe that the instigation of the banks' behavior comes from outside, that certain events induce them to pump more fiduciary media into circulation and that they would behave differently if these circumstances failed to appear. I was also inclined to this view in the first edition of my book on monetary theory.[5] I could not understand why the banks didn't learn from experience. I thought they would certainly persist in a policy of caution and restraint, if they were not led by outside circumstances to abandon it. Only later did I become convinced that it was useless to look to an outside stimulus for the change in the conduct of the banks. Only later did I also become convinced that fluctuations in general business conditions were completely dependent on the relationship of the quantity of fiduciary media in circulation to demand.

---

[5]See *Theorie des Geldes und der Umlaufsmittel* (1912), pp. 433ff. I had been deeply impressed by the fact that Lord Overstone was also apparently inclined to this interpretation. See his *Reflections,* op. cit., pp. 32ff. LvM. [NOTE: These paragraphs were deleted from the 2nd German edition (1924) from which was made the H. E. Batson English translation, *The Theory of Money and Credit,* published 1934, 1953 and 1971.]

136   ON THE MANIPULATION OF MONEY AND CREDIT

Each new issue of fiduciary media has the consequences described above. First of all, it depresses the loan rate and then it reduces the monetary unit's purchasing power. Every subsequent issue brings the same result. The establishment of new banks of issue and their step-by-step expansion of circulation credit provides the means for a business boom and, as a result, leads to the crisis with its accompanying decline. We can readily understand that the banks issuing fiduciary media, in order to improve their chances for profit, may be ready to expand the volume of credit granted and the number of notes issued. What calls for special explanation is why attempts are made again and again to improve general economic conditions by the expansion of circulation credit in spite of the spectacular failure of such efforts in the past.

The answer must run as follows: According to the prevailing ideology of businessman and economist-politician, the reduction of the interest rate is considered an essential goal of economic policy. Moreover, the expansion of circulation credit is assumed to be the appropriate means to achieve this goal.

4. The Mania for Lower Interest Rates

The naive inflationist theory of the 17th and 18th centuries could not stand up in the long run against the criticism of economics. In the 19th century, that doctrine was held only by obscure authors who had no connection with scientific inquiry or practical economic policy. For purely political reasons, the school of empirical and historical "Realism" did not pay attention to problems of economic theory. It was due only to this neglect of theory that the naive theory of inflation was once more able to gain prestige temporarily during the World War, especially in Germany.

The doctrine of inflationism by way of fiduciary media was more durable. Adam Smith had battered it severely, as had others even before him, especially the American William Douglass.[6] Many, notably in the Currency School, had fol-

---

[6]William Douglass (1691-1752), a renowned physician, came to America in 1716. His "A Discourse Concerning the Currencies of the British Plantations in America" (1739) first appeared anonymously.

lowed. But then came a reversal. The Banking School confused the situation. Its founders failed to see the error in their doctrine. They failed to see that the expansion of circulation credit lowered the interest rate. They even argued that it was impossible to expand credit beyond the "needs of business." So there are seeds in the Banking Theory which need only to be developed to reach the conclusion that the interest rate can be reduced by the conduct of the banks. At the very least, it must be admitted that those who dealt with those problems did not sufficiently understand the reasons for opposing credit expansion to be able to overcome the public clamor for the banks to provide "cheap money."

In discussions of the rate of interest, the economic press adopted the questionable jargon of the business world, speaking of a "scarcity" or an "abundance" of money and calling the short term loan market the "money market." Banks issuing fiduciary media, warned by experience to be cautious, practiced discretion and hesitated to indulge the universal desire of the press, political parties, parliaments, governments, entrepreneurs, landowners and workers for cheaper credit. Their reluctance to expand credit was falsely attributed to reprehensible motives. Even newspapers, that knew better, and politicians, who should have known better, never tired of asserting that the banks of issue could certainly discount larger sums more cheaply if they were not trying to hold the interest rate as high as possible out of concern for their own profitability and the interests of their controlling capitalists.

Almost without exception, the great European banks of issue on the continent were established with the expectation that the loan rate could be reduced by issuing fiduciary media. Under the influence of the Currency School doctrine, at first in England and then in other countries where old laws did not restrict the issue of notes, arrangements were made to limit the expansion of circulation credit, at least of that part granted through the issue of uncovered banknotes. Still, the Currency Theory lost out as a result of criticism by Tooke (1774-1858) and his followers. Although it was considered risky to abolish the laws which restricted the issue of notes, no harm was seen in circumventing them. Actually, the letter of the banking laws provided for a concentration of the nation's supply of precious metals in the vaults of banks of issue. This permitted an increase in the issue of fiduciary media and played an important role in the expansion of the gold exchange standard.

Before the war [1914], there was no hesitation in Germany in openly advocating withdrawal of gold from trade so that the Reichsbank might issue sixty marks in notes for every twenty marks in gold added to its stock. Propaganda was also made for expanding the use of payments by check with the explanation that this was a means to lower the interest rate substantially.[7] The situation was similar elsewhere, although perhaps more cautiously expressed.

Every single fluctuation in general business conditions—the upswing to the peak of the wave and the decline into the trough which follows—is prompted by the attempt of the banks of issue to reduce the loan rate and thus expand the volume of circulation credit through an increase in the supply of fiduciary media (i.e., banknotes and checking accounts not fully backed by money). The fact that these efforts are resumed again and again in spite of their widely deplored consequences, causing one business cycle after another, can be attributed to the predominance of an ideology—an ideology which regards rising commodity prices and especially a low rate of interest as goals of economic policy. The theory is that even this second goal may be attained by the expansion of fiduciary media. Both crisis and depression are lamented. Yet, because the causal connection between the behavior of the banks of issue and the evils complained about is not correctly interpreted, a policy with respect to interest is advocated which, in the last analysis, must necessarily always lead to crisis and depression.

5. Free Banking

Every deviation from the prices, wage rates and interest rates which would prevail on the unhampered market must

---

[7]See the examples cited in *The Theory of Money and Credit* (pp. 387ff.). LvM.

lead to disturbances of the economic "equilibrium."[8] This disturbance, brought about by attempts to depress the interest rate artificially, is precisely the cause of the crisis.

The ultimate cause, therefore, of the phenomenon of wave after wave of economic ups and downs is ideological in character. The cycles will not disappear so long as people believe that the rate of interest may be reduced, not through the accumulation of capital, but by banking policy.

Even if governments had never concerned themselves with the issue of fiduciary media, there would still be banks of issue and fiduciary media in the form of notes as well as checking accounts. There would then be no legal limitation on the issue of fiduciary media. Free banking would prevail. However, banks would have to be especially cautious because of the sensitivity to loss of reputation of their fiduciary media, which no one would be forced to accept. In the course of time, the inhabitants of capitalistic countries would learn to differentiate between good and bad banks. Those living in "undeveloped" countries would distrust all banks. No government would exert pressure on the banks to discount on easier terms than the banks themselves could justify. However, the managers of solvent and highly respected banks, the only banks whose fiduciary media would enjoy the general confidence essential for money-substitute quality, would have learned from past experiences. Even if they scarcely detected the deeper correlations, they would nevertheless know how far they might go without precipitating the danger of a breakdown.

The cautious policy of restraint on the part of respected and well-established banks would compel the more irresponsible managers of other banks to follow suit, however much they might want to discount more generously. For the expansion of circulation credit can never be the act of one individual bank alone, nor even of a group of individual banks. It always requires that the fiduciary media be *generally* accepted as a money substitute. If several banks of issue, each enjoying

---

[8]See above p. 124n.

140   ON THE MANIPULATION OF MONEY AND CREDIT

equal rights, existed side by side, and if some of them sought
to expand the volume of circulation credit while the others did
not alter their conduct, then at every bank clearing, demand
balances would regularly appear in favor of the conservative
enterprises. As a result of the presentation of notes for redemption and withdrawal of their cash balances, the expanding
banks would very quickly be compelled once more to limit the
scale of their emissions.

In the course of the development of a banking system with
fiduciary media, crises could not have been avoided. However,
as soon as bankers recognized the dangers of expanding
circulation credit, they would have done their utmost, in their
own interests, to avoid the crisis. They would then have taken
the only course leading to this goal: extreme restraint in the
issue of fiduciary media.

6. Government Intervention in Banking

The fact that the development of fiduciary media banking
took a different turn may be attributed entirely to the circumstance that the issue of banknotes (which for a long time
were the only form of fiduciary media and are today [1928] still
the more important, even in the United States and England)
became a public concern. The private bankers and joint-stock
banks were supplanted by the politically privileged banks of
issue because the governments favored the expansion of
circulation credit for reasons of fiscal and credit policy. The
privileged institutions could proceed unhesitatingly in the
granting of credit, not only because they usually held a
monopoly in the issue of notes, but also because they could
rely on the government's help in an emergency. The private
banker would go bankrupt, if he ventured too far in the issue of
credit. The privileged bank received permission to suspend
payments and its notes were made legal tender at face value.

If the knowledge derived from the Currency Theory had led
to the conclusion that fiduciary media should be deprived of
all special privileges and placed, like other claims, under
general law in every respect and without exception, this would
probably have contributed more toward eliminating the threat

of crises than was actually accomplished by establishing rigid proportions[9] for the issue of fiduciary media in the form of notes and restricting the freedom of banks to issue fiduciary media in the form of checking accounts. The principle of free banking was limited to the field of checking accounts. In fact, it could not function here to bring about restraint on the part of banks and bankers. Public opinion decreed that government should be guided by a different policy—a policy of coming to the assistance of the central banks of issue in times of crises. To permit the Bank of England to lend a helping hand to banks which had gotten into trouble by expanding circulation credit, the Peel Act was suspended in 1847, 1857 and 1866. Such assistance, in one form or another, has been offered time and again everywhere.

In the United States, national banking legislation made it technically difficult, if not entirely impossible, to grant such aid. The system was considered especially unsatisfactory, precisely because of the legal obstacles it placed in the path of helping grantors of credit who became insolvent and of supporting the value of circulation credit they had granted. Among the reasons leading to the significant revision of the American banking system [i.e., the Federal Reserve Act of 1913], the most important was the belief that provisions must be made for times of crises. In other words, just as the emergency institution of Clearing House Certificates was able to save expanding banks, so should technical expedients be used to prevent the breakdown of the banks and bankers whose conduct had led to the crisis. It was usually considered especially important to shield the banks which expanded circulation credit from the consequences of their conduct. One of the chief tasks of the central banks of issue was to jump into this breach. It was also considered the duty of those other banks who, thanks to foresight, had succeeded in preserving their solvency, even in the general crisis, to help fellow banks in difficulty.

---

[9]Of fractional reserves against notes and demand deposit liabilities.

142   ON THE MANIPULATION OF MONEY AND CREDIT

7. Intervention No Remedy

It may well be asked whether the damage inflicted by misguiding entrepreneurial activity by artificially lowering the loan rate would be greater if the crisis were permitted to run its course. Certainly many saved by the intervention would be sacrificed in the panic, but if such enterprises were permitted to fail, others would prosper. Still the total loss brought about by the "boom" (which the crisis did not produce, but only made evident) is largely due to the fact that factors of production were expended for fixed investments which, in the light of economic conditions, were not the most urgent. As a result, these factors of production are now lacking for more urgent uses. If intervention prevents the transfer of goods from the hands of imprudent entrepreneurs to those who would now take over because they have evidenced better foresight, this imbalance becomes neither less significant nor less perceptible.

In any event, the practice of intervening for the benefit of banks, rendered insolvent by the crisis, and of the customers of these banks, has resulted in suspending the market forces which could serve to prevent a return of the expansion, in the form of a new boom, and the crisis which inevitably follows. If the banks emerge from the crisis unscathed, or only slightly weakened, what remains to restrain them from embarking once more on an attempt to reduce artificially the interest rate on loans and expand circulation credit? If the crisis were ruthlessly permitted to run its course, bringing about the destruction of enterprises which were unable to meet their obligations, then all entrepreneurs—not only banks but also other businessmen—would exhibit more caution in granting and using credit in the future. Instead, public opinion approves of giving assistance in the crisis. Then, no sooner is the worst over, than the banks are spurred on to a new expansion of circulation credit.

To the businessman, it appears most natural and understandable that the banks should satisfy his demand for credit by the creation of fiduciary media. The banks, he believes,

MONETARY STABILIZATION AND CYCLICAL POLICY   143

should have the task and the duty to "stand by" business and trade. There is no dispute but what the expansion of circulation credit furthers the accumulation of capital within the narrow limits of the "forced savings" it brings about and to that extent permits an increase in productivity. Still it can be argued that, given the situation, each step in this direction steers business activity, in the manner described above, on a "wrong" course. The discrepancy between what the entrepreneurs do and what the unhampered market would have prescribed becomes evident in the crisis. The fact that each crisis, with its unpleasant consequences, is followed once more by a new "boom," which must eventually expend itself as another crisis, is due only to the circumstances that the ideology which dominates all influential groups—political economists, politicians, statesmen, the press and the business world—not only sanctions, but also demands, the expansion of circulation credit.

IV
THE CRISIS POLICY OF
THE CURRENCY SCHOOL

1. The Inadequacy of the Currency School

Every advance toward explaining the problem of business fluctuations to date is due to the Currency School. We are also indebted to this School alone for the ideas responsible for policies aimed at eliminating business fluctuations. The fatal error of the Currency School consisted in the fact that it failed to recognize the similarity between banknotes and bank demand deposits as money substitutes and, thus, as money certificates and fiduciary media. In their eyes, only the banknote was a money substitute. In their view, therefore, the circulation of pure metallic money could only be adulterated by the introduction of a banknote not covered by money.

Consequently, they thought that the only thing that needed to be done to prevent the periodic return of crises was to set a rigid limit for the issue of banknotes not backed by metal. The issue of fiduciary media in the form of demand deposits not covered by metal was left free.[1] Since nothing stood in the way of granting circulation credit through bank deposits, the policy of expanding circulation credit could be continued even in England. When technical difficulties limited further bank loans and precipitated a crisis, it became customary to come to the assistance of the banks and their customers with special

---

[1] Even the countries that have followed different procedures in this respect have, for all practical purposes, placed no obstacle in the way of the development of fiduciary media in the form of bank deposits. LvM.

MONETARY STABILIZATION AND CYCLICAL POLICY   145

issues of notes. The practice of restricting the notes in circulation not covered by metal, by limiting the ratio of such notes to metal, systematized this procedure. Banks could expand the volume of credit with ease if they could count on the support of the bank of issue in an emergency.

If all further expansion of fiduciary media had been forbidden in any form, that is, if the banks had been obliged to hold full reserves for both the additional notes issued and increases in customers' demand deposits subject to check or similar claim—or at least had not been permitted to increase the quantity of fiduciary media beyond a strictly limited ratio— prices would have declined sharply, especially at times when the increased demand for money surpassed the increase in its quantity. The economy would then not only have lacked the drive contributed by any "forced savings," it would also have temporarily suffered from the consequences of a rise in the monetary unit's purchasing power [i.e., falling prices]. Capital accumulation would then have been slowed down, although certainly not stopped. In any case, the economy surely would not then have experienced periods of stormy upswings followed by dramatic reversals of the upswings into crises and declines.

There is little sense in discussing whether it would have been better to restrict, in this way, the issue of fiduciary media by the banks than it was to pursue the policy actually followed. The alternatives are not merely restriction or freedom in the issue of fiduciary media. The alternatives are, or at least were, privilege in the granting of fiduciary media or true free banking.

The possibility of free banking has scarcely even been suggested. Intervention cast its first shadow over the capitalistic system when banking policy came to the forefront of economic and political discussion. To be sure, some authors, who defended free banking, appeared on the scene. However, their voices were overpowered. The desired goal was to protect the noteholders against the banks. It was forgotten that those hurt by the dangerous suspension of payments by the banks of issue are always the very ones the law was intended

146   ON THE MANIPULATION OF MONEY AND CREDIT

to help. No matter how severe the consequences one may
anticipate from a breakdown of the banks under a system of
absolutely free banking, one would have to admit that they
could never even remotely approach the severity of those
brought about by the war and postwar banking policies of the
three European empires.[2]

2. "Booms" Favored

In the last two generations, hardly anyone, who has given
this matter some thought, can fail to know that a crisis follows
a boom. Nevertheless, it would have been impossible for even
the sharpest and cleverest banker to suppress in time the
expansion of circulation credit. Public opinion stood in the
way. The fact that business conditions fluctuated violently was
generally assumed to be inherent in the capitalistic system.
Under the influence of the Banking Theory, it was thought
that the banks merely went along with the upswing and that
their conduct had nothing to do with bringing it about or
advancing it. If, after a long period of stagnation, the banks
again began to respond to the general demand for easier credit,
public opinion was always delighted by the signs of the start of
a boom.

In view of the prevailing ideology, it would have been
completely unthinkable for the banks to apply the brakes at
the start of such a boom. If business conditions continued to
improve, then, in conformity with the principles of Lord
Overstone, prophecies of a reaction certainly increased in
number. However, even those who gave this warning usually
did not call for a rigorous halt to all further expansion of
circulation credit. They asked only for moderation and for
restricting newly granted credits to "non-speculative" businesses.

Then finally, if the banks changed their policy and the crisis
came, it was always easy to find culprits. But there was no

---

[2]According to Professor Mises, the "three European empires" were Austria-
Hungary, Germany and Russia. This designation probably comes from the "Three
Emperors' League" (1872), an informal alliance among these governments. Its
effectiveness was declining by 1890, and World War I dealt it a final blow.

desire to locate the real offender—the false theoretical doctrine. So no changes were made in traditional procedures. Economic waves continued to follow one another.

The managers of the banks of issue have carried out their policy without reflecting very much on its basis. If the expansion of circulation credit began to alarm them, they proceeded, not always very skillfully, to raise the discount rate. Thus, they exposed themselves to public censure for having initiated the crisis by their behavior. It is clear that the crisis must come sooner or later. It is also clear that the crisis must always be caused, primarily and directly, by the change in the conduct of the banks. If we speak of error on the part of the banks, however, we must point to the wrong they do in encouraging the upswing. The fault lies, not with the policy of raising the interest rate, but only with the fact that it was raised too late.

[2]

A Proposal For Free Banking

Gary S. Becker

I wrote this paper on free banking in 1956 as a reaction to the 100 per cent reserve proposals that were then popular, especially at the University of Chicago. The paper argues that a 100 per cent reserve system requirement is an undesirable regulation, indeed, the theme of the essay is that the banking industry was already overregulated.

Among other things, I reject government deposit insurance as an unwarranted intervention in the banking industry. That was a very minority opinion at the time, but the failure of numerous S&Ls and other banks in recent years converted many economists to this view.

The paper was never published because I wanted to revise the analysis, but I did not get around to doing this. I was bothered by my conclusion that the Federal Government should retain a monopoly over currency. A truly 'free' banking system would permit banks to issue notes that circulate, and such a system might not even need government currency. I reluctantly accepted a common argument at that time that the supply of notes would increase without bound if they were issued only by a competitive banking system. I also tentatively accepted the allegation – I state in the paper that I have 'the impression' – that the public would have difficulty determining the relative qualities of notes issued by many banks.

But I was not convinced. Recent work argues that reputational considerations can limit the amount of currency issued by competitive banks, although this issue is not fully resolved. I am no longer persuaded that information about private currencies would be more difficult to acquire than information about the qualities of many other products and services. Indeed, I now believe that private currencies should be permitted, although that conclusion does not necessarily imply that government currency is undesirable.

The paper obviously needs a thorough rewriting, partly to bring the treatment of macroeconomic policy up to date. I would eliminate most of what I had said about multiplier effects and aggregate externalities. But I decided to leave the paper as it was written because its value is as a document that provided a fresh perspective on the banking industry relative to accepted views in the 1950s. I am happy for this opportunity to publish a paper written 35 years ago.

This paper presents a proposal to reform the banking system. First the proposal is presented; afterwards arguments for and against are evaluated. At the end it is compared with the 100 per cent reserve scheme.

The proposal is:

1. The Federal Government will retain its monopoly of the printing of currency or notes.
2. Otherwise there will be essentially free banking. Banks will be free to set themselves up and establish their own reserve ratios, interest rates, lending policies, and so on. That is, banking will be considered in industry like any other, and competition rather than Government will be the controlling mechanism.
3. There will be some *overall* countercyclical policy. This might take the form of stabiliz-

ing some index, either through discretionary open-market operations or through an automatic commodity reserve system, or it might be an automatic policy of the stable budget variety.[1]

This proposal takes government out of the lending and checking industries. With it are removed the inflexibilities which government intervention bring. It implicitly argues that the proper role of Government in combating cyclical movements is through overall, general, policies and *not* through specific ones.

Evaluation

(a) Fiat currency is a means of conserving the quantity of real resources used in facilitating transactions. Competitive private enterprise alone cannot provide this currency, for profit incentives would reduce this to a pure commodity standard. In other words, the equilibrium price level would be infinity.[2] This implies that a finite, relatively stable price level can be maintained only if the government issues notes.

Suppose private banks were also permitted to issue non-interest-bearing notes. Some of these banks would guarantee to convert their notes on demand into government notes. The necessity of doing this would limit the amount of notes they chose to issue. Some banks might refuse to convert their notes into other notes. With *knowledge of this*, individuals would refuse to accept these notes, and the issuing banks would be forced out of business. They could remain in business if they paid interest on these notes, with the interest payable in (say) government notes. But then these notes would be equivalent to a private consol, and for our purposes this shall not be treated as currency.

With perfect knowledge under this system, then the currency would consist of government notes and private notes convertible on demand into government notes. The reason I would prevent a private note issue is based on the impression that knowledge is particularly apt to be imperfect in this area. With thousands of banks issuing notes, it would be relatively easy to begin counterfeiting; a counterfeiting firm is essentially a bank that issues notes and refuses to convert them into 'good' notes. Among other things this means that many resources will have to be allocated to apprehending counterfeiters and to informing the public as to the quality of different notes. Since the conserving of resources used to facilitate transactions is one motivation for fiat currency, it seems somewhat desirable to outlaw private bank notes.[3]

(b) There will be institutions with deposits subject to check. Some of these will be demand obligations, some might have finite maturities, and some might have infinite maturities ('checking consols'). A 'counterfeit' checking deposit is a deposit with infinite maturity and which pays zero interest in terms of government notes. Since counterfeiting seems relatively difficult in this activity, we shall ignore it in our subsequent discussion.[4]

Moreover, since the analysis of these different contracts is very similar, for simplicity we shall concentrate on checking institutions with demand liabilities. This means that the institution contracts to convert deposits on demand into government notes (or currency). This possibility of conversion would induce banks to hold some of their assets in currency.

Various considerations would determine the appropriate reserve ratio: type of depositors, stage of the business cycle, investment opportunities, etc. The appropriate reserve ratio in turn determines the amount of deposits that can be created. Let me emphasize that the necessity of converting deposits into government notes leads to a finite nominal value of deposits, and hence to a finite price level.

One criticism of this free banking proposal is concerned with shifts in the desired ratio of currency to checking deposits. It is argued that even a relatively small increase in the desired ratio of currency to deposits will have serious depressive effects. Since a serious multiple contraction in checking deposits will result, I do not deny that there may be some depressive effect from this source but its magnitude and interpretation are subject to the following comments:

1. If the shift is generally expected to be temporary, banks will temporarily shift below their normal reserve ration. This is why seasonal shifts will not have significant depressive effects. More generally, by eliminating legal reserve requirements, one eliminates most of the inflexibilities caused by this requirement. Under my proposal a bank is free to alter its reserve ratio if circumstances dictate, and circumstances will so dictate when temporary shifts into currency take place.
2. If the change into currency is not clearly of a temporary kind, banks will adjust in other directions; for example, they will raise the interest paid on checking deposits. Increasing the return on deposits induces individuals to hold more deposits relative to currency; hence the equilibrium change in currency relative to deposits is smaller than the initial change. This makes the adjustment in checking deposits less than seemed necessary at first. The greater the elasticity of substitution between currency and deposits, the more important is the interest rate adjustment.[5]

(c) It is not denied that there may be some effect on the stock of 'money' and hence on economic activity when there is a shift between currency and checking deposits. But shifting between other short-term assets and currency will likewise have an effect on activity. For example, shifting from time deposits or from the granting of book credit affects the firms with these short-run liabilities. Their cash reserves will be generally only a small fraction of their total short-run liabilities. If their creditors demand cash their reserves will be run down, and to some extent this probably will force them to contract their lending (or spending as the case may be). Consequently there will be depressive effects on income and employment.

So it would seem that individuals who are worried by the ill effects of shifts between currency and checking deposits must likewise be worried by the ill effects of a shift between currency and other short-run assets. Any proposal to curtail or control the former must, to be logical, be applicable to the latter. However, at this point it may be argued that there is an important difference in degree; namely, that checking deposits are a much better substitute for currency than other short-run assets. Thus random forces impinging on the relative desirability of currency relative to checking deposits cause relatively large shifts in the desired ratio of checking deposits and currency. The greater substitutability may be granted, but it does not necessarily follow that the changes in the equilibrium ratio of currency to checking deposits are larger than the changes between the equilibrium ratios of currency and other assets. This should be clear from the footnote above: the reason is that small changes in the interest rate paid to depositors will greatly affect the supply of currency to banks, and thus a given shift to the left in the supply curve will affect bank reserves much less than the reserves of firms producing assets that are poor substitutes for currency. Therefore it seems that the substitutability argument is not a reason for putting checking deposits into a special category.

(d) It is argued that when an individual shifts between currency and checking deposits he merely wishes to alter the *form* in which his 'money' is held. But because of fractional reserve banking this shift affects the total stock of 'money,' and hence prices and employment. Since the latter changes affect other individuals, there is an argument based on the discrepancy between social and private costs for government control of the effects of this shift. Let it be noted, however, that shifts between currency and other short-run assets have the same kind of effect. More generally, any shift from goods or debt into currency imposes, through the multiplier or velocity mechanisms, social costs that are not completely borne by those doing the shifting. This, indeed, is the major argument for active government participation in fighting cyclical movements. It is not, in and of itself, reason for government intervention to prevent or control specific kinds of transactions. Indeed, for those who believe in general kinds of government intervention in combating depressions there are strong reasons against this kind of specific action.

(e) It may be asked: would it not be wise to complement my proposal with a system of government insurance of bank deposits so that banking panics such as the one which occurred during the Great Depression would be prevented? This proposal initially seemed desirable but I finally decided to reject it. One of the motivations for my scheme is the desire to get the government out of the banking business. If government insured they would necessarily influence reserve ratios, lending activity, etc. The desire to avoid this partly led me to reject the inclusion of government insurance in the scheme. I was also influenced by the argument that if the government insures checking deposits, why don't they also insure time deposits, book credit, private insurance firms, and so on endlessly? Of course there still could be private insurance of bank deposits, but this would not prevent panics as well as government insurance could.[6]

Bank failures due to panicky attempts to convert deposits into currency are not very different from failures of other kinds of firms due to attempts by creditors to obtain cash. Both kinds will have adverse effects on the economy. Moreover, both tend to occur on a large scale at about the same time: sometimes bank failures precede and sometimes they follow failures of other firms. Both, moreover, seem to be symptoms as well as causes of generally bad times with large price declines and mass unemployment.

To keep both kinds within tolerable limits is the purpose of general countercyclical activity of the government. If banks or other firms fail without having any significant effect on economic activity, this is probably a healthy adjustment to unwise decisions. Once again there does not seem to be any rationale for specific kinds of intervention. An effective general countercyclical policy would probably be sufficient to prevent any large-scale panic.

Evaluation of the 100 Per Cent Reserve Schemes

The 100 per cent reserve scheme as usually presented provides for 100 per cent reserves against deposits subject to check, and government monopoly of the note issue. This means that substitution of currency for checking deposits has no effect on the sum of currency and checking deposits. One of the arguments for the 100 per cent reserve scheme has been that it takes government intervention out of the industry of lending and borrowing. Our scheme goes further than this and also takes government intervention out of the checking deposit industry. So on the grounds of minimizing direct government control our proposal is desirable.

The two proposals can be compared from another point of view. The 100 per cent scheme as usually presented means that there will be freely determined reserve ratios for all private obligations other than checking deposit liabilities. For checking deposits and for currency 100 per cent reserves would be required. Our scheme says that there will be freely determined reserve ratios for *all private* liabilities, and that note issue would be a government monopoly with, of course, 100 per cent reserves existing against them.

If the analysis above is correct it follows that there is little reason to draw the free reserve line before checking deposits. Neither from the point of view of controlling cyclical movements nor from the point of view of conserving resources used in transactions (i.e., controlling 'counterfeiting' does it seem wise to treat checking deposits differently from other short-run assets. In order to conserve resources and prevent counterfeiting it does make sense to draw a distinction between notes and other liabilities and, accordingly, to establish a government monopoly of the note issue. Essentially this means that there will be 100 per cent reserves against notes. For the rest, however, it is best to use general countercyclical policy to combat depressions and inflations since there is no reason to interfere directly with the checking industry. If these arguments are accepted our proposal would seem to be definitely superior to the usual form of the 100 per cent reserve schemes. Either proposal seems much superior to the present intermediate position.

Notes

1. The appropriate countercyclical policy will not be discussed much in this paper. My own preferences are for a two-part policy: an automatic scheme like the stable budget plan if a price or employment index remains within say 10 per cent of desired levels; open-market operations or some other discretionary policy to supplement the automatic scheme when the index moves outside this band. Discretionary policies are less destabilizing the larger in magnitude and duration are the cyclical movements being combated.
2. This assumes that there is competition in the note-issuing industry. If there were monopoly the equilibrium would be a moving one with prices rising at a constant rate per unit time.
3. There still is a problem of preventing counterfeiting of government notes. But as our experience shows this is not a major problem. If it was, this would be a telling argument against a fiat currency. To put this in other words, counterfeiting under these circumstances would virtually reduce a fiat currency to a pure commodity currency.
4. However, note that a bank which fails has, to some extent, counterfeited deposits. This aspect of 'counterfeiting' will be discussed more fully later on.
5. More generally it also depends on the elasticity of demand for loans from banks. For example,

let $D(P)$ be the bank's demand for reserves from the public as a function of the cost P per unit of the reserves, $S(P,u)$ be the supply of reserves, and u be a shift parameter, with $\partial S/\partial u < 0$. Competitive equilibrium exists if $D(P) = S(P,u)$. Let us differentiate the equilibrium conditions with respect to u. Then

$$\frac{\partial D}{\partial P}\frac{\partial P}{\partial u} = \frac{\partial S}{\partial P}\frac{\partial P}{\partial u} + \partial S/\partial u,$$

or

$$\frac{\partial P}{\partial u} = \frac{\dfrac{\partial S}{\partial u}}{\dfrac{\partial D}{\partial P} - \dfrac{\partial S}{\partial P}}$$

This formula implies that the change in bank reserves as a result of a shift to the left of the supply curve is smaller the more inelastic is the demand and the more elastic is the supply of these reserves.

6. Under a gold standard with fractional reserve banking, government and private insurance firms would have access to the same amount of gold; namely, ultimately the world stock. Under a fiat currency the government has access to unlimited amounts of paper currency, and private insurance firms are limited to the amount in circulation. Hence with a fiat currency system government insurance could be more effective in preventing panics than private insurance could be.

[3]

THE EVOLUTION OF A FREE BANKING
SYSTEM

GEORGE A. SELGIN and LAWRENCE H. WHITE*

The institutional features of models of unregulated monetary systems have often been arbitrarily and implausibly assumed. This paper instead provides realistic grounding for important features by constructing a logical evolutionary account of free banking. Sophisticated and orderly arrangements are shown to emerge from competition and the pursuit of less costly methods of payment. The emergence of standardized commodity money is followed by the development, in turn, of basic money-transfer banking, easily transferable bank liabilities, and clearinghouses. The features of an evolved free banking system differ from those assumed in recent models of competitive payments systems.

I. INTRODUCTION

In recent years monetary theorists have produced a substantial literature on the properties of a completely unregulated monetary system.[1] Their assumptions concerning the institutional features of such a system have ranged from the proliferation of numerous competing private fiat currencies at one extreme to the complete disappearance of money at the other. While these assumptions have generated clear-cut and provocative conclusions, their plausibility or realism in light of historical experience is open to serious doubt. These doubts may unfortunately suggest that any discussion of an unregulated monetary system (or "free banking" system) must be tenuous and highly speculative. This paper shows, to the contrary, that important institutional features of a free banking system, in particular the nature of payment media, can be realistically grounded by constructing a logical explanation of its evolution.

The method of logical evolutionary explanation has previously been applied to monetary institutions by Hicks [1967] and Menger [1892], among others. The present study integrates and extends work along their lines. The method is employed here in the belief that it has been unduly neglected in recent work, not that it is the only valid method for theoretically explaining institutional arrangements. The more standard method of building explicit transactions costs or informational imperfections or asymmetries into an optimization model has unquestionably been useful in the task of explaining why banks exist as intermediaries (Santomero [1984, 577–80] surveys this literature).

* The authors are indebted to the Institute for Humane Studies for the opportunity to work together on this article, and to Chris Fauvelais, David Glasner, Israel Kirzner, Hu McCulloch, Mario Rizzo, Kurt Schuler, Richard J. Sweeney, and anonymous referees for useful comments. White's research is supported by the Scaife Foundation. The usual disclaimer applies.

1. See for example Black [1970], Klein [1974], Hayek [1978], Fama [1980], Greenfield and Yeager [1983], Wallace [1983], White [1984b], O'Driscoll [1985a], and Yeager [1985].

439

Our investigation derives arrangements that would have arisen had state intervention never occurred. The results should therefore help to identify the degree to which features of current monetary and banking institutions are rooted in market forces and the degree to which they have grown out of regulatory intervention. Such information gives important clues about how future deregulation would modify institutions. We show that sophisticated monetary arrangements, whose institutional features are described, emerge in the absence of regulation. No strong claims are advanced here about the welfare properties of these arrangements.[2] We aim to establish the most credible path for unrestricted monetary evolution, but certainly not the only possible path. Economists who find other institutional outcomes more plausible for an unregulated system will, we hope, similarly try to explain why and how those outcomes would emerge.

The evolution of a free banking system, following the emergence of standardized commodity money, proceeds through three stages. These are, first, the development of basic money-transfer services which substitute for the physical transportation of specie; second, the emergence of easily assignable and negotiable bank demand liabilities (inside money); and third, the development of arrangements for the routine exchange ("clearing") of inside monies among rival banks. The historical time separating these stages is not crucial. The path of development, rather than being one of steady progress as pictured here, may in practice involve false starts or creative leaps. What is essential is that each stage is the logical invisible-hand outgrowth of the circumstances that preceded it. In other words, each successive step in the process of evolution originates in individuals' discovery of new ways to promote their self-interest, with the outcome an arrangement at which no individual consciously aims.

II. COMMODITY MONEY

Because the use of money logically and historically precedes the emergence of banking firms, we begin with an account of the origin of money. Our account follows that of Menger [1892], who furnished an invisible-hand explanation, consistent with historical and anthropological evidence, of how money originated as a product of undesigned or spontaneous evolution.[3] Menger's theory shows that no state intervention is necessary in order to establish a basic medium of exchange or unit of account. It also provides a useful prototype for our explanations of how subsequent banking institutions evolve in spontaneous fashion.

In premonetary society, traders relying upon barter initially offer goods in exchange only for other goods directly entering their consumption or household production plans. The number of bargains struck this way is small, owing to

2. We have each made normative evaluations of free banking elsewhere: Selgin [1987, chs. 8–10]; White [1984a, ch. 5; 1984b].

3. See also Menger [1981, 260–62]. The same view appears in Carlisle [1901, 5], and Ridgeway [1892, 47]. A more recent version of Menger's theory is Jones [1976]. For a secondary account of Menger's theory see O'Driscoll [1985b].

SELGIN & WHITE: EVOLUTION OF FREE BANKING 441

the well-known problem of finding what Jevons termed a "double coincidence of wants." Before long some frustrated barterer realizes that he can increase his chances for success by adopting a two-stage procedure. He can trade his wares for some good, regardless of its direct usefulness to him, which will more easily find a taker among those selling what he ultimately wants. It follows that the earliest media of exchange are simply goods perceived to be in relatively widespread demand. The widening of demand for these things owing to their use as media of exchange reinforces their superior salability. Other traders eventually recognize the gains achieved by those using indirect exchange, and emulate them, even though they may be unaware of the reason for the advantages from using a medium of exchange. This emulation further enhances the acceptance of the most widely accepted media, elevating one or two goods above all others in salability. The snowballing of salability results in the spontaneous appearance of generally accepted media of exchange. Eventually traders throughout an economy converge on using a single commodity as a generally accepted medium of exchange, i.e., as money.

Historical evidence on primitive monies indicates that cattle were often the most frequently exchanged commodity, and that a standardized "cow" was the earliest unit of account. Cattle were a poor general medium of exchange, however, because of their relative nontransportability and nonuniformity. Not until the discovery of metals and of methods for working them did the use of money replace barter widely.[4] According to Jacques Melitz [1974, 95], common attributions of moneyness to primitive media, especially nonmetallic "moneys" (with the exception of cowries in China), warrant skepticism because many of these media (e.g., the Yap stones of Melanesia) do not meet any reasonably strict definition of money.

The emergence of coinage can also be explained as a spontaneous development, an unplanned result of merchants' attempts to minimize the necessity for assessing and weighing amounts of commodity money received in exchange. Merchants may at first mark irregular metallic nuggets or pieces after having assessed their quality. A merchant recognizing his own or another's mark can then avoid the trouble and cost of reassessment. Marking gives way to stamping or punching, which eventually leads to specialists' making coins in their modern form. Techniques for milling coin edges and covering the entire surface with type provide safeguards against clipping and sweating and so allow coinage to serve as a guarantee of weight as well as of quality. Arthur R. Burns [1927a, 297–304; 1927b, 59] has illustrated this process with evidence from ancient Lydia, where coins of electrum (a naturally occurring silver-gold alloy) coins came into early use.

Absent state interference, coinage is a private industry encompassing various competing brands. Under competition coins are valued according to bullion content plus a premium equal to the marginal cost of mintage. The demand

---

4. See Menger [1981, 263–66]; Ridgeway [1892, 6–11]; and Burns [1927a, 286–88]. On some alleged nonmetallic monies of primitive peoples see Quiggin [1963].

for readily exchangeable coins promotes the emergence of standard weights and fineness. Nonstandard coins must circulate at a discount because of the extra computational burden they impose, so that their production is unprofitable. States seem to have monopolized coinage early in history, but not by outcompeting private mints. Rather, the evidence suggests that state coinage monopolies were regularly established by legal compulsion and for reasons of propaganda and monopoly profit. State-minted coins functioned both as a symbol of rule and as a source of profits from shaving, clipping, and seignorage. For these reasons coinage became a state function throughout the world by the end of the seventh century [Burns 1927a, 308; 1927b, 78].

III. BANKING FIRMS

The counting and transporting of coin entail considerable inconvenience. Traders, particularly those frequently making large or distant exchanges, will naturally seek lower-cost means of transferring ownership of money. One likely locus for development of such means is the market where local coins are exchanged for foreign coins. Standard coins may differ interlocally even in the absence of local state interventions because of geographic diseconomies in reputation building for mints. A coin-exchange market then naturally arises with interlocal trade. A trader who uses a money changer must initially count and carry in local coin each time he wants to acquire foreign coin, or vice versa. He can reduce his costs by establishing a standing account balance, to build up at his convenience and draw upon as desired. The money changer's inventories equip him to provide such accounts, which constitute demand deposits, and even to allow overdrafts. These deposits may originally be non-transferable. But it will soon be apparent, where one customer withdraws coins in order to pay a recipient who redeposits them with the same exchange banker, that the transfer is more easily made at the banker's place of business, or more easily yet by persuading the banker to make the transfer on his books without any handling of coins. Thus trading individuals come to keep money balances with agencies which can make payments by ledger-account transfers.

Money-transfer services of this sort, provided by money changers and bill brokers in twelfth century Genoa and at medieval trade fairs in Champagne, mark the earliest recorded forms of banking.[5] In time all the major European trading centers had "transfer banks," as Raymond de Roover [1974, 184] calls them; he comments that "deposit banking grew out of [money-changing] activity, because the money changers developed a system of local payments by book transfer." In our view, however, the taking of deposits on at least a small scale logically *precedes* the development of book-transfer methods of payment.

Money-transfer services may also develop in connection with deposits made for safekeeping rather than for money changing. The well-known story of the

---

5. See Usher [1943], de Roover [1974, chs. 4–5], and Lopez [1979].

origins of goldsmith banking in seventeenth century England illustrates this development. Wealthy persons may temporarily lodge commodity money with scriveners, goldsmiths, mintmasters, and other reputable vault-owners for safe-keeping. Coin and bullion thus lodged must be physically withdrawn and transferred for its owner to use it as a means of payment. Exchanges in which the recipient redeposits it in the same vault (like redeposits with a money changer or bill broker) create obvious advantages in making the transfer at the vault, or better yet in simply notifying the vault's custodian to make the transfer on his books. In England, scriveners were the earliest pioneers in the banking trade; in Stuart times they were almost entirely displaced by goldsmith bankers. English goldsmiths evidently became transfer bankers during the seventeenth century, when they "began to keep a 'running cash' for the convenience of merchants and country gentlemen" [de Roover 1974, 83–4]. The confiscation by Charles I of gold deposited for safekeeping at the royal mint ended that institution's participation in the process of banking development. Private mints, had they been permitted, would have been logical sites for early banking activities.

Transfer banking is not connected with intermediation between borrowers and lenders when the banker acts strictly as a warehouseman, giving deposit receipts which are regular warehouse dockets. The strict warehouse banker is a bailee rather than a debtor to his depositors and can make loans only out of his personal wealth. Two conditions make it possible, however, to take advantage of the interest income available from lending out depositors' balances, even while satisfying depositors' desire to have their funds withdrawable on demand: (1) money is fungible, which allows a depositor to be repaid in coin and bullion not identical to that he brought in, and (2) the law of large numbers with random withdrawals and deposits makes a fractional reserve sufficient to meet actual withdrawal demands with high probability even though any single account may be removed without notice. (Interestingly, these conditions may also be met in the warehousing of standard-quality grain, so that fractional reserve "banking" can likewise develop there, as Williams [1984] has shown.) The lending of depositors' balances is an innovation that taps a vast new source of loanable funds and alters fundamentally the relationship of the banker to his depositor customers.

Historically in England, according to Richards [1965, 223], "the bailee . . . developed into the debtor of the depositor; and the depositor became an investor who loaned his money . . . for a consideration." Money "warehouse receipts" became merely ready promissory notes. W. R. Bisschop [1910, 50n] reports that English warehouse bankers had become intermediaries by the time of Charles II (1660–85): "Any deposit made in any other shape than ornament was looked upon by them as a free loan." Competition for deposits prompted the payment of interest on deposits, and the attractiveness of interest on safe and accessible deposits in turn apparently made the practice of depositing widespread among all ranks of people [Powell 1966, 56–57].

IV. TRANSFERABLE INSTRUMENTS

Under these circumstances the effective money supply obviously becomes greater than the existing stock of specie alone. The most important banking procedures and devices, however, have yet to develop. Many purchases are still made with actual coin. Bank depositors, in order to satisfy changing needs for money at hand, make frequent withdrawals from and deposits into their bank balances. These actions may in the aggregate largely cancel out through the law of large numbers. But they require the banks to hold greater precautionary commodity money reserves, and consequently to maintain a larger spread between deposit and loan rates of interest, than is necessary when payments practices become more sophisticated. Greater sophistication comes with the emergence of negotiable bank instruments, able to pass easily in exchange from one person to another, which replace coin and nonnegotiable deposit receipts in transactions balances. The use of coin is also superceded by the development of more efficient means for the bank-mediated transfer of deposits.

Assignability and negotiability may develop through several steps. Initially the assignment of deposited money (whether "warehoused" or entrusted to the banker for lending at interest) by the depositor to another party may require the presence of all three parties to the exchange or their attorneys. Money "warehouse receipts" (or promissory notes) and running deposit balances cannot be assigned by the owner's endorsement without the banker acting as witness. An important innovation is the development of bank-issued promissory notes transferable by endorsement. Assignable notes in turn give way to fully negotiable bank notes assigned to no one in particular but instead payable to the bearer on demand. A parallel development is the nonnegotiable check enabling the depositor to transfer balances to a specific party, in turn giving way to the negotiable check which can be repeatedly endorsed or made out "to cash."[6] Thus the modern forms of inside money—redeemable bearer bank notes and checkable deposits—are established. Once this stage is reached it is not difficult for bankers to conceive what Hartley Withers [1920, 24] has called "the epoch-making notion"—in our view it is only an incremental step— of giving inside money not only to depositors of metal but also to borrowers of money. The use of inside money enhances both customer and bank profits, so that only the possible reluctance of courts to enforce obligations represented by assigned or bearer paper stands in the way of its rapid development.

In England bearer notes were first recognized during the reign of Charles II, about the time when warehouse banking was giving way to fractional reserve transfer banking. At first the courts gave their grudging approval to the growing practice of repeated endorsement of promissory notes. Then after some controversy, fully negotiable notes were recognized by Act of Parliament. In France, Holland, and Italy during the sixteenth century merchants' checks

---

6. On the historical development of bank notes and checks in Europe see Usher [1943, 7–8, 23].

SELGIN & WHITE: EVOLUTION OF FREE BANKING   445

"drawn in blank" circulated within limited circles and may have cleared the way for the appearance of bank notes [Usher 1943, 189; Richards 1965, 46, 225].

V. REGULAR NOTE-EXCHANGE

Further economies in the use of commodity money require more complete circulation of inside money in place of commodity money, and more complete development of bank note and check clearing facilities to reduce the need for commodity money reserves. It is relatively straightforward to show that bankers and other agents pursuing their self-interest are indeed led to improve the acceptability of inside money and the efficiency of banking operations.

At this stage, although bank notes are less cumbersome than coin, and checkable deposits are both convenient for certain transactions and interest paying, some coin still remains in circulation. Consumers trust a local bank's notes more than a distant bank's notes because they are more aware of the local notes' likelihood of being honored and more familiar with their appearance (hence less prone to accepting forgeries). It follows that the cost to a bank of building a reputation for its issues—particularly regarding note convertibility—is higher in places further from the place of issue and redemption. The establishment of a network of bank branches for redemption is limited by transportation and communication costs. In the early stages of banking development the par circulation of every bank's notes and checks is therefore geographically relatively limited.[7] People who generally hold the inside money of a local bank but who do business in distant towns must either take the trouble to redeem some of their holdings for gold and incur the inconvenience of transporting coin, or suffer a loss in value on their notes by carrying them to a locale where they are accepted only at a discount, if at all. (The alternative practice of keeping on hand notes from each locality they deal with is likely to be prohibitively costly in terms of foregone interest.) In general, a brand of inside money will initially be used only for transactions in the vicinity of the issuer, and coin will continue to be held alongside notes of like denomination. The use of commodity money in circulation requires banks to hold commodity reserves greater than those required by the transfer of inside money, because the withdrawal of commodity money for spending generates more volatile reserve outflows than the spending of notes or deposits.

In this situation, profit opportunities arise which prompt actions leading to more general acceptance of particular inside monies. The discounting of notes outside the neighborhood of the issuing bank's office creates an arbitrage opportunity when the par value of notes (i.e., their face redemption value in commodity money) exceeds the price at which they can be purchased for commodity money or local issues in a distant town plus (secularly falling) transaction and transportation costs. As interlocal trade grows, "note brokers"

---

7. See White (1984a, 84–85) for nineteenth century views on geographic diseconomies in note circulation.

with specialized knowledge of distant banks can make a business, just as retail foreign currency brokers do today, of buying discounted nonlocal notes and transporting them to their par circulation areas or reselling them to travelers bound for those areas. Competition eventually reduces note discounts to the level of transaction and transportation costs plus a factor for redemption risk. By accepting the notes of unfamiliar banks at minimal commission rates, brokers unintentionally increase the general acceptability of notes, and promote their use in place of commodity money.

To this point we have implicitly assumed that banks refuse to accept one another's notes. This is not unreasonable; banks have as many reasons as other individuals do to refuse notes unfamiliar to them or difficult to redeem. They have in addition a further incentive for refusing to accept notes from rival banks, which is that by doing so they help to limit the acceptability of these notes, thereby enhancing the demand for their own issues. To cite just one historical illustration of this, the Bank of Scotland and the Royal Bank of Scotland—the first two banks of issue located in Edinburgh—refused to accept the notes of "provincial" banks of issue for a number of years (see Checkland [1975, 126]).

Nevertheless note brokerage presents opportunities for profit to bankers. Banks can out-compete other brokers because, unlike other brokers, they can issue their own notes (or deposit balances) to purchase "foreign" notes and need not hold costly till money. Each bank has an additional incentive to accept rival notes: larger interest earnings. If the notes acquired are redeemed sooner than the notes issued, interest-earning assets can be purchased and held in the interim. This profit from "float" can be continually renewed. In other words, a bank can maintain a permanently larger circulation of its own notes by continually replacing other notes with its own, and correspondingly can hold more earning assets than it otherwise could. If other banks are simultaneously replacing Bank A's notes with their own, there may be no absolute increase in A's circulation compared to the situation in which no bank accepts rival notes. But there will be an increase compared to Bank A not accepting, given whatever policies rivals are following, so that the incentive remains. (We argue below that in fact an indirect consequence of *other* banks' par acceptance of Bank A notes will be an absolute increase in A-note-holding in place of specie-holding.) Where transaction and transportation costs and risks are low enough, competition for circulation will narrow the brokerage fee to zero, that is, will lead the banks to general acceptance of one another's notes at par. The development of par acceptance by this route does not require that the banks explicitly and mutually agree to such a policy.

An alternative scenario, which assumes strategic behavior by the banks, leads to the same result. A bank may aggressively purchase foreign notes in the markets, and then suddenly return large quantities to their issuers for redemption in commodity money, hoping to force an unprepared issuer to suspend payments. The aggressor hopes to gain market share by damaging a rival's reputation or even forcing it into liquidation. These tactics, historically

known as "note-picking" and "note-duelling," initially provoke the other issuers to respond in kind. Collecting and redeeming the first bank's notes not
only returns the damage, but helps replenish the other banks' reserves. Purchasing its rivals' notes at par allows a bank to collect them in greater quantities,
and may therefore be adopted. (Arbitrage-redemption of notes paid out pre-
cludes paying a price above par.) In the long run, nonaggression among banks
should emerge, being less costly for all sides. Note-picking and note-duelling
are costly and ineffectual ways to promote circulation when others do likewise.
Banks thus find it profitable to take rivals' notes only as these are brought to
them for deposit or exchange, and to return the collected notes to their issuers
promptly in exchange for commodity money reserves. This result is contrary
to Eugene Fama's [1983, 19] suggestion that note-duelling will persist indefinitely. It is an example of the "tit for tat" strategy, as discussed by Robert
Axelrod [1984], proving dominant in a repeated-game setting.[8] Again, no
explicitly negotiated pact is necessary. It only takes a single bank acting without
cooperation from other banks to nudge the rest towards par acceptance (zero
brokerage fees) as a defensive measure to maintain their reserves and circulation.

In New England at the beginning of the nineteenth century the Boston
banks gave the nudge that put the whole region—with its multitude of "country" banks of issue far removed from the city—on a par-acceptance basis
[Trivoli 1979]. In Scotland the Royal Bank, when it opened for business in
1727, immediately began accepting at par the notes of the Bank of Scotland,
at that time its only rival, and instigated a short-lived note duel. One response
by the Bank of Scotland, later widely adopted, is notable: the Bank inserted
a clause into its notes giving it the option (which it did not normally exercise)
of delaying redemption for six months, in which event it would pay a bonus
amounting to 5 percent per annum [Checkland 1975, 60, 67–8]. In both places
established banks, even after they had begun accepting each other's notes at
par, sometimes refused to take the notes of new entrants. They soon changed
their policies because the new banks that accepted and redeemed their notes
were draining their reserves, while the established banks could not offset this
without engaging in the same practice.

Banks that accept other banks' notes at par improve the market for their
own notes and, unintentionally, for the notes that they accept. This makes a
third scenario possible: if two banks both understand these circulation gains,
they may explicitly enter a mutual par-acceptance arrangement. Others will
emulate them, leading to general par acceptance. This explanation, previously
offered by White [1984a, 19–21], assumes slightly more knowledge on the part
of banks than the first two scenarios. Historical evidence of such explicit
arrangements in Scotland is provided by Munn [1975].

Statistics from Boston dramatically illustrate the mutual circulation gains

8. An example of the explicit adoption of "tit for tat" by an exhausted note-duelling bank is
given by Munn [1981, 24].

from acceptance arrangements. From 1824 to 1833 the note circulation of the Boston banks increased 57 percent, but the Boston circulation of country banks increased 148 percent, despite the Boston banks' intent to drive the country banks out of business [Lake 1947, 186; Trivoli 1979, 10–12]. There is room for all banks to gain because the spread of par acceptance makes inside money more attractive to hold relative to commodity money. Since notes from one town are now accepted in a distant town at par, there is no longer good reason to lug around commodity money. As par note acceptance developed in Scotland, Canada, and New England—places where note issue was least restricted—during the nineteenth century, gold virtually disappeared from circulation. (Small amounts of gold coin were still used in these places at least in part because of restrictions upon the issue of "token" coin and of small denomination notes. In an entirely free system, such restrictions would not exist.) In England and the rest of the United States, where banking (and note issue in particular) were less free, gold remained in circulation.

Even the complete displacement of commodity money in circulation by inside money does not, however, exhaust the possibilities for economizing on commodity money. Much of the specie formerly used in circulation to settle exchanges outside the banks may still be needed to settle clearings among them. Banks can substantially reduce their prudentially required holdings of commodity money by making regular note exchanges which allow them to offset their mutual obligations. Only net clearings rather than gross clearings are then settled in commodity money. The probability of any given-sized reserve loss in a given period is accordingly reduced (by the law of large numbers) and each bank can prudently reduce its ratio of reserves to demand liabilities.

The gains to be had from rationalization of note exchange are illustrated by the provincial Scottish banks before 1771, which practiced par acceptance without regular exchange. Note duelling among these banks was not uncommon [Leslie 1950, 8–9; Munn 1981, 23–24], and to guard against redemption raids they had to keep substantial reserves. Munn's figures [1981, 141] show that their reserves during this period were typically above 10 percent of total liabilities. This contrasts with reserve ratios of around 2 percent that were typical after note clearings became routine. The advantages of regular note exchange are great enough to have secured its eventual adoption in every historical instance of relatively free plural note issue.

VI. CLEARINGHOUSES

The most readily made arrangements for note exchange are bilateral. In a system of more than two issuers, however, multilateral note exchange provides even greater economies. Reserve-holding economies result from the offsetting of claims that would otherwise be settled in specie. Multilateral clearing also allows savings in time and transportation costs by allowing all debts to be settled in one place and during one meeting rather than in numerous scattered meetings.

SELGIN & WHITE: EVOLUTION OF FREE BANKING   449

The institutional embodiment of multilateral note and deposit exchange, the clearinghouse, may evolve gradually from simpler note-exchange arrangements. For example, the note-exchange agents of banks A and B may accidentally meet each other at the counter of bank C. The greater the number of banks exchanging bilaterally, the less likely it is that such an encounter could be avoided. It would be natural for these two agents to recognize the savings in simple time and shoe-leather costs from settling their own exchange then and there, and from agreeing to do it again next time out, and then regularly. From a set of three pairwise settlements around one table it is not a large step toward the computation and settlement of combined net clearing balances. Once the advantages of this become clear to management, particularly the reserve holding economies which may not have concerned the note porters, the institution will spread. Fourth, fifth, and subsequent banks may join later meetings. Or similar regular few-sided exchanges may be formed among other groups of banks, either independently or by one of the first three banks, whose meetings are later combined with the meetings of the original group. Eventually all the banks within an economy will be connected through one or a small number of clearinghouses.

The histories of the best-known early clearinghouses, in London, Edinburgh, and New York, all conform to this general pattern. Gibbons [1858, 292] reports that in New York the impetus for change from numerous bilateral exchanges to combined multilateral exchange came from note porters who "crossed and re-crossed each other's footsteps constantly." Among the London check porters, as related by Bisschop [1910, 160], "occasional encounters developed into daily meetings at a certain fixed place. At length the bankers themselves resolved to organize these meetings on a regular basis in a room specially reserved for this purpose."

The settlement of interbank obligations is initially made by physical transfer of commodity money at the conclusion of clearing sessions. Banks will soon find it economical to settle instead by means of transferable reserve accounts kept on the books of the clearinghouse, echoing the original development of transfer banking. These accounts may be deposits or equity shares denominated in currency units. As a transfer bank, the clearinghouse need not hold 100 percent reserves, and can safely pay its members a return (net of operating costs) by holding safe earning assets. This development reduces a member bank's cost of holding reserves, but does not eliminate it because alternative assets yield a higher return. Unless regulated directly by the clearinghouse, a bank's reserve ratio is determined by precautionary liquidity considerations depending mainly on the volume and volatility of net clearings and the clearinghouse penalty for reserve deficiency (see Baltensperger [1980, 4–9] and Santomero [1984, 584–86]).

Once established, a clearinghouse may serve several purposes beyond the economical exchange and settlement of interbank obligations. It can become, in the words of James G. Cannon [1908, 97], "a medium for united action among the banks in ways that did not exist even in the imagination of those who were instrumental in its inception." One task the clearinghouse may take on is to serve as a credit information bureau for its members; by pooling their records, banks can learn whether loan applicants have had bad debts in the past or are overextended to other banks at present, and can then take appropriate precautions [Cannon 1910, 135]. Through the clearinghouse banks can also share information concerning bounced checks, forgeries, and the like.

The clearinghouse may also police the soundness of each member bank in order to assure the other member banks that notes and deposits are safe to accept for clearing. As part of this function, banks may be required to furnish financial statements and may have their books audited by clearinghouse examiners. The Chicago clearinghouse insisted on statements as early as 1867, and in 1876 gained the right to carry out comprehensive examinations whenever desired, to determine any member's financial condition [James 1938, 372–73, 499]. Regular examinations began in 1906 [Cannon 1910, 138–39]. Other clearinghouses, such as the Suffolk Bank and the Edinburgh clearinghouse, took their bearings mainly from the trends of members' clearing balances and traditional canons of sound banking practice. Those two clearinghouses enjoyed such high repute as certifying agencies that to be taken off their lists of members in good standing meant a serious loss in reputation and hence business for an offending bank [Trivoli 1979, 20; Graham 1911, 59].

It is possible that a clearinghouse may attempt to organize collusive agreements on interest rates, exchange rates, and fee schedules for its members. However, rates inconsistent with the results of competition would tend to break down under unregulated conditions, for the standard reason that secretly underbidding a cartel has concentrated benefits and largely external costs. A clear example of this comes from Scottish experience [Checkland 1975, 391–427]. The Edinburgh banks set up a committee in 1828 to set borrowing and lending rates. The Glasgow banks joined a new version of the committee in 1836, at which time it represented the preponderance of Scottish banks in number and in total assets. Though not a clearinghouse association itself, the committee had much the same membership as the Edinburgh clearinghouse. In spite of repeated formal agreements, the committee could not hold members to its recommended interest rates. Not until after entry to the industry was closed in 1844 did the agreements become at all effective.

Perhaps the most interesting of all the roles a clearinghouse may perform is to assist its members in times of crisis (see Cannon [1910, 24]). If a bank or group of banks is temporarily unable to pay its clearing balances, or if it experiences a run on its commodity money reserves, the clearinghouse can serve as a medium through which more liquid banks lend to less liquid ones. It provides the framework for an intermittent, short term credit market similar to the continuous federal funds market from which reserve-deficient American banks presently borrow. Another possible emergency function of clearinghouses is note issue. This function is called for when member banks are artificially restricted from issuing, as for example U.S. banks were by the bond collateral requirements of the National Banking Acts, so that the banks are not able independently to fulfill all of their depositors' requests for hand-to-hand means of payment. Currency shortages occurred frequently in the United States during the second half of the nineteenth century, and clearinghouses helped to fill the void caused by deficient note issues of the National Banks.[9]

VII. THE MATURE FREE BANKING SYSTEM

We have now reached the stage of mature development of a stylized free banking system, insofar as historical evidence illuminates its likely structural and operational characteristics. Evidence on industry structure from Scotland, Canada, Sweden, and elsewhere indicates that unregulated development does not produce natural monopoly, but rather an industry consisting of numerous competing banking firms, most having widespread branches, all of which are joined through one or more clearinghouses. In Scotland there were nineteen banks of issue in 1844, the final year of free entry. The largest four banks supplied 46.7 percent of the note circulation. In addition to their head offices the banks had 363 branch offices, 43.5 percent of which were owned by the largest (measured again by note issue) four banks.[10]

The banks in the mature system issue inside money in the shape of paper notes and demand deposit accounts (checkable either by paper or electronic means) that circulate routinely at par. Banks may also issue redeemable token coins, more durable but lighter and cheaper, to take the place of full-bodied coins as small change. Each bank's notes and tokens bear distinct brand-names identification marks and are issued in the denominations the public is most willing to hold. Because of the computational costs that would be involved in each transfer, interest is not likely to accrue on commonly used denominations of bank notes or tokens, contrary to the hypothesis of Neil Wallace [1983] that all currency would bear interest under laissez faire.[11] Checkable accounts, however, provide a competitive yield reflecting rates available on interest-earning assets issued outside the banking system.

Checkable bank accounts are most familiarly structured as demand deposits, i.e., liabilities having a predetermined payoff payable on demand. An important reason for this structure is that historically a debt contract has been easier for the depositor to monitor and enforce than an equity contract which ties the account's payoff to the performance of a costly-to-observe asset portfolio. The predetermined payoff feature, however, raises the possibility of insolvency and consequently of a run on the bank if depositors fear that the last in line will receive less than a full payoff. One method of forestalling runs that may prevail in an unregulated banking system is the advertised holding of a large equity cushion, either on the bank's books or off them in the form of extended liability for bank shareholders. If this method were inadequate to assure depositors, banks might provide an alternative solution by linking checkability

9. See Cannon [1908], Andrew [1908], Smith [1936], Timberlake [1984], and Gorton [1985a].
10. These figures are based on data in White [1984a, 37]. A recent econometric study of economies of scale in banking is Benston, Hanweck, and Humphrey [1982].
11. See White [1984a, 8–9; 1987].

to equity or mutual-fund-type accounts with postdetermined rather than pre-determined payoffs. The obstacles to such accounts (asset-monitoring and en-forcement costs) have been eroded over the centuries by the emergence of easy-to-observe assets, namely publicly traded securities. Insolvency is ruled out for a balance sheet without debt liabilities, and the incentive to redeem ahead of other account holders is eliminated. An institution that linked check-ability to equity accounts would operate like a contemporary money-market mutual fund, except that it would be directly tied into the clearing system (rather than having to clear via a deposit bank). Its optimal reserve holdings would be determined in the same way as those of a standard bank.

The assets of unregulated banks would presumably include short-term com-mercial paper, bonds of corporations and government agencies, and loans on various types of collateral. Without particular information on the assets avail-able in the economy, the structure of asset portfolios cannot be characterized in detail, except to say that the banks presumably strive to maximize the present value of their interest earnings, net of operating and liquidity costs, discounted at risk-adjusted rates. The declining probability of larger liquidity needs, and the trade-off at the margin between liquidity and interest yield, suggest a spectrum of assets ranging from perfectly liquid reserves, to highly liquid interest-earning investments (these constitute a "secondary reserve"), to less liquid higher-earning assets. Thus far, because the focus has been on monetary arrangements, the only bank liabilities discussed have been notes and checking accounts. Unregulated banks would almost certainly diversify on the liability side by offering a variety of time deposits and also travelers' checks. Some banks would probably become involved in such related lines of business as the production of bullion and token fractional coins, issue of credit cards, and management of mutual funds. Such banks would fulfill the con-temporary ideal of the "financial supermarket," with the additional feature of issuing bank notes.

Commodity money seldom if ever appears in circulation in the mature system, virtually all of it (outside numismatic collections) having been offered to the banks in exchange for inside money. Some commodity money will continue to be held by clearinghouses so long as it is the ultimate settlement asset among them. In the limit, if inter-clearinghouse settlements were made entirely with other assets (perhaps claims on a super-clearinghouse which itself holds negligible commodity money), and if the public were completely weaned from holding commodity money, the active demand for the old-fashioned money commodity would be wholly nonmonetary. The flow supply formerly sent to the mints would be devoted to industrial and other uses. Markets for those uses would determine the relative price of the commodity. The pur-chasing power of monetary instruments would continue to be fixed by the holder's contractual right (even if never exercised) to redeem them for phys-ically specified quantities of the money commodity. The problem of meeting any significant redemption request (e.g., a "run" on a bank) could be con-tractually handled, as it was historically during note-duelling episodes, by

SELGIN & WHITE: EVOLUTION OF FREE BANKING   453

invoking an "option clause" that allows the bank a specified period of time to gather the necessary commodity money while compensating the redeeming party for the delay. The clause need not (and historically did not) impair the par circulation of bank liabilities.

This picture of an unregulated banking system differs significantly in its institutional features from the visions presented in some of the recent literature on competitive payments systems. The system described here has assets fitting standard definitions of money. Banks and clearinghouses hold (except in the limit), and are contractually obligated to provide at request, high-powered reserve money (commodity money or deposits at the clearinghouse), and they issue debt liabilities (inside money) with which payments are generally made. These features contrast with the situation envisioned by Black [1970] and Fama [1980], in which "banks" hold no reserve assets and the payments mechanism operates by transferring equities or mutual fund shares unlinked to any money.

Bank reserves do not disappear in the evolution of a free banking system, as analyzed here, because the existence of bank liabilities that are promises to pay presupposes some more fundamental means of payment that is the thing promised. Individuals may forego actual redemption of promises, preferring to hold them instead of commodity money, so long as they believe that they will receive high-powered money if they ask for it. Banks, on the other hand, have a competitive incentive to redeem one another's liabilities regularly. So long as net clearing balances have a positive probability of being nonzero, reserves will continue to be held. In a system without reserve money it is not clear what would be used to settle clearing balances. In an evolved system, the scarcity of the money commodity and the costliness of holding reserves moreover serve to pin down the price level and to limit the quantity of inside money. In a moneyless system it is not clear what forces limit the expansion of payment media nor what pins down the price level. Nor are these things clear, at the other extreme, in a model of multiple competing fiat monies.[12]

Our analysis indicates that commodity-based money would persist in the absence of intervention, for the reason that the supreme salability of the particular money good is self-reinforcing. This result contradicts recent views (see Black [1970], Fama [1980], Greenfield and Yeager [1983], Yeager [1985]) that associate complete deregulation with the replacement of monetary exchange by a sophisticated form of barter. (To be sure, Greenfield and Yeager recognize that their system would be unlikely to emerge without deliberate action by government, particularly given a government-dominated monetary system as the starting point.) In a commodity-based-money economy, prices are stated in terms of a unit of the money commodity, so the question of using an abstract unit of account does not arise as it does in a sophisticated barter setting.[13] Even if actual commodity money were to disappear from reserves

12. Taub [1985] has shown that a dynamic inconsistency facing issuers in Klein's [1974] model will lead them to hyperinflate.

13. This point is emphasized by White [1984c]. For additional criticism of the Black-Fama-Yeager literature see O'Driscoll [1985a], Hoover [1985], and McCallum [1984].

and circulation, the media of exchange would not be "divorced" from the commodity unit of account; they would be linked by redeemability contracts. We can see no force severing this link. Contrary to Woolsey [1985], the renunciation of commodity redemption obligations is not compelled by economization of reserves. Thus we find no basis for the spontaneous emergence of a multicommodity monetary standard or of any pure fiat monetary standard, such as contemplated in works by Hall [1982], Woolsey [1984], Klein [1974], and Hayek [1978]. In short, unregulated banking would be much less radically unconventional, and much more akin to existing financial institutions than recent literature on the topic suggests.

One important contemporary financial institution is nonetheless missing from our account, namely the central bank. We find no market forces leading to the spontaneous emergence of a central bank, in contrast to the view of Charles Goodhart. (For this discussion a central bank is closely enough defined, following Goodhart [1985, 3–8], as an agency with two related powers: monetary policy, and external regulation of the banking system.) Goodhart [1985, 76] argues that the development of a central bank is "natural" because "the natural process of centralization of inter-bank deposits with leading commercial banks tends toward the development of a banks' club" which then needs an independent arbiter. But even on his own account the forces that historically promoted centralized inter-bank deposits were *not* "natural" in any laissez faire sense. They stemmed crucially from legal restrictions, particularly the awarding of a monopoly of note issue or the suppression of branch banking. Where no legislation inhibits the growth of branched banking firms with direct access to investment markets in the economy's financial center, and able to issue their own notes, it is not at all apparent that profit seeking compels any significant inter-bank depositing of reserves. Walter Bagehot [1873, 66–68] argued persuasively that "the natural system—that which would have sprung up if Government had let banking alone—is that of many banks of equal or not altogether unequal size" and that in such a system no bank "gets so much before the others that the others voluntarily place their reserves in its keeping." None of the relevant historical cases (Scotland, Canada, Sweden) shows any significant tendency toward inter-bank deposits.

We have seen that reserves do tend to centralize, on the other hand, in the clearinghouses. And clearinghouses, as Gorton [1985a, 277, 283; 1985b, 274] has recently emphasized, may take on functions that are today associated with national central banks: holding reserves for clearing purposes, establishing and policing safety and soundness standards for member banks, and managing panics should they arise. But these functional similarities should not be taken to indicate that clearinghouses have (or would have) freely evolved into central banks. The similarities instead reflect the pre-emption of clearinghouse functions by legally privileged banks or, particularly in the founding of the Federal Reserve System [Gorton 1985a, 277; Timberlake 1984], the deliberate nationalization of clearinghouse functions. Central banks have emerged from leg-

SELGIN & WHITE: EVOLUTION OF FREE BANKING   455

islation contravening, not complementing, spontaneous market developments.[14]

REFERENCES

Andrew, A. Piatt. "Substitutes for Cash in the Panic of 1907." *Quarterly Journal of Economics*, August 1908, 497–516.

Axelrod, Robert. *The Evolution of Cooperation*. New York: Basic Books, 1984.

Baltensperger, Ernst. "Alternative Approaches to the Theory of the Banking Firm." *Journal of Monetary Economics*, January 1980, 1–37.

Benston, George J., Gerald A. Hanweck, and David B. Humphrey. "Scale Economies in Banking: A Restructuring and Reassessment." *Journal of Money, Credit, and Banking*, November 1982, 435–54.

Black, Fischer. "Banking and Interest Rates in a World Without Money: The Effects of Uncontrolled Banking." *Journal of Bank Research*, Autumn 1970, 9–20.

Bisschop, W. R. *The Rise of the London Money Market, 1640–1826*. London: P. S. King & Son, 1910.

Bordo, Michael and Angela Redish. "Why Did the Bank of Canada Emerge in 1935?" Unpublished manuscript, 1985.

Burns, A. R. "Early Stages in the Development of Money and Coins," in *London Essays in Economics in Honour of Edwin Cannan*, edited by T. E. Gregory and Hugh Dalton. London: George Routledge & Sons, 1927a.

———. *Money and Monetary Policy in Early Times*. New York: Alfred E. Knopf, 1927b.

Cannon, James G. "Clearing Houses and the Currency," in *The Currency Problem and the Present Financial Situation*, edited by New York: Columbia University Press, 1908.

———. *Clearing Houses*. Washington: Government Printing Office, 1910.

Carlisle, William. *The Evolution of Modern Money*. London: Macmillan, 1901.

Checkland, S. G. *Scottish Banking: A History, 1695–1973*. Glasgow: Collins, 1975.

de Roover, Raymond. *Business, Banking, and Economic Thought in Late Medieval and Early Modern Europe*, edited by Julius Kirshner. Chicago: University of Chicago Press, 1974.

Fama, Eugene F. "Banking in the Theory of Finance." *Journal of Monetary Economics*, January 1980, 39–57.

———. "Financial Intermediation and Price Level Control." *Journal of Monetary Economics*, July 1983, 7–28.

Gibbons, J. S. *The Banks of New York, Their Dealers, the Clearing House, and the Panic of 1857*. New York: D. Appleton Co., 1858.

Goodhart, Charles. *The Evolution of Central Banks: A Natural Development?* London: Suntory-Toyota International Centre for Economics and Related Disciplines/London School of Economics and Political Science, 1985.

Gorton, Gary. "Clearinghouses and the Origin of Central Banking in the United States." *Journal of Economic History*, June 1985a, 277–83.

———. "Banking Theory and Free Banking History: A Review Essay." *Journal of Monetary Economics*, September 1985b, 267–76.

14. On the appearance of central banks in several nations see Smith [1936]; on Canada in particular see Bordo and Redish [1985].

456   ECONOMIC INQUIRY

Graham, William. *The One Pound Note in the History of Banking in Great Britain*, 2nd ed. Edinburgh: James Thin, 1911.

Greenfield, Robert L. and Leland B. Yeager. "A Laissez Faire Approach to Monetary Stability." *Journal of Money, Credit and Banking*, August 1983, 302–15.

Hall, Robert. "Explorations in the Gold Standard and Related Policies for Stabilizing the Dollar," in *Inflation Causes and Effects*, edited by Robert Hall. Chicago: University of Chicago Press for the National Bureau of Economic Research, 1982.

Hayek, F. A. *Denationalisation of Money*, 2nd ed. London: Institute of Economic Affairs, 1978.

Hicks, John. "The Two Triads, Lecture I," in *Critical Essays in Monetary Theory*. Oxford: Clarendon Press, 1967.

Hoover, Kevin D. "Causality and Invariance in the Money Supply Process." Doctoral dissertation, Oxford University, 1985.

James, F. Cyril. *The Growth of Chicago Banks*. New York: Harper & Brothers, 1938.

Jones, Robert. "The Origin and Development of Media of Exchange." *Journal of Political Economy*, November 1976, 757–75.

Klein, Benjamin. "The Competitive Supply of Money." *Journal of Money, Credit, and Banking*, November 1974, 423–53.

Lake, Wilfred S. "The End of the Suffolk System." *Journal of Economic History*, November 1947, 183–207.

Leslie, J. O. *The Note Exchange and Clearing House Systems*. Edinburgh: William Blackwood, 1950.

Lopez, Robert S. "The Dawn of Medieval Banking," in *The Dawn of Modern Banking*. New Haven: Yale University Press, 1979.

McCallum, Bennett T. "Bank Deregulation, Accounting Systems of Exchange, and the Unit of Account: A Critical Review." Carnegie-Rochester Conference Series on Public Policy, Autumn 1984, 13–45.

Melitz, Jacques. *Primitive and Modern Money*. Reading, MA: Addison-Wesley, 1974.

Menger, Carl. "The Origin of Money." *Economic Journal*, June 1892, 239–55.

————. *Principles of Economics* [1871]. New York: New York University Press, 1981.

Munn, Charles W. "The Origins of the Scottish Note Exchange." *Three Banks Review* 107, 1975, 45–60.

————. *The Scottish Provincial Banking Companies, 1747–1864*. Edinburgh: John Donald, 1981.

O'Driscoll, Gerald P., Jr. "Money in a Deregulated Financial System." *Economic Review*, Federal Reserve Bank of Dallas, May 1985a, 1–12.

————. "Money: Menger's Evolutionary Theory." Unpublished manuscript, Federal Reserve Bank of Dallas, 1985b.

Powell, Ellis T. *The Evolution of the Money Market, 1385–1915*. New York: Augustus M. Kelley, 1966.

Quiggin, A. Hingston. *A Survey of Primitive Money: The Beginning of Currency*. London: Methuen, 1963.

Richards, R. D. *The Early History of Banking in England*. New York: Augustus M. Kelley, 1965.

Ridgeway, William. *The Origin of Metallic Currency and Weight Standards*. Cambridge: Cambridge University Press, 1892.

Santomero, Anthony M. "Modeling the Banking Firm: A Survey." *Journal of Money, Credit, and Banking*, November 1984, 576–602.

Selgin, George A. *The Theory of Free Banking*. Totowa, N.J.: Rowman and Littlefield, 1987.

Smith, Vera C. *The Rationale of Central Banking*. London: P. S. King, 1936.

Taub, Bart. "Private Fiat Money with Many Suppliers." *Journal of Monetary Economics*, September 1985, 195–208.

Timberlake, R. H. "The Central Banking Role of Clearing-House Associations." *Journal of Money, Credit, and Banking*, February 1984, 1–15.

Trivoli, George. *The Suffolk Bank: A Study of a Free-Enterprise Clearing System*. London: Adam Smith Institute, 1979.

Usher, Abbott Payson. *The Early History of Deposit Banking in Mediterranean Europe*. Cambridge: Harvard University Press, 1943.

Wallace, Neil. "A Legal Restrictions Theory of the Demand for 'Money' and the Role of Monetary Policy." Federal Reserve Bank of Minneapolis *Quarterly Review*, Winter 1983, 1–7.

White, Lawrence H. *Free Banking in Britain: Theory, Experience, and Debate, 1800–1845*. Cambridge: Cambridge University Press, 1984a.

———. "Free Banking as an Alternative Monetary System," in *Money in Crisis*, edited by Barry N. Siegel. San Francisco: Pacific Institute, 1984b.

———. "Competitive Payments Systems and the Unit of Account." *American Economic Review*, September 1984c, 699–712.

———. "Accounting for Non-Interest-Bearing Currency: A Critique of the 'Legal Restrictions' Theory of Money." *Journal of Money, Credit and Banking*, 1987, forthcoming.

Williams, Jeffrey C. "Fractional Reserve Banking in Grain." *Journal of Money, Credit, and Banking*, November 1984, 488–96.

Withers, Hartley. *The Meaning of Money*. London: John Murray, 1920.

Woolsey, Warren W. "The Multiple Standard and the Means of Exchange." Unpublished manuscript, Talladega College, Talladega, Al, 1984.

———. "Competitive Payments Systems: Comment," Unpublished manuscript, Talladega College, 1985.

Yeager, Leland B. "Deregulation and Monetary Reform." *American Economic Review*, May 1985, 103–7.

[4]

Journal of Institutional and Theoretical Economics (JITE), 143 (1987), 435–456
Zeitschrift für die gesamte Staatswissenschaft

The Stability and Efficiency of Money Supply Under Free Banking

by

GEORGE A. SELGIN *

1. Introduction

Recent research has produced a spate of works re-examing the historical performance of more-or-less unregulated banking systems. [1] The overall conclusion of these studies is that the absence of regulation – and of centralized control in particular – did not result in the great monetary instability or other undesirable consequences that conventional thinking would predict. In addition to these historical works there have also been exercises in pure theory, showing how hypothetical, unregulated banking systems might avoid some macroeconomic shortcomings of existing arrangements. [2] Unfortunately, a wide gap separates these theoretical studies from the aforementioned historical works: the theorists generally deal with "moneyless" or fiat-money producing banking systems that differ radically from any unregulated "free banking" system of the past. The present paper attempts to close this gap by explaining the operation of a money-based, unregulated fractional-reserve banking system. [3] It shows that such a system promotes monetary stability, and in doing so reaffirms some of the well-known (but still controversial) conclusions of CANNAN [1935] and TOBIN [1963]. However, it also extends these conclusions by emphasizing the crucial role of competition in currency supply. It is because such competition is absent in central banking systems that they (and not free banking) *are*

---

* I wish to thank Clive Bull, Richard Ebeling, Kurt Schuler, Anna J. Schwartz, Richard H. Timberlake, Jr., and Lawrence H. White for their help.
[1] The most relevant of these are JONUNG [1985], ROCKOFF [1974], ROLNICK and WEBER [1982, 1983], WHITE [1984b], and VAUBEL [1984].
[2] See for example BLACK [1970], FAMA [1980], GREENFIELD and YEAGER [1983], SARGENT and WALLACE [1982], and WALLACE [1983]. HAYEK [1978] and KLEIN [1974] offer theories of the competitive production of irredeemable fiat monies.
[3] The arguments in this study are developed in much greater detail in SELGIN [1987]. Other theoretical studies of free banking which, however, fail to recognize some of its important properties are WHITE [1984b], Chapter 1 and WHITE [1984a]. There are also some scattered remarks in SMITH [1936].

"inherently unstable."[4] The difference made by competition is especially evident when a commodity-money based system in which note issue is monopolized is compared to one in which numerous banks compete in the unregulated issue of redeemable notes.

Because this study deals with the case of a commodity base money it should be viewed as a theoretical exercise intended to shed light on certain episodes of monetary history, and not as a ready proposal for monetary reform.

2. General Assumptions

To examine in depth the creation of bank-money under free banking, and to render comparisons with centralized banking most meaningful, a closed or "world" system of competing note issuers will be compared to one in which a single bank possesses a world monopoly of note issue.[5] Apart from these differences in the conditions of note issue no other special constraints are assumed to exist in either system;[6] it is only assumed that in both systems there exists a commodity "outside" money into which all monetary bank liabilities are convertible upon demand. This assumption is justified by historical precedent as well as by consideration of the evolutionary process, discussed below, by which bank money emerges in an unregulated system. No assumptions are made concerning the exact nature of the outside-money commodity except that it is scarce and reproducible only under increasing average costs.[7]

3. The Evolution of Bank Money

To motivate further assumptions, we turn to the evolutionary origins of bank money.[8] Typically, banking originates with the issuance of 100%-backed

---

[4] It is important to recall in this connection that in most instances monopolization of currency supply historically preceded the idea of centralized money-supply management. Thus, it is not accurate to say that central banking developed in response to the instability of *decentralized* banking; typically it developed in response to the instability of already centralized systems that lacked any systematic mechanism for regulating monopolistic institutions. In other cases it was imposed as an instrument of state finance. On this see SMITH [1936].

[5] Discussion of a world monopoly issuer is all the more relevant in that some present-day theorists advocate such a system. See for example MUNDELL [1983], pp. 207–209.

[6] Of course, this is not to suggest that particular *policies* of credit expansion on the part of monopoly issuers will not be considered.

[7] The "money commodity" could even be a defunct fiat money, in which case costs of production (absent counterfeiting) are infinite once all specimens have been unearthed.

[8] A more detailed discussion of the subject of this section is offered in SELGIN and WHITE (forthcoming).

"money certificates" by goldsmiths or bill-brokers who receive deposits of commodity money.[9] Such deposits take the form of *bailments*, for safekeeping; they are not intended to be at the goldsmith's or bill-broker's disposal. The depositors must pay a storage fee, since this is the only source of compensation to the providers of the bailment service.

Out of such primitive arrangements two important innovations arise. First, the deposit keepers discover that they can safely lend a portion of their deposits at interest and, second, the depositors find that their money certificates can serve in place of money proper as media of exchange. The two innovations complement one another: the first involves the discovery that depositors' holdings of bank-promises can be a source of loanable funds; the second means a general increase in the use of such promises. The modern institution of fractional-reserve banking grows out of these innovations. Its effect is to dramatically alter the status of the "depositor" of money: rather than being a *bailee*, he becomes a *lender* of funds to his bank, and what had formerly been money certificates in his possession become instruments of credit. Modern forms of bank money are matched on the balance sheet almost entirely by bank lending. The modern banker receives his revenues from interest on loans and investments; the "depositor", rather than paying a fee for the safekeeping of his money, becomes under competitive circumstances the chief recipient of this interest revenue.

Thus even in its earliest stages of development a free bank – i.e. a fractional-reserve bank free from regulation – performs an intermediary function. It recognizes credit granted to it by holders of its bank money (notes and demand deposits) and makes the involved funds available for loans and investments.[10] As confidence in the demand liabilities of individual banks grows, the entire demand for media of exchange may be fulfilled by them, so that all commodity money is withdrawn from circulation and placed at the disposal of the banks.[11] This leads to a decline in the real demand for and exchange value of the money commodity. Stock equilibrium is reached when the demand for the money commodity for non-circulation purposes (i.e., for bank reserves and industrial/consumptive uses) is sufficient to absorb the surplus created by the use of bank money. The size of the stock of bank money (denominated in commodity units) is then determined by the demand to hold bank money at the new (lower) equilibrium value of the money commodity. From this stage additional supplies

---

[9] See POWELL [1966], pp. 56ff. and RICHARDS [1965], Chapters II and IX.

[10] The controversial "pure intermediary" view of banking institutions is defended here and in what follows *only* for the free banking case. GURLEY and SHAW [1955, 1956] have attempted a more universal application of the "pure intermediary" approach. Their views are ably criticized in ASCHHEIM [1959]. The best general discussions of the intermediary role of commercial banks are POINDEXTER [1946] and TOBIN [1963].

[11] The issue of notes of small denominations and token coins (for use in the making of change) is necessary for the complete displacement of commodity money from circulation.

of bank money will appear only insofar as the aggregate demand for real balances happens to expand. (This is demonstrated in Section 6, below.)

It will be assumed hereafter that all users of media of exchange prefer bank money to commodity money and have enough confidence in the monies of *particular* banks to enable them to hold these liabilities instead of holding clumsier commodity money. Therefore, the public demand for media of exchange or for real money balances is equivalent to the demand to hold quantities of bank money. It is assumed, however, that banks continue to demand commodity money for their reserves. Another important assumption is that free banks routinely send the notes of rival banks back to their issuers for redemption. The reasons for this are similar to those responsible for the routine clearing of checks: by returning its rivals' notes, a bank only gives up assets that do not earn interest, and in return receives either its own notes held by other banks (which protects it from unexpected redemptions) or, alternatively, commodity money, which is a more liquid and risk-free asset. The implications of this assumption are far-reaching and form a large part of the analysis to follow.

4. The Law of Adverse Clearings

In the standard theory of a central banking system the creation of new demand deposits by an individual bank is limited by the bank's holdings of excess reserves. The system as a whole, however, is able to expand its liabilities by some multiple of the total of this amount. In a free banking system, the availability of excess reserves limits both individual banks' expansion of demand deposits and their ability to extend credit via the issue of bank notes. It will be shown here that 1) the scope for the existence of excess reserves is much smaller under free banking than under monopoly issue; and 2) when there is competitive note issue the value of the reserve multiplier adjusts to accommodate changes in the public's demand for bank-money balances.

The fundamental principle governing expansion of liabilities under free banking may be dubbed the "law of adverse clearings". According to this law, any bank that creates demand liabilities in *any* form in excess of the demand to *hold* such liabilities at a given price level is soon faced with adverse clearings and, hence, with a loss of commodity-money reserves equal to its overissue. The principle at work here is routinely acknowledged in discussions of the creation of demand deposits. [12] It applies equally, however, to the issue of bank notes: at any moment, with a given price level, there exists a limited demand to hold bank money in general and the bank money of any individual bank in particular. Suppose these demands are entirely satisfied. Then any notes received from a free bank as a result of additional credit granted by it represent excess bank money balances and are therefore spent. These notes rapidly find their way into

---

[12] E.g. PHILLIPS [1920].

the hands of banks competing with the issuing bank, because clients of competing banks who receive the notes exchange them for their own banks' liabilities. As was shown above, the recipient banks are driven by considerations of profit to return the notes to their issuer in exchange for commodity money. The issuing bank then suffers a loss of reserves which (unless it had excess reserves to sponsor the additional note issue in the first place) compels it to contract credit in compensation for its previous overissues. [13] Once a free bank reaches its optimum reserve level it can profit from new note issues only to the extent that the notes remain in some individual's balances; that is, only to the extent that they do not enter the clearing mechanism by being deposited or exchanged at competing banks.

An important implication of the law of adverse clearings is that no individual free bank can profitably undertake a loan pricing policy cheaper than its competitors simply by issuing notes gratuitously. It can accomplish nothing by attracting additional borrowers via cheap lending rates except the exhaustion of its liquid reserves and, ultimately, of its capital. There will be more to say regarding this in a later section.

The law of adverse clearings does not apply to a monopoly note issuer. This is what gives monopoly issuers their special influence on total money supply. Consider a system where note issue is monopolized but demand deposit creation is competitive. Not all of the demand for bank money can be satisfied by way of demand deposits; there is a need for currency (e.g. bank notes) as well, since currency can be used for transactions where checks are not acceptable. Thus the public will want to hold a definite portion of its bank money balances as currency. The division of its holdings between currency and demand deposits is, moreover, subject to change. [14] In order to fulfill their clients' demands for currency all the non-issuing banks must therefore always have on hand a ready supply of the notes of the monopoly issuer. A contest for the notes (and deposits convertible into notes) of the monopoly bank takes the place of the contest for commodity money that occurs under free banking. As a result, the deposit banks are able to settle clearings with notes or deposit-credits from the monopoly issuer. [15] If there is no public demand for commodity money, the deposit banks' reserves can consist entirely of the monopoly bank's demand liabilities. Commodity money can then be released for industrial and consumptive uses, with consequent impact upon its exchange value.

Under such conditions the law of adverse clearings cannot influence a monopoly note issuer's creation of demand liabilities. The notes and demand

---

[13] The extent and rapidity of the reserve drain is usually less for notes than for deposits (how much less depends upon particular conditions). Nevertheless, under all but the most improbable assumptions it will be adequate to deter overexpansion.

[14] Problems that arise under monopoly issue as a consequence of variations in this proportion are discussed in Section 11.

[15] See RIST [1966], p. 208. Note that this argument does not rest upon the presence of "legal tender" status for the notes of the monopoly issuer.

deposits of such a bank are treated as reserve *assets* by the deposit banks; there
is no reason for banks to request their redemption, even if they are issued
without regard to the monetary needs of the public. A world monopoly bank
of issue would for this reason be able to expand its demand liabilities without
any immediate limit.[16] To do so it merely has to add to its investments or
attract additional borrowers by lowering its loan interest rates or credit standards. It need not fear a clearing loss because the new liabilities thus created
become lodged in the reserves of the deposit banks. The resulting multiplicative
expansion of system-wide deposit balances is not restrained by the public's
limited demand to hold bank money at the existing price level. In the long run
there will be a general upward shift of the price level together with all nominal
magnitudes (although under present assumptions the nominal "price" of
commodity-money – the conversion rate – remains the same). Thus the supply
of bank money is not promptly self-regulating under monopoly issue. To be
effectively limited it must be controlled by way of special rules and restrictions
applied to the issuer. In other words, monopolized note issue creates the need
for a monetary policy.

The remaining sections of this paper examine the implications of the law of
adverse clearings under free banking and offer criticism of monetary policies
based upon monopolized note issue.

5. The Market for Bank Money and the Market for Credit

In a mature free banking system, a tight link connects the market for bank
liabilities to the market for bank assets (loanable funds). The exact nature of
this connection has often been misunderstood: often the demand for loanable
funds has been confounded with the demand for bank money. The demand for
loanable funds is for the most part a demand to acquire producers' and consumers' goods, with bank money serving only as a go-between. The true demand for bank money as such is the demand to *hold* it as a particular form of
wealth.[17]

Under free banking, the demand to hold bank money is far from being the
same as a demand for loanable funds. On the contrary, it represents a contribution to the *supply* of loanable funds: every holder of demand liabilities issued
by a free bank grants that bank a loan for the value of his holdings. According-

---

[16] Eventually a check occurs in the shape of an increased industrial demand for gold
prompted by the fall in its relative price. This "internal drain" is analogous to the
"price-specie-flow" that confronts monopoly overissuers of convertible liabilities in an
open system. These are long-run sources of restraint, which operate only once prices have
been generally influenced.

[17] This crucial point is emphasized by CANNAN [1921]. See also ROTHBARD [1970],
pp. 118–23 and 662–67.

143/3 (1987)   *Money Supply Under Free Banking*   441

ly, any increase in the public's willingness to hold bank money (*given* some level of nominal income and prices) is tantamount to an outward shift in the supply schedule of loanable funds to be intermediated by the banking system. [18]

It is true that the time dimension of loans made to banks by money-holding individuals is not formally stipulated. The estimation of the average duration of such loans is a practical problem that confronts bank management. The banker must be prepared to deal with adverse clearings that will result when his clients dispose of the bank's liabilities by exchanging them for goods and, eventually, for the liabilities of other banks. Such adverse clearings represent former liability-holders' termination of their loans. Older banking literature summarized the problem confronted by bank management as one of "matching the maturity dates of assets and liabilities". A similar problem is involved in the management of passbook savings accounts: although a formal stipulation of minimal loan duration typically exists (the "notice of withdrawal" clause), it is rarely used in actual practice, since it is inconsistent with customer convenience and hence with competitive policy. In practice passbook savings accounts, while not checkable, are nonetheless withdrawable upon demand; the difference in duration between them and demand deposits is merely one of degree.

Because the demand to hold bank money represents a granting of credit by individuals it follows that any issue of bank money consistent with this demand accords with the availability of voluntarily supplied, real savings. In other words, if a credit expansion under free banking is consistent with equilibrium in the market for bank money – that is, if the supply of liabilities does not (at given prices) exceed or fall short of the quantity demanded – then it does not disturb equilibrium in the market for loanable funds. To adopt Wicksell's terminology, interest rates remain at their "natural" levels. [19] The same circumstances that prevent free banks from issuing greater quantities of bank money than the public is willing to hold also ensure that the terms under which free banks extend credit are in agreement with wealthholders' willingness to lend funds. Once again it is the law of adverse clearings that ensures these results. This law, it has been shown, does not apply to a monpoly bank of issue.

The maintenance of loan market and bank money market equilibria under free banking has important implications. In the market for bank money it means that individuals never hold insufficient or excessive balances of bank money in the aggregate. In the loan market it means that banks make loans and investments only on the basis of voluntary (planned or *ex ante*) savings, so that there is no redirection of the means of production due to forced savings or false profit signals (based upon distorted bank rates of interest) that disappear once

---

[18] See BROWN [1910].

[19] It is assumed here that the non-commercial bank segment of the loanable funds market is not a source of disequilibrium. This reflects the standard view that only commercial banks can "create" (or destroy) loanable funds independent of the ex-ante savings of individuals. See ASCHHEIM [1959].

the redundancy or deficiency of bank money has had its effect upon nominal magnitudes. The disequilibrium situations depicted by monetary business cycle theories, such as HAYEK's [1935] are avoided. The long-run implication for both markets is that alterations of commodity prices (both absolute and relative) due to monetary disequilibrium are avoided.

In summary, competitive banks of issue are usually not independent sources of nominal demand for goods and services. This means that they cannot be independent generators of demand for bank money either, because their issues do not influence the general level of prices. Under free banking there is no "Wicksellian indeterminancy" of prices or of demand for money. The same is not true of an unregulated system based upon monopolized note issue.[20]

6. Changes in the Demand for Bank Money[21]

So far we have described the self-correcting responses in a free banking system to the creation of bank money in excess of some *given* demand for it. We must now consider how a free banking system responds to changes, positive or negative, in the aggregate demand for bank money balances; that is, we will examine the mechanisms of dynamic adjustment of demand liabilities under competitive note issue.

Consider first a circumstance where the demand for bank money has grown. It is useful to think of individual demands as "sumps" or "reservoirs" along a flowing stream of bank-money income. An increase in demand is analogous to a deepening of these reservoirs (an intensification of existing demands) or to an increase in their number (a multiplication of money-holding firms and individuals). In either case, the existence of greater demand for bank money means that the community will absorb further fiduciary issues without causing such issues to overflow into the stream of nominal income. Consequently, such new issues do not find their way into the clearing mechanism. They do not result in reserve losses to the banks responsible for them. In this case banks are able to lend profitably beyond what they previously considered their excess reserves.

Persons are not indifferent among various bank monies; everyone tends to hold a definite portfolio of monies. For illustrative purposes we assume that each person prefers the liabilities of one bank with which he does business. We must investigate the circumstances that allow a competitive bank of issue to take advantage of an extension of demands for its money. The most obvious

---

[20] WICKSELL himself ([1935], pp. 188–189) practically acknowledges this in his criticism of the views of Adolf Wagner. Wagner's position, which depends on the clearing mechanism, is of course vitiated if banks expand credit in unison via formal agreements. Yet such agreements are not, Wicksell concedes, (ibid, p. 190) in evidence. So Wicksell undermines his own criticism of Wagner.

[21] This section draws heavily upon CANNAN [1935]. Cannan's reasoning may be accepted without qualification only for the special case of competitive note issue.

place to begin is with the bank's borrower-customers. Most bank demand liabilities come into being via new loans and asset purchases. Clearly, to the extent that bank borrowers *hold* their borrowed balances rather than spend them, the bank that creates the balances suffers no negative clearings from them. Such balances include "compensating balance requirements" and are the simplest instance of bank money creation that does not lead to adverse clearings. [22]

A less trivial case is where borrowers' expenditures of bank money find their way into the hands of other indivduals who are or who choose to become clients of the issuing bank. This factor is only relevant when there is an actual increase in "permanent" money holdings; otherwise, the issuing bank soon suffers a clearing loss. When bank money demand has not permanently increased – that is, when a marginal increase in bank issues would lead to an increase in aggregate, nominal incomes as excess issues are spent off – the only asset that is suitable backing for the new liabilities is commodity money. We thus return to the traditional case where only receipt of new outside money by the system will make possible further issues of bank money.

What has been said regarding the expansion of liabilities of individual banks also applies to the free banking system as a whole: Whenever there is a *general* decline in the rate of turnover of bank money, as follows an increase in the demand to hold it, the banks are able to expand their total outstanding liabilities relative to their holdings of outside money reserves. In other words, there is an increase in the reserve multiplier. Bank money creation can continue only when there are unexploited "reservoirs" of bank demand. Any issues beyond this lead to additions to the stream of payments, and hence to an increase in total bank clearings and reserve needs. [23]

Now consider what happens when there is a reduction in demand for bank money. Just as new extensions of credit are the occasion for expansion of bank liabilities, retirements of loans and investments are the occasion for their extinction. Bank demand liabilities are reduced whenever new issues cannot offset the absorption of previous liabilities via loan repayments because a fallen demand for bank money renders new issues (or even the "rolling over" of old credits) unsustainable. Let us examine this process at the level of the individual bank of issue.

First of all, a reduction in the demand to hold the bank's liabilities is postulated. Suppose that the surplus liabilities are paid over to someone who is indebted to the issuing bank, who in turn uses them to repay his loan. What is the net result of these transactions? The bank suffers no clearing loss (i.e., no loss of reserves) and no change in its volume of clearings; however, the sum of

---

[22] Borrowers, insofar as they hold rather than spend borrowed bank money balances, are simultaneously debtors and creditors to the lending bank. On compensating balances see DAVIS and GUTTENTAG [1962].

[23] The determinants of economic reserve requirements are discussed in Section 7.

its outstanding liabilities falls. If it attempts to recover its previous business by extending new credit it suffers adverse clearings to the extend of the new issues. Since its reserve holdings were at the optimum determined by the volume and variance of clearings it faced, such new extensions of credit are unprofitable. Similar results follow if the liabilities of one bank are used to repay loans at another bank when there is a decline in the demand for the liabilities of the first bank with no offsetting increase in the demand to hold the liabilities of its rival.

The process described in the preceding example operates as well when there is a *general* reduction in the demand for bank money. Here there is a system-wide increase in the rate of turnover of demand liabilities, which means that bank assets must be made to "turn over" more rapidly as well. The liquidity needs of the banking system increase, and higher ratios of reserves to liabilities are needed. The reserve multiplier falls because of reduced demand for bank money balances.

7. Confusion About the "Reserve Ratio"

The individual bank of issue must monitor two statistics related to bank clearings: the *average* of net clearings over a given period and the *variance* of net clearings over the same period. The variance indicates minimum long-run reserve needs. Its value tends to increase absolutely (albeit as a decreasing percentage) with increases in gross bank clearings even if average net clearings remain constant. [24] This means that a bank must add to its reserves, other things being equal, whenever its gross clearings with other banks increase. Otherwise it faces a higher risk of failing to meet the adverse clearings it suffers on any particular day. The banking *system*, in turn, can only sustain an increase in its gross clearings if it improves the efficiency of its clearing arrangements (thereby reducing minimum reserve needs relative to clearings) or if it increases its total holdings of outside commodity money (the primary means of interbank settlement under free banking).

Textbook and other discussions of banking theory tend to devote undue attention to the ratio of reserves to total bank money as a limit to fiduciary issues by individual banks and by the banking system. This emphasis is partly due to focus on legal reserve requirements (which are often stipulated in terms of this ratio) rather than economic reserve requirements. The latter have only an indirect relationship to the total amount of bank money; they are not linked to it by a constant ratio. While total bank clearings (and their variance) are not unrelated to total outstanding liabilities, changes in money demand make it possible for total liabilities to change without at all affecting total clearings. These changes do not alter the banking system's total reserve needs. Therefore, the ratio of reserves to bank money (and hence, the reserve multiplier) in a free

---

[24] By the law of large numbers. See EDGEWORTH [1888] and ORR and MELLON [1961].

143/3 (1987)   *Money Supply Under Free Banking*   445

banking system alters in response to consumer demands. Variations would be apparent in comparing different banks of issue cross-sectionally and in observing an individual bank (or the banking system) over time.[25] The amount of bank money outstanding is determined, both for individual banks and for the banking system, by the public's demand to hold bank money, through the influence of money demand on optimal bank reserve holdings. Reserve-demand will not rise in step with the volume of bank money when the latter grows in response to increased demand to hold bank money. Other things being equal, increased demand to hold bank money leads to a transitional *fall* in individuals' expenditures relative to their total income. This in turn reduces total bank clearings, inviting a compensating expansion of liabilities. Decreased demand to hold bank money has the opposite effect. In these circumstances bank clearings and the demand to hold bank money move in opposite directions. To maintain an optimal ratio of reserves to total *clearings* the banks must allow their ratios of reserves to total *liabilities* to change.[26]

In the theory of monopoly issue or central banking it is customary to overlook changes in the reserve multiplier. This multiplier is treated as a constant. Attention is then drawn to what happens when the monopoly issuer's liabilities expand and the excess comes into the deposit banks' possession. The resulting change in the *system*'s demand liabilities is supply-determined. The chain of causation is (1) expansion of monopoly bank liabilities, (2) multiple expansion of deposit bank liabilities to the extent allowed by a fixed reserve multiplier, (3) increased spending prompted by an excess supply of money, (4) higher prices, (5) greater (nominal) demand to hold bank money, and, finally, (6) a new equilibrium with all nominal magnitudes proportionately scaled upward. Under free banking supply-induced expansions of bank money do not occur except when there are expansions in the stock of the commodity money.[27] The chain of causation generally appropriate to monetary expansion under free banking is (1) increased demand to hold bank money, (2) a change in the reserve multiplier, (3) expansion of bank demand liabilities, and (4) a new equilibrium with the scale of prices unchanged. For example, imagine a free banking system with commodity money reserves of $1000. Suppose that the supply of bank money is $50,000, which equals the public's initial demand for bank money. The reserve multiplier is, therefore, 50. Now imagine that the demand for bank money falls by $10,000, to $40,000. Bank demand liabilities

---

[25] For evidence on cross-sectional and temporal variation in Scottish free banks' reserve ratios see MUNN [1981].

[26] For an argument, within the context of central banking, for allowing *legal* reserve requirements to vary with differing rates of (deposit) turnover, see JACOBY [1963]. Jacoby does not note any connection between his recommended legal requirements and the economic requirements of an unregulated system.

[27] Increases in the stock of monetary gold are only disequilibrating if they involve shifts in its supply-schedule. In fact, many historic "discoveries" of gold were movements along, not of, the long-run gold supply curve. See ROCKOFF [1984].

will then be forced to contract by $10,000, so that the reserve multiplier falls
to 40; that is, the ratio of reserves to demand liabilities rises from 2% to 2.5%.

The above arguments could have been stated in terms of changes in the
"income velocity of circulation" of bank money (which is simply another means
of referring to the demand for bank money relative to expenditure), or in terms
of the determinants of equilibrium in the market for loanable funds. As has
been shown, changes in the demand to hold bank money affect the availability
of loanable funds: when more bank money is demanded, the supply of loanable
funds is increased, and competitive banks of issue can reduce their lending rates
until the demand for credit is sufficient to absorb the greater supply. Opposite
adjustments take place when the demand for bank money falls.

That the supply of bank money in a free banking system responds automatically to changes in demand to hold bank money means that equilibrium in both
the market for loanable funds and the market for media of exchange is maintained with minimal disturbance of prices from their initial positions even when
the demand for bank money changes. The "invisible hand" adjusts supply to
demand in a free banking system just as it does in other industries where goods
are produced on a competitive basis.

8. Credit Expansion "In Concert"

The arguments raised in the last section also help to refute the traditional view
that, if all banks (in an unregulated setting) expand credit "in concert", they
will not face any liquidity constraint, and so can expand credit without limit.
Picture a situation where every bank has *average* net clearings equal to zero,
because every bank's share of the market for bank money is stable, and no bank
is expanding "out of step" with its competitors. Assume, furthermore, that the
total supply of bank money is at first equal to the wants of the public. Do the
banks hold reserves in such a circumstance? They do hold *precautionary* reserves, because although net debit clearings for any bank have a *mean value* of
zero, they also tend to vary from this mean over the course of any series of
clearings. Therefore every bank holds reserves to protect itself against the
possibility of above average adverse clearings it may suffer in any one clearing
session. The demand for precautionary reserves is what limits expansion for the
system as a whole.

Now imagine that, starting from the above equilibrium situation, all the
banks expand their balance sheets in unison by an equal amount, although the
demand to hold bank money (and its distribution across banks) has not
changed. The "in concert" expansion might be a result of formal agreements,
or it might be spontaneous. Will it leave the banks unscathed? It will not,
because, although every bank would find its *average* clearinghouse credits and
debits increased by the same amount over the course of numerous clearing
sessions, the *variance* of net debit and net credit clearings faced by any bank

would also increase, by a factor approximately equal to the square-root of the percentage increase in *gross* clearings. In consequence, each bank would soon discover that its precautionary reserve holdings, though formerly adequate to protect it against above-average adverse clearings in any one clearing session, are no longer sufficient. The increased clearing activity brings with it a greater probability of single-session net debit clearings exceeding a bank's reserves. For this reason, "in concert" expansion will not be profitable or sustainable (assuming banks insist on spot payment of clearing balances). Therefore, each bank will have to reduce its liabilities to their previous equilibrium level. Moreover, only *one* bank has to determine that by expanding with the others it has overstretched its precautionary reserves, since contraction by any one bank will immediately force some of its rivals to contract as well, setting off a system-wide correction.

9. Stability of the Monetary Unit

Because the supply of bank money under free banking is demand-elastic, changes in prices that would otherwise arise from changes in demands for real money balances are avoided. The exchange value of the money commodity (and, therefore, of the unit of account) is stabilized. This stabilization takes place without displacement of relative prices or bank interest rates from their equilibrium levels. It is guided by the banks' desires to maximize profits, which inspire them to take advantage of any opportunity to safely expand their liabilities. The law of adverse clearings, in turn, ensures that any bank expanding credit without warrant suffers an unsustainable drain of reserves.

A second important implication of demand-elastic bank money supply under free banking is that any sharp general increase in individuals' bank money demand (i.e., any "hoarding" of bank money) need not result in a short-run interruption of bank-money income flows with consequent involuntary accumulation of goods inventories and trade disruption. Instead, hoarding (because it constitutes an increase in the supply of loanable funds), is met by the expansion of bank loans and liabilities. Otherwise bank loan rates would be forced temporarily *above* their equilibrium levels (the excess demand for money would imply an excess supply of bonds) until a general decline of incomes and prices led to a downward adjustment of the nominal demand for loanable funds, thereby returning the rates to their appropriate levels. Under free banking, not only is loan-market disequilibrium avoided, but the total supply of loanable funds (in real terms) is greater than it would be were the supply of bank money demand-inelastic. (There will be more to say about this in the next section).

The above results depend upon the operation of the law of adverse clearings; none of them apply to systems of discretionary monopoly note issue. Whether monopoly is preferable depends on whether deliberate State management of a monopoly issuer (that is, central banking and monetary policy) can duplicate or improve upon results achieved automatically by a free banking system.

Many theorists believe that a central bank can properly regulate its issues by stabilizing the general price level (as measured by some price index).[28] Since a monopoly issuer can generate excess or deficient supplies of bank money, and since these excess or deficient supplies should, *ceteris paribus,* reveal themselves in changes in prices of many goods and services, these theorists reason that eliminating changes in the general price level is equivalent to eliminating central bank under- and overexpansion. They fail to recognize that changes in the price level may occur for reasons other than maladjustment of the supply of bank liabilities to demand. Most important are price level changes due to changes in production per capita, which reflect changes in unit cost-of-production of goods. Attempts to offset, by money supply changes, movements in the price level stemming from such non-monetary causes are actually disruptive. Because unwarranted monetary injections never affect prices uniformly or simultaneously, they add to or subtract from aggregate nominal income, temporarily prevent relative prices from reaching their equilibrium levels, and disrupt the flow of goods and investment.[29, 30]

Some advocates of central banking realize that changes in the price level are not always due to exogenous changes in the demand for bank money. Accordingly, they have suggested formulae or "rules" for managing the supply of central bank money based on estimates of secular growth in aggregate demand. The most famous, of course, is Milton Friedman's – although Friedman himself has recently become a proponent of free banking.[31] Sometimes these rules reflect a rough estimate of population growth; other times they are based on much more elaborate estimates from econometric models. Unfortunately, such methods provide only a very crude and unsatisfactory alternative to a demand-elastic supply of bank money.[32] Most of them do not even attempt to deal with seasonal or cyclical changes in demand.

Rules for monetary management generally lead to disequilibrating price disturbances; in particular, an improper supply of central bank money disturbs interest rates, because the extension of loanable funds by the banking system ceases to agree with the voluntary savings decisions of individuals. This particular variety of relative-price distortion, a distortion of intertemporal rates of exchange, results either in a boom-and-bust cycle (inflationary case)[33] or in

---

[28] See for example HALL [1984].

[29] This is not to deny that movement in prices due, for example, to increased production do not themselves *influence* the nominal demand for bank money. For one thing, there is a "real balance" effect. However, with respect to it the necessary adjustment of demand liabilities (in the case of falling prices) is *downwards.*

[30] See FISHER [1935] and HAYEK [1935].

[31] See FRIEDMAN and SCHWARTZ [1986].

[32] The search for a stable money demand function to guide monetary policy has been among the more frustrated enterprises of contemporary monetary economics. See JUDD and SCADDING [1982], and COOLEY and LEROY [1981].

[33] As in HAYEK [1935].

more immediate depression (deflationary case). Obviously, advocates of a monetary rule desire neither consequence.

If it were true that the public's demand for money could always be satisfied with demand deposits, so that "free" deposit banking could by itself secure a demand-elastic supply of bank money, then one could make a system founded on monopoly note issue function satisfactorily simply by doing away with the issue and use of currency altogether.[34] Automatic alterations in the sum of deposits would then meet needs for money balances. There would be no problems of disequilibrium in either the bank money or the credit markets of such a system.

Unfortunately, not all demands for money can be satisfied by deposit balances: a definite portion of money demand is wanted in the form of currency, and the size of this portion changes frequently. The challenge of monopoly issue is to meet this specific demand for currency notes as it fluctuates seasonally and secularly without unnecessarily altering deposit bank reserves and without thereby causing a multiplicative (inflationary or deflationary) change in the *total* supply of bank money.[35]

Successful monetary management requires some means for identifying changes in the public's demand for bank money, so that bank liabilities expand as demand increases, and diminish as it subsides. Under central banking automatic adjustments will not occur. Overextensions of credit by the monopoly issuer do not reveal themselves by way of adverse clearings suffered by any of the deposit banks. Underexpansion by the monopoly issuer does not invite compensating expansion by the deposit banks because the latter cannot independently fulfill that part of the demand for money consisting of demand for currency. Thus, in a monopolized system the demand for money often must adjust to supply, rather than *vice versa*. No predetermined rule for monetary management can enable banks in a monopolized system to find the proper limits of credit expansion. Monopolization of currency issue destroys the adverse-clearing mechanism and in doing so creates a vast calculation problem that no a priori formula can solve.

To summarize: a demand-elastic supply of bank money has desirable properties. Free banking provides it automatically; monopolized banking cannot. Central banks and monetary management, usually supposed to solve the problem of controlling the supply of bank money, instead create the problem.

---

[34] A "freeze" on currency-issue, even if accompanied by a freeze on deposit creation by the monopoly issuer, would not by itself be adequate, because currency could still influence the supply of credit independently of demand as it passed in and out of bank vaults. On this see Section 11.

[35] The full extent of this challenge for monopoly issue is outlined in Section 11.

10. The Efficiency of Bank Money Supply Under Free Banking

A further consequence of the demand-elastic supply of bank money under free banking is that the use of resources in producing the basic money commodity is less affected by changes in the demand for media of exchange. Elimination of the public's demand for commodity money means significant reductions in the production of the money commodity for monetary uses. Here is the most important secular advantage of the use of fiduciary media under free banking: would-be investments in the money commodity become investments in other things. They are transformed via bank-money holdings into increased supplies of loanable funds. Savings that would, in a 100% reserve system, accumulate as commodity money manifest themselves instead as holdings of credit instruments (which, in the case of demand deposits, are interest-bearing). This continuing spur to capital accumulation comes in addition to the initial, once-and-for-all savings associated with the adoption of fiduciary media and resulting release of the money commodity for non-monetary uses. The once-and-for-all savings can, as was noted earlier, actually be increased by monopolizing note issue (since, ideally, *no* commodity money reserves are needed to settle clearings in a monopoly system). However, against this one-time gain must be weighed the costs that result from a monopoly bank's frequent under- and overissue of fiduciary media. (These costs are further discussed below.) Moreover, the absolute value of the gain is not great, since the reserve needs of a developed free banking system are modest to begin with,[36] and tend to diminish over time as clearing arrangements improve. Such improvements proceed whenever their marginal contributions to bank revenues exceed their marginal costs.

So far we are still operating under the assumption that bank money has completely replaced commodity (outside) money in circulation, and that individuals' confidence in bank money is absolute. To complete our analysis it is necessary to relax this assumption.

If commodity money still circulates, note-issuing bankers consider three margins when deciding the volume of their investments: (1) the marginal cost of attracting new deposits or permanent note-holdings; (2) the marginal cost of reducing holdings of non-earning reserve assets (e.g. by running higher risks or by improving the clearing system); and (3) the marginal gain in interest revenues from acquiring earning assets. Ultimately, it is the demanders of media of exchange who determine the direction and extent of economies undertaken with respect to commodity money, through their desires for interest-yielding *versus* low-risk money balances. The investments made by free bankers are, therefore, cost-minimizing from the consumers' point of view. In this

[36] In the Scottish free banking era, reserve ratios of between 2 and 10 percent were typical, and banks occasionally operated with ratios as low as .5 percent. Were it not for prohibitions upon the issue of small notes the figures might even be lower. See WHITE [1984b], p. 148.

143/3 (1987)   *Money Supply Under Free Banking*   451

(subjective) sense the use of bank money under free banking is efficient: bank money is employed (or "produced") instead of commodity money only so far as the anticipated marginal benefits exceed the anticipated marginal opportunity costs; and the banks are driven to supply bank money at the least possible expense. The first conclusion, at least, does *not* apply in the case of monopoly issue: a monopolized system can create excess bank money, and the monopoly issuer will maximize its profits by doing so. Since such an excess does not contribute to the flow of real goods and services (and may even obstruct this flow by disturbing the price system), its production is inefficient even though the direct resource costs involved (paper, ink, etc.) are minor. The overissue is not in accord with the public's desired portfolio mix of commodity money and bank money. In a world of less than complete confidence in bank money this might lead people to redeem excess bank money holdings. This could necessitate a multiplicative contraction of bank demand liabilities as deposit banks seek to protect their reserves, undoing some of the economies that were achieved using fiduciary media. *Under*issues of bank money under monopoly issue are also inefficient, because they cause the exchange value of the money commodity to rise directly, intensifying production of it. To these costs connected with unnecessary production of the money commodity must be added the costs of disequilibrium resource allocation due to displacement of prices and interest rates.

11. The Specific Demand for Currency

So far we have dealt with problems of supply and demand respecting bank money in general. Now it is necessary to consider the implications of a change in the demand for one form of bank money – currency – assuming the *total* demand for bank money remains unchanged. The specific demand for currency increases whenever the proportion of payments that can be made by check declines.[37]

The directors of a competitive bank of issue have no special difficulty meeting their clients' demands for currency. If a depositor wants to convert a portion or even all of his balance, the bank has only to supply him with notes from its own printing press, as it were. If many customers come forward for the same reason, the bank prints more notes for the occasion. What matters to a free bank is not the form of its demand liabilities but their total value. When customers convert existing deposits into notes, there is merely a reduction of

---

[37] An extreme case would be a general loss of confidence in "checkbook" money, which is to be distinguished from a loss of confidence in bank money in the broad sense. The former involves distrust of individual check writers; the latter would imply distrust of the banks of issue themselves. For a statistical analysis of variations in the specific demand for currency see CAGAN [1958].

one balance sheet item and an equivalent increase in another. Assuming that the total demand for money remains unchanged, and that the variance of note and deposit clearings is the same at the margin, there need be no change in the bank's total clearings nor in its reserve holdings.

Under monopoly note issue the situation is radically different. When clients of a competitive deposit bank in a currency monopoly system convert portions of their balances into currency, what they receive is not the bank's own currency (which it is prohibited from issuing) but rather the notes of the monopoly bank of issue. These notes are also the deposit bank's reserve media. To pay out notes to its customers, a deposit bank must acquire them in the interbank market, or from the bank of issue. If no additional notes are made available from the issuing bank to the system as a whole (e.g. if the "discount window" is closed or the rate charged is prohibitively high), reserves become deficient and the banks must contract their liabilities to avoid default on clearing balances. In this event the supply of loanable funds is curtailed, and lending rates rise above their equilibrium levels. A scarcity of credit results even though individuals' demand to hold bank money in the broad sense has not changed.

If the monopoly bank of issue provides the desired "reserve compensation" it prevents a credit shortage from happening. [38] However, there is no guarantee that a monopoly issuer will cooperate, especially if it is bound by a statute or rule limiting its ability to create reserves. And if the statute or rule is relaxed. so that the monopoly bank of issue can provide the needed notes, how can the issuer ensure that notes issued for emergency reasons are *retired* once the public no longer needs them? Unless it can take this precaution the surplus notes may return to the vaults of the deposit banks, where they will serve as the basis for a multiplicative, inflationary expansion of bank credit.

The problem of note supply for reserve compensation under monopoly issue may not be insuperable. Nevertheless it is certainly too complex to be solved by any simple rule or formula. It calls for an element of disrection, which creates dangers of its own. In contrast, this same problem simply does not arise under free banking.

12. The Inadequacy of "Knowledge Surrogates" Under Monopoly Issue [39]

The general problem of economic calculation is one of discovering individuals' and firms' demands for particular services and commodities. Where there are

---

[38] Of course, if what is "compensated" is not a true "currency drain" but only a transfer of funds from one bank to another, overissue of credit is involved. Under monopoly issue it is not always possible to tell, even *ex-post*, whether a currency withdrawal warrants reserve compensation or not. Under free banking, notes withdrawn for use in circulation do not cause reserve losses; those withdrawn for redeposit in other banks do.

[39] On the general problem of economic "knowledge administration" as faced by central planners see HAYEK [1948].

143/3 (1987) *Money Supply Under Free Banking* 453

market prices this problem is solved by entrepreneurial reactions to signals of profit and loss. Price and profit signals act as "knowledge surrogates", that is, they lead entrepreneurs and producers to adjust their actions *as if* they actually knew consumers' preferences.

The particular calculation problem that a well-managed banking system is supposed to solve involves estimating the demand for bank money (including the specific demand for currency). Under free banking the incidence of clearings, through its influence upon profits and losses, makes these demands known to banks: the clearing mechanism leads profit-maximizing free banks to adjust their outstanding loans and investments *as if* they had direct knowledge of individuals' willingness to hold bank money, via their attempts to maintain optimal reserves with respect to notes and deposits. Consequently interest rates are made to reflect the true state of individuals' time-preference.

Under monopoly note issue the clearing mechanism is undermined, since excess issues by the monopoly bank are treated as reserve assets by deposit banks instead of being redeemed by them. In a monopoly system there are no spontaneous knowledge surrogates to guide production. Thus conscious, centralized planning of the supply of bank money becomes necessary. Such planning suffers from an inherent incapacity for using localized (dispersed) information. Monetary policy is nothing more than a crude, makeshift knowledge surrogate erected in place of the vastly more effective knowledge surrogates that function under free banking, and most monetary reform proposals (e.g. "price rules", velocity adjusted money growth rate rules) offer only different makeshifts and not a solution. Rather then encouraging more complete use of available information, the adoption of central banking in place of free banking results in the complete abandonment of adequate means for gauging the demands for bank money.

A defender of central banking might point out that a central bank has access to information *superior* to that available to competitive banks of issue, including such things as elaborate econometric estimates of money demand and of seasonal fluctuations in the demand for currency. But this would be beside the point. Although free banks may not avail themselves of such information, they also do not *need* it; their attention to reserve drains is sufficient to guide them to supply bank money precisely in accordance with consumers' demand for it.

The absence of adequate knowledge surrogates under monopoly note issue leads to errors that are far more serious than those that would follow from centralized administration of any other industry. This is because money enters into practically all exchange and economic calculation, so that its disequilibrium supply distorts a wide array of price and profit signals, i.e., distorts other knowledge surrogates. The dislocation of interest rates is perhaps the most important example of this.

In summary, the clearing mechanism enables competitive banks of issue to discover their clients' demand for bank money. It rapidly translates banks' errors of judgment into suboptimal reserve positions and thereby into economic losses. A central bank cannot avail itself of a similar discovery procedure; it must rely upon knowledge surrogates of a decidedly inferior sort.

13. Conclusion

Although several writers in the past have stressed a pure intermediary view of commercial banking, few would argue that banking systems today function according to the pure intermediary ideal or that they do not require centralized supervision of one kind or another. Moreover, traditional textbook treatments do not question the need for central management of the money supply even though (and several economists, notably Friedman, have made this point) it is the central bank itself, and not commercial banks, that is a major source of monetary instability. The present paper has attempted to show that a free banking system is a perfect embodiment of the pure intermediary view of money supply processes. In comparison, central banking systems are inherently unable to function in the manner suggested by the pure intermediary view. These results suggest the need for a radical revision of conventional views on free *versus* central banking. Free banking should be regarded as a potential solution to monetary instability, and not as a likely cause of such instability. In contrast, centralized currency supply should be regarded as a likely cause of instability and not as a cure.

Summary

Though some theorists have expounded a "pure intermediary" view of banking institutions, few argue that present-day, regulated and centralized banking systems fulfill this pure-intermediary ideal. This paper examines the stability and efficiency of "free banking" – banking with competitive note issue and without government regulation – and shows how it, but not central banking, approaches the pure-intermediary ideal. In particular, it argues that the nominal money supply adjusts under free banking to changes in the demand for money balances. This avoids unnecessary changes in prices and interest rates.

Zusammenfassung
Stabilität und Effizienz des Geldangebots bei Bankfreiheit

Obwohl einige Theoretiker die Ansicht vertreten, daß Banken eine reine Mittlerrolle ausüben, behaupten nur wenige, daß das gegenwärtig bestehende regulierte und zentralisierte Bankensystem dem Ideal der reinen Mittlerrolle entspricht. In diesem Aufsatz wird die Stabilität und Effizienz der Bankfreiheit untersucht – mit konkurrierender Notenemission und ohne staatliche Regulierung – und gezeigt, wie es sich, im Unterschied zu einem System mit Zentralbank, dem Idealfall des reinen Mittlers annähert. Insbesondere wird argumentiert, daß sich das nominelle Geldangebot bei Bankfreiheit Änderungen in der Bargeldnachfrage anpaßt. Dadurch werden unnötige Preis- und Zinsänderungen vermieden.

References

ASCHHEIM, J. [1959], "Commercial Banks and Financial Intermediaries, Fallacies and Policy Implications", *Journal of Political Economy*, 67, 59–71.

BLACK, F. [1970], "Banking and Interest Rates in a World Without Money: The Effects of Uncontrolled Banking", *Journal of Bank Research*, 1, 9–20.

BROWN, H. G. [1910], "Commercial Banking and the Rate of Interest", *Quarterly Journal of Economics*, 24, 743–749.

CAGAN, P. [1958], "The Demand for Currency Relative to Total Money Supply", *Journal of Political Economy*, 66, 303–328.

CANNAN, E. [1921], "The Application of the Theoretical Apparatus of Supply and Demand to Units of Currency", *Economic Journal*, 31, 453–461.

– – [1935], "Growth and Fluctuations of Bankers' Liabilities to Customers," *The Manchester School*, 6, 2–17.

COOLEY, T. F., and LEROY, S. F. [1981], "Identification and Estimation of Money Demand", *American Economic Review*, 71, 825–844.

DAVIS, R. G. and GUTTENTAG, J. M. [1962], "Are Compensating Balance Requirements Irrational?" *Journal of Finance*, 17, 121–126.

EDGEWORTH, F. Y. [1888], "The Mathematical Theory of Banking", *Journal of the Royal Statistical Association*, 51, 113–127.

FAMA, E. [1980], "Banking in the Theory of Finance", *Journal of Monetary Economics*, 6, 39–57.

FISHER, A. G. B. [1935], "Does an Increase in Volume of Production Call for a Corresponding Increase in Volume of Money?", *American Economic Review*, 25, 197–211.

FRIEDMAN, M. and SCHWARTZ, A. [1986], "Has Government any Role in Money?", *Journal of Monetary Economics*, 17, 37–62.

GREENFIELD, R. L. and YEAGER, L. B. [1983], "A Laissez-Faire Approach to Monetary Stability", *Journal of Money, Credit, and Banking*, 15, 302–315.

GURLEY, J. G. and SHAW, E. S. [1965], "Financial Intermediaries and the Savings Investment Process", *Journal of Finance*, 11, 257–276.

HALL, R. E. [1984], "A Free-Market Policy to Stabilize the Purchasing Power of the Dollar", pp. 303–321, in: B. N. Siegel (ed.), *Money in Crisis*, San Francisco.

HAYEK, F. A. [1935], *Prices and Production*, London.

– – [1948], "The Use of Knowledge in Society," Ch. 4 of: *Individualism and Economic Order*, Chicago.

– – [1976], *Choice in Currency: A Way to Stop Inflation*, London.

– – [1978], *Denationalisation of Money – The Argument Refined*, 2nd, ed., London.

JACOBY, N. [1963], "The Structure and Use of Variable Bank Reserve Requirements", pp. 213–233, in: D. Carson (ed.), *Banking and Monetary Studies*, Homewood, Il.

JONUNG, L. [1985], "The Economics of Private Money: The Experience of Private Notes in Sweden, 1831–1902", *Paper presented at the Monetary History Group Meeting, London, Sept. 27, 1985*.

JUDD, J. P. and SCADDING J. L [1982], "The Search for a Stable Money Demand Function: A Survey of the Post-1973 Literature", *Journal of Economic Literature*, 20, 993–1023.

KLEIN, B. [1974], "The Competitive Supply of Money", *Journal of Money, Credit and Banking*, 6, 423–453.

MUNDELL, R. A. [1983], "International Monetary Options", *Cato Journal* 3, 189–210.

MUNN, C. [1981], *The Scottish Provincial Banking Companies, 1747–1864*, Edinburgh.

ORR, D. and MELLON, W. G. [1961], "Stochastic Reserve Losses and Expansion of Bank Credit", *American Economic Review*, 51, 614–623.

PHILLIPS, C. A. [1920], *Bank Credit*, New York.

POINDEXTER, J. C. [1946], "Some Misconceptions of Banking and Interest Theory", *Southern Economic Journal*, 13, 132–145.

POWELL, E. T. [1966], *The Evolution of the Money Market*, New York.

RICHARDS, R. D. [1965], *The Early History of Banking in England*, New York.

RIST, C. [1966], *History of Monetary and Credit Theory from John Law to the Present Day*, trans. Jane Degras, New York.

ROCKOFF, H. [1974], "The Free-Banking Era: A Re-Examination", *Journal of Money, Credit, and Banking*, 6, 141–167.

–– [1984], "Some Evidence on the Real Price of Gold, Its Costs of Production, and Commodity Prices", pp. 613–649, in: D. Bordo and A. J. Schwartz (eds.), *A Retrospective on the Classical Gold Standard, 1821–1931*, Chicago.

ROLNICK, A. J. and WEBER, W. E. [1982], "Free Banking, Wildcat Banking, and Shinplasters", *Federal Reserve Bank of Minneapolis Quarterly Review*, 6, 10–19.

–– [1983], "New Evidence on Laissez-Faire Banking", *American Economic Review*, 73, 1080–1091.

ROTHBARD, M. N. [1970], *Man. Economy, and State*, Los Angeles.

SARGENT, T. J. and WALLACE, N. [1982], "The Real-Bills Doctrine versus the Quantity Theory: A Reconsideration", *Journal of Political Economy*, 90, 1212–1236.

SELGIN, G. [1987], *The Theory of Free Banking: Money Supply Under Competitive Note Issue*, Totowa, N.J.

–– and WHITE, L. H. "The Evolution of a Free Banking System", forthcoming in *Economic Inquiry*.

SMITH, V. [1936], *The Rationale of Central Banking*, London.

TOBIN, J. [1963], "Commercial Banks as Creators of Money", pp. 408–419, in: Deane (ed.), *Banking and Monetary Studies*, Homewood, Il.

VAUBEL, R. [1984], "Private Competitive Note Issue in Monetary History", pp. 59–73, in: P. Salin (ed.), *Currency Competition and Monetary Union*, The Hague.

WALLACE, N. [1983], "A Legal Restrictions Theory of the Demand for 'Money' and the Role of Monetary Policy", *Federal Reserve Bank of Minneapolis Quarterly Review*, 7, 1–7.

WHITE, L. H. [1984a], "Free Banking as an Alternative Monetary System", pp. 269–302, in: B. Siegel (ed.), *Money in Crisis*, San Francisco.

–– [1984b], *Free Banking in Britain: Theory, History, and Debate, 1800–1845*, Cambridge, U.K.

WICKSELL, K. [1935], *Lectures on Political Economy Vol. 2*, London.

Professor George A. Selgin
Department of Economics
4400 University Drive
Fairfax, VA 22030
U.S.A.

[5]

Journal of Financial Services Research, 1: 319–333 (1988)
© 1988 Kluwer Academic Publishers

Option Clauses and the Stability of a Laisser Faire Monetary System

KEVIN DOWD
Department of Economics
University of Nottingham, Nottingham NG7 2RD, UK

Abstract

This article examines the potential of option clauses to stabilize a banking system with multiple banks of issue and convertible banknotes. It suggests that under laisser faire, banks will introduce option clauses and the public will be willing to accept them even when fully convertible notes are also available. This will be in the interest of both parties since option clauses protect banks against a liquidity crisis. The article then examines the historical experience of option clauses in Scotland in 1730–1765 and finds it to be broadly consistent with our prior expectations.

1. Introduction

This article explores a neglected topic in monetary economics: option clauses on convertible notes issued by competitive banks. These give banks the option of deferring redemption of their notes provided that they later pay compensation to the noteholders whose demands for redemption are deferred. They therefore allow banks to protect their liquidity if they are faced with an unexpected increase in demands for redemption. In addition, the knowledge that the banks had this protection would reassure the public that the banks were not likely to become illiquid, and this would reduce the likelihood of a bank run occurring in the first place. Option clauses are therefore a potentially important form of protection for banks that have redeemable liabilities and operate on a fractional-reserve.

Despite these potential benefits, option clauses have received very little attention from economists, and most of that has been unfavorable. Adam Smith condemned them in the *Wealth of Nations* (1776, pp. 290–291), and most succeeding economists who have discussed the issue have agreed with him (e.g., Graham (1886, p. 65), Kerr (1918, p. 74), MacLeod (1896, pp. 188–189), and Whittick (1896, pp. 67–69), to mention only four. Significantly, though, the only writer to examine the issue in any detail at all was Meulen (1934),[1] and he was unequivocally in favor

The author would like to thank Dave Chappell, Alec Chrystal, Jack Gilbert, Charles Goodhart, Neil Wallace, Larry White, John Zube, and an anonymous referee for their very helpful comments on an earlier draft. The usual disclaimer applies.

of them. He argued that option clauses would stabilize a free banking system as well as promote the replacement of gold by paper and thereby encourage the further spread of credit. This article takes up where Meulen left off and analyzes further the potential of option clauses to stabilize the banking system. The article first outlines how a laisser faire banking system driven purely by private interest might develop the option clause to deal with the problem of potential illiquidity to which fractional-reserve banking is otherwise subject. It then suggests reasons why individual noteholders would be prepared to accept option-clause notes in preference to notes convertible on demand—an important point which Meulen glossed over—and discusses how option clauses would both protect the banking system against liquidity crises and reduce the probability of such crises occurring in the first place. It then goes on to consider the historical experience of option clauses in Scotland in the period 1730–1765. This clearly confirms the claim that option clauses would be acceptable to the public and is not obviously inconsistent with the claim that option clauses would help to stabilize the monetary system.

2. The development of a free banking system with convertible notes

To discuss the theory of option-clause notes we consider the evolution of a free banking system from the following hypothetical primitive economy. Let us suppose that people originally use gold as their medium of exchange, but the use of gold is attended by various cost of storage and portability (i.e., it is expensive to keep it safe, and it wears holes in pockets because of its weight). Now suppose that there exist individuals ("goldsmiths") who already have the means of keeping gold safe (i.e., they have strongrooms). Both members of the public and the goldsmiths are assumed to be concerned only with their own private self-interest and not at all with any broader notions of "social interest." Let us also suppose that there is a legal system capable of enforcing any contracts entered into by private agents, and that people wish to avoid the penalty for default which involves having one's assets sold off to pay one's debts.

A banking system starts to evolve from this initial state of society when members of the public begin to pay goldsmiths to store their gold for them. Individuals will be ready to deposit their gold with a goldsmith provided that the fee is not too high and they are sufficiently confident that the goldsmith will not default while he has their gold. The goldsmiths will be prepared to accept the gold provided that the fee is above their marginal costs which we would expect to be low anyway. Hence there is some potential for mutually beneficial gains from trade. The practice of making gold deposits then gradually spreads, and the goldsmiths start to notice that withdrawals and deposits will be closely matched over time, and that over a given period the net loss in gold is likely to be quite small. They will realize that they could lend out some of the gold deposited with them and earn interest on it. They will then start competing with each other for deposits to lend out. The practice of charging depositors fees will die out, and goldsmiths will start offering depositors interest payments to attract them. At the same time, it will increasingly be the case in private trade that when one person withdraws gold to pay a debt the payee will simply deposit the gold again. Provided that both parties "trust" the goldsmith, they would both save time and trouble if the goldsmith's receipt were simply handed over instead. In this way these receipts/banknotes would start to circulate as media of exchange in their own right. This would reduce demands for redemption even more, and enable the goldsmith/bankers to expand their lending further.

We therefore arrive at a situation where competitive banks issue their own redeemable notes. Let us suppose that it is not feasible to pay interest on notes.[2] Let us also suppose that a market evolves in which agents can borrow gold on a short-term basis. If one likes, one could view this market as arising originally from agents' inability to predict their future cash needs with certainty. Over any given period some agents will find themselves with more cash than they anticipated, and some with less. It would then be mutually beneficial for the former to lend to the latter, and a short-term liquidity market would develop.

3. Convertibility on demand and potential illiquidity

To stay in business a bank would have to persuade people to accept its notes. (For simplicity, we shall ignore deposit banking throughout.) To do that it will try to reassure people that its notes would retain their value. The most effective way to do that would probably be for the bank to make a legally binding commitment to redeem its notes under certain specified conditions. The question then arises as to what those conditions might be. An "obvious" commitment the bank could make would be to redeem on demand without notice, that is, to make its notes "fully convertible." If the banks developed originally from goldsmiths it is quite likely that they started off by offering this kind of guarantee. Such a guarantee would give the public more flexibility and cost the goldsmiths little because they would operate with a 100 percent reserve ratio, to begin with at least. Once they start to lend out, however, they would not be able to honor more than a fraction of their note liabilities over any given (short) period, and this would expose them to the danger of defaulting on their legal obligations. This danger arises from the combination of a typical bank earning much of its income from borrowing short to lend long and its legally enforceable obligation to redeem any notes presented to it. Given sufficient time it could liquidate enough assets to meet any demand for redemption—assuming it was solvent—but the danger of default arises because it would not get the notice it might need.

These demands for redemption could come from various sources. One source is the general public, members of which might want to redeem their notes if they believed that the bank was insolvent (i.e., if its net value was negative). They might also demand redemption if they believed—rightly or wrongly—that there was some danger of the bank becoming illiquid. They might want to avoid holding the notes of a potentially illiquid bank because they might fear that other people would be reluctant to accept the notes of a bank that suspended, or because they thought that such notes would only be accepted at a discount. Such fears might lead to noteholders demanding redemption "just in case," and this gives rise to the possibility that the public's expectations of a bank run could become "self-fulfilling" in the sense that any intrinsically irrelevant event could trigger off a bank run if it made sufficiently many noteholders apprehensive about one (see, e.g., Diamond and Dybvig (1983)). Demands for redemption might also come from other banks: if a bank were committed to redemption on demand, a competitor might be tempted to collect a large amount of its notes and present them without warning for redemption to make it default. These "note duels" were a significant feature of early banking in Scotland, for instance, and we shall return to them below.

A possible solution to this potential illiquidity problem would be to modify the convertibility contract. Instead of promising to redeem on demand without notice, the bank might insert clauses into its notes giving it the option to defer redemption provided it later paid compensation to the noteholders. These "option clauses" would have two distinctive features: a period over which redemption could be deferred, and a compensatory (or penalty) interest rate, both of which would be specified in the contract.

Other things being equal, the bank would generally prefer a longer deferment period to give it more time to replenish reserves (which it could then do more cheaply), and it would obviously prefer a low penalty rate of interest to a higher one. In designing an option clause, however, a bank would have to make sure that it did not lose its noteholders to other banks. The first bank to introduce them would have to make sure that its new option clause (OC) notes were at least as attractive as the fully convertible (FC) notes issued by the other banks. If it failed to do this it would be outcompeted by its rivals. The bank might reason that noteholders would prefer low deferment periods (because they presumably prefer assets that could be redeemed more quickly) and high penalty rates (since a higher penalty rate would imply a larger claim to compensation if the option were invoked). Assuming appropriate convexity conditions, these preferences can be represented as in figure 1. The diagram shows those combinations of higher deferment periods and higher penalty interest rates that define the indifference map of the representative noteholder. The upper contour set (area A) is the set of combinations of deferment period and penalty rate which the public would prefer to FC notes, and the lower contour set (area B) shows those combinations at which the public would prefer FC notes. The figure also shows the isoprofit line of a representative bank. The problem for the bank is to select a combination (T, r^p) which is not in B to maximize its profits. This is shown as the point x in the figure. The bank would then replace its FC notes with OC notes with these particular features and its profit would rise from O to π_1.

This analysis suggests at perhaps a slightly superficial level that noteholders might be prepared to accept OC notes, and we clearly need to examine the issue in

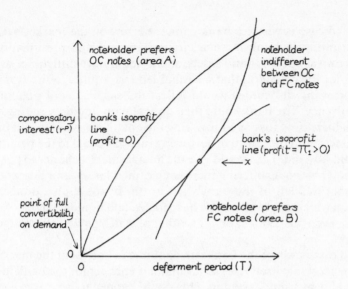

Fig. 1. The (ex ante) benefits of option clauses.

more depth. To do this we shall first discuss how a bank might use the option clause if it could get people to accept it. We then suggest reasons why this could be expected to make noteholders better off and can then reasonably safely conclude that rational noteholders could be expected to accept OC notes.

4. How an individual bank would use the option clause

Let us suppose that an individual bank has managed to persuade its noteholders to accept notes with option clauses on them. Since the bank is concerned purely with its own private interest, it would invoke the option whenever that provided a cheaper way to remain liquid than borrowing liquidity on the short-term market. There seem to be three situations in which this might be the case.

The first is if the bank were suddenly presented with a large amount of notes for redemption by a rival bank. In that case the demand might be so large and unexpected that it might not be feasible to borrow on the short-term market and the bank would have to suspend. One should add, however, that much of the temptation to engage in these duels comes from the prospect of forcing a rival to default, and a bank contemplating such an attack would not expect to destroy its rival if it were protected by an option clause. It would also appreciate that an attempt to collect notes and present them for redemption would invite the other bank to retaliate at a later date. A bank might thus choose to exercise its option clause if it found itself under attack from another bank, but the chances of that happening are likely to be reduced precisely because it has that option.

The second case is where a bank cannot borrow on the market because of its poor credit rating. A bank in such circumstances would presumably have exhausted its own supply of liquid assets, and it would have difficulties using its illiquid assets for the collateral that potential lenders would require from it. In this case its borrowing difficulties would reflect the suspicions of potential lenders about its solvency. The bank could then only remain liquid by selling off illiquid assets at an increasing loss or by invoking the option clause. It would presumably liquidate assets until the effective borrowing rate was equal to the penalty rate and then it would suspend. This would give the management a chance to put the bank's affairs in order without suffering increasing capital losses, and this would help to preserve what was left of the bank's net worth. It would also protect the bank against a run which might otherwise have forced it to liquidate more of its remaining assets or even pushed it to default, either of which could inflict large losses on its creditors.[3]

The third case is where the bank can continue to borrow at the market rate, but where the market rate itself rises so far that it is cheaper for the bank to obtain (or retain) liquidity by using its option. This would happen if there were a systemwide liquidity crisis. A bank would continue to redeem on demand for as long as it was cheaper to do so. Once interest rates reached a threshold level, however, it would exercise its option and suspend convertibility. It would do so because it could make arbitrage profits by lending its reserves on the short-term markets and realize the difference between market interest rates and the penalty rate it was paying on its funds. In doing so it would not only be acting to preserve its own liquidity but it would also be channelling liquidity to where the demand for it was greatest, and thereby would help to alleviate the rise in interest rates.

5. Would noteholders accept OC notes?

We can now address the question we raised earlier: would noteholders accept OC notes given their expectations of how they would be used? There are several reasons why noteholders might expect to be at least as well off accepting these notes as they would be with FC notes.

The first stems from the fact that a bank protected by option clauses would face little if any danger from either note duels or self-fulfilling bank runs. With FC notes, as we have seen, there is always the danger that a rival might try to destroy it in a note duel, or that an intrinsically irrelevant event might trigger off a bank run which would be fuelled by the public's knowledge that the bank could not redeem all its notes on demand. These sudden demands for redemption would harm noteholders insofar as notes that would normally be widely acceptable might only be accepted at a discount, or they might be refused outright. They would also harm noteholders if they led to capital losses on notes as a result of the bank defaulting. The prospect of a note duel or a "self-fulfilling" bank run thus increases the probability of noteholders suffering losses, and noteholders might prefer OC notes because they help substantially to avoid these dangers.

OC notes offer noteholders an additional potential advantage. A bank that introduced option clauses would effectively relax the liquidity constraint under which it operated. This would make certain lending opportunities profitable that would otherwise have been unworthwhile. The bank's prospective profits would rise and increase the valuation of its stock. Other things being equal, this would reduce the probability of bankruptcy and hence make the notes safer. The higher expected profits of the bank therefore indirectly help the noteholders even if the bank cannot pass on some of that profit by paying them direct pecuniary returns.

There is, however, a possible drawback of OC notes that noteholders would have to take into consideration. It is possible that an insolvent bank might invoke the option clause to "buy time" and take risks in the hope of salvaging an otherwise bankrupt organization. If this happened, the bank would be able to take gambles at the expense of its noteholders, and they would be deprived of the normal recourse of demanding instant redemption. We must bear in mind, however, that the bank would be aware of this, and it has a clear incentive to provide noteholders with a credible reassurance that this would not happen. The bank could do this by "bonding" shareholders' capital. In Scotland, for instance, the shareholders of some banks assumed unlimited liability, while in the early United States the custom was for shareholders to assume "double liability." Provided shareholders still have something to lose, they have an incentive to avoid wild risks even if the bank has a negative net worth. Knowing this, rational noteholders would presumably discount the likelihood of the bank becoming insolvent and taking wild risks at their expense.

6. The banking system with OC notes

I have given some reasons why it might be in the private interest of a bank to introduce option clauses on its notes, and why it might be in the private interest of its customers to prefer them to FC notes. If this is so, a bank which introduced OC notes would have a competitive advantage over others. In the context of figure 1, such a bank would only have to choose a point (T, r^p) in the set A to outcompete its rivals. The latter would be forced to introduce option clauses of their own to stay in business. The banks that introduced successful option clauses first would make higher profits, but when equilibrium is restored all banks would make zero profits again. The situation is illustrated in figure 2. The set of possible long-run equilibrium points is given by the line xy; x would be an equilibrium point if the banks' shares were traded on the stock market and their prices rose to capitalize the expected future profits. In this case the people who owned the shares initially would get the economic surplus. The opposite polar extreme is illustrated by y at which all the surplus goes to the noteholders and none to the shareholders. In general we

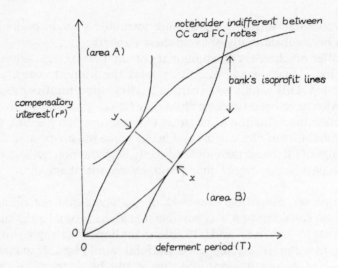

Fig. 2. The option-clause equilibrium.

can only say that the surplus is divided between the shareholders and the noteholders, but without additional information we cannot say what the proportions of the share-out would be. We cannot, therefore, say what the resulting (T, r^p) equilibrium point would be. For the sake of simplicity we shall leave aside the issue of how this point is determined and we shall assume that it is the same for each bank.

7. The stability of the OC equilibrium

Suppose that there is a sudden, unanticipated, but temporary increase in the demand for to convert notes into specie (i.e., a "liquidity crisis"). This will be reflected in the short-term rate of interest which would rise steeply above "normal" levels. By hypothesis, the extra demand is temporary so people could reasonably expect interest rates to fall back again in the short-to-medium term. This implies that bill prices are currently low and falling, but that in the longer run people expect them to rise back to normal levels. Consider now the position of an operator in the short-term liquidity market. He can be reasonably sure that in the longer run he should buy bills, but in the very short run it might be worthwhile to sell them instead. He might therefore sell bills and thereby bid up interest rates even further. As this continues, other people would be encouraged to enter the market and bet on the prospects of medium-term capital gains by buying bills. These people would, therefore, run down their stocks of gold, demand redemption of their notes, and import gold with the intention of lending it out in the short-term market. This

bullish activity might be enough to satisfy the demand for liquidity and bring interest rates down, but there is no telling just when the market will turn around.

This situation could be very dangerous for the banks if they were obliged to
redeem on demand. Noteholders might be tempted to demand redemption either
because they wished to make a profit by lending the gold or because they feared
that the banks would default. If the demand for liquidity continued unabated the
banks might eventually default and the banking system could collapse. This
would not happen if the banks were protected by option clauses. In that case, if interest rates continued to rise they would eventually reach a "threshold" level at
which it would be cheaper for banks to remain liquid by exercising their options
than by borrowing on the short-term market. As this point was the same for all
banks they would invoke their options simultaneously and immediately stop the
liquidity "drain" they were facing from noteholders demanding redemption. Once
the interest rate passes this threshold level it would become worthwhile for the
banks to lend their reserves on the short-term market. These arbitrage activities
would continue to be profitable for as long as market interest rates remained
above the penalty rate, and so the banks' intervention would bring market rates
down to this level. The demand for liquidity would be satisfied, the panic would
subside, and the interest rate would return to normal levels. In this way the panic
would be corrected by the banks acting to maximize their profits with no thought
at all of any wider "social interest." It is also worth noting that there would be no
need at all for any "lender of last resort" to stand above the banking system to protect it against a liquidity crisis: this suggests the lender of last resort function would
be redundant in a laisser faire monetary system.

This is still not the whole story. The discussion so far has ignored the possibility
that the banks' intervention might have been anticipated. However, it seems
reasonable to suppose that their intervention would be anticipated because the
public could calculate the threshold level of the short-term interest rate at which
the banks would suspend and intervene. It follows that as interest continued to
rise, a rational bear speculator would estimate that the chances of it going
significantly above that threshold rate would be very low. He would therefore appreciate that the threshold put an effective floor to expected bill prices. As bill
prices approached that floor, our speculator would estimate that his chances of
making further profits by selling bills would diminish very considerably while the
probability of capital loss would increase. At some point before the threshold was
reached he would almost certainly decide that further risks were not worth taking,
and buy instead to take his capital gains. He would be further encouraged to do so
by the knowledge that other people were making the same calculation, and he
would be anxious to avoid being short on bills when their price started to rise. The
demand for liquidity would therefore almost certainly "break" before interest rates
hit the threshold level because of the banks' anticipated intervention. This shows
that option clauses can be effective even if they are never actually invoked. In most
cases one would expect that the mere prospect that they might be invoked would
suffice to stabilize the panic and protect the banking system from collapse.

8. Option clauses in Scotland, 1730–1765

It would be interesting to compare the speculations above with an empirical example of OC notes under free banking. Unfortunately, such examples are hard to find. Historical instances of "free banking" are rare, but instances of option clauses being tolerated under free banking are rarer still, and the only recorded case seems to be in Scotland during the period 1730–1765.

Option clauses in Scotland were introduced by the Bank of Scotland in 1730, after it had fought a note duel with a newly established rival, the Royal Bank of Scotland, and been forced to suspend convertibility. The Bank inserted option clauses on its notes to protect itself when it later reopened. These clauses gave the Bank the option to defer redemption for six months provided it paid compensation of sixpence in the pound on redemption (i.e., 5 percent per annum).[4] The Bank announced the reason for the innovation, and its notes continued to circulate at par afterwards. The Royal Bank refused to imitate it and advertised the fact that its notes were redeemable on demand at all times, but these attempts to persuade the Bank's noteholders to abandon it were not successful, and the two notes circulated side by side at par. This shows that option clauses can be acceptable to the public even when FC notes are also available.

The next 30 years saw a rapid growth of banking in Scotland. The Bank of Scotland and the Royal Bank continued to wage war on each other for most of the period, as well as on new banks that were set up in the meantime. The business of banking was a new one to everyone, so it took the banks a long time to develop appropriate rules of thumb to guide them. They had to learn by trial and error the reserve ratios to observe, how to respond to specie shortages, how to deal with each other, and so on. Despite all this, the banking system was relatively stable during these years, and the option clause was apparently never invoked.

This changed in the early 1760s. As Checkland (1975, p. 109) explains:

> A good deal of money from England had been lent in Scotland at 4% between 1748 and 1757; much of this was now withdrawn, for under war conditions it could be more profitably placed at home ... The Edinburgh exchange on London became very adverse. Bills on London rose to a premium of 4½ or 5%. It was well known that when this rate reached 2–3% specie would be carried south ... The banks were faced with a major liquidity crisis.

This had two major effects on the Scottish banking system. The first was that banks started looking for ways to protect their liquidity. By June 1762 all of them had adopted option clauses. In addition they resorted to a number of other expedients. One such expedient was to borrow gold from London at a heavy loss. This involved heavy costs of both exchange and conversion which together amounted to over 5 percent of the value of the specie (Checkland, 1975, p. 109). It was also pointless because the gold simply found its way south again where returns were higher: "while in this state, bringing gold into the country was like pouring water into a sieve" (MacLeod, 1896, p. 189). One must bear in mind, however, that this was the first time the Scottish banks had experienced a major drain, and the banks presumably had to learn through experience which measures were effective and which were not. The banks also contracted credit and raised deposit interest rates to cut gold outflows. The Bank of Scotland and the Royal Bank began doing this in January 1762, but at the cost of some public criticism (Checkland. 1975, pp. 109–110). In contracting credit the banks were particularly careful to refuse credits to "badly disposed people" like specie exporters and those who aided them. The banks also discouraged people from demanding redemption by offering to grant requests for redemption in part only, and by threatening to invoke the option clause and give them no gold at all if noteholders insisted on more gold than the banks were willing to part with. Measures like these were effective, but they were resented and helped make the option clause unpopular. Fortunately for the banks these measures appeared to work, and normality seemed to be returning in the early part of 1763.

The second effect of the shortage of specie was an increase in the demand for small denomination notes to replace coins. For reasons that remain unclear, the major banks refused to satisfy this demand. Many private individuals therefore began to issue notes of their own. Clapham (1970, p. 241) talks of a "grotesque multitude of small notes, not issued by regular bankers" for different sums, to be redeemable into various goods, while Checkland (p. 1975, 105) talks of the provision of substitutes for coin being left to "petty tradesmen." The public accepted these notes for lack of any alternative in the same way that they used to accept similar substitutes in the past whenever coins were scarce. Nonetheless, the dubious status of the issuers gave small notes a bad name and paved the way for their later suppression.

The pressure on reserves started to mount again in August 1763. It was occasioned by the failure of an Amsterdam bank which had been engaged in speculation toward the end of the seven years' war. This failure triggered off a general collapse of banks across the continent and a flight toward specie. The increased demand for specie again pushed up interest rates in London, and all the banks experienced a renewed shortage of liquidity. The pressure became so intense that the Bank of Scotland and the Royal Bank were obliged to exercise their option clauses in March 1764. They also cut back credit and increased deposit rates (Checkland, 1975, pp. 121–2).

In the meantime there was much public dissatisfaction with small notes, the contraction of credit, and the way the banks were threatening and sometimes using option clauses. Public meetings up and down the country in 1763–1764 petitioned Parliament to legislate. The government indicated it was sympathetic to these requests so the banks lobbied to influence the legislation. The two big Edinburgh banks had been reconciled with each other since 1752 and lobbied for a legislated duopoly to eliminate their opposition. In return they were prepared to pay an annual sum of £1500 each and surrender their rights to the option clause. The main Glasgow banks lobbied instead for free banking to protect their rights to

330   KEVIN DOWD

issue notes. The government would have none of the Edinburgh banks' attempts to do away with the opposition and was also concerned to protect people from what it perceived as the abuse of small notes and option clauses. The result was an Act of 1765 which guaranteed the freedom of entry to the Scottish banking industry, but which prohibited option clauses and Scottish notes of less than £1. And so the Scottish experiment with option clauses was suppressed only 35 years after it had begun.

9. Is the Scottish experience consistent with our prior expectations?

Our discussion of the theory of option clauses suggested two main "empirical predictions." The first is that there would be some conditions under which option clauses would be accepted by the public, and the second is that the adoption of option clauses promotes monetary stability. Are these consistent with the Scottish experience?

The first prediction obviously is. Noteholders in Scotland were clearly prepared to accept OC notes even when they could have chosen FC notes instead. As Meulen (1934, p. 132) states, "The one fact which is firmly established . . . is that option-clause notes were issued by the foremost banks in Scotland, and in these cases were freely circulated, at par."

The second predition is much more difficult to assess. Part of the problem is that the Scottish banking system was developing rapidly throughout the brief option clause period. Banking was a new business that the bankers were still trying to learn and the public trying to become used to. Mistakes were frequent, and it took time for bankers to realize where their true interests lay. This is well illustrated by the length of time it took the banks to agree to a note exchange. A note exchange was in each bank's own interest because it promoted the demand for its notes,[5] and yet the note exchange was only established in 1771. Another example seems to be the regular banks' reluctance to meet the demand for small notes. If private individuals found it worthwhile to issue notes, the regular banks would certainly have, and they would have had a comparative advantage at it. Why they failed even to try is a mystery. Considerations like these suggest that the Scottish banking system of the early 1760s had not yet settled into the "OC equilibrium" discussed earlier, and so any inferences drawn from a comparison of the two must be very cautious ones.

Several inferences can, however, be made. Opponents of option clauses made much of the depreciation of the OC notes relative to FC notes or gold when the option was exercised, and used this to suggest that OC notes destabilized the value of money. Adam Smith (1776, pp. 290–291), for example, cited the example of a Dumfries bank whose notes were at a considerable discount in Carlisle relative to FC notes. However, as Meulen (p. 132) points out:

... the option clause was introduced only in order to stave off outside demands for gold. The ordinary customers of banks needed only exchange medium, not necessarily gold, and they were quite content to accept the option-clause notes of a reliable bank. Those who desired to obtain gold for export, however, would undoubtedly differentiate between option-clause notes and those which were redeemable in gold on demand, and this would undoubtedly be twisted ... into an evidence of "depreciation" of Scottish paper ...

One might extend this argument further. During a crisis interest rates rise because of the increased demand for gold relative to notes and other goods, and the exercise of the option clause temporarily breaks the link between the value of the notes and gold. This helps to stabilize the value of the notes in terms of goods, and thus to insulate day-to-day trade from the monetary shock. The exercise of the option also stabilizes trade by protecting the banks' liquidity, thus reducing the danger of a run, as we discussed earlier. In this context it is worth noting that there was apparently no major public concern about the danger of bank runs in Scotland during this period. It is also possible that the exercise of the option helped to stabilize interest rates in Scotland, although we have very little evidence about this. In short, the very fact that OC notes fell to a discount against gold when the option was used may well have helped to stabilize the Scottish economy because it was an essential part of the mechanism through which the domestic economy was insulated from the external shock. If this is what happened, it would lend further support to our second prediction that option clauses would help to stabilize the banking system. Given the very tenuous nature of the evidence, however, it would be safer to conclude that this prediction is not obviously at variance with the Scottish experience.

10. Some limitations and conclusions

Our discussion of option clauses has left a number of issues unresolved. Some of these center around the option clause itself. We have not discussed how banks would choose a penalty rate and deferment period, for example. One possibility is that banks might choose these using the formula "x percent above the short-term market rate of interest prevailing over the last y months," but even if the banks use this formula, we would still have to explain how x and y would be chosen. A related issue is how banks would "compete" with different option clauses. If the option clause is used only rarely, or possibly never, then one has to explain the process whereby the public and the banks settle down on a particular kind (of kinds) of option clause contract. Also, we have only considered "simple" option clauses which give the bank two options only. It might be worth their while for the banks to introduce more "sophisticated" option clauses which would give them more options. It is interesting to note that White (1984, p. 29) reports an instance of a "triple" op-

332   KEVIN DOWD

tion clause in Scotland in the early 1760s. The idea did not catch on, but that may be because option clauses were banned so soon after.

Option clauses also have important implications for the lender of last resort and our perception of the "inherent" instability of a fractional-reserve banking system. Our discussion indicates that private profit-maximizing banks can and will protect themselves adequately against shocks that threaten their liquidity. All they appear to need is a legal framework that allows them to do so, and this suggests that the lender of last resort function is redundant in a laisser faire monetary system.

Another issue is how option clauses relate to current commercial banking arrangements. I have examined option clauses on notes, but option clauses could also be inserted into the contracts governing deposits as well. In the recent past banks in both the United States and United Kingdom frequently inserted "notice of withdrawal" clauses into deposit contracts but seldom if ever invoked them. It is not clear why banks do not write these clauses into their deposit contracts more than they appear to do. Perhaps it is because they believe they can get the reserve media they might need from other banks or the central bank.

A final limitation of this article is that is relies on heuristic reasoning and does not use a formal theoretical framework. Since demands for redemption are formally similar to queuing problems, it seems one could model option clauses using an application of queuing theory. I hope to be able to report the results of such an exercise in the near future.

Notes

1. Meulen was the last in a line of "underground" British free bankers, most of whom were active toward the end of the last century, and of whom the best known is Herbert Spencer. While some of his views seem questionable, there is no doubt that his work has not received the attention it deserves. Meulen's principal discussions of option clauses occur in his 1934 book on pp. 81–83, 87–88, and 127–132. One should note that many of the ideas in this book were previously published in an earlier edition *Industrial Justice Through Banking Reform* (1917) and a pamphlet "Banking and the Social Problem" (Wadsworth and Co., Keighley, 1909).

One might also add that this article concentrates on the stabilizing properties of option clauses and does not deal with the implications of option clauses for the long-run efficiency of the economy. Meulen stressed repeatedly that option clauses helped to promote economic efficiency by promoting the replacement of gold by paper, thereby economizing on holdings of "dead" (i.e., noninterest-bearing) specie.

2. Our task would be much easier if we assumed that banks could pay interest on their notes, since banks could then encourage people to hold OC notes simply by increasing the interest rate on them, but unfortunately there are reasons to believe that the transactions and/or accounting costs of doing so do not make it feasible. I refer the reader to White (1987).

3. There is, however, a possible counterargument here. It is possible that a badly run bank might use the "breathing space" provided by the exercise of the option clause to run the bank further into the ground. This is discussed on p. 319 below.

4. MacLeod (1896, p. 18). Note that this was the maximum permissible legal rate of interest. It is not clear what effect usury laws might have had on option clauses.

5. See, for example, White (1984).

References

Checkland, S. G. *Scottish Banking: A History.* Glasgow and London: Collins, 1975.

Clapham, Sir J. *The Bank of England: A History,* Vol. I 1694–1797. Cambridge: Cambridge University Press, 1970.

Diamond, D. W. & Dybvig, P. H. Bank Runs, Deposit Insurance, and Liquidity. *Journal of Political Economy* (Vol. 91, 1983), pp. 401–419.

Graham, W. *The One Pound Note.* Edinburgh: James Thin, 1886.

Kerr, Andrew W. *History of Banking in Scotland,* 3rd ed., London: A. & C. Black Ltd., 1918.

MacLeod, H. D. *A History of Banking in Great Britain,* (1896) in Vol. III of *A History of Banking in All the Leading Nations,* edited by W. G. Sumner, reprinted by Augustus M. Kelley. New York: 1971.

Meulen, H. *Free Banking: An Outline of a Policy of Individualism,* London: Macmillan, 1934.

Smith, A. *An Inquiry into the Nature and Causes of the Wealth of Nations* (1776), edited by E. R. A. Seligman and reprinted by J. M. Dent and Sons, Ltd., London, and E. P. Dutton and Co., New York, 1911.

White, L. H. *Free Banking in Britain: Theory, Experience, and Debate, 1800–1845,* Cambridge: Cambridge University Press, 1984.

White, L. H. Accounting for Non-Interest-Bearing Currency: A Critique of the "Legal Restrictions" Theory of Money, *Journal of Money, Credit, and Banking* (Vol. 19, 1987), pp. 448–456.

Whittick, W. A. *Value and an Invariable Standard of Value.* Philadelphia: J. B. Lippincott, 1896.

Part II
Competing Non-Commodity
Base Monies

[6]

BENJAMIN KLEIN*

The Competitive Supply of Money

FEW AREAS OF ECONOMIC ACTIVITY can claim as long and unanimous a record of agreement on the appropriateness of governmental intervention as the supply of money.[1] Very early in our history money was recognized by policy makers to be "special," and individuals fearful of government influence in other areas of economic life readily acknowledged that government had a primary role in controlling monetary arrangements. Free market advocates who now argue for, among other things, unregulated entry and the elimination of all interest rate and portfolio restrictions do not opt for a completely unregulated money industry, but recognize that money has unique characteristics which require that it not be supplied freely as an ordinary good. The monetary role of government is agreed to include, at a minimum, the monopolistic supply of a currency, into which all privately supplied demand deposits should be convertible. In

*This paper was presented at the American Bankers Association Conference of University Professors held at Lake Arrowhead California, September 1970. Publication of the article and comments to it are made possible by the support of the Center for Research in Government Policy and Business, University of Rochester.

The essential argument of this paper was originally presented at a University of Chicago Money workshop in June, 1968. I am especially indebted to Armen Alchian and also to Stephen Friedberg, Milton Friedman, Levis Kochin, Roger Kormendi, Edward Lazear, Mather Lindsay, Joseph Ostroy, Sam Peltzman, Douglas Shetler, and Earl Thompson for useful comments and discussions on the succeeding drafts of the paper. I would also like to gratefully acknowledge research support from the Lilly Endowment, Inc. grant to UCLA for the study of property rights and from the UCLA Research Program in Business Economics and Policy. I alone should be held responsible for the views expressed and for the remaining errors.

[1] A major exception was Herbert Spencer, who advocated a completely laissez-faire policy towards money [35, pp. 354-360]. Rothbard [33] has more recently advocated, on fundamentally ethical grounds, the adoption of an unregulated gold money supply.

BENJAMIN KLEIN *is associate professor of economics at the University of California, Los Angeles.*

424 : MONEY, CREDIT, AND BANKING

addition, reserve requirements are often considered appropriate. This paper is an attempt to begin to identify the peculiar characteristics of money that necessitate this expanded governmental responsibility in the money industry.

Section 1 starts from the "money is a good" theoretical framework, i.e., assumes that a demand for money exists. We initially assume that all money supply changes are fully anticipated and therefore the nominal quantity of each competitive firm's money (and the price level in terms of each particular money) is in metastable equilibrium. Within this context Friedman's argument that unregulated competitive production of money will lead to an infinite price level is examined. The argument is shown to use an improper concept of competition by implicitly assuming that competitive firms are producing indistinguishable monies. If product quality is a function of total supply, then consumers must be able to distinguish between the products of different firms if a competitive market is to function. In Section 2 we introduce information costs regarding money supply changes and therefore the possibility that firms may "deceive" their customers by supplying more money than anticipated. But it is shown that if consumers and producers make the same estimate of the short-run profits from a policy of deception, then the equilibrium quantity of brand-name capital will insure that firms will not excessively overissue. In the process the distinction between "commodity" and "fiduciary" money is blurred. In Section 3 we examine actual monetary arrangements to determine the applicability of the analysis, and implications for international monetary relations are drawn. Finally, in Section 4 an attempt to rationalize the government's role in the money industry is made.

I. The Competitive Supply of Monetary Services

A. The Price of Monetary Services

If money is considered to be a durable good yielding a service flow, the stock of money must be distinguished from the flow of "monetary services." Whatever the service flow from *holding* money consists of, its services depend on the eventual or possible *spending* of money and therefore on the exchange rate of money for real commodities. Hence, the real monetary-service stream N yielded to an individual holding M_j nominal units of the jth money-producing firm's money is negatively related to the price level P_j of goods and services in terms of the jth money and is assumed homogeneous of degree zero in money prices; viz,

$$N = N((M/P)_j, \beta_j),$$ (1)

where β_j represents the "confidence" (to be defined later) the individual has in the future exchange value of the jth money and each individual is assumed to hold only one firm's money.

Assume that the jth money also yields an explicit pecuniary rate of return (or interest payments) of $(r_M)_j$. Assume further that there are financial assets, called "bonds," which are claims to a future nominal unit of the jth money and which yield no nonpecuniary monetary-service returns but do yield pecuniary interest payments in terms of the jth money at the rate of i_j. The pecuniary alternative cost per unit time, in terms of the jth money, of holding a unit of the jth money is therefore $(i - r_M)_j$. In equilibrium, $(i - r_M)_j$ must equal the value of the monetary-service stream from a marginal unit of the jth money and will be the rental price of holding a unit of the jth money. The real rental price of a unit of monetary services produced by jth money holdings is therefore, in equilibrium, given by:

$$(P_N)_j / P_j = (i - r_M)_j / [(\partial N / \partial M_j) \cdot P_j], \tag{2}$$

where $(\partial N / \partial M_j)$ is the marginal product in monetary services of the jth money and (if the individual is assumed to be a price taker with respect to changes in his own money holdings) is equal to $(\partial N / \partial (M/P)_j) (1/P_j)$.

B. Competitive Equilibrium

Assume that there is a perfectly competitive unregulated monetary service industry operating under conditions where consumers costlessly possess perfect information regarding future money supply and price level changes. Let C_j represent the jth firm's real costs of producing monetary services, where

$$C_j = C_j(N). \tag{3}$$

Each firm producing money faces an infinitely elastic demand curve with respect to the real price of its monetary services, and therefore, in equilibrium, the real rental price of monetary services will equal the firm's real marginal cost of producing monetary services, dC_j / dN:

$$(P_N)_j / P_j = dC_j / dN \equiv [\partial C_j / \partial (M/P)_j][d(M/P)_j / dN]$$

$$+ [\partial C_j / \partial \beta_j][d\beta_j / dN]. \tag{4}$$

Under conditions of fully anticipated money supply changes, consumer confidence β_j can be assumed to be unlimited and therefore the competitive equilibrium (4) becomes

$$(i - r_M)_j = dC_j / d(M/P)_j ;\tag{5}$$

i.e., the alternative cost of holding a unit of the jth firm's money is equal to the jth firm's real marginal cost of producing real cash balances.[2]

Assuming each firm has identical costs of producing monetary services, equilibrium condition (5) yields the competitive equilibrium quantity of monetary services and real cash balances produced by an individual firm and the competitive interest payment on money. And given the market demand for monetary services, the equilibrium determines the total rate of monetary services supplied and the number of firms in the money industry. If the real costs of producing real cash balances are assumed to be zero, then competitive interest payments on money will equal "the" interest rate and the number of firms in the industry is indeterminate. Demanders can be assumed to differentiate between firms, and therefore the market is shared among firms, on the basis of nonprice factors.

C. Finite Price Levels

It is commonly asserted that "fiduciary" (zero marginal production cost) money cannot be supplied under conditions of unregulated laissez-faire competition without leading to an infinite price level. However, the competitive equilibrium described above does not imply an infinite price level. First, since each firm produces a different, distinguishable money, the concept "price level" is ambiguous; with many monies circulating side by side at flexible market exchange rates, we can only unambiguously talk about the price level in terms of a particular money.

If we assume that all money supply changes are anticipated, then the quantity of each particular money and the price level in terms of that money may be indeterminately large or small, but this metastable equilibrium with respect to each firm's nominal quantity of money is of no importance. The initial nominal quantity of each firm's money is assumed to be arbitrarily determined and is analogous to the question of what to call the particular monetary unit.[3] And perfectly foreseen changes in the supply of a firm's money will not change its profit or the cost to the consumer.

If a money-producing firm increases its outstanding nominal money by purchase of real goods and services or of bonds denominated in another firm's money, then it may (erroneously) appear that the real value of

---

[2]This statement is somewhat difficult to interpret since a firm only indirectly "produces" $(M/P)_j$ by altering $(i - r_M)_j$ and β_j, i.e., by altering the amount demanded. Real output is conceptually not a control variable of the firm but ultimately determined on the demand side—a unique characteristic of the money industry.

[3]In a more realistic information-scarce world, the denomination of a monetary unit may have important effects on consumer confidence. Consider, in this context, the many currency reforms which countries undertake and the number of currencies that are called "dollar" or "pound."

the firm's net wealth will increase with its supply of money. A money supply increase will reduce the real value of the money stock obtained by customers in previous exchanges without changing the real value of what the previous customers exchanged for the money. Wealth maximization would seem to imply an unlimited once-and-for-all increase in the firm's money and an infinite price level. But such a conclusion follows only if all money supply increases are unanticipated. The money firm would then be "deceiving" its previous money holders by depreciating the value of their holdings when no future money increase and depreciation were anticipated and contracted for at the time of the earlier exchanges. We have, however, here assumed that such unanticipated changes in the supply of a money were impossible. Therefore, the present price of the monetary services from a particular money reflects all future changes in the supply of the particular money. The wealth-maximizing actual (and anticipated) level of the nominal stock of money will therefore not be unique.[4]

The competitive *rate of change* of each individual firm's nominal money supply and price level is also not unique. Our perfectly competitive anticipated money supply world implies that the actual rate of change of the jth firm's money $(\dot{M}/M)_j$ equals the anticipated rate of change of the jth firm's money $(\dot{M}/M)_j^*$ and also equals the actual $(\dot{P}/P)_j$ and anticipated $(\dot{P}/P)_j^*$ rate of change of prices in terms of the jth firm's money. The higher the anticipated rate of change of any firm's money (and therefore the higher the anticipated rate of change of prices in terms of its money), the higher "the" nominal rate of interest in terms of the firm's money and therefore the higher the anticipated and actual cost to consumers of holding the firm's money. If the firm is to make any sales, it must now pay a higher rate of interest on its money to keep the alternative cost of holding its money $(i - r_M)_j$ constant.[5] Consumers are indifferent between monies of varying anticipated rates of price change and interest yields as long as the implied rental price of monetary services from a unit of money is identical. And money producers are also indifferent between different combinations of $(\dot{M}/M)_j$ and $(r_M)_j$ as long as they all imply identical $(i - r_M)_j$ values. Given costless information regarding future money supply changes, distinguishable monies, and interest payments on money,

---

[4]The usual competitive model is often said to implicitly assume that all contracts are enforced costlessly. It may be more enlightening to say that the usual model implicitly assumes perfect information and therefore parties to a contract know when a contract will be broken; *unanticipated* broken contracts are not possible. The implicit economic (as opposed to common usage) concept of "contract" refers to anticipated outcomes, not to verbal or written agreements; and therefore, with perfect information, "contracts" cannot be broken.

[5]Real interest payments on money must equal "the" real rate of interest minus the real marginal costs of producing real cash balances. And since all money changes are anticipated and equal to price changes, $(r_M)_j = \rho - [dC_j/d(M/P)_j] + (\dot{M}/M)_j$; where ρ is "the" real rate of interest. A money producing firm therefore cannot make interest payments on its money simply by increasing its money supply. Interest payments on money must be greater than the rate of increase of the firm's money supply by $\rho - [dC_j/d(M/P)_j]$.

428 : MONEY, CREDIT, AND BANKING

there is no unique profit-maximizing rate of increase in the supply of a competitive firm's money. A condition of metastable equilibrium exists with regard to nominal magnitudes.

D. Previous Arguments

Economists have earlier argued that unregulated competition in the supply of fiduciary money would lead to an infinite price level. For example, Boris Pesek [29, p. 889] has recently argued that if the marginal cost of producing money were zero, competition in the money industry would be "self-defeating" because it would result in a situation where "money is 'so abundant' as to sell for a zero price and be a free good. . . . This guarantees further retrogression into full-time barter since free money is worthless money, incapable of performing its task of facilitating exchanges of goods among persons." (Also see Pesek and Saving [31, pp. 86-87].)

Pesek confuses the rental price of the monetary services derived from holding money with the exchange value of the money asset.[6] A zero rental price of monetary services from a money is not necessarily associated with an infinite price level in terms of the money, i.e., a worthless money asset. A zero price of monetary services from a money implies, instead, that individuals will hold a quantity of *real* money at which the marginal value of monetary services is zero. If there are zero marginal costs of producing *real* money balances (which is what Pesek must be referring to in the context of the optimal monetary growth models in which he makes his comment), the competitive equilibrium supply of monetary services implies a supply of *real* cash balances which are "so abundant" as to make the monetary services from them a free good, but would not imply a value for the supply of *nominal* money. The competitive equilibrium nominal quantity of a money and hence the price level in terms of the money must be determined elsewhere.[7]

---

[6]This distinction between the opportunity cost of monetary services to holders of money and the purchasing power of money has been emphasized by Johnson [16].

[7]The optimum quantity of money literature generally ignores the distinction between the marginal cost of producing additional nominal money and the marginal cost of producing real cash balances. The fact that it is costless to "add a zero" implies nothing about the marginal cost of producing real cash balances (or monetary services). Note that Pesek and Saving [30] make the additional analytical error of asserting that if $(r_M)_j = i_j$, then the quantity of money would vanish. They are confusing two distinct theoretical concepts: the capitalized value of the monetary service stream from money and the nominal quantity of money. The marginal value of the monetary service stream from money, and hence the former concept, could equal zero without the quantity of money vanishing. Their error is analogous to the more general mistake of measuring the quantity of capital in terms of its market value. The quantity of money should be defined in nominal units (e.g., the number of dollars) and distinguished from the capitalized value of the monetary services from the units. $(r_M)_j = i_j$ implies that the capitalized marginal value of the monetary service stream from a unit of the money is zero but it does not imply that the money is "worthless." The capitalized value of all the returns on the margin from a unit of a money, the interest payments and the monetary services $[(r_M)_j + (\partial N/\partial M_j) (P_N)_j]$, must, of course, always equal one unit of the money. If all costs and returns are measured properly, then money, like every other asset held and exchanged in the economy, must yield "the" interest rate.

In our model, equilibrium nominal stocks of monies (and their rates of change) are arbitrarily determined, irrelevant magnitudes. Others have asserted, however, that if there are zero marginal costs of producing *nominal* money balances, then competition in the money industry would yield an infinite quantity of money and therefore an infinite price level. Friedman [9, p. 7] makes an especially lucid statement of this latter argument:

> So long as the fiduciary currency has a value greater than its cost of production—which under conditions can be compressed close to the cost of the paper on which it is printed—any individual issuer has an incentive to issue additional amounts. A fiduciary currency would thus probably tend through increased issue to degenerate into a commodity currency—into a literal paper standard—there being no stable equilibrium price level short of that at which the money value of currency is no greater than that of the paper it contains. And in view of the negligible cost of adding zeros, it is not clear that there is any finite price level for which this is the case.

Friedman's conclusion, while similar to Pesek's in claiming that competition forces the exchange value (what Friedman calls "the market value") of money to zero or the price level to infinity, does not confuse the price of monetary services from a unit of nominal money with its exchange value. His argument is correctly based on the competitive determinants of the nominal, not real, supply of money and hence of the price level. The argument is based, however, on the implicit assumption that a necessary condition for the existence of "competition" is the sale by all firms in an industry of *indistinguishable* homogeneous products. Acceptance of this condition for the money industry would lead to an infinite price level equilibrium. But if individual producers of money differentiate their products (e.g., by placing their names on the money they issue), profit maximization will not induce each producer to expand his money production without limit.

It is true that if, for example, a new money producer could issue money that was indistinguishable from an established money, competition would lead to an overissue of the particular money and the destruction of its value. The new firm's increase in the supply of money would cause prices in terms of that money to rise and, if anticipated, leave real profit derived from the total production of the money unchanged. But there has been a distribution effect—a fall in the established firm's real wealth and a rise in the new firm's real wealth. The larger the new firm's money issue the greater its profit; therefore profit maximization implies that the new firm will make unlimited increases in the supply of the money, reducing the established firm's profit share close to zero (unless it too expands).

If the established firm legally possesses a trademark on its money, this "externality" of the new firm's production represents a violation of the established firm's property right and is called counterfeiting. Lack of enforcement of an individual's firm's property right to his particular name will permit unlimited competitive counterfeiting and lead to an infinite

430 : MONEY, CREDIT, AND BANKING

price level. This merely points up the difficulties in the usual specification
of competitive conditions. If buyers are unable to distinguish between
the products of competing firms in an industry, competition will lead each
firm to reduce the quality of the product it sells since the costs of such
an action will be borne mainly by the other firms in the industry. Competition
will therefore, via a form of Gresham's Law, drive firms that do not
reduce the quality of their products out of business and lead to the complete
depreciation of the quality of product that is marketed in the industry.

But indistinguishability of the output of competing firms will lead to
product quality depreciation in *any* industry.[8] In the money industry these
problems are merely exaggerated. Consumers may distinguish between
outputs in an industry (and thereby form an expectation about the quality
of a product that may differ from the industry-expected product quality)
by either directly examining the technical characteristics of the product
or by noting the name on the product. Consumers generally rely on both
of these methods when attempting to determine the quality of products
they are purchasing. The greater the costs of judging quality by directly
examining the technical characteristics of the product, the more consumers
will rely on brand names.

For fiduciary money consumers must rely solely on the brand-name
method of obtaining information about quality since the monetary service
flow from a money is assumed to be independent of any technical
characteristic of the money (e.g., the size or color of a currency).[9] If
property rights to a firm's name are not enforced consumers will not be
able to distinguish between the output of different firms, and the quality
of money sold will be destroyed.[10] Hence brand-name differentiated output
is necessary for the competitive production and sale of money.

Friedman implicitly assumes that firms in a perfectly competitive industry
produce output that is not differentiated by brand names. This condition,

___

[8]Goldman [11] observes that Soviet Union economic planners have recognized the necessity
of requiring producers to imprint their individual "production marks" on their output to
maintain quality.

[9]If consumers could costlessly examine and thereby costlessly obtain information regarding
the quality of products, the lack of brand names would have no effects. But for money
(and insurance policies, bonds, theater tickets, and anything else purchased solely on the
"promise" of future performance) inspection is irrelevant.

[10]This is not entirely correct. A producer may rely on some unique physical characteristic
of his money that, although it produces no monetary services, differentiates his output from
that of other firms. The characteristic becomes his trade name. But if property rights are
not enforced on this physical characteristic other firms will imitate it. This phenomenon
can now be observed in the illegal drug industry where lack of producer trade name enforcement
results in attempts to physically differentiate products and competitive "counterfeiting."
Buyers rely almost completely on the reputation of (distinguishable) retailers. The major
difference between money and other goods may be that the lack of examinable technical
monetary service producing characteristics, combined with the high costs for firms to determine
and rely on the reputations of their many money-using customers, makes the costs of producing
indistinguishable substitutes (relative to the market exchange value of the product) much
lower for money than for other goods and therefore increases the incentive for counterfeit
production.

when applied to a product with high costs of determining quality by direct inspection of technical characteristics, will result in a higher price per unit service flow; when applied to money, a product with essentially infinite costs of determining quality by direct inspection of technical characteristics, it implies an infinite equilibrium price level. A more meaningful way to stipulate "perfect" competition is to assume costless consumer identifiability of sellers and to refer solely to the elasticity of demand facing individual sellers. We will therefore assume that each firm (*a*) possesses a distinct "brand name" (formally represented by the subscript *j*) and (*b*) is a price taker. No costs need be borne by anyone to enable buyers to identify the producer of a product, nor for the government to police and enforce property rights and prevent forgery. The many different monies may be completely homogeneous with regard to physical characteristics and are distinguishable only in the sense of having unique uncopyable names, none of which (given our assumption concerning costless knowledge of future money supply changes and therefore the absence of any "confidence" problems) have any value. The names merely permit consumers to costlessly distinguish between the output of competing firms. Although consumers have desired ratios for different real money holdings to one another (determined by nonprice factors), the monies are assumed to be perfect substitutes for one another on the margin and each firm faces an infinitely elastic demand for monetary services curve.[11]

E. Fixed Versus Flexible Exchange Rates

Friedman's contention that competitive equilibrium in the money industry implies an infinite price level is therefore seen to be based on the implicit and misleading assumption that all monies are indistinguishable. A more general statement of this critical assumption is that the different monies are convertible into one another by all producers and consumers at unchanging *fixed* exchange rates. Our competitive model assumes, on the contrary, that different monies exchange with one another in the market at freely determined *flexible* exchange rates. Gresham's Law, in the form stated above, is therefore not applicable.

If every money-producing firm guaranteed to convert its money into every other firm's money at a given fixed exchange rate, then competition would lead each firm to attempt to inflate at a higher rate than all other firms. Each firm would want to run a "deficit" in its trade clearing accounts with all other firms, financed by the increased holdings by the other firms

---

[11] My colleague Earl Thompson [38] has independently characterized a competitive money production equilibrium in a similar way. He, however, relies on a unique physical characteristic of each firm's money (e.g., a particular color) as the necessary identification mark analogous to my "brand name." In this context both are merely devices relied upon by consumers to distinguish between the output of competing firms.

432 : MONEY, CREDIT, AND BANKING

of its costlessly produced money. Indistinguishability of different monies merely strengthens the argument by eliminating the *possibility* of ever changing the fixed exchange rate peg between the different monies. If, however, the multiple monies circulated at market-determined flexible exchange rates, changes in the supply of any one money relative to another money would alter the exchange rate between the monies. Anticipated money supply changes and distinguishability of individual monies is sufficient to guarantee that deficits between firms would not arise. The incentive for each firm to inflate at a higher rate than competing firms is eliminated.

II. CONSUMER CONFIDENCE

In this section we continue to assume that distinguishable competitive monies circulate at flexible exchange rates with one another and that the costs of distinguishing the monies and enforcing property rights are zero (and therefore counterfeiting is impossible). But we introduce information costs regarding future money supply changes and therefore the possibility that money-supplying firms may "deceive" their consumers by overissuing (i.e., by increasing money more than anticipated). Given this uncertainty, consumer confidence regarding the future exchange value of a money now becomes a factor in the production of monetary services.

A. Brand Names and Consumer Confidence

If information about future performance is costly, information is a valuable product. The brand name of a firm is then not only an identification mark but also a capital asset. The market value of the firm's "reputation" reflects the confidence consumers have that the actual quality of the product, when consumed, will equal the quality that is anticipated, and therefore paid for, when the product is purchased. Reliance on brand names is a means that consumers use to decrease the costs of judging credibility of fulfillment of contract.

Define the anticipated quality of a nominal unit of a money over a particular time period as a negative function of the mean of the anticipated rate of price change distribution of the money over the period. Assume that this is the quality of money consumers pay for when they purchase monetary services; i.e., it is the mean anticipated rate of price change that is embodied in the market rate of interest in terms of the money i_j.

In a costly information world individuals realize that the actual rate of change of prices may not equal the mean anticipated rate of price change; i.e., the anticipated rate of price change probability distribution has a variance. Assume that the real market value of the jth firm's brand-name capital, represented by β_j, is negatively related to the variance of the anticipated rate of change of prices in terms of the jth firm's money. The value of the brand name of, or consumer confidence in, a money is therefore assumed to be related to the anticipated *predictability* of the future price level in terms of the money, while the quality of a nominal unit of money is assumed to be related to the anticipated *stability* of the future price level in terms of the money.

We previously concluded that if competitive interest payments were made on monies, then consumers would be indifferent between monies of differing quality, as long as the alternative costs of holding the different monies $(i - r_M)_j$ were identical. However, given the possibility of unanticipated money supply changes, an increase in the predictability of a money's future exchange price will increase the monetary service flow from a given real quantity of the money and lower the money's implied price of monetary services. The demand in real terms for a particular firm's money is therefore not only a negative function of the alternative cost of holding the money but is now assumed to be also a positive function of the consumer confidence in the money. Therefore at a given alternative cost of holding different monies, high confidence monies will drive out low confidence monies.[12]

The existence of information costs and hence valuable firm brand names does *not* imply that the model must now be considered under the rubric of "monopolistic competition." We must distinguish between imperfect information and a less than perfectly elastic demand curve. Although some firms may be supplying higher confidence monies at higher alternative costs than other firms, our representative individual analysis assumes that there is a unique scalar measure of the monetary service flow. Therefore we are not prohibited from assuming that every firm faces an infinitely elastic demand for its monetary services and that all charge identical real rental prices for monetary services.[13]

[12] "Jevons (in *Money and Mechanism of Exchange*, pp. 64, 82) has called attention to the theory of Herbert Spencer that if private coinage were established, the honest coiner would gain possession of the circulation and drive out inferior coins" (quoted in Laughlin [21, p. 52].)

An increase in the confidence of a money has two different effects on the demand for the money: (1) a decrease in the demand for money because $(M/P)_j$ and β_j are substitutes in the production of monetary services (an increase in β_j implies that less $(M/P)_j$ is demanded to produce a given monetary service flow), and (2) an increase in the demand for money because real cash balances and monetary services are complements in consumption (an increase in β_j may decrease $(P_N)_j$ and hence increase the desired monetary service flow). Since firms are assumed to be facing an infinitely elastic demand for monetary services, the second effect is assumed to predominate. See Klein [18] for a more complete discussion.

[13] It is noteworthy that Chamberlin [6, Appendix E] advocated a policy of permitting imitation and infringement of "trade marks." Protection of property rights on a trade mark could be justified, he asserted, if trade marks merely "identified" products; but they also "differentiate" products. Therefore, for the consumer "the name stands for a certain quality, a certain product not a certain producer, and to permit only one producer to use the name is to grant him a monopoly of this product" (p. 272). Our analysis more nearly conforms to the ideas of Knight who, nearly fifty years ago, stated that "the buyer being the judge of his own wants, if the name makes a difference to him, it constitutes a peculiarity in

B. The Equilibrium Quantity of Brand-Name Capital

Reliable information about anticipated performance is costly to produce and therefore consumer confidence is not a free good. Commodity money produces consumer confidence by placing a *physical* constraint on money production and hence on the possible unanticipated depreciation. "Guaranteed" convertibility of a money into a commodity (or into another more predictable money) is another way to obtain consumer confidence, and any stocks of the commodity (or the high confidence money) held as reserves to increase that assurance should also be considered an investment by the firm in brand name capital. Other confidence-producing expenditures may take the form, for example, of advertising, luxurious offices, an impressive vault, employment of responsible individuals, and payments made to a certifying or insurance agency. A competitive firm optimally invests in brand name capital by trading off these expenditures which increase the productivity of its real cash balances with the reduced real interest payments that must be made on its money to maintain a constant rental price of monetary services. On the margin an efficient investment in brand name capital (e.g., in renting a gold stock) will increase the present discounted value of the firm's profit stream by the value of the resources expended.

Under these conditions, competitive equilibrium, equation (4), is unchanged. But with information costs and the costs of creating consumer confidence, the alternative cost of holding individual monies will be greater than the marginal cost of producing the real cash balances; i.e., equation (5) no longer holds. Even if the costs of producing real cash balances were zero, the firm's average profit rate $(i - r_M)_j (M/P)_j$ will be positive and represent a return on the firm's brand-name capital.[14]

If the individual firm's brand-name capital is measured properly as a residual element earning a normal real rate of return, then the average brand name "costs" must be such as to make the net real "pure profit" zero. If the costs of producing real cash balances were zero, then zero profit implies that $(i - r_M)_j (M/P)_j - \rho \beta_j$ equals zero, or

---

the commodity, however similar it may be in physical properties to competing wares. And the difference from physical equivalent goods may be very real, in the way of confidence in what one is getting" [20, p. 185]. Also note Hayek's statement [14, pp. 96-97]: "Especially remarkable in this connection is the explicit and complete exclusion from the theory of perfect competition of all personal relationships between the parties. In actual life the fact that our inadequate knowledge of the available commodities or services is made up for by our experience with the persons or firms supplying them—that competition is in a large measure competition for reputation or good will—is one of the most important facts which enables us to solve our daily problems. The function of competition is here precisely to teach us *who* will serve us well."

[14] The cost of brand name capital, which includes the confidence created expenditures, can be thought of as the cost of "selling" (as opposed to "producing") real cash balances. The difference between what we define as "profit" and these "selling costs" can be considered to be a pure rent on the firm's brand name capital.

$$\beta_j = \left[\frac{(i - r_M)_j}{\rho} \right] (M/P)_j. \tag{6}$$

The ratio of the alternative cost of holding the jth money to "the" real rate of interest (or one minus the ratio of real interest payments on the jth money to the real rate of interest) can therefore be thought of as the jth firm's brand-name capital (or net wealth) "backing" per unit of its money. If interest payments on the jth money equal the anticipated rate of change of prices in terms of the jth money (real interest payments on the jth money equal zero), then the jth firm's brand name capital equals the real quantity of its money outstanding and the firm's money can be considered to be entirely net wealth. If confidence were completely costless to produce, the value of the jth firm's brand-name capital and the net wealth value of the firm's money would vanish and competitive interest payments on its money would equal "the" market rate of interest. We would then once again be operating in a world where money supply changes were perfectly and costlessly anticipated and brand-names would be merely valueless identification marks. [15]

Given the presence of information costs regarding future money supply changes, we can no longer assume that anticipations are correct. Firms can now "deceive" consumers by increasing money faster than anticipated and it may seem at first thought that the firm's equilibrium rate of change of money is infinite.

Redefine the firm's current profit equation to take account of the fact that current actual and anticipated values are not necessarily equal. It is $(\dot{P}/P)_j^*$ which is an element of i_j and hence a determinant of the demand for the jth firm's real cash balances, but it is $(\dot{P}/P)_j$ which is the actual rate of cost to individuals of holding the jth money and $(\dot{M}/M)_j$ which is the actual rate of return to the jth firm from new money issues. Therefore, assuming that the costs of producing real cash balances are zero, the jth

---

[15] Harry G. Johnson [15] makes a similar distinction between competitive-interest bearing and noninterest bearing money as representing the distinction between "inside" and "outside" money. Unfortunately he identifies the equity of a commercial bank, which permits it to borrow at a rate of interest less than "the" market rate at which it lends, solely with government regulation in the money industry. But repeal of all legal restrictions would still leave some proportion of bank deposits as "outside" money if monetary services are costly to produce. Competitive interest paid by banks on deposits would remain below "the" rate of interest on assets yielding no monetary services. In Johnson's analysis, confidence is implicitly assumed to be created costlessly and therefore commodity money is merely a deadweight social cost and fiduciary money is merely a costless invention which someone happens to think of. His analysis should be correctly thought of as providing an estimate of the maximum social saving of moving from a commodity to a fiduciary monetary system. But if confidence for fiduciary money costs as much to produce as the commodity, the social saving would be zero. A reasonable explanation of why credit money did not replace commodity money before it did may not be because someone did not happen to think of the credit money idea, but rather may be because commodity money was, at the time, the cheapest way to produce confidence; i.e., a forced movement from commodity to fiduciary money would have implied a negative social saving.

436 : MONEY, CREDIT, AND BANKING

firm's current real profit (or rent on its given brand-name capital) per unit time is

$$(\pi/P)_j = (i - r_M)_j (M/P)_j + [(\dot{M}/M)_j - (\dot{P}/P)_j^*] (M/P)_j. \qquad (7)$$

If we assume that there are lags in the adjustment of anticipations so that $d(P/P)_j^* / d(\dot{M}/M)_j$ is less than one, then, on the margin, an increase in the current rate of change of money increases the extent of current deceiving; i.e., $d[\dot{M}/M)_j - (\dot{P}/P)_j^*] / d(\dot{M}/M)_j$ is greater than zero, and the profit-maximizing rate of inflation would appear to be infinite.

To see this, differentiate the firm's current real profit rate with respect to the current rate of change of its money. If the demand for the firm's real money is assumed to be solely a function of $(i - r_M)_j$, which the firm is assumed to hold constant as $(M/M)_j$ is varied, then

$$\frac{d(\pi/P)_j}{d(\dot{M}/M)_j} = (M/P)_j \left(1 - \frac{d(\dot{P}/P)_j^*}{d(\dot{M}/M)_j} \right). \qquad (8)$$

If $d(\dot{P}/P)_j^* / d(\dot{M}/M)_j$ is less than one, then $d(\pi/P)_j / d(\dot{M}/M)_j$ is always positive, and therefore the firm can make its current profit rate as large as it wants by merely making $(\dot{M}/M)_j$ arbitrarily large while increasing interest payments on money to keep pace with price anticipations. The profit-maximizing rate of increase of money is therefore infinite. The money-producing firm could theoretically obtain all the wealth of its customers. The only constraint on the extent of the firm's profit rate is the existence of some rising costs of increasing $(\dot{M}/M)_j$ which places a limit on the rate at which a firm can profitably increase the supply of its money in circulation.[16]

However, this argument assumes that the money firm's brand-name capital is constant and so fails to consider the effect on consumer confidence and the firm's demand from a policy of "deceiving" customers. A major method by which a firm invests (or disinvests) in brand-name capital is by successful (or unsuccessful) performance. If the actual rate of change of money is greater than the anticipated rate, then the firm is supplying a product the quality of which is less than buyers anticipated and therefore

---

[16] In the antebellum banking period the head cashier of each bank was required by law to sign all bank notes. This requirement was a major constraint on the rate of increase of notes that could, in principle, be circulated by an individual bank. See Hammond [13, pp. 172–80] for a discussion of the first U.S. bank failure in 1809 and the limitation this requirement placed on the extent of the intentional overissue of bank notes that was possible. Note that I am assuming here that money producers but not consumers make the calculations implied by equations (7) and (8). If consumers also so calculated, they would know that the firm would deceive and therefore would certainly refuse to hold any money since demanding any real amount would represent a lien on all their wealth. The exchange value of each firm's money would under these circumstances necessarily be zero.

paid for. The higher the actual rate compared to the anticipated rate, i.e., the greater the extent of deceiving that is occurring, the lower will be consumer confidence. As β_j falls, $\partial N/\partial (M/P)_j$ can be assumed to fall and $(i - r_M)_j$ must also fall to keep $(P_N)_j/P_j$ constant.[17] Differentiating (7), taking account of this effect, yields

$$\frac{d(\pi/P)_j}{d(\dot{M}/M)_j} = (M/P)_j \left[1 - \frac{d(\dot{P}/P)_j^*}{d(\dot{M}/M)_j} + \frac{d(i - r_M)_j}{d(\dot{M}/M)_j} \right]. \qquad (9)$$

The profit-maximizing rate of growth of money is determined at the point where

$$\frac{d(\dot{P}/P)_j^*}{d(\dot{M}/M)_j} - \frac{d(i - r_M)_j}{d(\dot{M}/M)_j} = 1. \qquad (10)$$

It may seem that the profit-maximizing rate of growth of the firm's money can still be infinite. But $d\beta_j/d(\dot{M}/M)_j$, and hence $d(i - r_M)_j/d(\dot{M}/M)_j$, is partially determined by consumers. The smaller (in absolute value) an assumed given elasticity of depreciation of brand-name capital to alternative rates of monetary growth, the more brand-name capital will be demanded and the greater (in absolute value) will be $d\beta_j/d(\dot{M}/M)_j$ at alternative rates of monetary growth. Consumers can (and will) control $d(i - r_M)_j/d(\dot{M}/M)_j$ to prevent an infinite rate of growth of money. In this one-period model consumers will therefore trade off higher levels of β_j, with correspondingly higher costs of holding cash balances $(i - r_M)_j$, against higher levels of unanticipated $(\dot{M}/M)_j$. Given the production function for confidence, an equilibrium quantity of brand-name capital will be supplied and a finite rate of unanticipated inflation implied; i.e., in equilibrium the prior probability expected rate of price change distribution will have a variance.[18]

---

[17] This negative effect of overissuing on the market value of a money issuing firm's reputation has been noted previously. "When Philip of Valois swore the officers of his mint to conceal the debasement of the coinage and to endeavor to make the merchants believe that the gold and silver pieces were of full value, he thought that, although perhaps unprincipled, such a measure would be vastly profitable. And so no doubt believed the other kings, who, in the 'good old times,' almost universally did the like. . . . [However], the loss of their reputation for honesty made them afterward unable to borrow money, except at proportionately high rates of interest, to cover the risk ran by the lender. So that they . . . put themselves at a great disadvantage for the future" (Spencer [35, pp. 43–44].)

Note that we are assuming throughout our argument no lag in the adjustment of the firm's brand name capital to alternative rates of growth of its money. If there is a lag, i.e., *future* consumer confidence and the firm's *future* demand is decreased by a policy of *currently* deceiving consumers, then once again only the existence of costs of increasing $(\dot{M}/M)_j$ prevents the firm from inflating at an infinite rate and obtaining all the wealth of its customers.

[18] The real total payments per unit time by consumers therefore consists of two parts: $(i - r_M)_j (M/P)_j$ and $[(\dot{M}/M)_j - (\dot{M}/M)_j^*] (M/P)_j$. Given costs of unanticipated price

438 : MONEY, CREDIT, AND BANKING

More generally, if the firm maximizes the present discounted value of its profit stream, rather than its current profit rate, then it must choose a $(\dot{M}/M)_j$ time path rather than a unique $(\dot{M}/M)_j$. In any case, a policy of intentionally depreciating the exchange value of its money to zero will not be wealth maximizing. The equilibrium value of the firm brand names in a particular industry and their rate of depreciation from unsuccessful performance will be determined by consumer estimates of the possible gain to producers from "deceiving." The greater the consumer estimate of the possible gain from deceiving, (e.g., the greater is the cost of detecting and reacting to less than anticipated quality), the greater the quantity of brand-name capital they will demand and pay for in a higher alternative cost, and therefore the more the firm potentially has to lose from a policy of deceiving consumers. A firm's brand-name capital is a type of collateral that it loses if it performs below anticipations.[19]

If consumers and producers make the same estimate of what can be gained by short-run deceiving then the equilibrium quantity of confidence collateral supplied will imply that wealth-maximizing firms will not inflate at an infinite rate. (If an infinite inflation rate were implied, i.e., if the absolute value of $d(i - r_M)_j/d(\dot{M}/M)_j$ never reached $1 - d(\dot{P}/P)_j^*/d$ $(\dot{M}/M)_j$, then consumers would not hold any money.) Only if the consumer estimate of the short-run profit from deceiving is less than the producer estimate will less than the equilibrium quantity of brand-name capital be demanded and supplied and will wealth maximization yield greater than anticipated deception and the possibility of an infinite inflation rate.

In a strict sense, therefore, competitive costly information equilibrium implies that all money is at least partially "commodity" money. On the margin, an unanticipated increase in the nominal quantity of a firm's money implies the real marginal (private and social) cost because of the loss of consumer confidence. In equilibrium the alternative cost to the firm of consumer confidence, in the sense of what the brand-name asset could be "sold" for to consumers via depreciation, is equal to the present value of the firm's nondeceiving "profit" stream.

---

movements consumers would prefer to make this total payment entirely in a higher $(i - r_M)_j$ with producers agreeing not to deceive at all. But, although producers should be indifferent to these two arrangements, this higher $(i - r_M)_j$ payment would not imply a high enough level of β_j to insure no deception. Under our information conditions, producers would collect this higher $(i - r_M)_j$ and still engage in some (although less) deception; i.e., such a contract would not be enforced. If confidence were costless, such a contract would certainly be fulfilled. But then deception and $(i - r_M)_j$ would both equal zero.

[19] Although the capital lost is not transferred to consumers; there is not a redistribution of wealth, as with other forms of collateral, but a net wealth loss.

III. "COMPETITIVE" MONETARY ARRANGEMENTS

A. Historical Examples

Historical examples of competitive producers of a single money or of different monies convertible into one another at fixed exchange rates are rare, but the available examples reveal the incentive to overissue. One major U.S. historical example of competing convertible monies is the New England colonial monetary arrangements in the first half of the eighteenth century, when separate paper money issues of each of the New England colonies (Massachusetts, Connecticut, Rhode Island, and New Hampshire) were accepted at par in each of the other New England colonies in payment of taxes and in general exchange. "This peculiar arrangement, with no central control or direction, eventually led the New England colonies to compete with one another in issuing quantities of paper money" (Lester [22, p. 7]) and produced a significantly greater depreciation of the New England monies than the monies of the middle colonies (Lester [22, pp. 7-10, 24]).

Another U.S. example of a similar competitively destructive arrangement was the requirement adopted by the Second Bank of the United States in 1816 that any branch of the Bank was obligated to redeem at par the notes issued by any other branch. This arrangement is not entirely analogous to the convertible competitive monies case since the different notes were not just convertible into one another but were also convertible into gold. However, competition did lead western and southern branches of the Bank to overissue bank notes which were redeemed in the East until the practice of redeemability of all notes at all branches was discontinued in 1818.[20]

The classic U.S. example of competitive domestic monies circulating at *flexible* exchange rates is usually taken to be the antebellum "free banking" experience.[21] Many distinguishable bank notes circulated at the time side

---

[20] Temin [37, pp. 31-36] discusses why bank notes normally flowed from the West and South to the East and how the monetary arrangements could therefore be abused by the western and southern branches. Rather than base the argument on the "natural" flow of bank notes, an alternative explanation could be based on the incentive by the western and southern branches to take advantage of (i.e., consume) the superior reputation of the established, more reputable, eastern branches and thereby overissue. In the short run this would cause them to experience a balance of payments deficit with the eastern branches, financed at least partially by the flow of bank notes from the West and South to the East. This incentive for the (relatively small) western and southern branches to overissue will be magnified if the redemption of bank notes is related to the size and location of a branch while bank note issuance is independent of either.

[21] "Free banking" is somewhat of a misnomer. The period was one of relatively unrestricted entry into banking. Prior to this period private banks issued their own distinguishable notes which circulated freely at varying discounts with one another.

Other historical examples of multiple monies circulating side-by-side domestically at flexible exchange rates are gold and greenbacks in the U.S. during the Civil War, foreign exchange

440 : MONEY, CREDIT, AND BANKING

by side at varying discounts in terms of specie and were freely exchanged for one another by merchants and brokers in the major financial centers. These bank note exchange rates were frequently published in newspapers and in bank note reporters.[22] Monetary arrangements during the nineteenth century free banking era, however, were much closer to multiple monies circulating at fixed exchange rates than to multiple monies circulating at flexible exchange rates. The private bank notes that circulated at the time were all denominated in dollars, where "dollar" denoted a particular weight of gold. But each bank placed its particular name on its notes. That is, gold was the single dominant unit of account and all the private notes were convertible into gold at fixed exchange rates. The name of the note merely represented the probability that the particular firm would fulfill its convertibility contract. And the great majority of banking firms did normally maintain convertibility. Bank notes generally circulated at par or differed from par at a particular geographical point by the transportation costs of shipping the notes from the point of quotation to the redemption point and the costs of shipping the gold back. There were banking panics and liquidity crises, at which time all banks suspended convertibility and the discounts on all bank notes rose significantly. But universal suspension of payments was temporary, and competitive forces were such that banks had to resume payments and generally maintain convertibility or fail. The overwhelming bulk of bank notes did not generally fluctuate widely in terms of one another nor in terms of specie.[23]

Fiat or irredeemable bank notes were not generally acceptable in exchange, no matter how substantial the discount.[24] Although most state governments seldom enforced bank note gold-convertibility contracts, private competitive institutions policed convertibility and thereby kept bank notes circulating at or near par. Money brokers bought out-of-town bank notes at a discount and presented them to the issuing bank for payment in specie, and publishers of bank note reporters and counterfeit detectors kept individuals informed about the market value of different bank notes together with a description of counterfeit, altered, and spuriously signed notes. In addition, banks would demand payment in specie for the notes of competing banking firms

and marks in Germany after World War I, imperial rubles and revolutionary rubles in Russia after World War I, ordinary currency and special new currency issues in times of hyperinflation, and silver and copper in China from about 1650 to 1850. All of these examples, except the flexible bimetallic exchange rates in China, were temporary arrangements which existed for brief critical periods and should be considered exceptional.

[22] One of the earliest issues of a bank note reporter, dated 1830, listed the current New York City quotation of the discount rate in terms of gold on approximately five hundred different bank notes together with historical information on the reliability of particular banks (Dillistin [8, p. 99]). An analogous, highly reputable, service for nearly one hundred different national currencies is currently provided by Franz Pick [32].

[23] For sketchy evidence on the general level and movement of nineteenth century bank note discounts, see Van Fensternmaker [40, pp. 77-95], Berry [2] and Macesich [24].

[24] The bank notes of Kentucky and Tennessee were relatively unimportant exceptions. (Van Fensternmaker [40, p. 95]).

they received, and many banks became members of private protective and certifying agencies, which performed some functions similar to present-day central banks.[25]

B. Multiple Monies Convertible into a Dominant Money

The foregoing monetary arrangement will be called a "dominant" money arrangement. It is an arrangement where all money producers maintain convertibility on demand of their distinguishable monies at a one-to-one fixed exchange rate into a single (dominant) money which serves as the unit of account. The dominant money supplier does not maintain convertibility of his money into any other money. It is a *one-to-one* fixed exchange rate arrangement based on *one-way* convertibility agreements. This monetary arrangement implies that all the monies must inflate at the same rate as the dominant money, but it does not eliminate the possibility of competition between the different monies via interest payments. Competitive equilibrium will still imply that all (nondominant) monies pay a real rate of interest equal to "the" real rate of interest minus the marginal costs of producing a unit of real cash balances.

The unique inflation rate is determined by changes in the supply of the dominant money, and, given the one-way convertibility arrangements, there appears to be an incentive for a profit-maximizing dominant money supplier to overissue. It is therefore claimed that a competitively determined dominant money must be a commodity money. This argument, however, ignores the fact that the dominant money-producing firm will lose wealth (and its dominant position) if it overissues. But since the possible short-run gain to an established dominant money supplier from overissuing is enormous (see fn. 41), a competitively determined dominant money will possess a very valuable brand name and sell, in nondeceiving equilibrium, at a high alternative cost. This necessary brand-name backing implies that the money is, in a sense, "commodity" money.

Present U.S. domestic monetary arrangements can usefully be described

---

[25] Biddle is sometimes said to have performed the valuable social service of preventing unlimited inflation by returning all notes received by the Second Bank of the United States to the issuing bank for redemption. This far-sighted social policy conveniently coincided with profit maximization by the Second Bank and a similar policy was also followed by many nonfederally chartered private banks.

Very early in our banking history, firms joined cooperative associations, similar to what later became Clearing Houses, to sustain each others notes and demand payment from nonmembers. The Suffolk Bank of Boston provided this service very efficiently in New England from 1818–66 and redeemed on demand the notes of the banks that did not maintain a balance at the Suffolk Bank. Formal Clearing Houses were established in New York in 1853, in Boston in 1856 and in Philadelphia in 1858 and provided the particularly valuable service of examining member bank accounts and publishing the information. In this way individual banks were prevented from overissuing, even in times of general restriction of payments. (Cf. Hammond [13, pp. 705–6]. Temin [37, p. 117] discusses a similar cooperative action in the pre-Clearing House period).

in terms of this model of multiple monies convertible into a single dominant money at fixed exchange rates. There is one dominant money (currency supplied by a government monopoly) and many privately produced nondominant monies (deposits supplied by different commercial banks). All the private monies are denominated in the same units as the government's money and legally convertible into the government's money by the private money issuers. Given the general acceptance of the different monies at fixed exchange rates, the governmental intervention which prevents the money supply and the price level from approaching infinity is the strict enforcement of the requirement that the private monies be convertible into the government money; it is independent of any legal or economic reserve requirements. Even if commercial banks held no reserves of the dominant money, enforcement of the requirement that each bank maintain convertibility of its money into the dominant money will imply that the total money supply and the price level is determined by the government supply of the dominant money and consumer preferences among the different monies. As long as there is some demand for the government's dominant money, commercial bank reserve requirements are unnecessary for a determinate finite price level.[26] Legal reserve requirements appear in this context to constitute merely an excise tax on private money production, if less than a competitive rate of interest is paid on the government money held by private banks. And as long as the convertibility requirement is present, even government monopolization of the supply of currency is unnecessary for a finite equilibrium price level; monopolization appears in this context to represent merely nationalization of a particular industry. From this perspective the crucial distinguishing characteristic of present U.S. monetary arrangements is the legally imposed convertibility requirement that ties all the monies at fixed exchange rates to a governmentally supplied dominant money.[27]

C. Information and Transaction Costs

Flexible exchange rates between monies in a domestic money market has not been a common historical experience. Even when a legal fixed

[26]Our analysis here, that the existence of distinguishable monies on the demand side combined with a convertibility requirement on the supply side places a limit on the nominal quantity of non-dominant monies, is analogous to the analysis in Tobin [39].

[27]Pesek and Saving are among the few economists who explicitly assume that this convertibility requirement is a necessary characteristic of monetary institutions and call the requirement an "instant repurchase clause" [30, p. 80]. Pesek and Saving do not explicitly define dominant money other than to say that it is "the coin of the Realm" and beg the important question of whether dominant money must necessarily be supplied by the government.

It is interesting to note that Pesek and Saving's stated intention is to analyze money with the standard economic tools used in analyzing any economic good. This, however, is the second legally imposed institutional arrangement upon which their analysis is based; the first was the prohibition of interest payments on money (see fn. 7 above).

exchange rate requirement has been absent, private contractual relationships achieved the same result. Monetary arrangements have almost always consisted of a single money or of multiple monies convertible into a single dominant money.[28] To explain the almost universal existence of fixed exchange rate monetary arrangements, we must explicitly consider the information and transaction costs of competitive multiple independent monies. The reasons why such a monetary arrangement appears not to be viable are related to the theory of optimal currency areas.

Our competitive model, with many distinguishable monies circulating side by side at flexible market-determined rates, is essentially equivalent to the complete absence of any currency area. Mundell [27], in his original formulation of the optimum currency area problem, argues that "the costs of valuation and money changing tend to increase with the number of currencies." If there are many monies and many sets of prices, the unit of account and medium of exchange functions of money are hampered. Money exchange rates are now necessary to determine relative values, and there are now the added transactions costs involved in currency conversions. These computational-conversion costs increase with the number of independent monies within a market. However, money changing and valuation costs are present even if the different monies are tied together at fixed exchange rates; their magnitude depends on the specific form of the fixed exchange rate arrangement adopted. The smaller the number of different fixed exchange rates, the lower these transaction costs will be. If, for example, the fixed exchange rates between all the monies are one to one, then the different monies would essentially be denominated in the same units and the computational-conversion costs would be substantially eliminated. Minimization of money changing and valuation costs implies a single currency, not a single currency area, and in a multiple money context is an argument not merely for fixed exchange rates but for a dominant money arrangement with its uniform unit of account.

McKinnon [26] extended Mundell's analysis by considering the store of value function of money and the costs of future price level uncertainty. McKinnon assumed that the maintenance of stability of a money's value in terms of a representative bundle of economic goods reduces these costs and facilitates efficient resource allocation. If the producer of every distinguishable currency maintains a stable price level in terms of its currency of essentially the same bundle of goods, then "each currency will be pegged to the other" [26, p. 722].[29]

---

[28]Cipolla [7, ch. 2] documents the fact that dominant monies existed over large areas and long time periods as early as the fifth century when the Byzantine gold solidus had a dominant position throughout the Mediterranean.

[29]This conclusion is misleadingly stated. Given the assumptions, exchange rates between the competing monies will remain unchanged. But we must distinguish between *constant* market exchange rates and convertibility of currencies at unchanging *fixed* or pegged exchange rates. McKinnon implicitly recognizes this distinction and the inherent continuum between

444 : MONEY, CREDIT, AND BANKING

But the crucial information costs reducing characteristic of monetary arrangements is the *predictability* of exchange rate changes. Similarly, it is the *predictability*, and not necessarily the stability, of prices in terms of a money which reduces information costs and provides store-of-value liquidity services. There is therefore no theoretical reason to expect even constant exchange rates between competing monies to be an optimal solution. Stability may facilitate prediction; but consider the possibility of a monetary arrangement where each individual money were inflating at a different perfectly stable (and predictable) *rate* and money exchange rates were changing at a stable (and predictable) rate.

More important, these information cost considerations argue for fixed exchange rates, but not necessarily for a dominant money. To explain the existence of a dominant monetary arrangement we must more carefully consider the nature of the production function for consumer confidence. Significant economies of scale probably exist in the production of information about reliability of a money.[30] In addition, the costs of disseminating information about a particular industry are smaller the smaller the number of independent firms in the industry. The greater the homogeneity of products in an industry, the smaller the variance of the anticipated quality distribution in the industry (cf. Alchian [1, p. 124]). Since information about anticipated quality (predictability of prices) is a major determinant of the monetary-service flow from a money, we can therefore expect these considerations to be paramount and the value of a single quality product in the industry to be substantial.

D. International Monetary Implications

There are implications of this analysis for the international money market, where confidence remains as a significant problem and where different countries supplying distinguishable monies can usefully be thought of as

monetary exchange rate systems categorized as fixed and those categorized as flexible when he states that to "maintain the liquidity value of individual currencies for small areas," the currencies must be pegged "convincingly." The coincidental historical maintenance of stable prices in terms of many different monies does not imply that the currencies are "convincingly pegged" together and part of a single currency area. Given information costs, the distinction between fixed and flexible exchange rates hinges upon *anticipations* concerning *future* exchange rate changes. A currency area can be meaningfully defined as an arrangement where the probability of an exchange rate change between currencies is essentially zero. Exchange rates between two currencies may be legally "fixed," but the anticipated probability of an exchange rate change can be significant. Present (1970) international monetary arrangements among the major currencies should be thought of as lying much closer to the flexible exchange rate than to the fixed exchange rate benchmark. Frequent devaluations in the past have significantly increased consumer estimates of probability of future exchange rate changes and forward rates, which are highly significant for international trade, are frequently outside the "guaranteed" band of the spot rate.

[30] "Since the cost of collection of information is (approximately) independent of its use (although the cost of dissemination is not), there is a strong tendency toward monopoly in the provision of information; in general, there will be a "standard" source for trade information" (Stigler [36, pp. 181-2]).

analogous to competing firms in an unregulated money industry. Present (1970) international monetary arrangements are often described as being (or moving toward) a fixed exchange rate dollar standard system—with all monies tied to the dominant U.S. dollar. This arrangement is based not on any regulation but on the dollar's valuable brand name. There is open entry into the dominant international money business and we can expect the dollar brand name to depreciate if the dollar's performance is unexpectedly poor. This essentially is the balance of payments constraint under which the United States is currently operating. The profit or "seigniorage" currently being earned on foreign holdings of high-powered dollars should be thought of as payment by foreigners for the use of the U.S. confidence and as a normal return on the dollar brand-name capital. On the margin the alternative cost to the owners of the dollar brand-name capital of an unanticipated increase in the quantity of dollars is the decrease in the value of the brand-name capital and hence future profit stream that can be earned. [31]

International monetary reform is now seen to be closely related to the transaction-information costs associated with multiple money exchange arrangements. If the dollar is the dominant international money, the adoption of flexible exchange rates may substantially reduce the monetary services yielded by a given real quantity of nondollar monies and result in increased holdings of dollars and dollar denominated assets. This would increase the real value of the U.S. dollar's brand name. However, the dollar's dominant position is not completely secure and flexibility may in fact create a competitive dominant money (e.g., the mark) or group of monies and decrease the international demand for dollars. Therefore, *if* U.S. monetary authorities were attempting to maximize the value of the dollar brand name capital, it is unclear whether they should support a movement towards greater flexibility at this time.

But what is difficult to understand in this context is the advocacy by U.S. authorities of the creation of SDRs, a new competitor for the dollar in the international money business. This does not appear to be a policy that would increase the demand for dollars and hence the value of the dollar brand-name capital. [32] A possible explanation for the U.S. government's behavior is that it is hoping SDRs will reduce the monetary usefulness of gold, an important competitor of the dollar, while not displacing

[31] Estimates of the current profit (return on brand-name capital) being earned on the dollar should not assume that confidence capital necessarily has a zero cost of creation and maintenance (as, e.g., Grubel [12] and Johnson [17] do).

[32] Discussions of the creation of "paper gold" have often implicitly assumed that the IMF has unlimited brand name capital. A stationary equilibrium measure of the IMF's limited brand name capital can be obtained by multiplying the difference between "the" market interest rate and the rate that is paid on SDR's by the real value of the SDRs "in circulation" (the quantity effectively demanded, i.e., voluntarily held by countries in payment for a balance of payments surplus—not IMF "allocations"). And even this finite value of the brand name of SDR's is based, to some extent, on the willingness of the U.S. to accept them.

446 : MONEY, CREDIT, AND BANKING

foreign dollar holdings. Another possible explanation is that the U.S. monetary authorities want to decrease foreign dollar holdings because they do not recognize that to a large extent the postwar increase in foreign holdings of dollar assets has resulted from the relative rise of the dollar brand name. If monetary services were considered to be a good, voluntary increases of dollar holdings by foreign individuals and governments should be recognized as exports and not as a balance of payments "deficit." Going one step further, even "involuntary" holdings of dollars may represent payment by foreign governments for U.S. protection and other services. The only economic definition of a "deficit," other than upward pressure on the foreign exchange rate, involves the depreciation of the brand name of a money—i.e., the use (or "sale") by a government of some of its brand name capital in international exchange. Long-term movements in U.S. foreign exchange rates "unexplained" by relative inflation rates may therefore be due to appreciation or depreciation of the dollar's brand name as an international currency.

IV. Government Intervention in the Money Industry

The transaction and information cost effects considered above suggest some reasons for the existence of monetary arrangements where individual monies are convertible at a fixed one-to-one exchange rate into a dominant money. But we have not yet specified the efficient role of government within such monetary arrangements. U.S. history suggests that contracts guaranteeing convertibility into a single dominant money will arise and generally be honored under conditions of free unregulated competition. What peculiarities of money, then, justify present government intervention (*a*) to supply the dominant money and require all private monies to maintain convertibility, (*b*) to require producers of private monies to maintain reserves in the government money, and (*c*) to monopolize the supply of currency? We will now discuss some possible rationalizations for this intervention.

Money differs from other durable consumer goods in the importance of its resale value as a determinant of its service flow. As a result, future supply and demand significantly affects the quality of money an individual purchases now.[33] This characteristic of money plus the fact that fraud

[33] This property may be considered unique to money. Although the current cost of other durable goods may be related to their future resale value, the real (non-liquidity) service flow from other goods is independent of their exchange value. The service flow from a money, on the contrary, is related solely to its market exchange value. An individual may, for example, consider a refrigerator to be of very high quality and be correct—independent of how anyone else values the refrigerator, while an individual's estimate of the quality of a money that completely disagrees with the market estimate must be incorrect. If everyone thinks a money is worthless, it necessarily is and therefore yields no monetary services. Increased future supply of other durable goods will decrease the value, *but not the quantity*, of the service flow yielded by goods currently purchased.

(unanticipated changes in the quantity of a firm's money) is costly to detect and react to in the money industry implies that consumer confidence and therefore firm brand names are of exceptional value relative to other inputs in the money industry. Gains from government intervention, however, are not yet implied.

Government control of the supply of dominant money may be related to macroeconomic stabilization policy. If a government is to engage in monetary policy, it must be able to control the supply of (or demand for) dominant money. If a private producer supplies the dominant money into which the government's money is convertible, then a government cannot inflate at a rate different from that of the dominant money. But this loss of domestic money supply control refers only to the long-run secular rate of change of money. A government can always engage in short-run stabilization policy by inflating at a rate greater than (or less than) the dominant money's, thereby losing (or gaining) reserves of dominant money. The only added cost to a government is the inventory costs of holding reserves of the privately supplied dominant money.

Alternatively, the government may supply the dominant money because of natural monopoly characteristics of the industry. Given declining costs of supplying information, a single firm or private trade association would be efficient in producing confidence for a group of monies. The monopolistic or cooperative association could provide a dominant money and implicit or explicit insurance to consumers of member firms, similar to the use of warranties for other durable goods. However, such an arrangement increases distinguishability costs and therefore the incentive for individual member firms to overissue and consume the brand-name capital of other firms in the association. The association would therefore have to assume some control over member firm production decisions to internalize what would otherwise by unheeded externalities. If any firm in the money industry can take advantage of general consumer confidence and significantly damage the reputation of other producers, the economic forces for compulsory membership and highly regulated or monopolistic organization will be magnified. But other industries that are natural monopolies often lead to governmental franchises and public regulation instead of governmental monopoly production.

Perhaps governmental monopoly of the supply of dominant money, rather than regulated private production, is based on a governmental advantage in supplying confidence. If indeed such an advantage exists, then the government would control production of the dominant money even if entry into the industry were permitted. But such an advantage should not be assumed to exist for all governments at all times. Before 1933 the U.S. government was promising to convert on demand its money into a private competitively produced money—gold. Rather than always having a monopoly in the supply of monetary confidence, historically governments entered the money business to supply legal sanction (and at times certification) to preexisting privately developed monetary arrangements.[34] And although private producers have taken advantage of the confidence placed in their monies, it is difficult to find a government that has not betrayed consumer trust.[35]

If some governments do have a cost advantage over private firms in producing monetary confidence, we must still determine *what* enables them to be more efficient. It is sometimes asserted that the advantage is based on the government's coercive power, for example, the governmental ability to declare its money "legal tender."[36] But this authority is neither necessary nor sufficient for the supply of monetary confidence[37] and may not even be important. The designation "legal tender" means that debtors cannot legally refuse the money as payment and amounts to the assertion by the government that individuals may use the government courts and police to force acceptance of its money in discharge of debts.[38] But this unique legal sanction possessed by the government's money in the enforcement of contracts may not even be a crucial attribute. Macauley [23] provides evidence that relatively informal legally unenforceable contractual practices predominate in business and that reliance on explicit legal sanctions is extremely rare. Business firms are said to generally rely on effective nonlegal sanctions, such as the appreciation or depreciation of a firm's goodwill from fulfillment or nonfulfillment of contracts.

Another possible advantage for the government may be that the production of monetary confidence is highly complementary with the production of

[34] "The first attempts to secure confidence of metallic money came from private individuals, bankers, goldsmiths, or great merchants who imprinted on the metals their particular marks" (Laughlin [21, p. 47]). For historical evidence of the role of government in the development of money see Burns [3, chs. 4 and 17], Carlile [5] and Nussbaum [28, pp. 32-45].

[35] Examples of private "abuses" are very well known. Examples of private reliability in the supply of money are not sensational or newsworthy and therefore are less well known. An outstanding example of a reliable private money in the U.S. was George Smith money. It was issued by the Wisconsin Marine and Fire Insurance Co. and was the major money in circulation in the Midwest during the 1840s. (See Hammond [13, pp. 613-14]). Government depreciation of monetary confidence occurred as long ago as the third century B.C. with the intentional debasement of metallic coins. (Laughlin [21, pp. 61-68]).

[36] The most extreme version of this assertion states that money is merely what government declares it to be and can be traced back to Knapp [19] who begins his book: "Money is a creature of law. A theory of money must therefore deal with legal history." Menger [25, p. 255], on the other hand, notes that "Money has not been generated by law. In its origin it is a social, and not a state-institution." Von Mises [41, pp. 68-78] and Nussbaum [28, pp. 5-10] also believe that it is the voluntary usage in commercial transactions based on the custom and confidence of the people that makes things money.

[37] There is overwhelming historical evidence on the existence of nonlegal tender circulating monies (and nonmonetary legal tenders); cf. Nussbaum [28, pp. 508, 46-48 and 54-55]. Federal Reserve notes, for example, were not made legal tender until 1933.

[38] See, for example, Nussbaum [28, pp. 45-55]. Alternatively, the government may only legally obligate itself to accept its money as payment for taxes. (The money is then said to possess "public receivability"; cf. Nussbaum [28, pp. 57-58]). But, for example, Ford Motor Company, if it were a private supplier of money, could similarly guarantee that its money would always be acceptable in payment, for example, of Ford cars. These promises amount to very little and are not analogous to guaranteed convertibility of a money into a commodity since the price of the Ford or the taxes is not fixed in terms of the money.

other goods that the government generally supplies. The production of national defense, for example, may be complementary with supplying monetary confidence. Positive technical externalities appear to go both ways; i.e., production of national defense not only yields some monetary confidence as a by-product, but production of monetary confidence also yields national defense services. Control of a country's dominant money supply carries with it the ability to quickly gain control of a significant quantity of the country's resources. To a government such control represents a very large potential tax that can quickly be levied and collected in a broad based and efficient way—without market or democratic tests. If the government holds its coercion capital in such a highly liquid form the asset can then be conveniently used for national defense purposes. England, for example, exhausted a large part of the pound sterling brand-name capital, built up over more than two centuries of successful performance, to fight World War II. [39]

Governmental depreciation of its monetary confidence asset to fight a war points up a peculiar difficulty with governmental control of money production. Government officials do not own the monetary brand-name capital and therefore have less incentive to conserve it. They will more generally tolerate its destruction to maintain their political power than would owners of a private firm. The creation of stable price expectations appears to be such a long-term investment that politicians, particularly those whose positions are not secure, will not undertake its current costs and will consume inherited brand-name capital. [40]

The U.S. has attempted to create institutions in which semi-independent officials control the money supply. These officials are subject to less immediate political pressure and therefore have less short-run incentive to inflate and consume monetary confidence capital than do elected officials. Present U.S. monetary arrangements also attempt to separate individuals who control the dominant money supply from the beneficiaries of the income earned on the dollar brand-name capital. If competitive interest

[39] Intentional monetary depreciation during wars appears, at first glance, to be rational governmental policy in that we would expect it to be optimal to use on the margin some of all forms of a nation's wealth, including monetary confidence capital. But the loss of brand-name capital is a social cost that accompanies the transfer of wealth from money consumers to money producers and this cost must be explicitly taken account of when considering the efficiency of various taxes. If foreigners hold some of the money then unanticipated inflation produces more than merely a redistribution of wealth among citizens of the country; it yields the country additional net resources for current use. Therefore the decision by England after World War II to adopt a policy of devaluation with a resulting loss of brand-name capital rather than a policy of decrease in the rate of growth of money to "repay" the borrowings it made against its brand-name capital during the war (when it credited foreign accounts at the Bank of England in exchange for resources) may have been rational.

[40] Throughout this discussion we are assuming that political power is not an endowed saleable asset. If government officials possessed private property rights to their political power, they would experience a wealth loss if they depreciated monetary brand-name capital and the incentive to overissue would be reduced.

payments are made by private financial institutions, then solely the Federal Reserve earns income on the dollar brand-name capital, which it then passes on to the Treasury as "interest" on Federal Reserve notes. The short-run incentives for overissue are thereby reduced compared to direct governmental control. But, still, Federal Reserve officials do not have private property rights to the confidence capital embodied in the dollar brand name and therefore the arrangement is less effective in this respect than a private property right arrangement.

Alternatively, if the government were to regulate a private dominant money supplier, many of the beneficial incentive effects from private ownership of brand-name capital would still vanish. If the government does not permit the firm to set a profit-maximizing rental price for the dominant money, the private firm will have an incentive to overissue. Given the natural monopoly characteristics in the production of monetary confidence and the costs of switching to a new dominant money, we can expect the profit-maximizing price in a nondeceiving equilibrium to be very high.[41] If the government is to prevent the firm from setting such a high price and also from overissuing, regulation must include price and quantity and the situation is closer to public ownership.

None of the arguments we have considered justify legal monopolization by the government of the supply of currency. Furthermore, although all dominant monies may in fact have to be currencies, all currencies need not be dominant monies. Why should not the government allow many different private currencies to circulate, all convertible on demand into the government's dominant currency (as with travelers checks)? A possible answer is related to the efficiency that one currency permits in prevention of counterfeiting. During the free banking era, counterfeit bank notes were a more significant problem than the fraud associated with overissue and bank failures. The entry into the market of additional currencies creates social information-transaction costs associated with detecting counterfeits and therefore a single currency must be established.[42]

---

[41] An indication of the costs of switching to a new dominant money is the continued use of the established money within a country during a hyperinflation, even though regulations against the use of foreign currencies often did not exist. Cagan [4] notes that of the seven hyperinflations he studied only in 1923 Germany did substantial amounts of unauthorized currencies issued by local governments and private organizations circulate, and these illegal currencies were denominated in the hyperinflating unit (p. 101). His estimates of the constant (anticipated) rate of change in the quantity of money and prices that would maximize the government's revenue ranged from 12 to 54 percent *per month* (p. 81).

[42] Small denomination notes were particularly easy to counterfeit and difficult to control during the free banking period since it did not pay to examine them carefully, and some states therefore prohibited their issuance (cf. Gallantin [10, p. 301], Hammond [13, p. 186] and Temin [37, p. 188]). The Bank of England did not issue notes under £20 until 1759 and bank notes were not commonly used in everyday exchange but circulated primarily between specializing money dealers (cf. Smith [34, pp. 306-8]). An interesting fact that may provide some evidence on the reduced costs of preventing counterfeiting when only a single major currency exists is that Bank of England paper notes circulated for 64 years before the first counterfeit appeared while counterfeits appeared in the U.S. soon after paper money was introduced (Dillistin [8, p. 10]).

BENJAMIN KLEIN : 451

These conjectures about present domestic monetary arrangements await verification in future research on the fundamental unanswered questions regarding the nature of the monetary service stream and the production function for monetary confidence. An increase in our understanding of the economic attributes of money and its role in facilitating exchange combined with knowledge of the historical development of monetary brand names and the part government played in the process is essential before we can hope to determine the optimal set of institutions and government regulations for the money industry.

LITERATURE CITED

1. ALCHIAN, ARMEN A. "Information Costs, Pricing, and Resource Unemployment." *Western Economic Journal,* 7 (June, 1969), 109-28.

2. BERRY, THOMAS S. *Western Prices Before 1861.* Cambridge: Harvard University Press, 1943.

3. BURNS, ARTHUR R. *Money and Monetary Policy in Early Times.* New York: Knopf, 1927.

4. CAGAN, PHILLIP. "The Monetary Dynamics of Hyperinflation." In Milton Friedman, ed., *Studies in the Quantity Theory of Money.* Chicago: University of Chicago Press, 1950. PP. 25-117.

5. CARLILE, WILLIAM W. *The Evolution of Modern Money.* London: Macmillan, 1901.

6. CHAMBERLIN, EDWARD H. *The Theory of Monopolistic Competition.* 8th ed. Cambridge: Harvard University Press, 1965.

7. CIPOLLA, CARLO M. *Money, Prices and Civilization in the Mediterranean World: Fifth to Seventeenth Century.* New York: Gordian Press, 1967.

8. DILLISTIN, WILLIAM H. *Bank Note Reporters and Counterfeit Detectors,* 1826-1866. New York: The American Numismatic Society, 1949.

9. FRIEDMAN, MILTON. *A Program for Monetary Stability.* New York: Fordham University Press, 1959.

10. GALLATIN, ALBERT. "Considerations on the Currency and Banking System of the United States," (1831) in H. Adams, ed., *The Writings of Albert Gallatin,* vol. 3. Philadelphia: Lippincott, 1879. Pp. 231-364.

11. GOLDMAN, MARSHALL I. "Product Differentiation and Advertising: Some Lessons from Soviet Experience." *Journal of Political Economy,* 68 (August, 1960), 346-57.

12. GRUBEL, HERBERT G. "The Distribution of Seigniorage from International Liquidity Creation." In R. A. Mundell and A. K. Swoboda, eds., *Monetary Problems of the International Economy.* Chicago: University of Chicago Press, 1969. Pp. 269-82.

13. HAMMOND, BRAY. *Banks and Politics in America from the Revolution to the Civil War.* Princeton, N.J.: Princeton University Press, 1957.

14. HAYEK, FRIEDRICH A. "The Meaning of Competition." In *Individualism and Economic Order.* Chicago: University of Chicago Press, 1948. Pp. 92-106.

452 : MONEY, CREDIT, AND BANKING

15. JOHNSON, HARRY G. "Inside Money, Outside Money, Income, Wealth, and Welfare in Monetary Theory." *Journal of Money, Credit, and Banking*, 1 (February, 1969), 30-45.

16. _____. "Pesek and Saving's Theory of Money and Wealth: A Comment." *Journal of Money, Credit, and Banking*, 1 (August, 1969), 535-37.

17. _____. "A Note On Seigniorage and the Social Saving from Substituting Credit for Commodity Money." In R. A. Mundell and A. K. Swoboda, eds., *Monetary Problems of the International Economy.* Chicago: University of Chicago Press, 1969. Pp. 323-29.

18. KLEIN, BENJAMIN. "The Demand for Quality Adjusted Cash Balances." Unpublished manuscript.

19. KNAPP, GEORGE FRIEDRICH. *The State Theory of Money.* London: Macmillan, 1924.

20. KNIGHT, FRANK H. *Risk, Uncertainty and Profit.* 1921; rpt. New York: Kelley, 1964.

21. LAUGHLIN, J. LAWRENCE. "A New Exposition of Money, Credit, and Prices," vol. 1, *The Evolution of the Standard.* Chicago: University of Chicago Press, 1931.

22. LESTER, RICHARD A. *Monetary Experiments: Early American and Recent Scandinavian.* Princeton: Princeton University Press, 1939.

23. MACAULEY, STEWART. "Non-Contractual Relations in Business: A Preliminary Study." *American Sociological Review*, 28 (February, 1963), 55-69.

24. MACESICH, GEORGE. "Monetary Disturbances in the United States, 1834-45." Unpublished Ph.D. dissertation, University of Chicago, June, 1958.

25. MENGER, KARL. "On the Origin of Money." *The Economic Journal*, 2 (June, 1892), 239-55.

26. McKINNON, RONALD I. "Optimum Currency Areas." *American Economic Review*, 53 (September, 1963), 717-25.

27. MUNDELL, ROBERT A. "A Theory of Optimum Currency Areas." *American Economic Review*, 51 (September, 1961), 657-65.

28. NUSSBAUM, ARTHUR. *Money in the Law: National and International.* Brooklyn, N.Y.: Foundation Press, 1950.

29. PESEK, BORIS P. "Comment." *Journal of Political Economy*, 76 (August, 1968 supplement) 885-92.

30. PESEK, BORIS P., and THOMAS R. SAVING. *Money, Wealth and Economic Theory.* New York: Macmillan, 1967.

31. _____. *The Foundations of Money and Banking.* New York: Macmillan, 1968.

32. PICK, FRANZ. *Pick's Currency Yearbook.* New York: Pick Publishing Corporation, annually.

33. ROTHBARD, MURRAY N. "The Case for A 100 Percent Gold Dollar." In Leland B. Yeager, ed., *In Search of a Monetary Constitution.* Cambridge: Harvard University Press, 1962. Pp. 94-136.

34. SMITH, ADAM. *An Inquiry Into the Nature and Causes of the Wealth of Nations.* 1776; rpt. New York: The Modern Library, 1937.

35. SPENCER, HERBERT. *Social Statics.* 1877; rpt. New York: Robert Schalkenbach Foundation, 1954.

36. STIGLER, GEORGE J. "The Economics of Information." In *The Organization of Industry.* Homewood, Ill.: Irwin, 1968. Pp. 171-90 (Reprinted from *Journal of Political Economy*, 69 [June 1961]).

37. TEMIN, PETER. *The Jacksonian Economy.* New York: W. W. Norton, 1969.
38. THOMPSON, EARL A. "The Theory of Money and Income Consistent with Orthodox Value Theory." Unpublished manuscript.
39. TOBIN, JAMES. "Commercial Banks as Creators of 'Money'." In Dean Carson, ed., *Banking and Monetary Studies.* Homewood, Ill.: Irwin, 1963. Pp. 408-19.
40. VAN FENSTERNMAKER, J. *The Development of American Commercial Banking, 1787-1837.* Kent, Ohio: Kent State University, 1965.
41. VON MISES, LUDWIG. *The Theory of Money and Credit.* New Haven: Yale University Press, 1953.

[7]

LANCE GIRTON
DON ROPER*

Theory and Implications of
Currency Substitution

Thus if currency notes were to be deprived of their liquidity-premium by the stamping system, a long series of substitutes would step into their shoes—bank-money,
debts at call, foreign money, jewelery and the precious metals generally, and so forth.
(John M. Keynes [18, p. 358])

MONETARY THEORY HAS TRADITIONALLY ASSUMED that one
currency circulates in each country. The relaxation of the one-currency-per-country
assumption allows currency questions to be separated from questions dealing
primarily with international and interregional trade. Just as the pure theory of
international trade abstracts from monetary phenomena, the pure theory of multiple
currencies can be investigated independently of the number of countries or regions.

The theory of substitutable monies developed here is applicable to several monies
circulating in one country and to several monies circulating internationally. Consideration of issues involving CS (currency substitution) cuts across the usual distinction (based on political or governmental jurisdictions) between "domestic" and
"international" monetary economics. Consequently, the literature on substitutable

*This paper has benefited from helpful suggestions from Dale Henderson, Tom Grennes, George
Moore (for material in Appendix B), Stephen Turnovsky, and two anonymous referees. The authors
appreciate the comments and support from members of the IIES (Institute for International Economic
Studies) at the University of Stockholm, where the first draft of the paper was completed in 1974.
Helpful discussions over subsequent drafts followed seminars at ANU, Chase Manhattan Bank, University of North Carolina, Monash University, Princeton University, and UCLA. Our work was
stimulated by conversations with Russell Boyer at the Federal Reserve Board in the summers of
1972 and 1973. An earlier version of the paper was circulated under the same title in 1976.

LANCE GIRTON AND DON ROPER *are professors of economics, University of Utah.*

0022-2879/81/0281-0012$00.50/0   ©1981 Ohio State University Press
JOURNAL OF MONEY, CREDIT, AND BANKING, vol. 13, no. 1 (February 1981)

monies comes from domestic monetary economics [e.g., 2, 4, 20, 25, 32] and international monetary economics [e.g., 3, 5, 15, 16, 19, 21, 22, 23, 24, 28, 33]. A brief survey is given in [6].

The paper is organized as follows: In section 1 a two-currency model of the exchange rate is developed under the assumption that (the paths of) the quantities of monies are exogenous. The exchange rate between monies is shown to be "unstable" in the sense that movements in the exchange rate necessary to maintain monetary equilibrium become larger without limit as CS increases. In addition, the exchange rate is indeterminate with perfect CS. In contrast with CS, an increase in substitution between bonds does not produce an "unstable" bond-exchange rate and perfect bond substitution does not produce indeterminacy. CS is different from substitution between other financial assets because the yield on money is independent of the value of money. This independence is, as argued in section 2, due to the choice of units in which financial contracts are specified. The fact that the interest payment on money is denominated in terms of itself (money) and that the interest payment on bonds is not denominated in terms of bonds provides a distinction between money and bonds which, we argue, is more fundamental than the usual view of the money-bond distinction. In section 3 the behavior of money issuers in response to CS is characterized as the choice between fixing exchange rates or competing in the production of monies. It is shown that there is no externality in the production of money such that the usual implication of competition, allocative efficiency, is as applicable to money as to other commodities. When the behavior of money issuers is endogenized, the presence of CS is found to eliminate rather than cause exchange rate instability. In the summary it is concluded that the usual fixed-money-growth rule will lead to an inferior, depreciating money if the public is offered competitively produced substitutes.

1. AN ASSET DEMAND MODEL OF CURRENCY SUBSTITUTION

The model of CS developed here contains two money-demand functions which, together with exogenous money supplies, are used to analyze the money exchange rate. A third nonmonetary asset is implicit in the model, but the balance sheet constraint makes the market equilibrium condition for this asset redundant.

CS can be modeled by the inclusion of real returns on both monies in both money-demand functions. Defining r_1 and r_2 as the anticipated real returns on monies one and two, the demands for real balances can be expressed as

$$M_k/P_k = L_k(r_1, r_2, r, w), \qquad (k = 1,2) \tag{1}$$

where M_k is the nominal quantity of currency k, P_k is the price of goods in terms of currency k, r is the anticipated real return on the nonmonetary asset, and w is a scale variable such as real wealth. w and r are taken as exogenous. Money holders are

14 : MONEY, CREDIT, AND BANKING

assumed to hold both monies so the same scale variable, w, is used in both L_1 and L_2.[1]

In keeping with standard specifications, money-demands are assumed to depend on differential returns:

$$L_1(r_1-r, r_1-r_2, w) \quad \text{and} \quad L_2(r_2-r, r_2-r_1, w). \tag{2}$$

To simplify the argument, the demand functions are assumed to have exponential specifications. The equilibrium condition for currency one is,[2]

$$M_1/P_1 = \theta_1(w) \exp[\alpha_1(r_1-r) + \sigma_1(r_1-r_2)], \quad (\alpha_1, \sigma_1 > 0) \tag{3}$$

where σ_1 is a coefficient of substitution between monies one and two and α_1 is a coefficient of substitution between money one and the nonmonetary asset.

The monetary equilibrium conditions in logarithmic form are

$$\ln M_1 - \ln P_1 = \ln \theta_1 + \alpha_1(r_1-r) + \sigma_1(r_1-r_2) \tag{4a}$$

$$\ln M_2 - \ln P_2 = \ln \theta_2 + \alpha_2(r_2-r) + \sigma_2(r_2-r_1). \tag{4b}$$

Implications of CS can be obtained by focusing on the relative values of the two monies. To find the expression determining the relative value of the monies, subtract (4b) from (4a) and rearrange terms to obtain

$$\ln(P_1/P_2) = \ln[(M_1/\theta_1)/(M_2/\theta_2)] - \alpha(r_1 - r_2) - 2\sigma(r_1 - r_2), \tag{5}$$

where the following symmetry conditions have been imposed: $\alpha_1 = \alpha_2 = \alpha$ and $\sigma_1 = \sigma_2 = \sigma$. The assumption $\sigma_1 = \sigma_2$ identifies CS with the single parameter, σ, and the condition $\alpha_1 = \alpha_2$ makes the relative value of monies invariant to changes in r, the yield on the nonmonetary asset.

Equation (5) can be used to determine the exchange rate between the two monies if some relation between P_1/P_2 and E (the exchange market price of money two in

---

[1]The money-demand functions L_1 and L_2 are defined by currency, not by country. Most BOP (balance of payments) models are based on the assumption of one currency-per-country and therefore do not distinguish between money demand defined by country of residence and money demand defined by currency. When defined by country, money-demand functions are appropriate for explaining the multiregional or interregional BOP. When defined by currency, they are appropriate for explaining the multicurrency concept of exchange market pressure, defined as that combination of reserve and exchange rate changes that is independent of central bank intervention. A measure of EMP with equal weights is given in [11].

Standard BOP accounting does not distinguish between these two concepts of the BOP. Data is collected for above-the-line-entries on the basis of country residency. The official settlements definition of the BOP, a measure (when the exchange rate is fixed) of exchange market pressure, is entered below the line.

[2]$\alpha_1(r_1-r)$ is the usual interest rate term found in money-demand functions. This becomes clear if r_1 is expressed as the difference between the market or nominal interest rate on money one, i_1, and the anticipated rate of inflation in terms of money one, π_1. Substituting $i_1-\pi_1$ for r_1 converts $\alpha_1(r_1-r)$ to $-\alpha_1(r+\pi_1) + \alpha_1 i_1$, where $\alpha_1 i_1$ is usually assumed constant and therefore suppressed. Equation (3), therefore, is a typical *LM* equation with the addition of the substitution effect between the two monies.

terms of money one) is imposed. The obvious condition to use is that $E = P_1/P_2$. This looks like and might well be regarded as purchasing power parity, but it is not based on the usual arbitrage assumption associated with PPP. Rather than the usual condition that arbitrage takes place across space or between regions, the multicurrency version of PPP requires that arbitrage take place between currencies. This condition means that neither money is discriminated against, or discounted relative to the other, when used as a medium of exchange. When two prices are quoted for the same good, the ratio of the prices must equal the rate at which the currencies are traded in the exchange market.

Defining $e = \ln E$ and imposing the condition that $e = \ln(P_1/P_2)$, equation (5) can be expressed as

$$e = \tilde{e} - \eta\,\delta, \tag{6}$$

where $\tilde{e} = \ln[(M_1/\theta_1)/(M_2/\theta_2)]$, $\eta = \alpha + 2\sigma$, and $\delta = r_1 - r_2$. Exogenous money supplies and demand factors are contained in the term $\tilde{e}$.[3] CS is reflected in the σ-parameter such that η will vary from α to infinity as CS ranges from zero to infinity.

The differential anticipated real return on monies is equal to the differential nominal return minus the differential anticipated rate of inflation:

$$\begin{aligned} \delta = r_1 - r_2 &= (i_1 - \pi_1) - (i_2 - \pi_2) \\ &= (i_1 - i_2) - (\pi_1 - \pi_2). \end{aligned} \tag{7}$$

Assuming anticipations are formed in a manner consistent with (the multicurrency version of) PPP, the anticipated rate of change in the exchange rate, x, will equal the difference between the anticipated inflation rates such that equation (7) can be expressed as

$$\delta = i_1 - i_2 - x. \tag{7'}$$

Substituting this expression for δ into the exchange rate equation (6) produces

$$e = \tilde{e} - \eta(i_1 - i_2 - x). \tag{8}$$

Since equation (8) will be used to derive implications of CS, it is worth summarizing the assumptions used in the derivation of this relationship. First, the nominal interest rates on monies, i_1 and i_2, are assumed fixed. This assumption will be discussed in section 2. Second, the money supplies are taken as exogenous and are contained in $\tilde{e}$. The assumption of exogenous money supplies will be relaxed in

---

[3]We are assuming that $\tilde{e}$ is independent of e. A sufficient condition to assure this independence is that any exchange-rate induced wealth effects have proportional impacts on θ_1 and θ_2.

In contrast to an arbitrage version of PPP, we could have assumed the neutrality version of PPP, viz., the real exchange rate is independent of nominal variables. This would complicate the definition of $\tilde{e}$ but leave the conclusions unaffected.

16 : MONEY, CREDIT, AND BANKING

section 3. Third, the anticipated rate of change of the exchange rate x is taken as exogenous. When x is endogenized using rational expectations in Appendix A or using adaptive expectations in [10], the results are consistent with the conclusions of this section.

There are two basic implications of CS, given the assumptions of this section. One implication relates directly to a policy issue and the other concerns the foundations of monetary theory. First, CS will cause exchange rate "instability" in the sense that shifts in the anticipated rate of change of the exchange rate lead to larger exchange rate movements with greater degrees of CS. Second, perfect CS implies that the exchange rate is indeterminate.

Consider first the impact of a shift in the anticipated rate of change of the exchange rate x. Taking the derivative of expression (8),

$$\partial e/\partial x = \eta = \alpha + 2\sigma. \tag{8'}$$

The greater the degree of CS (i.e., the larger the value of σ), the larger the change in e needed to satisfy monetary equilibrium for a given shift in x. The movement in the exchange rate needed to satisfy the monetary equilibrium conditions approaches infinity as substitution becomes perfect (i.e., as η approaches infinity).

From equation (8), the impact of $\bar{e}$ on e, given by $\partial e/\partial \bar{e} = 1$, holds for all finite value of CS. Since money supplies are included in $\bar{e}$, changes in the supplies or composition of monies have a proportional impact on the exchange rate for all finite degrees of CS. CS increases the impact of x (or δ) on e but leaves the impact of money supplies on e unaffected, so exchange market intervention becomes a relatively less effective instrument for offsetting shifts in x. The fact that e is more sensitive to i_1 and i_2 as CS increases motivates the assumption in section 3 that, when money issuers compete for larger market shares, they do so by offering more attractive rates on their liabilities.

The second implication concerns the theoretical question of exchange rate determination under perfect CS.[4] In order for both monies to circulate, their values (in terms of goods) must be finite. This means the exchange rate must be nonzero and finite. In order for the exchange rate to be finite and greater than zero, the rate of return δ must be zero. But equal real returns do not impose any condition on the exchange rate because δ is independent of P_1 and P_2 and, therefore, of the exchange rate. The remaining condition to which one might appeal is $e = \bar{e}$. But with perfect CS, the individual money-demands in $\bar{e}$ are no longer defined. Consequently, any exchange rate is an equilibrium rate when CS is perfect.[5]

[4] The implications of perfect CS for exchange rate determination are also found in [2, 3, 10, 15, 16]. We assume that monies (like other financial assets) are distinguished by issuer, and counterfeiting is effectively prohibited. (See [20, 33, 12].) Perfect substitution does not imply indistinguishability.
[5] It should be noted that there is no inconsistency in the proposition that, when CS is perfect, the exchange rate is both unstable and indeterminate. Instability does not presuppose determinacy as can be seen with the following argument: Suppose that two perfectly substitutable currencies have the same initial real yields and are exchangeable at some initial finite exchange rate, e^0. Now suppose that δ is changed from its initial zero value. This shock will cause e to go to plus or minus infinity (E will go to plus infinity or to zero). The infinite movement in e reflects instability under perfect CS. But e^0 was completely arbitrary. It is not necessary to determine the initial value of e to determine that the (limit of the) derivative $\partial e/\partial x$, is infinite.

To see that these implications of CS are peculiar to money, per se, we will contrast CS with bond substitution. With slight changes in the expression for δ, equation (8) can be used to examine substitution between two bonds, A and B. The only assumption that makes the preceding specification of δ unique to money is that the market yields i_1 and i_2 have been taken as exogenous. Rather than being fixed, bond market yields vary inversely with the values of the bonds. For convenience, the bonds are assumed to be perpetuities paying a constant and continuous stream of interest denoted as C_a and C_b. The market yields on the bonds are

$$i_a = C_a/Q_a \quad \text{and} \quad i_b = C_b/Q_b,$$

where Q_a and Q_b are the bond prices. Both bond prices and their stream of interest payments are measured in terms of a single background numeraire needing no further specification for our purposes.

Retaining the symbols η and x from the money-equation (8), the counterpart bond-equation is

$$R = \bar{R} - \eta(C_a/Q_a - C_b/Q_b - x), \tag{8b}$$

where R is the (log of the) bond-exchange rate, $\ln(Q_b/Q_a)$, and x is the anticipated rate of change of R. Supply and demand factors are embedded in $\bar{R}$ exactly as they were in $\bar{e}$ such that $\bar{R}$ is the value of R when the anticipated differential return is zero.

It is clear from the construction of the money-equation (8) and the bond-equation (8b) that the only difference between the determination of the money-exchange rate (e) and the bond-exchange rate (R) is that the values of bonds effect the differential bond yield whereas the values of monies do not influence the differential money yield.

Equation (8b) can be used to contrast the implications of CS with the implications of bond substitution. First, we found that the change in e necessary to accommodate a change in the anticipated rate of change of e, as given by $\partial e/\partial x$, approaches infinity as CS becomes perfect. In contrast, the change in R necessary to accommodate a change in the differential bond return is

$$\partial R/\partial x = \eta/(1+\eta i), \tag{9}$$

where the derivative has been simplified by evaluating it at the point where $C_a/Q_a = C_b/Q_b = i$. The derivative $\partial R/\partial x$ approaches $1/i$ as bond substitution becomes perfect. Thus, changes in x have a limited impact on the bond-exchange rate. If, for example, bond holders suddenly expect bond B to appreciate relative to bond A, their effort to sell A and purchase B increases the yield on A and decreases the yield on B until holders are satisfied with the existing quantities of bonds. This is not the case for two monies since values of monies have no influence on the market yields on monies.

Finally, consider the determination of the bond-exchange rate, R, when bonds A

18 : MONEY, CREDIT, AND BANKING

and B are perfect substitutes. Just as individual money demands are no longer defined ($\bar{e}$ is undefined) when CS is perfect, individual bond demands are no longer defined ($\bar{R}$ is undefined) when bond substitution is perfect. But in the case of perfect bond substitution, R is determined by the requirement that the differential return is zero. Setting the parenthesis on the right-hand side of (8b) to zero constrains the bond-exchange rate since Q_a and Q_b are determinants of the differential yield. In contrast, P_1 and P_2 did not appear in the differential yield formula for monies. For perpetuity bonds with continuous interest payments, the bond-exchange rate equals the ratio of interest payments, that is, $Q_b/Q_a = C_b/C_a$.[6] Perfect bond substitution rigidly fixes the bond-exchange rate whereas perfect CS leaves the money-exchange rate indeterminate.

Although indeterminacy is a logical implication of a model that utilizes widely accepted money-demand functions, we regard it as a consequence of abstracting from transactions costs and not of immediate concern for policy. The macro model used in this section abstracts from the costs of posting multiple prices or converting prices stated in one money to another money. Examples of *perfect* substitution of which we are aware, for example, Federal Reserve notes of different districts, exhibit *unitary* exchange rates. This suggests that transactions costs at exchange rates other than unity (or perhaps multiples of ten) may be an important constraint on the rate of exchange between perfectly substitutable currencies.

2. THE DISTINCTION BETWEEN MONEY AND BONDS

In the preceding section the implications of CS were contrasted with the implications of bond substitution. It was emphasized that the peculiarity of the CS implications is due to the invariance of the market yields on monies with respect to their values. The economic rationale for this distinguishing characteristic of money will be examined in this section.

It will be sufficient to focus on only one bond and one money. The analysis is simplified with the assumption of perfect foresight. With this assumption, r_m and r_b are used to represent both the anticipated and actual real returns on the money and the bond, respectively. The procedure will be to examine the yield formulas for r_b and r_m to determine exactly why r_b depends on the value of the bond and why r_m does not depend on the value of money.

The formula for the instantaneous real return on a bond can be expressed as

$$r_b = C_b/Q_b + g, \tag{10}$$

---

[6]With perfect substitution between bonds A and B, their anticipated real yields will be equal, which implies that

$$C_a/Q_a + g_a = C_b/Q_b + g_b,$$

where g_a and g_b are the capital gains. If capital gains are equal, the equality of real yields immediately implies that the bond-exchange rate equals the ratio of the interest payments. This solution is also derived in Appendix B, where the capital gains are not assumed equal.

where g represents the capital gain against goods (which could be decomposed into the appreciation of the money price of the bond minus the rate of change of the money price of goods). Using π to represent the rate of inflation, the instantaneous real yield on money is

$$r_m = i_m - \pi. \tag{11}$$

To understand why i_m is "constant" requires explicit recognition of the difference between the interest *payment* and the interest *rate* on money.[7] By denoting the money value of the interest payment as C_m, formula (11) can be expressed as

$$r_m = C_m/1 - \pi, \tag{12}$$

where $-\pi$ is, like g in equation (10), the capital gain against goods. C_m is the (fraction of) units of money paid per time period per unit of money. The price of money that must be used to deflate C_m is, as the dimensions indicate, the price of money in terms of itself, viz., unity.

A comparison of the yield formulas (10) and (12) reemphasizes the earlier argument that the yield on a bond depends inversely on its value Q_b, whereas the yield on money does not depend on its value (whether measured in terms of goods P^{-1}, or in terms of bonds Q_b^{-1}). To explain the difference between money and bonds, we will briefly consider how the yield formulas would be written if the interest payments on both bonds and money were tied to the price level or indexed against inflation. Suppose that the interest payment on a bond were indexed against inflation such that the real interest payment were constant. Then the appropriate expression for the real bond return would be

$$r_b = c_b/q_b + g, \tag{10'}$$

where $c_b = C_b/P$, $q_b = Q_b/P$, and P is the money price of goods. If c_b is constant, then (10') shows that r_b depends not on Q_b per se, but on q_b.

Similarly, if the coupon or interest payment on money were fixed in real terms, then the appropriate real return formula for money would be

$$r_m = c_m/P^{-1} - \pi, \tag{12'}$$

where c_m is the constant real interest payment. The denominator P^{-1} is the goods value of money. Equation (12'), in contrast to (12), shows that the yield on money *does* depend on the (goods) value of money when the interest payment is contracted

---

[7]In this section we assume that the interest *payment* on money is fixed and use the fixed interest payment to explain the fixed interest rate i_m. In a broader analysis in which other variables are endogenized, neither the interest rate nor the interest payment would need to be fixed. i_m could vary but, if the model were neutral (with respect to the level of nominal variables), then r_m and, therefore, i_m would be independent of P. The invariance of i_m with respect to P is consistent with the observable, positive relation between bank deposit rates (that are not subject to ceilings) and the *rate-of-change* of P.

20 : MONEY, CREDIT, AND BANKING

in terms of goods. When contrasted with (10) and (12), equations (10') and (12') show that the yield on an asset depends inversely on the value of the asset measured in the units in which the interest payments are fixed.

One observes that most contractual obligations are specified in terms of the units in which the medium of exchange is measured. Escalated contracts and other forms of indexation are the exceptions, not the rule. Interest payments on money, when they are nonzero, are specified in terms of money units.[8] Interest payments on bonds are not specified in bond units. As Keynes pointed out, "it is the essence of debt [in contrast to what Keynes called "money proper"] to be enforceable in terms of something other than itself" [17, p. 6]. Conversely, it is the essence of money that its own return be contracted in the same units used to measure the asset itself. And this defining characteristic of money explains the differences in the implications generated by CS and those generated by bond substitution.

The distinction developed here between money and bonds contrasts sharply with the current view in the theoretical literature. A widely accepted statement of the money-bond distinction is given by Tobin [30, 31]. According to Tobin, the nominal interest rate on money is "exogenously fixed." But the only items fixed are the coupons or interest payments on both money and bonds. And the interest *rate* on money is "fixed" (i.e., invariant to the value of money), not because the interest payment is fixed, but because interest on money is specified in terms of itself. It is not the fixity of the interest payment but the units in which it is fixed that makes i_m invariant to the value of money. If the interest payment on money were fixed in terms of any other commodity or asset, then money, like other assets, would have a market yield dependent on its value and the implications of CS would be similar to the implications of substitution between other financial assets. Further research should provide more insight into why contracts are specified in units in which the medium of exchange is measured.[9] But it is unnecessary to accept the invariance of i_m as an institutional datum.

3. IMPLICATIONS OF CS FOR THE BEHAVIOR OF MONEY ISSUERS

In section 1 CS was associated with instability in the sense that, for a given shift in anticipated exchange rate movements, greater CS produced larger exchange rate

---

[8] We have thus far considered only the pecuniary yield on money. To determine the relation between the value of money and its *total* return, it is necessary to consider the nonpecuniary yield on money and payments in kind (e.g., bank services to large depositors). As long as real behavioral functions are homogeneous of degree zero in nominal variables, these considerations do not alter the invariance of money's return to the value of money.

[9] Opinions differ over priority of the unit-of-account and medium-of-exchange properties of money. We conjecture that the medium-of-exchange property is fundamental to the unit-of-account because creditors can be paid off in any exchange medium as long as the market value of the medium satisfies the contract. If this is true, then, contrary to prevailing opinion, the medium-of-exchange property *is* embedded in models of the financial sector through the standard assumption that i_m is fixed. If the medium-of-exchange property is fundamental, then it is both the source of indeterminacy (through its determination of the units in which interest-payment contracts are specified) and a source of resolution of the indeterminacy issue (through the transactions costs of using more than one exchange media without unitary exchange rates).

Other authors (e.g., Keynes [17]) have argued that the unit-of-account property is fundamental to the medium-of-exchange property. Resolution of this question is outside the scope of this paper.

fluctuations. One of the crucial assumptions underlying the model in section 1 was that money issuers were assumed to alter neither the nomi nal quantity of money, M, nor the nominal yield on money, i_m, in response to exchange rate fluctuations. By altering either the explicit interest paid on money or the quantity of money (and imposing a capital gain or loss on money holders), a money issuer could alter the real return (r_m) and induce the changes in currency demand necessary to eliminate or at least dampen fluctuations in the exchange rate. It is particularly appropriate for an issuer of substitutable money to use the real money yield as the monetary control variable because, as was shown in section 1, the impact of a change in r_m on the exchange rate becomes greater as CS increases. In this section, the behavior of money issuers is endogenized and their response to demand shifts is shown to eliminate the instability associated with CS in the model of section 1.

There are a multitude of objectives leading money issuers to respond to exchange market pressure. With an increase in CS, the role of profit or seigniorage considerations should become more important in the determination of monetary policy. Central banks with policies more expansionary than the average would find their monetary control seriously eroded if they acted as if their seigniorage position was unimportant when their liabilities are substitutes with other currencies. The model developed in this section will, consequently, assume profit-maximization.

With substitutable monies, market pressure will force individual money issuers to make their monies attractive relative to alternative monies available to money holders. But the implications of CS will depend on the market structure in which substitutable monies are issued. Of particular interest are a competitive market structure and a cartel market structure.[10]

Money issuers may cooperatively determine a joint monetary policy through a cartel agreement to retain market shares.[11] To reduce the incentive for money holders to shift between monies, a formal cartel would likely include a fixed exchange rate agreement to help ensure that cartel members property coordinate their policies. If, for example, one member bank attempted to pursue a less inflationary policy (and pay a higher real yield), the demand for its currency would increase. In order to keep its currency from appreciating against member currencies, the bank would have to reverse its tight policy and create money against the purchase of the weaker currencies. Similarly, commercial banks' traditional commitment to maintain a fixed exchange rate between their deposit liabilities and central bank money restrains competition between the central and commercial banks. A cartel would stabilize exchange rates without providing money holders lower inflation rates or higher real yields.

A primary purpose of this section is to develop the implications of competitively supplied money.[12] Authors such as Friedman [7] and Pesek and Saving [26] have

---

[10]Rather than compete or form a cartel, money issuers could be protected through the institution of currency controls. The absence of such controls was implicitly assumed in section 1 when (the multicurrency version of) purchasing-power-parity was introduced, and that assumption is continued here. If governments protect central banks' monopoly position by prohibiting the use of "foreign" monies, then the arbitrage condition underlying PPP will be violated.

[11]As we have argued in [13], the European Monetary Union is an example of monetary cooperation facilitated through the use of a fixed-exchange-rate regime.

[12]Monetary competition has been introduced in a general neoclassical framework by Thompson [29].

argued that competition in the production of money is not viable because the value of money will be driven to its marginal cost of physical production. If this occurred, a commodity money would be the result and the advantages of a fiduciary system would be lost.

Since the marginal cost of paper and ink or maintenance of accounting entries necessary to physically produce other debt instruments (e.g., bonds) is, like money, near zero, we should ask why a similar conclusion has not been deduced for the supply of other financial instruments. The primary cost of producing a bond is, obviously, the interest and principal obligation, not the trivial cost of paper and ink. But the contractual payments represent a cost to a bond issuer only because the coupons are fixed in terms of another asset, usually money. On the other hand, the physical cost of production appears as the only cost for a monopoly issuer of fiat money because money holders must accept interest payments determined by contracts expressed in units of the money issuers own liability, if interest is paid at all. The fact that contracts are traditionally specified in money units explains why it is frequently argued that competitively supplied money will be issued until it becomes worthless and why a similar argument is not (to our knowledge) generally made for competition in the supply of other debt instruments.

Money holders choose between monies on the basis of anticipated real rates of return and, consequently, banks compete through their offers of real returns. Since the real return on money is $r_m = i_m - \pi$, a bank can change its real return by altering either the nominal yield i_m or the capital gain or loss on money, π. The theoretical results of this section are independent of the particular way a money issuer chooses to offer a given real return. But the institutional arrangements for rate-of-return competition are interesting in their own right. A brief discussion of possible arrangements will motivate a key assumption in the model that follows.

Under existing institutional arrangements, the monetary liabilities of commercial banks are convertible into the liabilities of a national central bank. But if commercial banks were not required to link their deposits to central bank liabilities, they could make their deposits convertible into any assets or goods they might choose. A bank concerned with seigniorage would choose assets that would have the greatest appeal to money holders. Since money holders are presumed interested in real rather than nominal values, they would prefer convertibility into real assets or assets with stable purchasing power. If the bank were able to, in effect, hold a portfolio of real assets, then the convertibility of the bank's deposit liabilities into real assets would insure depositors against real capital loss.[13] In short, profit considerations would induce banks to offer monetary liabilities convertible into assets with stable real values. This would be a return to a real (but not necessarily gold) standard.

At the abstract level of the model developed here the assets available for the banks of issue to hold are limited to capital goods paying a real yield of r. The assumption that banks maintain convertibility of their deposit liabilities into bank-

---

[13]Banks would presumably hold correspondent balances at other banks and deposit withdrawals could take the form of checks on other banks rather than convertibility into the actual assets of the first bank. The convertibility arrangement would be like a modern open-ended mutual fund or money market fund.

held assets implies that the bank's monetary liabilities are fixed against (capital) goods. This implies that the value of bank liabilities are guaranteed against capital loss in terms of goods.[14]

To make our model compatible with previous work on the revenue from inflation, we assume the nominal interest payment on money is zero ($i_m = 0$) such that the entire real return r_m is paid through deflation. This is equivalent to the institutional arrangement described above (in which money issuers maintain convertibility of their liabilities into assets with stable real purchasing power) if the convertibility feature is modified. Rather than maintaining a fixed parity between its liabilities and its (real) assets, a bank maintains convertibility at a price changing at a constant rate, $r_m = -\pi$. The bank of issue stands ready to redeem its liabilities at a price-path whose slope is (minus) the real return that the bank offers on its monetary liabilities.[15]

A profit-maximizing model for the behavior of a single money issuer will be developed for all degrees of CS. We depart from earlier literature on the revenue from inflation by dividing the flow of earnings into two parts. The first is the flow of net real income from issuing new money. The gross flow is M/P. Part of the new money issued is used to purchase and hold real assets to provide a redemption fund to back the liabilities being created. Thus, the flow of net real income is $\dot{M}/P - \dot{m}$ = πm where $\dot{m} = d(M/P)/dt$. The second part of the bank's earnings is the return on the redemption fund, rm. Total net real revenue at time t, measured as an instantaneous rate is, therefore,

$$\pi m + rm = im, \tag{13}$$

where im is the area under the usual liquidity preference schedule. The area is a maximum (or minimum) where the elasticity of the demand for real balances with respect to the market rate on the alternative asset is (minus) unity.[16] The elasticity, $m'(i)[i/m]$, is unitary when

[14]According to Friedman [8], it is not feasible for monetary policy to stabilize a price index given the current state of economic knowledge; hence, a stable rate of monetary growth is preferable to an active policy to stabilize P. Friedman is implicitly assuming that money issuers hold nominal assets. As we argue in the text, a bank that is serious about controlling the real value of its monetary liabilities would hold real, not nominal, assets. Just as money issuers once maintained the gold value of their liabilities by holding gold assets, they can maintain the real value of their liabilities by holding real assets. This would allow for price stabilization at the present state of economic knowledge.

[15]The assumption that the bank of issue guarantees a price path is equivalent to Auernheimer's [1] concept of an "honest" bank.

The question of the honesty or deception of money issuers in a competitive market has been given detailed attention by Klein [20]. He treats money as a consumer durable and argues that a long-run profit maximizing bank will limit current deception and hold down the current inflation rate in order to not erode consumer confidence in its money. Banks will act to create (what Klein calls) "brand name capital." In Klein's model with costly information it will be profitable, even under conditions of perfect competition, to have nonzero deception. We differ from Klein in that we assume banks can costlessly write binding contracts if they so desire, these contracts can be costlessly enforced, and default can be insured against. Under these conditions only firms that offer a goods-back-guarantee (along a price path) will be able to attract money holders.

[16]The present value of a bank offering a return $r_m = -\pi$ and facing an initial money-demand, $m(i,w(0))$, is $\int im(i,w(\tau))\exp(-r\tau)d\tau$, where integration is from zero to T, w is real wealth growing at an exogenous rate γ, and r is assumed greater than γ to assure convergence. Auernheimer [1] has a

$$i = m/m'\ (i) \quad \text{or} \quad \pi = m/m' - r. \tag{14}$$

A maximum is assured (i.e., $\partial^2[im(i)]/\partial i^2 < 0$) when an exponential specification for the demand for money is used. Assuming market interest rates on other monies are unchanged, the exponential specification used in section 1 (equation (3)) implies the relation $m'(i) = -(\alpha + \sigma)m$. Substituting this relation into (14) yields

$$i = 1/(\alpha + \sigma) \quad \text{or} \quad \pi = 1/(\alpha+\sigma) - r. \tag{15}$$

Several implications of CS follow immediately from equation (15). Beginning from a position in which each bank has a complete monopoly ($\sigma = 0$), equation (15) implies $\pi = 1/\alpha - r$, a result which has been derived by Phelps [27] and Auernheimer [1].

With substitution between the liabilities of money issuers, their ability to maintain monopolies in segmented markets is undermined. As inspection of equation (15) shows, the profit-maximizing inflation rate falls with larger values of σ. The greater the degree of CS, the more easily a money issuer can capture a larger share of the market by offering a lower rate of inflation. As substitution between monies becomes perfect ($\sigma \to \infty$), a competitive money issuer engineers a deflation equal to the alternative real return, r. Another way to express the condition is that the alternative asset's nominal yield is zero, that is, $r + \pi = 0$. With perfect CS, therefore, the opportunity cost of holding money becomes equal to the (assumed) zero marginal cost of production. This condition was introduced by Friedman [9] for an optimal quantity of real money balances.[17] Resource allocation between money creation and other activities should be efficient when money issuers compete and their liabilities are perfect substitutes in demand.[18]

---

similar present value formula for the limiting case, $T \to \infty$. As long as $m(i,w)$ is "separable" in i and w as in equation (3) of section 1, then the maximization of the flow, $im(i,w(t))$, at every point in time will assure the maximization of its present value. The discussion in the text is based on this assumption.

The upper limit of integration, T, is the date at which the bank is assumed to retire all of its liabilities outstanding. The preceding present value expression equals

$$m(0) + \int(\dot{M}/P)\exp(-r\tau)d\tau - m(T)\exp(-rT),$$

where integration is from 0 to T, $m(T)$ is short hand for $m(i,w(T))$, and the last term is the present value of the cost of converting $M(T)$ into $m(T)$ goods at the price $P(T) = P(0)\exp(\pi T)$. When the partial derivative of the present value is taken with respect to π and set to zero, the result is equation (14), which is independent of the value of T.

The assumption of an explicit redemption fund is expositionally convenient but not logically necessary. Regardless of the resources a bank might or might not retain in order to be able to maintain convertibility along the announced price path, the discounted value of the monetary liability, $m(T)\exp(-rT)$, must be substracted out to correctly ascertain the firm's net worth.

[17]Literature on the optimum quantity of money is usually expressed in terms of *the* optimum quantity of money. But the marginal conditions for Pareto efficiency can hold for different levels of real balances if other variables, such as the distribution of wealth, are considered. Consequently, it is more accurate to refer to the marginal conditions for *an* optimum quantity of money. The marginal condition ($i = 0$) assures efficiency in the production of money if efficiency conditions are not violated elsewhere, and, in particular, if other sources of government revenue are nondistorting. These issues are dealt with in an optimal tax framework by Phelps [27].

[18]Competition does not produce efficiency if, as has been argued, there is an externality involved in the holding of money. The usual argument (e.g., Friedman [9]) is that an individual who increases his cash balances must forgo consumption. Given a fixed nominal quantity of money, others in the community are able to temporarily consume more than their income as the value of their real balances is increased. Thus,

The solution found for no CS or for a monopoly bank, viz., that $\pi = 1/\alpha - r$, is also applicable to a cartel of money issuers whose liabilities are linked with fixed rates. A cartel produces money with a low or negative real return and suboptimal real balances.

The results of this section can be cast in more general terms by relaxing the assumption that the bank pays no explicit interest on its liabilities. The market or nominal yield on the alternative nonmonetary asset can be represented by $i = r + \pi$. If no interest is paid on money, then i is equal to the differential real yield. In symbols,

$$r - r_m = (i - \pi) - (i_m - \pi) = i - i_m \tag{16}$$

is equal to i if i_m is zero. If the more general expression $r - r_m$ is substituted for i in the profit-maximizing condition (15), the result is

$$r_m = r - 1/(\alpha + \sigma). \tag{15'}$$

If the interest payment on money is not taken as exogenous, then i_m and π can take on an infinity of values without violating the competitive profit-maximizing condition (15'). (*cf.* also [20].) When there are no exogenous nominal rates, a homogeneous model such as ours determines the difference in nominal rates but not their absolute levels.[19]

If the nominal returns on monies are equal, whether at zero or otherwise, then the equality of real returns assures equal inflation rates and secularly stable exchange rates.[20] The regime of fixed rates imposed by a cartel bears only a superficial

---

the person who acquires more real balances confers an external benefit on others in the community for which he receives no compensation. This argument is based on the assumption of an exogenous money supply.

When money is endogenized with the assumption that the bank of issue accommodates any changes in real demand, it becomes clear that an externality is not inherent in the holding of money. The bank issues more fiduciary currency in return for the goods (or equities) that the first person sells to acquire more cash balances. The individual must consume less only if the bank is not competitive. If the bank is competitive, money holders receive the real rate of return, r, and the individual's consumption does not fall. In short, there is no externality involved in the holding of money. What has appeared as an externality is due to the fixed money supply assumption. (A similar point has been developed in [33].)

[19]The original revenue function (13) can be redeveloped under the assumption that i_m is nonzero. The gross revenue is $M/P - i_m m$ and the net flow of real revenue is $M/P - i_m m - \dot{m}$ which equals $-r_m m$. The stream of real returns from the redemption fund remains $r \cdot m$ such that the total net flow of real revenue is

$$-r_m m + rm = [r - r_m] \cdot m(r - r_m). \tag{13'}$$

Maximization of (13') with respect to the differential real return yields (15').

Our results are consistent with Hayek's [14] argument that competition in the provision of currencies (that he calls "concurrent currencies") will produce a stable price level if it is assumed that i_m is equal to r. If there is no explicit interest on money, then competition should produce deflation rather than stable prices.

[20]With only one real asset in our model, the banks offer the same real return on their monetary liabilities and hold only the single real asset. An extended model would allow for many goods and diversity of tastes among money holders. In the more complex model, banks might offer monies with different characteristics and hold different assets. With the possibility of banks holding different asset bundles and offering real returns measured against different bundles of goods, the exchange rate between monies would vary as the relative price indices of the different bundles of goods changed.

resemblance to the stable rates under competition. While the real returns on monies will be equal in either situation, the level of the returns will be very different.

4. SUMMARY

Two fundamental implications of CS were derived in section 1. CS was found to produce instability in the sense that shifts in the anticipated rate of exchange rate change produce larger movements in the exchange rate and these movements are unbounded as CS increases. The second implication was that, if two monies are perfect substitutes in demand, their rate of exchange is indeterminate.

The indeterminacy of the exchange rate between two perfectly substitutable monies is a logical consequence of an asset-demand model utilizing standard money-demand assumptions. But we suspect that the exchange rate would be determinate (probably at the value of unity) if transactions costs were developed more fully in aggregate money-demand functions. Further research appears necessary before policy prescriptions can be based on the finding of indeterminacy.

The instability found in section 1 was eliminated when the behavior of money issuers was endogenized in section 3. The original instability was implied by a model with exogenous nominal returns and exogenous nominal money supplies. When the response of money issuers to CS is incorporated in the analysis, the nominal returns and/or nominal supplies change in response to demand shifts. The pressures of CS induce coordination of monetary policies or rate-of-return competition. In either case, the exchange rate should be stable or follow a stable path. In the absence of CS, money issuers can engage in independent monetary policies resulting in fluctuating exchange rates. It is the absence of CS, not its presence, that allows for unstable exchange rates.

Boyer [3] and Kareken and Wallace [15] have argued, and some of the remarks by Mundell [23, 24] suggest, that the instability associated with CS should be countered with fixed exchange rates. But as was shown in section 3, fixing exchange rates is a method whereby money issuers agree to coordinate monetary policies to avoid market pressure and maintain market shares. The chief disadvantage of the cartel solution is that it allows money issuers, by collective action, to frustrate money holders' search for superior monies and is consistent with the high inflation rates experienced with the demise of the gold standard.

It is widely believed that one solution to the problem of inflation is to replace discretionary monetary policy with a rule for a fixed money growth rate. In the absence of CS, such a rule might eliminate exchange rate instability. But in the presence of CS, money-growth rate rules (in conjunction with fixed nominal yields on monies) would, as shown in section 1, cause exchange rate instability. Moreover, monies with fixed growth rates would be seen as inferior to competitively supplied currencies. Interestingly enough, these rules have come from economists (e.g., Milton Friedman and Henry Simons) who have been staunch advocates of the free market. The fear of eliminating government supported monopolies in the production of money stems from the view that competitively supplied money would be issued in such quantities that it would become valueless. But to attract ultimate wealth holders faced with a choice in monies, banks would have to issue monies convertible into real assets to assure money holders against capital loss. Rather than the competively supplied money becoming worthless, it would be convertible into real goods such that risk against capital loss would be minimal. A fixed money growth rule can be applied to a monopoly or a cartel. But a money supplied at a fixed rate of growth would be driven from circulation if the public is offered substitutable convertible currencies.

APPENDIX A

The Exchange Rate with Rational Expectations

In the text the expected rate of change in the exchange rate x is taken as exogenous. In this appendix the expected rate of change of the exchange rate is endogenized using the assumption of rational expectations, that is, the expected rate of change in the exchange rate is equal to the rate of change in the exchange rate determined in the model. It will be demonstrated that if dynamic stability is assumed, the rational expectations assumption is a special case of the model developed in the text.

The assumption of rational expectations can be imposed by substituting $\dot{e}$ for x in equation (8) of the text:

$$e(t) = \tilde{e}(t) - \eta(i_1 - i_2) + \eta\dot{e}(t), \tag{A1}$$

where e and $\tilde{e}$ are written as explicit functions of time. In order to solve the differential equation (A1) we need to specify how $\tilde{e}(t) = \ln[(M_1(t)/\theta_1(t))/(M_2(t)/\theta_2(t))]$ moves over time. We assume that $\tilde{e}(t)$ is a linear function of time,

$$\tilde{e}(t) = \tilde{e}(0) + kt. \tag{A2}$$

Substituting (A2) into (A1) we obtain

$$e(t) = \tilde{e}(0) + kt - \eta(i_1 - i_2) + \eta\dot{e}(t), \tag{A3}$$

which is a nonautonomous, linear differential equation with constant coefficients.
The general solution of (A3) is

$$e(t) = [\tilde{e}(0) - \eta(i_1 - i_2) + \eta k] + kt + C\exp(t/\eta), \tag{A4}$$

where

$$\dot{e}(t) = k + (C/\eta)\exp(t/\eta).$$

28   :   MONEY, CREDIT, AND BANKING

The characteristic root is positive, $1/\eta > 0$, so the autonomous part of the solution for $e(t)$ (A4) is unstable unless $C = 0$. The initial condition implies $C = e(0) - [\bar{e}(0) - \eta(i_1 - i_2 - k)]$. Thus for the exchange rate to be on a nonexplosive time path $e(0) = \bar{e}(0) - \eta(i_1 - i_2 - k)$. That is, stability requires that the level of the exchange rate jump instantaneously to its equilibrium value, $e(0)$, following any shock to the system. Dynamic stability implies the time path of e is given by

$$e(t) = [\bar{e}(0) + kt] - \eta(i_1 - i_2 - k), \tag{A5}$$

where

$$\dot{e}(t) = k.$$

Equation (A5) produces the same implications as equations (8) in the text, with the proviso that x is equal to k, rather than being set arbitrarily, and where $\bar{e}(t)$ is separated into the level of $\bar{e}(t)$ at time zero, $\bar{e}(0)$, and the growth of $\bar{e}(t)$ after $t = 0$, $kt = (\bar{e}(t) - \bar{e}(0))$. Monetary changes are then separated into jumps in the levels of money supplies (and exogenous components of money demands), and changes in the rate of growth of $\bar{e}(t)$:

$$de(t) = d\bar{e}(t) - \eta d(i_1 - i_2) + \eta dk. \tag{A6}$$

As in the text, jumps in $\bar{e}$ (exogenous changes in money supplies and demands) produce proportional changes in e independently of the degree of CS. Changes in the anticipated relative rate of return (changes in the is and in k) produce effects on e in proportion to the CS parameter η. In particular higher degrees of CS require larger jumps in e for given changes in the anticipated differential rate of return.

APPENDIX B

Determination of the Bond-Exchange Rate

The bond-exchange rate is the ratio Q_b/Q_a, where Q_a and Q_b are found as the capitalized values of the streams of future interest payments. Since the instantaneous bond yields may vary over time, a variable-yield capitalization formula must be used to determine Q_a and Q_b.

The instantaneous capital gain on bonds A and B will be denoted as $\hat{Q}_a$ and $\hat{Q}_b$, where $\hat{\ }$ indicates the percent change or instantaneous logarithmic time derivative. By definition, $x = (\hat{Q}_b - \hat{Q}_a)^*$ and we assume that the latter term is equal to $\hat{Q}_b^* - \hat{Q}_a^*$, where * represents an anticipated magnitude. The condition that $\delta = 0$ for all t therefore implies that $C_a/Q_a + \hat{Q}_a^* = C_b/Q_b + \hat{Q}_b^*$ for all t. The instantaneous yields are inclusive of capital gains and will be denoted as

$$\hat{\phi}_j(t) = d\ln\phi_j/dt = C_j/Q_j + \hat{Q}^*, \qquad (j = a,b),$$

where ϕ_j is the discount factor used in the capitalization formula, and

$$Q_j(t) = \int C_j \phi_j(\tau) \, d\tau \, / \, \phi_j(t), \qquad (j = a,b)$$

where integration is from t to infinity and the discount factor has the initial condition $\phi_j(0) = 1$. Perfect bond-substitution implies that $\phi_a(t) = \phi_b(t)$ holds for all t. Consequently, the ratio of $Q_b(t)$ to $Q_a(t)$, both found from the capitalization formula, equals C_b/C_a. Were the bonds not perpetuities, the bond-exchange rate would not generally equal the ratio of the interest payments, but it would nevertheless be fully determinate.

LITERATURE CITED

1. Auernheimer, Leonardo. "The Honest Government's Guide to the Revenue from the Creation of Money." *Journal of Political Economy*, 82 (May/June 1974), 598–606.

2. Boyer, Russell S. "Nickles and Dimes." Unpublished manuscript, Federal Reserve Board, 1972.

3. _____. "Currency Mobility and Balance of Payments Adjustment." In *The Monetary Approach to International Adjustment*, edited by Bluford H. Putnam and D. Sykes Wilford, pp. 184–98. New York: Praeger, 1978.

4. Bronfenbrenner, Martin. "The Currency-Choice Defense." *Challenge*, 22 (January/February 1980), 31–36.

5. Calvo, Guillermo A., and Carlos A. Rodriguez. "A Model of Exchange Rate Determination Under Currency Substitution and Rational Expectations." *Journal of Political Economy*, 85 (June 1977), 617–25.

6. Connolly, Michael. "The Monetary Approach to an Open Economy: The Fundamental Theory." In *The Monetary Approach to International Adjustment*, edited by Bluford H. Putnam and D. Sykes Wilford, pp. 6–18. New York: Praeger, 1978.

7. Friedman, Milton. *A Program for Monetary Stability*. New York: Fordham University Press, 1959.

8. _____. "The Role of Monetary Policy." *American Economic Review*, 58 (March 1968), 1–17.

9. _____. "The Optimum Quantity of Money." In *The Optimum Quantity of Money and Other Essays*, edited by Milton Friedman, pp. 1–50. Chicago: Aldine, 1969.

10. Girton, Lance, and Don Roper. "Theory and Implications of Currency Substitution." *International Financial Discussion Papers*, Federal Reserve Board, 1976.

11. _____. "A Monetary Model of Exchange Market Pressure Applied to the Post-War Canadian Experience." *American Economic Review*, 67 (September 1977), 537–48.

12. _____. "Substitutable Monies and the Monetary Standard." In *The Political Economy of Policy Making*, edited by Michael Dooley, Herbert Kaufman, and Raymond Lombra, pp. 233–46. Beverly Hills, Calif.: Sage, 1979.

13. _____. "A Theory of Currency Substitution and Monetary Unification." *Economie Appliquee*, 1980.

14. Hayek, Frederick A. *Denationalization of Money: An Analysis of the Theory and Practice of Concurrent Currencies*. London: Institute of Economic Affairs, 1976.

15. Kareken, John, and Neil Wallace. "Samuelson's Consumption-Loan Model with Country-Specific Fiat Monies." *Staff Report*, No. 24, Federal Reserve Bank of Minneapolis, July 1978.

16. _____. "International Monetary Reform: The Feasible Alternatives." *Quarterly Review*, Federal Reserve Bank of Minneapolis, Summer 1978.

17. Keynes, John Maynard. *A Treatise on Money: The Pure Theory of Money*. London: Macmillan, 1930.

18. _____. *The General Theory of Employment Interest and Money*. New York: Harcourt, Brace and Company, 1936.

19. King, David, Bluford H. Putnam, and D. Sykes Wilford. "A Currency Portfolio Approach to Exchange Rate Determination: Exchange Rate Stability and the Independence of Monetary Policy." In *The Monetary Approach to International Adjustment*, edited by Bluford H. Putnam and D. Sykes Wilford, pp. 119–214. New York: Praeger, 1978.

20. Klein, Benjamin. "The Competitive Supply of Money." *Journal of Money, Credit, and Banking*, 6 (November 1974), 423–53.

21. Miles, Marc A. "Currency Substitution, Flexible Exchange Rates, and Monetary Independence." *American Economic Review*, 68 (June 1978), 428–36.

22. _____. "Currency Substitution: Perspective, Implications, and Empirical Evidence." In *The Monetary Approach to International Adjustment*, edited by Bluford H. Putnam and D. Sykes Wilford, pp. 170–83. New York: Praeger, 1978.

23. Mundell, Robert A. *International Economics*. New York: Macmillan, 1968.

24. _____. *Monetary Theory; Inflation, Interest, and Growth in the World's Economy*. Pacific Palisades; Calif.: Goodyear, 1971.

25. Parkin, Michael. "Price and Output Determination in an Economy with Two Media of Exchange and a Separate Unit of Account." In *Recent Issues in Monetary Economics*, edited by Emil Claassen and Pascal Salin, pp. 74–98. Amsterdam: North-Holland, 1976.

26. Pesek, Boris P., and Thomas R. Saving. *Money, Wealth, and Economic Theory*. New York: Macmillan, 1967.

27. Phelps, Edmund S. "Inflation in the Theory of Public Finance." *Swedish Journal of Economics*, 75 (March 1973), 67–82.

28. Takayama, Akira, and Y. N. Shieh. "Flexible Exchange Rates Under Currency Substitution and Rational Expectations—Two Approaches to the Balance of Payments." Texas A&M University, manuscript, 1980.

29. Thompson, Earl. "The Theory of Money and Income Consistent with Orthodox Value Theory." In *Trade Stability and Macroeconomics*, edited by George Horwich and Paul A. Samuelson, pp. 427–51. New York: Academic Press, 1974.

30. Tobin, James. "Commercial Banks as Creators of Money." In *Banking and Monetary Studies*, edited by Deane Carson, pp. 408–19. Homewood, Ill.: Irwin, 1963.

31. _____. "A General Equilibrium Approach to Monetary Theory." *Journal of Money, Credit, and Banking*, 1 (February 1969), 15–29.

32. Tullock, Gordon. "Competing Monies." *Journal of Money, Credit, and Banking*, 7 (November 1975), 491–97.

33. Vaubel, Roland. "Free Currency Competition." *Weltwirtschaftliches Archiv*, 113 (October 1977), 435–59.

[8]

Journal of Monetary Economics 16 (1985) 195–208. North-Holland

PRIVATE FIAT MONEY WITH MANY SUPPLIERS

Bart TAUB*

University of Virginia, Charlottesville, VA 22901, USA

A dynamic rational expectations model of money is used to investigate whether a Nash equilibrium of many firms, each supplying its own brand-name currency, will optimally deflate their currencies in Friedman's (1969) sense. The optimal deflation does arise under an open loop dynamic structure, but the equilibrium breaks down under a more realistic feedback control structure.

1. Introduction

Friedman (1969) argued that the optimal inflation would equate the rate of return on money with the internal rate of discount, but made no connection between the private competitive supply of money and its optimal supply. Klein (1975) and Hayek (1976) both reasoned that since competition in the supply of consumption goods yields efficient equilibria, it should do the same with money. Klein's model used an adaptive expectations framework to investigate this idea. The model presented here uses rational expectations in a framework in which money demand arises endogenously as a medium of exchange between the generations. Firms supply brand name currencies to demanders in a Nash equilibrium. Firms with excessive money growth relative to their competitors suffer a contraction of real balances demanded, and so temper their policies. The competitive outcome is generated as the number of firms grow large. The results confirm an earlier model [Taub (1984)] in which each firm behaves like a monopolist and a demand elasticity parameter is varied to generate competition.

If there is an initial period when each firm can choose its money growth rates for all following periods, then the Friedman rule is generated in the equilibrium. This dynamic structure is called open loop control [see Kydland (1977)]. Like other dynamic rational expectations with rational expectations and open loop control, the firms' policies are dynamically inconsistent: the firm wishes to renege on its commitment in every period, and hence requires an outside enforcement agent in order to work.

Under an alternative dynamic structure, feedback control, firms decide their policies anew each period. Under this more realistic structure the Friedman

*I thank an anonymous referee for useful suggestions.

rule is not generated by competition, and moreover, it is doubtful that money would even have value in the long run in such an equilibrium. This latter observation partly rationalizes the 'folk theorem' that money is a natural monopoly.

The following section describes the tastes and technology of the economy. The open loop equilibrium is developed in section 3. The feedback equilibrium is developed in section 4. Section 5 contains a discussion and concluding remarks.

2. Tastes and technology

2.1. Demand

Money demand arises in an overlapping generations framework descended from Samuelson's (1958) model. There is a continuum of individuals in each period of the infinitely-lived economy, each living for two periods. Individuals will be called young in their first period of life, old in the second. Each period a new generation is born, coexisting on that day with the old of the previous generation. There is no population growth and all individuals have identical tastes and endowments.

Individuals solve the following problem:

$$\max_{c,\,c'} \left\{ U(c) + V(c') \right\},\tag{1}$$

subject to

$$c \le y_0 - \sum_{i=1}^{N} M_i p_i,\tag{2}$$

$$c' \le y_1 + \sum_{i}^{N} M_i p_i',\tag{3}$$

$$M_i \ge 0,\tag{4}$$

$$c, c' \ge 0,\tag{5}$$

where

c, c' = consumption of perishable good when young and old,
y_0, y_1 = endowments of the perishable good when young and old,
M_i = nominal quantity of currency i purchased,
p_i = purchasing power of currency i, taken as given.

The utility functions U and V are concave, increasing and continuously differentiable, and have the following additional properties:

$$\frac{U'(y_0)}{V'(y_1)} < \frac{1}{1+\rho}, \quad U'(0) = \infty, \tag{6}$$

$$\frac{\mathrm{d}}{\mathrm{d}x}\left(xV'(x)\right) \geq 0, \tag{7}$$

where ρ is a fractional discount factor. Assumption (6) generates a desire to defer consumption. Assumption (7) will later guarantee the existence of an interior equilibrium.[1]

Substituting the constraints into (1) yields the set of first-order conditions

$$p_j U'(c) = p'_j V'(c'). \tag{8}$$

In equilibrium, the money and goods markets clear: denote the jth money supply by M_j.

Definition 1. A perfect foresight equilibrium is a sequence $\{p_{it}\}$, $t = 0,\ldots,$ $i = 1,\ldots, N$, such that

(i) eq. (8) and constraints (2)–(5) are satisfied,

(ii) $M_{jt} = M_{jt}$ for all j, t.

Goods market-clearing follows from Walras' law if (i) and (ii) are satisfied.

As is usual in such models, it is convenient to assume market clearing, convert nominal balances to real balances, and find an equilibrium sequence of real balances. The equilibrium price sequence is then trivially generated by dividing real balances by the supply of nominal balances.

Aggregate money growth in each currency follows the process

$$M'_j = M_j / R'_j. \tag{9}$$

The term R'_j is the inverse of the gross growth rate of money. The market clearing assumption then supposes that individuals do not receive lump sum redistributions of seignorage revenue. Multiplying (8) by M_j, substituting from (9) and denoting real balances $M_i p_i$ by m_i, (8) becomes a condition in real

---

[1] This assumption makes the marginal value of future consumption rise with consumption, and so with real balances as well. The condition is not necessary but makes it easier to sign derivatives in the stability analysis.

balances:

$$m_j U'\left(y_0 - \sum_{i=1}^{N} m_i \right) = R'_j m'_j V'\left(y_1 + \sum_{i=1}^{N} R'_i m'_i \right). \tag{8'}$$

An equilibrium consists of a sequence of $\{m_j(t)\}$, $j = 1, \ldots, N$ and $t = 0, \ldots,$ which satisfies these conditions.

It will be convenient to aggregate these equations so that aggregate real balances can be expressed as a function of an index of future real balances. Define

$$\hat{m} \equiv \sum_{i=1}^{N} m_i, \qquad \hat{q} \equiv \sum_{i=1}^{N} R_i m_i.$$

Aggregating (8), we have

$$\hat{m} U'(y_0 - \hat{m}) = \hat{q}' V'(y_1 + \hat{q}'). \tag{10}$$

Now assumptions (6) and (7) mean that the derivatives of the left- and right-hand sides of this equation will not vanish for interior $\hat{m}$ and $\hat{q}$, and so we can define the functions

$$\hat{m} \equiv \mu(\hat{q}'), \qquad \hat{q}' \equiv h(\hat{m}) = \mu^{-1}(\hat{m}).$$

2.2. Supply

Firms obtain seignorage profits by printing extra units of their brand of currency and purchasing consumption goods with it. Each period's profit is

$$(M_{jt} - M_{j,t-1}) p_{jt}.$$

Substituting from (9), this can be expressed as

$$(1 - R_{jt}) m_{jt}.$$

The firm's problem is to maximize the stream of discounted profits:

$$\max \sum_{s=0}^{\infty} \rho^s (1 - R_{j,t+s}) m_{j,t+s}, \tag{11}$$

subject to

$$R_{jt} \geq 0,$$

and subject to the demand conditions (8′), the reactions of other firms, and constraints on the control of the sequence of money growth policies $\{R_{j,t+s}\}$. These are developed in the following sections.

3. Open loop control

Under open loop control [see Kydland (1977)], the jth firm at time zero decides the entire sequence of current and future money growth factors for its currency, R_{jt}, $t = 0, 1 \ldots$. Since it is able to bind itself to future policies, the firm can choose different policies for each period. In the initial period each firm sells a stock of real balances and thereafter taxes that stock with an inflation tax, confirming the analysis of Auernheimer (1974).

The analysis is simplified by noting that the control of all future money growth factors, R_{jt}, is equivalent to the control of real balances held in each period. Eq. (8′) can therefore be written

$$R'_j m'_j = m_j \gamma(\hat{m}),\tag{12}$$

where

$$\gamma(\hat{m}) \equiv U'(y_0 - \hat{m})/V'(y_1 + h(\hat{m})).\tag{13}$$

Substituting into the firm's objective yields the modified objective

$$\max_{\{R_{j0},\{m_{jt}\}\}} \left\{ (1 - R_{j0}) m_{j0} + \rho \big(m_{j1} - m_{j0}\gamma(\hat{m}_0) \big) \right.$$

$$\left. + \rho^2 \big(m_{j2} - m_{j1}\gamma(\hat{m}_1) \big) + \ldots \right\}.\tag{14}$$

This problem can be solved if firms have Cournot–Nash reactions, that is they each assume other firms do not adjust real balances in response to their own choice of real balances:

Assumption 1. Firms assume $\partial m_{is}/\partial m_{jt} = 0$ for all $i \neq j, s, t$.

A direct consequence of the assumption is that $d\hat{m}/dm_{jt} = 1$, and so the sequence of first-order conditions is

$$R_{j0} = 0,\tag{15}$$

$$(1 - R_{j0}) - \rho \big(\gamma(\hat{m}_0) + m_{j0}\gamma'(\hat{m}_0) \big) = 0,\tag{16}$$

$$1 - \rho \big(\gamma(\hat{m}_t) + m_{jt}\gamma'(\hat{m}_t) \big) = 0, \quad t = 1, 2, \ldots.\tag{17}$$

Note that substitution of (15) into (16) yields (17) for $t = 0$. In the initial period, then, the firm has a currency reform, wiping out the value of any old currency and issuing a stock of new real balances, which it taxes thereafter.

Summing conditions (17) across firms yields

$$\gamma(\hat{m}_t) - 1 = -\frac{\hat{m}_t}{N}\gamma'(\hat{m}_t). \tag{18}$$

By implicitly differentiating (13), we find

$$\gamma'(\hat{m}) = -(U''V' - U'V''h')/(V')^2,$$

where

$$h' = (U' - \hat{m}U'')/(V' + \hat{q}V'').$$

By assumption (7), $h' > 0$ and so $\gamma'(\hat{m}) > 0$. Since the utility functions are increasing everywhere, and since $U'(c') < V'(y_1) < \infty$, it must be the case that $0 < \gamma'(\hat{m}) \leq \infty$.

Proposition 1.   An interior solution of (18) exists.

Proof.   Note first that $m = 0$ does not solve (18). It is straightforward to show that $0 < \gamma'(0) < \infty$, and so $\lim_{m \to 0} m\gamma'(m) = 0$. Also, since $U'(y_0) < V'(y_1)$ by assumption, $\rho\gamma(0) - 1 < 0$.

Next, divide both sides of (18) by $\gamma(m)$. Then $\lim h'(m) = \infty$ and so $\lim(m/N)(\gamma'/\gamma) = \infty$. Thus

$$\rho - \frac{1}{\gamma(y_0)} = \rho > -\frac{y_0}{N}\frac{\gamma'(y_0)}{\gamma(y_0)} = -\infty.$$

Since the inequality is reversed, and by the continuous differentiability of U and V, there exists an m which solves (18). This completes the proof.

The proposition is notable because, in dynamic monetary models, equilibria in which money is valueless or asymptotically valueless would appear: see for example Scheinkman (1980). The firms' abilities to control real balances rules out these solutions.[2]

While there are only stationary interior equilibria for aggregate real balances, it is possible for a particular firm's real balances to be non-stationary.

---

[2] Conditions (6) and (7) are not responsible for this outcome: compare Scheinkman's condition (7).

Inspection of condition (12) shows that if the firm's real balances are stationary, its money growth factor must equal the fixed aggregate money growth rate: this is in accord with the finding of Karaken and Wallace (1978). The distribution of firms' shares of aggregate real balances are therefore irrelevant to the aggregate equilibrium.

Define the average money growth factor by

$$\bar{R} \equiv \left(\sum R_{i,t+1} m_{i,t+1} \right) / \hat{m}_t.$$

By a straightforward application of Proposition 1, $\bar{R}$ is a constant. Firms in stationary equilibrium have this growth rate, i.e., if $m_{jt} = m_{j,t+1}$, then $R_j = \bar{R}$.

Proposition 2. As the number of firms grows large, the Friedman rule is attained:

$$\lim_{N \to \infty} \bar{R} = 1/\rho.$$

Proof. By summing (8′) across firms and recalling definition (12), eq. (18) can be expressed

$$\bar{R} = \frac{1}{\rho} - \frac{\hat{m}}{\rho N} \gamma'(\hat{m}).$$

Now suppose there is some $\bar{\gamma} < \infty$ such that $\gamma'(\hat{m}(N)) < \bar{\gamma}$ for all n. Then

$$\lim_{N \to \infty} \bar{R} = 1/\rho.$$

From (12) there is some m^*, $0 < m^* < y_0$, such that $\gamma(m^*) = 1/\rho$, and therefore $\gamma'(m^*)$ is bounded as conjectured.

The equality of the rate of return on money with the suppliers' discount factor, ρ, is equivalent to equality with the internal rate of discount, $1/\gamma$. This completes the proof.

The competitive rate of return on money is positive, so a deflation is being financed by the firms. A deflation is efficient in overlapping generations models [see Wallace (1980) for example]. Since firms cannot gain without withdrawing resources from the money demand economy, the equilibrium is efficient.

The equilibrium has the interpretation of allowing individuals in the money demanding economy to invest in productive opportunities in the supply economy. Their initial purchase of the stock of real balances is equivalent to a purchase of capital in the money supply economy, with the subsequent deflation equivalent to interest payments on that investment. Money and capital become equivalent, the original intent of the Friedman rule.

The rule is dynamically inconsistent. If firms were permitted to renege, they would institute a currency reform each period, that is, set $R_{jt} = 0$ for each t, and ineffectually plan deflations in the subsequent periods. It will be more realistic to suppose a weaker enforcement mechanism, and this is examined in the next section.

4. Feedback control

In this section firms have feedback control: rather than choosing an infinite sequence of money growth factors once and for all in the initial period, they are able to re-solve their maximum problems anew each period, taking past states and future solutions as given. Although firms still wish to choose an infinite sequence of policies, the control structure permits them to renege on all but a single period's policy. Such policies are dynamically consistent, but do not generate the Friedman rule and so are inefficient, even under competition.

4.1. Contemporaneous control

If the jth firm's control variable at time t is its contemporaneous money growth factor R_{jt}, then the solution to (11) is trivial: set $R_{jt} = 0$. This is equivalent to taxing away all real balances. Since this solution is anticipated by demanders, real balances will not be held in any period. This replicates Calvo's (1978) result for a single currency.

4.2. Pipeline control

The assumption that firms are completely unable to commit themselves to future behavior seems as extreme as the assumption that complete precommitment is possible: a realistic model lies between these extremes. Firms typically are able to commit themselves through contracts, but the enforceability of long-term contracts depreciates over time. A one-period lag between a firm's choice and implementation of a policy, and its inability to influence policy beyond the next period, crudely but tractably models this depreciation. Assume then that firms at time t choose the following period's money growth factor $R_{j,t+1}$, and take as given their contemporaneous money growth factor R_{jt}; it is in the 'pipeline'. Firms thus solve

$$\max_{R_{j,t+1}} \sum_{s=0}^{\infty} \rho^s (1 - R_{j,t+s}) m_{j,t+s}, \tag{19}$$

at each time t. The equilibrium demand for real balances of the jth firm's currency [see condition (12)] depends only on future money growth factors and real balances. Given any sequence of positive real balances $\{\{m_{i,t+1}\},$ $\{m_{i,t+2}\},\ldots\}$, $i = 1,\ldots,N$, the firm can set $m_{j,t}$ to any level by its choice of $R_{j,t+1}$, but will have no direct influence on the demand for real balances in period $t + 1$ and after. The solution of (19) is greatly simplified by reformulating it to reflect this fact.[3] Substituting from condition (12) for $R_{j,t+s}$, $s = 2,3,\ldots$, the firm's problem becomes

$$\max_{m_{jt}} \left\{ (1 - R_{jt})m_{jt} + \rho\left(m_{j,t+1} - m_{jt}\gamma(\hat{m}_{jt})\right) + \cdots \right\}, \tag{19'}$$

subject to

$$R_{jt}, \quad \{m_{j,t+1}, m_{j,t+2},\ldots\} \text{ given.} \tag{20}$$

Retaining the Cournot–Nash behavior of Assumption 1, the first-order conditions are

$$(1 - R_{jt}) - \rho\left[\gamma(\hat{m}_t) + m_j\gamma'(\hat{m}_t)\right] = 0. \tag{21}$$

Define $R_t^* \equiv (1/N)\sum R_{it}$. Then summing (21) across currencies yields

$$\rho\gamma(\hat{m}_t) - (1 - R_t^*) = -\rho\frac{\hat{m}_t}{N}\gamma'(\hat{m}_t). \tag{22}$$

Since $R_t^* = \overline{R}_t$ does not necessarily hold, the irrelevance of the aggregation in the open loop case does not carry over. In order to simplify the analysis, only those equilibria in which $R_t^* = \overline{R}_t$ will be examined.[4] In those cases we immediately have the following result:

Proposition 3. *As the number of firms grows large, the stationary money growth factor is bounded below one:*

$$\lim_{N \to \infty} \overline{R}_t = 1/(1 + \rho). \tag{23}$$

Proof. In a stationary equilibrium, $\gamma(\hat{m}_t) = R_{t+1}^* = R_t^*$. Substitute $\overline{R}_t = R_t^*$ in (22) and use the proof of Proposition 2.

[3] This reformulation is key, because in the original formulation, $R_{j,t+1}$ is a state variable for the problem solved at time $t + 1$, and so recursively for all future periods, greatly complicating the solution.

[4] In equilibria in which $R_t^* \neq \overline{R}_t$, firms' relative shares in real balances will shift over time. Whether there would be a trend toward equal shares, or toward the dominance of a single firm, is open to investigation. In a related paper [Taub (1984)], the dynamic stability of monopolistically supplied money suggests that the latter is true.

Proposition 4.   As the number of firms grows large, the competitive rate of return on real balances is greater than the return if there are only N firms.

Proof.   Rearranging (22) and substituting from (12) yields

$$\bar{R}_t = \frac{1}{1+\rho} - \frac{\rho}{1+\rho} \frac{\hat{m}_t}{N} \gamma'(\hat{m}_t).$$

Since $\gamma'(\hat{m}_t) > 0$, the result is proved.

Proposition 3 shows that even if there is competition, firms are not able to give a positive return on real balances: rather, inflation is always positive and firms continually collect real revenue from this tax. Fewer real balances are held than is efficient for the demand economy. Moreover, the firms would gain if they could commit themselves to an open loop scheme, but it is precisely this inability to commit themselves which forces the inefficient outcome.[5]

4.3. Entry consistency

In each period t, the jth firm takes its contemporaneous money growth factor R_{jt} as given: it is set by the firm in period $t-1$. In the initial period, $t = 0$, however, the firm has not been in existence in period $t = -1$, and so some other means of fixing R_{j0} must be used. The firm enters the industry in period zero, and the initial stock of real balances is sold to demanders at the time. As in section 3, this corresponds to $R_{j0} = 0$, and this fixes the initial conditions of the equilibrium system (21).

Substituting $R_{j0} = 0$ into (22) yields the period-zero first-order condition

$$\rho\gamma(\hat{m}_0) - 1 = -\rho \frac{\hat{m}_0}{N} \gamma'(\hat{m}_0). \tag{22'}$$

As N grows large, the initial money growth rate offered by firms, R_{j1}, is $1/\rho$ – the Friedman deflation. Firms subsidize their customers initially, but the subsidy does not last, as (22') is not consistent with a stationary equilibrium.

The stationary solution of Proposition 3 must therefore be attained asymptotically from the initial state characterized by (22') if at all. Whether this is

---

[5] The limiting rate of return, $1/(1+\rho)$, seems perverse in that the firms raise their inflation rate as their discount factor rises to unity. Since the discount factor, ρ, in the supply economy rises with the capital stock there, it is a Mundell–Tobin effect but with the causation going from capital to inflation rather than the reverse.

The discount factor, ρ, is also a function of the firm's horizon of control. If the time between periods is long, then ρ will be small, and as this horizon lengthens, ρ approaches zero, and the gross rate of return on real balances rises to unity. This is equivalent to a zero inflation rate and a zero net rate of return on real balances, and thus the optimal deflation of the open loop case is not approached, even with the extended horizon.

possible depends on the dynamic stability properties of the stationary equilibrium. If it is locally unstable, then there is no hope that it will be attained.

It is demonstrated in the appendix that the interior stationary point is in fact dynamically unstable. Moreover, there is another stationary equilibrium in which zero real balances are held. This equilibrium corresponds to complete autarky and so is inefficient relative to the already inefficient stationary equilibrium of Proposition 3. It is dynamically stable, however, and so it is the long-run equilibrium consistent with entry.[6]

5. Conclusion

The fundamental theorem of economics – that competition is efficient – has been confirmed for money, but only when an unrealistic dynamic structure is assumed. Under that structure, money bridges a capital-starved economy with a capital-rich one. The resultant equivalence of money and capital was the goal of Friedman's model.

When a more realistic control structure is introduced, in which firms can only temporarily commit themselves to fixed policies, the result breaks down: indeed, real balances are asymptotically zero. Competition is therefore not sufficient to overcome the inefficiency of dynamically consistent control structures, leaving monopolistically supplied money the default condition. Efficient deflations are therefore unlikely to be realized by the private market.

Appendix

This appendix derives the stability properties of the pipeline control equilibria set out in section 4.

First linearize the equilibrium system around the stationary state. Substituting for R_{jt} from (12) into (21) yields

$$m_{jt}\gamma(\hat{m}_t) = m_{j,t+1} - \rho\left[m_{j,t+1}\gamma(\hat{m}_{t+1}) + m_{j,t+1}^2\gamma'(\hat{m}_{t+1})\right]. \quad (A.1)$$

Differentiating yields

$$\gamma(\hat{m}_t)\,dm_{jt} + m_{jt}\gamma'(\hat{m}_t)\,d\hat{m}_t$$

$$= \left(1 - \rho\left[\gamma(\hat{m}_{t+1}) + 2m_{j,t+1}\gamma'(\hat{m}_{t+1})\right]\right)dm_{j,t+1}$$

$$- \rho\left[m_{j,t+1}\gamma'(\hat{m}_{t+1}) + m_{j,t+1}^2\gamma''(\hat{m}_{t+1})\right]d\hat{m}_{t+1}. \quad (A.2)$$

---

[6]Dynamic monetary models typically have asymptotically zero real balances equilibria in addition to stationary equilibria. The initial conditions of the model of section 4 exclude the non-asymptotic equilibria, in contrast to the section 3 model.

Defining the vector $\boldsymbol{m}_t \equiv (m_{1t}, m_{2t}, \ldots, m_{Nt})^T$ and $\iota \equiv (1, 1, \ldots, 1)^T$, we have the identity $\mathrm{d}\hat{m}_t = \iota^T \mathrm{d}\boldsymbol{m}_t$. We can then express the N versions of (A.2) as a matrix equation,

$$\left[\gamma(\hat{m}) I_N + \gamma'(\hat{m}) \boldsymbol{m}\iota^T \right] \mathrm{d}\boldsymbol{m}_t$$

$$= \left[(1 - \rho\gamma(\hat{m})) I_N - 2\rho\gamma'(\hat{m})[\mathrm{diag}(\boldsymbol{m})] \right.$$

$$\left. - \rho\gamma'(\hat{m})\boldsymbol{m}\iota^T - \rho\gamma''(\hat{m})[\mathrm{diag}(\boldsymbol{m})]\boldsymbol{m}\iota^T \right] \mathrm{d}\boldsymbol{m}_{t+1}. \tag{A.3}$$

Now consider the equilibrium in which all firms are identical. Each firm's real balances are then a fraction of the aggregate:

$$m_{jt} = \frac{1}{N}\hat{m}_t.$$

This simplifies (A.3):

$$K_3 \left[I_N + K_1 \iota^T \right] \mathrm{d}\boldsymbol{m}_t = \left[I_N - K_2 \iota^T \right] \mathrm{d}\boldsymbol{m}_{t+1}, \tag{A.4}$$

where

$$K_1 \equiv \frac{\hat{m}}{N} \frac{\gamma'}{\gamma},$$

$$K_2 \equiv \frac{\rho \left(\frac{\hat{m}}{N}\gamma' + \left(\frac{\hat{m}}{N} \right)^2 \gamma'' \right)}{1 - \rho\gamma - 2\rho\frac{\hat{m}}{N}\gamma'},$$

$$K_3 = \frac{\gamma}{1 - \rho\gamma - 2\rho\frac{\hat{m}}{N}\gamma'}.$$

A necessary condition for local stability is that all roots λ_i of the system (A.4) are such that $|\lambda_i| \le 1$. Taking advantage of the simple form of the left-hand-side matrix [Dhrymes (1978, proposition 33)], we have

$$\left[I - K_2\iota^T \right]^{-1} \left[I + K_1\iota^T \right] = \left[I + \frac{K_2}{1 - NK_2}\iota^T \right] \left[I + K_1\iota^T \right]$$

$$= \left[I + K_4\iota^T \right],$$

where

$$K_4 \equiv (K_1 + K_2)/(1 - NK_2).$$

The roots of eq. (A.4) thus solve the characteristic equation

$$|\lambda I - K_3[I + K_4 u^T]| = 0.$$

Defining $\lambda^* \equiv \lambda - K_3$, this equation is equivalent to

$$|\lambda^* I - K_3 K_4 u^T| = 0.$$

Since u^T has rank 1, then by a theorem from linear algebra [see Dhrymes (1978, corollary 5)],

$$\begin{aligned} \lambda_i^* &= 0 && \text{for } i = 1, \ldots, N - 1, \\ &= NK_3 K_4 && \text{for } i = N, \end{aligned}$$

and therefore

$$\begin{aligned} \lambda_i &= K_3 && \text{for } i = 1, \ldots, N - 1, \\ &= K_3(1 + NK_4) && \text{for } i = N. \end{aligned}$$

The magnitudes of these eigenvalues characterize the local stability of the steady states of the system.

Proposition A.1. The interior stationary equilibrium is not locally stable in the limit as the number of firms grows large, i.e., $\lim_{N \to \infty} |\lambda_i| \geq 1$.

Proof. The limiting behavior of K_3 is

$$\lim_{N \to \infty} K_3 = \gamma/(1 - \rho\gamma).$$

Substituting for γ from Proposition 3, the $N - 1$ roots are

$$\lim_{N \to \infty} \lambda_i = 1, \qquad i = 1, \ldots, N - 1.$$

We also have

$$\lim_{N \to \infty} NK_1 = m(\gamma'/\gamma), \qquad \lim_{N \to \infty} NK_2 = \rho\hat{m}\gamma'/(1 - \rho\gamma),$$

and so

$$\lim_{N \to \infty} (1 + NK_4) = (1 - \rho\gamma + \hat{m}\gamma')/(1 - \rho\gamma - \rho\hat{m}\gamma').$$

Again applying Proposition 3, this yields the root

$$\lim_{N \to \infty} \lambda_N = \left(1/(1 + \rho) + m\gamma'\right)/\left(1/(1 + \rho) - \rho m\gamma'\right).$$

It was demonstrated that $\gamma' > 0$ in the discussion of eq. (18), and so $|\lambda_N| > 1$. This completes the proof.

As is usually the case in dynamic monetary models, two stationary equilibria exist: one in which positive real balances exist, and one in which money is valueless and zero real balances are held.

Proposition A.2. The zero real balances solution is locally stable in the limit as the number of firms grows large, i.e., $\lim_{N \to \infty} |\lambda_i| \leq 1$, with strict inequality for some i.

Proof. Substituting $\hat{m} = 0$ in the expressions for K_3 and K_4, we have

$$\lim_{N \to \infty} K_3 = \gamma/(1 - \rho\gamma), \qquad \lim_{N \to \infty} K_4 = 1.$$

Since no real balances are held at the stationary point, $\gamma = U'(y_0)/V'(y_1)$, and by assumption (6), $\gamma < 1/(1 + \rho)$, and therefore $K_3 < 1$. This completes the proof.

References

Auenheimer, Leonardo, 1974, The welfare cost of inflationary finance, Journal of Political Economy 64, April.

Brock, William and José Scheinkman, 1980, Some remarks on monetary policy in an overlapping generations model, in: John H. Karaken and Neil Wallace, eds., Models of monetary economies (Federal Reserve Bank of Minneapolis, MN).

Calvo, Giullermo, 1978, Optimal seignorage from money creation, Journal of Monetary Economics 4, 503–517.

Dhrymes, Phoebus J., 1978, Mathematics for econometrics (Springer-Verlag, New York).

Friedman, Milton, 1969, The optimum quantity of money and other essays (Aldine Publishing Company, Chicago, IL).

Friedman, Milton, 1971, Government revenue from inflation, Journal of Political Economy 79, 846–856.

Hayek, F.A., 1976, The denationalization of money (Institute of Economic Affairs, London).

Karaken, John and Neil Wallace, 1978, Samuelson's consumption–loan model with country-specific fiat monies, Staff report no. 24 (Federal Reserve Bank of Minneapolis, MN).

Kydland, Finn, 1977, Equilibrium solutions in dynamic dominant-player models, Journal of Economic Theory 15, 307–324.

Samuelson, Paul, 1958, An exact consumption–loan model of interest with or without the social contrivance of money, Journal of Political Economy 66, Dec.

Scheinkman, José, 1978, Comment, in: John H. Karaken and Neil Wallace, eds., Models of monetary economies (Federal Reserve Bank of Minneapolis, MN).

Taub, Bart, 1984, Private fiat money and the Friedman rule, Working paper (Department of Economics, University of Virginia, Charlottesville, VA).

Part III
Competitive Payments Systems
Without Base Money

[9]

Excerpt from E.C. Riegel, in Spencer Heath MacCallum and George Morton (eds), *Flight From Inflation: The Monetary Alternative*, 47–63

Chapter 6

Toward a Natural Monetary System

Since money is but the mathematics of value, there is no more justification for the nations of the world to have separate monetary systems than separate systems of mathematics.

It has been said that a communist is a socialist in a hurry, to which it may be added that a fascist is a socialist dragging his feet. They all face in the same direction. All groups, whether they be called radicals or conservatives, progressives or reactionaries, have turned their backs upon personal enterprise and their faces, directly or obliquely, toward state dictatorship. All advocate state intervention in some form or degree.

Adam Smith in his political economy allocated the money power to the state, and thus he anteceded Marx as a socialist. It is his followers, unconscious socialists, and not those of Marx, who constitute the greatest peril to the social order. The Smith philosophy is taught in all our schools and colleges, and we are all indoctrinated with it, unaware that in its monetary concept it is antithetic to the true philosophy of personal enterprise.

The Smith and Marx philosophies are of the Old World, authoritarian. America, under the democratic ideal, must perfect the personal enterprise system by reserving to it all three essential factors, to wit, the means of exchange, the means of production, and the means of distribution. In the Old World structure of the enterprise system, monetary power, the keystone of the arch, has always been lacking, and thus the temple of personal enterprise has never withstood the political winds and storms.

"Political economy," the gospel of the so-called free world, is an assembly of speculations upon the behavior of man in political subjection. It offers no emancipation. It challenges no political presumptions, nor does it embody a fundamental concept of money, the life blood of economy. Hence its speculations are useless, for man's behavior must of necessity differ under a true monetary system than under a perverse one. An unnatural monetary system begets unnatural economic manifestations.

How can a free economy work with the monetary system socialized? As the very name suggests, *political economy* is an attempt to compound antitheses. The term is usually applied to the so-called classical school founded by Adam Smith, but it can be applied just as appropriately to the mercantilists, the physiocrats, and others that went before. All take the socialist approach; they differ on the extent and means of political intervention, but not on the principle. We search their literature in vain for any challenge to the basic socialistic doctrine of political money power.

With the modern world thus educated to think in terms of the political means of accomplishment, is there hope of salvation? Professional economists do not find the principle of separation of money and state in their textbooks, and to espouse it would require turning somersaults in public. If salvation depended altogether on reason, therefore, there might be none, for statism is deeply imbedded in the mores of the peoples of the earth. But it is not solely upon the rationality of the truth that we must depend; the irrationality of the existing order is being demonstrated by the collapse of the political monetary system. As we progress toward runaway world inflation and all that that signifies, there will come a public demand for an escape which political action cannot supply. Private, nonpolitical action alone can provide a true monetary system to which the peoples of all lands may turn for self preservation.

A monetary system is simply a system which facilitates the money issuing powers of its constituents and accounts for their monetary instruments. Personal enterprisers, which term includes employees as well as employers and the self-employed, have in their hands all the powers for the establishment and

and maintenance of such a true and stable system, while governments hold none. The substantive element of all money ever
issued has been supplied by personal enterprisers, hence it is
nothing new to propose that money be issued by them. What is
new is the idea that governments be excluded from the issue
power. Governments under such a system would be enabled to
collect and dispense money that had been created by personal
enterprisers, and they would also be enabled to borrow such
money, but they would not be permitted to undertake the
creation of money.

Whence will come this saving and liberating movement? It
might come through a worldwide effort of superstatesmen of
the business and financial spheres, or it might arise, instead,
from small local action in one or several locales with the humble
and modest purpose of preserving and promoting local trade. In
the former case, a world authority would be set up with a single
monetary unit and overall administration. In the latter case,
each locale would nominate its unit and govern itself until mer-
gers brought about unification under one unit and one administration.

Any sizable group anywhere, any day, could start a nonpolitical monetary unit and system. There is no law against it, and
no legislation need be invoked. The legal tender provision is
gratuitous window dressing, for any monetary unit that is not
acceptable in trade cannot be made so by law and, if acceptable,
needs none.

Since participants in a personal enterprise monetary system
will have to be drawn from the established political monetary
systems, its success will depend upon demonstrated merit. By
the test of competition, it will have to prove itself worthy of
universal acceptance by traders. Such a system will enjoy no
monopoly privilege. It will entail no political action. Therefore,
there will be no question of majorities—or minorities—denying
to any his right to trade with whatever medium is preferred by
him. If the system does not prove responsive to the needs and
preferences of all people, it will soon face competition from one
or more alternative systems. Because trade naturally tends to
unify and to adopt a single monetary language, one of these

systems, through sheer merit, must sooner or later become universal.

To avert the utter and complete disorder of a moneyless world, however, such a system must come into being before the present expires through total inflation. The present monetary units must not sink to complete worthlessness before a new unit and a true one becomes available. Not only must we act while exchange is still operating under the political monetary system, but we must also make it as easy as possible to exchange the old currencies for the new. To do this, it will be necessary also that we exchange old ideas for new.

The Valun Universal Monetary System

The valun plan for a nonpolitical, universal monetary system, represents a concrete effort to implement a new approach to freedom. It takes its name from *valun*, which is the name for any *value unit* that is established by a social compact of its users, who agree to bargain with one another in terms of it.* This proposed system will not be the only one devised or tried, nor need it be the one that ultimately prevails, but it provides a much needed starting place for thought and action. Free competition in the marketplaces of the world will be the ultimate arbitor, as it is in all things where free choice prevails.

The "built-in" features of the valun system have been limited to those considered indispensable to a successfully working monetary system, leaving to experience and the process of competition the selection of operating policies and details. The "built-in" principles are two:

a) All governments are excluded from the issue power.

b) The power to convert check drafts into currency shall not be limited.

The first principle, being basic to the whole thesis, needs no elaboration. The second is necessitated by the distinction made in the political monetary system between currency money and check money, a distinction which, as we have seen, puts a purely gratuitous hazard in the banking business. The political

* Dennis Riness, of Seal Beach, California, has suggested *Riegel* as an appropriate name for a new, wholly nonpolitical monetary unit. — Editors.

monetary system imposes artificial restraints upon the banks' ability to convert any or all bank deposits into currency. This is the reason for the recurrent bank crises of the past. Bank runs forced banks to resort to clearing house certificates or else fail, even though they were perfectly solvent but for the arbitrary distinction between currency and checks. This hazard in the banking business has been displaced in recent years by the yet greater evil of legal counterfeit. The banks have purchased so many Government securities that there is practically no possible demand for currency that they could not meet. A true monetary system, however, must preclude not only the major evil of counterfeiting, but the secondary evil of the business cycle as well. Hence the provision for the full interchangeability of checks and currency.

Let us now look beyond these bare-bones features which would obtain in any successful private enterprise monetary system, and envision how such a system actually might work in operation.

Organization of the Valun System

The valun system would be governed on a mutual participation basis. A board of governors would license the participating banks, and the board and member banks would be served by a separate service organization which, like the banks, would be organized and operated for profit. This basic structure is illustrated in Figure 4.

The board of governors would be a non-capitalized, mutual association of participating banks in which all members would have one vote. With the bank stocks, in turn, being held by personal enterprisers, the whole monetary system would thus be truly of, by and for personal enterprise. The banks would pay stipulated fees to the board, and any surplus accruing would be redistributed among the banks in proportion to their volume of valun business, probably with check clearances being the criterion.

The board would license new and existing banks to operate under the system, without distinction as to nationality or the monetary unit in which the latter normally transacted business. Valun banking would require merely a separate set of books. The operating licenses would stipulate rules of practice and provide for periodic examinations. Through its control of the name *valun,* the board would guarantee adherence to uniform standards by all banks in the system. The board would also authorize the printing of bills and minting of coins and provide for surveillance against counterfeiting of valun currency.

A chief responsibility of the board would be with respect to credit policy. The board could set what it deemed to be the most conservative policy and provide therefor a minimum percentage to be charged for loss insurance, and from there up graduations of more liberal policies, with appropriate percentages for loss insurance for each. Thus there would be no more need for standardizing the basis of credit in the valun system than in the present banking system. Each bank could choose its own credit policy. The appropriate loss insurance percentage would then be added to the check clearing charge made to the customers. In this way, customers of the various banks would pay more or less as the policy of their bank was less or more conservative. The insurance fund thus set up against defaults would be held by the board, subject to draft by any bank to cover any "loss" from credit default.

The service organization would be a profit corporation with capital adequate to promote the adoption of the system by banks and their depositors. In addition to negotiating licenses for the board, it would supply the banks with checks and other forms required by them, as well as any mechanical equipment desired. It would also supply valun currency in bills and coins, as authorized by the board. In view of the national and international potentialities of the valun system, it can be seen that the service organization would have the possibility of becoming a very profitable enterprise, expanding both in capital and income with the growth of the valun system.

The function of the banks would be to administer. for an appropriate service charge, the mutual credit of their account holders. The banks would provide credit facilities for the issuance and redemption of valuns by personal enterprisers, and

Figure 4

THE UNIVERSAL VALUN SYSTEM

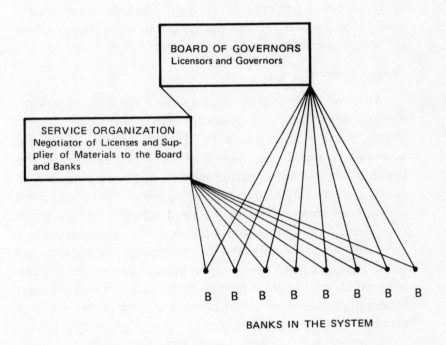

BANKS IN THE SYSTEM

would clear checks and render other appropriate banking services. There would, of course, be no interest charge for lines of credit, since the banks would take no credit risks. The credit would be extended by traders to one another, and the banks would not be involved except as administrators.

Hence, under the valun system, credit would be free, but not printing, bookkeeping, insurance and other expenses; service costs would be paid for by the account holders. The small percentage charge stipulated by the board of governors to set up reserves against credit "losses" might range from 1/20th to 1/10th of a per cent per month. Thus the valun system would save business the tremendous sums paid in interest under the speculative political monetary system.

Parity Provision

As noted, each bank would adopt and pursue its own credit policy under an insurance agreement whereunder a base, or minimum, premium rate would be charged, subject to increase according to that bank's "loss," or charge-off, experience, the board, of course, reserving the right to determine what constituted a charge-off. Under this arrangement, all valuns issued through all banks would be of equal validity. The insurance rate would compensate for all charge-offs, and the cost of insurance would be reflected in the charges for banking services. Thus, no matter how many banks were authorizing the issuance of valuns, nor wherever in the world their borrower-issuers might be, there could be no variation in the worth of valuns.

In other words, every issuer of valuns would be practically underwritten by the account holders of his bank, through the provision of reserve percentages adjusted to the "loss" experience of each bank. The board of governors might, for example, set a median rate of 1/10th of one per cent per month on debit balances, and then raise or lower this rate in accordance with the experience of each bank. Since these reserve percentages would affect the service charges of each bank, competition among banks would tend to deter laxness in the administration of credit. This credit, it will be remembered, would be based upon the debtor's potentiality of placing in the market, at the market price, the commodity or service that he dealt in, and not any specific, price-pegged commodity.

This insurance feature might better be called the *parity* provision. Unlike the Federal Deposit Insurance Corporation, its purpose would not be to insure depositors against default of the banks, but rather to preserve the parity of valun issues emitted through the various banks.

How much money might the banks permit each issuer to issue? As much as he could redeem, which means, as much as he might need to get a turnover in his business. This, admittedly, would vary with different lines. All lines, taken together, average about four turnovers a year. Thus, roughly speaking, business would need an issue power sufficient to span three months. This question will be dealt with more fully under "Credit Limits," below.

There would be no need for valun currency at first, because all existing currencies would be purchasable with valun checks at the going rate of exchange. When these currencies became so depreciated as to be inconvenient to use, then valun currency in bills and coins would be made available. These bills and coins would be uniform the world over and would be made of the cheapest serviceable material, without any suggestion of intrinsic value. Such currency would bear the certification of the board of governors and would be available from banks by check requisition, its author being, of course, the check writer from whose check it was converted.

Credit Limits

The major policy question to be resolved in valun banking would be the matter of credit limits, i.e. how much should the enterpriser be permitted to issue (to take goods and services out of the market) before being obliged to cancel out an equal sum (to recapture by sales). This could be worked out on the basis of the needs of various trades and professions, rather than passing upon the applications of each member thereof. On the other hand, account holders, once established, might be extended a line of credit based on a percentage of their previous year's business. This being done, each participant would be authorized to draw checks against his assigned credit without giving any note or other instrument. The credit would have no term, but would be in the nature of a call credit, since the pledge would be to deliver value on tender of money.

Different banks would have different needs, determined by whether they were largely agricultural, manufacturing, or mercantile. The nature of the prevailing industry and the degree of presence of reciprocating trades would determine the need for debit balances. For instance, a farmer who sold only once every six months or year, but who bought continuously, would need a longer debit line than a shopkeeper whose selling was more closely synchronized with his buying. A territory where the local product had to be transported a considerable distance before a sale could be effected would also need more time than one which was more integrated or self-sufficient.

The ideal issue policy would be that each customer of the bank be empowered to purchase equivalent to his capacity to sell and to emit sufficient money within such limitation. Whether this ideal could be determined would depend upon solution of the problem as to what constituted "capacity to sell," since value can be determined only in actual exchange and not prospective exchange. Whether the ideal would need to be attained, would depend upon the actual requirements of the money volume and its relation to total exchangeable wealth, of which the former can be determined only by experience and the latter can only be estimated.

Whenever men organize, there is always the possibility that their association may disadvantage some of their number or non-associates. If a debit policy is adopted that makes the money supply inadequate for some or all of the members, the ideal that animates the undertaking is defeated and conspiracy, in effect, exists against those adversely affected. For the money issuing function, although it is private, can be exerted only within the limits of the communal arrangement. There is an ideal debit policy, but it may have to be worked out by trial and error.

Launching the Valun

The determination of what value relativity a monetary unit should represent at the time of its adoption is a matter of choice. It might be the equivalent of a bushel of wheat, a bale of cotton, a pound of brass, or any other commodity. On the other hand, it could be placed on a parity with an existing political monetary unit which had attained a significance. It would be easier, obviously, to identify a unit in the public mind by making it at the outset equivalent to the current unit. Doubtless it was for this reason that the United States dollar was initiated at par with the Spanish dollar. For the same reason, therefore, the valun would be initiated at par with the United States dollar.

This does not imply constancy of parity; it merely means keynoting. All monetary units are, in practice, established by relativity to an existing unit. The relativity thereafter is subject to the issue policy governing each. Hence the valun would have an initial value of one dollar, which would be equal to the power of the dollar on the day of the valun's launching. Thereafter, it would be entirely dissociated from the dollar and independent of any subsequent fluctuations in value that the dollar might have.

Existing banks presumably could open valun departments without legal difficulty or political embarrassment, since under the valun system, they would extend no credit and therefore take no risks. Banks would merely administer the credit extended by the account holders to one another. A large bank such as the National City Bank could make the valun plan a world system overnight by offering it from all its far-flung branches.

The actual launching of the valun might be accomplished by enlisting a number of business concerns to pay their bills with *valdol* checks, which would offer the payee the option of accepting payment in valuns or dollars. The purpose of this would be to establish parity for the initial valun issues. It is expected that sufficient acceptances would be had that, from that point on, there would be a money exchange market for valuns in terms of dollars. After this, the free money market would be the guide to the values of the respective units and would govern the number of valuns required to pay for bills rendered in dollars.

The participating banks would open valdol accounts upon request, against which the holders could draw valdol checks. The valdol account would honor the payee's preference of payment in either valuns or dollars or both. In the case of a shortage of either valuns or dollars in an account, and there being an adequate balance of the other, the bank would be authorized to sell a sufficient amount of the long unit on the money market to offset the deficit in the short unit.

Valdol checks are proposed merely as an initial expedient. They would give non-valun account holders the option of accepting either valuns or dollars. Because of this option, these checks would be usable by participating banks in payment of any bill. This would extend invitations far and wide to others to become members of the valun system. Between valun account holders, however, such a form would not be needed, and a single-unit valun check would be used.

The face of the valdol check would carry spaces for the tender of either valuns or dollars, or half in each, and a place for the payee to state his preference and to add his signature. For the information of the recipient, the back of the check would carry the following notice:

> After stating your preference and signing on the face of this check, deposit in the regular way if your bank carries valdol accounts. If it does not, write your name and address here (space) and mail to us (name and address of issuing bank). We will immediately send signature card and, upon receipt thereof, will mail you a valdol checkbook.

Thus prospective valdol account holders, no matter where located, could bank by mail should there be no valdol bank in their locale.

The Money Exchange Market

All political monetary units are inflated and growing more so. There is no sound unit to which uneasy money can take

TOWARD A NATURAL MONETARY SYSTEM 59

flight. As inflation progresses, many will flee from the dollar into property, but it is exchange that produces income, and not the holding of property static. As the many retreat into a static situation, the volume of product will drop, thus aggravating the general inflation problem. The true and ideal accomplishment in an inflationary movement, for the individual as well as for society as a whole, is to keep active in exchange and thus produce income. Yet in order to continue in business without grave hazard, one must switch his exchange commitments to a stable monetary unit and convert his reserves and working capital to such a unit.

The valun, having no inflationary element and being secure against any, would naturally be desired by both the holders of idle funds and by active businesses that wanted to avoid the destruction of capital and profits. Since no valun could be issued except by a producer in the market, no inflationary units could enter into circulation, and the unit would remain stable. The valun user, therefore, would escape the storm; he would not be tossed about on a sea of confused costs and prices. Through the money quotations of the spot market, current remittances could be determined by translating dollar obligations into valuns. Through the futures market, manufacturers, importers, and exporters would be enabled to hedge against the inflationary decline of all national monetary units.

One of the most vexing problems of business is the difficulty of adjusting wages to the decline of the monetary unit. These troubles would be eliminated by employers paying wages with valdol checks. The employee would have his salary or wage stated on his check in both valuns and its equivalent in current dollars. Moreover, given the option to receive their pay in valuns, labor would not have to strike for cost-of-living raises. As inflation raised the dollar cost of living, each valun would purchase an additional corresponding amount of dollar currency.

With the exception of those who had joined the valun system and who thus, by mutual consent, were using the valun, pricing and billing at the outset would be in dollars. As the system spread, however, more and more business would be initiated in terms of valuns, first by manufacturers, then by wholesalers, and finally by retailers.

Once the valun system had started in the United States and the international money market had begun valun trading, check forms appropriate to the currencies of other nations, such as valmark, valpound, valfranc, etc., would be provided. As stated, between valun account holders, valun checks would be used for international as well as domestic payments.

As valun banking spread in this manner, the implications for world trade would be far-reaching. Since the valun would be a universal unit, it would be as much domestic to a nation as would be the unit of that nation. It would be issuable by the citizens of any nation, either through an internal bank or through one beyond the national boundaries. Thus the present obstructions to international monetary exchange would be removed. With monetary exchange operating internally between the national unit and the valun, the limitations on exchange between national units would no longer be restrictive of trade. Exporters and importers could operate with valuns. The valun would thus ameliorate trade restraints even if the national restrictions upon exchange between national units continued.

For these various reasons, therefore, it is believed that the valun would immediately take its place in the world as the monetary criterion, that the dollar would sell at a discount in valuns, and that all other units would be affected in relation to their dollar exchange value.

Universal Liquidation

It might seem impossible to liquidate the extant astronomical numbers of units of money by means of valuns, a unit that would have to start from scratch and that, at the outset, would be infinitessimal in volume. But the problem seems otherwise when we remember that money springs out of exchange, and not vice versa.

If the seller stipulates the unit that a transaction is to be expressed in, the buyer must provide payment accordingly. If he has bank credit in the stipulated unit, he creates the desired units. If he does not have the required bank credit in the unit stipulated, he uses available funds to buy the desired unit. Any unit that is not entirely worthless will buy any other unit at the market price.

Thus, demand for valuns would always be met by supply, either by bank credit in the purchase of goods or services, or by purchase of existing valuns by conversion from other units. As demand for valun bank credit increased, so would facilities therefor, either by expansion into a wider territory by the banks that already offered valun credit, or by new banks nearer to the locale of demand.

By the same token, supply of valuns would never exceed demand, even though there would be no credit limitations imposed upon member banks. The banks would be free to use their discretion, with the sole proviso that their parity insurance rate would be upped or lowered in accord with their loss experience. But with the freedom allowed valun bank credit, one must not visualize an irresponsible surfeit of valuns, for money can be issued only when it is bought into existence by a seller. To establish bank credit does not constitute issue. Issue is not effected until a tender has been accepted in exchange for value. In other words, money, to be issued, must be bought into circulation either with goods or services or by delivery of money of another name, which, being money, is a claim for goods or services. No issuer will issue money except for market value, and each, in turn, is under necessity of bidding for it to remain in business. Thus would the competitive system tend to maintain the parity of the valun unit both during and after liquidation of all political monetary units.

When May the Valun be Expected?

To put the valun theory into practice, it is not necessary to expand the number of theorists. It is no more necessary for men generally to understand the science of money than it is for them to understand the science of any other utility. Given a sufficient number of traders to participate initially, it will take only a few directing individuals to put the system into operation. These numbers of traders are as indispensable as the few theorists, however. One might understand the theory of baseball, be familiar with all the rules, have the diamond, the bats, the balls and gloves, but there would be no game until there were eighteen participants—nine on a side. Likewise there must be many times nine buyers and an equal number of sellers before the game of exchange can be played.

The simile may not seem a good one because the players of ball must be experts, while to predicate exchange upon expert participants would seem to be hopeless. Expertness in monetary exchange, however, does not imply comprehension of the theory of money. It means expertness in making up one's mind on what is wanted and what it is worth. Every person has this expertness. However much we may hear of super-scientific money management, there is no money management, just as there is no money creation, except by the buyer. Money management means spending for self gain, nothing more and nothing less.

To whom shall we look to start the valun? We must look to employers, for as we have seen, it is the buyer and not the seller who creates money. The common man begins his exchange activities by selling his services. He must do this to live, since he cannot apply his services directly to fashioning all his necessities. His psychology is really a buying psychology, since his selling is but the means of his buying. He visualizes the things he needs or desires, and hence, mentally buys before he sells, but chronologically he sells before he buys. The bit of paper or metal that intervenes between the sale of his services and the purchases of his wants, he calls *money*—if it works. He gives no further thought to the matter.

The first *buyer* in the chain of exchange is the employer. Therefore we must look to employers to start the valun, and employees have the right to expect it to be trustworthy. Employees will repose confidence in what employers profess to be an honest medium of exchange, and they will underwrite that medium with the basic commodity, the mother of all wealth, namely brain and brawn and sweat. If no one cheats—and in the valun system no one could cheat—the currency will circulate freely without popular understanding of the theory of its being. Let us understand clearly, therefore, that while we

TOWARD A NATURAL MONETARY SYSTEM 63

need numbers, we do not need understanding numbers. We need no educational crusade. We need but to comprehend the simple acquisitive instincts and how to serve them.

Banking and Interest Rates In a World Without Money

The Effects of Uncontrolled Banking

By Fischer Black

Associates In Finance

Belmont, Massachusetts

It is possible to imagine a world in which commercial banks and other financial institutions are free to offer checking accounts (and savings accounts) on any terms they might want to set, and in which there are no reserve requirements. Banks could pay interest on demand deposits, and might not choose to distinguish between demand deposits and time deposits. Since there would be no reserve requirements, there would be no reason for Federal Reserve open market operations.

In such a world, it would not be possible to give any reasonable definition of the quantity of money. The payments mechanism in such a world would be very efficient, but money in the usual sense would not exist. Thus neither the quantity theory of money nor the liquidity preference theory of money would be applicable.

Vickrey was one of the first writers to imagine such a world. He says [11, p. 113]:

"In passing it may be noted that the essentially institutional nature of monetary theory, including much of the basic notions of the quantity theory and of the liquidity-preference theory, is brought out by considering how far either of these theories would be applicable to a situation in which all transactions are executed by check or some similar instrument, in which banks cover their operating expenses entirely from service charges and pay interest on average balances at rates reflecting the return on their investments, and in which overdrafts are honored fairly freely, possibly at graduated interest rates. It seems likely that for application to such circumstances the theories would have to be rather radically modified, if indeed they did not become entirely inapplicable."

Vickrey does not explore the concept any further in this article, but he has a somewhat longer discussion in a later book [12, pp. 108-110]. There he emphasizes the fact that current monetary theory depends heavily on a rather restricted form of financial institution. He says that other institutional arrangements would make current monetary theory almost completely invalid.

Tobin comes close to saying the same thing several times. In "Commercial Banks as Creators of 'Money'," [8] he emphasizes the similarity between commercial banks and other financial intermediaries, and thus between the liabilities of commercial banks and the liabilities of other financial intermediaries. He says that the differences would tend to vanish in an unregulated, competitive financial world; and that even in today's world, the volume of liabilities of any financial institution is determined more by depositor preferences than by government and central bank actions. In [10], however, Tobin and Brainard say that the presence of uncontrolled banking reduces, but does not eliminate, the effec-

JBR

WORLD WITHOUT MONEY

tiveness of monetary control through changes in the volume of government debt.

In [9], Tobin points out some advantages, at least in a long run sense, of allowing interest on demand deposits, or allowing interest-bearing assets to serve as means of payment. He says [9, p. 846]:

> "Freeing means of payment from the legal limitations of zero interest would make it theoretically possible to have an efficient growth equilibrium without deflation—efficient in the sense that the real rate of interest is high enough to avoid over-capitalization and in the sense that real resources are not diverted into economizing means of payment."

Tobin comes closest to seeing the implications of uncontrolled banking in [7, p. 26]:

> "If the interest rate on money, as well as the rates on all other financial assets, were flexible and endogenous, then they would all simply adjust to the marginal efficiency of capital. There would be no room for discrepancies between market and natural rates of return on capital, between market valuation and reproduction cost. There would be no room for monetary policy to affect aggregate demand. The real economy would call the tune for the financial sector, with no feedback in the other direction. As previously observed, something like this occurs in the long run, where the influence of monetary policy is not on aggregate demand but on the relative supplies of monetary and real assets, to which all rates of return must adjust."

Gurley and Shaw [2, pp. 253-256] observe that with laissez-faire banking, the price level is not determinate, and suffers from "aimless drift". Patinkin [4, p. 303] also says that the price level is indeterminate when banks are not controlled:

> "Indeed, what we have here is the indeterminacy of Wicksell's 'pure credit' economy in which all transactions are carried out by checks, while banks hold no reserves. The economic interpretation of this indeterminacy is straightforward: In order for the absolute price level to be determined by market-equilibrating forces, changes in it must impinge on *real* behavior in *some* market, i.e., must create excess demands in some market."

Johnson [3] and Friedman and Schwartz [1], on the other hand, claim that uncontrolled banking will lead to an uncontrolled increase in prices. Friedman and Schwartz say [1, p 5]:

> "In the hypothetical world in which there are no costs of setting up a bank and running a bank, and

in which deposits transferable by check provide precisely the same services as dominant money, there would be no limit to this process short of a price level of infinity in terms of dominant money".

An even more extreme position is taken by Pesek and Saving [6], and by Pesek [5]. They say that making money a "free good" (by paying full interest on demand deposits) will make it a worthless good, and will cause a return to barter.

I maintain that the views expressed by Vickrey, Tobin, Gurley and Shaw, and Patinkin are the correct ones. In a world without controls on banking, the real sector will be independent of the financial sector, and the price level will be indeterminate. Traditional monetary theories will be inapplicable; in fact, it will not be possible to define the quantity of money in meaningful terms. Finally, I claim that this world would have several advantages, and few obvious disadvantages, over our present economic and monetary system.

A World Without Money

Let us imagine, then, a world in which money does not exist.

The major financial institutions in this world are banks. There are several competing major banks with branches in every state, as well as banks that are more limited geographically. Payments in this world are made by check. Because of economies of scale in check clearing, there may be only one major clearing corporation, which is operated either by the banks as a group or by the government. We might even imagine that checks have been replaced by an electronic payments mechanism; the discussion below would not be affected by this assumption.

Each bank is allowed to accept deposits under any conditions that it chooses to specify, and to pay any rate of interest on these deposits. In particular, the bank can allow transfers of credit by check between two interest-bearing accounts. Demand deposits will pay interest, and depositors are likely to be charged the full cost of transferring credit from one account to another. Almost all deposits will be in the form of demand deposits.

The banks will make loans to individuals, businesses and governments They will probably establish a schedule of interest charges for each borrower, and will then allow him to write checks on his account that increase the amount of his loan whenever he needs the money. The interest rate paid by a borrower will depend on such things as the amount he has borrowed, his wealth, his current income and his future income prospects. It will also depend on the extent to which he provides the bank with collateral for his loan. The banks will also probably set a maximum amount that they will lend to any individual, but this maximum is mainly to keep the borrower from running up a very large debt and then declaring bankruptcy. An individual who intends to repay his loans would not approach the maximum except in very unusual circumstances. Repayment will be flexible; so long as the bank is in touch with the borrower and is satisfied of his ability to repay, he will not need to make payments of principal or interest in any particular month or year. Interest will simply be charged against his account periodically and will serve to increase the amount of his loan.

There will be an active market in inter-bank funds. A bank that has more deposits than loans will deposit its excess funds with other banks that have more loans than deposits. There will be no special reason for an individual bank to have non-bank deposits equal to non-bank loans, since it can adjust any imbalance through transactions with other banks.

Banks will compete in setting schedules of interest rates on loans and in setting transactions charges. The interest rate on deposits will be a standard wholesale money rate. Individuals, corporations, governments and other banks will all receive the same interest rate on deposits.

Banks will make money on the administration of loans and on the handling of transactions. Their profits on loans will come from the difference between the rates they charge and the wholesale interest rate, minus their expenses. Their profits on transactions will come from the difference between their transactions charges and their costs in handling transactions.

A bank will be happy to bid a customer with positive balances away from another bank, even if it simply redeposits the customer's money with the original bank, because it gets that customer's transactions business (and possibly other business as well). A bank will be happy to bid a customer with negative balances away from another bank, even if it gets the deposits it needs to balance the new loan from the original bank, because it gets

both the customer's loan business and the customer's transactions business.

An individual, business or government will simply have an account at a bank; there will be no need to distinguish between accounts with positive balances (deposits) and accounts with negative balances (loans). An individual may write a check that converts his deposit into a loan, or he may receive a salary payment that converts his loan into a deposit. So long as his loan does not come to exceed the maximum permitted by the bank, there is no need to make special note of these transactions. If his average balance in the latest period is positive, his account will be credited with interest; if his average balance is negative, interest will be charged to his account. Thus there will be no reason for an individual to have both a loan and a deposit at the bank. Since he is allowed to write checks on either a positive or a negative account, and since the interest he pays on his negative account will be greater than the interest he receives on his positive account, he will be better off if he combines the two into a single account.

A business or government account will be handled in the same way as an individual account. The bank will establish a schedule of rates and a maximum loan size, and the account will be allowed to fluctuate freely so long as it does not become a loan larger than the maximum. The business or government can write checks against its account regardless of whether the account has a positive or negative balance.

For the federal government, the interest rate charged on loans will probably be independent of the size of the loan, since there is virtually no risk of default. And there will be no need for an individual bank to set a maximum loan size, since it will probably be happy to loan the government as much as it wants to borrow. The federal government will have very large negative balances at the banks, and will use these bank loans as a substitute for issuing bonds and notes. The total borrowing of the federal government will be limited by Congress, just as it is today. It will be determined by the relation between government outlays and income from taxes and other sources. Massive government spending that is not balanced by taxation would cause the financial system to break down, just as it would cause the existing financial system to break down.

Depositors will be protected in several ways.

JOURNAL OF BANK RESEARCH

JBR

WORLD WITHOUT MONEY

First of all, every bank will be required to have capital equal to a certain fraction of its loans, and any unusual losses on its loans will come out of that capital. Second, the major banks will be so large that their loan portfolios will be protected by vast diversification. A default on a single loan or on a single group of loans will not be dangerous because it will be such a small fraction of the bank's total portfolio. Finally, the government may provide deposit insurance to protect against catastrophic losses that affect a large fraction of the loans in all banks' portfolios.

Since the banks will not be restricted in making loans to businesses, they will be able to supply the bulk of the loans that businesses need, both short term and long term. There will be no reason for businesses to borrow directly by issuing debt securities on the open market; the banks can presumably offer loans at the same interest rate that the market would demand, and the cost of obtaining a bank loan is likely to be less than the cost of a public issue of debt securities. Businesses will obtain part of their capital from bank loans, and the rest from securities, especially common stock. There will be no fixed rule about how much of its capital a business obtains from bank loans; some businesses will have large loans, while others will have none at all. At any time a business can issue common stock to retire some of its loans, or expand its loans to retire some of its common stock.

For the moment, let us suppose that all payments in this simpler world are handled by check or credit card, and that currency is not used. In this world, money does not exist.

An individual has no currency. He has a bank account, but there is no distinction between demand deposits and time deposits. His bank account, if it is positive, represents all of his riskless savings. If it is negative, his bank account represents his borrowing. His bank account together with his holdings of securities and marketable real assets represent his total savings.

There is nothing in this simpler world that can meaningfully be called a quantity of money. Some might say that the total value of all positive bank accounts is the quantity of money. But this makes a completely arbitrary distinction between positive and negative bank accounts. And it means that the quantity of money will change every time an individual transfers credit from his negative bank account to another individual's positive bank account. Others might say that the net value of all bank accounts, both positive and negative, is the quantity of money. But the net value of all the accounts in a bank is simply the capital of that bank. It is equal to the assets of the bank (its loans) minus the liabilities of the bank (its deposits). Thus, the net value of all bank accounts is equal to the aggregate value of all bank securities. We would hardly want to call this the quantity of money.

Still others might say that the value of all potential additional loans in all accounts is the quantity of money. They would say the quantity of money in a positive account is the balance in the account plus the maximum amount the bank would allow the customer to borrow, and the quantity of money in a negative account is the difference between the maximum amount that can be borrowed and the actual amount borrowed. But the maximum size of the loan that is set for a bank customer is arbitrary, and is intended to keep him from intentionally spending himself into bankruptcy. It is not intended to limit the amount of debt he incurs that he will be able to repay. Virtually no individuals will borrow to the maximum, because they will want to have income and borrowing power available for future consumption. So the quantity of money defined in this way will generally have no economic meaning.

There are cases in which this definition of the quantity of money will have economic meaning, however. Suppose, for example, that the maximum loan amount for any individual is set equal to the estimated total value of his wealth, including real assets, financial assets and the present value of his future income. Then this last definition of the quantity of money will simply be equal to the total wealth of the community. Similarly, if the maximum loan amount is set at a standard percentage of the total value of his human and non-human wealth, this last definition of the quantity of money will be equal to a standard percentage of the total wealth of the community. So although the definition has economic meaning, it is not reasonable to call it the quantity of money.

There are no government bonds, because the government simply borrows from the banks in the same way that individuals and businesses borrow. There is no qualitative difference between government loans and other loans, so there is no reason to treat them differently. Thus, there is no

JBR

way to include government bonds as part of the quantity of money or the quantity of near money.

Since there is no quantity of money to control, there is no need for a Federal Reserve Board to control it. The banks are not restricted in the amount they can loan by reserve requirements, so there is no need to change their reserve positions through open market operations, or to make changes in the rules relating reserves to total bank assets. The banks may be subject to capital requirements, however. They may be required to have capital equal to some minimum percentage of their loans. But this is not a restriction on the total volume of loans that banks can make, because they can always issue new common stock to raise any additional amounts of capital they may need.

Since there is no quantity of money, it is clear that the quantity of money cannot affect the economy of this world in any way. The quantity of money cannot affect national income, employment or the rate of inflation, because it does not exist.

We can take one step in the direction of a more complex world by introducing currency. The federal government will print the currency, and will issue it to banks as requested. When a bank receives currency from the government, it will credit the government's account by the amount of currency received. The bank will then give the currency to individuals as requested. When a bank gives currency to an individual who has an account with the bank, it will simply reduce his balance by the amount given. When a bank gives currency to an individual in exchange for a check on another bank, it will reduce the balance of the other bank (or increase its balance with the other bank). Thus the amount of currency held by individuals and businesses will be determined by how much it is needed for small payments. So long as the interest rate on bank accounts is positive, an individual will want to hold down the amount of currency that he carries, because currency earns no interest. The amount of currency held by individuals and business will be determined by the volume of small payments, and by the cost and inconvenience of making payment by check or credit card.

JBR

WORLD WITHOUT MONEY

The amount of currency held by banks will be determined by the patterns of withdrawals and deposits of currency by individuals and businesses during the day, and by the cost of making transactions with the government. The government will issue currency or retire currency at any time. Thus the amount of currency outstanding at any time will be determined by the needs of individuals and businesses. There will be no need for any federal agency to fix the amount of currency outstanding.

Currency alone can hardly pass for the whole of money. The quantity of currency, in this world, will not be controlled by the central bank, and will not influence the economy. So even when currency is added to our model, the quantity of money can have no effect on output, employment or prices, because the quantity of money does not exist.

Evolution of the Means of Payment

In this section I want to start with a very simple economy and build up to the world without money described above. While there is no money in that world, there is a highly developed means of payment. In the paragraphs that follow I will use the word "money" as short for "means of payment," without meaning to imply that a quantity of money exists in any of these worlds.

1. Private Business and Commodity Money— In the simplest of all possible worlds there are no financial markets at all. Businesses are owned by individuals and may not be bought or sold. Transactions are made through barter, which is very costly, or through the use of some standard commodities that are compact, portable and don't deteriorate rapidly. A means of payment that requires transfer of physical commodities is costly because the transfer process is cumbersome, and is extra costly because the commodities, that have value in other uses, must be diverted from these uses to be used as means of payment. Transactions are expensive, and real resources must be tied up for use in making payments.

2. Common Stock and Portfolio Money—As soon as we introduce any financial market at all, we can eliminate the inefficiencies of barter and commodity money. For example, suppose we introduce common stock. We will allow an individual to sell shares in any businesses he owns, and

these shares will trade continuously on the stock market. Shares of common stock may now be used as a means of payment. While it may be possible to use the shares of any company that is traded in the stock market as means of payment, it may be practical to use a standard portfolio of stocks as the means of payment.

Goods may be priced in terms of a unit of account that does not fluctuate in value very much, and the means of payment may be priced in terms of the same unit of account. Thus the dollar price of a share of the standard portfolio will fluctuate from day to day, and even from hour to hour, while the dollar price of a commodity may be relatively stable. This means, of course, that the price of a commodity in terms of shares of the standard portfolio will be constantly fluctuating. This is a slight inconvenience, since it means that every business must be aware of the current dollar price of the standard portfolio, to know how many shares to take in payment for any item. Otherwise, this system would have no disadvantage as a means of payment. Currency could be issued representing shares and fractions of a share of the standard portfolio. The only problem would be the necessity of computing a price, in shares of the standard portfolio, at the time of sale. This price would simply be the dollar price of the item divided by the current dollar price of a share in the standard portfolio.

3. Borrowing, Lending and Note Money— While shares in a portfolio of common stocks would be quite satisfactory as a means of payment, they would be less satisfactory as the only intangible form of wealth. We would want to introduce borrowing and lending to provide a larger set of alternative forms of wealth, and at the same time we get a new form of means of payment that eliminates the disadvantage of a portfolio of common stocks. A principal reason for introducing borrowing and lending is for the transfer of risk. Some individuals, instead of holding their wealth in common stocks that fluctuate in value, would rather lend part of their wealth to other individuals at a fixed interest rate. Other individuals would want to borrow to increase their holdings of common stocks, if the borrowing rate were reasonable. In effect, the individuals who lend are paying the individuals who borrow to take over some of their risk. The expected return on equity of a lender will be lower than the expected return on equity of a borrower.

Another reason for introducing borrowing and lending is to allow some individuals to spend more than they are earning by borrowing against their future income, and to allow other individuals to spend less than they are earning, and lend the difference.

Business borrowing and lending adds nothing new; it is equivalent to borrowing and lending by the owners of the business. Whatever the reason for the borrowing and lending, we can assume that the borrower writes a personal note and gives it to the lender in exchange for certain assets. The initial lender may be simply the person from whom the borrower wants to buy. The notes that are created by borrowing and lending may now be used as means of payment. They are better as means of payment than shares in a portfolio of common stocks because they do not fluctuate very much in value (assuming that they are short term notes). On the other hand, notes have the disadvantage that the holder of a personal note can never be sure that it will be redeemed by the writer at maturity. There may be a significant risk of default, and a significant cost of collection of a personal note. (A note would be redeemed at maturity either in notes of other issuers or in common stock of equivalent value.)

4. Administration of Loans and Guaranteed Money—To get around the problem of default on personal notes, we can introduce "banks" that serve to administer loans and guarantee personal notes. These banks will neither make loans nor accept deposits. They will simply supervise each borrower, and will guarantee that if he doesn't pay off his notes, they will. In return the bank would charge a fee to cover administrative costs and the probability that a borrower will default on his notes. Thus the notes would bear interest at a lower rate than the rate paid by the borrower; the difference would be income to the supervising bank.

Banks would compete by offering low fees to issuers of notes, and by having a reputation for soundness among holders of notes that they have guaranteed. The government might help ensure a bank's solvency by requiring it to have capital equal to a certain percentage of the notes it has guaranteed. Otherwise, there would be no necessity for government regulation of banks.

Payments would be made using guaranteed notes. These notes would be a convenient, low-cost means of payment that would not fluctuate in value appreciably. But they would still have a few disadvantages. The value of a note would change from day to day due to the accrual of interest. The variety of different notes would be a disadvantage, and some notes might be more acceptable than others. The opportunity for theft might be great if individuals carried notes in large denominations from place to place, unless the notes were registered. But registration might be costly.

5. Checking Accounts and Bank Money—To solve these problems, we allow the banks to participate in the payments mechanism in a unique way. Instead of remaining outstanding, individual notes will be used only temporarily in making payments, and will then be extinguished. Individuals will have bank accounts that will have positive balances for lenders and negative balances for borrowers. Banks will credit interest to accounts with positive balances and will debit interest to accounts with negative balances. The individual will write a note whenever he wants to make a payment. This note will be either in the form of a check or in the form of a credit card purchase receipt. His note will serve to credit the balance of the seller and to debit his balance. It will also credit the balance of the seller's bank with his bank. This system will be a convenient, safe, low-cost means of payment.

In none of these five worlds was there any clearly defined quantity of money. The world of private business and commodity money came closest to having a money supply, but even there, a commodity used as means of payment also has other uses, and it may not be clear when it is to be counted as part of the money supply, and when it is to be counted as involved in one of its other uses. Once we introduce financial markets, however, and intangible means of payment, the idea of a "quantity of money" loses its meaning.

In none of these five worlds was there any role for a central bank. And the only effect that the financial sector had on the real sector was that as we go to successively more efficient means of payment, we reduce the cost of making payments and release real resources for other uses. In none of these worlds was there any mechanism that would cause uncontrolled inflation in the absence of a central bank.

JBR

WORLD WITHOUT MONEY

Evolution of Central Bank Control

In this section I want to build up the forms of central bank control over the banking system that are used in the United States. It is clear that each of these forms of control has some effect on the banking system; but it is not clear that any of them has any significant effect on the economy as a whole.

1. Maximum Interest Rates on Deposits—In the world without money described above, deposits earn interest at the wholesale money rate and banks earn a profit on their transactions charges. Competition will force a bank either to pay the wholesale rate on deposits or to compensate for a lower rate by reducing transactions charges. The wholesale rate will be more common, however, because a bank offering a lower rate and lower transactions charges will tend to attract depositors that keep small balances and have many transactions. Such a bank would tend to lose money on its deposit business.

If the central bank is allowed to establish maximum interest rates on deposits, then various distortions will be introduced. A maximum interest rate on deposits is a rather odd notion in this world, because a deposit is simply an account with a positive balance. What sense does it make to have a maximum interest rate on deposits (positive balances) but no maximum interest rate on loans (negative balances)?

If the maximum interest rate is below the natural level of the wholesale money rate, then an imbalance between supply and demand will be created. At that rate, many loans will seem profitable, but few deposits will come in. The economy will tend to revert to the use of individual and business notes for borrowing and lending, rather than the more efficient use of bank accounts. Because of this imbalance between demand for loans and supply of deposits, banks will try to evade the maximum rates by offering services instead of money interest on deposits. They will offer lower transactions charges, financial assistance to businesses, trust department services and lower rates on loans. This is rather inefficient, of course, and cannot completely eliminate the effects of maximum interest rates, but it seems to eliminate much of the impact of maximum interest rates in the United States, at least in normal times.

What would happen, though, if the maximum rates were effective on most sources of bank deposits? No bank would be able to attract additional funds from these sources by offering higher rates. So the supply of these funds would be strictly limited. To keep loan demand down to a level equal to the supply of funds, the wholesale money rate for banks would increase until the volume of profitable loans was equal to the volume of available deposits. And this is the rate that banks would offer to any sources of funds not subject to the maximum. The spread between the interest rate paid on most deposits and the wholesale money rate would represent an extra source of profit to the banks. So they might not object strenuously to the central bank's setting maximum interest rates on deposits.

It is sometimes claimed that if banks are not allowed to pay interest on deposits, and if there are no reserve requirements, they will create de-

posits to buy any asset with a positive expected return, thus bidding up the prices of all assets and causing massive inflation. It is claimed that once a bank creates a deposit, it can never be extinguished, so people will use it to try to buy things and will add to the inflationary pressure.

This argument makes no sense at all. First of all, banks cannot generally own real assets (except bank buildings and equipment) or common stocks. So they cannot simply bid up the prices of these assets. What banks can do is offer to make loans at low interest rates. In our world of positive and negative accounts, this would not work, because it would cause the demand for loans to exceed the supply of deposits. Recall that a borrower in this world simply writes a check that adds to his negative balance whenever he needs to make a payment. Making a loan does not involve the simultaneous creation of a negative balance and a positive balance.

Even in a world where checks can be written only on bank accounts with positive balances, banks cannot offer loans at low interest rates. When a bank creates a deposit larger than the individual wants to hold, he can always use it to pay off some of his loan. Or he can lend it to someone else who will pay off his bank loan. Bank deposits can always be extinguished; they can be used to pay off bank loans. If there are more deposits than people want to hold, the banks will discover that their deposits are being used to pay off their loans, and the volume of both will decline. Thus the banking system can be in equilibrium in a world with zero interest on deposits only if the interest rates on bank loans are high.

An individual bank offering lower interest rates on loans than other banks will be able to get loan customers away from the other banks. But to get money to lend to these customers, the bank will have to pay the wholesale interest rate, which will be high. Thus the bank will lose money by making these loans, and would not be tempted to do so.

2. Reserve Requirements—The central bank may require that each bank hold deposits at the central bank equal to some fraction of the individual bank's deposits or loans. It may do this even when it does not try to influence the total volume of bank deposits by controlling the volume of deposits with the central bank. If the central bank pays the wholesale money rate on the deposits of other banks with it, then this requirement will have no effect on the banking system. But if the central bank pays a lower rate than the wholesale money rate, this requirement will represent a tax on bank deposits. This tax will mean that banks will pay less than the wholesale rate on their deposits, too. It will cause the economy to revert somewhat to the use of personal and business notes for borrowing and lending.

3. Limited Reserves—If the central bank establishes reserve requirements in the form of deposits that each bank must carry with the central bank, and sets a rate of interest on these deposits, there will be a natural level of reserves. The higher the reserve requirements and the lower the rate of interest paid on reserves, the larger the tax on deposits, and the more the economy will revert to the use of personal and business notes for borrowing and lending. If, in addition, the central bank sets a maximum limit to the volume of reserves that is lower than the natural level of reserves, it will cause reserves to be worth more to banks than their face value. There is no way for the central bank to set a minimum limit on the volume of reserves other than by changing reserve requirements and the interest rate paid on reserves.

With the quantity of reserves limited to a level below its natural level, reserves take on a value greater than their nominal value. A bank with $1 million on deposit with the central bank might be able to sell its deposit to another bank for $1.5 million. This would increase the effective reserve requirements and reduce the effective rate of interest on reserves so that banks will be satisfied with the amount of reserves allowed by the central bank at the "black market" price. The central bank would have to be careful about accepting new deposits in this situation, since any deposit it accepts results in a windfall gain to the bank making the deposit, equal to the difference between the nominal value of the deposit and the market value of the deposit. The central bank would have to set up a system of rationing for accepting new deposits or for retiring existing deposits. Thus, this would be a very cumbersome system. Since limiting reserves has the same effect on the banking system as increasing reserve requirements or reducing the rate of interest on reserves, but requires rationing of changes in reserves, it is hard to see why this system would be used.

JOURNAL OF BANK RESEARCH

WORLD WITHOUT MONEY

4. Currency Reserves—If a central bank deposits and currency were both allowed as reserves, if the central bank allowed a bank to increase its deposits with the central bank by depositing currency and if the central bank limited the quantity of reserves below the natural level, then a very strange situation would be set up. Currency would be worth as much to a bank as deposits with the central bank; in particular, currency would be worth more than its face value to a bank. This means that banks would offer individuals more than face value for currency. An individual making a deposit of currency would have his account credited with the market value of the currency rather than with the face value of the currency. A two-price system would thus be established for all payments: One price for payment by check (the higher price) and one price for payment by currency (the lower price).

This would hardly be a desirable state of affairs. So if currency is to be equivalent to deposits with the central bank for use as reserves, the central bank must refrain from limiting the total supply of reserves to a level below its natural level. The central bank can control reserve requirements and the interest rate paid on reserves, but cannot, unless it wants either rationing or a two-price system, control the supply of reserves.

Since our present banking system allows the use of currency as reserves, and since we do not observe that banks are willing to pay more than face value for currency (in crediting a bank account), it seems likely that the Federal Reserve Board does not set the maximum quantity of reserves below its natural level. In other words, open market operations must be ineffective. If they were effective in controlling the quantity of reserves, then we would observe a two-price system. The only other possibility is that there is a profit opportunity that banks have not been exploiting, in paying more than face value for currency and central bank deposits.

All of these forms of central bank control tend to keep the total volume of banking below its optimal level. They all cause the economy to revert, in part, to the use of personal and business notes for borrowing and lending. Thus they make the financial system less efficient than it would otherwise be. Other than this, these forms of central bank control have no effect on the economy or on the price level.

Monopoly Banking

Even in a world with just one bank, there would be no money supply and the bank would have no significant influence on the real economy or on prices. The bank would not be forced by competition with other banks to offer high interest rates on deposits, but it would be influenced by other financial markets. If it offered very low rates on deposits, it might find that its deposits declined so much that it was more profitable to offer a higher rate and get more deposits. In any case, it is true that such a bank would charge more for transactions, would set higher interest rates on loans and might set lower interest rates on deposits, than a bank in competition with other banks.

It would not, however, be able to cause inflation by bidding up asset prices or by creating deposits that cannot be extinguished. First of all, it would not be allowed to own real assets or common stocks. And second, even if it were allowed to own such assets, it could not create deposits that could not be extinguished. A bank deposit can always be extinguished by being applied to reduction of a bank loan.

The Myth of Aggregate Demand

Those who believe that a central bank can influence the real sector of the economy often say that it does so by affecting aggregate demand for goods and services. In general, their argument is that the central bank can make loans easier to get or cheaper, which will expand aggregate demand, and that it can make loans harder to get or more expensive, which will contract aggregate demand. High aggregate demand is supposed to lead to low unemployment but rapid inflation; while low aggregate demand is supposed to lead to high unemployment but stable prices. Sometimes this argument centers on loans that businesses use to buy investment goods, and sometimes it centers on loans that individuals use to buy consumption goods.

What this argument overlooks is the fact that banks must have deposits for all their loans. When a bank allows one person to borrow, it must attract an additional deposit equal to the amount borrowed. When one individual decides to spend more, some other individual must decide to spend less. Borrowing must equal lending; an increase in one must be balanced by an increase in the other. Thus an added demand for consump-

JBR

tion goods by one individual must be balanced by a reduced demand for consumption goods by another individual. So aggregate demand is not affected.

Even when the central bank is able to affect the desired balance between consumption and investment, this does not mean that it is thereby able to affect aggregate demand. An increase in desired saving that is balanced by a decrease in desired consumption will leave aggregate demand unchanged. The central bank can increase borrowing only if it increases lending, and it can restrain borrowing only if it restrains lending. Restraining borrowing and lending will cause inefficiencies and misallocation of resources, but it is not clear that it will have any effect on aggregate demand.

The Quantity Theory of Money

In a world where transactions take place by the transfer of loans and deposits, the quantity theory has no place. As I have emphasized above, there is no reasonable definition of the quantity of money in such a world.

The quantity theory has a certain amount of plausibility in a world where the only means of payment is a commodity such as gold. If the supply of gold increases because new gold is found, then it seems fairly reasonable that the prices of other goods would rise relative to the price of gold. The quantity theory also has some plausibility in a world where the government creates currency in massive amounts and spends it for goods and services, as a substitute for direct taxation. However, there is a tendency in such a world for currency to lose its ability to serve as a means of payment. If this happens, then the quantity theory will no longer apply.

As soon as we get to a world where payments are made by transferring deposits and notes, the quantity theory becomes impossible even to formulate. Those who believe in the quantity theory are forced to argue in terms of a world with commodity money or a world where the government hands out massive amounts of currency or bonds, and then transfer their conclusions to an entirely different kind of world.

JOURNAL OF BANK RESEARCH

JBR

WORLD WITHOUT MONEY

The Liquidity Preference Theory

In a world where transactions take place by the transfer of loans, deposits and notes, the liquidity preference theory is just as inappropriate as the quantity theory. This is true whether we have competitive banking or monopoly banking, and whether banks are regulated by a central bank or are completely unregulated.

The general argument is similar to that of the quantity theory. When people have too much "money," they spend it, or they bid up the prices of financial assets, causing interest rates to fall, and stimulating business investment. When people have too little "money," they reduce their spending or sell financial assets, causing interest rates to rise and restraining business investment. Thus too much money increases aggregate demand, and too little money reduces aggregate demand.

But why should people do this? If they have too much money, in either currency or deposits, they can simply pay off their loans. If they have no loans, they can lend their deposits to someone who does, and charge him a little less interest than the bank would charge; he will then use the proceeds to pay off his loans with the bank.

An individual can adjust his portfolio of financial assets by trading with other individuals and by dealing with his bank. If he wants more currency, the bank will give it to him; if he wants less, the bank will take it back. If he wants more demand deposits, the bank will give him a loan (at some interest rate), and if he wants less, the bank will reduce his loans. If the bank will not do these things, other individuals or businesses will.

So transactions that affect portfolio composition are purely financial; they have no impact on the real sector or on the price level.

I am grateful for comments on earlier drafts of the paper by Myron Scholes, Franco Modigliani, Martin Bailey, James Lorie, John McQuown, Jack Treynor and Michael Jensen.

REFERENCES

1. Friedman, Milton, and Anna L. Schwartz, "The Definition of Money: Net Wealth and Neutrality as Criteria", *Journal of Money, Credit, and Banking* (February, 1969), pp. 1-14.
2. Gurley, John G. and Edward S. Shaw, *Money in a Theory of Finance*. Washington, D.C.: The Brookings Institution, 1960.
3. Johnson, Harry G., "Inside Money, Outside Money, Income, Wealth, and Welfare in Monetary Theory", *Journal of Money, Credit, and Banking* (February, 1969), pp. 30-45.
4. Patinkin, Don, *Money, Interest, and Prices*, 2nd. Edition. New York: Harper and Row, 1965.
5. Pesek, Boris P. "Comment", *Journal of Political Economy* (July/August, 1968), pp. 885-892.
6. Pesek, Boris P., and Thomas R. Saving, *Money, Wealth, and Economic Theory*. New York: Macmillan, 1967.
7. Tobin, James, "A General Equilibrium Approach to Monetary Theory", *Journal of Money, Credit, and Banking* (February, 1969), pp. 15-29.
8. Tobin, James, "Commercial Banks and Creators of 'Money' ", in Deane Carson, ed., *Banking and Monetary Studies*. Homewood, Illinois: Richard D. Irwin, Inc., 1963, pp. 408-419. Also in Donald D. Hester and James Tobin, eds., *Financial Markets and Economic Activity*, Cowles Foundation Monograph 21. New York: John Wiley & Sons, Inc., 1967, pp. 1-11.
9. Tobin, James, "Notes on Optimal Monetary Growth", *Journal of Political Economy* (July/August, 1968), pp. 833-859.
10. Tobin, James, and William C. Brainard, "Financial Intermediaries and the Effectiveness of Monetary Controls", *American Economic Review* (May, 1963) pp. 383-400. Also in Donald D. Hester and James Tobin, eds., *Financial Markets and Economic Activity*, Cowles Foundation Monograph 21. New York: John Wiley & Sons, Inc., 1967, pp. 55-93.
11. Vickrey, William S., "Stability Through Inflation", in Kenneth K. Kurihara, ed., *Post-Keynesian Economics*. London: George Allen and Unwin Ltd., 1955, pp. 89-122.
12. Vickrey, William S., *Metastatics and Macroeconomics*. New York: Harcourt, Brace & World, Inc., 1964.

[11]

ROBERT L. GREENFIELD
LELAND B. YEAGER*

A Laissez-Faire Approach to Monetary Stability

THIS PAPER DEVELOPS some diverse hints for a new monetary system offered separately by Fischer Black, Eugene Fama, and Robert E. Hall. (For reasons that will become evident, though, we should perhaps say "payments system" instead of monetary system.) None of the economists mentioned has actually proposed the particular system set forth here nor examined all its properties, and we call it the "BFH system" not to implicate them but only to give credit for some component ideas and to have a convenient label.[1] Regardless of who if anyone may actually advocate the system, contemplating it is instructive. It illuminates, by contrast, some characteristics of our existing and recent systems.

*The authors thank the Institute for Humane Studies for the opportunity to work together on this and related topics and James M. Buchanan, James P. Cover, and Kaj Areskoug for written comments on earlier drafts, Robert E. Hall, Joseph T. Salerno, and William Breit for discussion, and Lawrence H. White for large and valuable amounts of both. Buchanan suggested the story of the fungus that we shall use and contributed to explaining how what he called "indirect convertibility" might be said to characterize the BFH system.

[1]We do not claim to be offering an accurate summary or synthesis of particular persons' proposals. Instead, we are picking and choosing among ideas and modifying and extending them. (Incidentally, we would welcome suggestions for a name more descriptive than "BFH system.")

While Black and Fama do consider using commodities as numéraire (and Fama even considers using space-ship permits), they mainly discuss how an unregulated financial system would operate. While Hall also champions deregulation, he stresses his idea of a unit of account defined by a bundle of commodities. He would define the unit in terms of a small number of commodities whose amounts would be adjusted from time to time to stabilize a general price index. (He thus extends Irving Fisher's idea of a "compensated dollar" of adjustable gold content.) We, however, consider a unit defined once and for all in terms of so many commodities that its stability in terms of the unchanging bundle would come close to stability of its general purchasing power.

ROBERT L. GREENFIELD *is associate professor of economics and finance, Fairleigh Dickinson University, Madison.* LELAND B. YEAGER *is professor of economics, University of Virginia.*

Journal of Money, Credit, and Banking, Vol. 15, No. 3 (August 1983)
Copyright © 1983 by the Ohio State University Press

Briefly, the idea is to define the unit of account physically, in terms of many commodities, and not in terms of any medium of exchange whose value depends on regulation of its quantity or on its redeemability. (We use the terms "unit of account," "value unit," and "pricing unit" as synonyms, preferring one or another according to the particular emphasis intended.) Apart from defining the unit and enforcing contracts, the government would practice laissez faire toward the medium of exchange and the banking and financial system.

Remarks by readers of our drafts have alerted us to the danger of being misinterpreted, no matter how clearly we say what we mean. This danger is understandable. People absorb ideas, and even sense impressions, by classifying them in relation to their earlier experiences [8]. People then sometimes react more to the pigeonholes they use than to the ideas themselves. We must insist, therefore, that the system we describe does not fit into familiar pigeonholes. We must warn our readers against preconceptions and urge them to await what we actually say.

The BFH system is not a variant of the often-proposed composite-commodity or commodity-reserve money. It is not a variant of the tabular standard (widespread indexing). Questions about whether the BFH system involves convertible or inconvertible money—questions presupposing some familiar answer—are inapplicable to it. The definition of the BFH unit of account does not require "implementation" through convertibility of any familiar sort, any more than does maintenance of the defined length of the meter.

Although the BFH system would indeed lack money as we now know it, it would not entail the textbook inconveniences of barter. The advantages of having a definite unit of account and convenient methods of payment would be retained and enhanced.

Also false is the notion that the BFH system is impractical for somehow running counter to the natural evolution of monetary and financial institutions. Our existing system is far from the pure product of any such evolution. Dismantling it would require legislation, whose specific provisions would be bound to nudge subsequent developments one way or another. That is why it is not self-contradictory to assess alternative payments systems even from a laissez-faire position.

1. SYSTEMS COMPARED AND QUESTIONS ILLUMINATED

We gain better understanding of a given payments system by comparing it with alternatives. Walter Eucken [2, pp. 159–72] and Heinrich Rittershausen [9, pp. 57–69] have emphasized crucial differences between systems that unite and those that separate the unit of account and the medium of exchange. Separation, though familiar in the Middle Ages, is unfamiliar nowadays, a fact that makes the separated system we shall describe particularly instructive. In one type of monetary system, properly so called, the unit of account is the unit of the medium of exchange, whose value depends on the demand for it as such and on restriction of its quantity. This is our present system of fiat money. Under a second type of system, money is denominated in a unit kept equal in value to a definite quantity of some commodity by interconvertibility at a fixed ratio. The monetary commodity has a "natural" scarcity value; unlike fiat money, it cannot be simply printed or written into existence. This is the logic of the gold standard. The same logic applies, and more powerfully, to the often proposed composite-commodity or commodity-reserve standard, which would make the money unit interconvertible not with a single commodity but with a physically specified bundle of commodities.

A third type of payments system is the one examined here. It resembles the composite-commodity standard in its definition of the unit of account but differs from that standard in lacking any government-issued or government-specified medium of exchange and in lacking any claims obligatorily redeemable in bundles of the specific commodities defining the unit. One fundamental difference between this third (BFH) system and either ordinary system relates to the supply and demand that determine the value of the unit of account. Under both fiat money and an ordinary commodity standard, the unit's value is determined by supply of and demand for money or a monetary commodity, with the demand being wholly (for fiat money) or largely (for commodity money) of a monetary character. Under the BFH system, in contrast, the demand for the many commodities defining the unit is almost entirely nonmonetary. Under fiat money or an ordinary commodity standard, an imbalance between actual and desired money holdings can develop and (barring adroit remedial money-supply management) can call for adjustment of the real value of the unit of account. Pressures for this adjustment may work only sluggishly and therefore painfully because of stickiness in many individual prices and wages. Under the BFH system, in contrast, because of the almost wholly nonmonetary character of the demands for and supplies of the commodities defining the unit and because of the unit's separation from the medium of exchange, no monetary pressures can come to exert themselves, either sluggishly and painfully or otherwise, on the value of the unit. The BFH system offers much less scope than an ordinary monetary system for destructive monetary disequilibrium.

Comparison of the BFH system with others should help forestall misapplication of propositions true under one system to another system under which they do not apply. It should aid in pondering several interrelated questions. What are the possibilities and consequences of separating the unit of account and medium of exchange? What are the similarities and the differences between a unit of value and other units of weights and measures? What is necessary for an operationally meaningful definition of the pricing unit and for a determinate price level? By what processes does the value of the money unit change? Under what circumstances, if any, is the real-bills or needs-of-trade doctrine valid and is James Tobin's notion valid of a natural economic limit to the nominal size of the money and banking system? Under what circumstances and in what senses is it true that the supply of money tends to create its own demand and that the demand for money tends to create its own supply? What is the role of base money when the bulk of the circulating medium consists of demand obligations backed by fractional reserves of it? What market processes tend to forestall or correct an imbalance between money's supply and demand, and what circumstances impair these processes, permitting painful macroeconomic consequences? Most broadly, what are the merits and defects of different systems?

2. THE BLACK-FAMA-HALL SYSTEM

The BFH system would get rid of any distinct money existing in a definite quantity. The government would be forbidden to issue obligations fixed in value in the unit of account and especially suitable as media of exchange. It would not give legal-tender status to any particular means of payment but would simply enforce contracts in which the parties themselves had specified what would constitute fulfillment. No longer would there be any such thing as money whose purchasing power depended on limitation of its quantity. No longer, then, could there be too much of it, causing price inflation, or too little, causing depression, or a sequence of imbalances, causing stagflation. A wrong quantity of money could no longer cause problems because money would not exist.

But without money, how would prices be quoted, contracts expressed, and financial records kept? The answer is that there would be a defined unit of value, just as there are defined units of length, weight, volume, time, temperature, and energy. Business practice, left to itself, might eventually converge on a specific definition of the unit. The government could hasten and probably improve the choice, however, by noncoercively offering a definition, just as it does with weights and measures. The unit would be defined by a suitable bundle of commodities. Just as the meter is defined physically as 1,650,763.73 wavelengths of the orange-red radiation of krypton 86, so the value unit would be defined physically as the total market value of, say, 50 kg of ammonium nitrate + 40 kg of copper + 35 kg of aluminum + 80 square meters of plywood of a specified grade (the four commodities mentioned by Robert Hall) + definite amounts of still other commodities. The prices of the individual commodities would not be fixed and would remain free to vary in relation to one another. Only the bundle as a whole would, by definition, have the fixed price of 1 unit. (For a unit of convenient size, however, the bundle might be designated as worth 1 *thousand* units.) The bundle would be composed of precisely gradable, competitively traded, and industrially important commodities, and in amounts corresponding to their relative importance. Many would be materials used in the production of a wide range of goods so that adopting the bundle as the value unit would come close to stabilizing the general level of prices expressed in that unit.

The commodities defining the unit would have the characteristics envisaged in the composite-commodity or commodity-reserve proposal, with one exception. They would not have to be storable, that is, capable of being held as monetary reserves, since the BFH scheme does not require any direct convertibility of obligations into the particular commodities defining the value unit. This difference—this lack of dependence on any particular base money—deserves emphasis. The more familiar proposal calls for an ordinary commodity standard in the sense that standard commodity bundles would be exchangeable for newly issued money and money would be redeemable in bundles at a fixed ratio. That proposed system differs from the gold standard chiefly in that a bundle of commodities takes the place of a single one. It, like the gold standard, is vulnerable to abandonment or to devaluation of the money unit. When the gold standard is abandoned or the gold content of the money unit is cut, the old unit keeps its functions, and people regard gold as a commodity whose price has risen. Part of the beauty of the BFH system, in contrast, is that the value unit remains stable in terms of the designated commodity bundle because its value never did depend on direct convertibility into that bundle or any specific commodity. Instead, its value is fixed by definition. It is free of any link to issues of money that might become inflated.

The BFH system bears a superficial resemblance to the proposed tabular standard of value, that is, widespread indexing, in that both involve specifying a standard bundle of goods and services. The latter system, however, presupposes the continued existence of an ordinary medium of exchange whose unit also serves as the ordinary unit of account. The total price of the standard bundle quoted in that ordinary unit—or, rather, changes in that price level—is what the price index measures. Use of the index to calculate current ordinary-money equivalents of certain debts and payments erects a unit of constant purchasing power, corresponding to the price index employed and its commodity bundle, into a unit of account rivaling the ordinary money unit. This rival unit presumably serves mainly in contracts spanning substantial periods of time (it is a "standard of deferred payments," as the older textbooks used to say). The BFH system, in sharp contrast, abolishes any ordinary money in terms of which a price index might be calculated and so avoids any rivalry between distinct units of account.[2]

Robert Hall suggested an analogy between the yard and the proposed value unit (in his taped panel discussion; what follows here embroiders on what he actually said). Both are units of measurement—one of length, the other of value. Both are defined in physical terms. Neither unit has any quantitative existence. It is nonsense to ask how many yards or how many value units there are in existence. Another element of the analogy is that no one seeks to maintain the size of the yard or of the value unit by maintaining any direct convertibility, as between cloth and yardsticks or between money and specific commodities. (Issuers of demand obligations, like other debtors, would be concerned about maintaining the value of their own obligations, but that is not the same as their bearing responsibility for the real value of the unit of account itself.)

Of course, an analogy is just that and not an identity. There are differences between units of length and value, just as between units of length and weight. The key similarity is that both are *defined* units whose definitions do not change or stop being applicable because of changes in some quantity or because of other physical or economic events.

---

[2]Further discussion of the tabular standard and of why it is parasitical on the continued existence of ordinary money and unindexed prices appears in Yeager [15].

With no money quantitatively existing, people make payments by transferring other property. To buy a bicycle priced at 100 value units or pay a debt of 100 units, one transfers property having that total value. Although the BFH system is barter in that sense, it is not *crude* barter. People need not haggle over the particular goods to be accepted in each transaction. The profit motive will surely lead competing private firms to offer convenient methods of payment.

Under laissez faire, financial intermediaries blending the characteristics of present-day banks and mutual funds would presumably develop. People would make payments by writing checks (or doing the equivalent electronically) to transfer the appropriate amounts—value-unit-*worths*—of shares of ownership in these funds. (Convenience would dictate writing checks in numbers of value units, not in numbers of shares of heterogeneous funds.) The funds would invest in primary securities (business and personal loans and stocks and bonds) and perhaps in real estate and commodities. They would seek to attract customers (owners of their shares) by compiling records of high earnings, safety, and efficiency in administering the payments (checking) system. The funds would presumably charge for their checking services, so that investors would not be subsidizing customers using them mainly as checking accounts. Payment and investment institutions like these would arise unless entrepreneurs devised even more convenient ones that we have not been able to imagine. Different funds would specialize in different fields and services.

A customer's holding in his fund would not have to be fixed in size in value units. Apart from his adding to it or drawing it down, his holding would rise or fall in value as his fund received earnings and made capital gains or as it suffered losses on its asset portfolio. (In effect, holdings would bear interest or dividends at fluctuating rates, possibly sometimes negative.) Despite these fluctuations in value, the customer could watch his holding closely enough to avoid writing too big a volume of checks. He would probably be using the fund partly as an investment vehicle, anyway, and would not want to keep his holding down to the minimum required for transactions. Furthermore, funds might well arrange to honor overdraft checks by making automatic loans to their drawers.

Funds would have to make settlements with one another, as banks do nowadays, for the differences between the value-amounts of checks written on each one and of checks on others deposited with it. How would the funds do this? Remember, there is no base money—neither government-issued fiat money nor monetary stocks of particular commodities. Again, competition would favor efficient practices. Funds would presumably agree, under the auspices of their clearinghouses, on what portfolio assets—perhaps specified securities—would be acceptable in settlements.

The question of settlements leads into the question of what would happen if many owners of a particular fund wanted to get out of it. The departing owners would presumably write checks against their old fund and deposit them in their new funds. The shrinking fund would have to transfer assets to the growing ones. Loss of owners and of the value of assets and shareholdings would punish poor management. The discipline of competition would favor good performance.

What would serve as hand-to-hand currency? Fund shares of fluctuating value—

some of them—could take the physical form of coins and circulating paper. It would probably prove convenient, however, for currency to be denominated in the unit of account. (The distinction between *evaluation* and *denomination* deserves attention. All property can have its current value, changeable or not, measured in units of account. An asset so denominated, however—like a $10 bill of today—has its value *specified* as so many units.)

Nowadays, by way of a minor administrative detail or public-relations device, most money-market mutual funds fix the value of their shares at $1 each and take account of earnings (or losses) by adjusting the number of shares in each owner's holding. If, similarly, BFH funds kept their shares worth 1 unit of account each, then some bearer shares could circulate as coins and notes. Only a small fraction of all shares would presumably take that form, however, unless some convenient way were devised for adjusting not merely the number of book-entry shares but also the number of shares circulating as currency to reflect the earnings or losses of individual funds. Alternatively, instead of being ownership shares, the circulating currency (and also some deposits) could be debt instruments issued by funds and other organizations and denominated in units of account.

3. ADVANTAGES

Considering its possible advantages will serve further to contrast the BFH system with our existing system and to provide a focus for certain questions. Firstly, the system would provide a stable unit for pricing, invoicing, accounting, economic calculation, borrowing and lending, and writing contracts reaching into the future. The government, secondly, would come under financial discipline. It would have to borrow on the same basis as any other borrower and could no longer acquire resources by issuing money and otherwise imposing inflationary "taxation without representation." Competition under laissez faire, thirdly, would spur innovation in finance and the payments system and would exert discipline on banks and investment funds. Institutions would evolve, yes, but would no longer exhibit the socially unproductive instability hitherto associated with continual attempts to wriggle around changing government regulations.

A fourth set of advantages follows from the fact that the medium of exchange (i.e., readily transferable property) would not be redeemable in any particular base money, whether commodity money or government fiat money. No multiple expansions and contractions of ordinary money could occur in response to changes in the amount of any base money held as fractional reserves. No runs on financial institutions could occur of the self-aggravating type that used to be familiar (especially before government insurance of bank deposits, which, by the way, would be inappropriate under the BFH system). No scramble for base money of limited total quantity could make suspicion of particular institutions spread to others. Suspicion would be more nearly concentrated on poorly managed funds, holdings in which would depreciate in value, particularly as settlement of checks drawn by customers shifting to other funds stripped the shrinking funds of their most readily acceptable assets. Runs would be less catastrophic under the BFH system than under an ordinary banking system for reasons resembling the reasons for the differences between runs on national currencies under a system of pegged exchange rates and the more nearly self-restraining runs under floating exchange rates.

A related advantage is avoidance of multiple expansions and contractions of money supplies through the balance of payments. No longer could a payments deficit drain away base money and impose multiple deflation of a country's ordinary money supply. A country under the BFH system would have no fixed exchange rate (unless, quite exceptionally, and sacrificing key features of the system, it chose to define its unit of account as an amount of some foreign currency). Foreign currencies would be free to fluctuate in value against both the country's physically defined unit of account and its various media of exchange. A deficit on current account would necessarily mean either that foreigners were acquiring financial claims on the country or that its residents were disposing of financial claims on foreigners. No balance-of-payments surplus, to mention the opposite disorder, could impose imported inflation.

4. AVOIDING MACROECONOMIC DIFFICULTIES

Our existing monetary system is subject not only to inflation but also to stagflation, deflation, and depression because the unit of account and the medium of exchange are tied together and because the actual quantity of money can fail to correspond to the total of money holdings desired at the existing price level (or entrenched price trend). Market-clearing forces do not work very well to maintain or restore equilibrium between money's supply and demand because money does not have a single price of its own that can adjust on a market of its own. Instead, the medium of exchange has a fixed price in the unit of account (each dollar of the money supply has a price of exactly $1). With no specific price and market to impinge upon, imbalance between money's supply and demand must operate upon the dollar's purchasing power, that is, on the whole general price level. This process requires adjustments on the markets and in the prices of millions of individual goods and services, leaving scope for quantities traded and produced to be affected. Prices and wages respond far from promptly enough to absorb the full impact of imbalances; they are sticky—some more so than others—for reasons that make excellent sense from the standpoints of individual price-setters and wage-negotiators. Under these realistic circumstances, failure to keep the quantity of money correctly and steadily managed can have momentous consequences.[3]

Inadequate effective demand for goods and services is sometimes blamed on oversaving. That as such, we insist (without repeating in detail what we have written elsewhere), is not what threatens general deflation of economic activity. The trouble comes, rather, from attempts to save by acquiring money, a good for which

[3]To avoid repetition, we refer to four papers by Yeager.

excess demand can develop and persist because it has no price of its own that could adjust on a market of its own to equilibrate supply and demand. Since money routinely facilitates exchanges of goods for one another, impairment of its circulation obstructs those exchanges and in turn obstructs the production of goods to be exchanged. In these respects money has no close counterpart in the BFH system.

In avoiding these monetary difficulties, the BFH system offers yet a fifth set of advantages. The unit of account no longer has its value dependent on the quantity of the medium of exchange. The unit's general purchasing power, being practically fixed by definition, is never called upon to undergo adjustment through a process exposed to the hitches characteristic of our existing system. The very concepts of quantity of money and of possibly divergent actual and demanded quantities become inapplicable. What serves as the medium of exchange is indefinite, plastic, and subject to the desires of market participants. As in a barter world, no clear line separates media of exchange from other assets. Most owners of funds would be holding shares both as checking accounts and as investments. They could reclassify portions of their holdings as serving one purpose or the other as suited their changing circumstances and desires (if they ever bothered to make such a classification in the first place). Media of exchange would no longer have a fixed price in the unit of account (anyway, not all of them would). No longer could the pressures of imbalance between money's supply and demand be tending to change the purchasing power of the unit—but only sluggishly, with adverse side effects on quantities of goods and services traded and produced.

These macroeconomic advantages are worth a closer look. Actual quantities of media of exchange (liquid assets, readily transferable property) would adjust to the demand for them. In our existing world, by contrast, the nominal quantity of a country's medium of exchange is primarily determined on the supply side in the way described by the money-multiplier analysis of the money-and-banking textbooks (the analysis involving the quantity of base money and reserve and currency/deposit ratios). The real (purchasing-power) quantity of the medium of exchange does tend to be determined on the demand side, but through the roundabout and possibly sluggish and painful process of adjustment of the whole general price level. (For familiar reasons, this proposition about supply-side determination of the nominal quantity of money and demand-side determination of the real quantity applies strictly only to a closed economy, a country with a floating exchange rate, or a key-currency country in the special position that the United States enjoyed even under the Bretton Woods system. Under a fixed exchange rate regime, demands for money holdings can affect even the actual nominal quantity in a non-key-currency country through the balance of payments.)

In the BFH world, the (near-) fixity of the purchasing power of the unit of account obliterates any distinction between determination of real and determination of nominal quantities of assets usable as means of payment. No base money exists to constrain or support their quantities from the supply side. The fuzziness of the dividing line between these and other assets, furthermore, obviates the distinction that does hold in our actual world between the predominantly supply-side determination of nominal amounts of money and the supply-*and-demand* determination of nominal as well as real amounts of nearmoneys and nonmoneys.

5. RESPONSES OF QUANTITIES OF MEDIA OF EXCHANGE

With money of our present kind, the nominal quantity is determined on the supply side, with the nominal demand for it falling passively into line (subject to the standard exception for an open economy under fixed exchange rates). The unit's real size tends to adjust appropriately, but through a roundabout and possibly painful process.

With BFH fund shares serving as the media of exchange, their actual quantity, measured in units of account, is determined by interaction of demand with supply. Interest rates, broadly interpreted, play a role in the equilibration. By divorcing the unit of account and medium of exchange, the BFH system avoids supply-side determination of the latter's quantity. Just as even the nominal money supply is demand-determined in an open economy with a fixed exchange rate whose price level is dictated to it by the world market, so the volume of media of exchange is demand-determined in a BFH economy whose unit of account has a purchasing power dictated by its multicommodity definition.

Space permits only few examples of the process at work.[4] Suppose people's tastes shift away from holding fund shares and in favor of holding ''bonds.'' (Here we stretch the term to cover all primary securities—stocks, bonds, promissory notes, mortgage obligations, and the like issued by the users of the resources so obtained—and even to cover any real estate and other physical assets in which funds might invest.) Accordingly, the rate of return paid on fund shares rises, while the bond rate falls, the latter being an average rate of return on ''bonds'' in our stretched sense of the word. That is to say, the spread of the bond rate over the share rate—the price of intermediation services—falls, as is to be expected in consequence of the postulated decline in demand for those services. The unit-of-account volume of fund shares supplied goes down, matching the decline in demand for them.

For an example of an automatically accommodated increase in demand for media of exchange, suppose that some development expands the real size of the economy at full employment. Under an ordinary monetary system, an accommodating expansion of the nominal money supply is limited by the monetary base (as determined by policy or by the workings of a commodity standard) and by the determinants of the money multiplier. Under the BFH system, no such limitation or contingency impedes the expansion of fund shares. On the liability or equity side of their balance sheets, funds find their owners willing to hold more shares. On their asset side, funds find business firms willing to borrow more and issue more securities to

---

[4]Space constraints have forced deletion of our fuller discussion, as well as of our mathematical and graphical analysis. Copies of this material are available upon request from Greenfield.

finance taking advantage of the increased labor supply (if that, e.g., had been the element making for real growth) and of expanded markets for output.

Finally, let us suppose, or try to suppose, something analogous to expansion of an ordinary money supply at the initiative of issuers. Under our existing system, the central bank expands the stock of base money, the banking system responds, no one refuses payment in the newly created money, and spending and respending of the expanded money supply raises prices until it all is demanded as cash balances after all.

Under the BFH system, by way of an analogy that will prove incomplete, the funds step into the financial markets to grant loans and buy securities, paying with their own newly created shares. The more imprudently expanding funds face adverse clearing balances and the necessity of surrendering assets acceptable in interfund settlements. This happens not only because of their relatively great expansion of shares against which checks are now being written but also because doubts about their soundness lead owners to shift their holdings into more prudent funds. Both the asset portfolios of and shareholdings in the relatively imprudent funds decline not only in amount but also in price in terms of the unit of account, especially as those funds must part with their least dubious assets in interfund settlements. The settlement assets gained by the relatively prudent funds are not a close counterpart of base money under our existing system and cannot support a multiple expansion of assets and shares by those funds.

The crucial part of the story, however, is still to be told. As funds in general seek increased earnings by expanding at their own initiative, the firms and individuals borrowing from them or selling securities to them move to spend the shares thereby acquired. Shares accordingly depreciate against commodities, the unit of account, and funds' portfolio earnings. Just as would be the case were tastes simply to shift away from shareholdings and in favor of current consumption, share rates of return and then bond interest rates rise, discouraging the funds' supply of shares to the public and issuers' supply of primary securities to the funds. The funds' efforts to expand meet restraint after all.

Under both our existing system and the BFH system, the real volume of media of exchange is determined by demand (interacting with supply); and under the BFH system, fixity of the unit of account means that the volume measured in it, the nominal volume, is demand-determined also. This condition shields the BFH system from the macroeconomic disorder that does accompany an excess demand for or supply of money in our existing system. The BFH system has no clearly distinct medium of exchange that routinely flows to lubricate transactions in goods and services in such a way that expansion or restriction of its flow would do great damage. The medium of exchange—or a major part of it, shareholdings in funds— has a flexible price in terms of the stable-by-definition unit of account. (Recall the distinction between an asset's being denominated in a unit and its having a value expressible in that unit.) The total quantity of the medium of exchange—if that total is meaningful at all, in view of the vague and shiftable distinction between the exchange medium and investment assets—tends to adjust, as we have seen, to

ROBERT L. GREENFIELD AND LELAND B. YEAGER : 313

accommodate the demand for it. (Thus, the "natural economic limit" attributed by James Tobin [11], erroneously, to the nominal size of a money and banking system of our current type *would* operate under the BFH system.)

6. OPERATIONALITY AND DETERMINACY

Some readers may still be wondering whether the physical definition of the unit of account has operational meaning and whether the level of prices expressed in that unit is determinate. Determinacy, as Schumpeter [10] said of a monetary system, presupposes the specification from outside the market process of some "critical figure," some nominal magnitude (as by control of the number of money units in existence or, alternatively, by operational specification of the money price of some commodity or composite of commodities).

In the BFH system, that "critical figure" can only be the commodity-bundle definition of the unit of account. That definition leaves the individual prices of the items in the bundle free to respond to supply and demand changes. Could market conditions, then, establish prices that, when multiplied by the specified quantities, add up to more (or less) than 1 unit of account, contradicting the unit's definition?

Our reassuring answer does not rest on a circular argument. We do suppose—but on empirical grounds, namely, the tremendous convenience of a generally employed unit of account—that people take the government-suggested unit seriously in expressing prices, debts, and accounts. That unit has no plausible rivals. In an ordinary monetary system, the unit in which the medium of exchange is denominated remains available as an alternative to any proposed commodity-bundle unit. The BFH system, however, happily lacks any homogeneous medium of exchange denominated in units of itself.

Suppose that the BFH bundle were defined as 1 apple + 1 banana + 1 cherry. Prices are to be paid and debts settled in bundles-worths of convenient payment property. Now apples are struck by a fungus. What market forces arise to accomplish the appropriate changes in relative prices while still enforcing the unit's definition?

We know that apples should rise in price relative to miscellaneous goods and services and to bananas and cherries also. By hypothesis, bundles are now more difficult to obtain. And if it is more difficult to come by a BFH bundle, then it is more difficult to come by anything worth a BFH bundle. People therefore offer bundles—or bundles-worths of payment property—less eagerly than before in trying to buy miscellaneous commodities, whose prices therefore fall relative to the bundle itself.

Now, the banana and the cherry, besides being components of the bundle, are themselves desired commodities. They therefore number among the goods for which people bid less eagerly in view of the hypothesized increased difficulty of obtaining bundles and so bundles-worths of payment property. The resulting fall in the prices of bananas and cherries counterbalances the increased unit-of-account price of apples.

This view of the market process that maintains the commodity-bundle definition of the unit of account emphasizes the advantages of defining the BFH bundle in a more comprehensive way. In our simple example of a three-fruit bundle, the general price level comes under substantial downward pressure when apples are attacked by the fungus. Such pressure, confronting sluggishly adjusting disequilibrium prices, can impede exchange and so impede production and employment. This impediment, however, is a consequence of utilizing such a narrowly defined bundle.

If the bundle were more widely defined, the undisturbed supply conditions of the other items composing it would mitigate the deflationary impact of the worsened apple-supply conditions. Bundles and bundles-worths of property would become only marginally more difficult to come by, and as a result, the general price level would come under only slight deflationary pressure. Thus, the wider the definition of the bundle, the greater the degree to which appropriate changes in relative price are effected by change in the unit-of-account price of any particular bundle component struck by altered supply or demand conditions. A widely defined bundle thus concentrates the impact of such changes, avoiding widespread and possibly painful repercussions.

The absence of convertibility of a familiar type lacks the ominous consequences that it might have in a monetary system with a homogeneous medium of exchange. Under the often-proposed composite-commodity standard, for example, in which the paper dollar is set equal in value to a certain bundle of commodities, tension arises between regarding the paper dollar and regarding the commodity bundle as the unit of account. In such a system, two-way convertibility must be maintained to prevent a divergence of the two units. The BFH system, however, lacking as it does any paper dollar that might rival the commodity bundle as the unit of account, never permits such tension to arise. Absence of a rival unit makes the BFH system's lack of convertibility of the usual sort irrelevant to the system's operationality and determinacy. Worries about lack of convertibility reflect an understandable but inappropriate carry-over of concepts suited to existing monetary systems instead.

The BFH system of sophisticated barter does seem to avoid the disadvantages both of crude barter and of money as we have known it. We postpone considering a transition to the BFH system. It is a type of reform whose success does not hinge on its early adoption. (In contrast, one might plausibly argue that delay in adopting the program of today's monetarists threatens to entrench a situation in which rapid institutional change and the blurring of the very concept of money will have made that program no longer workable.) Regardless of whether the BFH system ever is adopted, the proposal offers a fresh slant on some crucial aspects of actual monetary systems.

LITERATURE CITED

1. Black, Fischer. "Banking and Interest Rates in a World without Money." *Journal of Bank Research* (Autumn 1970), 8–20.

2. Eucken, Walter. *The Foundations of Economics.* Translated by T. W. Hutchison. London: Hodge, 1950.

3. Fama, Eugene F. "Banking in the Theory of Finance." *Journal of Monetary Economics,* 6 (1980), 39–57.

4. Fisher, Irving. *Stabilizing the Dollar.* New York: Macmillan, 1920.

5. Hall, Robert E. "The Government and the Monetary Unit." Unpublished manuscript, 1981.

6. _____. "Monetary Strategies for Ending Inflation." Contribution to a panel discussion chaired by Michael R. Darby and also including Eugene F. Fama, Milton Friedman, and Roy W. Jastram at the meetings of the Western Economic Association, San Francisco, July 5, 1981, recorded on cassette tapes 18A and 18B by Audio-Stats, Marina del Rey, California.

7. _____. "Explorations in the Gold Standard and Related Policies for Stabilizing the Dollar." In *Inflation: Causes and Effects,* edited by Robert E. Hall, pp. 111–22. Chicago: University of Chicago Press for National Bureau of Economic Research, 1982.

8. Hayek, Friedrich A. *The Sensory Order.* London: Routledge & Kegan Paul, 1952.

9. Rittershausen, Heinrich. *Bankpolitik.* Frankfurt: Knapp, 1956.

10. Schumpeter, Joseph A. *Das Wesen des Geldes.* Edited from manuscript (mostly drafted by around 1930) and with an introduction by Fritz Karl Mann. Göttingen: Vandenhoeck & Ruprecht, 1970.

11. Tobin, James. "Commercial Banks as Creators of 'Money.' " In *Banking and Monetary Studies,* edited by Deane Carson, pp. 408–19. Homewood, Ill.: Irwin, 1963.

12. Yeager, Leland B. "Essential Properties of the Medium of Exchange." *Kyklos,* 21 (1968), 45–69. Reprinted in *Monetary Theory: Selected Readings,* edited by Robert W. Clower, pp. 37–60. Baltimore: Penguin, 1969.

13. _____. "What Are Banks?" *Atlantic Economic Journal,* 6 (December 1978), 1–14.

14. _____. "Sticky Prices or Equilibrium Always?" Presented at the meetings of the Western Economic Association, San Francisco, July 7, 1981.

15. _____. "Stable Money and Free-Market Currencies." Paper for a Cato Institute Conference of January 21–22, 1983. *Cato Journal,* 6 (Spring 1983).

ADDENDUM

On page 303, we warned against misinterpretations. Yet they continue to occur, making us wish that we had done better – somehow – in forestalling them despite a tight space constraint. The tentative name 'BFH system' seems to have given some readers the impression that we claimed to be faithfully reporting and combining the ideas of Fischer *B*lack, Eugene *F*ama, and Robert *H*all and endorsing anything these authors might have written. As we clearly stated, however, we were merely trying to give them due credit as we picked and chose from among their ideas, altered them, extended them, and recombined them. We were perhaps too casual in echoing some of these authors' remarks about abolition of money, even though we were referring to absence of 'money as we now know it', especially the absence of any base money. We stressed that the BFH system 'would not entail the textbook inconveniences of barter'; and we did envision banknotes, deposits, and checks denominated in the unit of account. Perhaps we put too much emphasis, relatively, on the use of checkable equity funds whose values would fluctuate in terms of the unit of account (although we continue to believe that such funds would have appealing advantages). None of our claims about the BFH system depends in any important way on how voluminous checkable equity funds turn out relative to notes and deposits denominated in the unit of account.

Remarks about 'separation' or 'divorce' of the unit of account and medium of exchange did not rule out notes and deposits denominated in the unit of account. These remarks precluded a unit of account *defined* by a particular medium of exchange (such as a coin of definite gold or silver content or a dollar bill of government fiat money). Under the BFH system, the unit of account is defined independently of any particular medium of exchange. Even so, quite understandably, most issuers of media of exchange will choose to denominate their notes and deposits in the unit of account and will undertake convertibility commitments to keep that denomination meaningful.[1]

Recent discussions of a supposed paradox of indirect convertibility, foreshadowed by a 1919 article of Knut Wicksell,[2] have stressed supposedly perverse movements in the price of the medium of redemption and interbank settlements (which might be designated securities, as in our article, or might be gold or some other commodity). These mistaken discussions have diverted attention away from a more genuine potential problem of a system of indirect rather than direct convertibility, a problem that recommends a unit of account defined by a broad bundle of goods and services, including ones with inherently flexible prices, rather than a unit defined by only one or even a few commodities. The discussion centering on our example of an apple fungus pertains to this problem and to its being largely, if not entirely, solved by a broad instead of a narrow bundle. Had we been allotted the necessary space and had we foreseen the worries about indirect convertibility that would come to the fore, we would have amplified this discussion.

One detail: the definition of the meter in terms of the radiation of krypton has been superseded by a definition in terms of the speed of light; see any recent large dictionary.

NOTES

1. Leland B. Yeager, 'A Competitive Payments System: Some Objections Considered', *Journal of Post Keynesian Economics* 11, Spring 1989, pp. 370–377, tries to clear up misconceptions about this and related matters.
2. Knut Wicksell, 'Ett angrep på kvantitetsteorien', *Ekonomisk Tidschrift* 21, no. 3, 1919, pp. 57–63. A manuscript by W. William Woolsey and Leland B. Yeager addresses the question 'Is There a Paradox of Indirect Convertibility?'

[12]

Competitive Payments Systems and the Unit of Account

By Lawrence H. White*

Recent competitive innovations in payment mechanisms, particularly the checkable money market mutual fund, seem to have blurred the edges of the category of assets properly called "money." These innovations have coincided with new attempts by economists to reconstruct monetary theory and policy using competitive models. Several authors have conceived of competitive payments systems seemingly devoid of any outside currency, base money, or standard medium of exchange.[1] The unit of account in these systems is evidently not a common currency unit established outside the banking industry. Yet it can be argued that the use of a common unit of account in decentralized economic calculation presupposes a general medium of exchange.

Lance Girton and Don Roper have recently written: "One observes that most contractual obligations are specified in terms of the units in which the medium of exchange is measured. Further research should provide more insight into why contracts are specified in units in which the medium of exchange is measured" (1981, p. 20). This paper attempts to provide some insight into this question. By examining whether the above-mentioned cashless competitive payments systems are coherent and operational, it explores the fundamental relationship of the unit of

account to the medium of exchange. It specifically examines the plausibility of competition divorcing the unit in which prices are specified (the unit of account) from the medium in which payment is typically made. The argument concludes that a payments system not based on convertibility into an outside currency should not be expected to arise in the absence of government intervention.

I. Cashless Competitive Payments Systems: A Brief Survey

A. Black

The belief that unrestricted competition would produce a payments mechanism devoid of outside money is expressed already in the title of Fischer Black's 1970 article, "Banking and Interest Rates in a World Without Money: The Effects of Uncontrolled Banking." Black claims that in the world he imagines "money in the usual sense would not exist" (p. 9). Initially he assumes that no currency is used; later he allows for currency, but supposes that its nominal quantity will be purely demand-determined, so that it does not serve as an outside money forming a base for bank liabilities.[2] Payments are made by transfer of this currency and bank liabilities. No mention is made of the redeemability of bank liabilities for this currency or any basic physical monetary asset produced outside the banking industry. I will for brevity's sake refer to such an asset as "outside currency" or "cash."

What serves as the unit of account? Black cannot say "the currency unit," for that is supposed to be subsidiary to the unit in which bank liabilities are denominated. Instead he says: "Goods may be priced in

*Assistant Professor of Economics, New York University, 269 Mercer St., New York, NY 10003. I am indebted for discussion and comments to Robert Greenfield, Leland Yeager, Fischer Black, Joseph Salerno, members of the colloquium on Austrian economics at New York University, and an anonymous referee. Research support from the U.S. Choice in Currency Commission (a private foundation) is gratefully acknowledged. Responsibility for the views expressed is mine alone.

[1] Fischer Black (1970), Eugene Fama (1980; 1982), Robert Hall (1981; 1982a,b), Robert Greenfield and Leland Yeager (1983). At the other extreme, F. A. Hayek (1978) and Benjamin Klein (1974) have conceived of a great multiplicity of parallel base monies and standards. Criticism of the latter models is left implicit in what follows.

[2] Currency in this world is supposed to be issued by the government, but only on request of the banks, in exchange for reduction of government debt with the banks. For criticism, see fn. 16 below.

699

terms of a unit of account that does not fluctuate in value very much, and means of payment may be priced in terms of the same unit of account" (1970, p. 14). The unit of account in Black's world is clearly not an outside currency unit as it is in our world. It is instead apparently a unit of a distinct numeraire commodity (or bundle of commodities) that does not itself serve as the means of payment. This is indicated by the remark that the means of payment is to be *priced* in terms of the unit of account rather than the unit of account being *defined* in terms of the means of payment. Thus Black's system divorces the unit of account from the characteristic units of the system's exchange media.

It is not at all clear in terms of what numeraire commodity the unit of account would be defined in Black's world, or how that numeraire would be selected. He conducts a thought experiment in which the means of payment successively assumes five forms: 1) barter; 2) shares of common stock; 3) corporate bonds; 4) corporate bonds certified by "banks"; 5) pure bank liabilities. The passage quoted above appears in his discussion of the second stage. There it was clear that the hypothesized unit of account was not the characteristic unit of the hypothesized means of payment (a share of a stock portfolio). At no later state is this divorce mended.

The logic of Black's construction receives fuller criticism below. But the following curious feature of Black's exposition deserves mention here. He speaks of "the dollar price" of a medium-of-exchange unit and "the dollar price" of a commodity, with "the dollar" clearly intended to designate the unit of account. He suggests that transactors in his system may use these "dollar" prices for the purpose of computing a commodity's price in terms of the medium of exchange. Yet there is nothing called "dollars" actually being traded against the commodities in the system, hence no mechanism for registering the prices of those commodities in terms of dollars. There are no dollar prices established on markets logically or temporally prior to establishment of medium-of-ex-

change prices.[3] The problem here is not that the unit of account is divorced from the medium of exchange, but that it is totally abstract, divorced from any traded good. Such an abstract unit of account, as Don Patinkin indicates (1965, p. 16), can have no operational significance for market participants. It can be meaningful only to a Walrasian auctioneer or other outside observer.

B. *Fama*

Black's article went uncited in the literature for a decade, until the appearance of Eugene Fama's "Banking in the Theory of Finance."[4] Fama, like Black, considers outside money inessential to the competitive payments mechanism he hypothesizes. He posits a "pure accounting system of exchange" (p. 42) in which the function of banks is to operate "a system of accounts in which transfers of wealth are carried out with bookkeeping entries" (p. 39). This method of wealth transfer is asserted to be "entirely different" in relevant respects from the use of cash. Fama claims that the transactions industry in the world he examines can dispense entirely with cash: "An accounting system works through bookkeeping entries, debits and credits, which do not require any physical medium or the concept of money" (p. 39). This means that in Fama's world, as in Black's, bank liabilities need not constitute claims to cash: "In a pure accounting system of exchange, the notion of a physical medium or temporary abode of purchasing power disappears" (p. 42).

Unlike Black, Fama is explicit in stipulating that the unit of account in his world should be thought of as the unit of a commodity that plays no medium-of-exchange role: "it could well be tons of fresh cut beef or barrels of crude oil" (p. 43). He explicitly recognizes that bank "deposits"— which would be heterogeneous, being essen-

---

[3] I am indebted to Robert Greenfield for this point.

[4] This result of a search through the literature (by Fama) was personally reported to me by Bob Hall. It evidently excludes self-citations by Black.

tially shares in various mutual funds and not claims to a common currency—are not a suitable candidate for numeraire.

Prices of commodities are stated in terms of the numeraire. Fama recognizes that an economy of this sort "is basically non-monetary." There is no question of price-level determination: since there is no money commodity trading against other goods, there is no money price level. There are only numeraire or relative prices to be determined. The determination of relative prices is apparently to be thought of as a performance of the Walrasian auctioneer. Fama speaks of the system posing "a standard problem concerning the existence of a stable general equilibrium in a non-monetary system" (1980, p. 44).

Like Black, Fama leaves the particular numeraire commodity ("some real good") and its method of selection both unspecified. This is of no concern so long as we take the auctioneer construct seriously. The auctioneer's choice of a numeraire is of no consequence. But Fama implicitly slips out of this construct. He suggests that agents in his world face genuine calculational problems, and that they deal with one another in decentralized markets rather than with the auctioneer alone. He says of the accounting system of exchange, for instance, that "its efficiency is improved when all prices are stated in units of a common numeraire" (1980, p. 43).

After analyzing banking in a nonmonetary setting, Fama introduces currency in the form of "a non-interest-bearing fiat currency produced monopolistically by the government" (1980, p. 50). The unit in which currency is measured may then serve as the economy's numeraire. The real value of a currency unit in terms of goods and services is determined in familiar fashion, as a determinate demand for real currency balances confronts a fixed nominal stock of currency.

Fama suggests that banks in the world with currency provide a "currency convertibility service" for their customers. But it is unclear whether he means "convertibility" in the usual sense of an obligation to *redeem* deposits on demand for outside currency.

Banks taking on such an obligation have an inventory demand to hold currency as reserves against stochastic redemption outflows.[5] Limitation of the quantity of reserve currency available to the banks then limits the quantity of deposits that banks can prudently create. Fama states that banks would indeed "inventory currency on behalf of depositors" (1980, p. 50), but at the same time implicitly denies that the banks of an unregulated system would hold any non-interest-bearing reserves. Yet a bank's vault cash should be considered the primary component of its reserves where its deposits are convertible in the usual sense of constituting sight claims to predetermined quantities of currency.[6] By "convertibility," Fama must mean only that the banks act in the manner of money market mutual funds. Bank liabilities in his analysis are not claims to outside currency, as they are today, but are on the order of shares in a mutual fund's portfolio of interest-bearing assets. These funds (or Fama's "banks") stand ready to liquidate their shares (his "deposits") on demand by selling the assets to which the deposits constitute a claim and then turning over the proceeds to the shareholder ("depositor"). Fama is explicit in a more recent paper that this is what he envisions. He states that in his world: "Deposits are just claims against other claims (securities, loans, etc.)" (1982, p. 6). That is, they are not redeemable claims to outside currency. Fama's propositions that "deposits issued competitively should not be called money" and that "the concept of

[5]See Ernst Baltensperger (1980, pp. 4–6). In the competitive banking system of Scotland prior to 1844, to give a historical example, banks held positive quantities of specie as reserves against redemptions of liabilities despite the absence of reserve requirements and despite the fact, consistent with Fama's hypothesis of how a competitive system would operate, that the banks settled claims among themselves by transfer of readily marketable interest-bearing assets, namely Exchequer bills. On this episode, see my 1984 book, ch. 2.

[6]By "predetermined" I do not mean that deposit interest rates never vary, but that rates are contractually set before the period to which they apply. They are not calculated afterwards based on portfolio performance, as in the case of mutual fund shares. For further discussion, see Section IIIA below.

money plays no role in the transactions services accessed through deposits' (1982, p. 7) both rest on deposits not being claims to outside currency. The significance of the difference between such assets and deposits in the usual sense is explored below.

It is clear from the "parable" with which Fama concludes his earlier article (1980, pp. 55–56) that he regards the existence of outside money as unnecessary for the operation of an accounting system of exchange. Outside money is to him simply one commodity that, if it exists, may serve as numeraire; however, there is no need for it to exist. Steel ingots or spaceship permits may as well serve as numeraire. This result is arguably not true of any plausible world. There are compelling reasons, discussed below, for outside money to exist and to serve as the unit of account.

C. Hall

In two recent papers Robert Hall, searching for monetary policies consistent with stable prices and full deregulation of banking and financial markets, has questioned the necessity and desirability of associating the unit of account with a medium-of-exchange currency unit. Citing Fama (1980), Hall states: "It is possible to define the monetary unit [the unit of account] as one unit of a resource called currency, but this is only one of many different definitions" (1981, p. 4). In general the unit is simply "a certain amount of some resource" specified by government; the resource need not be currency. As an example of a noncurrency monetary unit, Hall proposes "defining" the dollar in terms of a composite-commodity unit called the *ANCAP*, consisting of specified physical quantities of ammonium nitrate, copper, aluminum, and plywood. Beyond defining the dollar in such a way, government is to play no role in the payments industry.

The *ANCAP* unit was chosen by Hall for its stable purchasing power over the last thirty years. Presumably this stability was measured in terms of some price index. An obvious question therefore arises: why does Hall not suggest defining the dollar directly in terms of the commodity bundle making up the price index he desires to stabilize? The answer lies in the mechanism he im-

plicitly relies on for tying the value of the unit-of-account dollar to the specified commodity bundle. Only the commodity bundle is to be legal tender for dollar obligations. This means that all holders of contractual claims to receive dollars (or of obligations to pay dollars) are entitled to demand (or make) payment in the physical commodities defining the dollar. Any sufficiently wide divergence between the market price of the standard commodity bundle and one dollar will trigger demands by creditors to receive commodities rather than paper dollars (or deliveries by debtors of commodities in place of paper dollars). Transactors choosing to contract in *ANCAP* dollars would be exposing themselves to the risk of being forced to deliver, or to accept delivery of, physical bundles of the standard commodities. Every transactor would be taking on bank-like obligations. It is natural to doubt that many transactors would voluntarily do so. An *ANCAP* obligation seems to be clearly dominated for both creditor and debtor by an obligation indexed to the *ANCAP* bundle but contractually payable in a common medium of exchange, that is, explicitly ruling out the commodity-delivery possibility, given that a common medium of exchange is by definition more readily accepted than other commodities. The creditor would rather receive, and the debtor rather pay, readily spendable money than a bundle of commodities of equal market value. It is less implausible to suppose that specialized bank-like institutions might issue *ANCAP*-redeemable obligations. The question that then arises, to be answered below, is whether such obligations would gain currency in an unregulated environment.

D. Greenfield and Yeager

A recent paper by Robert Greenfield and Leland Yeager attempts to elaborate more explicitly the possible operation of a competitive mutual-funds-type payments system devoid of outside money. They attribute the inspiration behind the cashless competitive payments system to the three authors whose works I have just surveyed. In Greenfield and Yeager's view of that world, bank-like mutual funds would develop and operate a

VOL. 74 NO. 4

sophisticated barter system (pp. 305–08). The unit of account would be an arbitrarily chosen numeraire bundle of commodities; the means of payment would be primarily shares of ownership in mutual fund portfolios. They explicitly affirm both the nonexistence of any outside money in which funds' liabilities are redeemable and the divorce of the unit of account from these media of exchange.

Greenfield and Yeager do not examine the question of whether such a system could emerge or survive under competitive conditions. They do consider whether the system's unit of account "has operational meaning" and whether "the level of prices expressed in that unit is determinate" (p. 313). In both cases, they find in the affirmative. But this merely means that they find the concept of keeping track of relative prices by use of a numeraire unit not incoherent or self-contradictory. It remains to be considered whether economic agents in an unregulated world without a central auctioneer would be likely to converge on use of a unit of account that is not a unit of outside currency.

II. Competitive Payments Systems in Evolutionary Perspective

In past and present monetary systems of our world, the generally accepted media of exchange have been and are units of outside money and inside-money claims to outside money. Inside money is naturally denominated in units of the cash to which it is a claim, as each banknote or bank deposit is a claim to a particular number of units of outside money. The distinguishing feature of outside money is that it does not constitute a redeemable claim to any physical asset. Whatever may be the bookkeeping conventions with regard to the issue of fiat money, as a form of outside money it is not in actual fact a contractual debt liability of any agent or institution. The world has known both commodity outside money—gold and silver coins provide the most familiar example—and fiat outside money. The latter typically originated as monopoly issued inside money whose redeemability was suspended after it had gained currency. In all cases the outside monetary unit naturally functions as the unit of account. This is because prices are natu-

rally quoted in the units of the solitary item (or set of items, identically denominated because secondary members of the set are claims to a primary member) whose payment will routinely be accepted in exchange.

To mount a critique of cashless payments systems, one must give reasons for the emergence and prevalence of outside money as a generally accepted medium of exchange and unit of account. The reasons given here delve back to the origins of money.

A. The Origin of Commodity Money

The classic invisible hand explanation of the emergence of money from an initial state of barter was give by Carl Menger (1982). Under barter, each agent, attempting to transform his initial endowment into his desired final consumption bundle through direct exchange, confronts the problem of finding a second agent who both offers for sale what the first wishes to buy and is willing to accept in payment what the first has to sell. The typical agent can achieve his goal more economically if, instead of searching for this rare or even nonexistent match, he exchanges his endowment for more widely acceptable commodities that he may in turn readily exchange for the goods he ultimately wishes to consume. Accordingly he accumulates a trading inventory of highly saleable items. These allow him to economize on search costs by raising the probability that he may, in any given number of samplings among sellers, make desired purchases. In this situation the superior saleability of certain items becomes self-reinforcing: the knowledge that other traders will accept an item with high probability raises its acceptability to each particular trader. A network of traders will therefore converge on one or a small number of items as general media of exchange. Their supreme saleability then distinguishes these items from all other commodities. They have spontaneously become money.[7] Historically gold and silver emerged as money in eco-

---

[7]For a modern version of this theory, see Robert Jones (1976). See also Ludwig von Mises (1971, pp. 30–34). Menger defines "saleability" more or less as the narrowness of the effective bid-ask spread, but construes this broadly to include spatial and temporal dimensions.

nomically advanced nations through this process.

It should be readily apparent by extension of this perspective on the origin of money that a unit of account emerges together with and wedded to a medium of exchange. A seller pursues his self-interest by posting prices in terms of the media of exchange he is routinely willing to accept. This practice economizes on time spent in negotiation over what commodities are acceptable in payment and at what rate of exchange. More importantly, it economizes on the information necessary for the buyer's and the seller's economic calculation. Posting prices in terms of a numeraire commodity not routinely accepted in payment, by contrast, would force buyer and seller to know and agree upon the numeraire price of the payment media due. This numeraire price of the payment medium would naturally be subject to fluctuation, so that updated information would be necessary. A non-exchange-medium numeraire commodity would furthermore be subject to greater bid-ask spreads in barter against other commodities, as by hypothesis it is less saleable, than the medium of exchange. It would therefore serve less well as a tool of economic calculation.

It is worth emphasizing, as Menger emphasized with respect to the genesis of a general medium of exchange, that a collective decision is in no way necessary for the emergence of a clearly defined common unit of account. This point seems to have escaped those authors who consider monetary units to be the creatures of government proclamations.

B. *Coinage*

The evolution of monetary institutions does not, of course, stop with the emergence of commodity money. One may trace out further steps that take place in an unregulated competitive environment. Supposing that gold has emerged as primary money, the next logical step is economization of the costs of using the metal in transactions accomplished by the institution of coinage. Coined metal enjoys greater acceptability than uncoined metal (for example, gold dust)

due to the lower cost of determining its true bullion content. The ease of authentication is still further enhanced by the institution of brand names in minting: once a mint's products are trusted to be of the weight and fineness stated on their face, its coins may pass by tale. Transactors may then forego weighing and assaying each piece of metal tendered in payment. The demand for readily authenticated pieces of gold will therefore give rise to a market in minting services. Each mint strives to maintain a reputation for uniformly high quality, lest it lose customers to its rivals by imposing higher authentication costs.[8] In competitive equilibrium, the mintage fee will be just sufficient to earn each minter the normal rate of return on investment. Self-interest will lead all mints in an economy to denominate coins in terms of a unit of standard weight and fineness. A mint doing otherwise would inconvenience its customers. The precise definition of the unit is itself unimportant; it may be based on preexisting custom in measuring the bullion content of uncoined gold, or it may be adopted from the coinage of an early reputable mint. This unit then serves as the unit of account.

Competitive private minting industries have been comparatively rare historically. Governments have typically monopolized the supply of minting services. In a noncompetitive situation, where debased government-issued coins circulate, the bullion content of an earlier full-weight coin may continue to serve as unit of account though no existing coin measures up to that content. This is the phenomenon of "ghost money," which is sometimes misleadingly cited as an example of divorce between the unit of account and

---

[8] For examples of this process at work in the United States, where some three dozen private mints operated in the gold rush regions of the nineteenth century, see Donald Kagin (1981). Black (1972, p. 811) inaccurately identifies privately minted coins as a form of inside money. Armen Alchian's (1977) account of the selection of a commodity money relies solely on economization of authentication costs. In my view, this explains the emergence of standardized forms of money, but as far as the origin of money itself goes is subsidiary to economization of search costs through holding of highly saleable commodities. Easy authentication is simply one among several properties contributing to ready saleability.

the medium of exchange.[9] In fact, the unit of account and the medium of exchange both continue to be quantities of gold. The unit-of-account value of any particular coin in circulation is a question of its weight and fineness, not of variable market exchange rates. The unit of account and medium of exchange have not become distinct commodities, only distinct quantities of the same commodity. The informational difficulties posed by a non-payment-medium numeraire, whose exchange value may vary in terms of payment media, do not arise. The minor inconvenience that does arise may be attributed to the absence of competitive conditions. Under competitive conditions, a debasing mint would find that money users reject its products in favor of full-weight coins.

C. Bank Liabilities

The emergence of precious metals as money, and subsequently of coins as their common form, comes about in a free economy as the undesigned outcome of decentralized pursuit of self-interest. The genesis of inside monies may be similarly explained. Bank liabilities originate as claims to specie deposited with bankers (hence the term deposits; Fama's use of this term to denote money market fund shares is misleading). In medieval Italy the first bankers were money changers; in London they were goldsmiths.

Claims to specie assume a monetary character when bankers discover profit in the business of effecting the payments one depositor wishes to make to another by direct transfer of bank balances from the one to the other. Checks are today the common means of signalling the bank to perform a transfer of balances, but the emergence of paperless electronic means would do nothing to change

the essential nature of the transaction. Banknotes—claims to bank specie transferable without bank intervention and payable to the bearer on demand—similarly emerge as a means of payment.[10] Banknotes naturally find the greatest acceptance when denominated as round multiples of the specie unit that has previously become the standard unit of account. Money users find each form of redeemable claim to bank specie more economical to use for many purposes than actual specie. Bankers are recompensed for providing these instruments by the interest they earn on assets corresponding to the fraction of their liabilities not matched by specie on their balance sheets, or (in the case of deposits) by direct fees for the transfer service. In an unregulated system, the banks pay competitive rates of interest on their deposits. Due to the costliness of doing so, they are unlikely to pay interest on their notes.[11]

An invisible hand process can be shown (see my book, pp. 19–22) to account for the emergence of an interbank clearinghouse in a competitive banking system. Briefly, each member of a pair of banks profitably enhances the moneyness of its notes and deposits relative to specie by agreeing to accept one another's notes and deposits at face value as tendered by customers for deposit or loan repayment. Mutual acceptance of liabilities is naturally accompanied by an arrangement for periodic settlement of the claims each bank collects against the other. The potential gains from these pairwise arrangements are not exhausted until all banking companies in a region belong to a single clearinghouse system.

Members of the clearinghouse will, in the absence of regulation, be able to economize on specie transhipments by settling balances partly through the transfer of highly marketable interest-bearing assets. Specie redeemability remains essential to the economical functioning of the mutual acceptance ar-

[9]On "ghost monies," see Carlo Cipolla (1956, ch. 4). The misleading claim that these represent abstract units of account is made by Patinkin (p. 15). While it is true that a ghost money unit had no exact counterpart among existing coins, each of these coins bore a fixed value relationship to the unit based on relative bullion content. For purposes of pricing and calculation, the situation was similar in kind to that prevailing today in the Italian monetary system, where no one-lira coin or note circulates.

[10]On the early history of European banking, see Raymond de Roover (1956, ch. 5).
[11]See my book (pp. 8–9). Fama (1982, pp. 14–15) comes to the same conclusion for currency that is not a claim to outside money. Note that today's traveler's checks do not bear interest.

rangement, however, as the means by which all bank liabilities have their value fixed in terms of the unit of account. The acceptance of their notes at fixed par values spares banks' customers—and the banks themselves—exchange risk and calculational inconvenience, and is therefore integral to the function of acceptance arrangements in enhancing the moneyness of the participating banks' liabilities.

A competitive banking system of the following sort thus emerges in the absence of regulation. The stock of exchange media consists of specie in the hands of the public plus numerous brands of redeemable banknotes plus transferable bank deposits. The self-interest of issuers insures that notes circulate at par, that is, at unit-of-account values fully equal to the number of specie units to which they are claims.[12] Transferable deposits bear a competitive rate of interest, subject to competitive charges for transfer services. The nominal quantities of specie, notes, and transferable deposits held by the public are determined not by any central bank regulation of the monetary base, but by the real demand to hold those assets divided by the purchasing power of specie. Each bank's holdings of specie reserves are determined by its equating at the margin the cost of foregone interest to the benefit of reduced risk of illiquidity. Total specie reserves are simply a summation of these holdings across banks.[13]

The transition from a specie-based competitive banking system to a fiat-currency-based system is most readily made in two steps: government creation of a central bank, whose specie-redeemable liabilities displace specie as a commercial bank reserve asset; and suspension of redeemability for central bank liabilities. The supply of banking

services may continue to be competitive, but the nominal quantity of money is now scaled to central bank determination of the monetary base.

Note what happens to the unit of account in the transition to fiat money. At no point does it cease to be defined in units of the basic outside-money medium of exchange. The status of basic medium of exchange, however, passes from specie alone to a straddle between specie and a redeemable central bank currency denominated in specie units (dollars, pounds sterling, etc.), then to the no-longer-redeemable central bank currency (still bearing the same name) alone. In this way the economy arrives at a situation in which a noncommodity outside money has positive exchange value. Paper money is able to function as the basic medium of exchange because it previously functioned as a secondary medium of exchange.[14]

III. Cashless Competitive Payments Systems: Critique

In light of the evolution of money and banking, the problem confronting models of noncurrency-based payments systems is clear. Their applicability for modeling current institutions or predicting future arrangements awaits a coherent account of how a cashless system is consistent with or might emerge from the currency-based payments systems the world has known. This is not to deny that such models may serve to illuminate the monetary institutions of our world by contrast to the abstraction of a world without outside money. This is a use to which Greenfield and Yeager deliberately put their model. It is a role Fama may also have in mind, as he later introduces outside currency to his model after first abstracting from it. In a way, the models play this role in the present discussion: I hope to illuminate the importance of the causal-genetic processes behind monetary institutions, particularly the unit of account, by contrast to models seemingly inconsistent with these processes.

[12] That banknotes fell below par when they crossed state borders—reflecting risk and transportation costs of accomplishing redemption—in the American "free banking" era was due to the legal prohibition on interstate branch banking. In the freer Scottish system, no such inconvenience was experienced.

[13] This system is spelled out in my book (ch. 1). The statement of marginal conditions in the text assumes equal marginal operating costs of holding various assets. The basic paradigm of bank optimization is set forth by Baltensperger.

[14] This historical account may explain the fact that intrinsically useless fiat money has positive value more plausibly than the overlapping generations model of fiat money. For that model, see Neil Wallace (1980).

A. The Disappearance of Demand Deposits

Could a monetary system based on outside currency (specie or fiat currency) spontaneously evolve into a cashless competitive payments system of the sort envisioned by Black, Fama, and Greenfield-Yeager? Three steps are necessary to make the transition: 1) disappearance of redeemable inside money; 2) disappearance of outside money; and 3) redefinition of the unit of account in terms of a numeraire other than outside money. This section considers the first of these steps. For expositional convenience it focuses on demand deposits, though in the past banknotes have also been important as inside money. The term inside money here denotes ready claims to outside currency. These are distinct from shares in a managed portfolio of assets.

Fama envisions a world in which "competitive unregulated banks provide a wide variety of portfolios against which depositors can hold claims" (1982, p. 15). Bank deposits no longer constitute claims to cash, in other words, but are instead akin to transferable shares in mutual funds and hence "can be tailored to have the characteristics of any form of marketable wealth" (Fama, 1980, p. 43). Fama unfortunately fails to show that the outcome of unregulated competition would be the total domination of interest-bearing demand deposits by mutual fund shares. In fact this outcome is unlikely, even apart from the question of which can provide payments services more efficiently. Demand deposits, being ready debt claims, are potentially superior to mutual fund shares, which are equity claims, in at least one respect. The value of a deposit may be contractually guaranteed to increase over time at a preannounced rate of interest. Its unit-of-account value at a future date is certain so long as the bank continues to honor its obligation to redeem its deposits on demand. No such contractual guarantee may be made with respect to an equity claim. A mutual fund is obligated to pay out after the fact its actual earnings, so that the yield on fund shares cannot be predetermined. In the absence of deposit rate ceiling regulation, the range of anticipated possible returns from holding

fund shares need not lie entirely above the deposit interest rate. Risk-diversifying portfolio owners might therefore not divest themselves entirely of demand deposits even given a higher mean yield on mutual funds. It is true that the characteristic pledge of money market mutual funds to maintain a fixed share price, or rather the policy of investing exclusively in short-term highly reputable securities so that the pledge can be kept, makes fund shares akin to demand deposits in having near-zero risk of negative nominal yield over any period. The difference between predetermined and postdetermined yields—between debt and equity—nonetheless remains. The historical fact is that deposit banking did not naturally grow up on an equity basis.[15]

The more important reason why demand deposits would survive even under unregulated competition is that the payments system they provide is, given the conditions that lead to the emergence of money, less costly. This cost differential is suggested by the fact that a checkable money market fund today typically imposes a $500 minimum on checks written against shares in the fund. The comparative costliness of check writing against money market funds in their present form arises from the fact that checks written against a fund require it either 1) to incur the transactions costs of selling securities plus the cost of transmitting the receipts to the payee, or 2), what is presumably less costly and the method actually used, to draw against a demand deposit with a commercial bank held as one of the fund's assets.[16] In the latter case, it is evident that effecting a payment by writing a check against a fund, which in turn draws down its demand deposit, must be more costly than directly

---

[15] Though there was medieval banking in which bank deposits were treated as equity claims, this treatment was devised to evade church and state prohibitions against the payment of interest on debt. Again see de Roover (pp. 201–02).

[16] All funds whose prospectuses I have examined hold a small percentage of their assets (less than 1 percent) in the form of a demand deposit with a commercial bank for the purpose of honoring redemption checks (and purchasing securities).

effecting the payment by writing a check against the payer's own demand deposit. In the present world the checkable money market fund rides piggyback upon the banking system.

The check writing feature of money market mutual funds relies on a money-transfer system for the obvious reason that sellers of commodities generally wish to be paid in money and not in other assets. Checks written on a money market fund are generally acceptable in payment only because to the recipient they represent a transfer of inside money, that is, of cash-redeemable bank deposits. Its unique acceptability as a routine means of payment is, as we have seen, an essential property conferred on money by the Mengerian convergence process that engenders money. Every form of marketable wealth could serve generally as a medium of exchange only in a world where all forms of wealth begin and remain equally marketable. Outside a Walrasian general equilibrium setting, this is difficult to imagine.

There are no obstacles in principle to the spontaneous emergence of an interfund clearing system that does not rely on transfers of inside money. If mutual funds really could provide payments services efficiently, it would be natural to expect money market funds in the present system, unless prevented by law, to begin announcing bilateral or multilateral arrangements to permit check writing in any amount for purposes of transferring wealth to accounts in participating funds. By this device, each participating fund would enhance the spendability and hence desirability of its shares relative to nonparticipating shares and demand deposits. As yet this has not happened. At present, money market funds rarely allow check writing for unlimitedly small amounts, even for transfer of shares to another customer of the same fund. This is difficult to reconcile with the idea that fund shares are so routinely acceptable that they could dominate inside money as a means of payment.

This argument does not rule out mutual funds developing a money-transfer system and allowing cash withdrawals, or what would be identical, banks offering checkable mutual fund accounts with direct access to

an interbank clearing mechanism. The analytical question in this case—why money-transfer and cash-inventory services should be jointly produced with deposits at lower cost than with mutual fund shares—awaits further research. But it seems clear that the major impetus to the use of mutual funds for check writing purposes, a use negligible before 1974, has been Regulation Q's prohibition of competitive interest rates on checkable bank deposits. With this ceiling largely lifted, the rationale for joining money-tranfer services to mutual funds has largely disappeared.[17]

In a model competitive payments system devoid of cash or genuine demand deposits, payments effected via check writing against fund shares obviously do not work by transfers of money. Instead a check written against Fund A in favor of a customer of Fund B is supposed to occasion a transfer of nonmonetary assets from Fund A to Fund B via a clearing arrangement (Greenfield-Yeager, p. 307). These two funds must have previously entered a mutual acceptance arrangement of the sort (described earlier) arising in a free banking system. The clearing mechanism has to be slightly different, however, in the following respect. Fund B, in accepting checks written on Fund A, does not possess a claim to Fund A's vault cash of a specific quantity. Instead Fund B possesses a claim to Fund A's assets of a specific value. Checks are written, and interbank clearing balances computed in units of account, as at present. But a check no longer transfers a claim to so many physical units of outside currency; it instead transfers ownership of earning assets with a market value of so much. The interfund clearing arrangement has to specify

---

[17]Two caveats are in order. 1) The 1982 Garn-St. Germain Act authorizing Super NOW accounts (checking accounts with no legal interest ceiling) denies these accounts to business firms, leaving firms a reason for using money market fund or sweep accounts for check writing. 2) So long as demand deposits are in effect taxed by the imposition of reserve requirements, there remains a rationale for hybrid accounts. The reason why money market mutual funds (like banks) do not price their money-transfer services explicitly may be found in the taxation of explicit interest but nontaxation of gratuitous services.

VOL. 74 NO. 4 WHITE: COMPETITIVE PAYMENTS SYSTEMS 709

what types of assets are acceptable in settlement of adverse balances. So does an interbank clearing arrangement if it is to economize on physical transfers of non-interest bearing currency, of course, but this does not reduce its reliance on cash redeemability as the means by which the unit-of-account value of bank liabilities is fixed and their general acceptability maintained.

An apparent disadvantage of bank deposits in the form of ready claims to predetermined quantities of currency, in contrast to fund shares, is the possibility that a bank might become insolvent and thereby unable to honor all the claims presented to it for redemption. (Illiquidity is no greater problem for a bank than for a mutual fund that allows check writing and cash withdrawals.) A mutual fund cannot become insolvent: as it issues no liabilities in the strict sense, but only equities, it cannot have liabilities in excess of its assets. A money market fund can legally break its pledge to maintain a fixed share price if a sharp fall in the value of its assets makes a reduction necessary. A bank lacks the flexibility to reduce its deposit liabilities in a similar way without going into bankruptcy. In a *laissez-faire* monetary system, bank deposits would not be government insured. Depositor fears of insolvency might be adequately addressed, however, by high capital-asset ratios, by private deposit insurance, by forms of organization giving the bank's stockholders extended personal liability for its debts, or by some other means.[18] Hence it is not obvious that checkable mutual funds would dominate demand deposits on grounds of lesser risk. The debt form of deposits does insulate depositors from sharing in portfolio losses that leave equity positive.

The difference between demand deposits and fund shares, and the plausible nondisappearance of the former under freely competitive conditions, requires the revision of several propositions put forth by Fama (1982, pp. 2–8). 1) While outside currency and fund shares are indeed not perfect substitutes whose supplies may with any obvious sense be aggregated, and while outside currency and demand deposits are also not perfect substitutes, demand deposits (and banknotes) may sensibly be aggregated with outside currency held by the nonbank public in a measure of the quantity of money. The econometric use of this aggregate is a separate question. 2) The supply of demand deposits will likely be important in the determination of the price level for a closed economy with a competitive unregulated banking system. Even if the determination of the price level in that economy is most appropriately modeled in terms of the supply and demand for outside money alone, demand deposits are presumably a close substitute on the demand side. 3) The concept of money clearly does play a role in the transactions services made available through demand deposits. 4) A bank using the clearing mechanism of an unregulated banking system holds claims against the cash reserves of other banks, not against their portfolios.[19]

B. *The Disappearance of Outside Money*

Might outside money disappear with the evolution of competitive payments mechanisms? This boils down to the question of the disappearance of outside currency. In the present American banking system, the deposits of member banks with the Federal Reserve may be regarded as a form of outside money (though they are claims to Federal Reserve notes, their quantity is not regulated by the existing quantity of those notes). This form of outside money is an artifact of regulation, however; in an unregulated banking system with a private clearing mechanism and no central bank, outside currency (say, specie or fiat currency) would be the only form of outside money.

The authors whose models have been considered here all recognize that currency will continue in use so long as manual transfer of

---

[18] Unlimited liability was a feature of the Scottish free banking system. Depositors' losses due to bank insolvencies were completely negligible, as failures were rare and the losses fell upon shareholders.

[19] Only the last of these sentences rectifies an incorrect statement Fama makes about a banking system. The others contrast a banking system to his characterization of a payments system operated by mutual funds.

currency remains the least costly method for accomplishing certain transactions. Not only is currency 1) more convenient to use in small payments, but 2) its acceptance, unlike acceptance of personal checks, entails no risk that the payer's funds may be insufficient, and 3) its use leaves behind no possibly incriminating records of payment. These authors all think it coherent, however, to suppose that all currency is inside currency. Pieces of such currency would be akin to banknotes, except that they would constitute claims against the portfolios of the issuing funds rather than claims to cash.[20]

Cashlessness has an important implication. Bonds in the cashless world cannot be what they are in our world, claims to future streams of money payments. They must rather be claims to future payments of commodities or to other financial assets. These other financial assets must be equities or shares in a mutual fund portfolio of equities, as it would be circular for bonds to be exclusively claims to other bonds, either directly or indirectly via money market fund shares in bond portfolios. The present value of bonds in the cashless world must then be the discounted value of the commodities or equities to be received in future payments. This clearly would make bond pricing much more difficult than it is in our world were the future payments to be defined in units of the commodities or equities to be paid. Greenfield and Yeager understandably suggest that the quantity of payment property (as they call it, p. 313) to be received would be specified, like all other contractual payments, in numeraire value units rather than in the physical own-units of the property. Coupon payments would proceed in commodities or equities of specified worth in terms of the

numeraire. The bondholder nonetheless receives payment in commodities or equities. In general he will wish to sell these rather than hold his wealth in their form, so that he will prefer bonds whose coupon payments are made in the most readily saleable form of property. In our world the most saleable property is money; in the cashless world it is supposed to be shares in mutual fund bond portfolios. But this, as I have noted, creates a circularity problem. Hence one of two outcomes is possible: either bondholders are saddled with relatively high transactions costs in unloading payment property, or bond portfolio shares are not the dominant means of payment. In the latter case, say where shares in a mutual fund portfolio of common stocks were instead the dominant means of payment, the numeraire value of exchange-medium holdings would clearly be subject to significant fluctuation.

The natural question to ask from an evolutionary perspective is whether there is any plausible reason for outside currency to disappear in a payments system freed from anticompetitive regulation. I have explained above that the emergence of particular commodities as money is not wholly accidental, but a consequence of their superior saleability. Black (1970, p. 14) hypothesizes the use of shares of a portfolio of common stock as money, that is, as a generally accepted medium of exchange. There are good reasons, however, to doubt that such an item would ever become the most saleable in an economy. The primary reason is that the institution of common stock is unlikely to arise in a premonetary economy because the division of labor it presupposes would not exist there. Even were stock shares to emerge in a barter economy, it is difficult to conceive of their being more saleable than the most widely saleable of commodities. Arising in an already monetized economy (this is Black's scenario), shares of stock are from the outset routinely sold against money and not against any other good. They lack the saleability of money. And this inferior saleability is self-reinforcing: no trader routinely accepts shares of stock or shares of a portfolio of stocks when he cannot expect to be able to spend them easily. Each trader finds the use

---

[20]Fama (1982, pp. 9–11) and Greenfield-Yeager (pp. 307–08) clearly envision currency issued exclusively by mutual funds. Black (1970, pp. 13–14) introduces government-issued currency, but erroneously believes that the nominal quantity of this currency will be endogenously determined. He apparently fails to see or denies that an excess of supply of government currency at a given level of prices will be worked off through a rise in prices, not through retirement of the excess currency. In another paper (1972), Black advances a doctrine of the passivity of outside money.

of shares an inefficient medium of exchange due to high information and search costs. The "inefficiencies" of commodity money cited by Black would exceed the inefficiencies of common stock money only in a world in which common stock approached the saleability of commodity money.

For analogous reasons it should be apparent that a commodity reserve currency system, in which the basic money is redeemable for a basket of nonmonetary commodities, would not arise spontaneously in an unregulated setting. A claim to a basket of commodities would not originally emerge as money, since in a barter setting it would be less saleable then the most saleable of its components. Nor would it supplant the original monetary commodity. This is not to deny, however, that one money (say, silver or domestic fiat currency) may be spontaneously supplanted by another (say, gold or foreign fiat currency) in a region where both have been circulating internally, or where external trade with neighboring regions is conducted in their different money. A switch may come about because the transactions conducted in the second money grow in relative importance, or because the first money experiences an exogenously caused ongoing relative decline in purchasing power.

C. The Divorce of the Unit of Account from the Medium of Exchange

For reasons already suggested, a unit of account emerges wedded to a general medium of exchange. Prices are universally posted in the characteristic units of a medium or set of media that sellers are routinely prepared to accept in exchange. This process is self-reinforcing: a buyer or seller who communicated bid or ask offers in nonstandard units would impose calculation costs on potential trading partners. For this reason the unit of account remains wedded to the medium of exchange.

In an inflationary environment it is certainly possible for a unit of stable purchasing power to dispace the depreciating currency unit as the unit of account voluntarily adopted in contracts calling for payments at future dates. An example of a stable unit would be the "constant dollar" defined by a

base-year price index. There is no tendency for spot prices to be indexed in this way, however. Indeed the perpetuation of non-indexed spot prices is presupposed by indexing, which uses current nominal prices to compute the current-dollar equivalent of a constant-dollar sum.

The unit of account sticks with the medium of exchange even through the transition from commodity-based to fiat currency. A historical example is instructive here. In the suspension period of the Napoleonic Wars, 1797–1819 in Britain, Bank of England notes and deposits became the basic outside money.[21] Gold coins ceased to circulate. The unit of account, the pound sterling, stuck with the actual medium of exchange rather than with a now-abstract gold definition. The pounds-sterling price of gold fluctuated rather than the pounds-sterling price of Bank of England notes. Commodity prices rose with the expansion of Bank of England notes and deposits, while the unit-of-account value of a banknote or deposit remained fixed.

IV. Conclusion

In a decentralized and unregulated economy in which all property is not equally saleable, outside money emerges as most the saleable commodity and persists as a general medium of exchange. Inside monies arise and persist on the basis of their convertibility into outside money. The characteristic unit of outside money naturally defines the unit of account, as prices are natually posted by traders in terms of the item sellers will routinely accept in payment.

In a Walrasian world where the auctioneer renders all commodities equally saleable, and therefore equally suitable for use in indirect exchange, payment in any commodity could be accepted indifferently. Tatonnement may proceed without outside money. Any commodity or bundle of commodities could serve as unit of account, the auctioneer's choice of a unit of account being unconstrained by any economic considerations. The payments

[21] Technically they were not fiat money since resumption at a later data was both anticipated and realized. In von Mises' (p. 483) terminology they were credit money.

712   *THE AMERICAN ECONOMIC REVIEW*   *SEPTEMBER 1984*

system appropriate for such a world, however, is inappropriate in the present world of decentralized trade involving goods of unequal marketability. The convenience of traders in the present world dictates outside money whose units define the unit of account. Deregulation of the payments system in the present world does not imply disappearance of outside money, nor divorce of the unit of account from the basic outside-money medium of exchange.

REFERENCES

Alchian, Armen, "Why Money?," *Journal of Money, Credit and Banking*, February 1977, *9*, 133–40.

Baltensperger, Ernst, "Alternative Approaches to the Theory of the Banking Firm," *Journal of Monetary Economics*, January 1980, *6*, 1–37.

Black, Fischer, "Banking and Interest Rates in a World Without Money: The Effects of Uncontrolled Banking," *Journal of Bank Research*, Autumn 1970, *1*, 9–20.

_____, "Active and Passive Monetary Policy in a Neoclassical Model," *Journal of Finance*, September 1972, *27*, 801–14.

Cipolla, Carlo M., *Money, Prices, and Civilization in the Mediterranean World: Fifth to Seventeenth Century*, Princeton: Princeton University Press, 1956.

de Roover, Raymond, *Business, Banking, and Economic Thought in Late Medieval and Early Modern Europe*, Chicago: University of Chicago Press, 1956.

Fama, Eugene F., "Banking in the Theory of Finance," *Journal of Monetary Economics*, January 1980, *6*, 39–57.

_____, "Fiduciary Currency and Commodity Standards," mimeo., January 1982.

Girton, Lance and Roper, Don, "Theory and Implications of Currency Substitution," *Journal of Money, Credit and Banking*, February 1981, *13*, 12–30.

Greenfield, Robert L. and Yeager, Leland B., "A Laissez Faire Approach to Monetary Stability," *Journal of Money, Credit and Banking*, August 1983, *15*, 302–15.

Hall, Robert E., "The Government and the Monetary Unit," mimeo., 1981.

_____, (1982a) "Explorations in the Gold Standard and Related Policies for Stabilizing the Dollar," in his *Inflation: Causes and Effects*, Chicago: University of Chicago Press, 1982.

_____, (1982b) "*Monetary Trends in the United States and the United Kingdom*: A Review from the Perspective of New Developments in Monetary Economics," *Journal of Economic Literature*, December 1982, *20*, 1552–56.

Hayek, F. A., *Denationalisation of Money*, 2d ed., London: Institute of Economic Affairs, 1978.

Jones, Robert A., "The Origin and Development of Media of Exchange," *Journal of Political Economy*, November 1976, *84*, 757–75.

Kagin, Donald H., *Private Gold Coins and Patterns of the United States*, New York: Arco Publishing, 1981.

Klein, Benjamin, "The Competitive Supply of Money," *Journal of Money, Credit and Banking*, November 1974, *6*, 423–53.

Menger, Carl, "On the Origin of Money," *Economic Journal*, June 1982, *2*, 239–55.

Patinkin, Don, *Money, Interest, and Prices*, 2d ed., New York: Harper & Row, 1965.

von Mises, Ludwig, *The Theory of Money and Credit*, rev. ed., Irvington-on-Hudson: Foundation for Economic Education, 1971.

Wallace, Neil, "The Overlapping Generations Model of Fiat Money," in John H. Kareken and Neil Wallace, eds., *Models of Monetary Economies*, Minneapolis: Federal Reserve Bank of Minneapolis, 1980.

White, Lawrence H., *Free Banking in Britain: Theory, Experience, and Debate, 1800–1845*, Cambridge: Cambridge University Press, 1984.

[13]

Competitive Payments Systems: Comment

By ROBERT L. GREENFIELD AND LELAND B. YEAGER*

In the September 1984 issue of this *Review*, Lawrence H. White criticizes several recent proposals for monetary reform, including what we (1983) call the BFH system. Under this system, the government, precluded from issuing money, would merely define a new unit of account and encourage the unit's general adoption by using it in all its own, pricing, contracting, and accounting. The definition would run in terms of so comprehensive a bundle of precisely gradable items with continuously quoted prices that the new unit would have a stable general purchasing power.

According to White, our considering that the system's unit of account has operational meaning merely means that we "find the concept of keeping track of relative prices by use of a numeraire unit not incoherent or self-contradictory" (p. 703). But we see in the unit's operationality more than just the calculations of Walras's auctioneer. We use the term "operational" after having satisfied ourselves that in the course of honest-to-goodness market activity, the unit denominating privately issued notes and deposits would pose no threat of prying itself loose from its commodity-bundle definition. The absence of any dominant medium of exchange, or "cashlessness", to use White's term, ensures their adhesion.

The danger of the commodity-bundle-defined unit of account's falling into desuetude would exist if all things serving as media of exchange were essentially indistinguishable from one another. Quantities of a homogeneous medium of exchange would be measurable in a common unit distinct from the actual commodity bundle; and that common unit, the medium-of-exchange unit, might indeed rival the commodity bundle

itself as the unit of account. But under the BFH system, which would eschew government money, no such single homogeneous medium of exchange would exist, so no tension could arise between regarding a unit of it and regarding the commodity-bundle-defined unit as the unit of account. Notes and demand deposits, as well as checkable *equity* holdings in the institutions issuing them, would be distinguishable by their private issuers, who individually would face competitive pressures to keep their obligations *meaningful*.

These pressures would come to a focus at the clearinghouse. Convenience would dictate, however, that in settling clearinghouse balances due on account of notes and checks (checks drawn on both deposits and equity holdings), issuers transfer not quantities of the standard bundle itself, but redemption property *worth* as many standard bundles as the number of units to be settled. Issuers would thus keep their obligations meaningful by making them "indirectly" convertible, convertible into "bundles-worths," and so prevent the unit of account from losing contact with its commodity-bundle definition.

While retaining and enhancing the advantages of a single definite pricing and accounting unit and convenient methods of payment, the BFH system would avoid the absurdity of a unit of account whose size is the supply-and-demand-determined value of any medium of exchange. With the unit of account and media of exchange separated, the unit's value would be established by definition, leaving the quantities of the various media of exchange directly responsive to the demands for them. No longer could there be too much money, causing inflation, too little money, causing depression, or a temporal sequence of imbalances, causing stagflation.

Somehow thinking that we expect unit-of-account-denominated deposits to disappear even while outside money continues to

*Fairleigh Dickinson University, Madison, NJ 07940 and Auburn University, Auburn, AL 36849, respectively.

exist, White emphasizes today's "comparative costliness of check writing against money market funds" (p. 707). The BFH system, however, would dispense with outside money, from whose dominance that cost differential—if indeed one actually exists—might spring. People could choose between checkable equity holdings and checkable unit-denominated deposits. We conjecture that the former would play a prominent role, but the logic of the BFH system in no way presupposes their displacing unit-denominated deposits.

White (p. 710) says that deregulation does not imply the disappearance of outside money. Needless to say, it does not. But not only does he seem to say (p. 712) that we think it does, he considers "cashlessness" itself to do some violence to the very institution of credit. In White's view (p. 710), the BFH system is circular somehow, because bonds and interest on them are supposedly payable, ultimately, only in shares in portfolios of bonds. (Actually, we expect checks on equity funds to be used in payments also, but that is a side point only.)

What trouble does the supposed circularity cause? If White thinks the BFH system suffers from circularity, what does he think of our existing system, in which bonds are payable only in money—pieces of paper not payable in anything at all? Is White consoled because those pieces of paper count as outside money? In both the BFH system and our existing system, bondholders receive interest and repayment of principal in property, typically paper assets, that they can exchange for desired goods and services. (The processes that give actual exchange value to this payment property differ between the two systems, but that is a minor detail in-

sofar as White's tacitly taking redeemability as the criterion of noncircularity is concerned.) The longer people wait to consume goods and services, the more they can ultimately consume. That is what interest is about. Where is the difficulty?

White (p. 710) explains how money originated and how the unit of account has been linked to the medium of exchange. He says that the BFH system could not evolve in the same spontaneous fashion, as if this fact counted heavily against it. But why should an account of historical evolution, or conjectures about what might have spontaneously evolved or might still evolve, form the centerpiece of judgments about what is desirable now? Accumulated experience, new ideas for alternative systems, and advanced technology of communications, calculations, and record-keeping open up new possibilities. Why not take them into account in deciding where to proceed from here?

Any monetary reform must begin from where we are now. Dismantling government domination of the existing system will require deliberate policy actions, and the particular actions taken will unavoidably condition the successor system. Its capacity for emerging spontaneously is a spurious criterion of desirability.

REFERENCES

Greenfield, Robert L. and Yeager, Leland B., "A Laissez-Faire Approach to Monetary Stability," *Journal of Money, Credit and Banking*, August 1983, *15*, 302–15.

White, Lawrence H., "Competitive Payments Systems and the Unit of Account," *American Economic Review*, September 1984, *74*, 699–712.

[14]

Competitive Payments Systems: Reply

By Lawrence H. White*

My 1984 article critically reviewed the work of several authors who have conceived of competitive payments systems devoid of outside money and free of any link between payment media and the unit of account. I concluded that cashlessness, and the divorce of the unit of account from own-units of payment media, are not natural products of unrestricted competition. Further, some imagined systems incorporating these features suffer from internal incoherence. Robert Greenfield and Leland Yeager (1986) register three principal complaints about my treatment of their 1983 contribution to this literature. First, I did not appreciate just how operational they think the unit of account in their system (what they call a "BFH system") really is. Second, I made an argument, concerning the circularity of bonds payable only in bonds, which they find difficult to understand. Third, and evidently most importantly, they believe that I argued "as if" to question the desirability of their system as a serious proposal for monetary reform. I will respond to each of these complaints in turn.

I. Operationality

The issue of whether the unit of account in a Greenfield-Yeager system is operational, that is, fit for proper functioning, can be framed in various ways. The narrowest of these is whether a Walrasian auctioneer could coherently use the unit. Greenfield and Yeager apparently agree with me that an affirmative answer to that question does not establish very much, for they insist (justifiably) that they have framed the issue more broadly than that. They argue that "honest-to-goodness" decentralized trading would not pry the unit denominating payment accounts (demand deposits or checkable equity holdings) away from a commodity-bundle definition of the unit of account initially adopted. No divorce could come about, they say, because the only plausible alternative unit for denominating payment accounts would be some quantity of a common medium of exchange, and their system has no common medium of exchange.

Let us suppose, for the sake of argument, that a Greenfield-Yeager system has been established. Would market forces subsequently promote the emergence of a common medium of exchange, or would they prevent such a development? As far as I can tell, Greenfield and Yeager have not addressed this question. (Nor have I previously.) They do state that "under [our] system, which would eschew government money, no such single homogeneous medium of exchange would exist" (p. 848). But surely absence of government money does not insure absence of *any* homogeneous outside money: a specie standard with private mints and no government bank furnishes a conceptual counterexample.[1]

In Carl Menger's theory of the origin of money, which my article recounted, the needs of hand-to-hand traders promote the emergence of a common medium of exchange which eventually takes the form of an outside currency. For present purposes, however, I grant the assumption that in a sophisticated payments system the public can happily do without an outside currency. Market pressure for a common medium of exchange would instead be felt most strongly at the clearinghouse. (For simplicity, assume

*New York University, New York, NY 10003. I am thankful to members of the Austrian Economics colloquium at NYU for comments and discussion.

[1] Greenfield and Yeager (1986) add that payment account holdings would be nonhomogeneous, differing according to issuer. But this is logically unrelated, as the same counterexample shows, to the existence or nonexistence of a homogeneous outside money.

that a single clearinghouse covers the entire economy.) Greenfield and Yeager speak of clearing balances being settled by transfer of nonhomogeneous "redemption property" (1986, p. 848; 1983, p. 307). They do not further elaborate except to speculate that the settlement assets agreed upon by member funds might consist of "specified securities." Already this recognizes the crucial point that not all assets are equally acceptable to all traders as payment.

How then are settlement assets and their values agreed upon? Certainly it would not be feasible to negotiate each settlement individually. Suppose instead that there is a pre-approved list of specified securities. Who chooses the securities to be remitted in a particular day's settlement? It does not seem workable to let the paying member fund make the choice. Assuming end-of-day settlement using securities evaluated at closing prices, the fund would have an incentive to remit securities which up-to-the-minute news indicated would be likely to lose the most value between that day's (or the most recent market day's) closing and the next market day's opening. And it could profit the fund to bid up a closing security price in order to lock in an artificially high price at which to unload a great quantity of the security (including the quantity it had just purchased). There would be even graver problems with evaluation and choice of securities for purposes of intraday settlement, when the spread between bid and ask prices is obvious. For these reasons, there would be market pressure for a homogeneous settlement asset. The clearinghouse can provide such an asset by holding member fund redemption property on account, and pooling it, giving each fund homogeneous shares in the clearinghouse portfolio (hereafter *CP*). The clearinghouse can then make settlement instantaneously by transfer of *CP* shares between accounts. That ability is important in light of the fact that wire transfers account for approximately three-fourths of all transactions in the United States today in unit-of-account volume (Maxwell Fry and Raburn Williams, 1984, p. 6).

This arrangement makes the participating funds themselves owners of shares in a funds'

fund, just as clearing banks today own deposits at a bankers' bank. More importantly, it gives *CP* shares many of the characteristics of outside money. The *CP* shares are effectively a redemption medium for transfers among ordinary commercial payment accounts, just as deposits at the Federal Reserve are in the present American banking system. Over-the-counter redeemability might also emerge. *CP* shares are routinely accepted as a medium of exchange, because no one will refuse to accept the ultimate clearing asset. A question requiring further thought is whether *CP* shares can be spent into existence, and, if so, with what consequences.

Does the *CP* share constitute a unit which could rival the government-chosen commodity bundle as a unit of account? It does if the clearinghouse defines the *CP* share in "physical" terms, for example, one *CP* share equals 1.0 shares Alcoa common stock, 2.5 shares Burlington Northern stock, 1.7 shares Conoco stock, and so on down a list. The price of a *CP* share in terms of the government-stipulated numeraire would then vary day to day. Correspondingly, the *CP* share price of the commodity bundle to which all government accounting and obligations were indexed would vary from day to day. If, on the other hand, the clearinghouse were to denominate *CP* shares in unit-of-account terms, just as the typical money market mutual fund today fixes its share price at one dollar, then no rivalry would exist. The clearinghouse might well choose not to do so, however, in order to avoid the awkwardness of posting a price for acquisition and surrender of *CP* shares by funds, which could only be paid in bundles of primary securities, in units other than the units it would routinely accept and pay.

II. Circularity

I argued that there is a circularity problem in a Greenfield-Yeager system if two conditions simultaneously hold: 1) bonds are exclusively claims to streams of payment in fund shares; and 2) fund shares are claims to portfolios consisting exclusively of bonds. The problem may perhaps be grasped more clearly by considering the absurdity of consols which are exclusively claims to future streams of similar consols.[2] Who would want to buy such a claim? A transactor attempting to value it faces an infinite regress. I don't know how to make the difficulty any clearer. My conclusion was not that *every* cashless competitive payments system is inherently circular, but that to avoid circularity, conditions 1 and 2 could not both hold. Circularity would be avoided if either bonds were claims to streams of commodities or equities, or fund portfolios consisted of equities. (I argued that either of these arrangements would introduce other problems, however.) Present-day bonds payable in fiat money pose no circularity problem. To recognize this is not to find any great solace in fiat money's irredeemability. The apparent "bootstrap" paradox of fiat money itself having a positive value, I argued (p. 706), can be resolved by understanding the historical transition from redeemable to irredeemable central bank liabilities.

III. Reform

Contrary to the first sentence of Greenfield and Yeager's comment, I did not treat their 1983 piece as a proposal for monetary reform. I therefore did *not* intend my conjectures about spontaneous evolution to "form the centerpiece of judgments about what is desirable now," as they suppose (p. 000). Instead, I deliberately and explicitly limited my critique of their system, and of the cashless competitive payments systems of Black and Fama, to questioning "their applicability for modeling current arrangements or predicting future arrangements" (p. 706). I thought that a purely analytical approach was consistent with the approach of Greenfield and Yeager, who in their opening paragraph remark: "Regardless of who if anyone may actually advocate the system, contemplating it is instructive. It illuminates, by contrast, some characteristics of our existing and recent systems" (1983, p. 302). I

agree fully with that. And I would add that most readers will probably find the idea of a cashless competitive payments system easier to contemplate seriously when it is presented as an analytical construct than when it is presented as a reform proposal. But I am willing to deviate from my original purely analytical orientation in order to address briefly here the issues raised by cashlessness as a reform proposal.

I do not at all wish to question Greenfield and Yeager's preference for "Dismantling government domination of the existing system" (p. 849), that is, for moving to a private and unregulated payments system. (For what it is worth, I share that preference.) We agree that doing this entails deregulating banks and other financial institutions. There remains, however, the question of how to undo government's current control over the quantity of basic money. As they correctly insist, any approach requires deliberate policy actions that will condition the successor system. One avenue of reform (the one I happen to favor) is to take steps to enable private competitively issued money to supplant government fiat money. Commodity money, having historical precedent, is the most obvious form private outside money might take, but noncommodity monies as imagined by Hayek (1978) are also worth consideration. Greenfield and Yeager's alternative avenue is simply to abolish money.

In its starkest outlines, Greenfield and Yeager's argument for reform runs as follows. 1) Monetary payments systems inherently have important features which are socially undesirable. 2) Therefore it is desirable to abolish money. In advancing these two propositions their argument reminds me of S. Herbert Frankel's characterization of Keynes' outlook: "[I]t rests on the fear of money itself. ... Keynes ... sees money as distorting everything and wants the authority of the state to force money to reflect a less disturbing image" (1977, p. 3). Greenfield and Yeager, while fearing money, instead want the state to facilitate the abandonment of money. They propose that an effective and desirable way to abolish money is to have government announce and use a unit of account defined in terms of a bundle of

[2] I borrow this example from Kevin D. Hoover (1985, p. 55).

goods so wide as to be totally unusable as a medium of exchange.[3]

The logical gap between steps 1 and 2 should be obvious. Granting that the use of money carries with it certain social costs (foregone benefits of barter) does not compel one to conclude that its costs outweigh its benefits. One of my purposes in tracing the spontaneous evolution of money, and in emphasizing the supreme saleability of money, was to indicate that there are important benefits to using a common medium of exchange, namely in facilitating transaction. These benefits are never mentioned by Greenfield and Yeager, and seem to have been overlooked.[4] Such an oversight is surprising given that Yeager is the author of a classic account of "the essential properties of a medium of exchange" which emphasizes money's supreme saleability in comparison with other assets. In that paper, Yeager recognizes that money has uniquely low transactions costs, and explains that for an asset to have "the lowest transactions costs" means that "loosely speaking, it is the most convenient medium of exchange" (1968, p. 67). Surely the extra convenience of using money—of having a generally accepted asset or ultimate settlement—is a genuine benefit that ought not to be neglected in the evaluation of monetary vs. nonmonetary payments systems.

Most of the advantages that Greenfield and Yeager (1983, pp. 308–11) claim for their system may be attained, I believe, without abolishing money. Reasonable stability in the purchasing power of the numeraire, an end to inflationary finance, competitive innovation in payments insti-

tutions, resistance to financial panics, and mitigation of macroeconomic difficulties through a demand-elastic supply of particular forms of payment media, would all be promoted by deregulation of banking (including the private issue of currency) combined with freezing or denationalizing outright the supply of base money.[5] In addition, either freezing or denationalizing the monetary base (the latter by redeeming fiat dollars for some commodity presently stockpiled by government) avoids an important disadvantage of cashlessness: the transition to cashlessness implies significant wealth losses to relatively heavy base-money holders.

[5]George Selgin (1986) provides detailed arguments for these results, particularly the first, fourth, and fifth.

REFERENCES

Frankel, S. Herbert, *Money: Two Philosophies*, Oxford: Basil Blackwell, 1977.

Fry, Maxwell J. and Williams, Raburn M., *American Money and Banking*, New York: Wiley & Sons, 1984.

Greenfield, Robert L. and Yeager, Leland B., "A Laissez Faire Approach to Monetary Stability," *Journal of Money, Credit and Banking*, August 1983, *15*, 302–15.

_____ and _____, "Competitive Payments Systems: Comment," *American Economic Review*, September 1986, *76*, 848–49.

Hayek, F. A., *The Denationalisation of Money*, 2nd ed., London: Institute of Economic Affairs, 1978.

Hoover, Kevin D., "Causality and Invariance in the Money Supply Process," unpublished doctoral dissertation, Oxford University, 1985.

Selgin, George A., "The Theory of Free Banking," unpublished doctoral dissertation, New York University, 1986.

White, Lawrence H., "Competitive Payments Systems and the Unit of Account," *American Economics Review*, September 1984, *74*, 699–712.

Yeager, Leland B., "Essential Properties of a Medium of Exchange," *Kyklos*, 1968, *21*, 45–69.

---

[3]Greenfield and Yeager (1983, p. 303) explicitly eschew state force against money users. Presumably, however, citizens are to be forced to pay taxes in commodity-bundle-denominated media. It is nonetheless far from obvious, to anyone skeptical of the state theory of money, that these measures would be sufficient to make private traders abandon dollars in order to adopt the new system.

[4]Greenfield and Yeager do assert that their system would retain "convenient methods of payment" (1986, p. 848), for example, check writing, but they evidently see no convenience in a common *medium* of payment.

Part IV
The Legal Restrictions Theory

[15]

Federal Reserve Bank of Minneapolis Quarterly Review Winter 1983

A Legal Restrictions Theory of the Demand for "Money" and the Role of Monetary Policy*

Neil Wallace

Adviser
Research Department
Federal Reserve Bank of Minneapolis

and *Professor of Economics*
University of Minnesota

In this paper, I discuss a simple theory that explains the coexistence of alternative assets, some of which have significantly higher yields or returns than others.[1] The theory attributes such a paradoxical pattern of returns among assets to legal restrictions on private intermediation, an example being the widespread prohibition against private bank note issue. As I will show, this theory has as an almost immediate implication that monetary policy—central bank asset exchanges accomplished through open market operations or discount window lending—matters only in the presence of binding legal restrictions on private intermediation.[2]

In the first section, I describe obvious instances of paradoxical rate-of-return patterns and argue that these would disappear under laissez-faire—that is, in the absence of legal restrictions on private intermediation. The implication for monetary policy—that monetary policy under laissez-faire does not affect anything, not even the price level—is explained in the second section. In the third section, I discuss whether legal restrictions ought to be imposed. Although I do not arrive at a recommendation, I do discuss some of the considerations that are relevant to arriving at one.

Legal Restrictions and the Coexistence of High- and Low-Return Assets
An obvious instance of a paradoxical pattern of returns among assets is the coexistence of, on the one hand, U. S. Federal Reserve notes (U.S. currency) and, on the other

hand, interest-bearing securities that are default-free. By default-free, I mean that these securities, with complete certainty, entitle their owner to a stated amount of currency at some future date. Examples of such securities are U.S. savings bonds and Treasury bills. Our first task is to identify the features of these securities that prevent them from playing the same role in transactions as Federal Reserve notes. For if they could play that role, then it is hard to see why anyone would hold non-interest-bearing currency instead of the interest-bearing securities.

U.S. savings bonds, although issued in various and small denominations, are nonnegotiable. U.S. Treasury bills are negotiable and, until recently, were bearer securities, but they have always been issued in large denominations, for the most part in $10,000 denominations. I now argue that nonnegotiability in the case of savings bonds and large denomination in the case of bearer Treasury bills are *necessary* to explain why they cannot be substituted for Federal Reserve notes as alternative forms of currency.

---

*An earlier version of this paper was prepared for a November 1982 conference on interest rate deregulation and monetary policy sponsored by the Federal Reserve Bank of San Francisco.

[1] Hicks (1935) views this coexistence as the main puzzle facing monetary theory. He says (p. 5), "This, as I see it, is really the central issue in the pure theory of money. Either we have to give an explanation of the fact that people do hold money when rates of interest are positive, or we have to evade the difficulty somehow."

[2] See Fama 1980 and Hall 1982 for other discussions of the legal restrictions theory. Some other applications of the theory are listed in the box on page 3.

Consider what would happen if the Treasury started issuing bearer Treasury bills in small denominations—perhaps, $20s, $50s, and $100s. To be precise, suppose each such bill when issued says that the Treasury will pay the bearer at a date one year from the issue date or thereafter x dollars of Federal Reserve notes, where x is either 20, 50, or 100. Let us say that these bills are distinguishable from Federal Reserve notes because they are red, not green, but that they are the same physical size as Federal Reserve notes (and do not smell too much worse or have other obnoxious but inessential characteristics). If such bills were to coexist with Federal Reserve notes, then would they sell at a discount (so that they bear interest) or would they sell at par (and not bear interest)?

If these bills and Federal Reserve notes were to coexist, then they would sell at par and be used interchangeably with Federal Reserve notes in the same way that Lincoln and Indianhead pennies coexisted and were used interchangeably. To see this, consider what would happen at a date very close to the maturity date of the bills. If the bills were selling at a discount at such a date, then everyone would prefer them to Federal Reserve notes because the bills would surely appreciate and the Federal Reserve notes would not. But if everyone chose the bills, then the Federal Reserve notes would not be held, and the two would not coexist. Therefore, at a date sufficiently close to the maturity date of the bills, the bills would sell at par if they and Federal Reserves notes were to coexist. Now consider a somewhat earlier date. Since this date bears the same relationship to the first date we considered as the latter did to the maturity date and since we have concluded that the bills would sell at par at the date near maturity, we can apply the argument used above to the earlier date. Our conclusion is the same: small-denomination bearer Treasury bills would sell at par if they and Federal Reserve notes were to coexist. Repeated application of this argument—considering dates further and further from the maturity date of the bills and nearer and nearer to their issue date—shows that these bills would sell at par at every date.[3] Note, moreover, that if these small-denomination Treasury bills were selling at par, then there would be no incentive to turn them in at their maturity date; they would continue to circulate.

U.S. savings bonds differ from these hypothetical small-denomination Treasury bills only because they are very far from being bearer securities; they are nonnegotiable. Until very recently, when they ceased being bearer securities, U.S. Treasury bills differed only in their large denomination. That is why I claim that nonnegotiability in the case of savings bonds and large denomination in the case of bearer Treasury bills are necessary in order to explain how Federal Reserve notes can coexist with these securities while they bear substantial interest.

Our next task is to consider whether nonnegotiability and large denomination are *sufficient* for explaining the coexistence paradox. These features do explain why an individual with $10 or $20 in Federal Reserve notes does not switch them into savings bonds or Treasury bills even when those securities bear substantial interest. However, nonnegotiability and large denomination are not sufficient to explain the rate-of-return paradox because by themselves they fail to rule out arbitrage by financial institutions between such interest-bearing securities and small-denomination bearer notes. To see this, let us focus on denomination and begin with an analogy involving large and small packages of butter.

Suppose, for example, that we observe butter in one-pound packages selling for $1 per pound and butter in one-hundred-pound packages selling for 25 cents per pound. Is it an adequate explanation of this spread in prices per pound to say that individual households buy one-pound packages because they may not have or want to devote $25 to buying butter and they may not be able to transport or store one-hundred-pound packages? Obviously, such reasons are not adequate if there are sufficiently inexpensive ways to convert large packages into small packages and if there is free entry into the business of converting large packages into small packages.

If there is free entry into the business of converting large packages of butter into small packages, then the least costly technique for doing this sets an upper bound on the spread between prices per pound of large and small packages—that is, an upper bound on the quantity discount. Explanations of an observed quantity discount along the lines of individual households having small

---

[3] Liberty Bonds, which were issued during World War I as bearer securities in denominations as small as $50, actually seem to have circulated as currency from time to time. In August 1918, the secretary of the treasury, William Gibbs McAdoo, complained that merchants were accepting Liberty Bonds in exchange for merchandise (*New York Times*, August 23, 1918).

On September 20, 1920, Theodore Hardee, the director of the Treasury Department's Government Savings Organization for the Twelfth District, sent a statement from the secretary of the treasury entitled "On the Evils of Exchanging Merchandise for Liberty Bonds" to the Commonwealth Club in San Francisco. The statement began: "It has been brought to my attention that numbers of merchants throughout the country are offering to take Liberty Loan Bonds at par, or even in some cases at a premium, in exchange for merchandise."

Federal Reserve Bank of Minneapolis Quarterly Review / Winter 1983

Some Applications of the Legal Restrictions Theory

The legal restrictions theory described in this article has been applied to many issues in monetary theory and policy. A list and brief descriptions of some of these applications follow.

International Monetary Systems

Kareken and Wallace (1978,1981) and Wallace (1979) apply the legal restrictions theory to exchange rate systems. In a system of freely floating exchange rates among fiat currencies issued by different countries, legal restrictions that inhibit substitution among the currencies are necessary in order for exchange rates to be determined. Absent such restrictions, no natural forces determine exchange rates.

Multiple Government Liabilities

Most governments impose legal restrictions on private intermediaries and issue a variety of liabilities—for example, currency and bonds. Bryant and Wallace (1983) rationalize both in terms of price discrimination. Legal restrictions create separate markets for the different liabilities by preventing arbitrage among them; the composition of government liabilities determines relative sales by the government in the separated markets. Bryant and Wallace display circumstances in which these devices permit the levying of a discriminatory inflation tax that is preferable to the levying of a uniform inflation tax.

The Real Bills Doctrine

This doctrine asserts that the quantity of money ought to vary with the needs of trade and that it will vary appropriately if private credit markets are allowed to function without interference. Sargent and Wallace (1982) offer a defense of this much-criticized doctrine.

Commodity Money

Sargent and Wallace (1983) model commodity money as one of several of the storable goods (capital goods) in a growth model. Among the topics addressed are the nature of the inefficiency of commodity money; the validity of quantity-theory predictions for commodity money systems; the circumstances under which one commodity emerges naturally as the commodity money; and the role of inside money (money backed by private debt) in commodity money systems.

refrigerators are relevant only if barriers of one sort or another prevent the use of the least costly means or if individual household use of large packages is, in effect, the least costly way of carrying out such conversion. The latter seems unlikely.

Similar considerations apply in the case of the spread between the rate of return on Federal Reserve notes and that on default-free securities. In particular, consider a financial intermediary that does nothing but buy default-free securities—for example, U.S. Treasury bills—and issue bearer notes in small denominations with maturities that coincide with those of the default-free securities it holds. Such an intermediary is perfectly hedged so that, fraud aside, its bearer notes are as safe as the securities it holds as backing for them. It follows that such an activity gives rise to the same situation that prevails if the Treasury itself issues small-denomination bearer securities. If we suppose that, as part of its business, this intermediary takes actions that prevent fraud, then we conclude, exactly as we did for small-denomination bearer securities issued by the Treasury, that the bearer notes issued by such intermediaries would sell at par and be used interchange-ably with Federal Reserve notes if the two were to coexist.

Since the revenue for this intermediation business comes from buying default-free securities at a discount and issuing bearer notes at par, in an equilibrium with free entry the discount on default-free securities like Treasury bills must be small enough so that it is not profitable to expand this activity. That is the case when the discount is just sufficient to cover the costs of engaging in the business. In other words, in a laissez-faire system in which Federal Reserve notes and default-free securities like Treasury bills coexist, the yield or nominal rate of return on the latter is bounded above by the least costly way of operating such a financial intermediation business.

Rough estimates of the magnitude of this cost can be inferred from two sources: the cost of operating financial intermediaries in existing intermediary activities and the cost to the U.S. Treasury and Federal Reserve of issuing and maintaining the stock of Federal Reserve notes. Many financial intermediaries—common stock and money market mutual funds—operate at spreads of 1 percent or less. There is no reason to expect that the cost of intermediating securities like Treasury bills into bearer notes would be

3

much different from the cost of operating these intermediaries. This view is buttressed by the fact that, for all but the smallest denominations, the cost to the Treasury and Federal Reserve of maintaining Federal Reserve currency is a small fraction of 1 percent of the outstanding stock. These observations suggest that our hypothetical intermediary could operate with a discount that is close to zero and, hence, suggest that the upper bound on nominal interest rates on safe securities under laissez-faire would be close to zero.

Thus far my argument says that if Federal Reserve notes and default-free securities like Treasury bills coexist under laissez-faire, then nominal interest rates are close to zero. But they may not coexist. Laissez-faire means, among other things, no reserve requirements, no capital controls of the sort recently put into effect in Mexico, and so on. In other words, laissez-faire means the absence of legal restrictions that tend, among other things, to enhance the demand for a government's currency. Thus, the imposition of laissez-faire would almost certainly reduce the demand for government currency. It could even reduce it to zero. A zero demand for a government's currency should be interpreted as the abandonment of one monetary unit in favor of another—for example, the abandonment of the dollar in favor of one ounce of gold. Thus, my prediction of the effects of imposing laissez-faire takes the form of an either/or statement: either nominal interest rates go to zero or existing government currency becomes worthless.

While these possibilities seem extreme, they are not unfamiliar to economists. They match almost completely two possibilities described by Samuelson (1947, p. 123):

It is true that in a world involving no transaction friction and no uncertainty, there would be no reason for a spread between the yield on any two assets, and hence there would be no difference in the yield on money and on securities. Hicks concludes, therefore, that securities will not bear interest but will accommodate themselves to the yield on money. It is equally possible and more illuminating to suppose that under these conditions money adjusts itself to the yield of securities. In fact, in such a world securities themselves would circulate as money and be acceptable in transactions; demand bank deposits would bear interest, just as they often did in this country in the period of the twenties. And if money could not make the adjustment, as in the case of metal counters which Aristotle tells us are barren, it would pass out of use, wither away and die, become a free good.

What is added in my discussion is the claim that the only

significant frictions are those created by legal restrictions. Moreover, uncertainty seems not to be relevant because the hypothetical note-issuing intermediary described above is perfectly hedged.[4]

Legal Restrictions and Monetary Policy

In this section, let us make an additional assumption, which has already been hinted at above—namely, that a common and constant average-cost technology for the production and distribution of small-denomination bearer notes is available to the government and to potential private sector intermediaries. In terms of our butter analogy, this says that the government has neither a technological advantage nor a technological disadvantage relative to the private sector when it comes to converting large packages into small packages and that the cost per unit of producing small packages from large ones does not depend on the number produced. Under this assumption, my argument is that central bank intermediation activities, apart from outright credit subsidies, have no significant effects under laissez-faire.

In order to be concrete, I will discuss central bank intermediation in terms of an open market purchase of Treasury bills. This results in the private sector holding fewer bills and more Federal Reserve notes. Under laissez-faire, the equilibrium adjustment is a contraction in the scale of operations of private note-issuing intermediaries, a contraction that exactly offsets the open market purchase. If it is costly in terms of resources to carry out this private intermediation, then the contraction frees some resources—paper, people to run the presses, and so on. With technological symmetry between the private sector and the government, these are precisely the resources the government needs in order to provide and maintain the larger outstanding stock of government currency. In other words, under laissez-faire and technological symmetry,

---

[4]Some readers may wonder whether the coexistence in the U.S. of non-interest-bearing checking accounts and interest-bearing Treasury bills is an important counterexample to the claim that rate-of-return disparities are to be explained by legal restrictions. It is not, because government regulations and subsidies—interest ceilings, reserve requirements, zero marginal-cost check clearing by the Federal Reserve, and the failure to tax income in the form of transaction services—explain the way checking account services have been priced. In the absence of these forms of government interference, most observers predict that checking accounts would pay interest at the market rate with charges levied on a per transaction basis. (Note that under such pricing of demand deposit services, there would be no reason to distinguish the part of wealth that is subject to transfer by check from the part that is not, and checking accounts, whether distinguishable or not, could not be treated as part of the "cash" of inventory models of money demand. See, for example, Baumol 1952 and Tobin 1956.)

Federal Reserve Bank of Minneapolis Quarterly Review Winter 1983

the open market purchase does no more than change the location from the private sector to the government of a given quantity of an economic activity, the production of small-denomination bearer notes. Nothing else is affected, neither interest rates nor the price level nor the level of economic activity. A similar argument applies to open market sales.[5]

Matters are very different under binding legal restrictions on private intermediation. Let us discuss what would happen in terms of our butter analogy. Suppose the government has a legal monopoly on the business of converting large packages into small ones. Then much depends on the scale at which it chooses to operate. Under our assumptions, if the government chooses the output level that would have been produced in the absence of the legal monopoly, then the legal restriction does not matter. If it chooses a lower level of output, then it makes the legal restriction binding. An obvious measure of bindingness is the observed spread in prices per pound of small and large packages. How much greater is the observed spread than that which would obtain under laissez-faire?

The Federal Reserve does, of course, have a legal monopoly on the issue of small-denomination bearer notes in the United States. By its choice of an open market and discount window strategy, it determines how binding this legal restriction turns out to be. The appropriate measure of bindingness is the observed discount on Treasury bills. This corresponds exactly to the observed quantity discount on large packages of butter.

An important qualification is that the central bank not conduct its intermediation activities so as to incur losses. In terms of our butter analogy, if the government sells small packages at a price that does not permit it to cover costs, then even with free entry the government's operations clearly matter. To consider an intermediation example, suppose the central bank is allowed to incur losses and does so by granting both safe and risky loans at the laissez-faire interest rate on safe loans. Then, since risky loans would not otherwise be available at that rate, the central bank's lending has significant effects.

Thus, for a central bank constrained not to incur losses on average, our conclusion is that its intermediation matters if and only if there exist profitable arbitrage opportunities that the private sector cannot exploit because of legal restrictions.

The most objectionable of the assumptions used to obtain this result may be the constant-cost assumption. The provision of small-denomination bearer notes may be a decreasing average-cost activity, perhaps because the cost of inhibiting counterfeiting of the notes of a particular issuer does not increase in proportion to the value of the notes outstanding. If note issue is a decreasing cost activity, then the least costly way of providing small-denomination bearer notes is by way of a single supplier. Moreover, if there are decreasing average costs, then we cannot conclude that an open market operation under laissez-faire simply shifts the location of a given activity between the government and the private sector. We can, however, continue to conclude that under laissez-faire the cost structure for providing small-denomination bearer notes implies an upper bound on nominal interest rates on default-free securities when these and non–interest-bearing currency coexist. Also, we can continue to conclude that the degree to which legal restrictions are binding is to be judged by the magnitude of such interest rates.

Why Impose Legal Restrictions?

So far, nothing has been said about what legal restrictions, if any, ought to be imposed and what central bank intermediation strategy ought to be followed. Although I will not arrive at a recommendation, I will discuss some of the presumed costs and benefits of legal restrictions on private intermediation.

Legal restrictions on private intermediation give rise to costs that are similar to those that accompany barriers to trade in other contexts: resources tend to be misallocated under binding restrictions. For example, consider a prohibition on private note issue. If this prohibition is binding, then some borrowers face higher interest rates on loans than they would if they, directly or through "banks," were able to borrow by issuing small-denomination bearer notes. The prohibition puts a barrier between borrowers and lenders and, hence, inhibits the carrying out of some beneficial intertemporal trade.

The same point can be made in a slightly different way. We are familiar with proposals that urge that the quantities of certain private sector liabilities be controlled—for example, proposals that urge that the quantity of private bank notes should be zero or that the quantity of deposits subject to check should grow at some prescribed rate. But

---

[5]The result that central bank intermediation does not matter under laissez-faire also holds for central bank exchanges of Federal Reserve notes for other assets—risky mortgages, risky commercial loans, or common stock. It is a straightforward extension of a well-known finding in corporate finance called the Modigliani-Miller theorem. (See Stiglitz 1969 and Wallace 1981.)

what is so special about deposits subject to check and private bank notes? They are particular private credit instruments. If it makes sense to control their quantities, why not those of other credit instruments? For example, most economists would not favor a proposal to constrain the dollar volume of mortgages on single family residences to grow at a prescribed rate. Almost certainly, most would say that it is a necessary feature of a well-functioning credit system that the number of mortgages be determined in the market and not be set administratively. But if this is right for one set of private credit instruments, why is it not right for all? No satisfactory answer has ever been given.

One presumed benefit of legal restrictions that has played a prominent role in prior discussions rests on the notion that it would be much more difficult to control the price level were it not for restrictions on credit instruments like private bank notes and checking deposits. Since some forms of private debt are better substitutes than others for government currency—or, under a gold standard, gold coins—this notion may be valid. In particular, if there is a variable demand for forms of credit that under laissez-faire would compete closely with government currency or gold coins, then it can happen that the price level would be more variable under laissez-faire than under legal restrictions that limit or prohibit the issue of such forms of private debt.[6] Given that such restrictions, when they are binding, misallocate resources, it follows that there can be a tradeoff between achieving price level stability and achieving efficient resource allocation through credit markets.

However, this tradeoff presents a problem only if we accept price level stability as a goal, as an end in itself. That it should be a goal is not obvious. Although widely espoused as a goal, there exist no complete arguments leading to the conclusion that people are on average better off the more stable the price level, *given* the steps that have to be taken to attain greater stability of the price level. On the contrary, as Sargent and Wallace (1982) argue, the restrictions that make greater price level stability possible hurt some people and benefit others, while on average, in a certain sense, making all worse off.

I suspect that those who espouse price level stability as a goal do so partly because they think it is easy to attain; all that is needed is the right open market or intermediation strategy on the part of the central bank. That view, however, ignores what I argued above, namely, that central bank intermediation matters only in the presence of binding legal restrictions. Without such restrictions, it is no easier to achieve price level stability than it is to achieve stability of some relative price.

There is another potential benefit from legal restrictions on private intermediation that is less easy to dismiss. Such restrictions help governments tax asset holdings. Most legal restrictions on private intermediation have been and are the result of governments trying to enhance the demand for their liabilities. In general, such restrictions make it easier for governments to borrow and to tax by inflation. The fact that the restrictions misallocate resources is not decisive since the same can be said of virtually all taxes that are levied.

Finally, it should be noted that the above discussion does not deal with the transition from one set of restrictions to another. As with any major change in policy regime, substantial wealth redistribution may accompany alterations in legal restrictions on private intermediation.

Concluding Remarks

The theory I have described does two things. At a positive level, it suggests that we explain paradoxical rate-of-return patterns by way of legal restrictions on the kinds of assets and liabilities that the private sector can hold and issue. At a normative level, it suggests that we consider the consequences of alternative legal restrictions on the financial system in much the same way as we consider restrictions on trade in other contexts and, in particular, that we not be content with describing those consequences only in terms of their effects on variables like the price level and interest rates.

---

[6]For a complete example that exhibits this possibility, see Sargent and Wallace 1982.

Federal Reserve Bank of Minneapolis Quarterly Review. Winter 1983

References

Baumol, William J. 1952. The transactions demand for cash: An inventory theoretic approach. *Quarterly Journal of Economics* 66 (November): 545–56.

Bryant, John B., and Wallace, Neil. 1983. A price discrimination analysis of monetary policy. Research Department Staff Report 51. Federal Reserve Bank of Minneapolis.

Fama, Eugene. 1980. Banking in the theory of finance. *Journal of Monetary Economics* 6 (January): 39–57.

Hall, Robert E. 1982. *Monetary trends in the United States and the United Kingdom:* A review from the perspective of new developments in monetary economics. *Journal of Economic Literature* 20 (December): 1552–56.

Hicks, J. R. 1935. A suggestion for simplifying the theory of money. *Economica,* n. s. 2 (February): 1–19.

Kareken, John, and Wallace, Neil. 1978. International monetary reform: The feasible alternatives. *Federal Reserve Bank of Minneapolis Quarterly Review* 2(Summer): 2–7.

——————. 1981. On the indeterminancy of equilibrium exchange rates. *Quarterly Journal of Economics* 96 (May): 207–22.

Samuelson, Paul Anthony. 1947. *Foundations of economic analysis.* Cambridge: Harvard University Press.

Sargent, Thomas J., and Wallace, Neil. 1982. The real-bills doctrine versus the quantity theory: A reconsideration. *Journal of Political Economy* 90 (December): 1212–36.

——————. 1983. A model of commodity money. Research Department Staff Report 85. Federal Reserve Bank of Minneapolis.

Stiglitz, Joseph E. 1969. A re-examination of the Modigliani-Miller theorem. *American Economic Review* 59 (December): 784–93.

Tobin, James. 1956. The interest-elasticity of transactions demand for cash. *Review of Economics and Statistics* 38 (August): 241–47.

Wallace, Neil. 1979. Why markets in foreign exchange are different from other markets. *Federal Reserve Bank of Minneapolis Quarterly Review* 3 (Fall): 1–7.

——————. 1981. A Modigliani-Miller theorem for open-market operations. *American Economic Review* 71 (June): 267–74.

[16]

Deregulation and Monetary Reform

Gerald P. O'Driscoll, Jr.

Senior Economist and Policy Advisor
Federal Reserve Bank of Dallas

In recent years, deregulation has taken place in a number of economic activities. Deregulation of transportation modes, for instance, has increased freedom of entry and exit by competitors, permitted new services to be offered, and, in the case of air transportation, instituted rate-making freedom on domestic routes. Deregulation of financial services has been less dramatic but nonetheless substantial. The process of registering securities has been simplified, and new financial products have been introduced. In banking, a subset of financial services, noteworthy changes have occurred. Some of the changes in banking have even been dramatic, such as the elimination of interest-rate ceilings on all but certain transaction accounts.

Banking deregulation raises the issue of deregulation of the money creation process and, more generally, the question of monetary reform. Specifically, deregulation of deposits and interest rates makes it impossible for central banks to affect money supply growth through disintermediation. With deposits paying market rates of interest, financial intermediaries can acquire all the funds for which they are willing to pay. Some have argued that, as a result, deregulation may result in loss of monetary control. Others have suggested that the freeing up of the liability creation process may lead to a change in the monetary standard itself.

Recent analysis of unregulated monetary systems falls into two main classes: free-banking theory and the legal re-

striction theory. A free-banking system is one in which individuals need only comply with certain general legal requirements in order to start a bank. The system contrasts with one in which permission to open a bank either requires a specific legislative charter or is subject to the discretion of a chartering agency (for example, the Office of the Comptroller of the Currency). In the United States the first free-banking system was created in New York in 1838.[1] But even banks in free-banking states were subject to branching restrictions and restrictions on the assets they could purchase. These banks could, however, issue deposits and notes subject to regulations on the assets that the liabilities could be used to purchase. The Scottish system came much closer to being an "unregulated" banking system. Both systems were characterized by the absence of any central bank of issue.

In modern times, there have been only two major free-banking systems: Scotland before the first Peel Act (1844) and the United States before the National Banking Act (1864). Recent work on the American experience argues that observed cyclical instability in the 19th century reflected real shocks and flawed state banking regulations, rather than inherent instability of free banking. Work on the Scottish system of free banking both confirms the flaws in some American variants and supports the theoretical case for free banking.[2]

The legal restrictions theory constitutes an alternative approach to analyzing unregulated banking. The approach focuses on banks' role in providing accounting and transaction services. Since traditional approaches analyze banks as creators of money, banking deregulation immediately raises the question of the effects of deregulating the money creation process. In fact, the latter is the central issue in the long debates over free banking. In contrast, the legal restrictions theory questions whether money as we know it would exist in an unregulated banking system.

The legal restrictions theory concludes that non-interest-bearing money would not circulate in an unregulated monetary system. Taken to its logical conclusion, the theory predicts the disappearance of money as a distinctive financial asset. The argument is supported by the benchmark adopted by legal restrictions theorists for analyzing banks. Monetary theory has traditionally modeled banks as creators of money. Legal restrictions theorists view this function as secondary, contingent upon the existence of legal impediments to financial intermediation. They view the essential function of banks as the provision of accounting and transaction services. In an unregulated payments system, only the essential function would remain.

Supported by this theory, some authors have argued for reform to bring about a payments system without money. They contend that such a system would be an improvement over the present one. This article examines one such proposal. The major focus of the article is on the coherence and practicality of the reform proposal. In examining these issues, however, the article also analyzes some of the central propositions of the legal restrictions theory.

After briefly reviewing the legal restrictions theory and then introducing the proposed reform, I critically analyze the proposal. Two major conclusions are reached. First, I question the coherence of the proposal as well as the suggested methods for implementing the reform. Second, I adduce both demand and supply considerations for why non-interest-bearing money ("currency") would not disappear in an unregulated payments system. If eliminated, as is suggested in the reform proposal, currency will reemerge in a market process.

Legal restrictions theory of money

The legal restrictions theory begins by noting the apparent paradox that the very same entity, the U.S. Government, issues some default-free obligations that yield no interest (currency) and others that yield market rates of interest (bonds).[3] Legal restrictions theorists argue that, absent some legal compulsion, individuals would shun the government's non-interest-bearing liabilities and purchase only its

interest-bearing obligations.[4] One of two outcomes is then possible: either the government would no longer issue currency or the yield on bonds would be driven to zero. In the former case, individuals would presumably utilize government bonds as means of payment. In the latter case, bonds and currency become indistinguishable, leading to a similar result.

The logic of the argument is not merely that interest-bearing assets are preferred to non-interest-bearing assets (net of risk differences) but that so long as there is *any* interest-rate differential (net of specified transaction costs), money will be dominated by bonds. In other words, not only does non-interest-bearing money disappear but also any distinction between money and financial assets. This conclusion is incorporated explicitly by John Bryant and Neil Wallace in their work when they make the following assumptions:[5]

1. Assets are valued only in terms of their payoff distributions.

2. Anticipated payoff distributions are the same as actual payoff distributions.

3. Under laissez-faire, no transaction costs inhibit the operation of markets and, in particular, the law of one price.

Taken together, these assumptions lead to the conclusion that in the absence of legal restrictions, interest differentials between money and nonmoney financial assets will be arbitraged away. Since this has not happened, Bryant and Wallace postulate the presence of relevant legal restrictions. Wallace identifies these restrictions as (1) the nonnegotiability of some U.S. Treasury bonds (that is, savings bonds) and (2) the large denomination of other Treasury obligations (for example, Treasury bills). Neither would be a sufficient condition preventing arbitrage. The sufficient condition is that the U.S. Government is a monopolistic provider of currency. In other words, financial intermediation must be restricted.[6]

As indicated in the introduction, legal restrictions theorists have adopted a different benchmark for analyzing banks. Banks have traditionally been analyzed as creators of money. The alternative view propounded by legal restrictions theorists emphasizes that banks are financial intermediaries providing accounting and transaction services. The latter function is viewed as fundamental, while the creation of money by banks is viewed as contingent upon existing restrictions and institutions.[7] This approach to modeling banks rationalizes the separation of the unit of account from the means of payment—a characteristic proposition in the literature and the basis of the policy proposal examined in the next section.

For writers such as Bryant and Wallace, the legal restrictions theory is a modeling strategy. A piece of positive economic analysis, the theory is viewed as containing both explanatory and predictive power. Models applying the theory appear to explain anomalous phenomena, as well as predicting the consequences of completely deregulating banking. More generally, these models are viewed as providing insight into workings of the payments mechanism in a modern economy.

Robert Hall apparently was the first to utilize the theory to propose a reform of the payments system. If "money is exactly a creation of regulation,"[8] then further doses of deregulation will bring us a nonmonetary payments mechanism. Following Hall, Robert Greenfield and Leland Yeager have proposed a payments system incorporating ideas from the legal restrictions theory. In short, in the hands of Hall and of Greenfield and Yeager, positive economic analysis has been transformed into normative analysis; models of banking have become the basis for banking reform. This article focuses on the Greenfield-Yeager system, which constitutes a far-reaching reform proposal in the tradition of the legal restrictions theory. Moreover, consideration of the proposal highlights the issue of the separability of the means of payment and the unit of account.

Unregulated payments mechanisms

This section outlines a recent proposal for implementing an unregulated payments mechanism. (As will be evident, it would be misleading to call the mechanism a monetary system.) In a series of papers, Yeager offers elements of the analytical underpinnings of the proposal. An article coauthored with Greenfield provides the most complete statement of the proposal itself.[9]

The proposal. Yeager objects to the variability of the purchasing power of money. Our existing monetary standard is the "preposterous dollar," and the unit of account "is whatever value supply and demand fleetingly accord to the dollar of fiat money."[10] Problems arise because money alone has no market of its own. Maladjustments between the demand for and supply of money (a positive or negative excess demand for money) can only be cleared by costly adjustments in all other goods markets.[11]

By itself, the fact that money has no market of its own in which to clear an excess demand would not represent a unique problem. The interdependence of all markets ensures that an excess demand in one market "spills over" into others. Goods are connected by an intricate web of complementarities and substitutabilities. In a full general-equilibrium analysis, the demand for each good depends, in principle, on the prices of all other goods. Consequently, a

shock to one market affects all other markets. The fact, then, that money has no market of its own is a necessary but not a sufficient condition for macroeconomic problems.

Sticky prices cause monetary shocks to produce macroeconomic reverberations. The *downward* stickiness of prices is both a cause and an effect of the costliness of adjusting to changing demand conditions.

> Prices and wages respond far from promptly enough to absorb the full impact of imbalances; they are sticky—some more so than others—for reasons that make excellent sense from the standpoints of individual price-setters and wage-negotiators. Under these realistic circumstances, failure to keep the quantity of money correctly and steadily managed can have momentous consequences.[12]

If the supply of money adjusted automatically to changes in its demand, then Yeager-type macroeconomic problems (that is, those induced by demand shocks) could be avoided even in the presence of price and wage stickiness. Over the long run, commodity standards, like the gold standard, do provide such endogeneity to the money supply. In practice, however, the money supply under gold standards has not been highly elastic in the short run. Similarly, in theory, a perfectly managed fiat money system could accommodate short-run swings in money demand. In practice, however, monetary management has never been up to the task and probably never will be, given the informational requirements. In any case, Yeager believes that financial deregulation may have made monetary control impossible in the future.[13]

These considerations lead Greenfield and Yeager to recommend a payments system in which no money exists. In arguing for the system, they exploit the theoretical wedge driven by legal restrictions theorists between money, conceived as a means of payment, and the unit of account, conceived as a social accounting system. Greenfield and Yeager propose implementing a system with a unit of value "defined by a suitable bundle of commodities." They analogize the choice and measurement of a unit of value to the selection of a unit of weight and measurement. The government plays a role "by noncoercively offering a definition, just as it does with weights and measures."[14]

> Just as the meter is defined physically as 1,650,763.73 wavelengths of the orange-red radiation of krypton 86, so the value unit would be defined physically as the total market value of, say, 50 kg of ammonium nitrate + 40 kg of copper + 35 kg of aluminum + 80 square meters of

Development of the Legal Restrictions Theory

The modern statement of the legal restrictions theory can be traced to two articles, one by Fischer Black and the other by Eugene Fama.[1] Developments and elaborations have been provided by, among others, John Bryant, Robert Hall, and Neil Wallace.[2] Although different facets of the theory are emphasized by the various authors, it can be summarized concisely.[3]

Most generally, the theory connects the existence of certain institutions and financial assets with legal restrictions. Thus, banks and non-interest-bearing money (that is, currency) exist because of restrictions on the creation of liabilities by nonbank financial intermediaries. Wallace's analysis of why currency exists is exemplary.

Consolidating the central bank and U.S. Treasury accounts, Wallace identifies what he perceives to be a paradox. The same issuer provides default-free interest-bearing and non-interest-bearing liabilities (bonds and currency). To illustrate the paradox, Wallace considers the following example:

> Suppose, for example, that we observe butter in one-pound packages selling for $1 per pound and butter in one-hundred-pound packages selling for 25 cents per pound. Is it an adequate explanation of this spread in prices per pound to say that individual households buy one-pound packages because they may not have or want to devote $25 to buying butter and they may not be able to transport or store one-hundred-pound packages? Obviously, such reasons are not adequate if there are sufficiently inexpensive ways to convert large packages into small packages and if there is free entry into the business of converting large packages into small packages.[4]

Economic theory would predict that, in such circumstances, entrepreneurs would arbitrage between the two markets by purchasing butter in large quantities at 25 cents per pound and reselling it to consumers in 1-pound containers for less than $1. Competition ("free entry") ought to reduce the differential in the two markets to the actual costs of repackaging butter. Returns to retailing butter ought to be no greater than for any similar operations.

Mutual funds, banks, and other financial intermediaries constitute the retailers of a competitive financial system. Absent legal restrictions, financial retailers would purchase large-denomination, interest-bearing liabilities of the Treasury ("bonds") and repackage them into denominations small enough to circulate hand to hand as currency. Competition should drive down the yield differential between Treasury bonds and currency. As with butter, the yield differential should reflect only the costs of intermediating between large-denomination bonds and circulating currency.[5]

Citing money market mutual funds, Wallace estimates the cost of intermediating securities like Treasury bills into notes at 1 percent or less. He concludes that in an unregulated system, intermediaries "could operate with a discount that is close to zero and, hence, ... the upper bound on nominal interest rates on safe securities under laissez-faire would be close to zero."[6] This conclusion, however, has far-reaching implications for the government's present monopoly on currency creation.

> Laissez-faire means the absence of legal restrictions that tend, among other things, to enhance the demand for a government's currency. Thus, the imposition of laissez-faire would almost certainly reduce the demand for government currency. It could even reduce it to zero. A zero demand for a government's currency should be interpreted as the abandonment of one monetary unit in favor of another—for example, the abandonment of the dollar in favor of one ounce of gold. Thus, my prediction of the effects of imposing laissez-faire takes the form of an either/or statement: either nominal interest rates go to zero or existing government currency becomes worthless.[7]

Wallace's analysis implies not only the disappearance of currency as a distinctive asset but also the blurring of any distinction between bank and nonbank intermediaries. This is particularly true if banks are viewed as the institution creating a distinctive money. The typical intermediary in the unregulated world of the legal restrictions theory is a generic institution purchasing diverse assets and issuing diverse liabilities. In certain presentations, such as Wallace's, some of these liabilities circulate the same way today's currency does. In other presentations, such as Black's, there is no distinctive money as we know it.

If not money, what do "banks" (financial intermediaries) produce? As is clear in Greenfield and Yeager, banks' particular function would be to produce accounting and transaction services. These services would presumably be needed even in a world without money. They constitute the unit-of-account function that money now comprises (along with the medium-of-exchange function).

The change in the benchmark for analyzing banks reflects a specific assumption characterizing the legal restrictions theory. The assumption really has two parts. First, the medium-of-exchange function and the unit-of-account function are not only conceptually distinct but practically separable. Second, it is the latter, not the former, that is crucial for the operation of a developed market economy.

Legal restrictions theorists also emphasize that conventional monetary theories are special cases, whose applicability depends on the existence of legal restrictions. Since the existence of money as a distinct asset is, as it were, a contingent fact, so too is the applicability of conventional monetary theories. Existing monetary institutions and the relationship between the quantity of a subset of financial assets (namely, money) and key macroeconomic variables (such as the price level) depend on the existence of legal restrictions.[8]

Although I have dated the modern development of the theory from Black's 1970 article, Tyler Cowen and Randall Kroszner argue that the theory has a long history.[9] They trace the predecessors of Black, Fama, Wallace, and others back at least to the 18th century. They view the separability of the unit of account and medium of exchange as the central theoretical proposition in the literature, a judgment with which I concur. Nonetheless, it is useful to restate the theory's conclusions in terms of five propositions (Cowen and Kroszner find seven):

1. Money would not exist as a distinctive financial asset in the absence of legal restrictions.

2. Conventional monetary theories are applicable only to a specific set of financial institutions.

3. In an unregulated payments system, the provision of accounting and transaction services by banks would have no special effects on prices or macroeconomic activity.

4. The provision of accounting and transaction services—not the production of money—is the benchmark for analyzing banks.

5. The unit of account is separable from the means of payment.

Much of the literature involves drawing out further implications of these assumptions. In terms of the Greenfield and Yeager proposal, the fifth assumption is particularly important. If that assumption is questioned, their proposal cannot stand up.

---

1. Fischer Black, "Banking and Interest Rates in a World Without Money: The Effects of Uncontrolled Banking," *Journal of Bank Research* 1 (Autumn 1970): 8-20; and Eugene F. Fama, "Banking in the Theory of Finance," *Journal of Monetary Economics* 6 (January 1980): 39-57.

2. John Bryant and Neil Wallace, "The Inefficiency of Interest-bearing National Debt," *Journal of Political Economy* 87 (April 1979): 365-81, and "A Suggestion for Further Simplifying the Theory of Money" (Minneapolis, December 1980, Photocopy); Robert E. Hall, "Explorations in the Gold Standard and Related Policies for Stabilizing the Dollar," in *Inflation: Causes and Effects* (Chicago: University of Chicago Press for National Bureau of Economic Research, 1982), 111-22, and "Monetary Trends in the United States and the United Kingdom: A Review from the Perspective of New Developments in Monetary Economics," *Journal of Economic Literature* 20 (December 1982): 1552-56; and Neil Wallace, "A Legal Restrictions Theory of the Demand for 'Money' and the Role of Monetary Policy," *Federal Reserve Bank of Minneapolis Quarterly Review*, Winter 1983, 1-7.

3. The theory is more fully developed in Gerald P. O'Driscoll, Jr., "Money in a Deregulated Financial System," *Economic Review*, Federal Reserve Bank of Dallas, May 1985, and "Money, Deregulation and the Business Cycle," Federal Reserve Bank of Dallas Research Paper no. 8601 (Dallas, January 1986), 1-7.

4. "A Legal Restrictions Theory," 2.

5. Adding other kinds of financial assets would complicate matters by bringing in default but would not alter the thrust of Wallace's analysis.

6. Wallace, "A Legal Restrictions Theory," 4.

7. Wallace, "A Legal Restrictions Theory," 4.

8. The latter point is argued forcefully in Fama, "Banking in the Theory of Finance," 45-47; see also Wallace, "A Legal Restrictions Theory," 4-5. For an earlier criticism of this line of reasoning, see O'Driscoll, "Money, Deregulation and the Business Cycle," 18-26, "Money in a Deregulated Financial System," 6-12, and "Money: Menger's Evolutionary Theory," Federal Reserve Bank of Dallas Research Paper no. 8508 (Dallas, December 1985), 19-24.

9. Tyler Cowen and Randall Kroszner, "The Development of the 'New Monetary Economics'" (Cambridge, Mass., December 1985, Photocopy).

plywood of a specified grade . . . + definite amounts of still other commodities. . . . The bundle would be composed of precisely gradable, competitively traded, and industrially important commodities, and in amounts corresponding to their relative importance. Many would be materials used in the production of a wide range of goods so that adopting the bundle as the value unit would come close to stabilizing the general level of prices expressed in that unit.[15]

The crucial difference between their proposal and conventional commodity standards is that the commodities constituting the proposed unit of value would neither be stored nor need to be storable. Greenfield and Yeager place great emphasis on this point, which is crucial for understanding their proposal.[16]

A commodity standard is characterized by convertibility in fixed proportions between the commodity (for example, gold) and the national currency (for example, the U.S. dollar).[17] A composite-commodity standard involves convertibility in fixed proportions between a bundle of commodities and the national currency. Any commodity standard is subject, however, to the risk of devaluation or abandonment initiated by an excessive rate of growth in the national money supply. The reason is that excessive money growth eventually causes the nominal prices of all goods, including the price of the monetary commodity itself, to rise on open markets. If the market price of the monetary commodity is more than negligibly higher on organized markets than the official or conversion price, then the nation's mint simply becomes a source of the commodity at a subsidized price. Monetary reserves would be lost, and if the situation persisted, it would soon become untenable. One of three things would need to occur to remedy the situation:

1. Contraction or slowing in the growth rate of the money supply;
2. Devaluation of the currency unit;
3. Abandonment of the standard.

The first option involves precisely the kind of costly downward price adjustment that Greenfield and Yeager wish to avoid. The second and third choices, however, ratify the change in the purchasing power of the monetary unit. They also involve a partial or complete revision in the monetary standard itself, which is presumably costly. Greenfield and Yeager contend that all such costly adjustment processes are avoided in the proposed system:

> Part of the beauty of the . . . system, in contrast, is that the value unit remains stable in terms of the designated commodity bundle because its value never did depend on direct convertibility into that bundle or any specific commodity. Instead, its value is fixed by definition. It is free of any link to issues of money that might become inflated.[18]

The claim that nonconvertibility is advantageous is examined in the following section. At this juncture, it is important to note that there is a more fundamental reason why there is no link to money in the Greenfield-Yeager system: *there is no money.* Prices would be quoted, contracts expressed, and financial records kept in the defined unit of account.[19] Greenfield and Yeager have captured Fischer Black's vision of an unregulated financial system:

> In such a world, it would not be possible to give any reasonable definition of the quantity of money. The payments mechanism in such a world would be very efficient, but money in the usual sense would not exist.[20]

For Greenfield and Yeager, as for other writers in this tradition, it is the unit-of-account function of money (not its medium-of-exchange function) that permits the development of a complex market economy. The authors are not very clear, however, about how an accounting system without a medium of exchange would function. (The very distinction depends on the separability of the two functions, itself a controversial proposition.)

> With no money quantitatively existing, people make payments by transferring other property. To buy a bicycle priced at 100 value units or pay a debt of 100 units, one transfers property having that total value.[21]

The authors hypothesize that "financial intermediaries blending the characteristics of present-day banks and mutual funds would presumably develop. People would make payments by writing checks (or doing the equivalent electronically) to transfer the appropriate amounts— value-unit-*worths*—of shares of ownership in these funds."[22] They envision that funds offering payments services might invest in a wide variety of assets, including securities, real estate, and commodities. Fund shares might even circulate as hand-to-hand currency, but there would be no outside or base money in the system.[23] The authors envision payments occurring in fund shares and other financial liabilities, not in actual commodities.

Advantages. Greenfield and Yeager claim five advantages for their system over present monetary arrangements:[24]

1. The system offers a unit of account of stable value.

2. The government would come under "fiscal discipline."

3. The competitive aspects of the system would spur financial innovation.

4. The means of payment would not be redeemable in a base money.

5. The unit of account's value would no longer depend on the quantity of a medium of exchange.

The first advantage represents the chief goal of the proposal: to "provide a stable unit for pricing, invoicing, accounting, economic calculation, borrowing and lending, and writing contracts reaching into the future." The second advantage derives from the complete divorce of government from the payments system.[25] It is an advantage in their view because the government "would have to borrow on the same basis as any other borrower and could no longer acquire resources by issuing money and otherwise imposing inflationary 'taxation without representation.'" It should be noted that the second advantage is a characteristic of any commodity-based monetary system or, indeed, a managed money system constrained by an appropriate rule (such as a monetarist rule for a steady rate of growth in the money supply). In other words, abolishing money is not a necessary condition for attaining this advantage.

The third advantage derives from having a *competitive* payments system, rather than any of the particular characteristics of the Greenfield-Yeager proposal. The fourth advantage is a defining characteristic of the proposed system and can only be addressed in the overall evaluation of the next section. Finally, the fifth advantage is the means by which they propose to accomplish their chief goal, which, again, is captured in the first advantage.

The principal issue that must be addressed is determining the worthwhileness of the primary goal of the system. In doing so, one must also analyze whether the means proposed will achieve that goal. Finally, one must consider whether so radical a change in the payments system is necessary to achieve the stated goal. The next section examines these issues.

Critical assessment

This section analyzes the Greenfield-Yeager proposal, focusing on three issues: the evolution of standards and payments systems, the goal of a unit of account with a stable value, and the separability of the unit of account and the medium of exchange. My conclusions can be summarized as follows. First, Greenfield and Yeager disregard the evolutionary elements present in all monetary systems and are cavalier in their attitude toward the complexities of monetary reform. Second, the authors want to have both a stable unit of account and an unrestricted payments system. They

ignore, however, arguments adduced by other legal restrictions theorists that question both the value of strict price-level stability and its feasibility absent legal restrictions. Third, it is questionable whether the unit of account can be separated from a medium of exchange. Concretely, this implies reemergence of circulating currency. Money—an asset joining the medium of exchange to the unit of account—will evolve in their system for the same reasons it has evolved in virtually every other economy. Only legal restrictions could *prevent* money's evolution.

Unit of account. Greenfield and Yeager want to define the unit of account physically so as to give quantitative precision to the basic unit of value.[26] Moreover, they apparently view the choice of a unit of account as an essentially arbitrary decision.[27] Each viewpoint ignores both the origin and the significance of standards. Standards, be they units of weight, length, or value, have their origin in usage. Like language, they are evolved, not consciously created.[28]

In terms of its evolution, we can identify a standard only after it has been used for a sustained period of time. Without a sustained period of observation, we would not know whether a thing or action were "regularly and widely used, available, or supplied."[29] Further, the degree of precision of a standard tends to be enhanced only with the passage of time. This is certainly true for units of length, like the foot.[30] Similarly, in English at least, spelling standards have only solidified in this century. Indeed, in language, as is true generally, the concept of a "standard" must be dynamic; accepted usage and meaning are continually evolving.

Standards are sometimes codified. Even in these cases, however, codification often results from private not governmental action. Time zones represent an illustrative case.[31] Before 1883, every town had its own local time, based on when the sun passed over the meridian of the town. Until the coming of the railroad, this situation was not of great importance. In the 1870s the railroads began organizing to standardize time for their own operating purposes. On October 11, 1883, railroads adopted the present system of time zones at the General Time Convention. Railroad clocks and watches were set to the new standard at noon on Sunday, November 18, 1883.

In retrospect, it may seem natural that society at large eventually conformed to the operating standard of the dominant intercity transportation mode. The adoption of the railroad time system was the result, however, of innumerable individual, voluntary actions. It certainly did not reflect governmental action, since Congress only passed the Standard Time Act on March 19, 1918. Legislation thereby caught up with (codified) practice.

Standards typically emerge, then, from decentralized choices, not centralized ones. Standards are sometimes codified, but codification generally reflects use. Some users of a standard, like scientists, may require greater precision than the public at large. This is the origin of the precise, scientific definition of a meter. The definition, cited by Greenfield and Yeager, represents a spurious precision for most of us. For ordinary usage, no one need know the frequency definition to utilize the metric system. More to the point, the "definition" is simply the frequency distance of the meter as it already existed. The meter is 1,650,763.73 wavelengths of the orange-red radiation of krypton 86 because this figure exactly conforms to the length of the already standardized meter (and not the other way around, as Greenfield and Yeager seem to suggest).[32]

Up to this point, I have emphasized the private origin of standards. What if the government were to offer an alternative standard? In most such cases, either some coercion or subsidization is in fact present (thereby violating the assumption made by Greenfield and Yeager). Even in such cases, government efforts to alter, for example, linguistic standards have been more notable for their failures than for their successes. Policy actions sometimes influence at the margin but seldom determine standards. French governments have failed to maintain the "purity" of the language, and Irish governments have been unable to preserve Gaelic as a living language. In light of this experience, the idea that a governmental suggestion could alter the monetary standard is dubious.[33]

Even if Greenfield and Yeager's view of standards were not flawed, the analogy they draw is misapplied. Greenfield and Yeager maintain that money is a unit of measurement and, as such, it should have an invariant value just as the meter has an invariant length.[34] It is this assumption that leads them to view the existing monetary standard as "preposterous," because money's value varies with constantly changing demand and supply conditions. Even though it underpins both their analysis and proposal, the assumption is not really examined much less defended. Yet it is in fact dubious.

There is *only* an analogy between a monetary unit as a standard and a unit of length as a standard: they are alike in some respects (for example, both evolved) and unlike in other respects (for example, the latter is invariant and the former is not). Greenfield and Yeager do not ever demonstrate that the similarities are relevant and the differences inconsequential.[35]

The differences between the two types of standard are in fact fundamental, the most obvious one also being one of the most important. Money does not, nor did it ever, have

a fixed or even unique value. Its value (purchasing power) is inversely related to the exchange rates (prices) of all the goods that money can purchase. To estimate money's value, one must weight prices by the importance of the respective goods in an individual's purchases. In general, each individual purchases goods in different proportions, so that, even at a moment in time, the value of money varies across individuals. This variation is an inherent by-product of individual choice and will persist so long as the money good is an object of individual choice.[36] In contrast, an established standard of measurement is the same for everyone. Even more room for variation in money's value enters as time passes, since the value will be affected by every change in the demand and supply conditions for all other goods.

What I have just described is, of course, the characteristic of money to which Greenfield and Yeager object. Notice, however, that if this variability in value necessarily characterizes money, then money is not a standard of value in the same sense that a meter is a standard of length. That is, money is not an invariant measure of value.[37] "Standard" is being used equivocally, and the analogy made by Greenfield and Yeager draws its force from this equivocation.

The authors could argue that money (or the means of payment) *ought* to be standard in the same sense that the meter is. Instead of arguing for the position, however, they assume it. They then present a means for achieving a goal without ever having defended the goal. A crucial analytic step in the argument is thus simply missing—namely, the justification for the system they propose. Moreover, if one places any importance on institutions (or standards) as they have evolved and existed through time, the Greenfield-Yeager proposal must appear very odd indeed. It would endow a means of payment with a characteristic that it has never had.

Modern governments have certainly taken an activist role in monetary matters. The U.S. Government has intervened in many significant ways, the most notable case being the nationalization of private gold holdings in 1933.[38] Nonetheless, major features of the monetary system reflect evolutionary forces. The dollar itself was adopted in an evolutionary process by Americans before it ever became the official currency. Though Greenfield and Yeager are quite correct in pointing to the many monetary restrictions and interventions that have occurred, they all but ignore the evolutionary elements present in the current system. They accordingly beg the crucial question by implicitly treating all major features of the current monetary system as the result of policy interventions.[39] Moreover, they write as though money were invented, despite the fact that we have long known that "money is not the product of an agreement on the part of economizing men nor the product of legislative acts. No one invented it."[40]

Price level. Like many other monetary economists, Greenfield and Yeager prefer greater price stability. They believe that adopting an invariant standard of value will yield near-absolute price stability. It is important to note that "price stability" refers to the stability of the price level—an average of prices. Stability of *relative* prices is impossible and undesirable in a market economy. Changes in relative prices are sensitive indicators of the relative scarcity of goods; economic agents depend on these price signals for making allocational decisions.

What, then, is the case for stabilizing the price level? Given the degree of support for this position among economists, the arguments offered are surprisingly sketchy. We have already seen that the analogy on which Greenfield and Yeager rely—the invariance of a unit of length—breaks down. They do offer the more pragmatic argument of downward inflexibility of prices. Unfortunately, their argument proves too much. Consider the following passage:

> Elements of price and wage stickiness, though utterly rational from the individual points of view of the decision-makers involved, do keep downward price and wage adjustments from absorbing the full impact of the reduced willingness to spend associated with efforts to build or maintain cash balances. The rot snowballs, especially if people react to deteriorating business and growing uncertainty by trying to increase their money holdings relative to income and expenditure.[41]

The analysis overlooks the fact that nonmonetary factors—real shocks—are also capable of putting downward pressure on prices and wages in sectors of the economy. (The early-1986 fall in energy prices is a dramatic but relevant example.) Surely "the rot snowballs" in such cases too. A model incorporating reasonable lag could generate "deteriorating business and growing uncertainty," at least transitionally, as a consequence of a major real shock. More generally, save in a hyperinflation, some prices are always declining; if the economy cannot sustain downward pressure on key prices, then price stability is no solution. With the price level constant, many individual prices will be falling at any given time. Nothing but a policy of virtually unlimited inflation could prevent this.

Milton Friedman has suggested that stabilizing the general level of prices will diminish the number of price changes that need to be made overall. In this view, there is a given amount of price flexibility in the system, and policymakers ought to avoid placing excessive demands on this price

flexibility.[42] Unfortunately, Friedman does not offer an argument showing any direct connection between stabilizing a price level and minimizing the number of relative price changes. Others have argued that stabilizing the price level may cause disequilibrating relative price changes.[43] Since Friedman made his suggestion, an empirical literature has emerged that documents an apparent connection between the rate of change in the price level and the variance of relative prices.[44] The theory underlying this connection is not so well worked out, but, in any case, Friedman obviously did not rely on this literature.

Wallace contends that the legal restrictions theory calls into question the welfare argument for price stability:

> Although widely espoused as a goal, there exist no complete arguments leading to the conclusion that people are on average better off the more stable the price level, *given* the steps that have to be taken to attain greater stability of the price level.[45]

The argument assumes that in an unregulated financial system, private agents can create debt obligations, some of which will circulate as credit money. The variability in the supply of these money substitutes makes price-level control difficult. Only legal restrictions can ensure price-level stability. According to Wallace, then, the absence of legal restrictions is *inconsistent* with strict price-level control.

The Greenfield-Yeager system is susceptible to the Wallace critique. As they explicitly recognize, the funds in their system might issue debt instruments denominated in units of account.[46] If, as is argued below, circulating liabilities ("currency") are likely to be non-interest-bearing, then there is a fatal flaw in the system:

> In this case, . . . the banks (or funds) would always have an incentive to issue more of these paper Units, in effect using them to purchase interest-bearing assets. Indeed, the incentive to issue additional currency would prevail as long as the (nominal) interest rate on paper assets exceeded zero and the exchange value of Units exceeded the cost of printing paper Units. This, however, is a market force—and apparently a potent one—tending to undermine the scheme. One who believes that market forces are generally more effective than suggestions or expressions of sentiment by the government would then believe that the exchange value of the Unit would be driven far below that of a standard bundle.[47]

In other words, a circulating medium of exchange ("currency") would emerge once again in an unregulated payments system. One could forbid its issuance, but then the system would not be one in which "the government would practice laissez faire toward the medium of exchange and the banking and financial system."[48] Economic analysis suggests that architects of such a system will soon be faced with the choice of abandoning the scheme or forsaking the commitment to "laissez faire."

Non-interest-bearing money. Legal restrictions theorists believe that key features of our present monetary system have resulted from compulsion not competition. Greenfield and Yeager observe that "our existing system is far from the pure product of . . . evolution."[49] The observation is unquestionably true but does not address whether the features of the system relevant to the debate have evolved or are basically the product of intervention. Specifically, would non-interest-bearing currency exist in a completely unregulated payments system?

Though Greenfield and Yeager allow for some currency in their system, the issue is both the starting point and the major focus of the legal restrictions theory. Moreover, currency is the most distinctive monetary aggregate; it is least like nonmoney financial assets. Hence, an affirmative answer to the question would at least cast doubt on the broadest conclusion of the legal restrictions theory: namely, money would not exist as a distinct asset in a competitive payments system. On this broader issue, Greenfield and Yeager accept the conclusion of the legal restrictions theorists.

Elsewhere, I have developed the theoretical case for non-interest-bearing money in a competitive payments system. Basically, that case derives a *nonpecuniary* yield from holding money. The source of the yield is the transaction costs saved in utilizing a widely accepted medium of exchange in indirect exchange. In other words, money is more liquid than are nonmoney financial assets.[50]

This traditional argument addresses the demand for non-interest-bearing money (here, "currency"). Lawrence White has recently analyzed the cost or supply conditions of producing currency. His analysis strongly suggests the viability of currency even in a highly competitive payments system. White makes a rough calculation of the costs and benefits of paying interest on currency:

On a note whose initial value equals two hours' wages, held one week while yielding interest at 5 percent per annum, accumulated interest would amount to less than 7 seconds' wages. If the noteholder's wage rate indicates the opportunity cost of his time, then he will not find it worthwhile to compute and collect interest if to do so twice (once at the receiving end and once at the spending

end) takes 7 seconds or more, i.e. if it takes 3.5 seconds or more per note-transfer. To indicate the same point less generally, a $20 note held one week at 5 percent interest would yield less than 2 cents. Notes held in cash registers by retailers generally turn over much more rapidly than once a week, of course, so that the threshold denomination may well be extremely high.[51]

White's calculation ignores the cost of any capital equipment necessary to make such speedy calculations. For realistic wage rates, interest rates, and maximum denominations of currency, it is highly plausible that currency will continue to yield no interest. Non-interest-bearing money is the outcome of fundamental market forces, not legal compulsion.

Conclusion

The article began by considering the development of the legal restrictions theory. The theory constitutes positive economic analysis, and the models employing it implement a particular modeling strategy. It is fairly clear that Black believes that the system he outlines would emerge naturally. The same belief appears to characterize the work of Fama and Wallace. Greenfield and Yeager (and Hall) have advocated implementing the alternative payments system as a matter of public policy. Their papers represent a normative economic approach to the issues raised by the legal restrictions theory.

This article focused on the public policy proposal as put forth by Greenfield and Yeager. The coherence of their goal was questioned, as were the methods for attaining it. My criticism of that proposal does not directly address the legal restrictions theory as positive economic analysis. Nevertheless, one strong conclusion derives from both the theory and the policy proposal: the disappearance of money as a distinctive financial asset. This article strongly questions the soundness of the argument for that conclusion.

A number of important issues raised by the Greenfield-Yeager proposal have necessarily been left unresolved. For instance, Greenfield and Yeager believe that stability in the value of the unit of account can only be achieved in an unregulated payments system. Wallace, however, questions whether price-level control is attainable absent legal restrictions. Moreover, given the need for the restrictions, he questions the desirability of price-level control. It is not clear that banking deregulation necessarily obviates attainment of macroeconomic goals like price-level stabilization.[52] It does seem unlikely, however, that a monetary reform accelerating the move toward an unregulated payments system could increase the degree of control over the price level. With flaws in the Greenfield-Yeager proposal and continued disagreements among legal restrictions theorists, that remains an open question.

1. "Under this law any person or group had a *right* to start a bank. Under the old rule, the *privilege* of starting a bank had to be granted by special legislative act" (Ross M. Robertson, *History of the American Economy*, 3d ed. [New York: Harcourt Brace Jovanovich, 1973], 188n).

2. On the American system, see Hugh Rockoff, "The Free Banking Era: A Reexamination," *Journal of Money, Credit, and Banking* 6 (May 1974): 141-67; also, Arthur J. Rolnick and Warren E. Weber, "Free Banking, Wildcat Banking, and Shinplasters," *Federal Reserve Bank of Minneapolis Quarterly Review*, Fall 1982, 10-19, and "The Causes of Free Bank Failures: A Detailed Examination," *Journal of Monetary Economics* 14 (November 1984): 267-91. For the Scottish system, see Lawrence H. White, *Free Banking in Britain: Theory, Experience, and Debate, 1800-1845* (Cambridge and New York: Cambridge University Press, 1984).

3. In this usage, "bonds" comprise Treasury bills, notes, and bonds.

4. See Neil Wallace, "A Legal Restrictions Theory of the Demand for 'Money' and the Role of Monetary Policy," *Federal Reserve Bank of Minneapolis Quarterly Review*, Winter 1983, 1-7; and John Bryant, "Analyzing Deficit Finance in a Regime of Unbacked Government Paper," *Economic Review*, Federal Reserve Bank of Dallas, January 1985, 17-27.

5. John Bryant and Neil Wallace, "A Suggestion for Further Simplifying the Theory of Money" (Minneapolis, December 1980, Photocopy), 1.

6. Wallace, "A Legal Restrictions Theory," 1-4.

7. Eugene F. Fama, "Banking in the Theory of Finance," *Journal of Monetary Economics* 6 (January 1980): 55; also, his "Financial Intermediation and Price Level Control," *Journal of Monetary Economics* 12 (July 1983): 8.

8. Robert E. Hall, "Monetary Trends in the United States and the United Kingdom: A Review from the Perspective of New Developments in Monetary Economics," *Journal of Economic Literature* 20 (December 1982): 1554.

9. Leland B. Yeager, "Essential Properties of the Medium of Exchange," *Kyklos* 21, no. 1 (1968): 45-69; reprinted in R. W. Clower, ed., *Monetary Theory: Selected Readings* (Baltimore: Penguin Books, 1969), 37-60; "What Are Banks?" *Atlantic Economic Journal* 6 (December 1978): 1-14; "Sticky Prices or Equilibrium Always?" (Paper presented at the Western Economic Association meetings, San Francisco, 7 July 1981; "Stable Money and Free-Market Currencies," *Cato Journal* 3 (Spring 1983): 305-26; and Robert L. Greenfield and Leland B. Yeager, "A Laissez-Faire Approach to Monetary Stability," *Journal of Money, Credit, and Banking* 15 (August 1983): 302-15.

10. Yeager, "Stable Money and Free-Market Currencies," 305.

11. The classic statement of this view is in Yeager's "Essential Properties of the Medium of Exchange." See also his "Stable Money and Free-Market Currencies," 305-8, and Greenfield and Yeager, "A Laissez-Faire Approach to Monetary Stability," 309-11.

12. Greenfield and Yeager, "A Laissez-Faire Approach," 309. As in most such macroeconomic analysis of price setting, there is an asymmetry in the treatment of upward and downward price adjustments. From a micro-economic perspective, the asymmetry is troubling. This is especially true if adjustment costs reflect information costs or the value of price *stability*. In either case, prices ought to be sticky in *each* direction. In "Essential Properties of the Medium of Exchange," Yeager deals with inflation in a footnote, and then only with the special case of suppressed inflation (54n; cf. 57 n. 19).

13. "Recent and ongoing financial innovations (money-market funds, sweep accounts, overnight RPs, overnight Eurodollars, highly marketable credit instruments, cash management devices, and all the rest) are rendering the very concept of money hopelessly fuzzy and the velocity of whatever constitutes money hopelessly unstable and unpredictable. So, anyway, goes a view that I cannot confidently dismiss" (Yeager, "Stable Money and Free-Market Currencies," 308).

14. Greenfield and Yeager, "A Laissez-Faire Approach," 305.

15. Greenfield and Yeager, "A Laissez-Faire Approach," 305. In this quote, the authors refer to the four commodities constituting the monetary unit advocated by Robert E. Hall in "Explorations in the Gold Standard and Related Policies for Stabilizing the Dollar" (in *Inflation: Causes and Effects* [Chicago: University of Chicago Press for National Bureau of Economic Research, 1982], 111-22). Hall dubbed the unit "ANCAP" for its constituent parts: ammonium nitrate, copper, aluminum, and plywood. Some of the differences between the Greenfield-Yeager proposal and Hall's are explained in the text here.

16. According to Greenfield and Yeager, the commodities defining the unit "would not have to be storable, that is, capable of being held as monetary reserves, since the ... scheme does not require any direct convertibility of obligations into the particular commodities defining the value unit" ("A Laissez-Faire Approach," 305). The contention that the commodities need not be *storable* (as opposed to not actually being stored) is surely at odds with the requirement that the commodity bundle "would be composed of precisely gradable, competitively traded, and industrially important commodities." It is difficult to conceive of a commodity that is at once "precisely gradable, competitively traded, and industrially important" but not storable.

17. For this comparison, differences among various types of commodity standards can be sloughed over.

18. "A Laissez-Faire Approach," 306.

19. Greenfield and Yeager, "A Laissez-Faire Approach," 305.

20. Fischer Black, "Banking and Interest Rates in a World Without Money: The Effects of Uncontrolled Banking," *Journal of Bank Research* 1 (Autumn 1970): 9.

21. Greenfield and Yeager, "A Laissez-Faire Approach," 307.

22. Greenfield and Yeager, "A Laissez-Faire Approach," 307. Their account of the future payments mechanism adds little to Black's prophecy in "Banking and Interest Rates in a World Without Money."

23. Greenfield and Yeager, "A Laissez-Faire Approach," 307-8.

24. "A Laissez-Faire Approach," 308-11. The quotations here on the system's advantages are found on those pages.

25. "The government would be forbidden to issue obligations fixed in value in the unit of account and especially suitable as media of exchange" (Greenfield and Yeager, "A Laissez-Faire Approach," 305).

26. "A Laissez-Faire Approach," 303, 305.

27. Greenfield and Yeager, "A Laissez-Faire Approach," 306; cf. Yeager, "Stable Money and Free-Market Currencies," 324.

28. For an evolutionary theory of not only institutions but customs and even law, see F. A. Hayek, "The Results of Human Action but Not of Human Design," in *Studies in Philosophy, Politics and Economics* (New York: Simon and Schuster, Clarion Books, 1969), 96-105, and "Liberalism," in *New Studies in Philosophy, Politics, Economics and the History of Ideas* (Chicago: University of Chicago Press, 1978), 119-51.

29. *Webster's Ninth New Collegiate Dictionary*, s.v. "standard" (adjective).

30. A "foot" was originally the length of the terminal part of the reigning king's vertebrate leg.

31. This account of the episode is based on Larry Treiman, "Railroad Watches and Time Service," *National Railway Bulletin* 41, no. 1 (1976): 4.

32. Greenfield and Yeager chose an atypical and complex set of standards, the metric system. The metric system was indeed invented out of whole cloth. The meter was originally and arbitrarily defined as a fraction of the length (crudely measured) between the two poles of the earth. It later attained its more precise definition. The system was potentially useful, however, because of its conformity to customary units of length. (Richard Langlois kindly supplied me the history of this scientific unit of measurement.)

33. See Gerald P. O'Driscoll, Jr., and Mario J. Rizzo, *The Economics of Time and Ignorance* (Oxford and New York: Basil Blackwell, 1985), 195-98.

34. "A Laissez-Faire Approach," 306.

35. They come closest when they observe the following: "Of course, an analogy is just that and not an identity. There are differences between units of length and value, just as between units of length and weight. The key similarity is that both are *defined* units whose definitions do not change or stop being applicable because of changes in some quantity or because of other physical or economic events" ("A Laissez-Faire Approach," 306). Their explication of the differences does not meet the objection being raised here.

36. For a humorous demonstration of this point, see M. L. Burstein, *Money* (Cambridge, Mass.: Schenkman Publishing Co., 1963), 11-14; reprinted as "The Index-Number Problem," in R. W. Clower, ed., *Monetary Theory: Selected Readings* (Baltimore: Penguin Books, 1969), 61-64.

   Well-known price indices, like the consumer price index, certainly can provide useful information if properly utilized. Persistent or substantial changes in the indices typically indicate changes in the purchasing power of money confronting most individuals. Similarly, policymakers may use changes in the indices as information concerning the effects of recent policy actions.

37. The issue is actually an old one in the history of economics, one that was disposed of effectively by David Ricardo in the early 19th century. He examined whether there could be any "invariable standard" or "invariable measure" of value (David Ricardo, *On the Principles of Political Economy and Taxation*, vol. 1 of *The Works and Correspondence of David Ricardo*, ed. Piero Sraffa [Cambridge: Cambridge University Press, 1951], 14, 43). He concluded that "of such a measure it is impossible to be possessed" (p. 43). The reasons he gave against a commodity standard's being an invariable measure of value apply also to the unit of account proposed by Greenfield and Yeager. Indeed, at the end of their article, they evidence awareness of some of the problems. See

Greenfield and Yeager, "A Laissez-Faire Approach," 313-14. On this issue, see Gerald P. O'Driscoll, Jr., "Money, Deregulation and the Business Cycle," Federal Reserve Bank of Dallas Research Paper no. 8601 (Dallas, January 1986), 14-16.

38. See Steven L. Green, "The Abrogation of Gold Clauses in 1933 and Its Relation to Current Controversies in Monetary Economics," this *Economic Review*.

39. Greenfield and Yeager correctly observe that "our existing system is far from the pure product of . . . evolution" ("A Laissez-Faire Approach," 303). To justify their proposal within their own laissez-faire framework, however, they need to demonstrate that the major features of the existing monetary system reflect policy intervention. As argued in the text above, some variability in the value of money is an inherent feature of money. The search for an invariant measure of value is a quixotic quest. (See note 37.)

40. Carl Menger, *Principles of Economics*, trans. James Dingwall and Bert F. Hoselitz (1871; reprint, New York and London: New York University Press, 1981), 262.

41. Yeager, "Stable Money and Free-Market Currencies," 306.

42. According to Milton Friedman: "Under any conceivable institutional arrangements, and certainly under those that now prevail in the United States, there is only a limited amount of flexibility in prices and wages. We need to conserve this flexibility to achieve changes in relative prices and wages that are required to adjust to dynamic changes in tastes and technology. We should not dissipate it simply to achieve changes in the absolute level of prices that serve no economic function" ("The Role of Monetary Policy," in *The Optimum Quantity of Money and Other Essays* [Chicago: Aldine Publishing Company, 1969], 106).

43. Hayek argued that the actions necessary to stabilize the price level will generate *unsustainable* relative price changes. See Friedrich A. Hayek, *Prices and Production*, 2d ed. (London: George Routledge & Sons, 1935).

44. See, for instance, Michael David Bordo, "John E. Cairnes on the Effects of the Australian Gold Discoveries, 1851-73: An Early Application of the Methodology of Positive Economics," *History of Political Economy* 7 (Fall 1975): 337-59; "The Effects of Monetary Change on Relative Commodity Prices and the Role of Long-Term Contracts," *Journal of Political Economy* 88 (December 1980): 1088-1109; and "Some Aspects of the Monetary Economics of Richard Cantillon," *Journal of Monetary Economics* 12 (August 1983): 235-58. Also see Eugene F. Fama and G. William Schwert, "Inflation, Interest, and Relative Prices," *Journal of Business* 52 (April 1979): 183-209; Richard W. Parks, "Inflation and Relative Price Variability," *Journal of Political Economy* 86 (February 1978): 79-95; and John Spraos, "Why Inflation Is Not Relative Price-Neutral for Primary Products," *World Development* 5 (August 1977): 707-13.

45. "A Legal Restrictions Theory," 6.

46. Greenfield and Yeager, "A Laissez-Faire Approach," 307-8.

47. Bennett T. McCallum, "Bank Deregulation, Accounting Systems of Exchange, and the Unit of Account: A Critical Review," *Carnegie-Rochester Conference Series on Public Policy* 23 (Autumn 1985): 35-36. The argument brings into sharp relief the efficacy of any *noncoercive* suggestion by a government. The "standard bundle" refers to one unit of the composite-commodity bundle (for example, one ANCAP unit in Hall's system).

48. Greenfield and Yeager, "A Laissez-Faire Approach," 303.

49. "A Laissez-Faire Approach," 303.

50. See Gerald P. O'Driscoll, Jr., "Money in a Deregulated Financial System," *Economic Review*, Federal Reserve Bank of Dallas, May 1985, 11, and the references listed there. The original statement of this view was by Carl Menger; see Gerald P. O'Driscoll, Jr., "Money: Menger's Evolutionary Theory," Federal Reserve Bank of Dallas Research Paper no. 8508 (Dallas, December 1985). Also see Karl Brunner and Allan H. Meltzer, "The 'New Monetary Economics,' Fiscal Issues, and Unemployment," *Carnegie-Rochester Conference Series on Public Policy* 23 (Autumn 1985): 1-4.

51. Lawrence H. White, "Accounting for Non-interest-bearing Currency: A Critique of the 'Legal Restrictions' Theory of Money" (New York, February 1986, Photocopy), 8. White also presents an equilibrium model of competitive note creation with no interest payments; see *Free Banking in Britain*, 1-22.

52. See the discussion in O'Driscoll, "Money in a Deregulated Financial System."

[17]

LAWRENCE H. WHITE

Accounting for Non-interest-bearing Currency: A Critique of the Legal Restrictions Theory of Money

IN A SERIES OF ARTICLES, Neil Wallace and his collaborators have developed a "legal restrictions theory" of the demand for money which leads to several provocative conclusions.[1] The primary conclusion is that the difference between the rates of return on money and bonds is due entirely to certain legal restrictions on private intermediation, so that in the absence of legal restrictions the difference would go to zero. To put it another way, distinctive money would cease to exit under laissez faire. Two further conclusions follow: (1) because the effectiveness of open market operations depends on the existence of distinctive money, open market operations would have no effect on the price level in the absence of legal restrictions, and (2) the interest rate on Treasury bills measures the bindingness of the legal restrictions.

This note first attempts to reconstruct briefly the theory's primary conclusion, then cites historical evidence which indicates that the conclusion is empirically falsified. It next tries to explain where the theory goes wrong, and to account for

The author thanks Fernando Alvarez, John Bryant, Clive Bull, Ty Cowen, David Glasner, Robert Greenfield, Daniel Klein, Randy Kroszner, John Lott, Jr., Gerald O'Driscoll, Jr., Hugh Rockoff, George Selgin, Neil Wallace, seminar participants at Texas A&M University, and anonymous referees for comments. He also thanks the Scaife Foundation for research support, the Institute for Humane Studies for a congenial writing environment, and the C. V. Starr Center for Applied Economics for clerical support. None but the author is responsible for the views of the paper or for any errors or omissions.

[1]In particular see Wallace (1983). This article lists (p. 3) as "some applications of the legal restrictions theory" the following articles: Bryant and Wallace (1983), Karaken and Wallace (1978, 1981), Sargent and Wallace (1982, 1983), and Wallace (1979, 1981). An early and detailed presentation of the theory is offered by Bryant and Wallace (1980). Intellectual predecessors of the legal restrictions theory are surveyed by Cowen and Kroszner (1987).

LAWRENCE H. WHITE is assistant professor of economics, New York University.

Journal of Money, Credit, and Banking, Vol. 19, No. 4 (November 1987)

the "paradox" of non-interest-bearing currency coexisting with interest-bearing bonds even in the absence of the legal restrictions cited by Wallace. Conceivable future conditions are identified under which this account might no longer be valid, so that coexistence might indeed constitute a paradox. A final section restates the major points.

THE LEGAL RESTRICTIONS THEORY

In the legal restrictions framework, money and other assets "are valued only in terms of their payoff distributions" (Bryant and Wallace 1980), that is, only in terms of explicit pecuniary yields. It follows immediately from this assumption that a non-interest-yielding financial instrument of constant nominal value, for example, a $100 Federal Reserve note, is strictly dominated by an interest-yielding asset of the same denomination and with the same default risk and legal negotiability characteristics, e.g., a $100 Treasury bearer bond.[2] For Wallace (1983) "it is hard to see why anyone would hold non-interest-bearing currency instead of the interest-bearing securities" unless the securities were somehow legally prevented from playing the same role in transactions. He argues that securities in the United States today *are* legally prevented from playing a transactions role by virtue of the facts that (1) the Treasury has refused to issue any small-denomination bearer bonds, and (2) private firms are legally prohibited from issuing small-denomination bearer bonds.

The second of these facts prevents a form of intermediational arbitrage whereby a private firm could offer small-denomination bearer bonds presenting a default risk no greater (fraud aside) than that of the safest large-denomination bonds (e.g., Treasury bills) available in the economy. To do so a firm would hold as assets only such large-denomination bonds timed to mature simultaneously with its own small-denomination bonds. Wallace (1983) analogizes this sort of arbitrage to converting hundred-pound packages of butter into one-pound packages. Competition would force the interest rate paid on the small-denomination bonds to equal the rate on large-denomination bonds minus only the cost of intermediation, which he estimates to be less than one percent.

Were competition in this sort of intermediation allowed, Wallace argues, safe small-denomination interest-yielding bearer bonds would dominate and hence drive non-interest-yielding currency out of circulation. Non-interest-yielding currency could survive only if the yield on the small-denomination bonds were also zero, which would require that the yield on large-denomination securities be very close to zero (no greater than the cost of intermediation). Thus he concludes: "either nominal interest rates go to zero or existing government currency [which is non-interest-bearing, and no freer from default risk than private notes backed

---

[2]A "bearer bond" is a security conveyed without endorsement or supplementary documentation. In this respect it resembles a bank note.

exclusively by Treasury securities] becomes worthless."[3] The latter case implies adoption of a monetary unit other than the fiat dollar such as the gold ounce (Wallace 1983).

HISTORICAL EVIDENCE

The legal restrictions theory makes a clear and falsifiable prediction: non-interest-yielding paper currency should not be able to coexist with positive-interest-yielding securities carrying equal default risk in the absence of legal restrictions against the sort of intermediation that could produce interest-yielding bearer bonds backed by those same securities.[4] The prediction as stated here (though not by Wallace) specifies *paper* currency (or more precisely, non-commodity currency) because commodity money's complete freedom from default risk cannot be equalled, even assuming away fraud. The legal restrictions theory therefore does not imply the disappearance of commodity outside money.[5]

An obvious place to look for possible falsification of the non-coexistence prediction is in historical cases of laissez faire in money and banking. The clearest such case is the Scottish free banking system from 1716 to 1844 (see Checkland 1975 or White 1984). In examining Scottish experience, one finds that the non-coexistence prediction of the legal restrictions theory does appear to be falsified. Non-interest-yielding paper currency coexisted with interest-yielding assets, despite the absence of any legal impediments to entry into banking, to the issue of circulating liabilities (of £1 or larger), or, in particular, to the production of interest-yielding bearer bonds backed by interest-yielding assets. The typical private bank note promised only to be redeemable on demand for specie of a constant specified amount. Such a note neither paid coupon interest nor enjoyed any nominal appreciation. No law directly discouraged the payment of interest on bank notes. The bank-note-issuing Scottish banks did offer interest on demand deposit accounts, and Adam Smith (1981) reports that private bankers paid in-

---

[3]This statement suggests that free banking competition might itself force the risk-free interest rate on large securities down close to zero (i.e., down to the cost of intermediation), or, in other words, that the phenomenon of interest (beyond default risk and intermediation costs) may be simply a product of currency scarcity. Such a view is startling, but criticism of it here would require a major digression.

[4]Makinen and Woodward (1986) offer anecdotal evidence contradicting the legal restrictions theory in a different way, relating a case in which small-denomination French government-issued bearer bonds failed to circulate as a medium of exchange.

[5]Consequently Wallace (1983, p. 1, note 2) is not strictly correct in identifying Fama's (1980) and Hall's (1982) discussions of *purely* moneyless payments systems as "discussions of the legal restrictions theory."

A referee of this paper, agreeing that the coexistence of specie with interest-bearing assets is not inconsistent with the legal restrictions theory, argues that because bank notes are essentially default-free claims to specie, the coexistence of non-interesting-bearing bank notes is also consistent with the theory. The theory insists, however, that a note-issuing bank would be forced by competition to pay out to note-holders the anticipated net earnings on its asset portfolio. If there were literally no risk differential between specie and bank notes, then the theory moreover implies that specie would be dominated by such interest-bearing notes and could *not* coexist.

terest on promissory notes which were redeemable on demand. At the same time the banks' assets included essentially riskless government bonds yielding 3 to 4 percent annually, and high-quality short-term commercial bills of exchange yielding around 5 percent.[6] This conjunction of events represents a serious paradox for the legal restrictions theory.

Scotland was not an absolutely pure case of laissez faire banking, as two restrictions were placed on note issue by a Parliamentary Act of 1765. Neither restriction, however, eliminates the empirical challenge posed to the legal restrictions theory. First, the Act outlawed the use of an "optional clause" in bank notes. The clause had typically reserved to the issuer the option of delaying redemption for six months, in which case a 2.5 percent premium over par would be paid (Checkland 1975). By requiring that bank notes be redeemable on demand, the Act may have ruled out one method of paying interest, namely the circulation of postdated bearer instruments at a discount. (It is not clear whether a bank-issued bearer bond not redeemable on demand would have been considered an illegal bank note under the Act.) It left open the payment of interest by other means, such as promising redemption on demand for the note's initial value plus a premium that would grow over time. The latter method, to be sure, may not allow the perfectly maturity-matched intermediation that Wallace supposes possible. On the other hand, Scottish currency was non-interest-bearing before 1765 as well. Secondly, the Act prohibited bank notes smaller than £1, a sizable sum relative to per capital income. Large-denomination notes, however, should most clearly be interest-bearing under the legal restrictions theory.[7]

The paradox likewise appears in all other historical systems (e.g., nineteenth-century United States, Canada, Sweden, England) which, despite their other infringements of laissez faire, have allowed competitive note issue, have not banned interest-bearing notes, and yet have produced non-interest-bearing notes.

ACCOUNTING FOR THE "PARADOX" OF NON-INTEREST-BEARING CURRENCY

By assuming that money is valued only according to its risk-return characteristics and legal negotiability, the legal restrictions theory excludes consideration of the liquidity services or nonpecuniary yield provided by money.[8] If currency yields services that interest-bearing bonds do not, then non-interest-bearing currency (like non-interest-bearing oil paintings) can find willing holders and clearly

---

[6]Government bond yields and open market discount rates on short-term commercial bills in London are given by Homer (1977). The discount rate in Glasgow was 5 percent on the highest quality bills in 1800 (Anonymous 1960). The same figure is reported by Adam Smith (1981). Smith unfortunately does not provide details concerning the promissory notes of private (non-bank-note-issuing) bankers.

[7]In fact the "price discrimination" story told by Bryant and Wallace (1983) has large-denomination notes bearing interest even in the presence of legal restrictions.

[8]On the same score McCallum (1983, 1986) criticizes the overlapping-generations model of Sargent and Wallace (1982), and O'Driscoll (1985) criticizes cashless payments models.

can coexist with interest-bearing assets even in the absence of legal restrictions. One needs to explain, of course, the nature of these services and the inability of bearer securities to provide them. Well-known accounts of the nature and definition of money (e.g., Yeager 1968) have stressed money's supreme salability in comparison with all other assets. Money balances provide a liquidity service yield because, given that sums of money alone are generally or routinely accepted in exchange, their possession puts one in the position of being able to make any potential purchase with minimum inconvenience.[9]

This conception of the unique salability of money is fundamentally at odds with the legal restrictions approach. So, too, is the complementary theory of the origin of money whereby an invisible-hand market process elevates one commodity from superior salability under barter to the status of supreme salability or moneyness (Menger 1892, Jones 1976). Wallace implicitly assumes that all goods are equally salable, as, for example, they would be in a Walrasian general equilibrium setting where the auctioneer absorbs all the costs of finding a buyer at the most advantageous price available. In his view (1983) "the only significant frictions are those created by legal restrictions." In other words, in the absence of legal restrictions there are no greater transaction costs involved in spending securities than in spending money. Wallace sees no reason why interest-yielding bearer bonds would be any less readily exchangeable for goods than would non-interest-yielding currency (assuming like denomination and identical default risk).[10]

An obvious and credible reason for the superior salability of non-interest-yielding currency is surely the simplicity of transacting with it. Transacting with an interest-yielding bank note (or small-denomination bearer bond) requires both parties to perform a cumbersome calculation or other routine for discovering its present value at the moment of transfer. If the date of original issue, initial value, and stipulated rate of appreciation were stated on the note, accumulated interest would have to be calculated. If a date of redeemability and terminal value were stated, the present discounted value would have to be calculated using an agreed-upon discount rate.[11]

Alternative devices can also be imagined, but none would be costless to use. Fama (1983) hypothesizes currency denominated in portfolio-share units, with the (rising) numeraire redemption value of the unit reported daily in the newspapers, but he himself notes the inconvenience of having to check the up-to-date numeraire value of the unit. A calendar of nominal values at various dates might

[9]On this, see the important piece by Hutt (1956). Hutt contrasts the idea of a service yield from money balances with the idea that money is "barren." He shows that the latter idea has been endorsed by a long line of economists, to which we may add the legal restrictions theorists.

[10]Bryant and Wallace (1980) quite explicitly make the assumption of zero transactions costs part of their analytical framework: "Under laissez-faire, no transactions costs inhibit the operation of markets and, in particular, the law of one price." As they recognize, this assumption clearly contradicts the spirit of Hicks' 1935 article, which they in other respects aim to follow, and the title of which they appropriate.

[11]Bryant and Wallace (1980) suggest that unregulated bank notes could take the latter form: "titles to, say, $20 of U.S. currency payable to the bearer in, say, 30 days or thereafter." Wallace (1983) similarly hypothesizes bank notes with definite maturity dates.

be carried in small print on the back of a bank note, but then the current value would have to be tediously looked up. Cash registers might be equipped to read the necessary information concerning issue (or redemption) date and initial (or terminal) value from a "zebra" bar code on the face of a bank note, and to compute and display its present value, but some time would still be necessary to read the note by machine. The fixed cost of installing such a cash register furthermore suggests that it would not be economical to install one at every point of sale.

Under any of these technologies for paying interest on currency, the indicated calculations or operations would have to be performed not just once in each transaction, but separately for each note tendered by the buyer and for each note offered by the seller in change. This process recalls the inconvenience historically involved in transacting with coins each of which had to be tested for weight and possibly fineness.[12]

For competition to compel bank note issuers in practice to offer interest-bearing notes, bank note users must find the interest-bearing feature worthwhile. The expected interest receivable at each note-transfer occasion must at least compensate both the note-holder and the note-recipient for the time and trouble of computing and collecting it. Because the time cost of collecting interest is presumably the same for every denomination of bank note, whereas the benefit to the note holder declines proportionately with the size of the note, there must under any concrete set of circumstances be some threshold denomination of currency below which it will *not* pay an average-time-cost individual to bother about collecting interest.[13]

A thumbnail calculation indicates that this threshold value would in practice exceed historically common currency sizes, given historically common interest rates. On a note whose initial value equals two hours' wages, held one week while yielding interest at 5 percent per annum, accumulated interest would amount to less than 7 seconds' wages. If the note-holder's wage rate indicates the opportunity cost of his time, then he will not find it worthwhile to compute and collect interest if to do so twice (once at the receiving end and once at the spending end) takes 7 seconds or more, i.e., if it takes 3.5 seconds or more per note-transfer. To give a specific example, a $20 note held one week at 5 percent interest would yield less than 2 cents. Notes held in cash registers by retailers generally turn over much more rapidly than once a week, of course, so that the threshold denomination may well be extremely high.

The legal restrictions theorists simply overlook the significant costs involved in collecting interest on hand-to-hand currency. They do recognize a minor production cost to the intermediation which splits large interest-yielding assets into

---

[12]This cumbersome-transfer argument does not apply, however, to McCulloch's (1986) imaginative suggestion that interest in an expected-value sense could efficiently be paid on bank-notes by means of a periodic lottery on their serial numbers. Under that technology winning notes would be withdrawn from circulation, and remaining notes would presumably circulate at their face values. A version of the threshhold argument of the next two paragraphs does apply, but the relevant threshhold would be much lower. A (possibly minor) drawback of the scheme for the issuer is the incentive it gives for periodic surges and declines in bank note holding as the lottery date approaches and passes.

[13]Fama (1983) has arrived at a similar conclusion.

smaller assets. As a measure of this cost Bryant and Wallace (1980) and Wallace (1983) look to the spread at which competitive mutual funds presently operate, which is said to be 1 percent or less. This spread would be relevant for predicting the spread between bank asset yields and deposit yields under laissez faire, for the technology of paying interest on a bank deposit is not significantly different from that of adding earnings to a mutual fund account. Currency *is* different, however. Because the holder of a bank note at any moment is anonymous to the bank, it cannot simply make a bookkeeping entry to add interest to an account which it holds for him or her. Neither Bryant and Wallace (1980) nor Wallace (1983) recognizes any technological difference between demand deposits and currency with respect to the ease of paying interest. The only cost Wallace (1983) mentions with direct reference to currency is the cost to the issuer of replacing worn notes.

Two potential objections to the argument advanced here need to be addressed. First, the implication that paper currency under laissez faire would circulate at par might seem itself to be readily falsified by a historical example: the existence of variable discounts on bank notes, as recorded by "bank note reporter" publications, during the United States "free banking" period. Those publications only indicate, however, that discounts from par were charged by specialized brokers who purchased "foreign" notes with local notes or specie (Rockoff 1974). They do not indicate that notes routinely circulated at variable discounts. Indeed, the existence of the brokerage business reflects the fact that travelers needed to get hold of "current" money (accepted at par) for convenient local spending. That well-known brands of notes were not current across wide areas of the country (as they were in Scotland) is to be explained at least in part by the departures from laissez faire that prevented interlocal branch banking in the United States.

Second, it might be objected that unlimited profits are available to firms that hold interest-bearing assets and issue non-interest-bearing bank notes. On average and at the margin, of course, the profit from note issue must be zero in competitive equilibrium. The limiting factors are fixed costs and marginal diseconomies of scale in issuing notes and keeping them in circulation in the face of (non-price) competition from rival issuers. Outlays, which may rise at the margin, must be made on numerous services to attract note-holding customers: longer bank operating hours, more tellers and machines, and additional branch offices to make redemption easier; advertising to make notes more familiar or trusted; special engraving of notes to make them attractive and counterfeit-proof (White 1984). These services are similar to the familiar features of non-price competition among banks for depositors when interest rate ceilings are legally imposed on bank deposits.

Technological progress may one day render microchips and associated display equipment so cheap that tamper-proof chips may be economically implanted into currency (much as they are currently implanted at considerable cost into France's "smart" credit cards) which would enable an interest-bearing bank note to calculate and display its own present value continuously. On that day, which has certainly not yet arrived, the continued existence of non-interest-bearing currency might constitute a paradox. On the other hand, the simple ease of working with round denominations might well preserve a demand to hold non-interest-bearing notes, at least in the smaller denominations. If *all* pieces of currency were interest-bearing, locating exact change would become prohibitively costly or even impossible.

CONCLUSION

The legal restrictions theory of money accounts for the existence of non-interest-bearing paper currency by referring to legal barriers against certain forms of private intermediation. Yet we find that non-interest-bearing paper currency has existed historically even in the absence of such barriers. Non-interest-yielding paper currency can be accounted for without invoking legal restrictions on private intermediation once we drop the assumption that transaction and computation costs are universally zero. Interest is not worth collecting on at least some smaller denominations of currency because, given plausible technological assumptions, the collection of interest makes its transfer too cumbersome. Hence non-interest-bearing currency can survive even in the absence of legal restrictions.

LITERATURE CITED

Anonymous. "The Glasgow Financial Scene: Early Nineteenth Century." *Three Banks Review* 45 (March 1960), 33–44.

Bryant, John, and Neil Wallace. "A Suggestion for Further Simplifying the Theory of Money." Unpublished manuscript, Federal Reserve Bank of Minneapolis and University of Minnesota (December 1980).

———. "A Price Discrimination Analysis of Monetary Policy." Research Department Staff Report 51, Federal Reserve Bank of Minneapolis (1983).

Checkland, Sydney G. *Scottish Banking: A History 1695–1973*. Glasgow: Collins, 1975.

Cowen, Tyler, and Randall Kroszner. "The Development of the New Monetary Economics." *Journal of Political Economy* 95 (June 1987), 567–90.

Fama, Eugene. "Banking in the Theory of Finance." *Journal of Monetary Economics* 6 (January 1980), 39–57.

———. "Financial Intermediation and Price Level Control." *Journal of Monetary Economics* 12, July 1983, 7–28.

Hall, Robert. "Monetary Trends in the United States and the United Kingdom: A Review from the Perspective of New Developments in Monetary Economics." *Journal of Economic Literature* 20 (December 1982), 1552–56.

Hicks, John. "A Suggestion for Simplifying the Theory of Money." *Economica* (N. S.) 2 (February 1935), 1–19.

Homer, Sidney. *A History of Interest Rates*. 2nd ed. New Brunswick, N. J.: Rutgers University Press, 1977.

Hutt, W. H. "The Yield from Money Held." In *On Freedom and Free Enterprise*, edited by Mary Sennholz, pp. 196–223. Princeton: D. Van Nostrand, 1956.

456 : MONEY, CREDIT, AND BANKING

Jones, Robert A. "The Origin and Development of Media of Exchange." *Journal of Political Economy* 84 (November 1976), 757–75.

Karaken, John, and Neil Wallace. "International Monetary Reform: The Feasible Alternatives." Federal Reserve Bank of Minneapolis *Quarterly Review* 2 (Summer 1978), 2–7.

———. "On the Indeterminacy of Equilibrium Exchange Rates." *Quarterly Journal of Economics* 96 (May 1981), 207–22.

Makinen, Gail E., and G. Thomas Woodward. "Some Anecdotal Evidence Relating to the Legal Restrictions Theory of the Demand for Money." *Journal of Political Economy* 94 (April 1986), 260–65.

McCallum, Bennett T. "Comments [on Sargent and Wallace (1983)]." *Journal of Monetary Economics* 12 (July 1983), 189–96.

———. "Some Issues Concerning Interest Rate Pegging, Price Level Determinancy, and the Real Bills Doctrine." *Journal of Monetary Economics* 17 (January 1986), 135–60.

McCulloch, J. Huston. "Beyond the Historical Gold Standard." In *Alternative Monetary Regimes*, edited by Colin Campbell and William R. Dougan, pp. 73–81. Baltimore: Johns Hopkins University Press, 1986.

Menger, Carl. "On the Origin of Money," translated by Caroline A. Foley, *Economic Journal* 92 (June 1982), 239–55.

O'Driscoll, Gerald P., Jr. "Money in a Deregulated Financial System." *Economic Review*, Federal Reserve Bank of Dallas (May 1985), 1–12.

Rockoff, Hugh. "The Free Banking Era: A Reexamination." *Journal of Money, Credit, and Banking* 6 (May 1974), 141–67.

Samuelson, Paul A. *Foundations of Economic Analysis.* Cambridge: Harvard University Press, 1947.

Sargent, Thomas, and Neil Wallace. "The Real-Bills Doctrine versus the Quantity Theory: A Reconsideration." *Journal of Political Economy* 90 (December 1982), 1212–36.

———. "A Model of Commodity Money." *Journal of Monetary Economics* 12 (July 1983), 163–87.

Smith, Adam. *An Inquiry into the Nature and Causes of the Wealth of Nations,* edited by R. H. Campbell, A. S. Skinner, and W. B. Todd. Indianapolis: Liberty Classics, 1981.

Wallace, Neil. "Why Markets in Foreign Exchange are Different from Other Markets." Federal Reserve Bank of Minneapolis *Quarterly Review* 3 (Fall 1979), 1–7.

———. "A Modigliani-Miller Theorem for Open-Market Operations." *American Economic Review* 71 (June 1981), 267–74.

———. "A Legal Restrictions Theory of the Demand for 'Money' and the Role of Monetary Policy." Federal Reserve Bank of Minneapolis *Quarterly Review* (Winter 1983), 1–7.

White, Lawrence H. *Free Banking in Britain.* Cambridge: Cambridge University Press, 1984.

Yeager, Leland B. "Essential Properties of the Medium of Exchange." *Kyklos* 21 (1968), 45–69.

[18]

The Economic Journal, **98** (*Conference* 1988), 25–36
Printed in Great Britain

A SUGGESTION FOR OVERSIMPLIFYING
THE THEORY OF MONEY*

Neil Wallace

In his well-known paper 'A Suggestion for Simplifying the Theory of Money', Hicks (1935) said that the main challenge facing monetary theory is to face up to the frictions that lead people to hold low-yielding, monetary-like assets. Today I want to discuss ways of meeting a slightly revised version of that challenge: how do we go about building models which have equilibria in which some assets end up having a relatively low return?

One response is to say that it is easy to meet Hicks' challenge. For example, a model in which the real value of outside money is an argument of individuals' utility functions or one in which holdings of outside money are required to meet a Clower or cash-in-advance constraint will meet the challenge if the stock of outside money is somehow limited. However, such ways of meeting Hicks' challenge seem unconvincing.

Consider the money-in-the-utility-function model. Suppose someone could issue liabilities backed by holdings of interest-bearing securities that would compete with outside money in yielding utility. Such liabilities could be sold at a price that implies a yield lower than the market rate of interest on securities and so earn a profit for the issuer. The same possibility arises in the cash-in-advance model. As usually exposited (Helpman, 1981 and Lucas, 1982), in those models individuals face a sequence of two constraints at each date. First, outside money and securities are traded. Then, outside money and goods are traded. But, again, if securities bear interest and if someone in the first market, the money-securities market, could issue liabilities that would trade for goods in the second market, then there are potential profits to be earned by doing that. So we are left in these models with the question: what thwarts these profit opportunities?

A boorish response to these concerns consists of simply repeating the assumptions: outside money is an argument of utility functions not an aggregate of outside and inside money; outside money is needed in the goods market, not either outside or inside money. This is a boorish response, because it stops conversation and leaves us at an impasse. A more forthcoming response would display a willingness to discuss the properties of outside money that allow it to yield utility or to be used for goods purchases and that prevent inside money from playing those roles. Perhaps it is because outside money is trusted and inside money would not be. Or, perhaps such substitution of inside for outside money is limited because the inside money issuers would want to hold reserves in the form of outside money.

* The Harry G. Johnson Lecture. Financial support was provided by the Federal Reserve Bank of Minneapolis which, however, does not necessarily endorse the views expressed.

While more forthcoming, these responses are not satisfactory. As usually exposited, both money-in-the-utility function and cash-in-advance models have perfect securities markets in which individuals can borrow and lend. If trust is not a problem in those markets, why is it a problem for securities that are going to be exchanged for goods? Nor does there seem to be a need for inside money issuers to hold reserves in such models. In them, all the inside money issues would come due at the same time and could be paid from the proceeds of the assets held as backing. Thus, on the face of it, there is nothing in those models to explain imperfect substitution between outside and inside money.

The same difficulties arise in the context of models with transactions costs imposed on various market trades. Hicks seemed to advocate such an approach and indeed spelled out the main ingredients of inventory models of money demand. But in such models also, questions about possible substitution of inside for outside money are left unanswered.

It seems, therefore, that we should either abandon the imperfect substitution of inside for outside money or that we should somehow be explicit about the barriers to such substitution and in so doing abandon the perfect securities market assumption of those models. Either has important implications. The first turns those models into ones that do not meet the Hicksian challenge. The second gets us into a very different class of models in which, among other things, propositions like Ricardian equivalence fail because the perfect credit market has been abandoned. Today, I want to pursue the first route. My suggestion – which in the title is referred to as an oversimplifying suggestion – is that there are no *natural* barriers that limit substitution between privately issued inside money, on the one hand, and outside or government issued money, on the other hand. To explain it, I want to begin by describing in some detail the kind of private intermediation envisaged by this suggestion.

I. THE OVERSIMPLIFICATION

The kind of rate-of-return discrepancies that concern us are those between money-like assets and default-free securities. To begin, it is helpful to be specific and talk about currency, on the one hand, and certain kinds of government debt, on the other hand, debt which I will treat as being nominally default free – that is, as being sure titles to currency in the future. First, I want to identify features of such debt that would seem to make it a perfect substitute for currency. Then, given that actual debt does not satisfy those features, I want to consider whether private intermediation could produce those features.

Consider, then, government debt which is pure discount debt, which is payable-to-the-bearer, and whose face values match those of medium-size denomination currency. Let us also make this debt portable so that although distinguishable from currency, say, by its colour, it is of similar size and has similar wear and tear properties. As described, this debt differs from currency in only one objective respect; it consists of promises to currency at or after some specified future date, for example, a year from issue date. The question before us is as follows: Conditional on such debt and non-interest bearing currency coexisting, what would be the discount on the debt?

The answer I favour, is that such debt, if it coexisted with currency, would sell at face value, at no discount, and be used interchangably with currency. A loose argument for this answer goes like this. Consider first what happens at maturity. At maturity this debt is a demand claim on currency and, so, at that time becomes equivalent to currency. Given what I assumed about its physical characteristics, it should function as currency from then on. Consider next, what happens at a time very close to the maturity date, so close that few if any transactions occur between then and the maturity date. If the debt was going at a discount then, almost everyone would prefer it to acquiring actual currency at that time, because the debt will appreciate and the currency will not. Therefore, in order for such debt and currency to coexist at that time, the debt must be accepted at no discount. In other words, it takes on its currency-like character at some time prior to maturity. But if so, then we can repeat the argument and, working backwards, conclude that the debt takes on its currency-like character when it is issued.

In the United States, which is the only country I know a little about, the government does not issue the kind of debt I just described. (Of course, if I am right in what I just asserted, that is not at all surprising. Why go to so much trouble to issue what turns out to be another form of currency?) Until a few years ago, the United States issued Treasury bills which were like the debt described above except that they were issued in very large denominations, no smaller than $10,000. Now Treasury bills are all book entry. The United States also issues some small-denomination Savings bonds, but these are explicitly non-negotiable and, so, are certainly not payable-to-the-bearer.

Features like nonpayability-to-the-bearer and large-denomination are enough to explain why an individual does not regard such securities as close substitutes for the small amounts of currency that individuals typically hold. But stopping there and saying that that explains why the debt can bear substantial interest would be like saying that a very large per-pound discount on salt purchased in hundred pound sacks is explained by the fact that most people cannot lift a hundred pounds. An adequate explanation should take into account that the best way to break hundred pound sacks into reasonably sized packages does not involve each individual doing it at home in his or her kitchen. Analogously, the best way for substitution between government interest bearing debt and government currency to occur may not be by having individuals do it directly, but, instead, through the activities of financial intermediaries.

Suppose, then, that government debt is like U.S. Treasury bills – large-denomination, pure-discount debt – and consider a financial intermediary that operates as follows. It is like a money-market mutual fund in that it holds only Treasury bills as assets. Its liabilities, however, are designed to compete with government currency – they are small denomination, payable to the bearer, discount securities issued in maturities that match those of the Treasury bills held. Such an intermediary is perfectly hedged so that fraud aside and

even without reserves, its notes are as safe as the securities it holds as backing
for them. Therefore, if we continue to abstract from fraud, such an activity
gives rise to the same situation as prevails if the government itself issues small-
denomination, bearer securities. If we suppose that, as part of its business, this
intermediary takes actions that prevent fraud, then I conclude, exactly as I did
for small-denomination, bearer securities issued by the government, that the
bearer notes issued by such intermediaries would sell at par and be used
interchangably with currency, if the two were to coexist.

Since the revenue for this intermediation business comes from buying
default-free securities at a discount and issuing bearer notes at par, in an
equilibrium with free entry the discount on default-free securities like Treasury
bills must be small enough so that it is not profitable to expand this activity.
That is the case when the discount is just sufficient to cover the costs of engaging
in the business. In other words, in the presence of such intermediation, if
currency and government debt of the Treasury bill kind are to coexist, then the
yield or nominal rate of return on the latter is bounded above by the least costly
way of operating such a financial intermediation business.

Rough estimates of the magnitude of this cost can be inferred from two
sources: the cost of operating financial intermediaries in existing intermediary
activities and the cost of maintaining currency. Many financial intermediaries
– common stock and money market mutual funds – operate at spreads of one
percent or less. As for the cost of maintaining currency, in the United States,
for all but the smallest denominations the cost is less than 1% of the outstanding stock. These observations suggest that the upper bound on nominal
interest rates implied by our hypothetical intermediation is quite low,
on the order of 1 or 2% per year.

We generally do not observe nominal interest rates satisfying such a bound.
Nor do we generally observe the kind of intermediation I just described. An
obvious explanation of the latter is that it is explicitly prohibited in most
countries and has been at most times. I suspect that most countries have laws
or regulations that in intent and effect are similar to those of the following
Canadian statute:

> Every bank or other person who issues or reissues, makes, draws or
> endorses any bill, bond, note, check or other instrument, intended to
> circulate as money, or to be used as a substitute for money, is guilty of an
> offence against this act. (Banks and banking law revision act, 1980, 29,
> Eliz. 2, C.40, S311.1.

The oversimplifying suggestion ascribes to such restrictions the fact that
nominal interest rates do not always satisfy some low upper bound.

II. SOME POSITIVE IMPLICATIONS OF THE SUGGESTION

Now I want to describe some of the positive implications of this suggestion. The
sharp implications are those that are implied under *laissez-faire* in intermediation. They follow from noting that with nominal interest rates bounded
above by some rather low constant, real returns on all assets, including those

on objects we choose to call monies, must move together. Another way to put this is that under *laissez-faire*, an attempt to explain the values of all assets by store-of-value considerations should work well.

In some regards, a world with real returns on all assets forced into approximate equality seems bizarre. It is either a world in which currency as we know it – non-interest-bearing currency – continues to be valued and all real returns are driven down to approximately that on such currency, or it is a world in which currency as we know it disappears and the currency we use is different stuff, perhaps claims denominated in terms of some commodity like ounces of gold, and paying interest, perhaps by selling at a discount and appreciating as a maturity date is approached. Such extreme possibilities were described by Samuelson who, however, was not thinking of approximate rate-of-return equality being produced simply by *laissez-faire* in intermediation:

> It is true that in a world involving no transaction friction and no uncertainty, there would be no reason for a spread between the yield on any two assets, and hence there would be no difference in the yield on money and on securities. Hicks concludes, therefore, that securities will not bear interest but will accommodate themselves to the yield on money. It is equally possible and more illuminating to suppose that under these conditions money adjusts itself to the yield of securities. In fact, in such a world securities themselves would circulate as money and be acceptable in transactions; demand bank deposits would bear interest, just as they often did in this country in the period of the twenties. And if money could not make the adjustment, as in the case of metal counters which Aristotle tells us are barren, it would pass out of use, wither away and die, become a free good. [1947, p. 123.]

Each possibility may well seem strange. The view Samuelson favoured seems strange because we may have difficulty conceiving of what is, in effect, a cashless society with all transactions being accomplished by the use of interest-bearing instruments. While we can easily conceive of the widespread use of debit cards with debits and credits made against interest-bearing accounts, we may wonder about their use in all transactions. Would there not remain a demand for currency-like objects, at least for small transactions? And for small transactions, would it not be costly and bothersome to have these objects be interest-bearing? If we answer affirmatively, then we ought to entertain the Hicksian view that all yields fall to the yield on currency – net, however, of the costs of producing and maintaining the currency. In this regard, it should be noted that small denomination currency is somewhat costly to produce and maintain. In the United States, for example, the cost of maintaining the stock of one dollar bills – which remains in the form of paper despite attempts to introduce a one dollar coin – is approximately three percent of the stock per year. Thus, if currency consists entirely of quite small denomination objects, nominal interest rates higher than the 1 or 2% mentioned above are consistent with *laissez-faire* in intermediation. There are, moreover, other grounds for not dismissing too quickly the Hicksian view that, absent frictions, real returns would fall to the yield on currency. Although most economists tend to think in terms of intertemporal models – specifications of preferences and/or technologies – consistent with the Samuelson view, the evidence is far from clear-cut.

In the United States, there have been long periods of very low nominal interest rates. One such period was 1865 to 1913. During this period, National Banks could issue notes provided they held as backing certain eligible government bonds. Since these notes circulated as noninterest bearing currency, it is to be expected that the yield on the eligible bonds would have been driven down to a level consistent with zero profits on additional note issue. Yields on eligible bonds were quite low throughout the period. Moreover, throughout the period, some of the bonds eligible to be used as backing were held by the nonbank public, implying that market interest rates in general were tied to the yields on those eligible bonds. It is also to be noted that the period included both deflation and inflation – deflation from about 1873 to 1896, inflation at about 2% per year form 1896 to 1913. This suggests that real returns were adjusting to the real return on currency. Another period of very low nominal interest rates in the United States began in the 1930s and ended in the early 1950s.

Another kind of evidence that bears on whether preferences and technologies are consistent with all returns falling to the return on currency concerns holdings of gold. There is considerable casual evidence that some gold has almost always been held purely as a store of value. Certainly, gold is being held as a store of value today. This implies that preferences and technologies are now consistent with the rate-of-return on gold holding its own *vis-à-vis* that on other assets. That being so, it seems far fetched to say that these conditions did not hold at other times – when gold happened to also serve as a medium of exchange.

III. SOME NORMATIVE IMPLICATIONS OF THE SUGGESTION

I will now apply the Hicksian vision of a world without frictions – which I interpret as arising entirely from *laissez-faire* in intermediation – to consider two long-standing issues in monetary economics: the welfare effects of inflation and the inefficiency of commodity money. To do this one needs an intertemporal model which permits there to be equilibria in which all real returns are equal to the return on money. Overlapping generations models permit this to happen and the results I will be discussing should be understood as arising in the context of such models.

As regards to the inefficiency of commodity money, it is helpful to recall Friedman's remark which, paraphrasing slightly, is as follows: why expend resources to dig up gold simply in order to put it in a bank vault? (1960, p. 5). This remark captures the inefficiency of a commodity money if the only use of gold once it is dug up is as an asset. In this case, the gold is a costly to produce outside money and the inefficiency is measured by the resources used in digging it up. If, however, gold has other potential uses, as an input into the production of things that yield utility, then matters are less straightforward. If it is assumed that turning gold into a utility-yielding use now interferes with doing so at a later time, then the above paraphrase captures the inefficiency of commodity money only if it is interpreted to mean that the gold remains in the vault forever. An extreme technology of this sort was assumed in Sargent and Wallace (1983). We assumed that gold could at any time be turned into a non-durable consumption good, but that each unit of gold could be used this way only once. With this sort of technology and with gold holding its own in terms of rate of return, there is nothing inefficient or even suboptimal about an equilibrium path in which gold is held for a finite number of periods and then turned into consumption. Holding it *forever* is inefficient, because then there is some consumption which is sacrificed.

Notice that on this interpretation of the inefficiency of commodity money, the inefficiency is implied by an assumption about alternative uses of gold and the holding of gold forever and that it applies whether or not gold is a commodity money in the usual sense. Thus, if we interpret our world economy today as on a path where gold will be held in vaults forever, then we would conclude that that path is inefficient. This basis for attributing inefficiency to the holding of gold in vaults provides grounds for indicting a formal commodity money system only if we think that even more gold would be held *permanently* in vaults under such a system.

A similar proviso arises regarding the welfare effects of inflation in a world with fiat money in which we regard inflation as being produced by money-financed deficits. With money holding its own in terms of rate of return, the usual wedge-type arguments regarding inefficiency do not apply. Instead, non-optimality arises from all real returns being driven down below the natural growth rate permanently. In the context of a model with the usual one good neoclassical technology, nonoptimality is synonymous with a Tobin–Mundell effect that drives the capital-labour ratio beyond the golden rule point permanently. With money holding its own in terms of rate of return, no distortion accompanies an inflation known to be temporary.

Finally, I want to say a word about the implications of the view I have been discussing for open-market operations. Not surprisingly, the view I have been discussing leaves little scope for monetary policy in the sense of open-market operations. With private intermediation keeping nominal interest rates low, it is as if we have a liquidity trap, with the trap produced through variations in the amount of privately supplied inside money.

A more detailed picture of this lack of scope for open-market operations would go as follows. Suppose the money consists of small denomination, payable-to-bearer notes, and suppose there is a common and constant average-cost technology for producing and maintaining such notes – common to both the government and the private sector. Then, an open-market operation would do no more than shift the location of the intermediation between the private sector and the government or central bank. It would affect neither interest rates, the price level, nor anything else. In particular, there would not be any effects on the government's budgetary position. Thus, for example, if the government expands its intermediation, then its interest payments to the public fall, but the savings in interest payments are just matched by the increased costs of maintaining the higher real stock of government currency.

Now, admittedly, the common constant average cost assumption seems farfetched. It is, perhaps, more plausible that the provision of small denomination, bearer notes is a decreasing cost activity – maybe because the cost of inhibiting counterfeiting does not rise in proportion to the value of notes outstanding. While such considerations may justify a government monopoly on currency issue, they suggest that the problem of how the monopoly should be managed resembles the analogous problem for other decreasing costs industries.

IV. LEGAL RESTRICTIONS

So far I have been discussing what the oversimplifying suggestion says would occur under *laissez-faire*. Now I want to discuss why we hardly ever observe *laissez-faire* in intermediation – why legal restrictions have been so prevalent.

One obvious motivation for legal restrictions on private intermediation is to enhance seigniorage possibilities by increasing the demand for government currency. Many of the legal restrictions in place in the world today seem motivated by that consideration.

A related, but more subtle motivation for legal restrictions arises in settings in which there is a potential for earning seigniorage not only on currency, but also on other government liabilities. There is such a potential if the government can sell bonds with a real return less than the growth rate. Bryant and Wallace (1984) described one such setting – a stationary, pure exchange, overlapping generations model in which all private saving ends up being in the form of government liabilities. We showed that if a positive real deficit could be financed by money issue only, the usual kind of seigniorage, then there are Pareto Superior equilibria that have the same deficit being financed partly by bonds. The bonds are large denomination securities whose presence along with that of divisible money implies that savers face a nonconstant return schedule on savings, a schedule which is increasing in the amount saved. This non-constant schedule, which is synonymous with price discrimination, allows for better outcomes, given that the constant schedule would itself be distorting because a positive deficit is being financed. The non-constant schedule is achieved by bonds which are available only in a minimum denomination and which pay a higher rate-of-return than that on divisible currency and by a legal restriction against intermediation of government bonds. The legal restriction prevents savers from getting together and sharing the large denomination bonds. If they could, then according to the model, only a constant return schedule on government liabilities would be possible.

Seigniorage does not, however, seem to motivate all actual and suggested legal restrictions on private intermediation. It did not motivate Adam Smith's proposals that private banks be allowed to issue notes only in some substantial minimum denomination and only notes payable upon demand. Nor did it motivate proposals in the United States for high required reserves behind demand deposits or note issues. And it did not seem to motivate England's Bank Charter Act, often called Peel's Act, which gave the Bank of England a monopoly on note issue and set a marginal 100% reserve requirement against note issue. In a paper somewhat inaptly entitled 'The Real Bills Doctrine Versus the Quantity Theory: a Reconsideration', Sargent and Wallace (1982) poked fun at restrictions like those imposed by Peel's Act. We did so by interpreting the goal of the restrictions to be price stability and the restrictions themselves to be ones that force savings instruments for small savers to be 100% backed by outside money. In the context of an overlapping generations model, we imposed an endowment pattern that implied a fluctuating demand for private credit and showed that the restrictions would indeed stabilise the price level. They did so by separating the market for money, which had a stable demand under the restrictions, from the market for credit, which had a fluctuating demand. However, and this is the sense in which we poked fun at the restrictions, this stable price level outcome, which is accompanied by a fluctuating nominal interest rate, is not Pareto Optimal. In contrast, without the restrictions, there is an equilibrium with a fluctuating price level which is Pareto Optimal.

Of course, it is possible that our model was missing crucial features that justify the restrictions imposed by Peel's Act. Jevons in *Money and the Mechanism of Exchange* attempted to defend Peel's Act:

> The objectors to the Bank Charter Act urge that we want more currency, but they cannot really mean more metallic currency. We must not look to changes in the law to increase the amount of specie in the country, and, as I have remarked, any one can get sovereigns if he has the needful gold . . . . What the currency theorists want, then, is not more gold, but more promises to pay gold. The Free-Banking School especially argue that it is among the elementary rights of an individual to make promises, and that each banker should be allowed to issue as many notes as he can get his customers to take, keeping such a reserve of metallic money, as he thinks in his own private discretion, sufficient to enable him to redeem his promises. But this free issue of paper representative money does not at all meet the difficulty of the money market, which is a want of gold, not of paper; on the contrary, an unlimited issue of paper would tend to reduce the already narrow margin of gold upon which we erect an enormous system of trade. [1918, pp. 307-8.]

Jevons was right in saying that the Free-Banking School wanted more promises to pay gold. He may have been wrong in denying that such promises could meet the needs of the money market. The model just discussed has variable needs in the money market, which could arise from either a fluctuating demand for currency-like assets or from a fluctuating demand for credit. In it, allowing credit instruments to take a currency-like form would fill the needs of the money market. Admittedly, however, if fluctuations in the needs of the money market arise in other ways – for example, from fluctuations in the degree to which promises to pay gold are trusted – then that model is not applicable.

V. EVIDENCE

I now want to report and comment on some evidence concerning what is probably the weakest link in the private intermediation story I have told: the claim that the public would accept privately issued, payable-to-bearer claims on government currency or commodity currency *in the future* as perfect substitutes for the currency itself. Unfortunately, the evidence consists mainly of nonquantitative reports of what seem like relatively minor incidents.

Although there is considerable experience both in Great Britain and the United States with payable-to-bearer notes issued by private banks, almost all of the experience occurs under the restriction that the issuer redeem notes on demand. The most substantial exception of which I am aware concerns notes with option clauses issued by Scottish banks during the period from 1760 to 1764. (Such notes and notes in denominations smaller than one pound were eliminated by legislation in 1765.) According to Hugh Rockoff (1986), the option clause permitted banks to refuse immediate redemption and to repay later with interest. When banks chose to exercise the option, they would date notes brought in for payment to establish the final redemption date. Rockoff reports that notes subject to the option clause were readily accepted as currency. He does not, however, report directly on what happened to notes on which a bank chose to exercise the option.

Another kind of relevant evidence is experience with government securities that are payable-to-the-bearer and are titles to government currency in the future. Although such experience does not bear on whether the public would trust private promises to government currency in the future, it does throw light on how claims to currency in the future are treated. On this matter, the evidence is mixed.

One incident concerns the issue in India about four years ago of payable-to-the-bearer securities maturing in ten years and paying simple interest at 2 % a year. The main attraction of these securities was that they were exempt from all taxes. A newspaper reported that the bonds, which the government had expected to be discounted, began to command a premium of 20 % or more and passed from hand to hand in lieu of cash.

A related incident concerns US experience with Liberty Bonds, which were issued during World War I as bearer securities. In this case, the evidence that such bonds circulated as currency from time to time comes from complaints by the government. The Secretary of the Treasury issued a statement entitled 'On the Evils of Exchanging Merchandise for Liberty Bonds'. The statement began as follows. 'It has been brought to my attention that numbers of merchants throughout the country are offering to take Liberty Bonds at par, or even in some cases at a premium, in exchange for merchandise.' The statement went on to decry the practice, explaining that it was not the intent of the government that these bonds substitute for currency, but rather that the bond issues were intended to stimulate saving.

Finally, Makinen and Woodward (1986) report on some French experience with small denomination, payable-to-the-bearer government bonds. Beginning in 1915 and until 1927, the French government made available interest-bearing securities sold at discount and in a variety of denominations, including some quite small denominations, and with maturities of three months, six months, and one year. The authors report that notes could be obtained at the fixed discount prices at all banks, post offices, and numerous local offices of the finance ministry. They also report that in most years of their existence, the quantity outstanding was comparable to that of the currency, which consisted of notes of the Bank of France. The authors cite as evidence that the securities were not treated as perfect substitutes for Bank of France notes a reported incident in which it seemed impossible to carry out transactions using these securities. More damaging to the view I have been describing is the mere coexistence of these securities and Bank of France notes, with the former available at a discount. According to that view, either Bank of France notes should have disappeared – all of them being used to purchase the interest-bearing notes – or government offices should have run out of the interest-bearing notes and been unable to meet the demand for them. Neither seemed to happen.

I can offer only two possible explanations. First the interest-bearing notes were not well designed to circulate as currency at their face value because the prominent number of them and the one which was in a convenient denomination was their selling price, not their face value. More serious, perhaps, is the possibility that the discount notes were not viewed as default-free claims to Bank of France notes. The authors themselves suggest this when they remark that there were 'periodic crisis in the 1920s during which the interest-bearing notes were allowed by the public to run off and be replaced by Bank of France notes'.

VI. CONCLUDING REMARKS

I now want to, as it were, come clean and explain my qualms about the oversimplifying suggestion. Earlier, I criticised money-in-the-utility-function and cash-in-advance models because they were silent about the qualities an asset must possess in order that it yield utility or serve as a medium of exchange. Those theories simply assert that an outside or government money possesses those qualities and that other things do not. In a way, the oversimplifying suggestion does no better. It simply asserts that whatever are those qualities, they can be duplicated by privately provided inside money, by private intermediation. For example, in describing the oversimplifying suggestion, I repeatedly talked about properties like denomination and payability-to-the-bearer, but I did not describe an explicit model in which there was a demand for assets with these qualities. I did not because neither I nor anyone else, so far as I know, has such a model.

My concern can be put differently. I have at best described a one-blade-of-the-scissors theory of nominal interest rates – the one blade being a perfectly elastic supply curve of currency-like assets implied by private intermediation. If such a supply curve is operative, then much can be said about the nature of equilibrium without saying much about demand. However, this presumes what

36   THE ECONOMIC JOURNAL [CONFERENCE 1988]

is far from obvious: that it is legitimate to treat supply separately from demand
in the contexts under discussion. Such separate treatment is legitimate if one set
of features of the environment generate the demand for currency-like assets and
an independent set generates the supply of private liabilities than can meet that
demand. It is quite possible, though, that the features that generate a demand
for small-denomination, payable-to-the-bearer assets also have implications
for supply, and, in particular, imply that there are natural barriers to the
substitution of inside for outside currency-like assets. Given this possibility,
you can appreciate why I have chosen to label the one-blade theory an
*over*simplifying suggestion.

University of Minnesota and Federal Reserve Bank of Minneapolis

REFERENCES

Bryant, J. B. and Wallace, N. (1984). 'A price discrimination analysis of monetary policy.' *Review of Economic Studies*, vol. 51 (April) pp. 279–88.
Friedman, M. (1960). *A Program for Monetary Stability*. New York: Fordham University Press.
Helpman, E. (1981). 'An exploration in the theory of exchange rate regimes.' *Journal of Political Economy*, vol. 89 (October), pp. 865–90.
Hicks, J. R. (1935). A suggestion for simplifying the theory of money.' *Economica*.
Jevons, W. S. (1918). *Money and the Mechanisms of Exchange*, New York and London: D. Appleton.
Lucas, R. E., Jr (1982).'Interest rates and currency prices in a two-country world.' *Journal of Monetary Economics*, vol. 10, pp. 335–60.
Makinen, G. E. and Woodward, G. T. (1986). 'Some anecdotal evidence relating to the legal restrictions theory of the demand for money.' *Journal of Political Economy*, vol. 94 (April) pp. 260–5.
Rockoff, H. (1986). 'Institutional requirements for stable free banking.' *Cato Journal*, vol. 6 (Fall) pp. 617–34.
Samuelson, P. A. (1947). *Foundations of Economic Analysis*. Cambridge: Harvard University Press.
Sargent, T. and Wallace, N. (1982). 'The real-bills doctrine versus the quantity theory: a reconsideration.' *Journal of Political Economy*, vol. 90 (December), pp. 1212–36.
—— and —— (1983). 'A model of commodity money.' *Journal of Monetary Economics*, vol. 12, pp. 163–87.

[19]

Interest-Bearing Currency, Legal Restrictions, and the Rate of Return Dominance of Money

A Note by John Bryant

The rate of return dominance of money is the crucial anomaly of monetary theory. At least, this is the position taken by J. R. Hicks in his seminal paper "A Suggestion for Simplifying the Theory of Money" (1935). Hicks was concerned about the coexistence of non-interest-bearing money and real assets. Whether real assets, which are innately risky, actually dominate money is, of course, debatable, as Tobin (1958) points out. The dominance seems unambiguous, however, when the money is unbacked non-interest-bearing currency and the competing asset is default-free interest-bearing government bonds. Such bonds are promises to pay the unbacked currency, and the government is, typically, the sole legal provider of the unbacked currency. The promised currency being unbacked makes the default-free claim of the government more plausible. This paper considers various explanations of the rate of return dominance of money and defends the legal restrictions view.

The rate of return dominance of money has been explained by costs of trips to the bank. This explanation was the one put forward by Hicks. Baumol (1952) and Tobin (1956) developed this idea in the inventory model of money. This approach assumes that trade is carried out in a non-interest-bearing currency, and that trade directly using a bank's portfolio is impossible.

The rate of return dominance of money has been explained by costs of intermediation. Banks intermediate their portfolios into claims that are convenient for trade, but doing so is costly. Friedman (1969) considers the costly intermediation of bonds into interest-bearing demand deposits and currency, stating "competition among banks would force them to pay interest on deposits at a rate falling short of r_B [the bond rate] by the costs of running the banks. Competition would force banks also to pay interest on currency at a rate below the rate paid on deposits by the extra costs of administering the payment of interest on currency. They would, of course, have an incentive to devise an economical way to pay such interest" (p. 39). Bryant and Wallace (1979, 1980a) model the costly intermediation of government bonds into

The author thanks Peter Hartley, J. Huston McCulloch, and anonymous referees for very helpful comments. The Hoover Institution provided much appreciated support.

JOHN BRYANT *is professor of economics, Rice University.*

Journal of Money, Credit, and Banking, Vol. 21, No. 2 (May 1989)

demand deposits which are perfect substitutes for a government provided unbacked non-interest-bearing currency. The perfect-substitutes assumption was motivated by the common practice of defining money to be the sum of currency and demand deposits. Perfect substitution justifies the summation. The assumption of government provided unbacked non-interest-bearing currency was motivated by the observation that currencies typically take this form. Here the interest bill equals the cost of running the banks, as the demand deposits pay no interest.

The rate of return dominance of money has been explained by legal restrictions on intermediation. Friedman (1969) alludes to the role of legal restrictions in prohibiting the interest-bearing demand deposits and currency which he theorizes would result from competition. Bryant and Wallace (1980b, 1984) model the legal prohibition of the intermediation of bonds. This latter use of legal restrictions was motivated by the observation that actual intermediation costs do not seem high and variable enough to generate observed high and variable interest rates as required by the Bryant and Wallace (1979, 1980a) models. (See Wallace [1983] for a discussion of this point.) This rejection of intermediation costs in favor of legal restrictions as an explanation for the rate of return dominance of money might seem premature, at least for the case of currency. It may be very costly to pay interest on currency, and demand deposits may not be perfect substitutes for currency. (This point has been made by Lawrence White (1987), for example.) This paper argues that the rejection of intermediation costs in favor of legal restrictions was not premature. Costs of paying interest on currency are not sufficient to explain the rate of return dominance of currency.

Legal restrictions on intermediation may be necessary to explain the rate of return dominance of currency even if there are high costs of intermediation of bonds into interest-bearing currency. Fama (1983) briefly suggests deflating currencies. Such currencies would avoid the intermediation costs of paying interest on currency. However, Fama rejects his own suggestion on the basis of the costs of maintaining multiple currencies. On the other hand, Hayek (1978) argues at length that having multiple currencies is not very costly. This raises the possibility that Fama's suggestion should be taken more seriously. Currencies need not pay explicit interest, but only pay implicit interest through deflation. Friedman's "economical way to pay such interest" may be very economical indeed. The prohibition of private note issue may, then, be the crucial legal restriction for explaining the rate of return dominance of currency, as Friedman suggests.

National Bank Notes

The possibility of private, competitively provided, deflating, bond-backed bank note currencies is easily illustrated. The bank notes deflate relative to the government provided currency in the illustration. However, in terms of real goods, the bank notes actually inflate, but at a slower rate than does the government-provided currency. The bank notes have an implicit positive net nominal interest rate, but an implicit negative net real interest rate. The implicit negative net real interest rate on bank notes is caused by the costs of operating banks, analogous to the explicit interest-bearing currency regime considered by Friedman.[1]

Several simplifying assumptions are helpful for the illustration. A stationary economy is assumed in the illustration. A useful role for unbacked government paper is assumed in the illustration. It might well be that in the real world, absent legal restrictions, real assets dominate unbacked paper, as discussed above. However, for illustrative purposes, it is assumed here that this is not the case. The only "wedge" that needs to be explained is the one between currency and government bonds.[2] Thus, by assumption, the net safe real rate of interest on real assets is negative, and less than the net real rate of return on bank notes. Moreover, the net real rate of interest on government bonds is assumed to be zero.[3]

Hayek (1978) argues that unbacked paper can be efficiently provided by the private competitive market. Bryant (1981) disagrees, arguing that the competitive market has no mechanism for dissipating the rents generated by unbacked paper issue. In this paper, it is simply assumed that the government has a monopoly on unbacked paper issue, without justifying the monopoly.

Bond-backed bank notes are assumed to be a perfect substitute for the government's unbacked currency in the illustration. There are no costs associated with multiple currencies, and no costs associated with verifying a bank's backing of its currency—or at least all of these costs are incurred by the banks. Also the government accepts payments in bank notes. In the illustration the bank notes dominate the government's currency as they deflate relative to that currency. Consequently, the public has no demand for the government's currency. The government's currency is only used by banks to purchase the government's bonds. It is important to note that this does not imply that the government's currency becomes valueless. The banks use the entire supply of the government's currency to buy bonds, and the only entity holding that currency through time is the government. The government's currency becomes an accounting unit only.

It is assumed in the illustration that, as Friedman and Hayek argue, competition forces the banks to engage in the zero excess profit business of providing bank notes. Indeed, competition forces them to provide the identical backing for their notes, and to guarantee to continue to do so. One can imagine that the bank notes are denominated in terms of their backing. It is, then, conceivable that this multiple currency system is nearly costless as assumed, even without Hayek's arguments, although the assumption of costless verification of backing still is important. The regime is like a single currency of national bank notes.

Finally, the only useful role for government bonds is to back bank note currencies in the illustration. Naturally, one can well imagine that some private individuals might want to hold government bonds directly. For simplicity of exposition it is

---

[1] An open market sale of government bonds for bank notes by the Federal Reserve is *inflationary* and inefficient in this economy, as in Bryant and Wallace (1979, 1980a). Such an open market sale simply wastes resources in useless intermediation costs, just as in those papers.

[2] If the "wedge" is between currency and real assets, the argument still goes through. In this case, bank notes are backed by real assets. Deflation in the bank note currencies is achieved by banks' using interest payments on their portfolios, net of costs, to retire their bank notes.

[3] A government deficit would generate a negative net real rate of interest.

assumed here that this is not the case.

The details of the illustration of a national bank note regime follow. In particular, suppose the quantity of bank notes in circulation, B_t, satisfies

$$B_t = (1 + \alpha_b)^t B_o .$$ (1)

To hold real quantities stationary, the price level of bank notes, $P_{b,t}$ must satisfy

$$P_{b,t} = (1 + \alpha_b)^t P_{b,o} .$$ (2)

Similarly, the quantity of government currency, C_t, satisfies

$$C_t = (1 + \alpha_c)^t C_o .$$ (3)

and the price level of government currency, $P_{c,t}$, must satisfy

$$P_{c,t} = (1 + \alpha_c)^t P_{c,o} .$$ (4)

If $a_c > a_b$, bank notes dominate government currency. Only bank notes circulate. It remains to show that (1)–(4) and $a_c > a_b$ can be consistent with a coherent stationary economy.

The banking system in this stationary economy is assumed to be competitive, zero profit, and to exhibit constant returns to scale. Let K be the cost of operation of the entire banking system. Equations (1) and (2) determine the total real value of newly issued bank notes in a given period, $(B_t - B_{t-1})/P_{b,t}$. The banks finance their cost of operation by issuing new bank notes. It follows that

$$\frac{B_t - B_{t-1}}{P_{b,t}} = \frac{\alpha_b}{1 + \alpha_b} \frac{B_o}{P_{b,o}} = K .$$ (5)

The bank notes are backed by currency-denominated government bonds. These government bonds pay a net nominal rate of interest of α_c (generating that growth rate in currency and in the price level of currency). By assumption the only use of the government bonds is as backing for the bank notes. It follows that the backing rule used by the banks is that the ratio of the face value of their bond portfolio divided by their bank notes outstanding equals $(1 + \alpha_c)C_t/B_t$.[4] In terms of the ratio of the real current worth of their portfolio to the real worth of their bank notes this stationary rule is $[C_o/P_{c,o}]/[B_o/P_{c,o}]$. This rule is consistent with the banks' buying of government bonds to back bank notes absorbing the entire stock of government currency. This, in turn, is consistent with bank notes, and government bonds, dominating government currency.

As only bank notes circulate, the demand for real balances in the economy

---

[4] The bank notes are backed by a proportionate share of a bank's government bond portfolio, so that the note issue described in (5) "dilutes" the backing of the notes.

determines $B_o/P_{b,o} = B_t/P_{b,t}$. This and K then determine α_b from (5). Of course, in reality, the demand for real balances, K and α_b are determined simultaneously. From (2) we see that $-\alpha_b/[1 + \alpha_b]$ is the net real rate of return on bank notes, which presumably influences the demand for real balances. In turn, the cost of the banking system is proportional to the volume of real (bank note) balances supplied. The economy has parameters α_b, α_c, B_o, C_o, $P_{b,o}$, and $P_{c,o}$. The demand for real balances and (5) provide only two restrictions. This is not problematic. Rates of government currency inflation, α_c, greater than α_b do not affect government currency holders as there are no government currency holders, and do not affect bondholders (banks) as α_c is also the nominal rate of interest. Moreover, bank notes and unbacked government currency come in no natural units, and as there are no government currency holders, real government currency balances are indeterminate.

Concluding Comments

If the interest rate exceeds the rate of growth of bank notes necessary to sustain the banking system, the bank notes dominate government currency. These bank notes are not interest-bearing, but have deflation relative to government currency. This deflation is an implicit nominal interest payment on bank notes. Such implicit interest payments avoid the costs of explicit interest payments. In this bank note regime government "currency" is just an accounting unit. Bank notes alone circulate as the true currency. Indeed, as bank notes alone circulate, it is unnecessary to post two prices. The bank note regime does not impose additional pricing costs. One can imagine a transitional period in which banks would have to advertise the conversion schedule, and possibly retain government currency to "make the market." The interest rate would have to be high enough to warrant this activity.

The usefulness of such a circulating bank note regime to the economy probably depends upon costs. The clear alternative regime is the government's directly providing circulating currency and dispensing with bank notes and government bonds. The circulating bank note regime could be defended if the costs to the government of directly providing circulating currency exceeds the costs to the government of handling bonds plus the operating costs of the banking system. Perhaps this could be justified by agency problems. In any case, the purpose of the above example of a circulating bank note regime is not to advocate formation of such a regime. Rather, the purpose is to suggest that costs of paying interest on currency are not sufficient to explain the observed rate of return dominance of circulating currency. Competition would force banks to supply deflating bond backed bank note currencies.

Admittedly, the general assertion of no-transactions-costs is clearly untenable. The observation of financial institutions accounting for roughly 10 percent of GNP is grossly at variance with this general assertion. However, this observation may not be to the point. The legal restrictions theory may still be a useful abstraction for addressing such circumstances as a 15 percent treasury bill rate. In such circum-

NOTES, COMMENTS, REPLIES : 245

stances the question of why bank notes alone do not circulate as currency, absent legal restrictions, may be a legitimate one. In the example, how big is K in expression (5)?

LITERATURE CITED

Baumol, William J. "The Transactions Demand for Cash: An Inventory Theoretic Approach." *Quarterly Journal of Economics* 66 (November 1952), 545–56.

Bryant, John. "The Competitive Provision of Fiat Money." *Journal of Banking and Finance* 5 (December 1981), 587–93.

Bryant, John, and Neil Wallace. "The Inefficiency of Interest-Bearing National Debt." *Journal of Political Economy* 87 (April 1979), 365–81.

_____. "Open-Market Operations in a Model of Regulated, Insured Intermediaries." *Journal of Political Economy* 88 (February 1980), 146–73. (a)

_____. "A Suggestion for Further Simplifying the Theory of Money." Staff Report #62, Federal Reserve Bank of Minneapolis, 1980. (b)

_____. "A Price Discrimination Analysis of Monetary Policy." *Review of Economic Studies* 51 (April 1984),279–88.

Cowen, Tyler, and Randall Kroszner. "The Development of the New Monetary Economics." *Journal of Political Economy* 95 (June 1987), 567–90. (a)

_____. "Does the Scottish Banking Experience Provide a Model for Laissez-Faire?" Unpublished ms., University of California at Irvine, Harvard University, and Council of Economic Advisors, 1987. (b)

Fama, Eugene. "Financial Intermediation and Price Level Control." *Journal of Monetary Economics* 12 (July 1983), 7–28.

Friedman, Milton. *The Optimum Quantity of Money and Other Essays.* Chicago: Aldine Publishing, 1969.

Hayek, F. A. *Denationalisation of Money—The Argument Refined: An Analysis of the Theory and Practice of Concurrent Currencies.* 2nd edition. London: *The Institute of Economic Affairs,* 1978.

Hicks, J. R. "A Suggestion for Simplifying the Theory of Money." *Economica,* New Series, 2: 1–19.

Tobin, James. "The Interest Elasticity of Transactions Demand for Cash." *Review of Economics and Statistics* 38 (August 1956), 241–47.

_____. "Liquidity Preference as Behavior toward Risk." *Review of Economic Studies* 25 (February 1958), 65–86.

Wallace, Neil. "A Legal Restrictions Theory of the Demand for 'Money' and the Role of Monetary Policy." Federal Reserve Bank of Minneapolis *Quarterly Review* 7 (Winter 1983), 1–7.

White, Lawrence H. "Accounting for Non-interest-bearing Currency: A Critique of the Legal Restrictions Theory of Money." *Journal of Money, Credit, and Banking* 19 (November 1987), 448–56.

[20]

Journal of Economic Behavior and Organization 13 (1990) 117–124. North-Holland

LEGAL RESTRICTIONS AND MONETARY EVOLUTION

Karl WÄRNERYD*

Stockholm School of Economics, S-113 83 Stockholm, Sweden

Received June 1988, final version received March 1989

The 'legal restrictions' school of monetary theory hypothesizes that the use of ordinary currency would die out if legal tender laws were abolished. Instead, interest-bearing instruments would be used in transactions. This paper refutes the claim, as far as it applies to money as a medium of exchange. The network externality or coordination convention properties of a medium of exchange imply that the strategy of holding interest-bearing instruments is not necessarily individually dominant. There is a 'critical mass' of users that has to be assembled before a switch can occur.

1. Introduction

What is known as 'money' in present-day societies has several distinct functions. It is

- a store of value,
- a unit of account, and
- a commonly accepted medium of exchange (CAMOE).

A recent discussion [with important forerunners, see Cowen and Kroszner (1987)] questions the theoretical necessity and efficiency of these functions all being performed by the same good. In any case, care should be taken to point out which particular functions are intended to be covered when discussing the good 'money'. Different definitions of what is to be considered 'moneyness' may have radically different implications for modeling results.

In particular, the origins and peculiar functioning of a *medium of exchange* have often been neglected or misunderstood. What a CAMOE accomplishes has, of course, always been recognized. Money solves the problem of the 'double coincidence of wants' necessary for trade to take place in a pure barter economy. Until very recently [see Jones (1976), Kiyotaki and Wright (1988, 1989), and Oh (1989)], however, the modeling of this important function has eluded formal neoclassical theory. One reason for this lack is noted by

*I would like to thank Robert Clower, Richard H. Day, Lars Hörngren, Ulrich Witt, and an anonymous referee for helpful suggestions, and Jack High for my initial introduction to Carl Menger's theory of money.

Niehans (1978). This is the more fundamental problem that we do not even have a formal understanding of the workings of an actual auctioneer-less barter economy.

An example of confusing the CAMOE function with the store-of-value function is found in one of the claims of the 'legal restrictions' school of monetary theorists. According to Wallace (1983, p. 1):

> An obvious instance of a paradoxical pattern of returns among assets is the coexistence of, on the one hand, US Federal Reserve Notes (US currency) and, on the other hand, interest-bearing securities that are default-free. ... Examples of such securities are US savings bonds and Treasury bills. Our first task is to identify the features of these securities that prevent them from playing the same role in transactions as Federal Reserve notes. For if they could play that role, then it is hard to see why anyone would hold non-interest-bearing currency instead of the interest-bearing securities.

Wallace goes on to suggest that the use of non-interest-bearing money, i.e., ordinary currency, to carry out transactions would disappear in favor of interest-bearing instruments – such as government bonds – without legal tender laws. It is also apparent from the context that it is meant seriously as a statement about reality – not just about Walrasian general equilibrium models.

The Wallace hypothesis could be restated in the following form. It is in the interest of individuals to hold assets which yield positive rather than zero interest. Therefore, legal restrictions as to what may be used in exchanges must be what creates a demand for ordinary currency.

This paper is an attempt to bring a better understanding of the problem of medium-of-exchange choice in decntralized monetary anarchy to bear on this claim. This leads to a theoretical rejection of the claim, for the following reasons.

- A CAMOE is an institutional solution to a coordination problem. The crucial feature of such problems is that no action is individually dominant independently of what other people do. Therefore, the interest yields on various instruments are in an important sense irrelevant for their CAMOE potential.
- Indirect exchange in general, however, individually dominates direct exchange. Government intervention is not necessary to convey the CAMOE property on *something*.

In section 2, support is provided for the latter point by reference to 19th century Austrian economist Carl Menger's (1976) theory of the spontaneous origin of money. Section 3 then goes on to argue that for coordination conventions in general, and money in particular, switches to efficiency are not automatic.

Other important issues central to a more broadly defined 'legal restrictions' school of monetary economics are not dealt with here. An example would be the macro-stability of laissez-faire money.

2. The emergence of media of exchange

Early attempts at explaining the existence of CAMOE were typically 'legal restrictions' theories. They assumed that both the institution itself and the stability of a currency's value could only emerge and persist because of governmental enforcement. 'Social contract' theories provide a slightly more sophisticated, although obviously factually untrue, argument. Witness, for instance, Locke's (1967) praise for 'the *invention* of money, and the tacit *agreement of men* to put a value on it' (emphasis added). This naïve view is still prominent today.

Carl Menger pointed out that the social institution of a CAMOE can be explained by reference only to the decentralized actions of self-interested individuals. Invoking the deux ex machina of state power is not necessary. From a purely methodological point of view, as noted by, among others, Nozick (1974) and Ullmann-Margalit (1978) such *invisible hand* explanations are more satisfying than others. They are more parsimonious, particularly as regards assumptions about the information available to a central planner.

Menger considers a pure barter economy where there is some degree of division of labor. Agents do not themselves produce all the goods they ultimately wish to consume. Every week or so they venture out in search of someone to trade with. Assume agents initially do not trade until they have found someone who has something they want and who is also willing to accept what they offer in return.

Now some enterprising individual E may realize that his search time can be reduced. This is done by trading his original basket for one which he does not wish to consume, but contains goods for which comsumption demand is more wide-spread. Let there be a good M which many people desire for ultimate consumption. Then the probability of finding someone who has M and wants what E has and later finding another agent who wants M and has what E wants may be greater than the probability of finding a 'first-best' exchange opportunity. Let the *saleability* of a good or basket of goods mean the probability of finding someone who wishes to acquire it. Then we may say that M is more saleable than E's original basket. Assume this to be the case.

E in accepting M has discovered indirect exchange, and is using M as a medium of exchange. The story of the emergence of money now proceeds as follows.

(1) E's use of M as a medium of exchange lowers his total search time. This leaves him more time each week to pursue other interests.
(2) Other agents in E's immediate environment may be assumed to notice this improvement in E's conditions.
(3) Assume they can correctly identify the source of E's improved want-satisfaction as the use of a medium of exchange. They will then want to imitate this practice.
(4) Assuming that M was a highly saleable good when E started accepting it in indirect exchange, his doing so will increase its saleability even more. A transactions demand is added to final consumption demand for the good. Therefore, imitating agents will find M even more attractive.
(5) The choice of M by the second generation further increases its saleability.

This cumulative process may converge to M being the single good with supreme saleability. It would then be the generally accepted medium of exchange. Starting from less severe premises, several goods might acquire this property. In the real world, of course, there are no generally accepted media of exchange, but local CAMOE.

Two features of this story that are of particular interest to the present discussion are the following.

– Acquiring highly marketable goods in the absence of legal restrictions not for their direct consumption-value but to use them in indirect exchange is individually rational. This amounts to saying that a CAMOE is an equilibrium in a non-cooperative game, rather than being a cooperative institution. A non-cooperative equilibrium is self-enforcing. By definition nothing can be gained by unilaterally deviating from an equilibrium strategy. An external enforcement agency, e.g., government, is not necessary. Observe, however, that this is a theory of commodity money. A pure token money is one backed by nothing but expectations as to its common acceptance. Whether token money could ever emerge spontaneously in the decentralized manner suggested is a tricky issue. Once such an institution is in existence, though, we would expect it to be able to persist even if legal enforcement of it is abolished [see White (1984)].
– The Mengerian account suggests that global knowledge of the game structure and unbounded rationality in agents is not necessary for the emergence of money. The self-interested practices of a few innovative individuals are diffused through an evolutionary process of imitation of successful behavior.

The Mengerian theory of 'money' is a theory of a good that solves the double-coincidence-of-wants problem in a barter economy. An alternative version of this statement could serve as a definition of money. A money is whatever good an individual agent can reasonably expect will be commonly accepted in indirect exchange, i.e., a CAMOE. This subjectivist definition of money [see White (1986) for an in-depth discussion] radically departs from the still common textbook alternative. The latter locates moneyness in, on the one hand, the property of being legal tender, and, on the other, certain physical attributes of a good, such as its divisibility, storability, transportability, etc. While these attributes are often present, what serves as a CAMOE in a particular society at a particular time cannot be identified by looking for the good that satisfies a list of physical criteria best. Again, a CAMOE is *whatever* is commonly used for indirect exchange. Still, there is a long tradition in monetary theory of discussing at length the 'optimal' physical properties of a money. This is a curious feature of a discipline that has adopted a subjectivist viewpoint in most other areas. Money is not really all that different.

3. Media-of-exchange as conventions

The 'legal restrictions' idea has been subjected to various criticisms [see, e.g., White (1987) and O'Driscoll (1986)]. These more or less stay within the same general sort of contemporary macro-model framework that Wallace discusses. This framework may not be adequate, however. The Wallace claim addresses issues of monetary anarchy. This is done without a real theory of a situation where agents are (in principle) at liberty to use whatever takes their fancy as a medium of exchange.

I would like to suggest that a convincing theory of a medium of exchange must first be a theory of an actual exchange process. This is a setting where no central coordinator is present. Individuals engage in specialized production and then have to search for someone to trade with. In fact, indirect exchange has no meaning except in such a world. Many standard neoclassical texts start out by defining money as the most saleable good. But saleability is a meaningless concept in a general equilibrium world. What is meant is the fact that all individuals hold a special good 'money'. That this is not the same thing is easily checked by asking oneself which is the second most saleable, third, etc., in general equilibrium. Such a distinction makes no sense in that context.

Consider the decision problem facing a single individual when there is no enforced rule as to what can be used as a means of payment. An interest-bearing instrument can for our purposes be defined as something that always yields a payoff, regardless of whether it can be traded or not. A first implicit assumption of Wallace's now seems to be that interest-bearing instruments in some sense individually dominate non-interest-bearing money as media of exchange. This does not necessarily follow simply from the definition.

Note that the value of any good intended to be used as an instrument for indirect exchange is dependent on expectations concerning the commonness of its acceptance. There is a network externality aspect involved. The larger the 'installed base', or population proportion that accepts a particular good X in trade, the more attractive it is as a medium of indirect exchange. The probability of finding somebody who has something that you value directly and is also prepared to accept X is greater. Conversely, if nobody wished to accept X in exchange, it is of no use to you *as a medium of exchange.*

Whether the medium-of-exchange candidate X is interest-bearing or not is irrelevant in this case. The unlikely exception would be when the expected yield from holding X is larger than any payoff you might expect to gain from participating in trade. Switching to speaking Esperanto, which supposedly is a simpler and more logical language, does not pay off if the person you are speaking to does not know Esperanto. In exactly the same way it is not necessarily true that interest-bearing assets are better than others as media of exchange to the individual agent. Like natural language, the institution of a CAMOE is a convention in the sense of Lewis (1986), i.e., an equilibrium solution to a coordination game.

This immediately points to a problem with a second implicit assumption of the Wallace hypothesis. This is the (admittedly common) notion that efficient practices always become prevalent in situations where there is no outside interference. Even if we assume that everybody would be better off if everybody used bonds as a medium of exchange, without legal enforcement agents face a coordination problem. In a decentralized environment, where individuals are unable to all get together and explicitly agree on a CAMOE, an agent is instead forced to base his decision on the experience of himself and those with whom he interacts as to what practices happen to work out better than others. It is never the case that you choose yourself what should conventionally be considered a medium of exchange. Furthermore, whether the evolutionary selection process of imitation of successful behavior converges to 'efficiency' will depend on where it started from. If the means of transaction is deregulated when an 'inefficient' instrument is commonly used, the inefficient convention may very well persist because of wide-spread expectations of its persistence.

As a simple example, let $V_M(n_M)$ be the expected utility of holding ordinary currency for transactions purposes when the population proportion doing so is n_M. V_M is, of course, a non-decreasing function of n_M. If the only alternative is holding bonds, then the population proportion holding bonds is $n_B = 1 - n_M$, so the expected utility of bonds may be written $V_B(n_M)$, a non-increasing function. Agents are for simplicity assumed to hold either currency or bonds, but not both. Incidentally, to hold something you must acquire it from somewhere. A decision to hold bonds is therefore equivalent to a decision to accept them in exchange.

Holding bonds will be a dominant strategy only when $V_B(n_M) > V_M(n_M)$, $\forall n_M$.

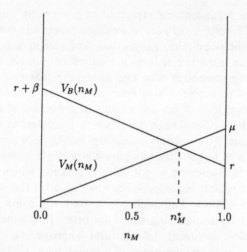

Fig. 1.   Two instruments with linear payoffs.

This condition would imply that $V_B(1) > V_M(1)$, or that holding bonds only for the interest paid on them, when nobody accepts them in exchange, is more profitable than taking part in exchanges. This is clearly an unreasonable assumption.

Ruling this case out, both $n_M = 1$ and $n_M = 0$ are non-cooperative equilibria. In both cases an agent would like to conform to whatever everyone else is doing. Now assume that universal use of bonds would in fact be efficient, i.e., that $V_B(0) > V_M(1)$. The payoff functions summarize the expected outcome of a search process, where an individual faces an entire economy of potential traders. Most of these he has never met before. It seems outrageous to assume that individuals would trust in the rationality of strangers to such a degree that they would automatically coordinate themselves to the efficient solution. Instead, individuals would switch to bonds only when a group of bond-holders sufficiently large to make the expected value of holding bonds greater than that of holding currency has somehow been assembled.

Assuming the V_M and V_B functions to be continuous, then in general there will be some n_M^* such that $V_M(n_M^*) = V_B(n_M^*)$. If the functions are strictly monotonic, it is trivial to prove that n_M^* is unique. It has the property that $V_M(n_M) > V_B(n_M)$ if $n_M > n_M^*$, and $V_M(n_M) < V_B(n_M)$ if $n_M < n_M^*$. Then $n_B^* = 1 - n_M^*$ is the 'critical mass' necessary for a switch from currency to bonds.

The relative efficiency of the two equilibria does not in general determine the size of n_B^*. It could be the case that the critical mass is large, for instance in the sense of being greater than 1/2, even though using bonds is the efficient equilibrium.

In the special case where the payoff functions are linear, n_B^* will be less than $1/2$ if using bonds is efficient. This case is illustrated in fig. 1, with $V_M(n_M) = \mu n_M$ and $V_B(n_M) = r + \beta n_B = r + \beta - \beta n_M$, where μ, β are parameters and r is the interest paid on bonds. Efficiency of bonds implies $r + \beta > \mu$.

A more detailed version of this simple model is given in Wärneryd (1989).

Finally, the 'legal restrictions' argument is clearly meant to suggest that certain goods cannot function as CAMOE without centralized enforcement. This essentially amounts to saying that the very existence of token money is a government conspiracy. That no theoretical necessity for enforcement exists was shown above.

References

Cowen, Tyler and Randall Kroszner, 1987, The development of the new monetary economics, Journal of Political Economy 95, 567–590.

Jones, Robert A, 1976, The origin and development of media of exchange, Journal of Political Economy 84, 757–775.

Kiyotaki, Nobuhiro and Randall Wright, 1988, Money and specialization, Working paper, University of Wisconsin-Madison.

Kiyotaki, Nobuhiro and Randall Wright, 1989, On money as a medium of exchange, Journal of Political Economy 97, 927–954.

Lewis, David K., 1986, Convention. A philosophical study (Basil Blackwell, Oxford).

Locke, John, 1967, Two treatises of government (Cambridge University Press, New York).

Menger, Carl, 1976, Principles of economics, trans James Dingwall and Bert F. Hoselitz (New York University Press, New York).

Niehans, Jürg, 1978, The theory of money (The Johns Hopkins University Press, Baltimore).

Nozick, Robert, 1974, Anarchy state and utopia (Basic Books, New York).

O'Driscoll, Gerald P., Jr., 1986, Money: Menger's evolutionary theory, History of Political Economy 18, 601–616.

Oh, Seonghwan, 1989, A theory of a generally acceptable medium of exchange and barter, Journal of Monetary Economics 23, 101–119.

Ullmann-Margalit, Edna, 1978, Invisible hand explanations, Synthèse 39, 263–291.

Wallace, Neil, 1983, A legal restrictions theory of the demand for 'money' and the role of monetary policy, Federal Reserve Bank of Minneapolis Quarterly Review 7, 1–7.

Wärneryd, Karl, 1989, Legal restrictions and the evolution of media of exchange, Journal of Institutional and Theoretical Economics, forthcoming.

White, Lawrence H., 1984, Competitive payments systems and the unit of account, American Economic Review 74, 699–712.

White, Lawrence H., 1986, A subjectivist perspective on the definition and identification of money, in: Israel M. Kirzner, ed., Subjectivism, intelligibility and economic understanding (New York University Press, New York).

White, Lawrence H., 1987, Accounting for non-interest-bearing currency: A critique of the legal restrictions theory of money, Journal of Money, Credit and Banking 19, 448–456.

Part V
Policy Implications

[21]

KYKLOS, Vol. 37 – 1984 – Fasc. 1, 27–58

The Government's Money Monopoly:
Externalities or Natural Monopoly?

ROLAND VAUBEL*

Several justifications have been given for the government's monopoly in the production of base money:
1. Competitive production of money by the private sector renders the price level indeterminate[1].
2. Private competitive supply of money is inflationary; the equilibrium price level may even be infinite[2].

* Institut für Weltwirtschaft, Universität Kiel, Bundesrepublik Deutschland. – This paper replies to the criticisms which CHARLES P. KINDLEBERGER has recently expressed in this journal [1983, especially pp. 383f.]. Helpful comments from the participants in the 13th Konstanz Seminar on Monetary Theory and Monetary Policy and the seminar members of the Public Choice Center, VPI, Blacksburg, are gratefully acknowledged. Thanks are also due to ROLF KNUDSEN for very efficient research assistance.

1. This view has been taken, e.g., by GURLEY and SHAW [1960, pp. 255ff.], PATINKIN [1961, p. 116] and McKINNON [1969, p. 316]. To be relevant from a welfare-theoretic point of view the argument would have to show that the rate of change of the price level is indeterminate as well.

2. See LUTZ [1936, pp. 4f.], FRIEDMAN [1959a, p. 7; 1969, p. 39], PESEK and SAVING [1967, p. 129], JOHNSON [1968, p. 976], MELTZER [1969, p. 35] and GEHRIG [1978, p. 454]. As KLEIN [1974] has shown, these analyses ignore that the demand for (distinguishable) money depends on inflation expectations. Insofar there may be a link with FRIEDMAN's early empirical work which de-emphasized the role of the interest rate in the money demand function [e.g., FRIEDMAN, 1959b]. In his more recent work [e.g., FRIEDMAN, 1981], he does not use this justification any longer but relies on a combination of the sixth and seventh argument.

KLEIN [1974, pp. 428–431] and GIRTON and ROPER [1981, pp. 21–24] have also demonstrated that a zero marginal cost of producing money would not imply a zero price of money (i.e., an infinite price level) in competitive equilibrium. It is not the price of money but the opportunity cost (price) of holding money that would be driven down to zero. As JOHNSON [1969] has shown, the same confusion between the price of money and the opportunity cost of holding money underlies the work of PESEK and SAVING [1967].

ROLAND VAUBEL

3. The banking system is inherently unstable.

4. The private non-bank sector is inherently unstable and has to be stabilized through monetary policy.

5. Monopolistic production of money by the state is an efficient way of raising government revenue[3].

6. The supply of money is a natural monopoly because of economies of scale in production or use.

7. Money exerts external effects; money may even be a public good.

This paper deals with the last two of these justifications. *Section I* is devoted to the question whether money is the extreme case of an externality which we call a public good. *Section II* examines the possibility that the holding of money or the decision to use a money have more limited, but nevertheless PARETO-relevant external effects. *Section III* discusses the natural monopoly argument. *Section IV* contains an empirical test for social economies of scale in the use of money. The last section summarizes the results of the paper.

I. IS MONEY A PUBLIC GOOD?

Whether money is a public good depends on the definition of a public good. There is no generally accepted definition. Most authors seem to consider non-rivalness a necessary and sufficient condition[4]. Others regard non-excludability as an alternative sufficient condition[5]. A few treat the term public good as synonymous with positive consumption externality[6].

In this paper we shall retain the benefit of being able to distinguish between the general concept of consumption externality and the polar case of a (pure) public good which, in terms of production units, is equally available to all members of the group in a quantity or quality that is independent of the size of the group (non-rivalness)[7]. We shall call a free good a good for which exclusion is not profitable (non-ex-

3. This raises the question why the collection of government seigniorage should be more efficient than the taxation of private money creation.
4. The seminal modern contribution is SAMUELSON [1954].
5. See notably MUSGRAVE [1959, p. 9].
6. SAMUELSON [1969].
7. This is essentially BUCHANAN's definition [1968, p. 54].

THE GOVERNMENT'S MONEY MONOPOLY

cludability). More limited consumption externalities will be discussed in *Section II*.

One group of authors ascribe a public good nature to money because 'any one agent, holding cash balances of a given average size, is less likely to incur the costs of temporarily running out of cash, the larger are the average balances of those with whom he trades'[8]. However, money balances do not satisfy the non-rivalness criterion (nor the non-excludability criterion): as long as one person holds a unit of money and benefits from its 'liquidity services', nobody else can own it and benefit from it. If he gives it away, he increases his own risk of temporarily running out of cash. Therefore, he will ask for a *quid pro quo* – a good, service or some other asset.

For the same reason, it is not true that 'the provision of a convertible currency is an international "public good"' because 'a convertible currency can be held and used by foreigners' [McKinnon 1979, p. 3] or that 'the dollar is an "international public good"' because 'the United States provides the world's reserve currency' [Schmidt 1979, p. 143]. Otherwise, any exportable good or asset which happens to be supplied by a government would be an international public good.

Kindleberger refers to 'the public good provided by money as a unit of account' [1972, p. 434] and 'standard of measurement' [1983, p. 383] and applies the term public good to 'money' [1978a, pp. 9–10], 'international money' [1976, p. 61; 1978b, p. 286], 'an international unit of account' and 'international monetary stability' [1972, p. 435]. International monetary stability in the sense of stability of purchasing power or exchange rate stability is not a good but a quality characteristic of the product money. Quality characteristics, it is true, meet the non-rivalness test: enjoyment by one does not detract from enjoyment by others (nor can they be excluded from them) provided they have bought the good itself. However, this applies to the quality characteristics of all goods. If the publicness of its characteristics made a good a public good, all goods that are sold to more than one person would be public goods.

It might be argued that the benefits of a unit of account (and a price index) can be enjoyed by a person independently of whether he holds and uses the money which it denominates [Yeager 1983, p. 321]. More

---

8. Laidler [1977, pp. 321f.]. A similar view seems to be taken by Kolm [1972, 1977] and Mundell [in: Claassen and Salin 1972, p. 97].

29

ROLAND VAUBEL

specifically, a person or organisation, by adopting a certain unit of account (and by publishing a price index for it), may convey information, a public good, to all others. This would imply that government should suggest a unit of account and publish a price index for it, but not that it should suppress the use of other units[9] or supply money, let alone the only (base) money[10].

BRUNNER and MELTZER [1964, 1971] have emphasized that money itself is a substitute for information because it also reduces transaction costs, and because transaction costs can largely be reduced to the costs of information about possible transaction chains, asset properties and exchange ratios between assets. Since money is a substitute for information and since information is a public good, HAMADA [1979, p. 7] and FRATIANNI [1982, p. 437] conclude, there is a 'public good nature of money'. However, to show that X is a substitute for a public good is not sufficient to prove that X is a public good. A fence, a dog and an alarm system are all to some extent substitutes for police protection but they are not public goods. What has to be shown is not that money is a substitute for information but that it provides the public good of information.

Several authors have argued that 'public consensus' or 'social agreement' on a common money is a way of creating generally useful knowledge and is thus a public good[11]. The knowledge in question is the predictability of individual behavior. What becomes predictable is not only the money which each individual accepts but also that each individual in the country accepts the same money.

Public decisions by definition meet the non-rivalness test. However, not all public decisions are public goods – they can be public bads [TULLOCK, 1971]. Since the aim of securing predictability of individual trading behavior, if taken to the extreme, may serve to justify the most far-reaching central planning by an omnipotent government [HIRSHLEIFER 1973, p. 132], the mere fact that a certain act of government generates knowledge is not a sufficient justification. It has to be shown that the knowledge in question is worth its cost and that it is provided more

9. KINDLEBERGER [1983, p. 383], for example, seems to object to competition from private units of account.

10. This conclusion is in fact reached by ENGELS [1981, pp. 10f.], HALL [1981, p. 21] and YEAGER [1983].

11. HAMADA [1977, p. 16], FRENKEL [1975, p. 217], TULLOCK [1976, p. 524] and, with respect to the unit of account, HALL [1983, p. 3].

THE GOVERNMENT'S MONEY MONOPOLY

efficiently by the government than by a competitive private sector. Both contentions are controversial.

The only operational proof that a common money is more efficient than currency competition and that the government is the most efficient provider of the common money would be to permit free currency competition. Such competition might even be desirable if the process were known to converge to the government's money; for the government may not know in advance what type of money to converge to[12]. Thus, the market can be a more efficient provider of knowledge than the government.

If a common money is optimal, this is because it minimizes transaction costs. The transaction costs that are avoided are the costs of conversion, either spot or forward, or the transaction costs of hedging. If these transaction costs tend to be borne by both partners to a (bilateral) contract, an individual who decides to use the same money as his contract partner, confers an external benefit upon the latter. Similarly, the decision by a money producer to maintain a fixed exchange rate *vis-à-vis* the currency of another money producer may generate a positive externality for the latter and the users of the money issued by the latter. Can it be maintained that money – even thought it is not a public good – gives rise to PARETO-relevant external effects, *i.e.*, that transaction cost is not only a necessary condition for the presence of PARETO-relevant externalities [COASE, 1960] but also a sufficient one?

II. DOES MONEY GIVE RISE TO PARETO-RELEVANT EXTERNAL EFFECTS?

The production, use and choice of money is supposed to generate at least three types of external effects: (i) transaction cost externalities, (ii) price level externalities, and (iii) confidence externalities. It will prove convenient to proceed in reverse order.

---

12. While BRUNNER and MELTZER [1971, pp. 801f.] argue that governmental restrictions can reduce, and have reduced, the social cost of the transition to new transaction arrangements, HAYEK wants to use competition as a mechanism of discovery: 'The monopoly of government of issuing money ... has ... deprived us of the only process by which we can find out what would be good money' [1978, p. 5]. See also BROWN [1982, pp. 30f., 35].

31

ROLAND VAUBEL

1. Confidence Externalities

Several authors have argued that overissue and/or failure of an individual issuer can exert 'external' or 'third-party effects' on other issuing banks[13]. However, not all third-party effects are PARETO-relevant. Externalities are not PARETO-relevant if they are 'merely precuniary', *i.e.*, due to interdependence through the market, more precisely: through the price mechanism[14].

Confidence externalities are potentially PARETO-relevant if confidence in bank A is an input for the production of bank B. In this case, however, bank B has an incentive to support bank A if there is a run on the latter. If it does so, the externality is appropriable and not PARETO-relevant. Even if, for some reason, the externality were not appropriable, it would not follow that government should produce money (let alone as a monopolist) rather than introduce a mandatory deposit insurance scheme or act as a lender of last resort by borrowing and lending private money[15].

2. Price-Level Externalities

Another group of authors suggest that an individual's demand for money exerts positive external effects on other money holders because it makes 'the price level slightly lower than it would otherwise be', thereby 'yielding capital gains to all other holders of money'[16].

13. *Cf.* FRIEDMAN [1959a, pp. 6f.], KOLM [1972, p. 205], KLEIN [1974, p. 447] and NIEHANS [1978, p. 282]. While FRIEDMAN concludes that 'those third-party effects give special urgency to the prevention of fraud in respect of promises to pay a monetary commodity and the enforcement of such contracts', KOLM argues that they call for a central bank acting as a lender of last resort. KLEIN suggests that 'the association (of private banks) would ... have to assume some control over member firm production decisions to internalize what would otherwise be unheeded externalities', whereas, according to NIEHANS, 'deposit insurance was designed to reduce the externalities of depositor confidence'.

14. For a demonstration of the PARETO-irrelevance of pecuniary externalities see, *e.g.*, VINER [1931], SCITOVSKY [1954], McKEAN [1958, Ch. 8], TULLOCK [1970, Ch. 7].

15. KLEIN [1974, pp. 48f.] mentions the possibility of another type of confidence externality: governmental money production may increase the credibility of the national defense posture. Obviously, this would only be so if inflationary war finance was superior to taxation and government borrowing.

16. FRIEDMAN [1969, p. 15]. The same view is expressed by KOLM [1972, pp. 191,

THE GOVERNMENT'S MONEY MONOPOLY

However, the capital gains to other money holders are not PARETO-relevant external effects but 'merely pecuniary externalities'. They result exclusively from the operation of the price mechanism. Capital gains accrue to the holders of any asset for which demand increases (unless the asset is in perfectly elastic supply). Since the capital gains are not PARETO-relevant externalities, they are not the reason for paying a rate of return equal to the rate of time preference on cash balances[17].

The advocates of free currency competition agree that price-level stability is probably desirable and that, for this reason, changes in real money demand should call forth equal changes in money supply. They believe, however, that a competitive supplier has a stronger incentive than a monopolist to maintain the purchasing power of his money by adjusting supply in this way.

3. Transaction Cost Externalities
a. Implications for the Demand for Money

If A decides to accept and use the same money (currency c) which B accepts and uses, he confers an external benefit on B. A's bank account in currency c generates a 'non-pecuniary' or 'technological' externality[18] because, like the size of real money balances, it enters B's utility function if B is a consumer, or B's production function if B is a producer[19]. It

206], NIEHANS [1978, p. 93], CASSEL and THIEME [1981, pp. 311, 314, 328], YEAGER [1983, p. 322] and implicitly by SAMUELSON [1968, pp. 9–10]. Possibly in a similar vein, HALL [1981, p. 1] suggests that 'maintenance of a stable price level carries significant positive externalities'. MUNDELL's view [in: CLAASSEN and SALIN, 1972, p. 97] may have to be interpreted in this sense as well.

17. NIEHANS [1978, p. 93] suggests that 'the standard remedy ... is a subsidy to counteract the externality', and that a return on cash balances equal to the rate of time preference would be such a subsidy. However, the reason for paying such a rate of return is not an externality but the condition that the opportunity cost of holding money should equal the opportunity cost of producing money. No subsidy is involved. On the contrary, the refusal to pay a market rate of return on base money can be viewed as a tax.

18. This view can also be found in NIEHANS [1971, p. 774], JONES [1976, p. 773], GRUBEL [1977, p. 449], SALIN [1980, p. 25], YEAGER [1983, p. 321] and implicitly in ADAM SMITH [1976, pp. 26f.].

19. See, *e.g.*, FRIEDMAN [1959b, pp. 333f.; 1969, p. 14], CHETTY [1969] and FISCHER [1974]. The justification for including money or accounts in the production function is that money and accounts are inputs which reduce the need for other factors of production (labour and capital allocated to search and exchange).

ROLAND VAUBEL

enters, it is true, through market interdependence but not through the price mechanism. It raises the quality of (the utility or product derived from) B's bank account and the money balances on it. To determine whether this technological externality is also PARETO-relevant[20] the nature of the interdependency has to be analysed in more detail.

The utility which each person derives from his real money balances in currency c depends on the number of persons who accept (here: have a bank account in) currency c and on their prospective volume of transactions with the person concerned. For simplicity, we shall initially assume that each person faces the same volume of transactions with each other person before the use of a common money and that the elasticity of the volume of transactions with respect to changes in transactions costs is identical for all. This permits us to focus entirely on the number of users of currency c (N_c) and to write A's utility function as

$$U^A = U^A (X_i^A, ..., X_n^A; \beta_c^A, m_c^A, N_c) \tag{1}$$

or more specifically as

$$U^A = U^A [X_i^A, ..., X_n^A; \beta_c^A N_c, \beta_c^A m_c^A \, f(N_c)] \tag{2}$$

where

m_c^A denotes the real money balances of currency c held by A,

β_c^A indicates whether A has a bank account in currency c ($\beta_c^A = 1$) or not ($\beta_c^A = 0$), and where

$X_i^A, ..., X_n^A$ are the quantities of other (private and public) goods consumed by A.

The term $\beta_c^A N_c$ indicates that possession of a bank account may be useful even if the balance is temporarily zero. Binary variables like β_c have previously been used in the utility function for 'access goods' such as telephone connections [ARTLE and AVEROUS, 1973; ROHLFS, 1974; RABENAU and STAHL, 1974] and club goods [NG, 1973].

The above utility functions make it tempting to classify money as a club good, and, indeed, HAMADA [1979, p. 6] has done so. The presence of the N term in the utility function is a distinguishing characteristic of club goods as defined in the seminal contribution by BUCHANAN [1965,

20. For the point that technological externalities need not be PARETO-relevant see BUCHANAN and STUBBLEBINE [1962].

THE GOVERNMENT'S MONEY MONOPOLY

p. 4]: it distinguishes club goods from public goods and from normal private goods. Moreover, club goods and money have in common that the system's cost per user declines as the number of users increases [BUCHANAN 1965, p. 7]; *i.e.*, both are subject to what MUNDELL [1970, pp. 13f.] calls 'social economies of scale'[21]. The cost of establishing a bank account might even be compared to a membership fee.

In spite of these superficial similarities, there are two crucial differences, however:

– whereas, in the case of BUCHANAN-type club goods (his example is a swimming pool), an increase in N at some point begins to reduce the utility which each member derives from the good (congestion), an increase in the number of users of currency c raises the utility which each user derives from his bank account and his real money balance in currency c;

– whereas BUCHANAN-type club goods permit exclusion, an additional user of c cannot exclude the other users of c from the benefits which his use of c will have for them except by denying himself the benefit of using c.

These differences are crucial from a welfare-theoretic point of view because they determine whether PARETO-relevant externalities are present or not. Since, for BUCHANAN-type club goods, the coefficient of N is negative at the margin, club members have an incentive to limit congestion. Since exclusion is feasible, they will make sure that new entrants pay for the cost they impose on the old members. In this way, the negative congestion effects are internalized with those who generate them. PARETO-relevant externalities are absent.

21. BAUMOL [1967, p. 424] and FELDMAN [1973, p. 463] have pointed out that social or agglomeration economies, especially in the case of money, tend to grow more than proportionately as the size of the group (N) increases. In applying BAUMOL's reasoning, we could say that the transaction cost which each user saves by using money is proportional to the number of users (KN) and that the cost saved by all users is therefore KN_c^2. As FELDMAN points out, the square rule results from the fact that transaction costs are proportional to the number of pairs in the group.

Goods like money, whose quality increases as more people use it have been called 'social relation goods' [ENGELS 1981, p. 124]; other examples would be telephones, locations and languages. For the analogy with languages see KINDLEBERGER [1967], for the one with transportation costs see NIEHANS [1969, p. 724, b. 15] and OSTROY [1973, p. 608]. The choice of location is more complicated because there exists a continuous spectrum of possibilities; the decision to use a money is a yes-or-no-decision.

35

ROLAND VAUBEL

Figure 1

Individual Demand for Money with Social Economies of Scale

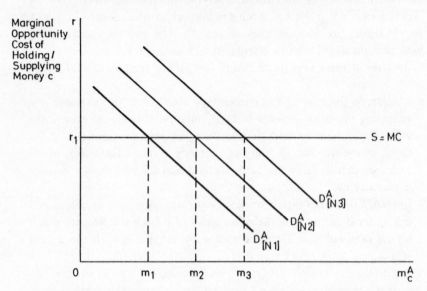

By contrast, if as in the case of money the coefficient of N is positive, it may be in the interest of group members to pay others for joining. However, the free-rider problem may be an obstacle to such payments. If the payments offered are too small, the decision to join is underproduced because its benefits would be partly external and cannot (fully) be internalized. Thus, it can be of crucial importance whether the marginal users have to pay the group (as in the case of BUCHANAN-type club goods) or whether the group may have to pay them (as in the case of money).

Since N enters the utility function with a positive coefficient, A's demand-for-money function (D^A) shifts outward as N increases: If the marginal cost of supplying additional real money balances is, for simplicity, assumed to be constant, A increases his holdings of m_e to m_2 and m_3 as N_e increases to N_2 and N_3.

Similarly, we can construct market demand curves (D_N) for different values of N_e: Assume that the supplier of currency c reduces the opportunity cost of holding his money from r_1 to r_2. This may increase the demand for real money balances in c in three ways. First, his traditional customers raise their demand by $m_2'' - m_1$ (movement along $D_{[N1]}$). Sec-

36

THE GOVERNMENT'S MONEY MONOPOLY

Figure 2

Market Demand for Money with Social Economies of Scale

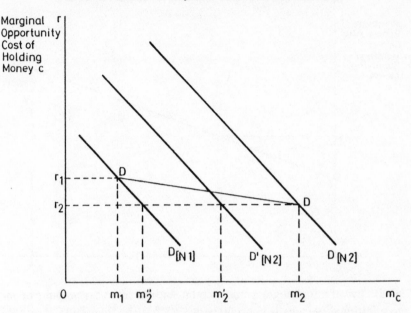

ond, additional users may be attracted who demand $m_2' - m_2''$. Third, the increase in the number of users induces the traditional users of currency c to raise their demand by an additional $m_2 - m_2'$. Thus, owing to the 'bandwagon effect'[22], the 'effective' demand curve (DD) is significantly more elastic (with respect to r) than it would otherwise be.

Our analysis implies that the opportunity cost of holding a given quantity of m_c which the users of c are willing to incur, increases as the number of users rises. Thus, if we replace m_c with N_c on the horizontal axis, we obtain an upward sloping 'demand curve' (DD'): If the mar-

---

22. This is the term used by LEIBENSTEIN [1950]. Although he subsumes also the case where 'A's demand is a function of the number of people that demand the commodity' (p. 190), his analysis is only concerned with the simpler case where 'the demand of consumer A (at given prices) [is] a function of the total demand of all others in the market collectively' (*ibid.*). The bandwagon effect is also noted by HIRSCHMAN [1970, p. 99]: 'Quality of a product is not invariant to the number of buyers or to the amount sold. The withdrawal of some members leads to lower quality'. He believes that, in such cases, 'loyalist behavior' is required (p. 100).

ROLAND VAUBEL

Figure 3

Market Demand for Money with Uniform Transaction Volumes

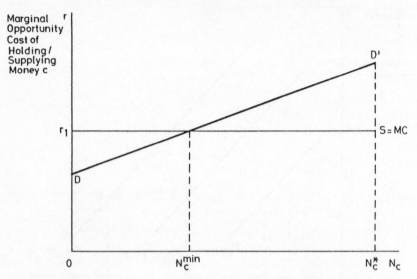

ginal cost of supplying a bank account and an identical amount of m_c to additional persons is constant at r_1, N_c^{min} is the 'minimum threshold size' or 'take-off point' [RABENAU and STAHL, 1974] or 'critical mass' [ROHLFS, 1974] which the system must attain to be viable. N_c^{min} is an equilibrium point but it is not stable. If N_c falls below N_c^{min}, the system collapses and $N_c = 0$ is the only stable equilibrium point. If N_c rises above N_c^{min}, the system expands up to the unique saturation level where everybody has a bank account ($N_c = N_c^*$). In contrast to normal private goods, the increase in market size is consistent with a constant or even increasing 'price' (opportunity cost).

So far we have greatly simplified by assuming that each person faces an identical volume of transactions and would hold an identical quantity of m_c, if he decided to open a bank account. This is analogous to what in the economics of telephone networks is called 'the uniform calling model' [ROHLFS, 1974]. We shall now enhance the realism of the analysis by allowing for differences in transaction volumes. This means that those with the largest volume of transactions would be the first to avail themselves of the services of money (if at all) and that the external benefits which additional users confer on those who do already use the money,

38

THE GOVERNMENT'S MONEY MONOPOLY

Figure 4

Market Demand for Money with Differing Transaction Volumes

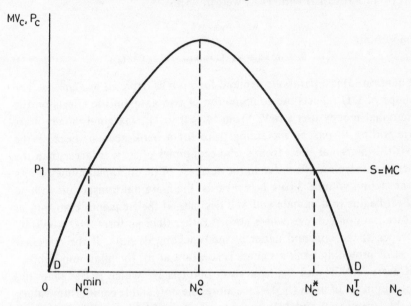

diminish as N_c increases[23]. To keep the analysis manageable, we shall assume that the frequency distribution of users between the minimum transaction volume ($T_{min} = 0$) and the maximum transaction volume (T_{max}) is uniform for all transaction volumes (T_i) and that each person is indifferent with whom to conduct his transactions. We can then apply ROHLFS' [1974] analysis to the case of money.

The demand curve for bank accounts in currency c is the locus of points where the price (P_c) of a bank account in currency c equals the value of a bank account to the marginal money user (MV_c), with both p_c and MV_c being measured in terms of some identical *numéraire*. MV_c can be viewed as the product of two factors: $MV_c = w_i \cdot f_c$ where

w_i is the value which a bank account would have for money user i if everybody had a bank account, and where

f_c is the fraction of the total population which has a bank account in currency c ($0 \leq f_c \leq 1$).

23. This is an application of LEIBENSTEIN's [1950] 'principle of diminishing marginal external consumption effect'.

39

ROLAND VAUBEL

If w_1 declines proportionately as the transaction volumes of additional money users and thus $1 - f_c$ decrease, and if w_{max} is used to denote the w_1 of an individual with T_{max}, we can write

$$w_1 = w_{max} \cdot (1 - f_c) \tag{3}$$

and obtain

$$P_c = MV_c = w_1 \cdot f_c = w_{max} \cdot (1 - f_c) \cdot f_c \tag{4}$$

Equation (4) is a parabolic demand function as depicted in *Figure 4*. The shape of DD reflects the combination of two antagonistic effects on the marginal money user's MV. From $N_c = 0$ to N_c^0, marginal money users are willing to pay an increasing price for a bank account because the positive marginal effect from social economies of scale is larger than the negative marginal effect due to the decrease of the marginal money user's transaction volume. From N_c^0 onwards, the marginal transaction volume effect begins to dominate and MV declines. If the frequency distribution of transaction volumes where normal rather than uniform, DD would be steeper at the tails and flatter at the (unchanged) peak. If the marginal cost of providing bank accounts is constant at p_1, the minimum number of users is N_c^{min} and the saturation point is N_c^* which is less than the total number of users (N_c^T). Once more, the only stable equilibrium values of N_c are $N_c = 0$ and N_c^*; however, there could be further stable local equilibria if the frequency distribution of T_1 is discontinuous.

Figures 3 and *4* imply that transaction cost externalities cannot be expected to prevent the use of money rather than barter[24]. If DD rises above MC at some point, the money can profitable be produced by private enterprise, and the threat of entry will push the producer to N_c^*. What is necessary is merely that he subsidizes bank accounts by the distance between the demand curve and the marginal cost curve while

---

24. They illustrate CARL MENGER's famous dictum that 'the economic interest of individual economic agents leads them ..., without any common agreement and without governmental coercion, without even any regard for the public interest, to sell their goods in exchange for other, more generally tradable goods, although they do not need the latter for their own direct consumption' and that this is although 'initially, only some economic agents will realize the advantages of money' [1871, pp. 253, 255]. For the opposite view see NIEHANS [1969, p. 724]: 'We cannot be sure that a medium of exchange will emerge whenever economic efficiency demands it, nor is there a guarantee that the "right" commodities will be chosen as media of exchange ... This may be the ultimate rationale for the notion ... that (the) adoption (of money) requires either command or convention'.

THE GOVERNMENT'S MONEY MONOPOLY

the number of his customers is still below the threshold N_c^{min}. As N_c rises above N_c^{min} he can recoup this temporary loss. A government subsidy for the first N_c^{min} bank accounts – let alone a government monopoly in the supply of money – is not required to get the network started, for the start-up costs can be covered from the future profits. This is how enterprises overcome the infant industry stage[25].

Although transaction cost externalities cannot be expected to prevent the use of money, they may render the number of money users smaller than optimal because the marginal non-users of money might be willing to use money if they were compensated for the positive transaction cost externalities which they would confer on those who use money anyway[26]. As *Figures 3* and *4* show, the number of users can but need not be suboptimal. However, where, like in the industrial countries, all economic agents do use money, the transaction cost externalities of using money cannot be PARETO-relevant. In less than fully monetized economies they would justify government subsidization of marginal bank accounts and of primary schools that teach the use of money, but not governmental money production.

b. *Implications for the Choice among Currencies*

Transaction cost externalities may not only affect the individual's choice between money and barter but also his choice among different monies. SWOBODA [1968, pp. 39 ff.] has shown that, in terms of transaction costs (though not necessarily in terms of portfolio balance), the individual money user will prefer the use of a single (foreign) money. Will the technological transaction externalities prevent him from picking the money that minimizes social transaction costs?

An individual who chooses currency X in place of currency Y, confers external benefits on the other users of currency X and withholds external benefits from the users of currency Y. The external benefits are

---

25. As FRIEDMAN [1981, p. 10] points out, the problem is more complicated if the start-up costs are costs of generating knowledge that facilitates the introduction of further monies. However, FRIEDMAN emphasizes that historical experience does not support the view that such information externalities are a crucial obstacle. If they were, there would be a case for governmental subsidization of such knowledge creation but not for governmental production of money.

26. For a similar view see JONES [1976, p. 773].

ROLAND VAUBEL

savings of currency conversion costs. Since currency conversion costs can be viewed as an excise tax on sales across currency boundaries, they are divided between buyer and seller, according to the theory of tax incidence, in the ratio of the elasticity of supply to the elasticity of demand. To simplify the exposition, let us distinguish three limiting cases[27]:

(i) If the individual (say, a seller) faces the same (weighted) elasticity of demand and the same fixed and variable rate of conversion cost in all currency domains, he will choose the currency of the currency domain with which he has most business (measured in terms of the number and the volume of transactions each weighted by the fixed and the variable rate of conversion cost, respectively). Since the elasticities of demand are assumed to be the same, the currency conversion cost borne by the seller is a fixed proportion of total currency conversion costs borne by seller and buyer together. Thus, the choice of currency which minimizes the seller's currency conversion cost also minimizes the total or social currency conversion costs. The external effect is not PARETO-relevant.

(ii) If the seller faces the same (weighted) elasticity of demand in all currency domains and if, in the absence of currency conversion costs, he would conduct the same number and volume of transactions with all currency domains, he will choose the currency for which the fixed and variable rate of conversion cost, each multiplied by the number and volume of transactions, respectively, yields the smallest currency conversion cost for him. Since the elasticities of demand are the same everywhere, his private currency conversion cost is a fixed proportion of social currency conversion cost. Thus, by minimizing private currency conversion cost, he also minimizes social currency conversion costs. Once more, the external effect is not PARETO-relevant.

(iii) If, in the absence of currency conversion costs, the seller would conduct the same volume and value of transactions with the members of all currency domains, if the fixed and variable conversion cost fee is the same between all pairs of currencies, but if the (weighted) elasticities of demand for the seller's products differ among currency domains, he will choose the currency domain with the highest price elasticity of demand for his product. Since currency conversion cost is small relative to the incomes and revenues of those who have to

27. For a more detailed exposition see VAUBEL [1978, pp. 80–82].

THE GOVERNMENT'S MONEY MONOPOLY

Figure 5

Individual Choice among Currencies

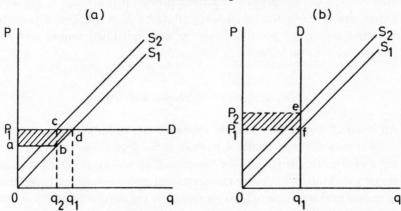

bear it, partial equilibrium analysis can be used for a simple geometric demonstration of the main point.

If demand is perfectly elastic (*Figure 5a*), our seller has to bear all currency conversion cost (rectangle p_1abc) and loses seller's surplus (triangle bcd). The social cost of currency conversion (p_1abd) is thus fully borne by the seller. If demand is perfectly inelastic (*Figure 5b*), all currency conversion cost is borne by the buyer (p_1p_2ef) at the expense of his surplus. His private currency conversion cost is identical with the social cost of currency conversion. As can be seen, the social cost of currency conversion is larger in panel (b) than in panel (a). However, the seller will choose the currency of those whose demand is most elastic (a) rather than the currency of those whose demand is least elastic (b). Thus, as far as elasticity differences are concerned, the seller's currency choice maximizes the social cost of currency conversion. The same can be shown for the buyer's currency choice.

The assumption that a seller faces a less than perfectly elastic demand, let alone a perfectly inelastic one (b), is of course, inconsistent with perfect or even imperfect competition. It implies that the seller acts, in some dealings, as a monopolist. If he considers himself an atomistic supplier, only *Figure 5a* applies, and since, in this case, the social cost of currency conversion is fully borne by him (at least he will believe so), he will minimize social cost by minimizing his private cost. The same can be shown for a buyer who faces (or believes to face) a perfectly elastic supply curve.

43

ROLAND VAUBEL

Thus, if perfect or imperfect competition prevails, transaction cost externalities do not lead to suboptimal currency choices. But even where monopolistic or oligopolistic situations prevail, it is difficult to see how government prescription of currency could be more efficient, especially if considerations of portfolio balance and individual unit-of-account preferences are also to be taken into account.

c. Implications for Exchange Rate Policy

An issuer of money who fixes the exchange rate of his currency *vis-à-vis* another currency may confer a positive technological externality on the users of the other currency (the 'dominant' currency), provided that he actually sticks to his exchange rate target and makes it sufficiently credible to reduce exchange rate risk (as measured by the deviations of the actual exchange rate from the exchange rate predicted in the past). To the extent that there are stochastic influences on the demand for money, an exchange rate target of this sort reduces exchange risk more than does an effective money supply target. If (and only if) the exchange rate is immutably fixed without any margins of fluctuations, the cost of information about the exchange rate is reduced as well.

However, the technological externalities of exchange-rate policy need not be PARETO-relevant, for they may be appropriable. A money issuer who adopts an exchange rate target can be compensated for any external benefits which he may confer on the users of the dominant currency. The compensation could come from the issuer of the dominant currency, for the users of the dominant currency would be willing to incur a correspondingly higher opportunity cost of holding the dominant currency. He would charge them for the compensation he is paying. In fact, transfers under multilateral exchange rate arrangements may have been motivated in this way. The subsidized credit facilities and the open resource transfers in the European Monetary System seem to be a case in point.

Even if no such transfers take place, the international public decision to maintain 'international monetary stability' or a 'monetary union' may not be underproduced as KINDLEBERGER [1972, 1976], HAMADA [1977, 1979] and FRENKEL [1975] suggest[28]. The reason is that the technological external effects of exchange rate targets may on balance be negative. To

28. For a critique see also VAUBEL [1978, pp. 20–21] and SALIN [1982, pp. 191 ff.].

44

THE GOVERNMENT'S MONEY MONOPOLY

fix exchange rates is to form a unit-of-account cartel among money producers. By reducing the opportunity for 'exit', the members of the cartel
can raise the opportunity cost of holding their monies. As a result of
collusion, the public good of the competitive order is in scarcer supply
and with it the knowledge and efficiency which it generates. If the imposition of a common national money can be a national public bad
(*Section I*), there is an even stronger possibility that international exchange rate arrangements are international public bads[29].

III. IS THE SUPPLY OF MONEY A NATURAL MONOPOLY?

Since externality theory fails to provide a convincing justification for the
government's monopoly in the production of (base) money, its rationale
may be sought in the existence of non-external economies of scale. Economies of scale is a conceptually distinct justification: they accrue only
from an increase in output, whereas external economies accrue to additional beneficiaries from a given output[30].

Economies of scale can relate to the use of money or to the production
of money. That the *use* of money is subject to social economies of scale
is apparent from the analysis in *Section II.3.a.* and has frequently been
stated in the literature[31]. As MUNDELL [1970, pp. 13f.] and BRUNNER
and MELTZER [1971, p. 792] have pointed out, there are also individual
economies of repetition ('temporal economies of scale') in the use of
money. Moreover, some authors[32] suggest that, at least over some range,
the *production* of money involves economies of scale because

29. For a detailed welfare-theoretic analysis of international monetary-policy coordination see VAUBEL [1983].

30. This distinction is blurred by writers like SAMUELSON [1969, p. 118] who treat
'decreasing cost phenomena as public goods'.

31. For the natural monopoly argument see notably KLEIN [1974, p. 450], VAUBEL
[1977, p. 458], CLAASSEN [1979, pp. 4–8], SALIN [1979], KLEIN and MELVIN [1982,
pp. 209ff.], STARBATTY [1982, pp. 397ff.], KING [1983, pp. 132f.]. According to MUN-
DELL [1970, p. 14] and ENGELS [1981, p. 9, 119], the currency unit is a natural monopoly. HAYEK, in the second edition [pp. 123–125] of his 1976b essay, considers
convergence to a single currency unit probable as well.

32. BELL and MURPHY [1968], BENSTON [1972], BALTENSPERGER [1972], KLEIN
[1974], LONGBRAKE and HASLEM [1975], GEHRIG [1978], NIEHANS [1978], CLAASSEN
[1979], SALIN [1979], KLEIN and MELVIN [1981].

45

ROLAND VAUBEL

- the variance of a bank's reserve losses rises less than proportionately as the number of depositors increases [BALTENSPERGER],
- fixed costs of reserve adjustment generate smaller deviations of actual from optimal reserves, the larger the bank [BALTENSPERGER],
- there are stochastic economies from diversification on the bank's asset side [BALTENSPERGER],
- more efficient technologies are available to larger banks [BELL and MURPHY],
- the creation of consumer confidence in a money is largely a fixed (sunk) cost [KLEIN], and
- the cost of disseminating information about a money declines, as the number of issuers decreases [KLEIN].

But the market uses a variety of means of payments: coins, notes, checks, traveller's checks, various types of bank account; it is only the standard of value which they have in common. As a store of value, economic agents may desire monetary assets denominated in a variety of standards of value (currencies) to spread their capital risk through diversification. In the presence of large relative price changes and large differences in consumption plans, different persons may also prefer different standards of value (here: standards of deferred payment) to minimize their purchasing-power risk. A particularly good example seems to be the century-long coexistence of a silver and a copper standard in different parts of China [CHEN, 1975]. For these reasons, the optimum currency area need not be the world.

It is true that, if money, or the currency unit, is a natural monopoly good, government production of money can be the optimal response, although the danger of X-inefficiency may lead one to prefer a regulated private monopoly, the auctioning of the monopoly license [DEMSETZ, 1968a], or even enforced fragmentation[33]. However, whichever solution is optimal in the present case, the optimum does not require restrictions on entry[34] or other forms of legal currency discrimination[35], not even

---

33. For a comparison of various alternatives to a government-owned natural monopoly see ROWLEY and PEACOCK [1975, pp. 176–180].

34. See also BRENNAN and BUCHANAN [1981, p. 56], LEWIN [1981] and WHITE [1983a, b].

35. For a discussion of legal tender laws and other forms of currency discrimination in selected countries see VAUBEL [1978, pp. 47–49].

46

THE GOVERNMENT'S MONEY MONOPOLY

with respect to the currency unit[36]. Since we do not know the characteristics of an optimal money (for instance, whether it should be of stable
or increasing purchasing power), there is a case against restrictions on
entry. Since, finally, we cannot even be sure that money or the currency
unit is a natural monopoly[37], the case against restrictions of entry is overwhelming. Only if a governmental producer of money can prevail in conditions of free entry and without discriminatory subsidies is he an efficient
natural monopolist[38].

IV. TESTING FOR SOCIAL ECONOMIES OF SCALE IN THE USE OF MONEY

If the usefulness of money as a means of payment depends exclusively
on the volume of transactions and if income is an adequate proxy for
the volume of transactions, social economies of scale in the use of money
are accounted for in the standard money demand functions. The volume
of transactions is an appropriate measure of the currency-conversion cost
that can be saved by using the same currency if currency-conversion cost
has only a variable component. If there is also a fixed cost per conversion,
as for instance SWOBODA [1968, pp. 39f.] assumes for the conversion of
domestic bonds into foreign cash, the usefulness of money as a medium
of exchange depends also on the number of transactions that can be conducted within the currency domain. The same will hold true if variable
transaction costs decrease with the number of transactions[39]. If the num-

36. ENGELS [1981, pp. 10f.] and HALL [1981, p. 21] suggest that the government
should prescribe the currency unit but refrain from money production itself.

37. Historically, competition has not tended to destroy itself in the money-
producing industry. See VAUBEL [1978, pp. 400f.], ENGELS [1981, p. 117], KING [1983,
p. 154], WHITE [1983b, p. 293].

38. This is also true if he has passed the point of minimum average cost; for in
this exceptional case, which SHARKEY [1982, Ch. 5] has emphasized, an efficient natural monopolist can produce the optimal quantity of output and sustain himself against
less efficient competitors if the government pays an equal amount of subsidy to all
producers who supply at least as much output. Under SHARKEY's assumptions, the
subsidy must be sufficient to keep the *net* average cost of the most efficient supplier
of optimal output at the minimum average cost attainable for the smaller quantity
of output.

39. DEMSETZ [1968b], has shown that bid-ask spreads in the New York Stock
Exchange decrease significantly with the number of transactions.

47

ROLAND VAUBEL

ber of transactions can be proxied by the number of members of a currency domain[40] rather than by the volume of transactions in that currency, the population of the currency domain should be an argument in the money demand function[41].

To test this hypothesis[42] in as simple a manner as possible, the following transformation of a money demand function has been estimated:

$$\ln(M_i/Y_i) = a + b_1 \ln i_i + b_2 \ln N_i + u_i \qquad (5)$$

where

M = a money supply aggregate
Y = nominal income
i = an interest rate index
N = population size.

Since population changes slowly over time, an international cross-section analysis has been preferred, *i.e.*, the subscript i denotes a country. The simplifying assumptions that nominal money balances and nominal income can be deflated by the same price index and that the income elasticity of the demand for money is unity[43], are chosen to avoid the thorny problem of international real income comparisons. As usual it is assumed that money demand equals money supply, *i.e.*, that the money market is in equilibrium. Since all data are five-year averages (1976–80), this assumption is especially realistic. Other simplifications concern the use of total population (rather than adult population) and the omission of other potentially relevant variables such as banking technology and restrictions on international capital movements and trade, which are difficult to proxy.

40. For the NYSE, DEMSETZ [1968b] found a highly significant correlation between the number of transactions and the number of stockholders.

41. CHANDLER [1959, p. 2], MUNDELL [1970, p. 13] and FELDMAN [1973, p. 463], for example, have suggested that social economies in the transacting process increase with the number of transactions and the size of the group.

42. The test is a joint test of three hypotheses:
– population size is a better proxy for the number of transactions than is the volume of transactions;
– currency conversion cost contains a fixed component per conversion;
– the demand for a money is larger, the more it saves transaction costs.

43. An income-elasticity close to unity is consistent with an inventory-theoretic approach to the demand for money if the cost of time is taken into account. See, *e.g.*, BARRO and SANTOMERO [1972, p. 408], DUTTON and GRAMM [1973, p. 664] and SAVING [1974].

48

THE GOVERNMENT'S MONEY MONOPOLY

Table 1

An International Cross-Section Analysis of the Demand for Money
(OLS Regressions)

Dependent Variable	Intercept	Explanatory Variables		R^2	S.E.E.	Sample Size
$\ln (M_1/Y)$	−1.41 (−1.59)	−0.101 $\ln i_L$ (−0.28)	+ 0.020 $\ln N$ (0.23)	0.01	0.464	18
$\ln (M_1/Y)$	−0.87 (−1.01)	−0.278 $\ln i_L$ (−0.79)	− 0.15 $\ln N$ (−0.17)	0.06	0.432	14
$\ln (M_2/Y)$		−0.305 $\ln i_L$ (−3.49*)	+ 0.016 $\ln N$ (0.25)	0.13	0.360	18
$\ln (M_2/Y)$		−0.287 $\ln i_L$ (−3.17*)	+ 0.0003 $\ln N$ (0.01)	0.23	0.312	14
$\ln (M_T/Y)$		−0.308 $\ln i_L$ (−3.54*)	+ 0.024 $\ln N$ (0.37)	0.14	0.358	18
$\ln (M_T/Y)$		−0.287 $\ln i_L$ (−3.19*)	+ 0.0068 $\ln N$ (0.11)	0.24	0.310	14
$\ln (M_T/Y)$		−0.283 $\ln i_S$ (−1.43)	+ 0.0022 $\ln N$ (0.02)	0.25	0.344	10
$\ln (M_X/T)$		−2.28 $\ln i_S$ (−3.96*)	+ 0.155 $\ln N$ (0.49)	0.41	1.00	10
$\ln (L_X/T)$		−2.21 $\ln i_S$ (−3.52*)	+ 0.551 $\ln N$ (1.60)	0.50	1.09	10

* = significant at the 1 per cent level.
t-values in parenthesis.

Equation (5) has been estimated for M_1, M_2 and M_T ('M-total') which in addition to M_2 comprises banks' domestic-currency and foreign-currency liabilities to foreign non-banks in currency i with a maturity of up to three months. The method of calculation and the sources are given in the appendix. Three sample sizes have been used:
– the 18 industrialized or semi-industrialized countries for which the IMF *International Financial Statistics* give values of M_1, M_2, GNP, N, and a long-term interest-rate index (line 61);
– the 14 of the 18 countries for which also a short-term market interest rate (line 60c or b) is given;

ROLAND VAUBEL

– the 10 of the 18 countries for whose currencies data on banks' foreign-currency and domestic-currency liabilities to foreigners are available.

The samples with 14 or 10 observations have been estimated with the long-term interest rate (i_L), the short-term interest rate (i_S), both, and with or without the value of the term-structure variable i_L–i_S. i_L and i_S have also been tried in unlogged form. All equations have been estimated with and without an intercept. Those results which yield a positive coefficient for N (if at all) and minimize the standard error of the estimate are reported in *Table 1* (first seven estimates).

As can be seen, the interest rate coefficients have a negative sign and are mostly significant at the 1 per cent level. Significantly negative interest-rate coefficients result also for ln (M_1/Y) if the intercept is omitted. The regression coefficient of ln N is always totally insignificant and in one case even never positive; nor is it ever close to 2 as BAUMOL's [1967] analysis of social economies would lead one to expect.

It is conceivable that these results are due to the omission of explanatory variables which swamp the population effect in the domestic context. In other words, it may be that currency-conversion costs per conversion are a significant factor only at the margin where a choice between different *foreign* currencies has to be made. To allow for this possibility the previous estimates have been replicated for foreigners' (*i.e.*, 'external') claims on banks, M_X and L_X. While M_{Xi} comprises only *short-term* claims of foreign *non-banks* in currency i ($M_{Xi} = M_{Ti} - M_{2i}$), L_{Xi} includes all claims of all foreigners in currency i[44].

The relevant volume of transactions (T_i) is now proxied by the sum of the country's exports and imports of goods and services.

The results are reported in *Table 1* (last two estimates). The coefficients of ln N are now less insignificant; the coefficient in ln (L_X/T) is almost significant at the 5 per cent level (the critical t-value is 1.86). The interest rate coefficients are again significant at the 1 per cent level; the coefficients of determination attain respectable levels.

The residuals for L_X/T [not: ln (L_X/T)] are listed in *Table 2*. It shows that, in comparison with our estimate, especially the Swiss Franc and even more so the U.S. dollar are overrepresented in international banking and that notably the Japanese Yen is underrepresented. A possible explanation, which is also consistent with the overrepresentation of the

44. For details see the *appendix*.

50

THE GOVERNMENT'S MONEY MONOPOLY

Table 2

Actual and Estimated Values of L_X/T

	Actual	Estimated	Residual
Belgium	0.044	0.039	+0.005
Canada	0.020	0.036	−0.016
France	0.057	0.065	−0.008
Germany	0.329	0.247	+0.082
Italy	0.013	0.027	−0.014
Japan	0.022	0.200	−0.178
Netherlands	0.095	0.053	+0.042
Switzerland	0.567	0.283	+0.284
U.K.	0.109	0.045	+0.064
U.S.	0.896	0.208	+0.688
Average	0.215		

Deutsche Mark and the Dutch Guilder and with the underrepresentation of the Italian Lira, would be the differences in the degree of international financial liberalisation.

Why does population size seem to play a role in the currency choice of all foreigners (*i.e.*, with respect to L_X) but not for the short-term claims of foreign non-banks (M_X)? Apparently, the cost of international interbank transactions is essentially a fixed currency-conversion cost per transaction, while non-banks are charged a variable currency-conversion cost as well.

APPENDIX: SAMPLES, SOURCES AND METHODS OF CALCULATION

The sample of 10 countries comprises Belgium, Canada, France, W. Germany, Italy, Japan, the Netherlands, Switzerland, the United Kingdom, and the United States.

The sample of 14 countries includes in addition Denmark, Ireland, Norway and South Africa.

The sample of 18 countries adds Australia, Austria, New Zealand and Portugal.

Yearly averages or end-of-year data of M_1, M_2, Y, i_L, i_S, N and T have been taken from IMF *International Financial Statistics*. The only exception is the short-term interest rate for the Swiss Franc (three-month euro-SF deposits) which had to be obtained from the *Monatsberichte* published by the Swiss Nationalbank.

End-of-year data about banks' domestic-currency and foreign-currency liabilities to foreigners have been taken from the *Annual Report* of the Bank for International Settlements. Data of banks' foreign-currency liabilities to non-banks are published

51

ROLAND VAUBEL

by the Bank for International Settlements in its quarterly *International Banking Developments*. The statistics about domestic-currency liabilities to foreign non-banks have been obtained from the Bank for International Settlements (except for the U.S. dollar and the Swiss Franc). The data for the U.S. dollar are published in the *Federal Reserve Bulletin*; the values for the Swiss Franc have been estimated: banks' SF-liabilities to all foreigners have been multiplied by the average non-bank share in the liabilities to all foreigners for all other currencies. The share of banks' foreign-currency liabilities to foreign non-banks with a maturity of up to 3 months is indicated, for the London eurocurrency market, in the *Quarterly Bulletin of the Bank of England*.

$M_{Xi} = M_{Ti} - M_{2i}$ has been calculated by multiplying the sum of banks' domestic-currency and foreign-currency liabilities to foreign non-banks in currency i by the share which London banks' foreign-currency liabilities to foreign non-banks with a maturity of up to three months occupy in their total foreign-currency liabilities to foreign non-banks.

REFERENCES

ARTLE, ROLAND and AVEROUS, CHRISTIAN: 'The Telephone System as a Public Good: Static and Dynamic Aspects', *The Bell Journal of Economics and Management Science*, Vol. 4 (1973), pp. 89–100.

BALTENSPERGER, ERNST: 'Economies of Scale, Firm Size, and Concentration in Banking', *Journal of Money, Credit and Banking*, Vol. 4 (1972), pp. 467–488.

BARRO, ROBERT J. and SANTOMERO, ANTHONY M.: 'Household Money Holdings and the Demand Deposit Rate', *Journal of Money, Credit and Banking*, Vol. 4 (1972), pp. 397–413.

BAUMOL, WILLIAM J.: 'Macroeconomics of Unbalanced Growth: The Anatomy of Urban Crisis', *American Economic Review*, Vol. 57 (1967), pp. 415–426.

BELL, FREDERICK W. and MURPHY, NEIL B.: 'Economies of Scale and the Division of Labor in Commercial Banking', *Southern Economic Journal*, Vol. 35 (1968), pp. 131–139.

BENSTON, GEORGE J.: 'Economies of Scale of Financial Institutions', *Journal of Money, Credit and Banking*, Vol. 4 (1972), pp. 312–341.

BILSON, JOHN F.O.: *A Proposal for Monetary Reform*, University of Chicago, unpubl. manuscript, 1981.

BRENNAN, GEOFFREY H. and BUCHANAN, JAMES M.: *Monopoly in Money and Inflation*, Institute of Economic Affairs, London: Hobart Paper, 88, 1981.

BROWN, PAMELA J.: 'Constitution or Competition? Alternative Views on Monetary Reform', *Literature of Liberty*, Autumn, 1982, pp. 7–52.

BRUNNER, KARL and MELTZER, ALLAN H.: 'Some Further Investigations of Demand and Supply Functions for Money', *Journal of Finance*, Vol. 19 (1964), pp. 240–283.

BRUNNER, KARL and MELTZER, ALLAN H.: 'The Uses of Money: Money in the Theory of an Exchange Economy', *American Economic Review*, Vol. 61 (1971), pp. 784–805.

BUCHANAN, JAMES M.: 'An Economic Theory of Clubs', *Economica*, Vol. 32 (1965), pp. 1–14.

THE GOVERNMENT'S MONEY MONOPOLY

BUCHANAN, JAMES M.: *The Demand and Supply of Public Goods*, Chicago, 1968.

BUCHANAN, JAMES M. and STUBBLEBINE, CRAIG WM.: 'Externality', *Economica*, Vol. 29 (1962), pp. 371–384.

CASSEL, DIETER H. and THIEME, JÖRG: 'Stabilitätspolitik', in: *Vahlens Kompendium der Wirtschaftstheorie und Wirtschaftspolitik*, Vol. 2, München, 1981.

CHANDLER, LESTER V.: *The Economics of Money and Banking*, New York, 1959.

CHEN, CHAU-NAN: 'Flexible Bimetallic Exchange Rates in China, 1650–1850: A Historical Example of Optimum Currency Areas', *Journal of Money, Credit and Banking*, Vol. 7 (1975), pp. 359–376.

CHETTY, KARUPPAN V.: 'On Measuring the Nearness of Near-moneys', *American Economic Review*, Vol. 59 (1969), pp. 270–281.

CLAASSEN, EMIL M.: *Monetary Integration and Monetary Stability: The Economic Criteria of the Monetary Constitution*, Paper presented at the Conference on 'New Economic Approaches to the Study of International Integration', Florence, May/June, 1979, revised.

CLAASSEN, EMIL M. and SALIN, PASCAL (eds.): *Stabilization Policies in Interdependent Economies*, Amsterdam/London, 1972.

COASE, RONALD: 'The Problem of Social Cost', *Journal of Law and Economics*, Vol. 3 (1960), pp. 1–44.

DEMSETZ, HAROLD: 'Why Regulate Utilities?', *Journal of Law and Economics*, Vol. 11 (1968a), pp. 55–65.

DEMSETZ, HAROLD: 'The Cost of Transacting', *Quarterly Journal of Economics*, Vol. 82 (1968b), pp. 33–53.

DEMSETZ, HAROLD: 'The Private Production of Public Goods', *Journal of Law and Economics*, Vol. 13 (1970), pp. 293–306.

DUTTON, DEAN S. and GRAMM, WILLIAM P.: 'Transactions Costs, the Wage Rate, and the Demand for Money', *American Economic Review*, Vol. 63 (1973), pp. 652–665.

ENGELS, WOLFRAM: *The Optimal Monetary Unit*, Frankfurt, 1981.

FELDMAN, ALLAN M.: 'Bilateral Trading Processes, Pairwise Optimality, and Pareto Optimality', *The Review of Economic Studies*, Vol. 40 (1973), pp. 463–473.

FISCHER, STANLEY: 'Money and the Production Function', *Economic Inquiry*, Vol. 12 (1974) pp. 517–533.

FRATIANNI, MICHELE: 'The Dollar and the ECU', in: DREYER, JACOB S.; HABERLER, GOTTFRIED and WILLETT, THOMAS D. (eds.): *The International Monetary System. A Time of Turbulence*, Washington, D.C., 1982.

FRENKEL, JACOB A.: 'Reflections on European Monetary Integration', *Weltwirtschaftliches Archiv*, Vol. 11 (1975), pp. 216–221.

FRIEDMAN, MILTON: *A Program for Monetary Stability*, New York, 1959a.

FRIEDMAN, MILTON: 'The Demand for Money: Some Theoretical and Empirical Results', *Journal of Political Economy*, Vol. 67 (1959), pp. 327–351.

FRIEDMAN, MILTON: *The Optimum Quantity of Money and Other Essays*, Chicago, 1969.

FRIEDMAN, MILTON: *Monetary System for a Free Society*, Hoover Institution, Stanford, unpubl. manuscript, 1981.

53

ROLAND VAUBEL

GEHRIG, BRUNO: 'Brauchen wir monopolistische Zentralbanken?', *Wirtschaft und Recht*, Vol. 30 (1978), pp. 452–464.

GIRTON, LANCE and ROPER, DON: 'Theory and Implications of Currency Substitution', *Journal of Money, Credit and Banking*, Vol. 13 (1981), pp. 12–30.

GRUBEL, HERBERT G.: *International Economics*, Homewood, Ill., 1977.

GURLEY, JOHN G. and SHAW, EDWARD S.: *Money in a Theory of Finance*, Washington, 1960.

HALL, ROBERT E.: *The Role of Government in Stabilizing Prices and Regulating Money*, Stanford University, unpubl. manuscript, 1981.

HALL, ROBERT: 'Optimal Fiduciary Monetary Systems', *Journal of Monetary Economics*, Vol. 12 (1983), pp. 33–50.

HAMADA, KOICHI: 'On the Political Economy of Monetary Integration: A Public Economics Approach', in: ALIBER, ROBERT Z. (ed.): *The Political Economy of Monetary Reform*, London/Basingstoke, 1977, pp. 13–31.

HAMADA, KOICHI: *On the Coordination of Monetary Policies in a Monetary Union*, Paper presented at the Conference on 'New Economic Approaches to the Study of International Integration', Florence, May/June, 1979.

HAYEK FRIEDRICH A.: *Choice in Currency: A Way to Stop Inflation*, Institute of Economic Affairs, London: Occasional Papers, 48, 1976a.

HAYEK, FRIEDRICH A.: *Denationalisation of Money*, Institute of Economic Affairs, London: Hobart Paper Special, 70, 1976b.

HAYEK, FRIEDRICH A.: 'Towards a Free Market Monetary System', *Journal of Libertarian Studies*, 1978.

HIRSCHMAN, ALBERT O.: *Exit, Voice, and Loyalty*, Cambridge, Mass., 1970.

HIRSHLEIFER, JACK: 'Exchange Theory: The Missing Chapter', *Western Economic Journal*, Vol. 11 (1973), pp. 129–146.

JOHNSON, HARRY G.: 'Problems of Efficiency in Monetary Management', *Journal of Political Economy*, Vol. 76 (1968), pp. 971–990.

JOHNSON, HARRY G.: 'Pesek and Saving's Theory of Money and Wealth', *Journal of Money, Credit and Banking*, Vol. 1 (1969), pp. 535–537.

JONES, ROBERT A.: 'The Origin and Development of Media of Exchange', *Journal of Political Economy*, Vol. 84 (1976), pp. 757–775.

KINDLEBERGER, CHARLES P.: *The Politics of International Money and World Language*, Essays in International Finance, 61, Princeton, 1967.

KINDLEBERGER, CHARLES P.: 'The Benefits of International Money', *Journal of International Economics*, Vol. 2 (1972), pp. 425–442.

KINDLEBERGER, CHARLES P.: 'Lessons from Floating Exchange Rates', in: BRUNNER, KARL and MELTZER, ALLAN H. (eds.): *Institutional Arrangements and the Inflation Problem*, Amsterdam/New York/Oxford, 1976, pp. 51–77.

KINDLEBERGER, CHARLES P.: *Manias, Panics and Crashes*, London/Basingstoke, 1978a.

KINDLEBERGER, CHARLES P.: 'Dominance and Leadership in the International Economy: Exploitation, Public Goods, and Free Rides', *Hommage à François Perroux*, Grenoble, 1978b, pp. 283–291.

THE GOVERNMENT'S MONEY MONOPOLY

KINDLEBERGER, CHARLES P.: 'Standards as Public, Collective and Private Goods', *Kyklos*, Vol. 36 (1983), pp. 377–396.

KING, ROBERT: 'On the Economics of Private Money', *Journal of Monetary Economics*, Vol. 12 (1983), pp. 127–158.

KLEIN, BENJAMIN: 'The Competitive Supply of Money', *Journal of Money, Credit and Banking*, Vol. 6 (1974), pp. 423–453.

KLEIN, BENJAMIN and MELVIN, MICHAEL: 'Competing International Monies and International Monetary Arrangements', in: CONNOLLY, MICHAEL B. (ed.): *The International Monetary System. Choices for the Future*, New York, 1982, pp. 199–225.

KOLM, SERGE-CHRISTOPHE: 'External Liquidity – A Study in Monetary Welfare Economics', in: SZEGÖ, GIORGIO P. and SHELL, KARL (eds.): *Mathematical Methods in Investment and Finance*, Amsterdam/London/New York, 1972, pp. 190–206.

KOLM, SERGE-CHRISTOPHE: 'Fondements de l'économie monétaire normative: seigneuriage, liquidité externe, impossibilité de rémunérer les espèces', *Revue Economique*, Vol. 28 (1977), pp. 1–35.

LAIDLER, DAVID E. W.: 'The Welfare Costs of Inflation in Neoclassical Theory – Some Unsettled Problems', in: LUNDBERG, ERIK (ed.): *Inflation Theory and Anti-Inflation Policy*, Boulder, Col., 1977, pp. 314–328.

LEIBENSTEIN, HARVEY: 'Bandwagon, Snob and Veblen Effects in the Theory of Consumers' Demand', *Quarterly Journal of Economics*, Vol. 64 (1950), pp. 183–207.

LEWIN, PETER: *The Denationalization of Money*, University of Texas, unpublished manuscript, Dallas, 1981.

LONGBRAKE, WILLIAM A. and HASLEM, JOHN A.: 'Productive Efficiency in Commercial Banking', *Journal of Money, Credit and Banking*, Vol. 7 (1975), pp. 317–330.

LUTZ, FRIEDRICH A.: *Das Grundproblem der Geldverfassung*, Berlin, 1936.

McKEAN, ROLAND N.: *Efficiency in Government through Systems Analysis*, New York, 1958.

McKINNON, RONALD I.: *Private and Official International Money: The Case for the Dollar*, Essays in International Finance, Princeton, 74, 1969.

McKINNON, RONALD I.: *Money in International Exchange*, New York/Oxford, 1979.

MELTZER, ALLAN H.: 'Money, Intermediation and Growth', *Journal of Economic Literature*, Vol. 7 (1969), pp. 27–56.

MENGER, CARL: *Grundsätze der Volkswirtschaftslehre*, Wien, 1871.

MUNDELL, ROBERT A.: *The Case for a European Currency*, unpubl. manuscript; published in French translation: 'Plan pour une monnaie européenne', in: SALIN, PASCAL (ed.): *L'Unification Monétaire Européenne*, Paris, 1970, pp. 165–209.

MUSGRAVE, RICHARD A.: *The Theory of Public Finance*, New York/Toronto/London, 1959.

NIEHANS, JÜRG: 'Money in a Static Theory of Optimal Payments Arrangements', *Journal of Money, Credit and Banking*, Vol. 1 (1969), pp. 706–726.

NIEHANS, JÜRG: 'Money and Barter in General Equilibrium with Transactions Costs', *American Economic Review*, Vol. 61 (1971), pp. 773–783.

NIEHANS, JÜRG: *The Theory of Money*, Baltimore/London, 1978.

NG, YEW-KWANG: 'The Economic Theory of Clubs: Pareto Optimality Conditions', *Economica*, Vol. 40 (1973), pp. 291–298.

55

ROLAND VAUBEL

OSTROY, JOSEPH M.: 'The Informational Efficiency of Monetary Exchange', *American Economic Review*, Vol. 63 (1973), pp. 597–610.

PATINKIN, DON: 'Financial Intermediaries and the Logical Structure of Monetary Theory', *American Economic Review*, Vol. 51 (1961), pp. 95–116.

PESEK, BORIS P. and SAVING, THOMAS R.: *Money, Wealth and Economic Theory*, London, 1967.

RABENAU, BURCKHARD VON and STAHL, KONRAD: 'Dynamic Aspects of Public Goods: A Further Analysis of the Telephone System', *The Bell Journal of Economics and Management Science*, Vol. 5 (1974), pp. 651–669.

ROHLFS, JEFFREY: 'A Theory of Interdependent Demand for a Communications Service', *The Bell Journal of Economics and Management Science*, Vol. 5 (1974), pp. 16–37.

ROWLEY, CHARLES K. and PEACOCK, ALAN T.: *Welfare Economics. A Liberal Restatement*, London, 1975.

SALIN, PASCAL: *The Political Economy of Alternative Approaches to Monetary Integration*, Paper presented at the Conference on 'New Economic Approaches to the Study of International Integration', Florence, May/June, 1979.

SALIN, PASCAL: *L'Unité Monétaire Européenne: au profit de qui?*, Paris, 1980.

SALIN, PASCAL: 'Lessons from the European Monetary System', in: CONNOLLY, M.B. (ed.): *The International Monetary System: Choices for the Future*, New York, 1982, pp. 175–198.

SAMUELSON, PAUL A.: 'The Pure Theory of Public Expenditure', *Review of Economics and Statistics*, Vol. 35 (1954), pp. 350–356.

SAMUELSON, PAUL A.: 'What Classical and Neoclassical Monetary Theory really was', *Canadian Journal of Economics*, Vol. 1 (1968), pp. 1–15.

SAMUELSON, PAUL A.: 'Pure Theory of Public Expenditure and Taxation', in: MARGOLIS, JULIUS and GUITTON, HENRI (eds.): *Public Economics*, London, 1969, pp. 98–123.

SAVING, THOMAS R.: 'The Value of Time and Economies of Scale in the Demand for Cash Balances', *Journal of Money, Credit and Banking*, Vol. 6 (1974), pp. 122–124.

SCHMIDT, WILSON E.: *The U.S. Balance of Payments and the Sinking Dollar*, New York, 1979.

SCITOVSKY, TIBOR: 'Two Concepts of External Economies', *Journal of Political Economy*, Vol. 62 (1954), pp. 143–151.

SHARKEY, WILLIAM W.: *The Theory of Natural Monopoly*, Cambridge, 1982.

SMITH, ADAM: *An Inquiry into the Nature and Causes of the Wealth of Nations*, in: CANNAN, EDWIN (ed.), Chicago, 1976.

SOLOW, ROBERT: 'On the Lender of Last Resort', in: KINDLEBERGER, CHARLES P. and LAFFARGUE, JEAN-PIERRE (eds.): *Financial Crises*, Cambridge/Paris, 1982, pp. 237–255.

STARBATTY, JOACHIM: 'Zur Umkehrung des Greshamschen Gesetzes bei Entnationalisierung des Geldes', *Kredit und Kapital*, Vol. 15 (1982), pp. 387–410.

STOCKMAN, ALAN C.: 'Comments on R.E.HALL's paper', *Journal of Monetary Economics*, Vol. 12 (1983), pp. 51–54.

SWOBODA, ALEXANDER K.: *The Eurodollar Market: An Interpretation*, Essays in International Finance, Princeton, 64, 1968.

56

THE GOVERNMENT'S MONEY MONOPOLY

TOBIN, JAMES: 'Discussion', in: KAREKEN, JOHN H. and WALLACE, NEIL (eds.): *Models of Monetary Economies*, Federal Reserve Bank of Minneapolis, pp. 83–90.

TULLOCK, GORDON: *Private Wants, Public Means*, New York/London, 1970.

TULLOCK, GORDON: 'Public Decisions as Public Goods', *Journal of Political Economy*, Vol. 79 (1971), pp. 913–918.

TULLOCK, GORDON: 'Competing Monies: A Reply', *Journal of Money, Credit and Banking*, Vol. 8 (1976), pp. 521–525.

VAUBEL, ROLAND: 'Free Currency Competition', *Weltwirtschaftliches Archiv*, Vol. 113 (1977), pp. 435–461.

VAUBEL, ROLAND: *Strategies for Currency Unification: The Economics of Currency Competition and the Case for a European Parallel Currency*, Tübingen, 1978.

VAUBEL, ROLAND: 'Coordination or Competition among National Macroeconomic Policies?', in: MACHLUP, F.; FELS, G. and MÜLLER-GROELING, H. (eds.): *Reflections on a Troubled World Economy: Essays in Honour of Herbert Giersch*, London/Basingstoke, 1983, pp. 3–28.

VINER, JACOB: 'Cost Curves and Supply Curves', *Zeitschrift für Nationalökonomie*, Vol. 3 (1931), pp. 23–46 [reprinted in: STIGLER, G.J. and BOULDING, K.E. (eds.): *Readings in Price Theory*, London, 1953].

WHITE, LAWRENCE H.: 'Free Banking as an Alternative Monetary System', in: JOHNSON, BRUCE M. and O'DRISCOLL, GERALD P. (eds.): *Inflation or Deflation*, Cambridge, Mass., 1983a.

WHITE, LAWRENCE H.: 'Competitive Money, Inside and Out', *Cato Journal*, Washington, D.C., Vol. 3 (1983b), pp. 281–300.

YEAGER, LELAND B.: 'Stable Money and Free Market Currencies', *Cato Journal*, Washington, D.C., Vol. 3 (1983), pp. 305–326.

SUMMARY

Does externality theory provide a basis for the government's monopoly in the production of base money? Money, as has been shown, is not a public good because it does not satisfy the non-rivalness criterion (nor the non-excludability criterion). Like any public decision, political agreement on a common money or unit of account (*i.e.*, exchange rate fixity) passes the non-rivalness test. However, whether the imposition of a common money or monetary unit is a public good or a public bad depends on whether money is a natural-monopoly good or not. Hence, there is no independent public-good justification for the government's money monopoly. The public good argument is redundant. Whether money is a natural monopoly good cannot be determined *a priori*, but only on the basis of experience. If governments are natural money monopolists, they should have gained their monopoly position by prevailing in the market. Historically, this is not the case. The only valid test of the natural monopoly argument is to abolish all barriers to entry and to admit free currency competition from private issuers on equal terms. An international cross-section estimate of money demand functions reveals only weak evidence of social economies of scale in the use of money. By contrast, choice among currencies is shown to be strongly affected by restrictions of convertibility.

[22]

Competing Currencies: The Case for Free Entry* **

By Roland Vaubel

After a brief overview of existing barriers to competition from private and foreign public money suppliers, the main arguments in favour of such barriers are analyzed and criticized. The concluding section surveys current forecasts of the monetary arrangements that would develop in conditions of free entry, and questions some of them.

I. Barriers to Currency Competition

Currency competition for the established national central banks can come from foreign central banks or from private money suppliers (at home or abroad). At present, currency competition from both sources is severely restricted in many countries, especially in the Federal Republic of Germany.

Currency competition from *foreign central banks* can be restricted in several ways:

— the currency issued by the national central bank can be prescribed as a private unit of account[1];

— contracts in foreign currencies can be prohibited by law or discouraged through discriminatory contract enforcement in the courts[2];

— governments can restrict or discourage the holding of foreign currencies by residents (or the holding of the domestic currency by foreigners) and thereby interfere with the choice of means of payments;

---

* Referat gehalten vor dem Ausschuß für Geldtheorie und Geldpolitik, Gesellschaft für Wirtschafts- und Sozialwissenschaften, Frankfurt, 25./26. Mai 1984.
** This paper is a synthesis of Vaubel (1976, 1977, 1978 a, b, 1980, 1982 a, b, 1983, 1984).

[1] For instance, the national currency is prescribed for the denomination of company capital in W. Germany, France, United Kingdom and for all obligations which enter the land register (W. Germany, France) or which have to be notarized (Belgium, France).

[2] In the United Kingdom, for example, the courts do not award foreign currency claims if the contract has been concluded between residents or in a "third" currency.

548 Roland Vaubel

— governments can refuse to accept any other currency than the one issued by their central bank.

In the Federal Republic, residents are free to hold foreign currencies (notes, coins, deposits) in unlimited amounts, but contracting in foreign currencies or international currency units (like the European Currency Unit) is restricted more severely than in any other major industrialized country[3]. The most far-reaching plan to admit a foreign currency (the US dollar) on equal terms was recently put forward by Yoram Aridor, Minister of Finance of Israel; his plan was rejected, and he had to resign.

Currency competition from *private money suppliers* is not admitted in any industrial country, but there have been many instances of such competition in monetary history (including German monetary history)[4]. To the extent that money may be issued by private enterprises at all, it must be denominated in the currency issued by the central bank. Moreover, with minor exceptions, private enterprises are not permitted to issue currency (notes and coins). Their supply of deposits is subject to reserve requirements and many other regulations.

In the Federal Republic of Germany, currency competition from private money suppliers is also suppressed most severely because the Bundesbank uses § 3 II Währungsgesetz to prohibit even DM deposits whose value is linked to a price index[5]. According to § 35 I Bundesbankgesetz, the unauthorized issuance of coins, notes or other certificates that are suited to be used as means of payments instead of the legally permitted coins and notes, and the unauthorized issuance of non-interest-bearing bearer securities can be punished with fines or imprisonment of up to five years, even if the competing money is not denomi-

---

[3] § 3 I of the German Währungsgesetz (enacted by the Allied Military Government on June 20, 1948) stipulates that all foreign currency contracts are subject to licencing by the authority responsible for foreign exchange controls. § 49 of the German Außenwirtschaftsgesetz specifies that this provision applies only to contracts between residents (I) and that applications for permission have to be submitted to the Deutsche Bundesbank (II). The rules which the Deutsche Bundesbank follows in permitting or prohibiting foreign-currency contracts between residents have been published in Bundesanzeiger No. 169, Sept. 12, 1969, and in Monatsberichte der Deutschen Bundesbank, April 1971, 29. As a rule, the Bundesbank does not permit foreign-currency contracts between residents unless they are directly connected with international contracts.

[4] See *Vaubel* (1978 a), 387 - 400. During the German hyperinflation of 1922 - 1924, for example, private enterprises issued inflation-proof emergency notes in competing currency units. In mid-November 1923, inflation-proof emergency money was issued by about 500 institutions and accounted for 37 per cent of the currency in circulation.

[5] The Bundesbank authorizes certain types of indexed contracts (in 1982 in 34.096 cases) but it does not permit the issuance of indexed monetary or capital market instruments.

nated in Deutsche Mark. The Bundesbank's domestic monopoly in the production of base money is not prescribed by the German Constitution. Art. 88 of the Grundgesetz merely obliges the Federal Government to establish a central bank that supplies money[6].

The existence of these barriers to entry raises three questions:

— What welfare-theoretic grounds are there to justify restrictions of currency competition from foreign central banks?

— If there is a case for free currency competition from foreign central banks, why doesn't this case extend to private banks as well?

— If private banks should be free to supply currencies of their own, why should the government (its central bank) supply money, or a monetary unit of account, at all?

These questions are the topics of the following three sections.

II. The Case for Free Currency Competition among Central Banks

The standard argument against barriers to entry is that they narrow the consumers' freedom of choice and that they raise the price, and reduce the supply and the quality, of the product in question. Prima facie, an increase in "price" and decrease of supply may seem to be desirable in the case of money. Do not a smaller supply and a higher "price" of money imply less inflation? This is a fallacy, for the argument confuses the price of acquiring money (the inverse of the price level) with the price (opportunity cost) of holding money[7] and overlooks the fact that holding demand for money is a demand for real balances. Since money is an asset to be held, demand for it depends on the price of holding it. The yield foregone by holding a money that bears no interest or is subject to non-interest bearing reserve requirements, is larger, the higher the expected inflation rate. An inflation-prone central bank loses real money demand to less inflation-prone foreign central banks[8]. In this way, it loses both revenue and its power to affect the national economy through monetary policy. Thus, the removal of barriers to entry encourages less inflationary monetary policies. In real terms, the standard case against barriers to entry applies to the product money as well: the removal of barriers raises the *real* quantity of money and reduces the relative price of *holding* it.

---

[6] For this view see notably *Suhr* (1982), 102 f.

[7] *Johnson* (1969) has pointed out the same confusion in the work of *Pesek /
Saving* (1967).

[8] In the absence of a forced or legal disequilibrium exchange rate, the less inflationary money prevails ultimately not only as a store of value but also as a means of payment. The conditions for the operation of "'Gresham's Law" are analyzed in *Vaubel* (1978 a), 82 - 89.

550   Roland Vaubel

If the standard case for competition applies, it implies not only removal of barriers to entry but also prevention of collusion among the public producers of money. Collusion is the international coordination of monetary policies[9]. In the extreme case, it takes the form of fixed exchange rates, an international holding-price cartel among money producers[10].

Competition among central banks reduces inflation in at least three ways:

1. *"Exit"*[11]: the world demand for money shifts from the currencies that are expected to depreciate and to be risky to currencies that are expected to appreciate and to be more stable.

2. *"Voice"*[11]: even if exit does not help, public opinion in the more inflation-ridden countries is impressed by the example of the less inflation-ridden countries. It makes the government (the central bank) responsible for its inferior performance. In politics, too, competition works as a mechanism of discovery and imitation.

3. *Acceleration Effect:* even in the absence of exit and voice, an inflationary monetary impulse in one country affects the price level faster than a simultaneous monetary expansion of equal size that is common to all, or several, countries. This is because the uncoordinated national monetary impulse affects the exchange rate, and to that extent the price level, almost immediately. By rendering the causal connection between money supply and price level more transparent, international currency competition reduces the likelihood of inflationary monetary policies.

In spite of these beneficial effects, free entry and, more generally, international currency competition are not usually advocated by national central banks, not even by the competitive ones. The Bundesbank, for example, launched a campaign in 1979 to convince the German public and foreign monetary authorities that everything had to be done to prevent the mark from taking over a larger part of the dollar's position as an international currency, especially as an official reserve currency. The Bundesbank gave three main reasons for its policy stance[12]:

---

[9] For a critical analysis of the welfare-theoretic arguments in favour of monetary-policy coordination see *Vaubel* (1983). *Vaubel* (1978 b) shows that, in 1969 - 1977, the average rate of European monetary expansion has always been negatively correlated with the dispersion of national rates of monetary expansion in the seven main countries.

[10] For a more detailed exposition see *Vaubel* (1978 a), 33 f.

[11] This is the terminology of *Hirschman* (1970).

[12] *Deutsche Bundesbank* (1979), Nov., 33: "The Deutsche Mark as an International Investment Currency" (Monthly Report). In a more recent article

1. "Owing to the limited capacity of our money and capital markets there would from the outset be a danger of the investment or withdrawal ... of DM reserves consistently putting an undue strain on the viability of these markets. This would entail fluctuations in liquidity and interest rates which would not be desirable for the domestic economy and which the Bundesbank would not always be able to offset. ... Germany's economic policy makers would eventually be faced with the choice either of allowing the exchange rate of the DM to rise consistently faster than was justified by the inflation differential and tolerating the resultant shifts in the structure of the domestic economy (which would have disastrous economic policy consequences...) or of restraining the movement of the exchange rate ... which would entail the risk of an inflationary expansion of the domestic money stock".

2. "Compared with the risks ... the possible advantages for a country (such as) Germany ... are rather questionable ... In the case of Germany ... the view that the country of issue ... derives seigniorage from its reserve role ... would be a highly theoretical notion. On the one hand, the assets held in DM would normally bear a considerable real rate of interest and therefore not be without cost. On the other, the reserve role of a currency is incompatible in the long run with deficits on current account ... Sustained large-scale current account deficits would very soon lead to a loss of confidence and thus preclude the build-up of a reserve currency from the start. So far Germany has derived no significant real economic benefit from the investment of monetary reserves in DM, if only because the German current account has almost always been in substantial surplus. ... Germany has thus relieved the diversifiers of the exchange risk on their dollar assets without receiving any quid pro quo."

3. "A 'system' of several reserve currencies, such as would be the outcome of an unrestrained diversification process, would be a highly unstable structure, exposed to the risks of constant exchange rate unrest and uncontrolled development of international liquidity. ... The limitation of the reserve role of the DM is therefore not only in the German interest; it seems to be desirable from an international point of view as well."

The first argument is correct in pointing to the greater difficulty of planning monetary expansion under currency competition. If the demand for money shifts among currencies, a simple x per cent rule for monetary expansion is not likely to be adequate. The forward premium and a world portfolio growth variable will have to be included in the money demand function[13], or the monetary target has to be formulated for the "world" money supply or some proxy thereof[14]. However, even if international shifts in the demand for money are not correctly identified, they will hardly have "disastrous consequences"; for their real

---

under the same title, the Bundesbank calls foreign holdings of DM assets "neither too large nor too small" (Monthly Report, January 1983, 13 of the German edition).

[13] For a theoretical and econometric implementation of this approach see *Vaubel* (1980).

[14] See the proposal by *McKinnon* (1983).

exchange rate effects do not last longer than the lag of price-level adjustment. They are strictly temporary.

More generally, the argument reveals a high degree of risk aversion. The Bundesbank's attitude resembles that of a (non-?)banker who refuses to accept deposits because banking involves intermediation risk. Still more generally, it resembles that of a (non-?)entrepreneur who refuses to produce (for example, money) because he may miss the optimal output. Even a spatial monopolist who would be competitive in the world market may dislike competition because he prefers a quiet life.

Second, as for the benefits for Germany, is it true that Germany would not earn more external seigniorage? Seigniorage gains are by no means confined to the issuers of assets that do not bear interest. Seigniorage is the "monopoly" profit from the production of money. Any money producer who faces a less than perfectly elastic demand for his product — that is, for whose product there are no perfect substitutes — can gain seigniorage. An increase in foreign demand for its currency or assets denominated in its currency enables the issuing country to borrow at a lower cost — that is, at a lower real interest rate — from foreign savers than it otherwise could[15]. The extent to which the increase in net short-term capital imports leads to an increase of private long-term capital exports or to an increase in net imports of goods is irrelevant to the seigniorage issue. An increase in income is an increase in income regardless of whether it is consumed or saved.

The extent to which the increase in foreigners' liquid DM claims on German residents would be offset by additional German next exports of capital or by additional German net imports of goods and services etc., would not affect international confidence in the mark if the Bundesbank limits the increase in DM supply to the increase in the demand for real DM balances.

Third, is international currency competition undesirable from an international point of view? It disciplines those who try to supply their product at too high a price. If international shifts in the demand for money have been responsible for the dollar's and sterling's weakness in the 1970s and for the weakness of the French Franc in 1981 - 83, they have played a crucial role in bringing about a correction. International shifts in the demand for money are not the cause of monetary instability but its consequence and symptom. They are part of the corrective feedback mechanism.

---

[15] In other words, its "terms of finance" improve.

Why then do even central banks that would be competitive object to international currency competition? It is tempting to adopt a public-economics approach: the benefits of currency competition accrue to private money holders and users (lower inflation tax and inflation risk) and to domestic taxpayers (larger external seigniorage), but the cost, the greater difficulty of determining the optimal rate of monetary expansion, has to be borne by the central bankers. After all, bureaucrats tend to be held responsible for the errors they commit rather than for the opportunities they miss.

III. Currency Competition from Private Suppliers: The Case for Free Entry

If free currency competition between the central banks of different countries has the salutary effect of reducing rates of inflation below the monopolistic rates, it is difficult to see why the case for a competitive supply of money should not also extend to competition from private banks of issue. From a present-day perspective, the suggestion of an unrestricted competitive supply of (distinguishable[16]) private high-powered money must be regarded as truly (counter-)revolutionary, and even Hayek needed more than half a year to proceed, in 1976, from the demand for "free choice in currency" to the case for the "denationalisation of money".

Several justifications have been given for the prohibition of currency competition from private suppliers:

1. Profit-maximizing private issuers would increase the supply of their money until its price equals the marginal cost of producing it, namely zero; the result would be hyperinflation[17].

2. Private competitive supply of money renders the price level indeterminate[18].

3. The private banking system is inherently unstable.

4. Monopolistic production of money by the state is an efficient way of raising government revenue.

5. The supply of money is a natural monopoly because of economies of scale in production or use.

---

[16] See *Klein* (1974).

[17] See *Lutz* (1936), 4 f., *Friedman* (1959 a), 7; (1969), 39, *Pesek/Saving* (1967), 129, *Johnson* (1968), 976, *Meltzer* (1969), 35 and *Gehrig* (1978), 454. This view has been criticized by *Klein* (1974), 428 - 31, *Vaubel* (1977), 449 - 52 and *Girton/Roper* (1981), 21 - 24.

[18] *Gurley/Shaw* (1960), 255 ff., *Patinkin* (1961), 116 and *McKinnon* (1969), 316.

554 Roland Vaubel

6. Money exerts positive external effects; money, or the currency unit, may even be a public good.

The first argument repeats the confusion noted above: it mistakes the price of acquiring money for the price (opportunity cost) of holding money. What private profit maximization reduces to almost zero is not the value of money but the opportunity cost of holding it.

Some authors have objected that private suppliers of money may choose to maximize their short run profits rather than their long run profits, thus opting for hyperinflation at the time of their greatest success, when the present value of their confidence capital is at its maximum. Klein (1974, p. 449) and Tullock (1975, pp. 496 f.) have replied that private enterprises tend to have a longer planning horizon than democratically elected governments and their central banks. However, this answer implies that central banks act as profit maximizers as well — in some cases a debatable assumption. The answer is rather that, if there is a danger of "profit snatching", money holders will prefer currencies that offer value guarantees. This point will be further developed in the concluding section.

The second argument is correct in pointing out that the price level is indeterminate — indeed, under any system of money production, for the initial supply of nominal balances is an arbitrarily chosen number. To serve as an objection to private currency competition, the argument would have to show that the rate of change of the price level is indeterminate as well under such a system.

The third argument may justify money production by governments, but it does not justify barriers to entry. Whether claims on the private banking system are excessively risky is a question which each money holder can be left to decide on his own depending on his individual degree of risk aversion.

Fourthly, even if a system of optimal taxation requires a tax on money balances in addition to the wealth tax, what reason is there to assume that the collection of government seigniorage is more efficient than the taxation of private money creation or of private money holdings?

Fifthly, if money is a natural-monopoly good, the central bank does not need a legal monopoly (although it may have to be subsidized[19]).

---

[19] Subsidies may be justified even if marginal cost pricing is not the aim (because the additional taxation required would create excessive distortions elsewhere in the economy). They may be justified if the natural monopolist has passed the point of minimum average cost; for in this exceptional case, which *Sharkey* (1982), Ch. 5 has emphasized, an efficient natural monopolist

Since we do not even know whether money is a natural monopoly good and what its optimal characteristics are (for instance, whether it should be of stable or increasing purchasing power), barriers to competition from private issuers prevent us from finding out; the mechanism of discovery is blocked. A governmental producer of money is not an efficient natural monopolist unless he can prevail in conditions of free entry and without discrimination[20]. Historically, the major central banks have not acquired their national monopoly position in this way[21].

Finally, if money exerts positive external effects or is even a public good, there may be a case for subsidization, or even for governmental production, of money, but not for barriers to entry. The private supply of money would be too small, not too large.

IV. Should Governments Supply Money?

The previous section has shown that governmental production of money may be justified, if (i) the private banking system is inherently unstable, and/or if money is a (ii) natural-monopoly good or (iii) a public good. Whether arguments (i) and (ii) apply is an empirical question which cannot be answered as long as free currency competition from private issuers is not permitted[22]. Monetary history does not provide a clear answer[23]. Whether money is a public good, as has often been claimed, is largely a matter of definition and needs to be clarified[24].

There is no generally accepted definition of a public good. However, most authors seem to consider non-rivalness a necessary and sufficient

---

may be unable to produce the optimal quantity of output and to sustain himself against less efficient competitors if the government does not pay him a subsidy (which it should offer to all producers who supply at least as much output). Under Sharkey's assumptions, the subsidy must be sufficient to keep the net-of-subsidy average cost of the most efficient supplier of optimal output at the minimum average cost attainable for any smaller quantity of output.

[20] Non-discrimination also implies that the government is willing to accept or pay any currency preferred by its private counterpart. Otherwise, a superior private money may not prevail in the market, merely because the government uses only its own money.

[21] The Bank of England, for example, was granted its monopoly not because it was gaining ground in the market but because it was losing out to the other joint-stock issuing banks which had emerged after the Bank's joint-stock monopoly had been abolished in 1826 (for details see *Vaubel* (1978 a), 389).

[22] For an econometric test of the natural-monopoly hypothesis and for a list of previous studies of this issue see *Vaubel* (1984). The results are not conclusive.

[23] *Vaubel* (1978 a), 387 - 401.

[24] The remainder of section IV is adapted from *Vaubel* (1984).

556   Roland Vaubel

condition[25]. Others regard non-excludability as an alternative sufficient condition[26]. A few treat the term public good as synonymous with positive consumption externality[27].

In this paper we shall retain the benefit of being able to distinguish between the general concept of consumption externality and the polar case of a (pure) public good which, in terms of production units, is equally available to all members of the group in a quantity or quality that is independent of the size of the group (non-rivalness)[28]. We shall call a free good a good for which exclusion is not profitable (non-excludability). More limited consumption externalities have been discussed in Vaubel (1984).

One group of authors ascribe a public good nature to money because "any one agent, holding cash balances of a given average size, is less likely to incur the costs of temporarily running out of cash, the larger are the average balances of those with whom he trades"[29]. However, money balances do not satisfy the non-rivalness criterion (nor the non-excludability criterion): as long as one person holds a unit of money and benefits from its "liquidity services", nobody else can own it and benefit from it. If he gives it away, he increases his own risk of temporarily running out of cash. Therefore, he will ask for a quid pro quo — a good, service or some other asset.

For the same reason, it is not true that "the provision of a convertible currency is an international 'public good'" because "a convertible currency can be held and used by foreigners"[30] or that "the dollar is an 'international public good'" because "the United States provides the world's reserve currency"[31]. Otherwise, any exportable good or asset which happens to be supplied by a government would be an international public good.

Kindleberger refers to "the public good provided by money as a unit of account"[32] and "standard of measurement"[33] and applies the term public good to "money"[34], "international money"[35], "an international

---

[25] The seminal modern contribution is *Samuelson* (1954).
[26] See notably *Musgrave* (1959), 9.
[27] *Samuelson* (1969).
[28] This is essentially *Buchanan's* definition (1968), 54.
[29] *Laidler* (1977, pp. 321 f.). A similar view seems to be taken by *Kolm* (1972, 1977) and *Mundell* (*Claassen/Salin*, (1972), 97).
[30] *McKinnon* (1979), 3.
[31] *Schmidt* (1979), 143.
[32] *Kindleberger* (1972), 434.
[33] *Ders.*, (1983), 383.
[34] *Ders.*, (1978 a), 9 - 10.
[35] *Ders.*, (1976), 61; (1978b), 286.

unit of account" and "international monetary stability"[36]. International monetary stability in the sense of stability of purchasing power or exchange rate stability is not a good but a quality characteristic of the product money. Quality charateristics, it is true, meet the non-rivalness test: enjoyment by one does not detract from enjoyment by others (nor can they be excluded from them) provided they have bought the good itself. However, this applies to the quality characteristics of all goods. If the publicness of its characteristics made a good a public good, all goods that are sold to more than one person would be public goods.

It might be argued that the benefits of a unit of account (and a price index) can be enjoyed by a person independently of whether he holds and uses the money which it denominates[37]. More specifically, a person or organisation, by adopting a certain unit of account (and by publishing a price index for it), may convey information, a public good, to all others. This would imply that government should suggest a unit of account and publish a price index for it, but not that it should supply money, let alone the only (base) money[38] or monetary unit.

Brunner and *Meltzer*[39] have emphasized that money itself is a substitute for information because it also reduces transaction costs, and because transaction costs can largely be reduced to the costs of information about possible transaction chains, asset properties and exchange ratios between assets. Since money is a substitute for information and since information is a public good, *Hamada*[40] and *Fratianni*[41] conclude, there is a "public good nature of money". However, to show that X is a substitute for a public good is not sufficient to prove that X is a public good. A fence, a dog and an alarm system are all to some extent substitutes for police protection but they are not public goods. What has to be shown is not that money is a substitute for information but that it provides the public good of information.

Several authors have argued that "public consensus" or "social agreement" on a common money is a way of creating generally useful knowledge and is thus a public good[42]. The knowledge in question is the predictability of individual behavior. What becomes predictable is not

[36] *Ders.*, (1972), 435.
[37] *Yeager* (1983), 321.
[38] This conclusion is in fact reached by *Engels* (1981), 10f., *Hall* (1981), 21, and *Yeager* (1983), 324 f.
[39] *Brunner/Meltzer* (1964), (1971).
[40] *Hamada* (1979), 7.
[41] *Fratianni* (1982), 437.
[42] *Hamada* (1977), 16, *Frenkel* (1975), 217, *Tullock* (1976), 524, *Tobin* (1980), 86 – 87 and, with respect to the unit of account, *Hall* (1983), 34, and *Stockman* (1983), 52.

only the money which each individual accepts but also that each individual in the country accepts the same money.

Public decisions by definition meet the non-rivalness test. However, not all public decisions are public goods — they can be public bads[43]. Since the aim of securing predictability of individual trading behavior, if taken to the extreme, may serve to justify the most far-reaching central planning by an omnipotent government[44], the mere fact that a certain act of government generates knowledge is not a sufficient justification. It has to be shown that the knowledge in question is worth its cost and that it is provided more efficiently by the government than by a competitive private sector. Both contentions are controversial.

The only operational proof that a common money is more efficient than currency competition and that the government is the most efficient provider of the common money would be to permit free currency competition. Whether the imposition of a common money or monetary unit is a public good or a public bad depends on whether money is a natural-monopoly good or not[45]. Hence, there is no independent public-good justification for the government's money monopoly. The public good argument is redundant.

V. Forecasting Monetary Arrangements under Free Currency Competition

If currency competition is to serve as a mechanism of discovery, government must not prescribe the characteristics of the privately issued currencies nor the organisation of the private issuing institutions. Contrary to some proposals[46], for example, it must not prescribe the monetary unit of account nor the types of assets that may be held by the issuing institutions.

Refusal to prescribe specific arrangements does not prevent us from trying to forecast monetary arrangements under free currency competi-

---

[43] *Tullock* (1971).

[44] *Hirshleifer* (1973), 132.

[45] Currency competition might even be desirable if the process were known to converge to the government's money; for the government may not know in advance what type of money to converge to: "The monopoly of government of issuing money ... has ... deprived us of the only process by which we can find out what would be good money" (*Hayek* (1978 b), 5).

[46] *Engels* (1981) suggests that the government "has the task of defining the monetary unit ... in terms of the market valuation of real assets ... and of securing the solvency of issuing banks" (pp. 9f.). *Hall* (1983) believes that private money must be denominated in an interest-bearing reserve certificate which is issued by the government and is indexed to the price level. For a critical review of Engels see *Vaubel* (1982 b).

tion; even *Hayek*[47] has done so. Hayek believes that private money would be stable in terms of "the prices of widely traded products such as raw materials, agricultural food stuffs and certain standardised semi-finished industrial products" (p. 71) and that "competition might lead to the extensive use of the same commodity base by a large number of issue banks" (p. 123). *Vaubel*[48] has suggested that "value guarantees ... are likely to be a necessary condition for acceptance of a competing money" and that "in the presence of unpredictable fluctuations in the determinants of the demand for money, value guarantees can only be maintained with precision and instantaneously, if they can be validated through exchange rate adjustment vis-à-vis another currency for which a price index is calculated". He believes that this reference currency, which cannot also be indexed (owing to the n-th currency problem), would be the money supplied and used by the government.

Another group of authors argues that the optimal money would appreciate relative to goods. Not all of them claim that the money which they regard as most efficient would also be most attractive to money users and prevail in the market, but this possibility should be considered. One variant is the so-called theory of the optimum quantity of money expounded by *Friedman* (1969), *Johnson* (1968), *Samuelson* (1963, 1969) and others; as *Mussa* (1977) has emphasized and criticized, it views money only as a store of value and ignores its standard of value function. According to another variant, which is due to *Alchian* and *Klein* (1973), the optimal monetary unit is stable in terms of a price index of all assets because the money cost of a given level of lifetime consumption utility ought to be held constant. Thirdly, *Engels* (1981) has recommended a real asset or pure equity standard because it would stabilize Tobin's q and thereby the business cycle. Engels suggests that such a unit would minimize the monetary risk for borrowers who invest in capital goods. However, the same is not likely to be true for all other debtors nor for all creditors. Finally, *Bilson* (1981) wants to transform money into an equity claim on a portfolio of real and nominal assets in order to render movements in the unanticipated rate of inflation countercyclical.

Whether privately issued money would appreciate relative to, or be stable in terms of, some composite of goods, cannot be predicted with certainty. However, experience with hyperinflation shows that the value of alternative monies, some of them private monies, tends to be linked to the price of one or more commodities. At times, e.g. in Germany in 1922/23, several commodity standards were used side by side.

---

[47] *Hayek* (1978 a), 70 ff., 122 ff.
[48] *Vaubel* (1977), 451.

560   Roland Vaubel

Chen (1975) reports a case in which this occurred over two centuries. Whether convergence toward a common standard of value and money is efficient and occurs depends on how similar the purchase and sale plans of different market agents are and how variable they expect the relative prices among commodities to be[49].

What assets are private issuing institutions likely to hold if they are not restricted by government? They would minimize their balance sheet risk by acquiring assets denominated in the money which they issue. The intermediation risk is zero in the case of equity or mutual-fund money, as suggested by Engels and Bilson. It is also zero in the case of commodity reserve money, however at the price of a zero real rate of return. The issuer of a money whose value is linked to a commodity price index can earn a positive real rate of return without incurring a monetary intermediation risk, if his assets are indexed as well; but he (and his creditors) cannot avoid a real intermediation risk. Thus, under free currency competition — even more than now — the composition of banks' assets will depend on the risk-yield preference trade-off of money users. Their degree of risk aversion is likely to differ, and it may vary over time. It cannot be reliably predicted — not even by governments.

Summary

In several respects, barriers to competition from private and foreign public money producers are higher in Germany than in any other major industrial country. The Bundesbank's defence of these barriers and the academic objections to currency competition are not convincing. The central bank's base money monopoly cannot be justified unless money is a natural monopoly good. In this case, however, there is no need for barriers to entry. Only if entry is free can we find out whether money is a natural monopoly good and what type(s) of money the market needs.

Zusammenfassung

Die Marktzutrittsbeschränkungen für private und ausländische öffentliche Geldproduzenten sind in der Bundesrepublik in mancherlei Hinsicht gravierender als in den anderen großen Industrieländern. Die Argumente, mit denen die Deutsche Bundesbank und zahlreiche Wissenschaftler derartige Beschränkungen verteidigen, sind bei näherem Hinsehen nicht überzeugend. Das Geldbasismonopol der Zentralbank kann nur dann gerechtfertigt sein, wenn Geld ein natürliches Monopolgut ist. In diesem Fall sind Marktzutrittsbeschränkungen überflüssig. Nur bei freiem Marktzutritt kann sich zeigen, ob Geld ein natürliches Monopolgut ist und was für Geld der Markt braucht.

---

[49] See *Vaubel* (1978 a, 1982 b).

Competing Currencies: The Case for Free Entry   561

References

Alchian, Armen A. and Benjamin *Klein* (1973), On a Correct Measure of Inflation. Journal of Money, Credit and Banking 5 (1), 173 - 191.

Bilson, John F. O. (1981), A Proposal for Monetary Reform. University of Chicago, unpubl. manuscript, Sept., 30 p.

Brunner, Karl und Allan H. *Meltzer* (1964), Some Further Investigations of Demand and Supply Functions for Money. Journal of Finance 19 (2), 240 - 283.

— / — (1971), The Uses of Money: Money in the Theory of an Exchange Economy. American Economic Review 61 (5), 784 - 805.

Buchanan, James M. (1968), The Demand and Supply of Public Goods. Chicago.

Chen, Chau-Nan (1975), Flexible Bimetallic Exchange Rates in China, 1650 - 1850: A Historical Example of Optimum Currency Areas. Journal of Money, Credit and Banking 7 (2), 359 - 376.

Claassen, Emil M. and Pascal *Salin* (Eds.) (1972), Stabilization Policies in Interdependent Economies. Amsterdam, London.

Deutsche Bundesbank (1979), Monthly Reports.

Engels, Wolfram (1981), The Optimal Monetary Unit. Frankfurt.

Fratianni, Michele (1982), The Dollar and the ECU, in: J. S. Dreyer / G. Haberler / T. D. Willet (Eds.), The International Monetary System: A Time of Turbulence. Washington, D.C., 430 - 453.

Frenkel, Jacob A. (1975), Reflections on European Monetary Integration. Weltwirtschaftliches Archiv 111 (2), 216 - 221.

Friedman, Milton (1959 a), A Program for Monetary Stability. New York.

— (1959 b), The Demand for Money: Some Theoretical and Empirical Results. Journal of Political Economy 67 (4), 327 - 351.

— (1969), The Optimum Quantity of Money and Other Essays. Chicago.

— (1981), Monetary System for a Free Society. Hoover Institution, Stanford, unpubl. manuscript, Nov., 14 p.

Gehrig, Bruno (1978), Brauchen wir monopolistische Zentralbanken? Wirtschaft und Recht 30 (4), 452 - 464.

Girton, Lance and Don *Roper* (1981), Theory and Implications of Currency Substitution. Journal of Money, Credit and Banking 13 (1), 12 - 30.

Gurley, John G. and Edward S. *Shaw* (1960), Money in a Theory of Finance. Washington.

Hall, Robert E. (1981), The Role of Government in Stabilizing Prices and Regulating Money. Stanford University, unpubl. manuscript, Jan., 34.

— (1983), Optimal Fiduciary Monetary Systems. Journal of Monetary Economics 12 (3), 33 - 50.

Hamada, Koichi (1977), On the Political Economy of Monetary Integration: A Public Economics Approach, in: Robert Z. Aliber (Ed.), The Political Economy of Monetary Reform. London, Basingstoke, 13 - 31.

562 Roland Vaubel

— (1979), On the Coordination of Monetary Policies in a Monetary Union. Paper presented at the Conference on New Economic Approaches to the Study of International Integration, Florence, May/June, 32.

Hayek, Friedrich A. (1976 a), Choice in Currency. A Way to Stop Inflation. Institute of Economic Affairs, London. Occasional Papers, 48.

— (1976 b, 1978 a), Denationalisation of Money. Institute of Economic Affairs, London. Hobart Paper Special, 70.

— (1978 b), Towards a Free Market Monetary System. Journal of Libertarian Studies 3, 1 - 8.

Hirschman, Albert O. (1970), Exit, Voice, and Loyalty. Cambridge, Mass.

Hirshleifer, Jack (1973), Exchange Theory: The Missing Chapter. Western Economic Journal 11 (2), 129 - 146.

Johnson, Harry G. (1968), Problems of Efficiency in Monetary Management. Journal of Political Economy 76 (5), 971 - 990.

— (1969), Pesek and Saving's Theory of Money and Wealth. Journal of Money, Credit and Banking 1 (3), 535 - 537.

Kindleberger, Charles P. (1972), The Benefits of International Money. Journal of International Economics 2 (3), 425 - 442.

— (1976), Lessons from Floating Exchange Rates, in: Karl Brunner / Allan H. Meltzer (Eds.), Institutional Arrangements and the Inflation Problem. Amsterdam, New York, Oxford, 51 - 77.

— (1978 a), Manias, Panics and Crashes. London, Basingstoke.

— (1978 b), Dominance and Leadership in the International Economy: Exploitation, Public Goods, and Free Rides. Hommage a François Perroux. Grenoble, 283 - 291.

— (1983), Standards as Public, Collective and Private Goods. Kyklos 36 (3), 377 - 396.

Klein, Benjamin (1974), The Competitive Supply of Money. Journal of Money, Credit and Banking 6 (4), 423 - 453.

Kolm, Serge-Christophe (1972), External Liquidity — A Study in Monetary Welfare Economics, in: Giorgio P. Szegö / Karl Shell (Eds.), Mathematical Methods in Investment and Finance. Amsterdam, London, New York, 190 - 206.

— (1977), Fondements de l'économie monétaire normative: seigneurage, liquidité externe, impossibilité de rémunérer les espèces. Revue Economique, 28 (1), 1 - 35.

Laidler, David E. W. (1977), The Welfare Costs of Inflation in Neoclassical Theory — Some Unsettled Problems, in: Erik Lundberg (Ed.), Inflation Theory and Anti-Inflation Policy. Boulder, Col., 314 - 328.

Lutz, Friedrich A. (1936), Das Grundproblem der Geldverfassung. Berlin.

McKinnon, Ronald I. (1969), Private and Official International Money: The Case for the Dollar. Essays in International Finance. Princeton, 74.

— (1979), Money in International Exchange. New York, Oxford.

— (1983), A New International Standard for Monetary Stabilization. Institute for International Economics, Washington, D.C.

Competing Currencies: The Case for Free Entry   563

Meltzer, Allan H. (1969), Money, Intermediation and Growth. Journal of Economic Literature 7 (1), 27 - 56.

Mussa, Michael (1977), The Welfare Cost of Inflation and the Role of Money as a Unit of Account. Journal of Money, Credit and Banking, 9 (2), 276 - 286.

Musgrave, Richard A. (1959), The Theory of Public Finance. New York, Toronto, London.

Patinkin, Don (1961), Financial Intermediaries and the Logical Structure of Monetary Theory. American Economic Review 51 (1), 95 - 116.

Pesek, Boris P. and Thomas R. *Saving* (1967), Money, Wealth and Economic Theory. London.

Samuelson, Paul A. (1954), The Pure Theory of Public Expenditure. Review of Economics and Statistics 35 (4), 387 - 389.

— (1963), D. H. Robertson (1890 - 1963). Quarterly Journal of Economics 77 (4), 517 - 536.

— (1969), Pure Theory of Public Expenditures and Taxation, in: Julius Margolis / Henri Guitton (Eds.), Public Economics. London, 98 - 123.

Schmidt, Wilson E. (1979), The U.S. Balance of Payments and the Sinking Dollar. New York.

Sharkey, William W. (1982), The Theory of Natural Monopoly. Cambridge.

Stockman, Alan C. (1983), Comments on R. E. Hall's Paper. Journal of Monetary Economics 12 (1), 51 - 54.

Suhr, Dieter (1982), Die Geldordnung aus verfassungsrechtlicher Sicht, Geldordnung und Geldpolitik in einer freiheitlichen Gesellschaft. Wirtschaftswissenschaftliche und wirtschaftsrechtliche Untersuchungen, 18. Tuebingen.

Tobin, James (1980), Discussion, in: J. H. Kareken / N. Wallace (Eds.), Models of Monetary Economies. Federal Reserve Bank of Minneapolis, 83 - 90.

Tullock, Gordon (1971), Public Decisions as Public Goods. Journal of Political Economy 79 (4), 913 - 918.

— (1975), Competing Monies. Journal of Money, Credit and Banking 7 (4), 491 - 497.

— (1976), Competing Monies: A Reply. Journal of Money, Credit and Banking 8 (4), 521 - 525.

Vaubel, Roland (1976), Freier Wettbewerb zwischen Währungen? Wirtschaftsdienst (Hamburg), 56 (8), 422 - 428.

— (1977), Free Currency Competition. Weltwirtschaftliches Archiv 113 (3), 435 - 461.

— (1978 a), Strategies for Currency Unification: The Economics of Currency Competition and the Case for a European Parallel Currency. Tuebingen.

— (1978 b), The Money Supply in Europe: Why EMS may make inflation worse. Euromoney, Dec., 139 - 142.

— (1980), International Shifts in the Demand for Money, their Effects on Exchange Rates and Price Levels, and their Implications for the Preannouncement of Monetary Expansion. Weltwirtschaftliches Archiv 116 (1), 1 - 44.

564   Roland Vaubel

— (1982 a), West Germany's and Switzerland's Experience with Exchange-Rate Flexibility, in: J. S. Dreyer / G. Haberler / T. D. Willett (Eds.), The International Monetary System: A Time of Turbulence. Washington, D.C., 180 - 222.

— (1982 b), Private Geldproduktion und Optimale Währungseinheit (Review of 'The Optimal Monetary Unit' by Wolfram Engels). Weltwirtschaftliches Archiv 581 - 585.

— (1983), Coordination or Competition among National Macroeconomic Policies?, in: F. Machlup / G. Fels / H. Müller-Groeling (Eds.), Reflections on a Troubled World Economy. Essays in Honour of Herbert Giersch. London, 3 - 28.

— (1984), The Government's Money Monopoly: Externalities or Natural Monopoly? Kyklos 37 (1), 27 - 58.

Yeager, Leland B. (1983), Stable Money and Free Market Currencies. Cato Journal 3 (1), 305 - 326.

[23]

What do we know about Currency Competition?

By Martin F. Hellwig*

The paper presents a critical analysis of the proposals of Hayek and Vaubel for unregulated competition among private money suppliers. Because of externalities, time inconsistencies and moral hazard, these proposals are detrimental for outside money and, at best, dubious for inside money.

I am skeptical about the price theoretical foundations of Vaubel's[1] policy recommendations. This skepticism extends to the work of von Hayek (1976, 1977), which initiated our current concern with the optimal monetary constitution. Specifically, I have the following problems with the Hayek-Vaubel analysis.

A. Both, Hayek and Vaubel, neglect the distinction between inside and outside money. Their discussion of competition among outside monies is based on an invalid premise.

B. There are Pareto-relevant externalities in money demand decisions which justify the use of lumpsum taxation to create a real return on money.

C. In contrast to the market for an inside money, the market for an outside money is destroyed by the coexistence of more than one firm in the market.

D. Vaubel and Hayek fail to distinguish between the dynamic problem of time inconsistency and the static problem of monopoly power. In the absence of binding money supply announcements, the time inconsistency of profit maximizing policies rules out *any* unregulated private organization of the market for outside money.

E. The analysis of competing inside monies pays too little attention to the problems of uncertainty, information asymmetries, and time inconsistency that are endemic to debtor-creditor relations.

In the following, I shall discuss these points one by one.

* This paper was presented as a comment on *Vaubel* (1985) at the May 1984 meeting of the Ausschuß für Geldtheorie und Geldpolitik of the Verein für Socialpolitik. I thank Michael Rey for research assistance and the Deutsche Forschungsgemeinschaft for financial support through Sonderforschungsbereiche 21 and 303.
[1] Vaubel's analysis of external effects in the money market is presented in *Vaubel* (1984). My comments here cover that analysis as well because at the May 1984 meeting, it was presented as an integral part of the argument.

566   Martin F. Hellwig

1. Inside versus Outside Money

We must distinguish between *inside money*, which gives its bearer a
legal claim against the issuer, and *outside money*, which entails no such
claim. Suppliers of inside money are constrained by the need to fulfill
their obligations or else go bankrupt. Suppliers of outside money are
under no such constraint. Presumably then, the behaviour of a money
supplier will depend on whether he issues inside or outside money.[2]

The distinction between inside and outside money will also affect the
demand for money. My willingness to hold paper outside money depends
only on the prospect of selling this paper outside money to somebody
else, who in turn is willing to pay a positive price only because he hopes
to resell it to a third agent, who ... In contrast, the decision to pay a
positive price for inside money is at least partly motivated by the prospect of calling the claim on the issuer. The shopkeeper accepts my
check — not because he expects to resell it to his wholesaler, but because
he will present it to my bank. Whereas the real value of outside money
is *exclusively* determined by resale considerations, i.e. by expectations
of its real value in future transactions, the real value of inside money
will depend on the "fundamentals" of the underlying claim against the
issuer.

Any positive or normative analysis of the monetary constitution must
take account of this difference. Hayek and Vaubel neglect it, apparently
because they believe that the existence of outside money itself is merely
a consequence of government interference with the monetary system.
According to this view, unregulated currency competition would lead
to the disappearance of outside money and its replacement by inside
money as a superior asset.[3]

However, as far as I can see, this point remains to be proved. Moreover, it is not clear that such an outcome is in fact desirable. For the
economy as a whole, the use of paper money may be advantageous
because it economizes on the holding of real assets. In a pure inside
money economy, this advantage is partly lost because the supplier of
money must hold a reserve against the claims on him. In the absence of
outside money, this reserve will consist of real assets such as gold,

---

[2] In stressing this distinction, I do *not* take issue with *Johnson's* (1969)
proposition that "the real theoretical difference to be drawn is between
interest-bearing and noninterest-bearing money". Johnson was concerned
with the determination of the economy's net wealth rather than the behaviour of money suppliers. Even in the context of his analysis, the distinction
between inside and outside money is apparent in the inside money suppliers'
need to hold reserves against withdrawels.

[3] This proposition was explicity asserted by Vaubel in the oral discussion
following the presentation of his paper and my comments.

machines, shares, etc. Quite possibly then, the pure inside money economy may be inefficient because it involves an *over*accumulation of real assets.

To make this point precise, consider the precautionary money holding model of *Bewley* (1980, 1982) and *myself* (1980, 1982). In this model, agents with uncertain commodity endowments save and hold assets for self-insurance against future endowment fluctuations. These agents' portfolio choices between money and commodity inventories depend on their expectations about real rates of return. Agents will be indifferent between money and inventories if both assets have a zero own rate of return and if prices are nonrandom and constant over time. A monetary rational expectations equilibrium with nonrandom, constant prices does in fact exist if the endowment risks of different individuals cancel out so that all economic aggregates are nonrandom.

In this equilibrium, the use of paper money as a store of value enables the system to economize on commodity inventories. This substitution of money for inventories is useful because commodity inventories require a deferral of consumption and thereby involve a real cost.

Up to this point, the argument does not depend on whether we are dealing with an outside money which happens to have a nonrandom, constant purchasing power or an inside money whose purchasing power is supported by an instant repurchase promise of the issuer. In the absence of aggregate fluctuations, the inside money issuer need not hold any inventories because in each period, the public's demand for his money just balances the available supply.[4]

However, if money does not bear interest, the private incentives for holding money are too small for Pareto optimality.[5] In the present context, the use of non-interest-bearing money as a buffer stock does not yield perfect insurance of individual risks even though such perfect insurance would be feasible. If we are dealing with a government supplied outside money, then the allocation can be improved by using the government's power to tax in order to create a positive real return on money.[6] This device is not available for a privately supplied inside

---

[4] The substitution of a money without backing for a money with backing is perhaps best illustrated in the story, told by Peter Kenen, of the island which used sardine cans for money. A tourist once opened a can, found the sardines inedible, and complained to the person who had given him the can. The answer was: "There is nothing to complain about. I gave you money sardines. If you wanted food sardines, you should have gone to the supermarket!"

[5] *Friedman* (1969), *Johnson* (1969), (1970).

[6] *Hellwig* (1982).

568   Martin F. Hellwig

money. Such a non-interest-bearing inside money would in fact be displaced by any government supplied outside money which has a positive
real return.[7]

Furthermore, even without interest payments on money, the equivalence of inside and outside money disappears if the underlying uncertainty involves collective as well as individual risks. In this case, the
real quantity of money that the economy wants to hold will fluctuate
with the collective endowment realization. Therefore, the supplier of
an inside money must expect that with positive probability the claims
on him will be called. If the inside money represents a claim to real
commodities, he must be prepared to actually deliver these commodities.
If he wants to be sure to avoid bankruptcy — i.e. a default on his promise — then he typically needs to hold a 100 % reserve against his
money issue.[8] In equilibrium then, inside money will have the same
return structure as the underlying real asset to which it is a claim.
Whether such an inside money can coexist with a non-interest-bearing
outside money depends on (i) the extent of collective risk and (ii) the
own rate of return and the carrying cost of inventories. The non-interest-bearing outside money is displaced by inventories or an inside
money backed by inventories if the own rate of return on inventories
is zero; it is not so displaced if inventories have a high carrying cost so
that their own rate of return is close to -100 %.[9] Even in those instances in which a non-interest-bearing outside money is displaced by
an inside money with a value guarantee or repurchase clause, this result
is socially undesirable. In this case, the portfolio choice between outside
money and inventory-backed inside money is biased against the former despite the potential allocational role of paper outside money as a
socially costless buffer stock against individual, i.e. insurable endowment risks. As in the case of purely individual risks, welfare would be
increased by the introduction of a tax-financed real return on outside
money.

---

[7] The argument in the text is based on the assumption that commodity
inventories with a zero own rate of return are the only asset in the model.
If we introduce real capital with a neoclassical production function, the
argument must be modified along the following lines (due to Truman Bewley
in private correspondence): *Any* non-interest-bearing money is displaced by
real capital or by an inside money which promises the same real return as
real capital and is backed by real capital. However, because of the precautionary demand for saving, there would be an *overaccumulation* of capital to
a point where the net marginal product of capital is less than the rate of time
preference in consumption. Again, welfare can be increased by the introduction of an interest-bearing outside money which is backed by the government's power to tax.

[8] The problem of default by an issuer of inside money, which is neglected
by Hayek and Vaubel will be taken up in Section 6 below.

[9] *Hellwig* (1980).

What do we know about Currency Competition?   569

In summary, if we are interested in the impact of competition on the monetary system, we must consider both, outside and inside monies, and we must be careful to draw the distinction between them.

2. Competition among Outside Monies

Both *Hayek* (1976) and *Vaubel* address the problem of competition among outside monies when they consider "the case for free currency competition among central banks". They claim that such competition "encourages less inflationary monetary policies" because the currency with the lowest inflation rate will be the most attractive to a public that is free to choose among the different currencies.

This claim rests on the implicit assumption that each issuing bank can at least partially control the inflation rate of its own currency through its supply behaviour. This premise is invalid.

To illustrate the basic problem, I consider an example of competition among two "currencies" that is taken from the recent past. The first

Table 1

| | Annual Growth Rates over Preceding Year | | Relative Price |
	"Currency 1"	"Currency 2"	
1970	6,6	0,6	2
1971	9,5	1,8	2
1972	13,6	6,9	2
1973	5,3	− 1,2	2
1974	9,1	2,0	2
1975	9,1	3,5	2
1976	6,2	2,7	2
1977	12,0	6,0	2
1978	11,7	7,2	2
1979	5,0	2,0	2
1980	5,0	2,3	2
1981	0,1	− 0,7	2
Cumulative Growth 1970 – 1981	128 %	38 %	

Source: Statistisches Jahrbuch für die Bundesrepublik Deutschland.

two columns of Table 1 show the evolution of the outstanding quantities of the two "currencies". Over the period 1970 to 1981, "currency 1" grew by more than three times as much as "currency 2". Yet the last column shows that the relative price of the two "currencies" did not change. In each period, two units of "currency 2" were treated as a perfect substitute for one unit of "currency 1". In accordance with the Hicks-Leontief aggregation theorem, both "currencies" were in fact treated as parts of a single composite currency: Inflation concerned this composite currency as a whole rather than its individual components. The above average growth rate of "currency 1" probably raised the inflation rate of the composite currency and hence the common inflation rates of *all* individual components; it did *not* induce an above average inflation for "currency 1".

In this example, "currency 1" are blue pieces of paper on which the Bundesbank has printed the number "100"; "currency 2" are brown pieces of paper on which the Bundesbank has printed the number "50". We must now see to what extent the analysis of this example can also be applied to outside monies that are issued by different agencies which compete with each other.

First we need to note that the relative price of two DM 50,— bills for one DM 100,— bill is in fact a market price. One might object that DM 100,— is twice DM 50,— merely as a matter of arithmetic. However, here we are not concerned with arithmetic but with the price at which blue and brown pieces of paper, i.e. different physical objects, are exchanged in actual transactions. If you need to make an emergency phone call from a public phone booth at night, you may find yourself willing to part with a DM 10,— bill for much less than the ten DM 1,— coins that would be indicated by arithmetic.[10] Similarly, the scarcity of Italian 5 and 10 lire pieces is due to the fact that the central bank's arithmetic stands in no relation to the value of the nickel contained in these coins.

Once the relative price of DM 100,— and DM 50,— bills is seen as a market price, we must ask why the market seems to conform so well to the Bundesbank's arithmetic. The Bundesbank's readiness to intervene in support of the exchange rate of two DM 50,— bills for one DM 100,— bill provides only part of the explanation for this phenomenon. After all, there was a time when the Bundesbank also stood ready to support an exchange rate of DM 4,— for 1,— US $. It was significantly less suc-

---

[10] At the time of the opening of the then ultramodern Dallas-Fort Worth airport, the airport administration tried to cash in on this observation by installing money-change machines that returned 90 c in coins for a 1 $ bill. After considerable public protest, they had to abandon the idea.

cessfull then. Moreover, we observe that the Bundesbank hardly even needs to intervene in the market of DM 50,— for DM 100,— bills. What would happen, if it did not intervene at all? I submit that even in the absence of current or expected future interventions by the Bundesbank, the market might clear at the constant relative price of two DM 50,— bills for one DM 100,— bill. For consider any agent who expects two paper outside monies to have a relative price x in all future transactions. This agent will regard x units of one currency as a prefect substitute for one unit of the other currency. If the *current* relative price of the two currencies is also x, he will be indifferent between them; if the current relative price differs from x, the agent will have a strict preference for one of the two currencies. If the expected price x is the same for all agents, the current *equilibrium* price must also be x since otherwise no agent would be willing to hold the currency that is too expensive. If at all times all agents expect two DM 50,— bills to exchange for one DM 100,— bill in all future transactions, then two DM 50,— bills will exchange for one DM 100,— bill in all *actual* transactions even if the Bundesbank does not intervene at all. Thus the fixed exchange rate of two DM 50,— bills for one DM 100,— bill will correspond to a *rational expectations equilibrium*.

However, the same argument shows that if there is no Bundesbank intervention, then any other fixed exchange rate beween DM 50,— and DM 100,— bills will also correspond to a rational expectations equilibrium. More generally, *any economy with multiple fiat monies whose use in different transactions is not subject to exogenous constraints will have multiple rational expectations equilibria* (provided it has any rational expectations equilibrium at all). For any vector of exchange rates $x \geq 0$, *such an economy will have an equilibrium in which all transactions take place at the fixed exchange rates x.*[11]

This analysis is directly applicable to the Hayek-Vaubel discussion of currency competition among central banks. At present of course, a dollar bill and a DM coin cannot be used side by side in all transactions. However, the Hayek-Vaubel proposal aims precisely at lifting those restrictions which limit the use of dollars in Germany and of marks in the United States. If this proposal is realized, then the two currencies will circulate side by side and their relative acceptability in an individual transaction will depend *only* on the participants' expectations about their relative resale value in future transactions. In such a world, *there can be no systematic differences in inflation rates between outside monies*: Any anticipation that the mark will be relatively worthless in the future must make it relatively worthless today already.

---

[11] Formal analyses of this principle are presented by *Girton / Roper* (1981), *Hellwig* (1976), *Kareken* and *Wallace* (1981).

3. External Effects in Money Demand[12]

I now consider the question whether money gives rise to Pareto-relevant external effects. It will be convenient to distinguish between the external effects in money demand and the external effects in the decision to use money rather than barter.

First, I must take issue with both *Friedman's* (1969) formulation and Vaubel's criticism of the price-level externality of money demand. Both authors use the language and the tools of *static equilibrium theory* for what is essentially a *non-static, sequential problem.* Unlike a refrigerator, money is not an asset that one buys once in order to hold it forever and to enjoy the "liquidity services" that it yields. Instead, money is traded back and forth: one acquires it, then resells it, acquires it again, etc. "Liquidity services" do not arise from the possession of money as such, but from the ease with which money can be resold. If one expects that with probability one, one will never actually use this resale opportunity, then one has no reason to hold money in the first place. The use of money must therefore be analysed in a framework of *sequential, incomplete markets* rather than the usual set of simultaneous, complete markets. In the sequential framework, the different periods and occasions in which agents trade money must be tied together by the concept of a rational expectations equilibrium, i.e. an *"equilibrium of plans, prices, and price expectations".*[13]

In such a non-static setting, there is no presumption that pecuniary externalities are Pareto-irrelevant.[14, 15] For consider the effects of an increase in some individual's demand for money in period t. From the perspective of period t, this demand increase raises the value of money in that period, thereby conferring a positive pecuniary externality on all net sellers and a negative pecuniary externality on all net buyers of money in money in period t. Ceteris paribus, Vaubel is right in observing — against the formulation of *Friedman* (1969) — that these pecuniary externalities are Pareto-irrelevant.

However, from the perspective of period $t - 1$, the increase in the (real) value of (nominal) money in period t serves to raise the indirect expected utility associated with money holdings at the end of period $t - 1$. In terms of the temporary equilibrium of period $t - 1$, this effect is a non-pecuniary externality and is definitely Pareto-relevant. It tends to raise the equilibrium value of money in period $t - 1$, which in

---

[12] See Footnote 1.
[13] *Radner* (1972).
[14] See, e. g., *Scitovsky* (1954), 184 f.
[15] Contrary to footnote 14 in *Vaubel* (1984), a main point of Scitovsky's classic paper is the *Pareto-relevance* of pecuniary externalities outside the narrow framework of static equilibrium theory.

turn has further repercussions for period $t - 2$, etc. In a rational expectations model, an increase in the demand for money in some period thus has Pareto-relevant positive externalities in all prior periods. Because of the externalities, a permanent increase in the demand for money, i.e. an increase in all periods that is generated, e.g., by the creation of a real return on money can improve the allocation of resources.[16]

For a specific example, I again refer to the precautionary money holding models that were discussed in Section 1. In these models, agents with positive time preference are willing to accumulate money to the point where the marginal self-insurance benefit of additional money holdings just compensates for the difference between time preference and the return on money, i.e. the net opportunity cost of deferring consumption to hold money. If the net real rate of return on money is zero, agents' long run equilibrium real money holdings are finite and provide less than perfect insurance of individual endowment risks. The creation of a real return on money raises the real demand for money and hence the equilibrium value of money in all periods. In real terms, each individual then has larger buffer stocks, which provide better insurance against his endowment risks. Through the externality described above, the creation of a real return on money improves the allocation of resources by ensuring a better exploitation of the available insurance opportunities.[17]

Contrary to Vaubel's claims then, the demand for outside paper money involves a Pareto-relevant externality which justifies the creation of a real return that is financed from lump sum taxation. In general

---

[16] This is of course *Friedman's* main point. In terms of his (1969) formulation of money as an asset that yields "liquidity services" as it is held, the non-pecuniary externality arises because the liquidity services of money depend on its purchasing power. Money may then be compared to a refrigerator whose refrigerating power depends on its market price. A permanent increase in the demand for such an asset raises its price and, by a technological (!) external effect, changes the services per unit that it yields.

[17] *Vaubel* (1984) himself seems to accept this possibility when in footnote 17, he mentions "the condition that the (private?) opportunity cost of holding (real?) money should equal the (social?) opportunity cost of producing (real?) money" (my insertions) as the rationale for "creating a return on cash balances". However, he is mistaken when he claims that this rationale is not based on an externality and that "no subsidy is involved". The mistake arises from a confusion between the rate of time preference in consumption and the market rate of return on assets other than money. In the precautionary money holding model without real capital, the rate of return on inventories as the alternative asset is zero. With positive time preference, the condition that the opportunity cost of holding money be zero (the cost of producing real money balances) requires that money be subsidized and that the rate of return on money be *larger* than the return on inventories. In the model with real capital, money must again be subsidized to bring the common rate of return on money and real capital up to the rate of time preference (see fn. 7).

this measure requires a government intervention though not necessarily a government control of the money supply.

Vaubel himself concentrates his analysis of external effects on the choice between money and barter. The externality here is the same as the one in telephone networks: The more people own a telephone, the more people I can call, and the more attractive it is for myself to own a telephone. Similarly, the more people accept money as a medium of exchange, the more willing am I myself to accept it.[18]

However, if we talk about currency *competition,* it makes more sense to analyse this externality in terms of choices between different currencies and between different transactions networks rather than between money and barter. If there is, say, a postal giro system and a bank giro system, then my joining one or the other enhances the attractiveness of the one I choose for other agents. If there are costs to switching from one system to the other, it may be advisable to have a single transactions network rather than several networks that compete with each other. Once we consider the choice between different currencies and transactions networks, we can no longer accept Vaubel's conclusion that "where ... all economic agents use money, the transaction cost externalities of using money cannot be Pareto-relevant" (1984, 41).

4. The Supply of Outside Paper Money under Binding Precommitments

I now consider the behaviour of private suppliers of outside money. From the preceding discussion, it is clear that the analysis cannot be limited to a single period. The seigniorage that suppliers of money receive in the initial period depends on the market's expectation of the value of money in later periods, which in turn depends on the money supply in subsequent periods. In this section, I assume that *before the first period, each supplier of money makes a binding announcement of what quantities of his money he will supply to the market in periods* $t = 0, 1, 2, \ldots$ Given these announcements, the market finds a rational expectations equilibrium which determines the revenues of the different money suppliers.

4.1 Private Monopoly

Suppose first that outside money is supplied by a private monopoly. The monopolist chooses a sequence $M_t, t = 0, 1, 2, \ldots$ of money supplies. This sequence determines a sequence of real values of money $\pi_t, t =$

---

[18] It is, however, unclear whether this effect is at all different from the externality generated by (my anticipation of) somebody else's future demand for money as discussed in the first part of this section.

$0, 1, 2, \ldots$ in the corresponding rational expectations equilibrium. The monopolist's revenues in periods $t = 0, 1, 2, \ldots$ are then given as $\pi_t (M_t - M_{t-1})$.

Under standard assumptions about the absence of money illusion in the economy, the sequence $\{\pi_t\}$ is homogeneous of degree minus one, and the sequence $\{\pi_t (M_t - M_{t-1})\}$ is homogeneous of degree zero in the sequence $\{M_t\}$. Thus a proportional change in the money supply sequence has no effect on the sequence of real revenues $\{\pi_t (M_t - M_{t-1})\}$.

If the marginal cost of producing paper money were positive, the monopolist's problem would have no solution. Clearly, $M_t = 0$ for all t cannot be a solution because this sequence yields zero revenues. On the other hand, any nonzero sequence $\{M_t\}$ would be dominated by the sequence $\{\frac{1}{2} M_t\}$, which for each t yields the same revenue at a lower production cost.[19]

The monopolist's problem typically does have a solution if the marginal cost of producing paper money is zero. In this case the monopolist is indifferent between all sequences $\{M_t\}$ that differ only by a constant of proportionality. He will only be concerned about the sequence of money growth rates $\mu_t = (M_t - M_{t-1})/M_{t-1}$ which is to be applied to an (arbitrary) initial money supply M_0. Under standard assumptions, an optimal sequence of money growth rates will exist.

The qualitative properties, in particular the welfare properties of the monopoly solution are unknown. In general, the solution will very much depend on the real structure of the economy, in particular on the alternative assets that are available.

As an example, consider again the precautionary money holding model. For any money supply policy in this model, the equilibrium real rate of return on money in any period cannot be less than the own rate of return on commodity inventories. Hence the rate of price inflation $\left(\dfrac{1}{\pi_{t+1}} - \dfrac{1}{\pi_t} \right) \Big/ \dfrac{1}{\pi_t}$ is bounded by the rate of inventory depreciation. If inventories do not depreciate at all, i.e. if the net own rate of return on inventories is zero, then there can be no price inflation, i.e. the value of money π_t cannot fall over time.

Given that the equilibrium rate of return on money is no less than the rate of return on inventories, we may suppose that in any period t, the economy's savings are all invested in money.[20] Hence the real value

---

[19] Technically, the problem arises from the discontinuity in the product $\pi_t M_t$ as $M_t \to 0$ and $\pi_t \to \infty$.

[20] If the rate of return on money is strictly greater than that on inventories, no inventories are held. If the two rates are equal, both the monopolist and the rest of the economy are indifferent between them. Hence

576 Martin F. Hellwig

of money $\pi_t M_t$ in period t is just equal to the economy's real precautionary savings S_t. The monopolist's real revenues $\pi_t (M_t - M_{t-1})$ are equal to S_0 in period 0 and to $\dfrac{\mu_t}{1 + \mu_t} S_t$ in periods $t = 1, 2, \ldots$ Depending on his own intertemporal tradeoffs, he cooses the money growth rates $\mu_1, \mu_2, \ldots$ to maximize some function of S_0 and $\dfrac{\mu_t}{1 + \mu_t} S_t$, $t = 1, 2, \ldots$, taking account of the dependence of S_t on all future inflation rates and of the constraint that the inflation rate must never exceed the bound given by the rate of inventory depreciation.[21]

If the rate of inventory depreciation is zero so that there can be no price inflation, the monopolist simply chooses the largest money growth rates that are compatible with constant prices. For many specifications of savings behaviours, this involves setting $\mu_t = 0$ for all t. Typically, the optimal policy for the monopolist involves an exchange of the money's real assets S_0 against money in period 0 followed by zero money growth in all subsequent periods. It turns out that in the absence of taxes and subsidies that could finance the payment of interest on money, this policy actually is the "second best" welfare maximizing policy.

However, if the rate of inventory depreciation is positive, the monopolist will typically *not* hold the money supply constant. A sufficiently small growth of the money supply is now compatible with the bound on the rate of price inflation. This growth yields the seigniorage $\dfrac{\mu_t}{1 + \mu_t} S_t$ in period t at the expense of adverse effects on savings and hence on the revenues S_0 in period 0 and $\dfrac{\mu_\tau}{1 + \mu_\tau} S_\tau$ in periods $\tau = 1, 2, \ldots, t - 1$. Unless the adverse effects on S_0 and $\dfrac{\mu_\tau}{1 + \mu_\tau} S_\tau$ for $\tau = 1, \ldots, t - 1$ are very strong, the monopolist will choose $\mu_t > 0$ in period t to enjoy the seigniorage income from further money growth. In this case, the policy chosen by the monopolist will *not* coincide with the "second best" welfare maximizing policy of zero money growth.

In summary, the behaviour of an unregulated private monopoly in the supply of outside money is extremely sensitive to the specification of the model. There is, however, no presumption that the policy chosen by

there is no loss of generality in assuming that in each period the monopolist issues enough money so that the rest of the economy holds no inventories. If the monopolist is impatient, he will actually have a preference for this.

[21] From the equation $\pi_t M_t = S_t$, this constraint may be written as

$$\mu_t + (1 + \mu_t) \frac{S_{t-1} - S_t}{S_t} \leq \frac{\delta}{1 - \delta},$$

where δ is the rate of depreciation on inventories. For $\delta = 0$, this constraint requires $\mu_t \leq 0$ unless savings are increasing over time.

such a monopoly will be in any sense desirable. On the contrary, one must expect that *the monopolist's desire for seigniorage income induces him to have "too much" inflation from a welfare point of view.*

4.2 Actual Competition

As an alternative to monopoly, consider a world with many outside money suppliers. Each outside money supplier f chooses a sequence of money supplies m_t^f for $t = 0, 1, 2, \ldots$ In view of the discussion of Section 2, I assume that the market implements a rational expectations equilibrium for which there exists a vector $x \geq 0$ such that in all periods, the monies supplied by suppliers f and f' exchange at the relative price $x_f/x_{f'}$. By the Hicks-Leontief aggregation theorem, outside money then may be regarded as a single composite commodity with the aggregate quantity $M_t = \sum_f x_f m_t^f$ for $t = 0, 1, 2 \ldots$ If π_t again is an index of the real value of this aggregate in period t, then supplier f's revenues in period t are equal to $\pi_t x_f (m_t^f - m_{t-1}^f)$.

Suppose first that every supplier f takes the prices $\pi_t x_f$, $t = 0, 1, 2, \ldots$, of his money as given. If production costs are zero and if $\pi_t x_f > 0$, then his profit "maximizing" flow money supply $(m_t^f - m_{t-1}^f)$ is infinite. Since the economy's real resources are finite, this cannot be an equilibrium. In equilibrium, it must be the case that $\pi_t x_f = 0$ for all t and all price-taking money suppliers f. Then the equilibrium real value of the aggregate quantity of money $\pi_t M_t = \sum_f \pi_t x_f m_t^f$ is equal to zero for all t. *Far from remedying the evils of monopoly, the introduction of competition with many price-taking money suppliers merely destroys the use of outside money altogether.*

This conclusion is well known.[22] Vaubel's assertion to the contrary is again due to his failure to distinguish between inside and outside money.[23] An inside money supplier looks not only at the price $\pi_t x_f$ at which he can sell his money, but also at the cost of fulfilling whatever promise he makes to his clients. If this cost is too large, he will not be in the market at all even though $\pi_t x_f$ may be positive. Inside money suppliers therefore compete on the relation between the content of the promise they make and the price $\pi_t x_f$ that they get. As Vaubel correctly notes, this type of competition drives the market's opportunity cost of holding money to zero, but the price of inside money remains positive. However, this conclusion breaks down for outside money which does not involve any claim of the holder on the issuer. For this case, the

---

[22] See, e. g., *Pesek / Saving* (1967), 69 ff.
[23] See *Vaubel* (1985) 3, 9.

analysis above shows that competition among price-taking money suppliers cannot work.[24]

The preceding conclusion even holds for the case of a finite number of (non-price-taking) Cournot oligopolists. If there is no money illusion in the economy, the real quantity of money $\pi_t M_t$ in period t is equal to a real variable S_t, which depends on rates of return and relative prices, but *not* on the nominal quantity of money. A Cournot oligopolist will thus evaluate his revenues in period t as $S_t x_f (m_t^f - m_{t-1}^f)/M_t = S_t x_f (m_t^f - m_{t-1}^f)/\sum_{f'} x_{f'} m_t^{f'}$. No matter what the constellation of supply policies is, he finds that he can always increase his revenues by raising m_t^f and hence his share in the aggregate money supply M_t. In the absence of production costs, the oligopolist's profit "maximizing" supply of outside money is again infinite. *Hence Cournot oligopoly also destroys the use of outside money.*

These results suggest that the *supply of outside money should be regarded as a natural monopoly* not in the technical sense of a subadditive cost function, but in the looser sense that any other organization of the market will destroy the market itself.

4.3 Potential Competition

Even if one accepts the conclusion that outside money should be supplied by a single firm, it is not clear that one must put up with an unregulated monopoly. The preceding analysis shows that *actual* competition among several firms will not work. However, the recent work of *Baumol, Panzar* and *Willig* (1982) on contestable markets shows that quite often the threat of *potential* competition is enough to discipline an otherwise unregulated monopolist.

Drawing on these authors' ideas, we may consider the following scheme. Consider a regulation whereby the supply of outside money is subject to a franchise. If no more than one money supplier is enfranchized, this regulation will prohibit the actual coexistence of different firms in the market.

However, competition may now be introduced by having different potential money suppliers bid for the franchise. Their bids must specify both a sequence of money supplies $\{M_t\}$ that they are going to implement and a sequence of seigniorage taxes $\{T_t\}$ that they are willing to pay in order to get the franchise.

[24] *Vaubel* (1985, p. 3) draws attention to the confusion between the price of money and the opportunity cost of holding money in the work of *Pesek / Saving* (1967). Their work was flawed because they indiscriminately applied to an inside money economy the conclusions that they had first obtained for an outside money economy. The reverse procedure is also problematic.

The question is how the franchise is to be awarded. If there is no conflict about the ranking of any two bids $\{M_t^1, T_t^1\}$ and $\{M_t^2, T_t^2\}$, then the regulatory commission should simply award the franchise to the bidder whose bid is (unanimously) ranked highest. The bidders are thus involved in a type of Bertrand game in which they make "contract" offers and "the public" chooses whichever contract maximizes its utility. The usual Bertrand argument shows that in an equilibrium of this game, the winning bid must be the one that is most highly ranked among *all* those that are technically feasible and do not impose a net loss on the bidder.

In contrast to the unregulated monopoly, the approach would *always* lead to the second best monetary policy, i.e. the one that is best among all policies that do not rely on the government's power to tax. Moreover, in this approach even the seigniorage would not stay with the winning bidder but would be channelled back to the economy through the seigniorage taxes T_t.

The preceding analysis has its weak spot in the assumption of unanimity among the users of money. In general, there is no reason to expect such unanimity. Different people with different tastes will have different views about monetary policies and the distribution of seigniorage. In this case, the criteria of the regulatory commission become problematic. However, the distributional conflicts that arise are no different than the distributional conflicts arising in any other area of collective choice, or, more narrowly, in any other regulatory problem. The problem of regulating the supply of outside money no longer is a problem *sui generis*, but it has been brought into the confines of traditional public choice and welfare analysis. Even if one is pessimistic about the possibility of resolving the distributional issues that arise, one may still expect that a commission of the sort that is suggested will pay rather more attention to the public's aversion to inflation and less attention to the money suppliers' desire for seigniorage than an entirely unregulated monopoly.

5. The Problem of Time Inconsistency

I now turn to what is probably the most important problem for any monetary constitution. Up to now, I assumed that the sequence of money supplies is announced before the first period and that this announcement cannot be revoked in any later period. In practice there is no reason why such initial announcements should be binding at later dates. The question then is how the money market behaves in the absence of binding announcements of future money supplies.

580   Martin F. Hellwig

If initial announcements are not binding, the optimal policy precommitment $\{M_t\}$ of an unregulated private monopoly that was discussed in Section 4.1 no longer is an equilibrium. This conclusion is obvious in those cases in which the money supplies M_t are constant and $\mu_t = 0$ for all t. With zero money growth, the monopolist earns the revenue $\pi_0 M_0$ in period zero and nothing thereafter. From the perspective of period 0, this may be a good policy because zero money growth and zero inflation in later periods enhance the real revenue $\pi_0 M_0$ in period 0. From the perspective of period 1, the revenue $\pi_0 M_0$ of period 0 is forever bygone and does not enter into the monopolist's considerations any more. From the perspective of period 1 the zero money growth policy continuation with zero revenues in all periods $t = 1$ is dominated by a policy of positive money growth and positive revenues in some periods.

More generally, let $\{M_t\}$ be the optimal policy precommitment of the private monopolist, and recall that this policy yields the real revenues S_0 in period 0 and $\dfrac{\mu_t}{1 + \mu_t} S_t$ in period $t \geq 1$, where $\mu_t = (M_t - M_{t-1})/M_{t-1}$ is the money growth rate and $S_0, S_1, \ldots$ are the economy's *real* money demands in periods $0, 1, \ldots$ at the given rates of return. For a given quantity of money M_0 in period 0 and given money growth rates μ_t for $t \geq 2$, the quantity of money M_1 in period 1 affects *only* the real money demand S_0 in period 0 and the seigniorage income $\dfrac{\mu_t}{1 + \mu_t} S_1$ in period 1. The seigniorage income is an *increasing* function of μ_1 and hence, for given M_0, of M_1. Nevertheless, from the perspective of period zero, it is not desirable to set $\mu_1 = \infty$ because a large value of M_1 entails a low real value of money $\pi_1 = S_1/M_1$ at date 1, and under rational expectations, a low real value of money π_0 at date 0. (If inventories have no carrying costs, arbitrage between inventories and money ensures $\pi_0 = \pi_1$; if arbitrage considerations impose no bound on the rate of inflation, intertemporal substitution will reduce S_0.) However, from the perspective of period 1, this consideration plays no role, and the revenue "maximizing" policy requires an infinite money growth rate.

The basic rationale of the argument is very simple: At any date t, a fixed pattern of money growth rates $\mu_{t+1}, \mu_{t+2}, \ldots$ induces a certain pattern of expected inflation rates, which determines the real resources S_t that the economy is willing to spend on its money holdings at the end of period t. These real resources S_t are shared between the monopolist and the previous holders of money in proportions $\dfrac{\mu_t}{1 + \mu_t}$ and $\dfrac{1}{1 + \mu_t}$. By making μ_t indefinitely *large*, the monopolist can dispropriate the previous money holders and raise his portion of the quantity S_t that goes into money.

What do we know about Currency Competition?   581

In general then, the monopolist's revenue-maximizing policy is *time-inconsistent*[25] because in later periods, the monopolist wants to deviate from this policy. It follows that the monopolist's initial announcement will not actually be *credible* unless he can devise an institution that makes this announcement binding.

Moreover, it is now easy to see that *in the absence of binding pre-commitments about future money supplies, there cannot be any equilibrium in which the value of money is positive.* The preceding arguments show that no matter what situation we are considering, as of period t, the monopolist has an incentive to make M_t and μ_t arbitrarily large (and hence π_t arbitrarily close to zero). Under rational expectations, this future behaviour of the monopolist is anticipated by the market. With this anticipation, the market sets $S_\tau = \pi_\tau = 0$ for $\tau < t$ because nobody wants to spend real resources on an asset that will be made worthless by the monopolist's future behaviour. In general $S_t = \pi_t = 0$ for all t is the only possible equilibrium.

In summary, an unregulated private monopoly without binding commitments destroys the use of outside paper money just as surely (and by almost the same argument) as the coexistence of several competing outside money supplies.[26] I conjecture that this conclusion does in fact hold for *any* unregulated private organization of a market for outside paper money.

I also believe that the problem of time inconsistency bedevils any government run or regulated monetary system. This is obvious if the government itself behaves like a revenue-maximizing monopolist. Most of *von Hayek's* (1977) historical overview illustrates the very conflict between the monetary stability that is promised to make money acceptable and the money growth that is generated later to raise revenues.

However, time inconsistency would probably be a problem even if the government were run by welfare economists who do not try to maximize seigniorage revenue *per se*. For consider again the model of Bertrand competition among potential money suppliers that was discussed in Section 4.3. Suppose that the regulatory commission has awarded the franchise to a firm with a bid $\{M_t, T_t\}_{t=0}^{\infty}$. In period 0,

---

[25] This time-inconsistency was first discussed by *Calvo* (1978). For the general problem of time-inconsistency of monopoly in a durable goods market, see *Coase* (1972) and *Stokey* (1981).

[26] See *Coase* (1972) on the analogy between the durable goods monopoly and perfect competition. Because of the peculiarity of money, the conclusion here is even stronger than Coase's, which holds only if the time span between subsequent market dates is small, see Stokey (1981).

38*

the initial money supply M_0 and seigniorage tax T_0 are implemented. Now in period 1, the winning firm (or some other firm) presents a new bid $\{\hat{M}_t, \hat{T}_t\}_{t=0}^{\infty}$ to the regulatory commission, which it finds preferable because the net seigniorage revenues $\hat{\pi}_t (\hat{M}_t - \hat{T}_t)$ under the new policy are higher than the net seigniorage revenues $\pi_t (M_t - T_t)$ under the old policy. How will the regulatory commission react to this new bid?

At this point, there is going to be an important *distributional conflict* in the economy: Those who have held money from period 0 will object to any increase in the quantity of money M_1 because it reduces the value of their own money holdings; those who do not hold any money will *not* object unless the new proposal also raises the inflation rate from period 1 to period 2 and thereby worsens the intertemporal price ratio with which they are faced. The latter agents will actually favour the proposed policy change if they can share in the spoils by obtaining a large portion of the seigniorage tax $\hat{T}_1$.

The regulatory commission's reaction to the proposed change in monetary policy will therefore depend on the commission's composition and on its rules of procedure. Specifically the question is how the commission's rules of procedure adjudicate the distributional conflict between money-holders and non-money-holders.[27] The most conservative rule would require *unanimity* for any changes in policy and would thereby give either group an effective veto. A unanimity requirement would probably eliminate the problem of time inconsistency by making it impossible to change monetary policy.

On the other hand, a unanimity requirement will make it hard to agree on a winning bid in the first place. Moreover, it might be desirable to discipline the firm that has been awarded the money supply franchise by threatening to give the franchise to another bank if it fails to comply with the terms of the contract. If such a move requires an unanimous agreement by all members of the commission, then the threat is not very effective, and the existing supplier of outside money can try to violate the terms of the winning bid without much fear of repercussions.

However, for any voting rule that does not require unanimity of decisions about monetary policy, time inconsistency is likely to be a problem. I suspect that time inconsistency is indeed the deepest and least solvable problem for the monetary constitution.

---

[27] In Section 4.3, this distributional conflict played no rule because prior to the determination of the winning bid there were not yet any money holders.

6. Competition among Inside Monies

To conclude the discussion, I briefly consider competition among inside monies, i.e. among monies whose issuers give their clients a claim
of some sort or other. In the simplest case, the holder of an inside
money has the right to obtain a certain specified quantity of a real
good, an asset, or another money upon demand or at some prespecified
date. The Hayek-Vaubel notion of a "value guarantee" is a bit more
complicated because it does not seem to involve a *legal* claim of the
money holder on the money issuer. Instead, the value guarantee is
publicly announced as the guiding principle for future policy.[28] However, as long as the money issuer fulfils his obligation, it does not
matter whether the obligation arises from a policy announcement or
from a legal claim. The distinction matters only when the money issuer
defaults on his promise and the question is how one can make him pay.

If we accept the usual treatment of demand deposits as "money", we
see that most countries already have some competition among inside
monies. However, this competition is rigidly regulated by the government. The Hayek-Vaubel proposal amounts to an outright abolition of
all government regulation of this sector. In particular, they want to
abolish the following regulations:

a) The ban on the issue of private bank notes that can circulate as
   money.

b) The requirement to hold (minimum) reserves in central bank money.

c) The requirement to denominate the private money issuer's obligation
   in units of central bank money.

I should wholeheartedly support these proposals if we lived in a
world in which all agents are completely informed about everything
and all contracts and promises are always honoured. Unfortunately, the
very use of money has to do with the fact that we do not live in such a
world. Given the imperfections and uncertainties of actual markets, I
see no conclusive evidence either against or for government regulation
of the banking system and the market for inside money. Economic
theory simply has too little to say on these matters to warrant any firm
conclusions of the sort Hayek and Vaubel want to draw.

The relation between the holder and the issuer of an inside money
is akin to that between a creditor and a debtor. This relation is problematic because when the contract is made the creditor surrenders a
real asset and gets no more than a piece of paper with a repayment
promise for the future. The whole creditor-debtor relation hinges on

---

[28] *Hayek* (1977), 31.

the question what this promise is going to be worth. In considering this question one must deal with a whole spectrum of difficulties arising from uncertainty, moral hazard, asymmetric information, and again time inconsistency. These difficulties which beset the theory of credit markets are just as important in the market for inside monies.

6.1 Uncertainty and Product Heterogeneity

The returns that the bank earns on its own investments are typically uncertain. Therefore, its own ability to fulfil its obligations to the holders of its money is uncertain. The returns on inside money will generally be uncertain and will depend on the bank's own investment policy. In consequence the inside monies issued by different banks will be less than perfect substitutes for each other. Inside monies must be regarded as a set of differentiated products rather than a single homogeneous product. Competition among inside monies then must be analysed as monopolistic competition in the sense of Chamberlin rather than perfect competition. In a world of Chamberlinian monopolistic competition, there is no presumption that the market outcome has any nice welfare properties.[29]

Both Vaubel and Hayek are aware that the market for inside monies must be analysed in terms of differentiated rather than homogeneous products. They do not seem to be aware that the welfare properties of monopolistic competition in a differentiated products market are quite unclear.

6.2 Moral Hazard and Bankruptcy

The return that an inside money holder eventually gets depends on the behaviour of the issuer of the money. If the issuer selects poor investments, the holder of the inside money gets a poor return — like those depositors who suffered from Herstatt's bad currency speculations. If the issuer embezzles the company's funds, the holder of the inside money gets a poor return — like those IOS certificate holders who suffered from Mr. Vesco's depleting the fund's assets. In principle, the contract between the issuer and holder of an inside money might prescribe the most careful behaviour on the side of the bank; in practice, the holder has no way of enforcing such a clause.

The recent literature on credit rationing and credit contracts shows that many institutional peculiarities in capital markets may be interpreted as devices that eliminate or reduce such instances of moral

---

[29] See, e. g. *Hart* (1983).

hazard. Thus, the standard debt contract with a fixed repayment obligation and bankruptcy if and only if the repayment obligation cannot be
met may be interpreted as the market's response to the moral hazard
that arises if the debtor (here the bank), but not the creditor (here the
money holder) can costlessly observe the realized return on the debtor's
investment.[30] In the same setting, banks as intermediaries may serve to
reduce the agency costs of financing final real investment.[31] Credit
rationing with bounds on both loan sizes and interest rates may serve
to induce less risky investment policies by debtors and banks.[32]

Such devices reduce, but do not eliminate the problem of moral
hazard in financial relations. The central issue is that the behaviour of
a debtor, in particular the issuer of an inside money, exerts an external
effect on the creditor, in particular the holder of the inside money.
Because of this external effect, market allocations will generally not
be more than n-th best, and it is unclear whether government intervention is harmful or useful.

To some extent, *Vaubel* seems to see that moral hazard might be a
problem. He suggests that the danger of "profit snatching" can be eliminated through value guarantees ((1985), 554).[33] However, he does not see
that such guarantees themselves might be subject to moral hazard and
therefore might not be credible. A value guarantee, debt obligation and
the like may eliminate moral hazard if the penalties for non-compliance
with one's obligation are very large. If as in the Vesco-IOS case, the
penalties are small in comparison to the gains from noncompliance,
then such obligations may simply be irrelevant.

Morever, even if the penalties are large enough to eliminate outright
dishonesty, they may still not be large enough to ensure an appropriate
investment policy ex ante.[34] Could it be the case that minimum reserve
requirements for banks or investment regulations for insurance companies are just one admittedly coarse way to "internalize" the effects
that these companies' decisions have on their financiers through the
risk of bankruptcy?

---

[30] *Gale / Hellwig* (1983).
[31] *Diamond* (1984).
[32] *Jaffee / Russell* (1976), *Stiglitz / Weiss* (1981).
[33] Vaubel himself dismisses the Klein-Tullock argument that moral hazard
is less of a problem in a repeated-game setting in which banks care about
their long run prospects. This argument requires that agents do not discount the future so that no matter how large the short turn gains from dis-
honest or negligent behaviour may be, they are always outweighed by the
infinite tail of continued future relations with one's creditors. At least Mr.
Vesco does seem to have had a positive discount rate.
[34] See, e. g. *Stiglitz / Weiss* (1981).

586   Martin F. Hellwig

6.3 Moral Hazard and Time Inconsistency

If a debtor tells his creditor that he cannot pay, does the creditor call
a bankruptcy or does he wait in the hope of sharing in the debtor's
better luck in the future? Given the moral hazard problems discussed
above, it seems desirable *ab initio* to threaten bankruptcy fairly quickly
in order to induce the debtor to take care to avoid bankruptcy. However, *after* it has been determined that the debtor cannot pay, at least
at present, the creditor may prefer to keep him alive. If bankruptcy is
called immediately, the creditor has to write off his claims on the
debtor. If bankruptcy is not called, there might be a time in the future
when these claims could be collected. The decision to call a bankruptcy
is thus subject to time inconsistency just like the optimal supply of
outside money.[35] Concrete examples of these considerations have been
observed in recent proceedings concerning the City of New York as well
as the so-called "International Debt Crisis".

In those cases where the debtor is a large bank and the debts are
inside money held by the public, the reluctance to call a bankruptcy
seems to be especially great. In the case of the Continental Illinois
Bank, it was made clear that because of adverse effects on the monetary
system, a large bank would not be allowed to go bankrupt no matter
how many bad loans it might have made. The problem is, of course,
that if the banks know this, then they have no reason to avoid making
bad loans. More generally, debtors who know that they will not be put
into bankruptcy have only weak incentives to manage their means
carefully so as to make sure that they can fulfil their obligations.

In summary, I believe that the markets for inside monies and the
larger set of capital markets of which they form part are so replete with
market imperfections, information asymmetries and problems of moral
hazard that we cannot make any firm assessment about the welfare
properties of the outcomes in such markets. Whether government regulation in these markets is warranted at all, whether it should take
the form it does take, is something that at present we do not know —
unless of course we start from the axiom that everything would be for
the best in the best of all possible worlds if only the government
ceased interfering. If we do not accept this axiom, we must admit that
we simply do not know very much about how competition among inside
monies works.

---

[35] *Hellwig* (1977).

Summary

The paper studies the proposals of Hayek and Vaubel for unregulated private competition in the money market. These proposals are shown to rest on an insufficient distinction between *inside* and *outside* money. The existence of an outside money without a backing is desirable on welfare grounds. However, *any* private supply of outside money in perfect competition, Cournot oligopoly or monopoly would actually destroy the use of outside money. The main problem is that of *time inconsistency* of the optimal money supply policy. Problems of time inconsistency and of moral hazard arise also in the market for inside money. Because of these problems, the appropriateness of unregulated competition in the market for inside money must also be doubted.

Zusammenfassung

Die Arbeit befaßt sich mit den Vorschlägen Hayeks und Vaubels zur Einführung des Wettbewerbs im Geldwesen. Es wird gezeigt, daß diese Vorschläge auf einer unzureichenden Unterscheidung zwischen *Außengeld* und *Innengeld* beruhen. Die Existenz eines Außengeldes ohne Deckung ist aus wohlfahrtstheoretischen Erwägungen wünschenswert. Ein privates Angebot an Außengeld im Wettbewerb, Cournot-Oligopol oder Monopol würde aber die Funktionsfähigkeit des Marktes für Außengeld zerstören. Zentrales Problem ist die *Zeitinkonsistenz* jeglicher Geldangebotspolitik. Zeitinkonsistenzprobleme in Verbindung mit „moral hazard" treten auch im Markt für Innengeld auf und lassen auch hier die Angemessenheit der Vorschläge von Hayek und Vaubel als zweifelhaft erscheinen.

References

Baumol, W., J. *Panzar* and R. *Willig* (1982), Contestable Markets and the Theory of Industry Structure. New York.

Bewley, T. (1980), The Optimum Quantity of Money, in: J. Kareken / N. Wallace, Models of Monetary Economics. Minneapolis.

— (1982), A Difficulty with the Optimum Quantity of Money. Econometrica 51, 1485 - 1504.

Calvo, G. (1978), Optimal Seigniorage from Money Creation. Journal of Monetary Economics 4, 503 - 517.

Coase, R. M. (1972), Monopoly and Durability. Journal of Law and Economics 15, 143 - 149.

Diamond, D. (1984), Financial Intermediation and Delegated Monitoring. Review of Economic Studies 51, 393 - 414.

Friedman, M. (1969), The Optimum Quantity of Money, in: M. Friedman, The Optimum Quantity of Money and Other Essays. Chicago.

Gale, D. and M. *Hellwig* (1983), Incentive Compatible Debt Contracts: The One-Period Problem. Discussion Paper No. 124, Sonderforschungsbereich 21. Bonn.

588   Martin F. Hellwig

Girton, L. and D. *Roper* (1981), Theory and Implications of Currency Substitution. Journal of Money, Credit, and Banking 13, 12 - 30.

Hart, O. D. (1983), Monopolistic Competition in the Spirit of Chamberlin: A General Model. Discussion Paper No. 83/82. ICERD, London.

Hayek, F. A. v. (1976), Choice in Currency: A Way to Stop Inflation. Institute of Economic Affairs, Occasional Paper 48. London.

— (1977), Entnationalisierung des Geldes. Tübingen.

Hellwig, M. F. (1976), A Model of Monetary Exchange. Discussion Paper No. 202, Econometric Research Program. Princeton.

— (1977), A Model of Borrowing and Lending with Bankruptcy. Econometrica 45, 1879 - 1906.

— (1980), Precautionary Asset Holding under Individual and Collective Risk. Paper presented at the World Congress of the Econometric Society.

— (1982), Precautionary Money Holding and the Payment of Interest on Money. Discussion Paper No. 92, Sonderforschungsbereich 21. Bonn.

Jaffee, D. W. and T. *Russell* (1976), Imperfect Information, Uncertainty and Credit Rationing. Quarterly Journal of Economics 90, 651 - 666.

Johnson, H. G. (1969), Inside Money, Outside Money, Income Wealth, and Welfare in Monetary Theory. Journal of Money, Credit, and Banking 1, 30 - 45.

— (1970), Is there an Optimal Money Supply? Journal of Finance 24, 435 - 442.

Kareken, J. and N. *Wallace* (1981), On the Interminancy of Equilibrium Exchange Rates. Quarterly Journal of Economics 96, 202 - 222.

Pesek, B.P. and T. *Saving* (1967), Money, Wealth and Economic Theory. London.

Radner, R. (1972), Existence of Equilibrium of Plans, Prices, and Price Expectations in a Sequence of Markets. Econometrica 40, 289 - 303.

Scitovsky, T. (1954), Two Concepts of Externalities. Journal of Political Economy 62, 143 - 151.

Stiglitz, J. and A. *Weiss* (1981), Credit Rationing in Markets with Imperfect Information. American Economic Review 71, 393 - 410.

Stokey, N. (1981), Rational Expectations and Durable Goods Pricing. Bell Journal of Economics 12 (1), 112 - 128.

Vaubel, R. (1984), The Government's Money Monopoly: Externalities or Natural Monopoly? Kyklos 37, 27 - 58.

— (1985), Competing Currencies: The Case for Free Entry. Zeitschrift für Wirtschafts- und Sozialwissenschaften 5, 547 - 564.

[24]

Journal of Monetary Economics 17 (1986) 37–62. North-Holland

HAS GOVERNMENT ANY ROLE IN MONEY?

Milton FRIEDMAN

Hoover Institution, Stanford, CA 94305, USA

Anna J. SCHWARTZ

National Bureau of Economic Research, New York, NY 10003, USA

Recent interest in monetary reform has been sparked by the emergence of a world irredeemable paper money system. In light of this interest, we review the current validity of four 'good reasons' Friedman advanced in 1960 to rationalize government intervention. We conclude that the forces that produced government involvement in the past will persist. Deregulation of financial intermediaries is desirable on grounds of market efficiency, though it is an open question whether government should continue as lender of last resort. We expect that the present world fiat money standard will neither degenerate into hyperinflation nor revert to a commodity standard.

1. Introduction

In recent years there has been a burst of scholarly interest in various aspects of monetary reform – not the conduct of current monetary policy, which has for decades been the object of active scholarly work, but the institutional structure of the monetary system. This interest has centered on three separate but related topics: (1) competition versus government monopoly in the creation of or control over outside or high-powered money, (2) so-called free banking, and (3) the determination of the unit of account and its relation to media of exchange. The topics are related because they all deal with what role, if any, government has in the monetary system.

This burst of interest has been a response to mutually reinforcing developments, some internal to the discipline of economics; others, external.

The internal developments were threefold. One is the emergence of the theory of public choice, which has produced a large-scale shift from a public-interest to a private-interest interpretation of government activity. Instead of regarding civil servants and legislators as disinterestedly pursuing the public interest, as they judged it – in sharp contrast to the behavior we have attributed to participants in business enterprises – economists have increasingly come to regard civil servants and legislators as pursuing their private interests, treated not as narrowly pecuniary or selfish but as encompassing whatever ends enter into their utility functions, not excluding concern for the public interest. This public choice perspective is extremely attractive intellectually because it aligns our interpretations of government and private activity. It has inevitably led to extensive research on the determinants of governmental behavior as well as to renewed attention to the kinds of institutions and policies, if any, that can make each participant in government as in a free market operate as if, in Adam Smith's famous phase, he were 'led by an invisible hand to promote an end that was no part of his intention', namely, the interest of the public. Monetary policy and the monetary authorities have been obvious candidates for attention.[1]

A second internal development is the rational expectations approach, particularly its stress on the effect of the institutional structure and changes in the institutional structure on the expectations of the public. In one sense, this approach is not new. For example, the effect of the existence of central banks on the behavior of commercial banks and the public had long been explicitly recognized in the monetary literature. Yet, the coining of a new name, the application of the idea by Lucas to the validity of econometric forecasts, and the explicit modelling of the role of expectations have all had a major impact on the profession's thinking and, incidentally, have promoted greater attention to institutional structures as compared with current policy formation.

A third internal development is the renewed interest in so-called 'Austrian Economics', with its emphasis on invisible-hand interpretations of the origin and development of economic institutions, and its interpretation of the business cycle as largely reflecting the effect of non-neutral money. The latter in turn produced a long 'Austrian' tradition of support for 'hard' money and opposition to discretionary money management. Hayek's proposal (1976, 1978) for denationalizing money was especially influential in reviving this tradition.

The key external development – the ultimate consequences of which are shrouded in uncertainty – was the emergence of a world monetary system that, we believe, is unprecedented: a system in which essentially every currency in the world is, directly or indirectly, on a pure fiat standard – directly, if the exchange rate of the currency is flexible though possibly manipulated; indirectly, if the exchange rate is effectively fixed in terms of another fiat-based currency (e.g., since 1983, the Hong Kong dollar). This system emerged gradually after World War I. From then to 1971, much of the world was effectively on a dollar standard, while the U.S., though ostensibly on a gold standard (except for a brief interval in 1933–34), was actually on a fiat standard combined with a government program for pegging the price of gold. The Bretton Woods agreement in the main simply ratified that situation, despite the lip service paid to the role of gold, and the provisions for changes in exchange rates. The end of Bretton Woods in 1971 removed both the formal

---

[1] See Acheson and Chant (1973), Brunner (1976), Buchanan (1984), Hetzel (1984) and Kane (1980).

links to the dollar and the pretense that the U.S. was on a gold standard. The stocks of gold listed on the books of the central books of the world are a relic of a bygone era, though a slim possibility remains that they will again become more than that at some future date.

The formal ending of Bretton Woods was precipitated by an inflationary surge in the U.S. in the 1960s and in turn helped to produce a continuation and acceleration of that surge in the 1970s. The inflation and the subsequent economic instability were more directly responsible for the burst of interest in monetary reform than the momentous change in the world's monetary system of which the inflation was both a cause and a manifestation. It did so in several ways. In the first place, it brought into sharp focus the poor performance of the monetary authorities – reinforcing the conclusions about prior policy that various scholars had reached, including ourselves in our *Monetary History*. Even granted the market failures that we and many other economists had attributed to a strictly laissez-faire policy in money and banking, the course of events encouraged the view that turning to government as an alternative was a cure that was worse than the disease, at least with existing government policies and institutions. Government failure might be worse than market failure.

In the second place, the rise in nominal interest rates produced by the rise in inflation converted government control of interest rates in the U.S. via Regulation Q from a minor to a serious impediment to the effective clearing of credit markets. One response was the invention of money market mutual funds as a way to avoid Regulation Q. The money market funds performed a valuable social function. Yet, from a broader perspective, their invention constituted social waste. If either the inflation had not occurred or banks had been free to respond to market forces, there would have been no demand for the services of money market funds, and the entrepreneurial talent and other resources absorbed by the money market mutuals could have been employed in socially more productive activities. The money market funds proved an entering wedge to financial innovations that forced a relaxation and near-abandonment of control over the interest rates that banks could pay, as well as over other regulations that restricted their activities. The deregulation of banking that has occurred came too late and has been too incomplete to prevent a sharp reduction in the role of banks, as traditionally defined, in the financial system as a whole.

In Friedman's *Program for Monetary Stability*, published a quarter of a century ago, he asked the question 'whether monetary and banking arrangements could be left to the market, subject only to the general rules applying to all other economic activity'.

'I am by no means certain', he wrote, 'that the answer is indubitably in the negative. What is clear is that monetary arrangements have seldom been left entirely to the market, even in societies following a thoroughly liberal policy in other respects, and that there are good reasons why this should have been the case' [Friedman (1959, p. 4)]. Those 'good reasons' were: '[1] the resource cost of a pure commodity currency and hence its tendency to become partly fiduciary; [2] the peculiar difficulty of enforcing contracts involving promises to pay that serve as a medium of exchange and of preventing fraud in respect to them; [3] the technical monopoly character of a pure fiduciary currency which makes essential the setting of some external limit on its amount; and finally, [4] the pervasive character of money which means that the issuance of money has important effects on parties other than those directly involved and gives special importance to the preceding features. Something like a moderately stable monetary framework seems an essential prerequisite for the effective operation of a private market economy. It is dubious that the market can by itself provide such a framework. Hence, the function of providing one is an essential governmental function on a par with the provision of a stable legal framework' [Friedman (1959, p. 8), numbers added].

Of course, recognition that there are 'good reasons' for government to intervene and that, as a matter of historical fact, governments, and especially modern governments, almost invariably have done so, does not mean that the actual interventions have promoted the public welfare, or that the modes of intervention have been wisely chosen. A major aim of our *Monetary History* was precisely to investigate this question for the U.S. for the period after the Civil War.

The evidence we assembled strongly suggests, indeed we believe demonstrates, that government intervention was at least as often a source of instability and inefficiency as the reverse, and that the major 'reform' during the period, the establishment of the Federal Reserve System, in practice did more harm than good. Our personal conclusion, reinforced by the evidence in that work though not stated therein, is that a rigid monetary rule is preferable to discretionary monetary management by the Federal Reserve.

The aim of this paper is to consider whether the new evidence and new arguments that have emerged in recent years justify a revision of the earlier summary of 'good reasons' why government has intervened, in particular of the conclusion that 'the market itself cannot provide' a 'stable monetary framework'. In the most extreme form, does the evidence justify an unqualified affirmative rather than negative answer to the question 'whether monetary and banking arrangements cannot [i.e., should not] be left to the market'?

This question in turn breaks down into three separate questions, the clear differentiation of which is one of the valuable contributions of recent writings:

(1) Can and should the determination of a unit of account linked with a medium of exchange and the provision of outside money itself be left to the market or do items [1], [3], and [4] of Friedman's good reasons justify a government role in defining the unit of account and providing an outside money?

(2) Given a well-defined outside money involving a unit of account and a medium of exchange, can and should strict laissez-faire be the rule for banking – broadly defined to include the issuance of inside money in the form of currency as well as deposits – except only for the general rules applied to all other economic activity? This is the so-called free-banking question, which bears particularly on items [2] and [4] of Friedman's 'good reasons'.

In terms of institutional and legal arrangements, the major sub-issues are:

(a) Should financial intermediaries be prohibited from issuing inside money in the form of hand-to-hand currency, i.e., should hand-to-hand currency be a government monopoly?

(b) Are governmental limitations on lending and investing by financial intermediaries necessary or desirable?

(c) Is a government 'lender of last resort' – a central bank – necessary or desirable?

(3) In the absence of legal obstacles, can, should, and would the unit of account be separated in practice from the medium of exchange function in the belief that financial innovation will render outside money unnecessary and obsolete? I.e., do financial innovations promise to make a 100 percent inside money the most efficient means of engaging in transactions?

It may be worth noting explicitly that the word 'can' as used in these questions admits of two very different interpretations. One is narrowly economic: is a given set of arrangements internally consistent so far as narrowly economic conditions are concerned; that is, would it generate a stable equilibrium, both static and dynamic? The other is broader. Would the set of arrangements generate a stable political as well as economic equilibrium; that is, is its existence consistent with the political constitution, or would it generate political forces leading to major changes in the arrangements?

We believe that failure to distinguish between these interpretations is responsible for much of the appearance of disagreement in the discussions of monetary reform.

Of the three questions posed, we propose to discuss the first two, since the third is much less related to our earlier work, and besides, has been dealt with recently, and in our opinion correctly, by others [McCallum (1985) and White (1984b)].

The first and third questions are new in a sense in which the second is not. Essentially all participants in the nineteenth- and early twentieth-century controversies about monetary and banking matters took for granted a specie standard, in which government's role was restricted to coinage or its equivalent (i.e., provision of warehouse receipts for specie); hence they never had occasion to consider the first and third questions. Suspension of specie payments was regarded as, and in fact generally was, a temporary expedient to meet a temporary difficulty. Any government-issued money (whether notes or deposits) in excess of specie reserves was, in modern terminology, regarded as inside money, not outside money, though it clearly became the latter during periods of suspension of specie payments. This common view no doubt reflected widespread agreement that historical experience showed, as Irving Fisher put it in 1911, that 'Irredeemable paper money has almost invariably proved a curse to the country employing it' [see Fisher (1929, p. 131)].

The disappearance of specie standards and the emergence of a world monetary system in which, for the first time, every country is, in Fisher's terms, on an 'irredeemable paper standard' has produced two very different streams of literature: one, scientific; the other, popular. The scientific literature is that already referred to, dealing with monetary reform and the government's role in providing outside money (section 2 below). The popular literature is alarmist and 'hard money', essentially all of it based on the proposition that Fisher's generalization will continue to hold and that the world is inevitably condemned to runaway inflation unless and until the leading nations adopt commodity standards.

There has been some, but limited, intersection between these two streams. The scientific literature has occasionally dealt with but mostly ignored the question raised by the popular literature. Have the conditions that have produced the current unprecedented monetary system also altered the likelihood that it will go the way of earlier paper standards? We consider that question in a tentative way in section 4 below.

By contrast with outside money, free banking was fully and exhaustively discussed in the nineteenth and early twentieth century. Recent literature has added much historical detail, discussed the arguments in terms of current monetary arrangements, and expressed old arguments in more formal and abstract terms. And we now have a much wider span of historical experience on which to base a judgment. Nonetheless, Vera Smith's 1936 *Rationale of Central Banking* provides, we believe, as accurate and complete a summary of recent theoretical arguments for and against 'free banking' as it does of the earlier arguments (section 3).

2. Outside money

Whether the government has a role in providing outside money, and what that role should be, is more basic than whether government should intervene in the provision of inside money by non-government banking institutions. Existing banking systems rest on the foundation of an outside money, and so did those 'free banking' systems, such as the Scottish, Canadian and early U.S., that have recently been subjected to reexamination and offered as object lessons. Historically, a single unit of account linked to a single dominant outside money has tended to emerge, initially via a market process of transactors settling on a particular commodity, followed almost invariably by government's exercising control over one or more aspects of the issuance of outside money – typically with the ostensible purpose of standardizing the coinage and certifying its quality (purity, fineness, etc.). Occasionally, two commodities, with a flexible rate of exchange between them, have simultaneously been outside moneys, one for small transactions, the other for large, as with silver and gold in the Middle Ages, or copper and silver in China.

Insofar as governments confined themselves to producing standardized coinage, the activity was a source of revenue because of the convenience to the public of using for transaction purposes coins with a stated face value rather than bullion. The mint could make a 'seignorage' charge for providing this service, and the government's visibility and authority gave it an advantage over private mints even when it did not prohibit them. However, governments have repeatedly gone farther and have used (or abused) their control over outside money to raise revenue by introducing fiat elements. Initially, this took the form of the debasement of the metallic coinage issued by the sovereign – that is, increasing the proportion of base metal in silver and gold coins, so that the stated face value of the coins exceeded the market value of the precious metal they contained. Such debasement was a source of revenue because of the lag in the adjustment of nominal prices to the lowered precious metal content of the coins. During this period, the base metal served, as it were, as inside money.

The introduction and subsequent widespread use of paper money and deposits, initially as warehouse receipts for specie, opened a broader range of possibilities, exploited both by private individuals or bankers who issued notes and deposits promising to pay specie on demand in excess of the amount of specie they held (private inside money, so long as the issuers honored the promise), and by governments that did the same (government inside money, subject to the same proviso).

As banking developed, commercial banks came to regard all non-interest bearing government issues – in the U.K., notes and deposits at the Bank of England; in the U.S., United States notes (greenbacks), national bank notes, silver certificates, Federal Reserve notes and deposits – as outside money. However, for the system as a whole, so long as convertibility into specie was maintained, only specie was in fact outside money; the excess of government issues over the government's specie holdings was government-created inside money. All such issues, however, became true outside money – pure fiat money – when convertibility was suspended, as it now has been throughout the world.

We still refer to government-issued non-interest bearing notes and deposits as government 'liabilities' or 'obligations', although that is not what they are, as is eminently clear in other contexts. We now take a pure fiat standard so much for granted that we no longer find any need to distinguish between the concepts of outside money relevant for the commercial banks and for the system as a whole. But that distinction remains important in judging proposals for monetary reform, and in interpreting historical experience.

That experience provides striking evidence of the value that communities attach to having a single unit of account and medium of exchange. The large revenue that governments have been able to extract by introducing fiat elements into outside money is one measure of the price that economic agents are willing to pay to preserve the unit of account and the medium of exchange to which they have become habituated. It takes truly major depreciation in the purchasing power of the dominant money before any substantial fraction of the community adopts alternatives, either with respect to the unit of account or the medium of exchange. Yet such alternatives have generally been available.

For example, students of money have repeatedly recommended what Alfred Marshall called a tabular standard, namely, the indexation of long-term contracts, so that for such contracts the unit of account becomes, to use one currency as an example, not the nominal dollar, but the real dollar, although the medium of exchange may remain the nominal dollar.[2] In most Western countries, nothing has prevented the private emergence of a tabular standard. Yet, a tabular standard has emerged on any widespread scale only in countries that have been subject to extreme movements in the price level, like some Latin American countries, Israel, etc. Indexation has been privately introduced on any substantial scale in the U.S. only with respect to labor contracts, and even there only occasionally and with respect to a minority of contracts.

Another alternative has been foreign currency, which has occasionally been resorted to both as unit of account and medium of circulation, but again only under extreme provocation.

The apparently great value to the economy of having a single unit of account linked with an (ultimate) medium of exchange does not mean that government must play any role, or that there need be a single producer of the medium of exchange. And indeed, historically, governments have entered the picture after the event, after the community had settled on a unit of account and private producers had produced media of exchange.

Two features of this history are striking. The first is that the unit of account has, invariably or nearly so, been linked to a commodity. We know of no example of an abstract unit of account – a fiduciary or fiat unit such as now

---

[2] In his rediscovery and advocacy of a tabular standard, R.W.R. White (1979), former governor of the Reserve Bank of New Zealand, proposed terming the corresponding unit of account, the 'Real'.

W. Stanley Jevons (1890, pp. 328,331), in recommending a tabular standard of which he says 'the difficulties in the way of such a scheme are not considerable', refers to a book by Joseph Lowe (*The Present State of England*) published in 1822 which contains a similar proposal.

prevails everywhere, having emerged spontaneously through its acceptance in private transactions. The second is how universally government has taken over, and how often it has established a monopoly in the certification or production of the outside money. In his explanation of this phenomenon, Friedman stressed considerations of economic efficiency – 'can' in the narrower economic sense. But this is clearly inadequate. The theory of public choice requires attention to the political forces that have produced this result and the kind of monetary constitution, if any, that can avoid it.[3] It is not enough to document the abuses that have arisen from government control of outside money, or to demonstrate the existence of alternative arrangements that are economically more satisfactory. We shall be evading our task of explanation unless we examine the political forces that established government control under a wide range of political and economic circumstances, superseding private certification and production of outside money. And, so far as reform is concerned, we shall simply be spitting in the wind, as economists have done for 200 years with respect to tariffs, unless we explore how effective political support can be mobilized for one or another solution. We hasten to add that the latter is not the task of this paper.[4]

Item [3] of Friedman's list of 'good reasons', the technical monopoly character of a *pure fiduciary* currency' (italics added) has been questioned, particularly by Benjamin Klein (1974). Klein's theoretical case, resting on the necessity for a producer of money to establish confidence in his money, and the increasing capital cost of creating such confidence, is impeccable, and has received wide acceptance. Yet it is not clear that his argument can be carried over to a 'pure fiduciary' currency.[5] Historically, producers of money have established confidence by promising convertibility into some dominant money, generally, specie. Many examples can be cited of fairly long-continued and successful producers of private moneys convertible into specie.[6] We do not know, however, of any example of the private production of purely inconvertible fiduciary moneys (except as temporary expedients, e.g., wooden nickels, clearing house certificates), or of the simultaneous existence in the same community of private producers of moneys convertible into different ultimate media, except for the previously mentioned case when two metals circulated

---

[3] See, for example, Brennan and Buchanan (1981).

[4] One of us has discussed elsewhere some of the issues involved, and possible reforms for the U.S. See Friedman (1984b).

[5] McCallum (1985, p. 25) also makes this point.

[6] E.g., George Smith money was a widely used medium of exchange in the Middle West of the U.S. in the 1840s and 1850s. However, when George Smith retired from control of the Wisconsin Marine and Fire Insurance Company, which he created to evade the state of Wisconsin's prohibition of banks of issue, George Smith money went the way of all money. His successors could not resist the temptation of dissipating for short-term gain the 'brand name capital' George Smith had built up. See Hammond (1957, p. 613). The Scottish banks discussed by White are another even more impressive example of a competitive issue of convertible money.

simultaneously at a flexible rate of exchange, and the somewhat similar case of the greenback period (1862–1878) in the U.S. when banks had both greenback and gold deposit liabilities. Yet Klein's argument would not seem to preclude the simultaneous existence in the same community of several dominant moneys produced by different private issuers.

Hayek, in his argument for the denationalization of money, believes that such an outcome is a real possibility, if the current legal obstacles to the production of competitive moneys were removed. In particular, he believes that private issuers who produced a medium of exchange with constant purchasing power (a 'real dollar') would become dominant. He recognizes that a single dominant money might tend to develop over large areas, but anticipates that different definitions of constant purchasing power would be appropriate for different areas or groups and hence that a 'number of different competitive money producers would survive, with extensive overlap in border areas' [Hayek (1978, p.112)].

Entirely aside from the question of the political forces that such arrangements would generate, we are skeptical of his conjecture, rather agreeing with Benjamin Klein's (1976, p. 514) early judgment that 'I do not think that adoption of Hayek's... policy recommendation of complete domestic freedom of choice in currency would significantly reduce the amount of monopoly power on currency issue currently possessed by each individual European government'.[7]

So far, neither Hayek's belief that privately produced constant purchasing power moneys would become dominant nor Klein's and our skepticism has any direct empirical basis, but derive rather from an interpretation of historical experience under very different monetary arrangements than those Hayek proposes. However, some direct evidence may emerge in the near future, because of developments within the present system that could facilitate the issuance of constant purchasing power money.

In the United States, the Federal Home Loan Bank Board in 1980 authorized federal savings and loan associations to make price-level-adjusted-mortgage (or PLAM) loans and, in 1982, to accept price-level-adjusted-deposits (PLAD). There seems no reason such deposits could not be readily transferable by checks or their equivalent, which would provide a medium of exchange as well as a unit of account of constant purchasing power. So far, apparently, no savings and loan has taken advantage of this possibility. However, since 1982 disinflation has been the rule, and confidence in a more stable future price level has grown rapidly. A real test will come when and if that confidence is shattered.[8]

---

[7]See also Martino (1984, especially p. 15).
[8]See McCulloch (1980).

Another U.S. development, in the course of being realized as this is written, is the introduction of futures markets in price index numbers [Friedman (1984a)]. The Coffee, Sugar & Cocoa Exchange has received permission from the Commodity Futures Trading Commission (the federal agency that regulates futures markets) to introduce a futures contract in the consumer price index. Trading in the contract began on June 21, 1985. Such futures markets would enable banks to accept deposits on a price-level adjusted basis and hedge their risk in the futures market rather than by matching price-level adjusted liabilities with price-level adjusted assets. This development seems to us the most promising of the recent innovations, in terms of its potential effect on the operation of the monetary system.

An earlier U.S. development was the removal in 1974 of the prohibition against the ownership, purchase and sale of gold by private persons. In principle, it has been possible since then for individuals in private dealings to use gold as a medium of exchange. And there have been some minor stirrings. The Gold Standard Corporation in Kansas City provides facilities for deposits denominated in gold and for the transfer of such deposits among persons by check. However, this is a warehousing operation -- a 100 percent reserve bank, as it were – rather than a private currency denominated in gold and issued on a fractional reserve basis. Unfortunately, there are currently legal obstacles to any developments that would enable gold to be used not only as a store of value or part of an asset portfolio but as a unit of account or a medium of circulation. Hence, the current situation provides little evidence on what would occur if those obstacles were removed.

In the U.K., the government now issues securities that link interest and principal to a price index number. Banks could use such securities as assets to match price-level adjusted deposits.

It remains to be seen whether any of these opportunities will be exploited. Our personal view is that they will be if and only if government monetary policy produces wide fluctuations in inflation, fluctuations even wider than those that occurred in the U.S. or the U.K. in recent decades. Moreover, even if they are, we conjecture that the use of a constant purchasing power of money as a unit of account and medium of circulation will be confined to large transactions involving long times delays, not to small or current transactions.

A further qualification is that the circumstance envisaged in the preceding paragraph – wide fluctuations in inflation in major countries – is not likely to prove stable and long-lasting. It is almost certain to produce political pressures for major monetary reform – in the extreme, after it has degenerated into hyperinflation; on a more hopeful note, long before.

Until recent years, true hyperinflation has occurred only in countries undergoing revolution or severe civil unrest or that have been defeated in a major war, with the possible exception of John Law's experiment of doubling the French bank-note issue in the four-year period 1716 to 1720. However, currently, several countries seem on the verge of hyperinflation under relatively peaceful circumstances – Bolivia, Argentina and Israel, to mention only the most prominent. The misfortune of these countries promises to provide us with some evidence on a so far rarely observed phenomenon.

Another recent hybrid development of considerable interest is the increased use of the ECU (European Currency Unit) in private transactions. The ECU is a composite of the separate national currencies of those Common Market countries participating in the European Monetary System – or, as it has come to be described, a basket containing specified numbers of units of each of the national currencies included in it. Its value in terms of any single national currency, including the dollar or any of the currencies composing it, is thus a weighted average of the market values in terms of that currency of the component ECU currencies. Though initially created for clearing intergovernmental balances, it has increasingly been used as a unit of account in private bond issues and other transactions [see Triffin (1984, especially pp. 150–163)], and banks in some countries have been offering ECU denominated deposits, though in others, such as Germany, they are currently not permitted to do so. So far, the ECU has been convertible into dollars and most other currencies. However, it has been in existence only since 1979, so it is still in the early stages of development. What role it will play in the future is highly uncertain.

The ECU is a governmentally created and issued currency. It is convertible only into other governmentally created and issued currencies, all of which are purely fiduciary, despite lip service still paid to gold by including gold, generally at an artificial price, as a 'reserve asset' in the balance sheets of the central banks. What is unique is its composite character, resembling in this respect the fiduciary counterpart to the symmetallic proposal by Marshall and the later commodity reserve proposals.[9]

It does offer an alternative to the separate national currencies and so does enhance currency competition. However, its growth and wider use would represent joint government action in the field of money along the lines of the International Monetary Fund, rather than private action. As with national currencies, private action would take the form of producing inside money convertible into the ECU as an outside money.

Items [3] and [4] of Friedman's list of 'good reasons', technical monopoly and external effects, have been questioned also by Roland Vaubel (1984) in a thoughtful article. He concludes that neither is a valid justification for a government monopoly in the production of base money.

With respect to natural monopoly, he concludes that 'the only valid test of the natural monopoly argument is to abolish all barriers to entry and to admit free currency competition from private issuers on equal terms' [Vaubel (1984,

---

[9]See Friedman (1951). Interestingly, F.A. Hayek (1943) was an early supporter of such a proposal.

p. 57)]. We agree with him entirely on this point while, as noted earlier, being highly skeptical that, given the starting point with a government currency firmly established, any private issuers would be likely to compete successfully – especially in producing a 'pure fiduciary' money. As already noted, there is no historical precedent. Historical experience suggests that the only plausible alternative to a government issued fiduciary currency is a commodity currency, with private issuers producing inside money convertible into the commodity. And we believe that even that outcome is highly unlikely unless there is a major collapse of national currencies – something approximating hyperinflation on a worldwide scale.

With respect to externalities, Vaubel's negative conclusion is a quibble with respect to the basic issue of whether government has a key role to play in the monetary system. Even if there are externalities, he says, it 'does not follow that government should produce money (let alone as a monopolist) rather than introduce a mandatory deposit insurance scheme or act as a lender of last resort by borrowing and lending private money' [Vaubel (1984, p. 32)]. But either of these policies would be a far cry from leaving 'money and banking arrangements... to the market'.

To summarize our answer to the first question: there is no economic reason why the determination of a unit of account linked with a medium of exchange and the provision of outside money cannot be left to the market. But history suggests both that any privately generated unit of account will be linked to a commodity and that government will not long keep aloof. Under a wide variety of economic and political circumstances, a monetary system has emerged that rests on a unit of account and on outside money at least certified, and generally more than that, by government. Such a system will not easily be dislodged or replaced by a strictly private system.

3. Free banking

A number of recent authors have argued that the historical experience with 'free banking' is less unfavorable than suggested by Friedman and other authors. Lawrence White has reexamined the experience in Scotland for the period up to 1845 and concluded that it supports 'the case for thorough deregulation' of banking [White (1984a, p. 148)]. Rockoff (1975), Rolnick and Weber (1983) and King (1983) have reexamined the experience in the United States prior to the Civil War and come to a similar conclusion, arguing that prior studies of this period have grossly exaggerated the quantitative importance of 'wildcat banking', overissue of depreciated bank notes, and the other ills generally associated with banking in that era.

The experience of Scotland, as most recently described by White, is surely the most favorable. For more than a century and a half Scotland had a system of free banking, with completely free entry and minimal governmental regulation or restraint. Scottish banks were banks of issue as well as of deposit. Their note issues circulated widely and were in practice the dominant medium of circulation. With minor exceptions the issues of different banks – numbering as many as 29 in 1826 and 19 in 1845, just before the end of the era of free banking – circulated at par with one another, thanks to an agreement among the banks to accept one another's notes [White (1984a, pp. 35, 37)]. Some banks did fail, but holders of their notes suffered negligible, if any, losses. And this system developed entirely by market forces, with government intervention consisting solely in the chartering of three of the banks.

However, before accepting the relevance of this experience to our current situation, it is important to note several special features of Scottish experience: first, it dealt only with inside money. Outside money consisted of either gold or, during the period of suspension of convertibility by the Bank of England (1797–1821), Bank of England notes. Second, as White stresses (1984a, p. 41), shareholders of banks assumed unlimited liability for the obligations of the banks.[10] As a result, bank depositors and holders of bank notes were sheltered from the failure of banks; the whole burden fell on the stockholders. Third, Scotland was an old, established community, with a relatively stable population, so that stockholders consisted in the main of persons who were well known, had considerable private wealth and valued their own reputations for probity highly enough to honor their obligations.[11] Fourth, while the only equivalent in Scotland itself of a central bank was the extent to which some of the larger banks served as bankers' banks, the Scottish banks had access to the London financial market, which performed the equivalent of some modern central bank functions for Scotland [see Goodhart (1985, sect. 5, note 3)].

For a contrast, consider the experience of the United States from, say, 1791 to 1836, the period spanning the first and second Banks of the United States. New England perhaps came closest to matching Scotland in some of its characteristics, particularly in containing substantial communities with long-settled prominent families possessing much wealth. It was taken for granted that specie was the dominant money and provided the appropriate unit of account. In the main, laissez-faire prevailed in banking, despite the existence of the two Federal banks, as Hammond (1957) calls them. There was nothing that prevented a system from developing along Scottish lines. Yet it did not. Numerous banks were established, which issued bank notes promising to pay specie on demand, yet a wide range of imaginative stratagems were adopted to postpone and impede redemption, and country bank notes circulated in Boston at varying discounts, leading Boston banks to adopt a succession of measures to enforce redemption. The end result was the famous Suffolk Bank system,

---

[10] Except for the three chartered banks.

[11] The extreme example was Adam Smith's patron, the Duke of Buccleigh, who was a stockholder in the ill-fated Ayr bank and suffered a major loss when it failed in 1772.

which developed gradually from about 1820 on. As Hammond (1957, pp. 554, 556) remarks: 'The Suffolk was in effect the central bank of New England.... The operators of the Suffolk Bank showed *laissez-faire* at its best'. But even here, laissez-faire did not lead to unlimited liability as a rule, though there must have been private bankers who subjected themselves to unlimited liability; it did not lead to the kind of orderly, efficient, monetary system that developed in Scotland.

And the experience of the rest of the country is even less favorable to regarding the Scottish experience as highly relevant to the circumstances of the U.S. in the early decades of the nineteenth century. Various degrees of laissez-faire prevailed in the several states, but nowhere did it lead to unlimited liability, freely interconvertible bank notes, security of both note holders and depositors from loss, and the other favorable characteristics of the Scottish banking system.

Rockoff, Rolnick and Weber, and King may well be right that wildcat banking in the first half of the nineteenth century was less widespread and extensive than earlier writers made it out to be. They may also be correct that the bank failures that occurred owed far more to the legal conditions imposed on bank note issues – namely, that they be 'backed' by state or U.S. bonds – and the subsequent depreciation in value of the bonds of a number of states than to irresponsible wildcat banking. Yet none of their evidence is directly relevant to the question of how banking and currency issue would have developed in the absence of state legislation.

Further, conditions have changed drastically in the past century and a half in ways that are particularly relevant to the question whether financial intermediaries should be prohibited from issuing inside money in the form of hand-to-hand currency [our point 2(a) in section 1]. We are no longer dealing with a sparsely settled country in which travel is slow and communication between distant points involves long delays. We now have instant communication and rapid means of transport. Book entries have replaced the physical transfer of currency or specie as the principal means of discharging monetary obligations. From being the primary medium of exchange, currency has become the counterpart of a minor fraction of aggregate transactions. Private institutions, both banks and non-banks, issue inside money in the form of traveler's checks redeemable on demand in outside money. The value of such traveler's checks outstanding is now included in the official estimates of all monetary aggregates broader than the monetary base (equal to outside money).[12] The possibility – and reality – of fraud by financial institutions remains, but under current conditions it seems unlikely to be more serious for hand-to-hand currency than for deposits.

---

[12] For banks, the Federal Reserve statistics include traveler's checks with demand deposits, so no separate estimate of their amount is available. Traveler's checks of non-bank issuers total about 3 percent of total currency, less than 1 percent of total M1.

What was a burning issue a century or two ago has therefore become a relatively minor issue today. Moreover, the arguments by Klein and Hayek discussed in the preceding section are far more persuasive with respect to permitting the issuance of hand-to-hand inside money than with respect to the possibility that the private market might produce fiduciary outside money, i.e., a non-commodity outside money. While we therefore see no reason currently to prohibit banks from issuing hand-to-hand currency, there is no pressure by banks or other groups to gain that privilege. The question of government monopoly of hand-to-hand currency is likely to remain a largely dead issue.

The more important questions currently are the other two under this heading: namely, the restrictions, if any, that government should impose on financial intermediaries and the necessity or desirability of a 'lender of last resort'. Whatever conclusions one may reach about these issues, it seems to us, would currently be valid regardless of the form of the liabilities issued by the financial intermediaries.

In respect of these questions, conditions have changed much less drastically – as the recent liquidity crises arising out of the problems of Continental Illinois Bank and the failure of Home State Savings in Ohio vividly illustrate. These liquidity crises are of the same genus as those that occurred repeatedly during the nineteenth century. Their very different outcomes – no significant spread to other institutions in the Continental Illinois episode; the permanent closing of many Ohio savings and loans and temporary closing of all of them in the quantitatively far smaller Ohio episode – reflect the different way they were handled – and that too evokes historical echoes.

Governor Celeste of Ohio would have benefited greatly from reading and following Walter Bagehot's (1873) famous advice on how to handle an 'internal drain': 'A panic', he wrote, 'in a word, is a species of neuralgia, and according to the rules of science you must not starve it. The holders of the cash reserve must be ready not only to keep it for their own liabilities, but to advance it most freely for the liabilities of others' [Bagehot (1873, p. 51)].

The run on the Ohio savings and loan associations precipitated by the failure of Home State Savings could have been promptly stemmed if Bagehot's advice had been followed. It was only necessary for Governor Celeste to arrange with the Federal Reserve Bank of Cleveland and the commercial banks of Ohio – who were apparently more than willing – to lend currency and its equivalent to the savings and loans on the collateral of their temporarily illiquid but sound assets. Once the savings and loans demonstrated their ability to meet all demands of depositors for cash, the unusual demand would have evaporated – as many historical examples demonstrate, including, most recently, the stemming of the liquidity crisis following the Continental Illinois episode.

Instead, Governor Celeste blundered by declaring a savings and loan holiday, repeating the mistaken Federal Reserve policies of 1931 to 1933, ending in the 1933 bank holiday. As in that case, the final result of not recognizing the differences between a liquidity and a solvency crisis will doubtless be the failure or liquidation of many savings and loans that would have been sound and solvent in the absence of the savings and loan holiday.

These episodes show that what used to be called 'the inherent instability' of a fractional reserve banking system is, unfortunately, still alive and well. What they do not show, and what is still an open question, is whether a government 'lender of last resort' – a central bank – is necessary and desirable as a cure. It did not prove to be a cure in the U.S. in the 1930s; it did in the Continental Illinois case, as well as in some earlier episodes. And, whether a satisfactory cure or not, is the emergence of a 'lender of last resort' a likely or unavoidable consequence of financial development?

In a recent paper, Charles Goodhart, after surveying a wide range of historical evidence, including the studies we have referred to earlier, concludes that the emergence of 'lenders of last resort' in the form of central banks was a natural and desirable development arising from the very characteristics of a fractional reserve banking system. The theoretical argument is straightforward and well-known. It rests on the distinction, already referred to, between a liquidity and solvency crisis. A bank or any other institution faces a problem of *solvency* if its liabilities exceed the value of its assets. The magnitude of the problem is measured by the difference between the two. That difference may be a small fraction of total liabilities, perhaps even less than the equity of the shareholders, so that if the assets could be liquidated in an orderly fashion the institution could pay off all other liabilities in full or for that matter continue as a going institution. The special feature of a fractional-reserve bank is that the bulk of its liabilities are payable on demand – either by contract or usage. Hence, even in the special case assumed, it will face a *liquidity* problem if its depositors demand payment. Moreover, the bank's liquidity problem will be far larger in magnitude than its solvency problem.[13] It cannot satisfy its depositors unless it can in some way convert its temporarily illiquid assets into cash.

A liquidity problem is not likely to remain confined to a single bank. The difficulty of one bank gives rise to fears about others, whose depositors, not well-informed about the banks' condition, seek to convert their deposits into cash. A full-blown liquidity crisis of major dimensions can be prevented only if depositors can somehow be reassured. An individual bank may be able to reassure its depositors by borrowing cash on the collateral of its sound assets from other banks and meeting all demands on it. But if the crisis is widespread, that recourse is not available. Some outside source of cash is necessary. A

---

[13] For example, Continental Illinois had total deposit liabilities of close to $30 billion as of December 31, 1983, and non-performing loans of less than $2 billion. Its solvency problem was still smaller, given the presence of an equity cushion.

central bank with the power to create outside money is potentially such a source.

After the Federal Reserve in the early 1930s failed to perform the function for which it had been established, the U.S. enacted Federal Deposit Insurance as an alternative way to reassure depositors and thereby prevent a widespread liquidity crisis. That device worked effectively for decades, so long as banks were closely regulated – and incidentally sheltered from competition – and so long as inflation remained moderate and relatively stable. It has become less and less effective as deregulation proceeded in an environment of high and variable inflation. In the Continental Illinois case, it had to be supplemented by the Federal Reserve as 'lender of last resort'.

Insurance of depositors against bank insolvency is of a magnitude that is well within the capacity of private casualty insurance. It could allow for differences among banks in the riskiness of their assets much more effectively than government insurance [see Ely (1985a, b)].

A liquidity crisis, whether or not it arises out of an insolvency crisis, as it did with Continental Illinois and Home State Savings of Ohio, and whether or not it spreads to solvent banks, is a different matter. In the U.S., prior to the Federal Reserve, it was dealt with by a concerted agreement among banks to suspend convertibility of deposits into cash – to pay deposits only 'through the clearing house'. In some other countries, such as Canada, nationwide branch banks (subject to extensive government regulation) have preserved confidence sufficiently to avoid liquidity crises.

The U.S. has been almost unique in preserving a unit banking system with numerous independent banks. The current pressures for deregulation and the widening competition in financial intermediation is changing that situation. The barriers against interstate banking are weakening and very likely will ultimately fall completely. Such 'non-banks' as Sears Roebuck, Merrill-Lynch, and so on, in most respects are the equivalent of nationwide branch banks. These developments, as they mature, will simultaneously lessen the probability of liquidity crises and increase the magnitude and severity of those that occur. It is therefore far from clear what implications they have for the 'lender of last resort' function.

Vera Smith (1936, p. 148) rightly concluded: 'A central bank is not a natural product of banking development. It is imposed from outside or comes into being as a result of Government favours.' However, as Goodhart's (1985) exhaustive survey of the historical experience indicates, a central bank or its equivalent, once established, reluctantly assumed the responsibility of serving as a lender of last resort because of the reality or possibility of a liquidity crisis. What is impressive about his evidence is the wide range of circumstances – in respect of political and economic arrangements – and the long span of time for which that has proved the outcome.

In practice, the lender of last resort function has been combined with control over government outside money. Such a combination has obvious advantages.

However, in principle the two functions could be separated, and some proposals for monetary reform would require such separation, if the government were to continue to serve as a lender of last resort.[14]

The existence of a lender of last resort has clearly enabled banks having access to the lender to operate on thinner margins of capital and cash reserves than they would otherwise have deemed prudent. This fact has been used as an argument both for and against the government assuming lender of last resort functions – for, as a way of lowering the cost of financial intermediation; against, as providing an implicit subsidy to financial intermediation. It has also led to the imposition of required reserve ratios, which has turned a subsidy into a tax by increasing the demand for non-interest bearing outside money.

Deregulation of financial intermediaries so that they are free to pay whatever interest is required to obtain funds and to offer a variety of services over broad geographical areas seems clearly desirable on grounds of market efficiency. The open question is whether that is feasible or desirable without a continued role for government in such matters as requiring registration, provision of information, and the imposition of capital or reserve requirements. Moreover, certainly during a transition period, deregulation increases the danger of liquidity crises and so may strengthen the case for a governmental 'lender of last resort'.[15] That role could perhaps be phased out if market developments provided protection through insurance or otherwise against the new risks that might arise in a deregulated financial system.

Goodhart's argument (1985) that such an outcome, whether desirable or not, is not achievable, can be put to the test, by enlarging the opportunities for private insurance of deposit liabilities. If such insurance became widespread, risk-adjusted premiums could render regulatory restrictions unnecessary. It is more difficult to envision the market arrangements that would eliminate the pressure for a government 'lender of last resort'.

4. The future of fiat money

As noted earlier, the nations of the world are for the first time in history essentially unanimously committed to a purely fiat monetary standard. Will Fisher's 1911 generalization that 'irredeemable paper money has almost invariably proved a curse to the country employing it' hold true for the current situation? In some ways that seems to us the most interesting and important current scientific question in the monetary area. How it is answered will

[14] For example, the proposal to freeze the amount of high-powered money. See Friedman (1984b, pp. 48–52).

[15] This point is stressed by Summers in his comment on King (1983). He contrasts the possible gain in micro-efficiency of private money with what he regards as the likely loss in macro-efficiency through increased economic instability. However, he simply takes it for granted that government control of money reduces rather than increases economic instability. That is, to put it mildly, far from clear on the basis of historical experience.

largely determine the relevance of the issues discussed in the preceding two sections.

We do not believe it is possible to give a confident and unambiguous answer. The experience of such countries as Argentina, Brazil, Chile, Mexico and Israel are contemporary examples of Fisher's generalization, but they are all lesser developed countries that except for chronology may have more in common with the countries Fisher had in mind than with the more advanced Western countries. The experience of those more advanced countries – Japan, the United States and the members of the Common Market – gives grounds for greater optimism. The pressures on government that led to the destruction of earlier irredeemable paper moneys are every bit as strong today in these countries than earlier – most clearly, the pressure to obtain resources for government use without levying explicit taxes. However, developments in the economy, and in financial markets in particular, have produced counter-pressures that reduce the political attractiveness of paper money inflation.

The most important such developments, we believe, are the greater sensitivity and sophistication of both the financial markets and the public at large. There has indeed been an information revolution, which has greatly reduced the cost of acquiring information and has enabled expectations to respond more rapidly and accurately to developments.

Historically, inflation has added to government resources in three ways: first, through the paper money issues themselves (i.e., the implicit inflation tax on outside money holdings); second, through the unvoted increase in explicit taxes as a result of bracket creep; third, by the reduction in the real value of outstanding debt issued at interest rates that did not include sufficient allowance for future inflation. The economic, political and financial developments of recent decades have eroded the potency of all three sources of revenue.

Though outside money remained remarkably constant at about 10 percent of national income from the middle of the past century to the Great Depression, and then rose sharply to a peak of about 25 percent in 1946, it has been on a declining trend since the end of World War II, and is currently about 7 percent of national income. However, for a modern society, with the current level of government taxes and spending, this component is perhaps the least important of the three. Even if outside money as a fraction of income did not decline as a result of inflation which it unquestionably would, a 10 percent per year increase in outside money would yield as revenue to the government only about seven-tenths of 1 percent of national income.

The second component of revenue has very likely been more important. Past rates of inflation have subjected low and moderate income persons to levels of personal income tax that could never have been voted explicitly. However, the result has been political pressure that has led to the indexation of the personal income tax schedule for inflation, which largely eliminates this source of revenue.

The third component has also been extremely important. At the end of World War II, the funded federal debt amounted to 6 percent more than a year's national income. By 1967 it was down to about 32 percent of national income despite repeated 'deficits' in the official federal budget. Since then it has risen as deficits have continued and increased, but even so only to about 36 percent currently. The reason for the decline in the deficit ratio was partly real growth but mostly the reduction through inflation in the real value of debt that has been issued at interest rates that *ex post* proved negative in real terms.

The potency of this source of revenue has been sharply eroded by the developments in the financial markets referred to earlier. Market pressures have made it difficult for the government to issue long-term debt at low nominal rates. One result is that the average term to maturity of the federal debt has tended to decline. Except under wartime conditions, it is far more difficult to convert interest rates on short-term debt into *ex post* negative real rates by unanticipated inflation than to do so for long-term debt. And for both short- and long-term debt, producing unanticipated inflation of any magnitude for any substantial period has become far more difficult after several decades of historically high and variable inflation than it was even a decade or so ago, when the public's perceptions still reflected the effect of a relatively stable price level over long periods.

In the U.K., the resort to government bonds adjusted for inflation eliminates more directly the possibility that government can benefit from *ex post* negative real interest rates. There have been pressures on the U.S. Treasury to issue similar securities. Those pressures would undoubtedly intensify if the U.S. were again to experience high and variable inflation.

Perhaps if, instead, we experienced several decades of a relatively stable long-run price level, asset holders would again be lulled into regarding nominal interest rates as equivalent to real interest rates. But that is certainly not the case today.

To summarize, inflation has become far less attractive as a political option. Given a voting public very sensitive to inflation, it may currently be politically profitable to establish monetary arrangements that will make the present inconvertible paper standard an exception to Fisher's generalization.

That is a source of promise; it is far from a guarantee that Fisher's generalization is obsolete. Governments have often acted under short-run pressures in ways that have had strongly adverse long-run consequences. Israel today offers a conspicuous example. It continues to resort to inflation under conditions that make inflation a poor source of revenue, if, indeed, not itself a drain.

5. Conclusion

To return to where we started, Friedman's list of the 'good reasons' why 'monetary arrangements have seldom been left to the market', what alterations are indicated by the experience and writings of the past quarter century?

58   *M. Friedman and A.J. Schwartz, Has government any role in money?*

Point [1], 'the resource cost of a pure commodity currency and hence its tendency to become purely fiduciary', has in one sense fully worked itself out. All money is now fiduciary. Yet the resource cost has not been eliminated; it remains present because private individuals hoard precious metals and gold and silver coins as a hedge against the inflation that they fear may result from a wholly fiduciary money. To go farther afield, a new resource cost has been added because a purely fiduciary currency reduces the long-run predictability of the price level. That cost takes the form of resources employed in futures and other financial markets to provide the additional hedging facilities demanded by individuals, business enterprises and governmental bodies. It would be a paradoxical reversal if these new forms of resource costs produced pressure for the reintroduction of commodity elements into money as a way to reduce the resource costs of the monetary system. We do not know of any study that has tried to compare the resource costs of the pre-World War I monetary system and the post-1971 monetary system. That is a challenging task for research [Friedman (1986)].

Point [2], 'the peculiar difficulty of enforcing contracts involving promises to pay that serve as a medium of exchange and of preventing fraud in respect of them', remains alive and well, as the recent Continental Illinois and Ohio Savings and Loan episodes demonstrate, and, more indirectly, the much publicized failures in the government bond market. However, the character of the difficulty has changed. It no longer seems any more serious for hand-to-hand currency than for deposits or other monetary or quasi-monetary promises to pay. Moreover, it is now taken for granted that governments (i.e., taxpayers) will completely shield holders of deposit liabilities from loss, whether due to fraud or other causes. The improvements in communication and in the extent and sophistication of financial markets have in some respects increased, in others decreased, the difficulty of enforcing contracts and preventing fraud. They have certainly made it more difficult politically for governments to remain uninvolved.

Point [3], 'the technical monopoly character of a pure fiduciary currency which makes essential the setting of some external limit on its amount', has been questioned, far more persuasively, we believe, for currencies convertible into a commodity, than for a pure fiduciary currency. We continue to believe that the possibility that private issuers can (in either sense of that term) provide competing, efficient and safe fiduciary currencies with no role for governmental monetary authorities remains to be demonstrated. As a result we believe that this is the most important challenge posed by the elimination of a commodity-based outside money.

Point [4], 'the pervasive character of money' and the 'important effects on parties other than those directly involved' in the issuance of money, has not been questioned. What has been questioned, and remains very much an open question, is what institutional arrangements would minimize those third party effects. A strong case can be made that government involvement has made matters worse rather than better both directly and indirectly because the failure of monetary authorities to pursue a stable non-inflationary policy renders performance by private intermediaries equally unstable. As yet, there has developed no consensus on desirable alternative arrangements, let alone any effective political movement to adopt alternative arrangements.

Our own conclusion – like that of Walter Bagehot and Vera Smith – is that leaving monetary and banking arrangements to the market would have produced a more satisfactory outcome than was actually achieved through governmental involvement. Nevertheless, we also believe that the same forces that prevented that outcome in the past will continue to prevent it in the future. Whether those forces produce or prevent major changes in monetary institutions will depend on developments in the monetary area in the next several decades – and that crystal ball is rendered even more murky than usual by our venture into largely unexplored monetary terrain.

The failure to recognize that we are in unexplored terrain gives an air of unreality and paradox to the whole discussion of private money and free banking. Its basis was well expressed by Walter Bagehot over a century ago, in the context of the free banking issue. Said Bagehot (1873, pp. 66–67, 68–69):

'We are so accustomed to a system of banking, dependent for its cardinal function on a single bank, that we can hardly conceive of any other. But the natural system – that which would have sprung up if Government had let banking alone – is that of many banks of equal or not altogether unequal size....

'I shall be at once asked – Do you propose a revolution? Do you propose to abandon the one-reserve system, and create anew a many-reserve system? My plain answer is, that I do not propose it: I know it would be childish...[A]n immense system of credit, founded on the Bank of England as its pivot and its basis, now exists. The English people and foreigners too, trust it implicitly...The whole rests on an instinctive confidence generated by use and years....[I]f some calamity swept it away, generations must elapse before at all the same trust would be placed in any other equivalent. A many-reserve system, if some miracle should put it down in Lombard Street, would seem monstrous there. Nobody would understand it, or confide in it. *Credit is a power which may grow, but cannot be constructed*' (italics added).

Substitute 'unit of account' or 'outside money' for 'credit' in the italicized sentence and it is directly relevant to the outside money issue. What has happened to the role of gold since Bagehot wrote, the way in which it has been replaced by a purely fiat money, is a striking application of Bagehot's proposition. It took 'generations' for confidence in gold 'generated by use and years' to erode and for confidence to develop in the pieces of paper which for many yers after it was meaningless continued to contain the promise that 'The United States of America will pay to the bearer on demand —— dollars', or words to that effect. Now they simply state 'Federal Reserve Note', 'One Dollar' or '—— Dollars' plus the statement 'This note is legal tender for all debts, public and private'. And even now, a half-century after the effective end of the domestic convertibility of government issued money into gold, the Federal Reserve still lists the 'Gold Stock', valued at an artificial 'legal' price among the 'Factors Supplying Reserve Funds'. Like old soldiers, gold does not die; it just fades away.

Similarly, as already noted, there are no effective legal obstacles currently in the U.S. to the development of a private 'real' (i.e., inflation adjusted) standard as an alternative to the paper dollar, yet, absent a major monetary catastrophe, it will take decades for such an alternative to become a serious competitor to the paper dollar, if it ever does.

The element of paradox arises particularly with respect to the views of Hayek [see especially Hayek (1979, vol. 3)]. His latest works have been devoted to explaining how gradual cultural evolution – a widespread invisible hand process – produces institutions and social arrangements that are far superior to those that are deliberately constructed by explicit human design. Yet he recommends in his recent publications on competitive currencies replacing the results of such an invisible hand process by a deliberate construct – the introduction of currency competition. This paradox affects us all. On the one hand, we are observers of the forces shaping society; on the other, we are participants and want ourselves to shape society.

If there is a resolution to this paradox, it occurs at times of crisis. Then and only then are major changes in monetary and other institutions likely or even possible. What changes then occur depend on the alternatives that are recog- nized as available. Decades of academic argument in favor of eliminating Regulation Q and, in a very different area, adopting flexible exchange rates had little or no impact on institutional arrangements until crises made major changes inevitable. The existence of well articulated cases for these changes made them realistic options.

Similarly, the wide-ranging discussion of possible major monetary reforms will have little effect on the course of events if the present fiat system into which the world has drifted operates in a reasonably satisfactory manner – producing neither major inflations nor major depressions. However, the possibility that it will not do so is very real – particularly that it will fall victim to Fisher's generalization and lead to major inflation. When and if it does, what happens will depend critically on the options that have been explored by the intellectual community and have become intellectually respec- table. That – the widening of the range of options and keeping them available – is, we believe, the major contribution of the burst of scholarly interest in monetary reform.

References

Acheson, K. and J. Chant, 1973, Bureaucratic theory and the choice of central bank goals: The case of the Bank of Canada, Journal of Money, Credit, and Banking 5, 637–655.
Bagehot, W., 1873, Lombard Street (P.S. King, London).
Brennan, G. and J.M. Buchanan, 1981, Monopoly in money and inflation (Institute of Economic Affairs, London).
Brunner, K., 1976, Programmatic suggestions for a 'political economy of inflation', in: Comment, Journal of Law and Economics 18, 851–857.
Buchanan, J.M., 1984, Can policy activism succeed? A public choice perspective, Paper presented at Federal Reserve Bank of St. Louis Conference on The Monetary vs. Fiscal Policy Debate.
Ely, B., 1985a, No deposit reform, no return to stable banking, Wall Street Journal, March 5.
Ely, B., 1985b, Yes – private sector depositor protection is a viable alternative to Federal Deposit Insurance, Paper presented at Conference on Bank Structure and Competition, Chicago, IL, May 2–3.
Fisher, I., 1929, The purchasing power of money, New ed. (Macmillan, New York).
Friedman, M., 1951, Commodity-reserve currency, Journal of Political Economy 59, 203–232. Reprinted in: M. Friedman, 1953, Essays in positive economics (University of Chicago Press, Chicago, IL) 204–250.
Friedman, M., 1959, A program for monetary stability (Fordham University Press, New York).
Friedman, M., 1984a, Financial futures markets and tabular standards, Journal of Political Economy 92, 165–167.
Friedman, M., 1984b, Monetary policy for the 1980s, in: J.H. Moore, ed., To promote prosperity: U.S. domestic policy in the mid-1980s (Hoover Institution Press, Stanford, CA) 40–54.
Friedman, M., 1986, The resource cost of irredeemable paper money, Journal of Political Economy, forthcoming.
Friedman, M. and A.J. Schwartz, 1963, A monetary history of the United States, 1867–1960 (Princeton University Press, Princeton, NJ).
Goodhart, C.A.E., 1985, The evolution of central banks: A natural development? Working paper (London School of Economics, London).
Hammond, B., 1957, Banks and politics in America (Princeton University Press, Princeton, NJ).
Hayek, F., 1943, A commodity reserve currency, Economic Journal 53, 176–184.
Hayek, F., 1976, Denationalization of money (Institute of Economic Affairs, London). 1978, 2nd extended ed.
Hayek, F., 1979, Law, legislation and liberty, especially vol. 3: The political order of a free people (University of Chicago Press, Chicago, IL).
Hetzel, R.L., 1984, The formulation of monetary policy, Working paper (Federal Reserve Bank of Richmond, VA).
Jevons, W.S., 1890, Money and the mechanism of exchange, 9th ed. (Kegan Paul, London).
Kane, E.J., 1980, Politics and Fed policymaking, Journal of Monetary Economics 6, 199–211.
King, R.G., 1983, On the economics of private money, Journal of Monetary Economics 12, 127–158.
Klein, B., 1974, The competitive supply of money, Journal of Money, Credit, and Banking 6, 423–453.
Klein, B., 1976, Competing monies, Journal of Money, Credit, and Banking 8, 513–519.
McCallum, B., 1985, Bank deregulation, accounting systems of exchange and the unit of account: A critical review, Working paper (National Bureau of Economic Research).
McCulloch, J.H., 1980, The ban on indexed bonds, 1973–77, American Economic Review 70, 1018–1021.
Martino, A., 1984, Toward monetary stability?, Economia Internazionale 37, 1–16.
Rockoff, H., 1975, The free banking era: A re-examination (Arno Press, New York).

Rolnick, A.J. and W.E. Weber, 1983, New evidence on the free banking era, American Economic Review 73, 1080–1091.

Smith, V.C., 1936, The rationale of central banking (P.S. King, London).

Summers, L.H., 1983, Comments, Journal of Monetary Economics 12, 159–162.

Triffin, R., 1984, The European monetary system: Tombstone or cornerstone? in: The international monetary system: Forty years after Bretton Woods, Conference series no. 28, 127–173 (Federal Reserve Bank of Boston, Boston, MA).

Vaubel, R., 1984, The government's money monopoly: Externalities or natural monopoly?, Kyklos 37, 27–58.

White, L.H. 1984a, Free banking in Britain: Theory, experience, and debate, 1800–1845 (Cambridge University Press, New York).

White, L.H., 1984b, Competitive payment systems and the unit of account, American Economic Review 74, 699–712.

White, R.W.R., 1979, Money and the New Zealand economy, Reserve Bank of New Zealand Bulletin, 371–374.

[25]

CENTRAL BANKING AND THE FED:
A PUBLIC CHOICE PERSPECTIVE
Richard E. Wagner

This paper examines central banking in general and the Federal Reserve system in particular from the perspective of the theory of public choice. It is common to rationalize central banking as being necessary to offset the market failures that would otherwise plague a competitive regime of free banking. By overcoming problems of public goods and externalities, central banking would raise the aggregate level of wealth in a society, in much the same manner as the effective governmental provision of security of property and contract would raise it.

The theory of public choice, however, explains that the mere development of a rationalization or justification for a regulation or institution is not the same thing as an explanation of what that regulation or institution actually accomplishes. What is actually accomplished, in economic regulation generally, as well as in banking regulation in particular, depends upon the incentives that characterize a particular institutional or constitutional framework. For instance, the development of central banking could represent an outcome of a rent-seeking political process. In this case the average level of wealth might be lower than it could be under some alternative institutional regime, but there would be a controlling subset of the population that would be better off under the present regime.

This paper first explores possible disparities between the apologetics of central banking and its actual accomplishments. It then examines the Federal Reserve system in particular, arguing that the support for central banking seems more likely to be explained by the economic theory of rent-seeking than by the theories of market failure and public goods.

Cato Journal, Vol. 6, No. 2 (Fall 1986). Copyright © Cato Institute. All rights reserved.
The author is Professor of Economics at Florida State University.

Rationalization, Explanation, and Central Banking

It is often claimed that a competitive system of free banking will be plagued by problems of public goods and externalities. The resulting market failure is then used to rationalize or justify government control over the money and banking industry. A rationalization for governmental involvement in the supply of money is not, of course, an explanation of the actual conduct of government with respect to the supply of money. Moreover, the efficiency basis for governmental involvement in the supply of money has some problematical aspects. These can be seen by considering four major elements in the rationalization of central banking, namely: the natural monopoly character of money; the social saving through the development of fiat money; the promotion of economic stability through an activist monetary policy; and the external diseconomies that would otherwise plague a competitive system of free banking.

The Natural Monopoly Rationalization

The assertion that communication becomes less costly as the number of languages in use declines seems to be intuitively obvious, much like the assertion that the sun rises in the east and sets in the west was long regarded as intuitively obvious. And the cognitive basis of the assertion about a common language may be no firmer than that of the movement of the sun. Nonetheless, it is something that is generally believed, and this same principle is commonly extended to money by asserting that exchange becomes less costly as the number of media of exchange in a society decreases. The argument that there is a saving in transaction costs through the adoption of a common medium of exchange is not, of course, a rationalization for governmental provision of that medium. As Carl Menger (1892) explains, money arose through ordinary economic processes and not through some collective act. While both money and lighthouses have often served as archetypical illustrations of public goods, the historical record shows clearly that both have been supplied through ordinary market institutions.[1]

There are numerous cases in which we are all better off by some degree of standardization, but for the most part that standardization arises naturally through competitive market processes. However, in some cases it might be possible to imagine improvements upon the standardization that results from competition. Typewriter keyboards might provide one such illustration. In the early days of typewriters

---

[1]See Coase (1974) for a discussion of the lighthouse example.

BANKING AND PUBLIC CHOICE

there were numerous arrangements of the keyboard. Gradually the present keyboard came to dominate. It was selected primarily for mechanical reasons of avoiding the jamming of keys; it is not the arrangement that would maximize typing speed if the jamming of keys were no concern, as it no longer is. However, such an act of imagination does not translate automatically into an explanation of reality. With respect to the typewriter, for instance, if the present value of the gain from the introduction of a new keyboard were substantial, there would surely exist profit opportunities for developing ways of marketing that superior product to beginning typists, even if not to experienced typists. And with the passage of time, the new keyboards would become increasingly dominant.

With respect to money, a claim that government is improving upon the money that has arisen through usage, while possibly correct, should likewise be examined carefully, for the introduction of that new money might serve quite different purposes. During the French Revolution, for example, the government offered what it called a monetary improvement, the assignat, but it encountered public resistance. As Andrew Dickson White (1912, pp. 78–79) observed:

> It [the Convention] decreed that any person selling gold or silver coin, or making any difference in any transaction between paper and specie, should be imprisoned in irons for six years; that anyone who refused to accept a payment in assignats, or accepted assignats at a discount, should pay a fine of three thousand francs; and that anyone commiting this crime a second time should pay a fine of six thousand francs and suffer imprisonment twenty years in irons. . . .[T]he Convention decreed, in May 1794, that the death penalty should be inflicted on any person convicted of "having asked, before a bargain was concluded, in what money payment was to be made.

Finally, Roland Vaubel (1986, p. 933) argues that if money production were a natural monopoly, there would be no need to restrict enrty by giving government a monopoly on high-powered money. The fact is, says Vaubel, that "we do not even know whether money is a natural monopoly good," and entry barriers "prevent us from finding out." This has certainly been the case in modern democratic states.

The Social Saving Rationalization

Even though money might arise through competitive market processes, there is a potential social saving from replacing specie with fiat. A system of free banking might well have developed in which bank notes represented claims on gold or some other commodity. Part of the stock of gold would have been held as reserves or base

CATO JOURNAL

money, with the remainder being used for nonmonetary purposes. The average wealth of the members of this society could be increased if the gold that was used for monetary purposes were replaced by what Luigi Einaudi (1953) characterized as imaginary or political money—so long as that replacement operated "perfectly." Under a perfectly working system of imaginary money, the society will experience a positive wealth effect as the stock of monetary gold is replaced by political fiat, thereby releasing that monetary gold for nonmonetary uses. The possibility of such a saving, however, does not imply the realization of that saving. Consider Einaudi's characterization of the replacement of real money with imaginary money: "Instead of a crude but certain monetary unit like the grain or gram or pure gold, it [imaginary money] established an abstract unit which the public fancied to be stable. Princes could manipulate this monetary device for their own advantage, although they acted as if it were for the benefit of the public" (p. 260).

Roger Garrison (1983) is correct in his observation that a perfectly working system of fiat money will be superior to a system based on commodity money. But what are the institutional requisites for such perfection (or even near-perfection)? The problem, of course, is one of trust and reliance. Suppose someone were to say that there would be a social saving from replacing our present system of personal security, in which resources are tied up in locks, guns, dogs, police, and the like, with a system of trust and love. This might be thought of as buffoonery, and it might provide material for political speeches or churchly sermons, but it would not be thought of as being grounded in reality. Merely pointing out the potential social saving that would result if people did not feel a need for investing in various forms of personal security does not imply that there is any way of realizing that saving.

Why is it any different in the case of money? Why is the claim that fiat money offers a potential social saving vis-à-vis a commodity standard not greeted in the same manner as the aforementioned claim about achieving a social saving by replacing locks and dogs with love and trust? Both propositions are certainly true, but do we know any more about how to achieve the social saving from replacing a commodity money with a fiat money than we know about achieving the social saving from replacing locks and dogs with love and trust?

In the case of commodity standards, there are various constraints grounded in self-interest that limit note issue and thereby make it reasonable for people to trust their banks. But this trust is purchased at a price: audits, financial reports, investigations, occasional bank failures, and the like are part of the process of the production of trust and reliability. The process for producing trust and reliability under a fiat standard encounters the problem of counterfeiting. If government fiat substitutes for a money commodity, what, if anything, is there to restrain the increase in monetary claims? Private counterfeiting is limited, though hardly eliminated, by a system of punishment for detection. But the interests that would lead to counterfeiting privately are exactly the same as those that would lead to counterfeiting publicly: counterfeiting will take place so long as the value of the claims to resources exceeds the cost of counterfeiting, which in turn includes both the punishment costs and the opportunity costs of the resources invested in counterfeiting.

The Economic Stability Rationalization

A further advantage often claimed for a regulated system of central banking over a competitive system is that a central bank's control over base money makes it possible to achieve economic stability. If people were suddenly to increase their demand for money, the real balance effect would operate as a corrective market process, of course, but in a system of competitive free banking there is no supplementary action that individual banks could take to speed the corrective process. It is often claimed, however, that a policy of monetary expansion by the central bank would speed that process of correction. Hence, an economic order characterized by a central bank would have a higher level of average wealth than one characterized by free banking, because there would be less wastage through economic disruption and discoordination.

Once again, however, merely to state a hypothetical case is not equivalent to making a real case. While the rational expectations analysis of anticipated policy measures raises serious questions about the scope for promoting stability through an activist policy, that line of analysis does not seem to go far enough in its critique of activist monetary policy, due perhaps to the highly aggregated nature of those models. To speak of "output" or "employment" and their stabilization neglects important questions of economic coordination within a complex, time-dependent structure of production. It is not sufficient to describe stability in terms of some aggregate output or employment; rather, it is necessary to describe the *pattern* of production and employment—and hence, the allocation of resources among competing uses. In other words, a policy that promotes stability is not a program that smooths out fluctuations in some single, homogeneous item called output, but rather is a program that promotes more fully the coordination of economic activities by millions of people scattered throughout the nation and even the world, in a setting in which it is impossible for any person or committee actually to orchestrate that coordination.

As Don Lavoie (1985) explains, the theory of economic calculation shows that a truly hierarchically organized economy is impossible. Although it is possible to understand the general processes by which we can feel assured about our ability to eat our morning's breakfast, it would be impossible for anyone even to describe the detailed, coordinated actions of everyone involved in making breakfast possible, let alone those involved in organizing more complicated activities. But if an activist policy of economic coordination, that is, central planning, is impossible, how is an activist monetary policy any more possible? At the very least, for an activist monetary policy to be possible, it would seem necessary to be able to describe in detail how the entire structure of economic activity is affected by various monetary changes.

The External Diseconomy Rationalization

It is commonly claimed that in a system of free banking one bank will be able to impose costs on other banks and depositors, with the result that people in general will be poorer under a system of free banking than they would under a central bank. This claim posits an individual bank that has issued an excessive amount of notes, and suggests that the inability of depositors of one or a few banks to redeem their deposits for specie will spread fear to other depositors. If individual depositors are relatively uninformed about the solvency of any particular bank, they might use the observation that one bank is insolvent as evidence that their own bank is insolvent, or at least is less solvent than they had previously believed. This is not to say that individual banks have any inherent tendency toward excessive note issue; the clearing of notes against bank reserves can be recognized as constraining the issue of notes by individual banks. Rather it is only to say that the issue of excessive notes by one or a few banks can threaten the stability of those banks that did not overissue bank notes, but which cannot convince their depositors that this is so.

The problem, at base, is one of uninformed depositors and banks with no means of convincing depositors to the contrary. Hence, a central bank is rationalized as being necessary to assure the solvency of the entire system by acting as a lender of last resort, as well as by regulating the individual banks to prevent excessive note issue. For such informational problems to arise, it must be impossible for banks readily to transmit knowledge about their solvency. The theoretical possibility of such inherent instability in free banking is one more conceptual illustration of the "lemon" problem described by George

BANKING AND PUBLIC CHOICE

Akerlof (1970). In the lemon model, the sellers of used cars know the quality of their cars but the buyers of cars know only the average quality of used cars and know nothing about the quality of any particular car. The persistence of such a state of asymmetric information is, of course, inconsistent with the existence of a market for used cars, for only "lemons" will be offered for sale. What is noteworthy about the lemon problem is its counterfactual character, for the market for used cars has developed—through the organization of dealerships and the development of diagnostic services, among other things—in such a way that the lemon problem is suppressed.

It is the same with competitive banking. If depositors have no knowledge about the solvency of different banks, and so assume that all banks are equally (in)solvent, they would interpret a failure of one bank to pay its depositors as evidence that most or all banks are in a similar state. In such a setting panics will surely erupt, assuming that a banking system already exists. More generally, of course, it is hard to reconcile the assumption of conditions that lead to such inherent instability in free banking with the emergence and development of free banking in the first place. And even if it were costly for depositors to investigate the solvency of banks, it would be in the banks' interest to provide such information reliably.

On this point, Richard Timberlake (1984a) shows that clearinghouse associations arose during the latter half of the 19th century as a market response to the problems of providing reliable information and coping with uncertainties in the timing of payments. Ross Watts and Jerold Zimmerman (1983) have shown that the development of independent auditing had nothing to do with governmental regulation or taxation, but rather arose out of the interest of corporations in demonstrating to potential investors the reliability of their financial reports. And with respect to free banking, Arthur Rolnick and Warren Weber (1984, 1985) have shown that knowledge about bank solvency was readily available in easily understandable form. For instance, bank notes in Indiana, New York, and Wisconsin were strongly backed and they exchanged at par, whereas in Minnesota bank notes that were backed by weak railroad bonds exchanged well below par. The presumption of insufficient knowledge about the solvency of different banks is distinctly counterfactual.

The Fed and the Theory of Bureaucracy

The cognitive basis of the common justifications for central banking seems even weaker now than it did at the time of Vera Smith's (1936) critique of those justifications. To some extent this is due to our

525

improved knowledge of how free banking systems actually operated, as well as to the effort of economists to develop explanatory theories of public choice processes. In particular, public choice theory has revealed the systematic incongruities between normative justifications for particular policy measures and the positive explanation of the actual choice of particular policy measures. The remainder of this paper explores the process of central banking and the Fed's behavior from a public choice perspective. This section and the next rely, in turn, upon the economic theories of bureaucracy and legislation to examine Fed policymaking.

While the literature on bureaucracy that has examined central banks is still comparatively sparse, the popularity of central banks as a subject of examination seems to be growing. Consistent with the central thrust of the literature on bureaucracy, Mark Toma (1982) and William Shughart and Robert Tollison (1983) ask whether there is any direct relation between the well-being of Fed officials and the type of policies the Fed pursues. They both select the Fed's method of financing as being of pivotal importance. The Fed is not financed directly by budgetary appropriations, but rather through its interest earnings on the Treasury debt it holds, although the Fed returns the bulk of those earnings to the Treasury. As compared with the case where the central bank was financed by budgetary appropriations, the effect of the present form of financing might seem to impart an inflationary bias to the Fed, because increases in its holdings of government debt would increase the size of its budget, unless it returned all of the additional interest earnings to the Treasury.

In a similar presumption about the dependence of central bank conduct upon the incentives it faces, though with somewhat different empirical results, Michael Parkin and Robin Bade (1978) attempt to relate the inflationary tendencies of central banks to the degree to which they are controlled by the government. They find significantly lower inflation in West Germany and Switzerland, which in their judgment have the greatest degree of central bank independence among the nations examined. Furthermore, what Parkin and Bade found to be important was not the method by which the central bank was financed, but the degree of independence the bank had in appointing its board and making policy.[2] Moreover, Parkin (forthcom-

---

[2]Evidence on how the conduct of a central bank depends on the type of incentives it faces is also presented in Santoni's (1984) examination of the Bank of England from 1694 to 1913. Between 1694 and 1793 the Bank of England's profit-maximizing conduct occurred with a zero rate of inflation, as it did also from 1822 to 1913. But between 1793 and 1821 the Parliament created accommodating, inflationary incentives by suspending specie payments and taking over control of the money supply. This occurred during the Napoleonic Wars, and while inflationary finance has been popular during wars, the British did fight the Seven Years' War (1755—63) without inflationary finance.

BANKING AND PUBLIC CHOICE

ing) suggests that a *truly* independent central bank, which means a central bank that unwaveringly pursues a policy of stable money growth, will both achieve monetary stability and constrain the government's creation of deficits. If the central bank sticks with a rule of constant money growth despite the government's creation of budget deficits, the government's ability to sell bonds will eventually be constrained by the willingness of the public to hold those bonds.

The relationship between the central bank and the Treasury or government has been portrayed in stark relief by the "Unpleasant Monetarist Arithmetic" of Thomas Sargent and Neil Wallace (1981), which draws out the implications of the dominance-subordinance relationship between the central bank and the government for the course of budget deficits and money creation. Their model is fully consistent with Parkin's analysis of the ability of a truly independent central bank—that is, one that had both the will and the means to promote stable monetary growth—to constrain both the inflation rate and the ability of the government to engage in deficit finance.

But suppose the government is dominant. Sargent and Wallace model this possibility by assuming that the size of the budget deficit is exogenous to the monetary authority. Even if the monetary authority initially follows a stable money growth rule, it will eventually have to shift to a policy of deficit accommodation, because the public will be unwilling to buy the government bonds the deficit requires. Although money might be tight now, it will have to be looser in the future, under the presumption that the deficit is exogenous. Their use of the term "unpleasant arithmetic" expresses the possibility that if individuals generally expect an increase in future money growth due to the deficit, a current policy of tight money could actually be accompanied by an increase in current prices. But even if prices do not rise now, they will fall by less than what they should have fallen, as judged by monetary models that fail to take into account the present value consequences of the future behavior that is implicit in present policy actions.

A truly independent central bank that was dedicated to the promotion of monetary stability would constrain both government deficits and inflation. On the other hand, a central bank that was ultimately controlled by the government would accommodate the government's fiscal policies.[3] In the latter case, monetary policy (inflation) falls in line with politics (deficits). Since central banking institutions are chosen as part of the regulatory apparatus of government, it would seem doubtful that a government in which the pursuit of political

[3]On this point, see Brunner (1986) and Jordan (1986).

interest led it in expansionary directions would choose banking regulations that both made monetary policy truly independent of politics
and created incentives and constraints that led the monetary authority to promote monetary stability. An independent Fed is, within our
present political regime, surely a wholly imaginary construction.
After all, Congress established the Fed, and it could always change
the Fed whenever and however it wanted. It is surely more reasonable to say that Congress chooses and sustains one form of organization over another because the form it chooses advances more fully
the interests of a dominant set of its members.

Although it is surely reasonable to seek to explain Fed conduct in
terms of the costs and gains of different courses of conduct, it is also
ultimately unsatisfactory to consider the conduct of bureaus without
considering the conduct of their legislative sponsors. Congress created and oversees the Fed, and Congress chooses the method by
which the central bank is financed and its governors chosen. If the
Fed were acting contrary to the interests of its sponsors, those sponsors, principally the House and Senate banking committees, would
have an incentive to modify the Fed's incentive structure. If the
congressional sponsor did not want an inflationary bias, for example,
it would change the method by which the Fed is financed. Alternatively, if Congress approved of the inflationary bias but did not want
the Fed to capture the gains from inflation, it would require the Fed
to return its inflationary gain to the Treasury. Congress could then
decide who would receive the gains from inflation through the appropriations process. Since it is clearly costly for a sponsor to monitor
agencies, monitoring will tend to focus on relatively visible activities
(Lindsay 1976). In the case of the Fed, such things as the number of
employees are relatively visible, so it seems unlikely that the Fed
would be able to pursue an inflationary expansion of the monetary
base beyond what Congress would desire as a way of increasing its
own staff.

Legislation, Rent Seeking, and the Fed

With few exceptions governments have been involved in the regulation if not the direct production of money. Of course, the same
thing could be said about economic activity in general. The thesis
that in undertaking such regulation governments are offsetting externalities or providing public goods does not seem to have much support. This leaves for consideration the other main type of government
activity, rent seeking, in which government serves as a means of
transferring wealth. The theory of rent seeking recognizes that

BANKING AND PUBLIC CHOICE

people can seek wealth not only by producing services that other people value, but also by transferring wealth to themselves from others, either directly as in tax and subsidy programs or indirectly as through securing favorable legislation that restricts competition.[4]

What holds for economic activity in general also should hold for the production of monetary services as one particular type of economic activity. It has, of course, long been recognized that inflation can serve as a form of taxation. In a commodity money system, however, this form of taxation would be relatively costly. If the government simply issued more notes through its own bank, and if that bank were simply one bank among many in a competitive banking industry, the government's bank would run the same risk of failure as would any private bank that engaged in excessive note issue. While the government's bank could probably suspend payment in specie without failing in the same sense that a private bank would fail, it would still bear a cost because customers would shift their patronage to more reliable banks.

Alternatively, the government could engage in such activities as the clipping and shaving of coins, and then re-issue debased coins. While governments have often debased commodity monies in this fashion, and for reasons that are perfectly understandable from the perspective of a theory of counterfeiting, it is surely more costly for government to engage in inflation or counterfeiting under a commodity money system than it would be under a fiat money system. Even in a fiat money system, government's ability to inflate will be limited by its need to maintain some credibility and acceptability, as evidenced by the lengths to which the French government went to secure acceptance for its assignats.

While a government that wanted to increase its command over resources through inflation would understandably want to replace a competitive system of free banking with some form of regulation or direct provision of banking, the existing Federal Reserve system does not seem consistent with the proposition that the Fed is part of a program for maximizing government's tax collections. Even setting aside questions about whether the actual inflation tax is one that maximizes government's tax take, the fractional reserve system of banking requires the government to share the seigniorage from monetary expansion with commercial banks. And the lower the required reserve ratio, the greater is the share captured by commercial banks.

---

[4]The seminal work is Tullock (1967). Many papers on rent seeking are collected in Buchanan, Tollison, and Tullock (1980). A thorough survey of the theory of rent seeking is provided by Tollison (1982).

CATO JOURNAL

Recognition of this sharing of seigniorage raises the possibility that the Fed represents not just a means of increasing taxes but also a method of cartelizing what would otherwise be a competitive banking industry.

Although, as Lawrence H. White (1984) explains in his study of free banking in Scotland in the 18th and 19th centuries, individual banks would be constrained in issuing notes by the demand for redemption by other banks and by individual note holders, all banks could engage in overissue if they could agree to reduce their demands for redemption. One method for doing this would be to replace individual bank notes with a common note, and to develop rules and procedures that would lead each bank to issue the amount of notes that would conform to the systemwide profit-maximizing supply of notes and loans. Reserve requirements can serve as a source of the necessary rules and procedures. This arrangement would seem to accomplish the same thing as an agreement not to redeem each other's notes, only perhaps in a less costly fashion.

An important part of the theory of regulation and rent seeking has developed around the demand by producers for cartels and the supply by legislatures of those cartels. The demand side of such legislation is relatively straightforward and is represented by the present value of the rents that could be captured by a cartel. Complications arise with respect to such things as promoting the durability of the cartel, restricting the development of substitute products, and constraining chiseling among the members, but the latent demand for cartels is straightforward and is no different for banks than it is for eggs, milk, clothing, and the like. The legislature is in the business of supplying legislation, and it will seek to produce a value-maximizing mix of legislation. Essentially this means that legislation will be sold to the highest bidders, although the production of one piece of legislation may raise or lower the value of other pieces. For example, the value of legislation that strengthens the monopoly position of dairy farmers would be diminished by legislation that reduces restrictions on the marketing of reconstituted milk.

As with any cartel there is a problem with the durability of rents, because what is individually rational for members of the cartel conflicts with what maximizes the aggregate wealth of the entire membership. And even if there is no chiseling among the members of the cartel, there is a problem of restraining entry. Moreover, the problem of chiseling is not easily resolved, because of the numerous margins along which it can occur.

A rent-seeking approach to the Fed does perhaps put the questions of the Fed's "independence" in somewhat different light. It is Congress that chooses whether the Fed will be "independent" or "dependent," and Congress presumably will make that choice on the basis of the organizational form that will maximize the value of legislation to buyers. To the extent control over the Fed is a matter of control over the initial receipt of new money, an independent Fed might raise the price that people will pay for such control. In any event, it is the distributional consequences of alternative monetary institutions and their processes of monetary expansion that will be the primary element in explaining the choice and persistence of particular institutions. Consider, for instance, a distributionally neutral increase in the stock of fiat money. Such an increase would be one in which each person's nominal money balance increased by the same percentage. In these days of computerization it would be relatively easy to implement this approach to monetary expansion. Each depositor's commercial bank account simply would be credited by the desired percentage growth rate. If the desired growth rate were .01 percent per day, as Richard Timberlake (1984b) suggests in a different context, this rate of credit would be applied to the average monthly balances of each depositor. Consistency with the reserve requirements of the Federal Reserve could be maintained by crediting each bank's reserve account with the Fed by the appropriate amount; the Fed could then increase its holdings of government debt as required. Monetary expansion, therefore, would take place in such a way that distributes the new money in proportion to existing money balances.

But monetary expansion does not take place in this manner. If it did it would correspond to a model of counterfeiting in which everyone counterfeited at the same rate and, hence, there would be no gain to counterfeiting. The gain to counterfeiting depends on its distributional effect. In this neutral expansionary process, the taxes that people pay through inflation are equal to the gains they experience as inflators. But there is no point to such a process of inflation; there would be no demand for such an institutional format, for it essentially would be no different from a competitive system of free banking, at least with respect to its distributional properties.

Central banking, as such, must contain distributional changes vis-à-vis a competitive system of free banking. The Fed would seem to be principally involved in the supply of counterfeiting, and to do so by virtue of a license from Congress. More particularly, it would seem fruitful to model the Fed as the agent of the House and Senate Banking committees, as Kevin Grier (1985) has done. Accordingly, the Fed's survival depends on whether alternative legislation becomes more valuable to some set of people than the value of maintaining the Fed is to those who would lose by its demise.

Any existing mode of operation that generates a particular level of rents will through time come to generate less rent for a variety of reasons. Chiseling might take place. Input monopolies could form to capture a share of the rents. Quality competition could arise. Substitute lines of business would be likely to develop. To the extent these things happen, the value of alternative legislation will rise relative to the present value of the present Fed legislation. The Civil Aeronautics Board (AB), which initially created rents for the domestic airline industry, is perhaps instructive on this point. Even though the CAB prevented entry, it could not prevent quality competition among carriers, as well as the participation of labor unions in the sharing of those cartel rents. As those rents eroded, the value of the cartel fell, thereby increasing the likelihood of its demise or replacement.

Monetary Reform Without Political Reform?

Both the academic division of labor and the sources of financing that sustain it lead naturally to a piecemeal approach to public policy issues. Thus monetary policy is approached separately from tax policy which is approached separately from housing policy, and so on. Although such a division of labor and knowledge is inescapable, this piecemeal approach to public policy issues has some serious limitations. Recognition that monetary instability originates ultimately in political processes must, I think, lead one to ponder the utility of discussing monetary reform in isolation from political reform. If the present pattern of monetary institutions and the economic characteristics they tend to promote are a product of individual self-interest operating within the existing political order, what is the survival value of sensible monetary reform without political reform?

It is possible for accidental forces to generate conditions under which some deregulation of money might take place. This happened with airlines and perhaps with trucking. But what I consider to be reasonable models of our present political regime suggest that free enterprise in air transportation as well as in trucking has low survival value. It is abjectly inconsistent to use an economic model of the market for legislation to explain the development of public regulation, and then to look upon deregulation as the sudden dominance of consumer interests over narrower interests, whether such interests are those of producers only or of some conjunction of producers and subsets of consumers.

BANKING AND PUBLIC CHOICE

Rather than being characterized as representing the sudden dominance of common-interest politics over special-interest politics, deregulation would seem better represented as a temporary confluence of dominant special interests. For instance, if the firms in an industry want regulations that raise prices while consumers want regulations that lower them, and if the value of this regulation is independent of the value of other pieces of legislation, the resulting outcome will depend on the relative valuations to the contending factions. If those valuations are equal, which admittedly is an assumption that clashes with the general presumption that concentration defeats diffusion, it is possible for the zero regulation, competitive output to result.

However, such an outcome would not be described as representing the transformation of a rent-seeking political process into some aggregate wealth-maximizing process; the same rent-seeking process remains in place, except that in this particular legislative market the value-maximizing outcome is, for now, zero legislation. This condition is fragile, however, for there is no reason to expect the roughly equal valuations to persist. For example, instead of producers being opposed by a unified group of consumers, there may be opportunities for transfers among consumers, as through cross-subsidization, in which the cartel gain is shared between producers and a subset of consumers, as well as by the politicians who establish and maintain the cartel. The sustainability of deregulation of money or anything else, as against the possible emergence of instances of deregulation as one possible outcome of rent-seeking politics, would seem to depend on some underlying political reform that diminishes the ability of legislatures to interfere with property rights and requires them instead to operate more consistently within the framework of those rights.

Recent scholarship in public choice, which is surveyed in William Mitchell (1983), has shown that there are systematic reasons for the substantial divergences between the rationalizations advanced for governmental activities and the actual consequences of those activities. While the rationalizations envision government as protecting rights and providing beneficial activities that cannot be provided efficiently through markets, much government activity seems to involve the injection of insecurity into ownership and the replacement of relatively efficient markets with less efficient government provision. Moreover, these outcomes are an understandable attribute of the incentive features of contemporary democratic institutions.

That democracies possess a latent tendency to degenerate into rent seeking has, of course, long been commonplace among students of

CATO JOURNAL

political theory and history. That possibility was central to James Madison's *Federalist* No. 10, and its control was a central concern in some of Madison's other essays in the *Federalist*. In the same vein, Alexander Tytler, an 18th century Scot historian, generalized from his study of democracy in ancient Greece:[5]

> A democracy cannot exist as a permanent form of government. It can only exist until a majority of voters discover that they can vote themselves largesse out of the public treasury. From that moment on, the majority always votes for the candidate who promises them the most benefits from the public treasury, with the result that democracy always collapses over a loose fiscal policy. . . .

Recent scholarship in public choice has extended and deepened our knowledge of the properties of majoritarian democracy, reaffirming in the process such insights as those of Madison and Tytler. Indeed, one of the major contributions of the recent literature on public choice has been a better recognition of how minority factions can dominate a system based on majority rule.[6]

It has been recognized for millenia that constitutional government faces strong and perhaps ultimately irresistible tendencies to confound *jurisdictio* and *gubernaculum*.[7] The central principle of constitutionally limited government is that a constitution is at base an antecedent agreement among a set of people to constitute a government, and it most clearly is *not* an act of government itself. Individual rights are not created by a constitution but rather are the basis upon which a constitution is established. Government governs *(gubernaculum)*, but it governs subject to the same rules of law *(jurisdictio)* that apply to all other persons and institutions in society. For instance, a strict interpretation of and adherence to the Fifth Amendment strictures on taking property without just compensation, perhaps as illustrated by *Pennsylvania Coal Co. v. Mahon*,[8] has the effect of forcing government to act by the same rules of law as all other participants in society: resources can be shifted from one use to another only with the consent of the owners of those resources.

The issue of what types of constitutional reform might be required to reestablish a more thoroughly constitutional democracy is well beyond the scope of this paper. My intention even in raising these questions of political reform, as against sticking more narrowly to a

[5]As quoted in Niskanen (1978, p. 159).
[6]See, for instance, the development of this theme in Aranson and Ordeshook (1977).
[7]For a careful historical survey of thought and practice on constitutional government, see McIlwain (1947) and, with respect to Great Britain, Dicey (1927).
[8]260 U.S. 393 (1921).

BANKING AND PUBLIC CHOICE

consideration of monetary reform, is not to advocate one constitutional order over another, but only to point out that the problems of monetary (dis)order we face are but one piece of a larger pattern of increasingly lawless democracy. There are myriad reflections of the same central phenomena. Monetary disorder is not independent of the growth of government spending and regulation. It is not independent of capital-eroding programs and policies. It is not even independent of such things as shifts in judicial rulings that reduce liability for the value consequences of one's actions, as, for instance, by the awarding of damages in tort actions to "victims" who clearly could have avoided the accident, but who confronted a wealthier defendant—as in the apparently not atypical case of someone who strapped a refrigerator to his back before entering a race and was awarded nearly $1 million when he injured himself.[9] All of these, and many more, are manifestations of a leveling, tax-and-transfer process that reflects the problematical aspect of democracy.

In noting these problems of political order, I would affirm, only in even more general fashion, the judgment reached by James Buchanan (1983, pp. 145—46):

> Unless we can get an effective change in regimes, we cannot expect our politicians or our central bankers to resolve the stagflation dilemma. Until and unless we begin to take the long-term perspective in our private and in our public capacities, including the adoption of new and binding constitutional constraints on the fiscal and monetary powers of government, we are doomed to remain mired in the muck of modern politics.

Conclusion

My purpose has been to examine some of the insights that the theory of public choice can bring to bear upon the persistence of central banking in general and the Federal Reserve system in particular; it has not been to advance or to discuss particular suggestions for reform. As for such reforms, it should be clear that I think both reason and historical evidence support the case for free banking. At the same time, I also acknowledge the arguments by such people as Michael Bordo and Anna Schwartz (1983), that nature does not make leaps and so, barring total monetary collapse, any reform we get is likely to retain considerable state regulation over the supply of money. But, to repeat, neither my purpose nor my main interest nor my competence lies in the practicalities of reform. What is raised most pertinently by the public choice perspective are some questions

[9]Several such cases are discussed in Andresky, Kuntz, and Kallen (1985).

about possibilities for reform that go beyond the technical merits of various proposals. The central message of this perspective is that the actual operation of any monetary institution will depend upon the pattern of costs and gains that exist for different courses of conduct. What gets produced is what rewards producers the most—in politics, in monetary institutions, and in economic life generally.

At the ultimate, constitutional level, monetary institutions are chosen as just one subset of outcomes of a political process, and it is unlikely that the particular institutions that are chosen with regard to money will diverge greatly from the essential characteristics of political outcomes in general. As political institutions increasingly reward rent-seeking activities over genuinely productive activities, as Terry Anderson and Peter Hill (1980) have shown to be the case for the United States, the prospects that those same political processes will generate monetary institutions that operate in contrary fashion surely weakens. Those who are interested in monetary reform should recognize that the circumstances they are concerned about reflect the outcome of people's pursuit of their interests within our existing constitutional order. Monetary reform without political reform to redress the rent-seeking excesses of prevailing political institutions seems likely to be a short-lived aberration.

References

Akerlof, George A. "The Market for 'Lemons': Quality, Uncertainty, and the Market Mechanism." *Quarterly Journal of Economics* 84 (August 1970): 488–500.

Anderson, Terry L., and Hill, Peter J. *The Birth of a Transfer Society.* Stanford, Calif.: Hoover Institution Press, 1980.

Andresky, Jill; Kuntz, Mary; and Kallen, Barbara. "A World without Insurance?" *Forbes* (15 July 1985): 40–43.

Aranson, Peter H., and Ordeshook, Peter C. "A Prolegomenon to a Theory of the Failure of Representative Democracy." In *American Re-evolution: Papers and Proceedings*, pp. 23–46. Edited by R. Auster and B. Sears. Tucson: University of Arizona Press, 1977.

Bordo, Michael D., and Schwartz, Anna J. "The Importance of Stable Money: Theory and Evidence." *Cato Journal* 3 (Spring 1983): 63–82.

Brunner, Karl. "Deficits, Interest Rates, and Monetary Policy." *Cato Journal* 5 (Winter 1986): 709–26.

Buchanan, James M. "Monetary Research, Monetary Rules, and Monetary Regimes." *Cato Journal* 3 (Spring 1983): 143–46.

Buchanan, James M.; Tollison, Robert D.; and Tullock, Gordon. *Toward a Theory of the Rent-Seeking Society.* College Station: Texas A&M University Press, 1980.

Coase, Ronald H. "The Lighthouse in Economics." *Journal of Law and Economics* 17 (October 1974): 357–76.

BANKING AND PUBLIC CHOICE

Dicey, Albert. *Introduction to the Study of the Law of the Constitution.* 8th ed. London: Macmillan, 1927.

Einaudi, Luigi. "The Theory of Imaginary Money from Charlemagne to the French Revolution." In *Enterprise and Secular Change*, pp. 229–61. Edited by Frederic C. Lane and Jelle C. Riemersma. Homewood, Ill: Richard D. Irwin, 1953.

Garrison, Roger. "Gold: A Standard and an Institution." *Cato Journal* 3 (Spring 1983): 233–38.

Grier, Kevin B. "Congressional Preference and Federal Reserve Policy." St. Louis: Center for the Study of American Business, Washington University, 1985.

Jordan, Jerry L. "Monetary Policy as a Fiscal Instrument." *Cato Journal* 5 (Winter 1986): 733–41.

Lavoie, Don. *National Economic Planning: What Is Left?* Cambridge, Mass.: Ballinger, 1985.

Lindsay, Cotton M. "A Theory of Government Enterprise." *Journal of Political Economy* 84 (October 1976): 1061–77.

McIlwain, Charles. *Constitutionalism: Ancient and Modern.* 2d ed. Ithaca, N.Y.: Cornell University Press, 1947.

Menger, Carl. 1892. "Geld." In *Carl Menger Gesammelte Werke.* Vol. 4, pp. 1–116. Tübingen: J. C. B. Mohr, 1970.

Mitchell, William C. "Fiscal Behavior of the Modern Democratic State: Public-Choice Perspectives and Contributions." In *Political Economy: Recent Views*, pp. 69–114. Edited by L. Wade. Los Angeles: Sage, 1983.

Niskanen, William A. "The Prospect for Liberal Democracy." In *Fiscal Responsibility in Constitutional Democracy*, pp. 157–74. Edited by James M. Buchanan and Richard E. Wagner. Leiden: Martinus Nijhoff, 1978.

Parkin, Michael. "Domestic Monetary Institutions and Fiscal Deficits." In *Toward a Political Economy of Deficits.* Edited by James M. Buchanan, Charles K. Rowley, and Robert D. Tollison. Oxford: Basil Blackwell, forthcoming.

Parkin, Michael, and Bade, Robin. "Central Bank Laws and Monetary Policies: A Preliminary Investigation." In *The Australian Monetary System in the 1970s*, pp. 24–39. Edited by Michael A. Porter. Melbourne: Monash University Press, 1978.

Rolnick, Arthur J., and Weber, Warren E. "Banking Instability and Regulation in the U.S. Free Banking Era." Federal Reserve Bank of Minneapolis *Quarterly Review* 9 (Summer 1985): 2–9.

Rolnick, Arthur J., and Weber, Warren E. "The Causes of Free Bank Failures: A Detailed Examination." *Journal of Monetary Economics* 14 (November 1984): 267–91.

Santoni, G. J. "A Private Central Bank: Some Olde English Lessons." Federal Reserve Bank of St. Louis *Review* 66 (April 1984): 12–22.

Sargent, Thomas J., and Wallace, Neil. "Some Unpleasant Monetarist Arithmetic." Federal Reserve Bank of Minneapolis *Quarterly Review* 5 (Fall 1981): 1–17.

Shughart, William F. II, and Tollison, Robert D. "Preliminary Evidence on the Use of Inputs by the Federal Reserve System." *American Economic Review* 73 (June 1983): 291–304.

Smith, Vera C. *The Rationale of Central Banking*. London: P. S. King, 1936.

Timberlake, Richard H. "The Central Banking Role of Clearinghouse Associations." *Journal of Money, Credit, and Banking* 16 (February 1984a): 1–15.

Timberlake, Richard H. "Federal Reserve Policy since 1945." In *Money in Crisis*, pp. 177–93. Edited by Barry N. Siegel. Cambridge, Mass.: Ballinger, 1984b.

Tollison, Robert D. "Rent Seeking: A Survey." *Kyklos* 35 (1981): 575–602.

Toma, Mark. "Inflationary Bias of the Federal Reserve System: A Bureaucratic Perspective." *Journal of Monetary Economics* 10 (September 1982): 163–90.

Tullock, Gordon. "The Welfare Costs of Tariffs, Monopolies, and Theft." *Economic Inquiry* 5 (June 1967): 224–32.

Vaubel, Roland. "Currency Competition versus Governmental Money Monopolies." *Cato Journal* 5 (Winter 1986): 927–42.

Watts, Ross L., and Zimmerman, Jerold L. "Agency Problems, Auditing, and the Theory of the Firm." *Journal of Law and Economics* 26 (October 1983): 613–33.

White, Andrew Dickson. *Fiat Money Inflation in France*. 1912. Irvington-on-Hudson: Foundation for Economic Education, 1959.

White, Lawrence H. *Free Banking in Britain*. Cambridge: Cambridge University Press, 1984.

Name Index